CW00739470

OXFORD MONOGRAPHS IN INTERNATIONAL LAW

General Editor: PROFESSOR VAUGHAN LOWE

Chichele Professor of Public International Law in the
University of Oxford and Fellow of
All Souls College, Oxford

The Collective Responsibility of States to Protect Refugees

OXFORD MONOGRAPHS IN INTERNATIONAL LAW

The aim of this series is to publish important and original pieces of research on all aspects of international law. Topics that are given particular prominence are those which, while of interest to the academic lawyer, also have important bearing on issues which touch upon the actual conduct of international relations. Nonetheless, the series is wide in scope and includes monographs on the history and philosophical foundations of international law.

RECENT TITLES IN THE SERIES

Jurisdiction in International Law
Cedric Ryngaert

The Interpretation of Acts and Rules in Public
International Law
Alexander Orakhelashvili

Targeted Killing in International Law
Nils Melzer

The Fair and Equitable Treatment Standard in International
Foreign Investment Law
Ioana Tudor

The Immunity of States and Their Officials in International Criminal Law
and International Human Rights Law
Rosanne van Alebeek

Defining Terrorism in International Law
Ben Saul

Diplomatic Protection
Chittharanjan F. Amerasinghe

Human Rights and Non-Discrimination in the 'War on Terror'
Daniel Moeckli

The Decolonization of International Law: State Succession and the
Law of Treaties
Matthew Craven

Investment Treaty Arbitration and Public Law
HHA Van Harten

The Collective Responsibility of States to Protect Refugees

AGNÈS HURWITZ

OXFORD

UNIVERSITY PRESS

OXFORD
UNIVERSITY PRESS

Great Clarendon Street, Oxford OX2 6DP

Oxford University Press is a department of the University of Oxford.
It furthers the University's objective of excellence in research, scholarship,
and education by publishing worldwide in

Oxford New York

Auckland   Cape Town Dar es Salaam   Hong Kong   Karachi
Kuala Lumpur Madrid Melbourne Mexico City   Nairobi
New Delhi Shanghai Taipei Toronto
With offices in
Argentina Austria Brazil Chile Czech Republic France Greece
Guatemala Hungary Italy Japan South Korea Poland Portugal
Singapore Switzerland Thailand Turkey Ukraine Vietnam

Oxford is a registered trade mark of Oxford University Press
in the UK and in certain other countries

Published in the United States
by Oxford University Press Inc., New York

ISBN 978-0-19-927838-1

Printed in the United Kingdom by
Lightning Source UK Ltd., Milton Keynes

To my grandfather, Walter Hurwitz, who like many other refugees then and now, managed to flee his country but was eventually returned to his persecutors and died in deportation after waiting in vain for a visa to travel to a safer place.

Foreword

The international regime of refugee protection and solutions typified by the 1951 Convention and 1967 Protocol relating to the Status of Refugees is criticized on many counts; among them, it is said to provide no protection against terrorism, or criminals, or those simply in search of a better life. None of these complaints in fact has much substance, for the drafters back in 1951 were not blind to State interests, or to the need for integrity in refugee protection. They thus provided for the exclusion of war criminals and other undeserving cases and, faced with a society of States then in principle committed to the reserved domain of domestic jurisdiction, they held back from seeking to regulate core sovereignty issues such as admission and asylum.

That reticence remains the source of much dispute, however, and is the subject of this book. For here the contested issue is that of responsibility—the responsibility of States to determine claims for refugee status, to grant asylum, to provide and to promote solutions. Here, too, competing interests seem to be in play. Historically, States have indeed combined to provide solutions to refugee problems, if not always consistently or sufficiently, but they have held back, at the international level, from pursuing answers to basic legal issues about responsibility, no matter how often the UN General Assembly and other competent bodies have urged co-operation between States and with the Office of the UN High Commissioner for Refugees.

It is this question of the *collective* responsibility to protect refugees that Dr Hurwitz tackles head on in this excellent study. As she notes, allocating responsibility for deciding refugee claims would be admirable, at least if asylum seekers were guaranteed a substantive hearing in accordance with appropriate, harmonized protection standards, and provided also that the system did not over-burden certain States. She shows, however, that the theory is not borne out in present-day practices, which tend to undermine the principles that are the very foundation of the refugee regime.

Drawing on her extensive research into and knowledge of the history of collective action, she explains convincingly how the will of States, particularly in Europe, has moved away from protection and individual needs, towards the better securing of State interests. Safe third country practices, readmission agreements, extra-territorial processing and regional initiatives, typified by the Dublin Convention/Regulation, combine now to work negative consequences on refugees, their families, and other States, without in any way contributing to efficiency, solidarity, or greater 'burden-sharing'.

The regime of refugee protection, of course, is not just about a few States or one particular region. Rather, it is a matter which brings the 147 States now party to the 1951 Convention/1967 Protocol together with a significant number of non-party States which have nevertheless committed themselves to protection and to its basic legal standards. Against this background and from the perspective of general international law, Dr Hurwitz casts closely reasoned doubt on the legality of some or all of the dimensions of modern practices, particularly as they push up against the limits of fundamental principles, such as *non-refoulement*. While there is some scope for future progress by way of judicial review in the European Union, there is nonetheless still a wider, pressing need for serious supervision of the international obligations accepted by States party to the refugee treaties or binding as a matter of customary international law.

This book is required reading for students of refugee displacement in all its dimensions, and for those charged with the implementation of international obligations. Dr Hurwitz demonstrates clearly and coherently how the effective working and durability of the refugee regime requires both good faith and good neighbourliness; in so doing, she points the way for more equitable and protection-effective laws and practices, and towards a regime in which collective responsibility can be a working reality.

Guy S. Goodwin-Gill
All Souls College
Oxford

Preface

This volume charters the development of safe third country practices and their implementation, with a view to assessing their validity under international law.

The sources cited to support this analysis include domestic, regional, and international legal instruments and jurisprudence. It was, however, not possible to include legal developments which took place after the manuscript was submitted to the publisher and this volume therefore attempts to state the law as it stood on 1 December 2008.

More recent developments that could not be addressed include, at the regional level, the presentation by the European Commission of a proposal amending the Dublin Regulation.[1] While this proposal does not fundamentally alter the Regulation's basic premise, namely, that unless family links exist, the 'Dublin State' responsible should be the one in which an asylum seeker first enters, legally or illegally,[2] some important improvements are suggested by the Commission. The scope of the Regulation would be expanded so as to include individuals applying for subsidiary protection.[3] The right to family reunification would be extended to the cases where a family member resides or enjoys subsidiary protection status in another Member State.[4] Family reunion would also be compulsory for 'dependent' relatives (thus no longer provided under the 'humanitarian' clause),[5] and enhanced protection for minors would be provided.[6] Another sensible amendment would be the 'merging' of the 'humanitarian' and 'sovereignty' clauses under the concept of 'discretionary clauses'.[7] Procedurally, more specific provisions on the duty to inform the applicant about the 'Dublin' procedure and on the remedies available to challenge a decision of transfer would be included.[8] Apart from these suggestions, the most significant change is the suggested inclusion of a 'safeguard' clause, allowing for the suspension of 'Dublin' transfers in case of particular pressure on a

---

[1] See European commission, 'Proposal for a Regulation of the European Parliament and the Council establishing the criteria and mechanisms for determining the Member State responsible for examining an application for international protection lodged in one of the Member States by a third-country national or a stateless person' COM (2008) 820, 3 December 2008.

[2] Ibid, 5.

[3] Ibid, 7.

[4] Ibid, 8.

[5] Ibid, 8-9.

[6] Ibid, 9.

[7] Ibid, 9.

[8] Ibid, 8.

responsible State with limited reception and absorption capacities or where there are concerns that applicants would not enjoy adequate standards of protection in that State.[9] At the same time as the presentation of the aforementioned proposal, the Commission also submitted amendments to the Eurodac Regulation, which are not, however, of great import for the present discussion.[10]

Also significant are the proposed amendment of the reception Directive,[11] and the Commission proposals for the establishment of a European Asylum Support Office.[12] The former clarifies the scope of the Directive, which would clearly apply to asylum seekers during the 'Dublin phase'.[13] The latter would arguably help alleviate existing discrepancies in the assessment by Members States of country of origin information,[14] even though it would not fully resolve the harmonization concerns raised in the present work, given that several 'Dublin States' are actually not members of the European Union.

Relevant regional jurisprudence since the manuscript's submission include the *KRS v United Kingdom* decision,[15] in which the European Court of Human Rights found that the United Kingdom would not violate Article 3 ECHR by returning an Iranian applicant to Greece.[16] In reaching such a conclusion, the Court relied on the fact that it was not Greece's practice to return Iranian asylum seekers to Iran, that Greece had recently modified its legislation to address the serious protection concerns previously raised by UNHCR and by non-governmental organizations.[17] Finally, it noted that the applicant would always have the opportunity to seek interim measures under Rule 39 of the Court's Rules, if the Greek authorities decided to return the asylum seeker to a country where there would be a substantial risk of ill-treatment contrary to Article 3 EHCR.[18] Thus, the Court, while reaffirming its previous case law in the *T.I.* case, decided to give particular credence to the assurances offered by Greece, based on the legislative changes that it had already implemented. It is not clear, therefore, that this case should be regarded as a shift in the Court's jurisprudence.[19]

---

[9] Ibid, 10.

[10] COM (2008) 825, 3 December 2008.

[11] Proposal for a Directive of the European Parliament and of the Council laying down minimum standards for the reception of asylum-seekers COM (2008) 815 final, 3 December 2008.

[12] Proposal for a Regulation of the European Parliament and of the Council on the Establishment of the European Asylum Support Office COM (2009) 66 final, 18 February 2009.

[13] Proposal for the amendment of the reception Directive, 4.

[14] Proposal for the Establishment of the European Asylum Support Office, 2.

[15] *KRS v United Kingdom* Appl. No. 32733/08, Decision on Admissibility, 2 December 2008

[16] Ibid, 17.

[17] See in this respect, Chapter 3, Section 3.3.5.

[18] Ibid, 17.

[19] It bears reminding, that in the *T.I.* case the Court, after setting out strict principles on States' responsibility for violations of the Convention irrespective of any arrangements concluded amongst States regarding the allocation of responsibility for the examination of asylum claims, nevertheless considered that the United Kingdom could return the asylum seeker to Germany without violating Article 3 ECHR; see in this respect Chapter 5, Section 5.1.2.1.2.

At the domestic level, it is worth noting that the *Nasseri* case was brought before the House of Lords, which upheld the Court of Appeal's finding and relied for this purpose on the aforementioned *KRS v United Kingdom* decision. It also noted that:

Parliament must have decided that the administrative convenience of having the list in primary legislation, to avoid administrative law challenges to the procedure for consideration of article 3 rights, or to the non-exercise of a discretionary power to remove a country from the list, outweighed the risk that there might be cases in which a court found that a listed country was in fact unsafe and made a declaration of incompatibility. It removed the decision-making process from administrative law and left only the bare Convention question of whether article 3 would in fact be infringed.[20]

It is also worth mentioning that the Supreme Court of Canada dismissed the application for leave to appeal the Judgment of the Federal Court of Appeal on the legality of the Safe Third Country Agreement concluded with the United States.[21]

As a final note, the author would like to emphasize that while several friends and colleagues have been kind enough to comment on specific draft chapters of this volume, she remains solely responsible for the views expressed herein, and for the errors and omissions as occur. Also, the views expressed are those of the author alone and do not reflect the views of the International Criminal Tribunal for the former Yugoslavia or the United Nations in general.

Agnès Hurwitz

---

[20] *Secretary of State for the Home Department v Nasseri* [2009] UKHL 23, para 22, 44; see Chapter 2 Section 2.1.2.3 and Chapter 5, Section 5.1.1.2 on the Court of Appeal's Decision.

[21] See Case No. 32820, Supreme Court of Canada Bulletin of Proceedings, 6 February 2009, available at http://scc.lexum.umontreal.ca/en/bulletin/2009/09-02-06.bul/09-02-06.bul.html See Chapter 2, Section 2.1.2.

Acknowledgements

There are many people and institutions I would like to thank for their invaluable support during the preparation of this volume.

Several institutions in Belgium and in the United Kingdom have offered essential financial backing during my doctoral studies. The fellowship from the 'Fonds National de la Recherche Scientifique' enabled me to begin my research, first at the Free University of Brussels and then during my first year at Oxford University. The Fondation Wiener-Anspach provided vital financial support throughout the doctorate research. The Arts and Humanities Research Board of the British Academy should also be acknowledged for covering my university and college fees during the last two years of the doctorate. Finally, I want to express my gratitude to Francoise Miot and the Rotary Club of Brussels EC for their help via a Rotary District grant in the final year of my doctorate.

I would also like to thank the academic institutions where I conducted research into the practice of various EU members States on safe third country regulations and the Dublin Convention. The University of Brussels, and in particular Professor Philippe De Bruycker offered ongoing support during my research. I am also grateful to the staff and researchers at the Max Planck Institute for Comparative Public Law and Public International Law in Heidelberg, and at the Centre for Migration Law at the University of Nijmegen, including Eva Woyczechowski Andreas Zimmerman, Elspelth Guild, Thomas Spijkerboer, and Karin Zwaan. Finally, I would like to thank the officials in national administrations, the European Union, and UNHCR, in particular Johannes van der Klaauw, Jean-Louis De Brouwer, Wenceslas de Lobkowicz, Guillaume Asselin, and Mr Goriya for accepting to be interviewed; their comments provided extremely useful insight into the intricacies of European Union and domestic decision-making processes in the asylum realm.

Gratitude and acknowledgements are also due to the many people who guided me towards the successful completion of this volume. I have been unbelievably fortunate to have had Professor Guy S. Goodwin-Gill as my doctoral supervisor; his unparalleled legal and academic expertise and personal kindness allowed me to pursue this project under the best possible conditions and his constant encouragement drove me to complete this volume after finishing my doctorate at Oxford University. I am also much indebted to Professor Philippe De Bruycker, whose commitment and energy greatly contributed to making this project a reality in the first place and I thank him for his invaluable advice and friendship throughout the years. I also want to express my appreciation to the academic staff at the Refugee Studies Centre, in particular, Dr Dawn Chatty, Dr Maryanne Loughry and Dr Matthew Gibney, for their encouragement and support in the last year of my doctorate. Nicolas Croquet, Jean-François Durieux, María-Teresa Gil-Bazo, James Milner, and Helen Toner provided invaluable comments on various draft chapters and I am deeply thankful to them. I am also indebted to Yvonne McDermott, who provided invaluable research and editorial assistance and whose attention to detail, efficiency, and enthusiasm undoubtedly contributed to the final completion of the manuscript. By the same token, I must extend my appreciation to OUP's editorial staff, in particular, Merel Alstein and Darcy Ahl, and Vimal Stephen at Cepha, for their impressive patience and professionalism. Let me finally thank all of those whose views and expertise on international law greatly enriched my understanding of a number of issues raised in this volume and who generously offered their support through some challenging times: H.E. Judge Fausto Pocar and Professor Laurence Boisson de Chazournes for their incredible kindness and legal erudition, and my colleagues and friends, Guido Acquaviva, Valeria Bolici, Andrea Carcano, Hannah Garry, and Jessica Salomon.

Most importantly, my love and appreciation goes to my amazing husband, Darius, my dear parents, Esther and Henri, my lovely sister Manuelle and her husband Philip, my fabulous aunt, Beatrice, my wonderful in-laws Karlene and Nader, and their children Manijeh, John, Kamran, and Taneda Farivar Sadri. Their love, patience, and unwavering support has been vital throughout this long process.

Contents

Table of Cases	xxi
Table of Treaties and Other International Instruments	xxix
List of Abbreviations	xxxiii

Introduction	1

**1 Origins and Developments of Arrangements to Allocate
Responsibility for the Protection of Refugees**   9

1.1 Fundamental Concepts   10
     1.1.1 The international legal framework of refugee protection:
       historical background   10
     1.1.2 The establishment of the United Nations High Commissioner
       for Refugees   12
     1.1.3 The 1951 Geneva Convention Relating to the Status of Refugees   13
     1.1.4 Refugees and asylum   15

1.2 The Refugee Situation at the End of the 1970s   17
     1.2.1 'Refugees in orbit'   20
     1.2.2 The 1977 United Nations' conference on territorial asylum   21
     1.2.3 Conclusions of the Executive Committee of the
       High Commissioner's Programme   23
     1.2.4 The Council of Europe   26

1.3 The European Union   30
     1.3.1 The European Commission's proposals   30
     1.3.2 The 1985 Schengen Agreement and the 1990
       Implementing Convention   33
     1.3.3 The elaboration of the Dublin Convention   35
     1.3.4 The Amsterdam Treaty and the 'Communitarisation' of
       visas, asylum, immigration, and other policies related to the
       movement of persons   36
       1.3.4.1 'An area of freedom, security and justice'   36
       1.3.4.2 Provisions on asylum, refugees, and displaced persons
          (Article 63.1 and 2 ECT): harmonizing asylum laws
          in the European Union   38
       1.3.4.3 The British/Irish and Danish 'opt-outs'   41
       1.3.4.4 The next stage: the Lisbon Treaty   43

1.4 Conclusion   44

2 Safe Third Country Practices, Readmission, and
   Extraterritorial Processing   45
   2.1 Safe Third Country Practices   46
        2.1.1 Definition   46
        2.1.2 Origins and development   47
               2.1.2.1 Effective protection   52
               2.1.2.2 Contact between the asylum seeker and the
                        third country and consent of the third state
                        to the removal   56
               2.1.2.3 Procedural issues concerning the application of the
                        safe third country concept   59
        2.1.3 Conclusion   66
   2.2 Readmission Agreements   67
        2.2.1 Definition   67
        2.2.2 Evolution of readmission agreements   67
        2.2.3 Characteristics   69
        2.2.4 Readmission as a component of the European Union's
               external dimension of asylum and immigration policies   71
   2.3 Extraterritorial Processing   78
        2.3.1 Origins   78
        2.3.2 European proposals for extraterritorial processing   78
        2.3.3 Analysis   81
   2.4 The Way Forward   83
   2.5 Conclusion   87

3 Allocation of Responsibility for Examining an Application
   for Asylum under the Dublin Regime   89
   3.1 Elaboration of the Dublin Regulation   90
   3.2 Principles   91
        3.2.1 Only one State is responsible for examining an application
               for asylum   92
        3.2.2 The State responsible is under the obligation to guarantee
               effective access to the asylum procedure   92
        3.2.3 Scope   94
   3.3 Criteria Determining the State Responsible   95
        3.3.1 Family unity   96
        3.3.2 Visa and residence permit   101
        3.3.3 Illegal crossing of the territory of a Member State   101
        3.3.4 Control of the entry of the alien into the territory
               of the Member States   102
        3.3.5 The humanitarian and 'sovereignty' clauses   102

3.4 Procedure 111
    3.4.1 Transfer of the asylum seeker to the responsible State   111
    3.4.2 Rules of evidence   115
    3.4.3 Identification of the asylum seeker: the Eurodac Regulation   117
3.5 Assessment 121
3.6 Conclusion 125

4 **The Impact of Safe Third Country Practices on Inter-State Relations** 127

4.1 Protection Elsewhere or Mere Transit: The Relevance and Scope of Article 31 CSR 127
4.2 International Cooperation to Protect Refugees: Solidarity, Burden-Sharing, and Good-Neighbourliness 138
    4.2.1 The principle of solidarity and burden-sharing   139
        4.2.1.1 International instruments   140
        4.2.1.2 Burden-sharing and *non-refoulement*   144
        4.2.1.3 International practice   146
            4.2.1.3.1 Fiscal burden-sharing   147
            4.2.1.3.2 Physical burden-sharing   150
            4.2.1.3.3 Comprehensive approaches   156
        4.2.1.4 The legal relevance of the principle of solidarity and burden-sharing   161
        4.2.1.5 Safe third country practices and burden-sharing   164
    4.2.2 The principle of good-neighbourliness   167
4.3 Conclusion 170

5 **States' Obligations Towards Refugees** 173

5.1 The Obligation of *Non-Refoulement* 173
    5.1.1 The obligation of *non-refoulement* under international refugee law   174
        5.1.1.1 Nature and scope of Article 33 CSR: the prohibition of expulsion or return ('*refoulement*')   174
        5.1.1.2 States' obligation to implement the Refugee Convention   181
    5.1.2 *Non-refoulement* under international human rights law   187
        5.1.2.1 *Non-refoulement* under the European Convention on Human Rights   189
            5.1.2.1.1 Applicable standard   191
            5.1.2.1.2 Jurisprudence of relevance to safe third country practices   194
        5.1.2.2 Article 3 of the Convention Against Torture   199
    5.1.3 *Non-refoulement* as a customary obligation   204

5.2 Other Human Rights Obligations   209

    5.2.1 The right to seek and enjoy asylum from persecution   209

    5.2.2 The right to leave one's country   212

    5.2.3 Other relevant international refugee law and human rights obligations   214

5.3 Removal to a Safe Third Country and States' Obligations: The Content and Scope of Effective Protection   217

5.4 Conclusion   221

6 Supervision at the Level of the European Union   223

6.1 The Court of Justice under the EC Treaty   224

    6.1.1 Remedies before the European Court of Justice   224

        6.1.1.1 Failure to comply with the Treaty: Articles 226 and 227 ECT   225

        6.1.1.2 Review of the legality of Community acts   227

            6.1.1.2.1 Reviewable acts   228

            6.1.1.2.2 Grounds for annulment   228

            6.1.1.2.3 Applicants   228

        6.1.1.3 Failure to act: Article 232 ECT   232

        6.1.1.4 Preliminary ruling: Article 68.1 ECT   232

        6.1.1.5 Competence to rule on the interpretation of Title IV ECT   236

    6.1.2 Consequences of the British/Irish and Danish 'Opt-out'   237

    6.1.3 Intervention of UNHCR in ECJ proceedings   237

    6.1.4 Assessment of existing remedies   238

6.2 The European Court of Justice and Fundamental Rights   240

    6.2.1 Fundamental rights as general principles of European Community law   240

    6.2.2 The European Court of Justice and the European Court of Human Rights   242

    6.2.3 Fundamental rights in European Treaties   245

    6.2.4 The latest twist: the Charter of Fundamental Rights   247

6.3 Conclusion   249

Chapter 7 International Supervision   251

7.1 Supervisory Mechanisms Relevant to the Protection of Refugees and Asylum Seekers   251

    7.1.1 Supervision by or on behalf of the organization   252

        7.1.1.1 The Executive Committee of the High Commissioner's Programme   252

        7.1.1.2 UNHCR's function of international protection   255

            7.1.1.2.1 The crisis of protection: UNHCR in the 1990s   257

7.1.1.2.2 UNHCR's position on safe third country
practices 258
7.1.1.3 Article 35 CSR 261
7.1.1.4 Advisory opinion from the International
Court of Justice 264
7.1.1.5 Human rights charter-based bodies 264
7.1.2 Supervision by States: Article 38 CSR 265
7.1.3 Supervision by individuals 266
7.2 Future Prospects 267
7.2.1 Supervision by or on behalf of UNHCR 267
7.2.1.1 UNHCR's international protection mandate 267
7.2.1.1.1 The Global Consultations and the Agenda
for Protection 267
7.2.1.1.2 Regulating secondary movements:
'Convention Plus' and other initiatives 271
7.2.1.1.3 Conclusion 275
7.2.1.2 The Executive Committee of the
High Commissioner's Programme 276
7.2.1.3 Establishment of an independent body to
examine State reports 278
7.2.2 Supervision by individuals 282
7.3 Conclusion 284

Conclusion 285

Select Bibliography 289
Index 335

Table of Cases

INTERNATIONAL CASE-LAW

1. International Court of Justice/Permanent Court of International Justice

Armed Activities on the Territory of the Congo (Democratic Republic of the
Congo v Uganda) (Judgment) (2005). 177
*Case Relating to the Territorial Jurisdiction of the International Commission of the River
Oder* (1929) 132
Corfu Channel Case (Merits) (1949) 168
International Status of South West Africa (Advisory Opinion) (1950) .137
Interpretation of Peace Treaties with Bulgaria, Hungary and Romania (Advisory
Opinion 2nd phase) (1950) 137
Legal Consequences of the Construction of the Wall in the Palestinian Occupied Territory
(Advisory Opinion) (2004). 177
Military and Paramilitary Activities in and Against Nicaragua (Merits) (1986) 204, 207
North Sea Continental Shelf (Judgment) (1969) 204
Reservations to the Convention on the Prevention and Punishment of Genocide
(Advisory Opinion) (1951). 266

2. Arbitration Tribunals

Eritrea-Ethiopia Boundary Arbitration (2002). 137
Lac Lanoux Arbitration (France v Spain) (1957) 168
Trail Smelter Arbitration (USA v Canada) (1941). 168

3. Human Rights Committee

Ahani v Canada, Communication No. 1051/2002 (29 March 2004) .189
ARJ v Australia, Communication No. 692/1996 (11 August 1997). 189
C v Australia, Communication No. 900/1999 (13 November 2002). .189
Cox v Canada, Communication No. 539/1993 (9 December 1994) 189
Kindler v Canada, Communication No. 470/1991 (30 July 1993) 189
Lopez Burgos v Uruguay Communication No. 52/79 (29 July 1981) .199
Ng v Canada, Communication No. 469/1991 (7 January 1994). 189

4. Committee Against Torture

Aemei v Switzerland, Communication No. 34/1995 (9 May 1997) 199, 201
Alan v Switzerland, Communication No. 21/1995 (13 May 1996) 200
Arana v France, Communication No. 63/1997 (5 June 2000) 199, 200, 203
Avedes Hamayak Korban v Sweden, Communication No. 88/1997 (16 November 1998). 200
Brada v France, Communication No. 195/2002 (24 May 2005) 203
C T and K M v Sweden, Communication No. 279/2005 (7 December 2006). 201
El Rgeig v Switzerland, Communication No. 280/2005 (30 November 2006) 200, 201
Falcon Rios v Canada, Communication No. 133/1999 (17 December 2004). 201
Iya v Switzerland, Communication No. 299/2006 (26 November 2007). 200, 201
Kamil Agiza v Sweden, Communication No. 233/2003 (20 May 2005). 200, 201, 203
Kaveh Yaragh Tala v Sweden, Communication No. 43/1996 (15 November 2006). 201
M B B v Sweden, Communication No. 104/1988 (5 May 1999). 200

M V v The Netherlands, Communication No. 201/2002 (19 May 2003) 201
Mutombo v Switzerland, Communication No. 13/1993 (17 April 1994) 200, 201
Paez v Sweden, Communication No. 39/1996 (28 April 1997) 199
Singh Sogi v Canada, Communication No. 297/2006 (29 November 2007) 203
T A v Sweden, Communication No. 226/2003 (27 May 2005) 201
T M v Sweden, Communication No. 228/2003 (2 December 2003) .200
Tebourski v France, Communication No. 300/2006 (11 May 2007) 200, 201, 203
V L v Switzerland, Communication No. 262/2005 (22 January 2007) 201

5. European Commission and Court of Human Rights

A v Switzerland, Appl. No. 11933/86 (1986) 46 DR 257 192
Abdulaziz and ors v United Kingdom, Appl. Nos. 9214/80; 9473/81; 9474/81,
 Judgment of 28 May 1985 105
Abdurrahim Incedursun v Netherlands, Appl. No. 33124/96, Judgment of
 22 June 1999 192
Ahmed v Austria, Appl. No. 25964/94, Judgment of 17 December 1996. . . . . .189, 191, 192, 193
Ahmet Özkan and ors v Turkey, Appl. No. 21689/93, Judgment of 6 April 2004 191
Amuur v France, Appl. No. 19776/92, Judgment of 25 June 1996. .195
Banković and ors v Belgium and 16 Other Contracting States, Appl. No. 52207/99,
 Admissibility Decision of 12 December 2001. 199
Bensaid v UK, Appl. No. 44599/98, Judgment of 6 February 2001 .107
Bosphorus Hava Yollari Turism Ve Ticaret Anonim Sirketi v Ireland, Appl. No. 45036/98,
 Judgment of 30 June 2005 244
CFDT v European Communities, Appl. No. 8030/77, Decision of 10 July 1978 243
Chahal v United Kingdom, Appl. No. 22414/93, Judgment of 25 October 1996. . . 189, 190, 191,
 192, 193
Conka v Belgium, Appl. No. 51564/99, Judgement of 5 February 2002 . . . . .66, 114, 198
Cruz Varas v Sweden, Appl. No. 15576/89, Judgment of 20 March 1991 . . . . .190, 191, 192
Denizci and ors v Cyprus, Appl. Nos. 25316-25321/94 and 27207/95,
 Judgement of 23 May 2001. 191
Dulas v Turkey, Appl. No. 25801/94, Judgement of 30 January 2001 191
Funke v France, Appl. No. 10828/84, Judgment of 25 February 1993. . . . . .242, 243
Gebremedhin v France, Appl. No. 25389/05, Judgment of 26 April 2007 . . . . .66, 114, 198
Giama v Belgium, Appl. 7612/76, (1980) 23 Yearbook of the European
 Convention of Human Rights 428 194
Harabi v the Netherlands, Appl. No. 10798/84, 5 March 1986 194
H.L.R. v France, Appl. No. 24573/94, Judgment of 29 April 1997 .192
Issa and ors v Turkey, Appl. No. 31821/96, Judgment of 16 November 2004. 199
Jabari v Turkey, Appl. No. 40035/98, Judgment of 11 July 2000 . . . . .18, 66, 114, 192, 198
M & Co v Federal Republic of Germany, Appl. No. 13258/87, 9 February 1990. 243
Mamatkulov and Askarov v Turkey, Appl. Nos. 46827/99 and 46951/99,
 Judgment of 4 February 2005. 189
Matthews v United Kingdom, Appl. No. 24833/94, Judgment of 18 February
 1999 ECHR 1999-I 244
NA v The United Kingdom, Appl. No. 25904/07, Judgment of 17 July 2008 192
Nazin Al-Kuzbari v Federal Republic of Germany, Appl. No. 1802/63, Decision
 of 26 March 1963 190
Niemetz v Germany, Appl. No. 13710/88, Judgment of 16 December 1992 242
Öcalan v Turkey, Appl. No. 46221/99, Judgment of 12 March 2003. 199
S v Federal Republic of Germany, Appl. No. 1465/62 190
Saadi v Italy, Appl. No. 37201/06, Judgment of
 28 February 2008. . . . . .189, 190, 191, 192, 193, 197, 198

Salah Sheekh v the Netherlands, Appl. No. 1948/04, Judgment of 11 January 2007 . . . . . . 192, 193
Salem and ors v Italy, Appl. No. 10171/05, 10601/05, 11593/05, 17165/05,
    Decision of 11 May 2006. . . . . .2, 80
Soering v United Kingdom, Appl. No. 14038/88, Judgment of 7 July 1989 . . . .189, 190, 191, 192
Sultani v France, Appl. No. 45223/05, Judgment of 20 December 2007. 192
T.I. v United Kingdom, Appl. No. 43844/98, Judgement of 7 March 2000 . . . . .84, 190, 195
Vilvarajah and ors v United Kingdom, Appl. Nos. 13163/87, 13164/87,
    13165/87, 13447/87, 13448/87 Judgment of 30 October 1991. . . . . .189, 191, 192
X v Austria and Yugoslavia, Appl. No. 2143/64, Decision of 30 June 1964 190
X v Belgium, Appl. No. 984/61, Decision of 29 May 1961 190
X v Germany, Appl. No. 7216/75, Decision of 20 May 1976 192
X v Germany, Appl. No. 7334/76, Decision of 9 March 1976. 192
X v Sweden, Appl. No. 434/58, Opinion of 30 June 1959. 190
X v the United Kingdom, Appl. 8581/79, Decision of 6 March 1980 .192

6. Court of Justice of the European Communities

Accession by the Community to the Convention for the Protection of Human Rights
    and Fundamental Freedoms, Opinion 2/94 . . . . .241, 246
Ahmed Adem and Hamrin Mosa Rashi v Federal Republic of Germany, Case C-178/08
A.M. & S. Europe Ltd v Commission, Case 155/79 . . . . .239, 241
Baustahlgewebe v Commission, Case C-185/95. 244
Biogen Inc v Smithkline Beecham Biologicals SA, Case C-181/95 236
Bostock, Case C-2/92. 241
Srl CILFIT and Lanifacio du Gavardo SpA v Ministry of Health, Case 283/81 . . . . .235, 236
Commission v Austria, Case C-102/06. 226
Commission v Belgium, Case 324/82 226
Commission v Belgium, Case C-389/06 226
Commission v Germany, Case 249/86 241
Commission v Germany, Case C-496/06. 226
Commission v Greece, Case C-476/04. 226
Commission v Greece, Case C-72/06. 226
Commission v Italy, Case C-462/04 227
Commission v Jégo Quéré & Cie SA Case C-263/02 P 230
Commission v Luxembourg, Case C-454/04 226
Commission v Luxembourg Case C-449/04. 226
Commission v Luxembourg, Case C-448/04 227
Commission v Luxembourg, Case C-47/06 226
Commission v Portugal, Case C-75/06 226
Commission v United Kingdom, Case 416/85 226
Commission v United Kingdom Case C-455/04 226
Da Costa en Schaake NV, Jacob Meyer NV and Hoechst-Holland NV v Nederlandse
    Belastingadministratie, Cases 28-30/62 235
Elgafaji v Staatssecretaris van Justitie (Advocate General's Opinion) Case
    C-465/07. . . . . .238, 239, 243
Elliniki Radiophonia Tileorassi AE v Dimotiki Etairia Pliroforissis and Sotirios Kouvelas,
    Case C-260/89. 241
ENU v Commission, Case C-107/91 232
Foglia (Pasquale) v Mariella Novello, Case 104/79 235
Foglia (Pasquale) v Mariella Novello, (No. 2) Case 244/80 235
Foto-Frost v Hauptzollamt Lübeck-Ost, Case 314/85 234
Germany v Council, Case C-280/93. 249
Germany v Council, Case C-122/95. 249

Grant v South West Trains Ltd, Case C-249/96 241
Hauer v Land Rheinland-Pfalz, Case 44/79 241
Hoechst AG v Commission, Cases 46/87 and 227/88 . . . . .241, 242
Hoffman-La Roche v Centrafarm, Case 107/76 233
International Business Machines Corporation v Commission, Case 60/81 228
Internationale Handelsgesellschaft v Einfuhr- und Vorratstelle für Getreide und Futtermittel,
    Case 11/70 240
Jégo-Quéré & Cie SA v Commission Case T-177/01 230
    Johnston v Chief Constable of the Royal Ulster Constabulary, Case 222/84 241
Kahn Scheepvart v Commission, Case T-398/94 232
KB v The National Health Service and the Secretary of State for Health, Case C-117/01 244
Lourenco Dias v Director da Alfandega do Porto, Case-343/90 235
Lyckesog Case C-99/00 233
Mannesmannröhren-Werke AG v Commission, Case T-112/98 243
Morson and Jhanjan v Netherlands, Joined Cases 35 and 36/82 233
National Panasonic v Commission, Case 136/79 242
Nold v Commission, Case 4/73 241
Netherlands v European Parliament and Council, Case C-377/98 241
Omega Spielhallen- und Automatenaufstellungs-GmbH v Oberbürgermeisterin der
    Bundesstadt Bonn, Case C-36/02 241
Orkem v Commission, Case 374/87 . . . . .241, 242
P v S and Cornwall County Council, Case C-13/94 241
Parfums Christian Dior, Case 337/95 233,
Parliament v Council, Case C-540/03 . . . . .241, 243, 248
Parliament v Council, Case C-133/06 . . . . .53, 93, 232
Parti écologiste 'Les Verts' v European Parliament, Case 294/83 236
Piraiki-Patraiki v Commission, Case 11/82 229
Plaumann & Co v Commission, Case 25/62 229
R v Kent Kirk, Case 63/83 241
Rombi and Arkopharma, Case C-107/97 241
Rutili v Minister for the Interior, Case 36/75 241
Star Fruit Company v Commission, Case 247/87 226
Stauder v City of Ulm, Case 29/69 240
Stichting Greenpeace Council (Greenpeace International) and ors v Commission,
    Case T-585/93 230
Telemarsicabruzzo SpA v Circostel, Ministerio delle Poste e Telecommunicazioni
    and Ministerio della Difesa, Case C-320-322/90 235
T Port GmbH & Co KG v Bundesanstalt für Landswirtschaft und Ernähung,
    Case C-68/95 242
TWD Textilwerke Deggendorf GmbH v Germany, Case 188/92 .229, 236
Union de Pequeños Agricultores v Council, Case C-50/00 P (Advocate General's
    Opinion) 229
Union de Pequeños Agricultores v Council, Case C-50/00 P 230
Wachauf v Germany, Case 5/88 . . . . .230, 241
Wienand Meilicke v ADV/ORGA F.A. Meyer AG, Case C-83/91 235

7. Miscellaneous

The Haitian Centre for Human Rights et al v United States, Case 10.675, Inter-American
    Commission on Human Rights 211
Organisation Mondiale contre la Torture and others v Rwanda Communications No. 27/89, 46/91,
    49/91, 99/93 Decision of the African Commission on Human and Peoples' Rights 212

NATIONAL CASE-LAW

1. Belgium

Judicial Courts

Cour d'appel, Arrêt of 29 June 1989 115
Tribunal de 1ère instance, Jugement of 24 December 1990 115

Conseil d'Etat

Arrêt No. 66.292 of 16 May 1997 103
Arrêt No. 67.538 of 22 July 1997 103
Arrêt No. 67.622 of 1 August 1997 103
Arrêt No. 67.710 of 14 August 1997 103
Arrêt No. 69.158 of 24 October 1997 106
Arrêt No. 69.232 of 28 October 1997 106
Arrêt No. 69.466 of 5 November 1997 106
Arrêt No. 69.578 of 13 November 1997 108
Arrêt No. 69.714 of 21 November 1997 124
Arrêt No. 70.163 of 11 December 1997 107
Arrêt No. 71.977 of 20 February 1998 107
Arrêt No. 73.085 of 14 April 1998 107
Arrêt No. 74.163 of 8 June 1998..111
Arrêt No. 75.497 of 31 July 1998 103
Arrêt No. 75.587 of 12 August 1998 109
Arrêt No. 75.628 of 28 August 1998 106
Arrêt No. 75.898 of 24 September 1998 109

2. Germany

Verwaltungsgericht Gießen, 25-01-1996.....................................103, 106
Verwaltungsgericht Schwerin, 3-05-96 ....103, 106
Bundesverfassungsgericht, 14-05-96 ....54, 92, 211
Verwaltungsgericht Berlin, 10-09-96 103
Verwaltungsgericht Berlin, 14-04-97 103
Verwaltungsgericht, 28-05-1998 97

3. The Netherlands

'Dublin' Case-Law

Den Haag 2-08-95 AWB 95/6192 103
Den Haag 4-12-95 AWB 95/10910 109
Pres Rechtb 's Gravenhage zp Zwolle 4-10-95 AWB 95/4126 98
Zwolle 25-10-95 AWB 95/4134 106
's-Gravenhage 17-11-95 AWB 95/10502 109
's-Gravenhage 17-11-95 AWB 95/10515...109
's Gravenhage 17-11-95 AWB 95/10544 en 95/10546 109
's-Gravenhage 17-11-1995 AWB 95/10607 108
's Gravenhage 5-12-95 AWB 95/5694 107
's-Gravenhage zp Zwolle 7-12-95 AWB 95/5371 107
Pres 's Gravenhage 8-12-95 AWB 95/11266 106
Zwolle 21-12-95 AWB 95/6004 109
's Gravenhage 21-12-95 AWB 95/6513 106
Rechtb Den Haag 22-12-95 AWB 95/12021 98

's Gravenhage 4-01-96 AWB 95/12042 106
's-Gravenhage 17-01-96 AWB 95/12477 109
's-Hertogenbosch 30-01-96 AWB 95/9408 109
's-Gravenhage 1-03-96 AWB 96/1098 ....108, 111
Pres Rb Den Haag 9-4-96 96/2281 98
's-Gravenhage 31-05-96 AWB 96/4192 ....108, 111
Zwolle 14-06-96 AWB 96/3460 105
's Gravenhage 11-09-1996 AWB 96/8273 108
Den Haag 11-09-96 AWB 96/8279 105
's Gravenhage 25-09-96 AWB 96/8727 92
's Gravenhage 7-10-96 AWB 96/9453 107
Zwolle 11-10-96 AWB 96/7163 and AWB 96/7323 98
Rechtseenheidskamer 19-12-96 AWB 96/9092 109
's Gravenhage 19-02-97 AWB 97/22 92
Zwolle 28-02-97 AWB 96/7502 98
Zwolle 7-03-97 AWB 97/56 109
's-Gravenhage 25-03-97 AWB 97/1760 107
Pres Rechtb 's-Gravenhage 10-12-97 AWB 97/6627 103
Pres Recht 's-Gravenhage 17-12-97 AWB 97/6172 98
's-Gravenhage zp Zwolle 30-1-98 AWB 97/6700 ....103, 108, 111
's-Gravenhage zp Zwolle 24-04-98 AWB 98/576 98/625 108
's-Gravenhage zp Zwolle 24-04-98 AWB 98/1203 116
's Gravenhage 20-05-98 AWB 98/3293 98/3308 109
Zwolle 15-07-98 AWB 98/2578 98
Zwolle 5-08-98 AWB 98/3760 103
Rechtb Den Haag 14-08-98 AWB 98/5139 108
Zwolle 18-09-98 AWB 98/3726 107
's Gravenhage zp Zwolle 9-10-98 AWB 98/4650 105
Zwolle 27-10-98 AWB 98/4848 108
's-Gravenhage 30-10-98 AWB 98/7771 98/7774 116
's-Gravenhage 30-10-98 AWB 98/7773 116
's Gravenhage 11-11-98 AWB 98/8090 117
Zwolle 18-11-98 AWB 98/5015 117
Zwolle 13-01-99 AWB 98/6636 108
's-Gravenhage zp Zwolle 19-01-99 AWB 98/6633...........................108
Zwolle 20-01-99 AWB 98/6948 109
's-Gravenhage zp Zwolle 17-02-99 AWB 99/172 109
's Gravenhage 26-02-99 AWB 99/425 109

Miscellaneous

Staat der Nederlanden v Hoge Raad Nederlands, 13 May 1988 175
Opinion of the Dutch *Raad van State* ('Council of State') of 8 April 1991
    No.WO2.91.0013 ....115, 183–4, 216, 239

4. United Kingdom

AH(Iran) Zego (Eritrea) Kadir (Iraq) v Secretary of State for the Home Department
    (CA) (2008)..110
Ahmed Gamel Haliq Abdulla v Secretary of State for the Home Department
    (CA) (1992)..54

Balbir Singh, Gurmail Singh, Parmjit Singh, Hardeep Singh, Satpal Singh v Secretary
    of State for the Home Department (CA) (1992) 54
Behluli v Secretary of State for the Home Department (CA) (1998).....................102
Bugdaycay and ors v Secretary of State for the Home Department (HL) (1987) 61, 181
EM (Lebanon) v Secretary of State for the Home Department (HL) (2008)..........56, 189, 216
Gulay Canbolat v Secretary of State for the Home Department (CA) (1997) 62
Huseyn Dursun v Secretary of State for the Home Department (CA) (1993) 54
In the Matter of an Application by Ngozi Christiana Okoye (QB) (2006) 107
Julia Martinas v a Special Adjudicator Secretary of State for the Home Department (CA) (1995)...54
Nasseri v Secretary of State for the Home Department (HC) (2007) 63, 109, 187
R (Nasseri) v Secretary of State for the Home Department (CA) (2008)......64, 109, 110, 187, 220
R v Asfaw (HL) (2008) 32, 129, 132, 211
R v Immigration Officer at Prague Airport and ors (Respondents) ex p European Roma
    Rights Centre and ors (Appellants) (HL) (2004) 179, 205
R v Secretary of State for the Home Department and Special adjudicators ex p Tania
    Luiza Stefan, Andrea Anca Chiper and Marius Ionel (QB) (1995) 220
R v Secretary of State for the Home Department ex p Adan and R v Secretary of State
    for the Home Department ex p Aitseguer (HL) (2000)..........................63, 186
R v Secretary of State for the Home Department ex p Adam Limbuela and Tesema
    (HL) (2005)..19
R v Secretary of State for the Home Department ex p Elshani and Berisha (QB)
    (1998) 54
R v Secretary of State for the Home Department ex p Hamid Aitsegeur (QB) (1999) 180, 185
R v Secretary of State for the Home Department ex p Khalil Yassine Rahma Yassine
    Mohammad El-Nacher Hicham Ali Hachem, Salam Bou Imad, Zouheir Bou Imad
    [1990] Imm AR 34 (QB) (1990) 58
R v Secretary of State for the Home Department ex p Lul Adan (QB) (1999)..................63
R v Secretary of State for the Home Department ex p Lul Omar Adan, Sittampalan
    Subaskaran and Hamid Aitseguer (CA) (1999)...........................185
R v Secretary of State for the Home Department ex p Mangal Singh (QB) (1992) 54
R v Secretary of State for the Home Department ex p Mehmet Tozlukaya (CA) (2006).........107
R v Secretary of State for the Home Department ex p Mohammed Kerrouche
    (QB) (1998)..185
R v Secretary of State for the Home Department ex p Razgar (HL) (2004)..........55, 107, 189
R v Secretary of State for the Home Department ex p Thangasara and R v Secretary of
    State for the Home Department ex p Yogathas (HL) (2002) 56, 63, 216,187
R v Secretary of State for the Home Department ex parte Senay Mehari Mohamed
    Ahmed Doreh Ali Abdi Hersi Fuat Celik Kuti Augusto (QB) (1994) 54, 58
R v Special Adjudicator ex p Linsam Kandasamy (QB) (1994) 57
R v Special Adjudicator ex parte Bekim Babatinca (QB) (1995).......................58
R v Special Adjudicator ex parte Vibulan Srikantharajah (QB) (1996).....................54
R v Special Adjudicators ex p Mehmet Turus, Adem Bostem, Awat Ammen, Adam
    Folly-Nostron, Selcuk Ururgul (QB) (1996) 62
R v Special Adjudicator ex p Ullah (HL) (2004) 55, 189
R v Uxbridge Magistrates' Court, ex p Adimi (QB) (2001)........................129, 132
RZ v Secretary of State for the Home Department (AIT) (2008) 120
Secretary of State for the Home Department v Razaq Mohd Saeid Abdu Abdel
    (Trib) (1992) 180, 181
Thayaparan Iyadurai v Secretary of State for the Home Department (CA) (1998) 63, 185

5. United States

Sale v Haitian Centers Council Inc (SC) 177

6. Canada

*Canadian Council for Refugees, Canadian Council of Churches, Amnesty International
and John Doe v R* (FC) 48, 54, 181, 187
*R v Canadian Council for Refugees, Canadian Council of Churches, Amnesty International
and John Doe* (FCA) 48, 220

Table of Treaties and Other International Instruments

1922 Arrangement with regard to the issue of Certificates of Identity to Russian Refugees . . . 10
1924 Plan for the Issue of a Certificate of Identity to Armenian Refugees 10
1926 Arrangement relating to the Issue of Identity Certificates to Russian and
Armenian Refugees 10
1928 Arrangement concerning the Extension to Other Categories of Refugees of Certain
Measures taken in favour of Russian and Armenian Refugees 10
1933 Convention relating to the International Status of Refugees 10, 174
1935 Plan for the Issue of a Certificate of Identity to Refugees from the Saar 10
1936 Provisional Arrangement concerning the Status of Refugees coming from Germany 10
1938 Convention concerning the Status of Refugees coming from Germany 10, 174
1939 Council Resolution on Refugees from Sudetenland 10
1939 Additional Protocol to the Provisional Arrangement and to the Convention
concerning the Status of Refugees coming from Germany 10
1945 Charter of the United Nations 138, 167, 264
1946 Constitution of the International Refugee Organisation 182
1948 Universal Declaration on Human Rights 16, 210, 212
1949 Convention (IV) Relative to the Protection of Civilian Persons in Time of War 204
1950 European Convention for the Protection of Human Rights and Fundamental
Freedoms 55, 98, 107, 114, 187, 188, 189, 190, 198,
230, 240–241, 242–245
1950 Statute of the Office of the High Commissioner for Refugees 12, 13, 150, 255–6
1951 Convention Relating to the Status of Refugees 9, 13–14, 37, 46–47, 56, 96,
114, 127–129, 132, 137, 174–187, 204,
214, 216–219, 223, 238, 252, 262, 282
1954 Caracas Convention on Territorial Asylum 16
1954 Convention Relating to the Status of Stateless Persons 204
1957 Convention concerning the Waiver of Passport Control at the Intra-Nordic
Frontiers 69
1959 European Agreement on the Abolition of Visas for Refugees 68
1960 Convention on the Transfer of Control of Persons to the External Frontiers of
Benelux Territory 69
1963 4th Protocol securing certain rights and freedoms other those already included in
the Convention and in the 1st Protocol thereto to the ECHR 70, 198, 212, 213
1966 Optional Protocol to the International Covenant on Civil and Political Rights 282
1966 Principles concerning Treatment of Refugees of the Asian African Legal
Consultative Committee 175
1966 UN Convention on the Elimination of all Forms of Racial
Discrimination 212, 280
1966 UN International Covenant on Civil and Political Rights 188, 212, 252, 241, 278
1967 Protocol relating to the Status of Refugees 14, 132, 261
1967 UN Declaration on Territorial Asylum 16, 21, 140, 175, 204, 209, 210
1969 American Convention on Human Rights 188, 204, 210, 212

1969   Convention governing the Specific Aspects of Refugee Problems in
        Africa 15–16, 21, 140, 175–176, 188, 204, 208, 210, 261
1969   Vienna Convention on the Law of Treaties 130
1970   Addendum to the Principles concerning Treatment of Refugees 141
1970   UN Declaration on Principles of International Law Concerning Friendly Relations
        and Cooperation among States 138
1972   Stockholm Declaration, UN Conference on the Human Environment 168
1979   Convention on the Elimination of All Forms of Discrimination Against Women 278
1981   African Charter on Human and People's Rights 210, 212
1984   Cartagena Declaration on Refugees 15, 141, 204, 261
1984   UN Convention Against Torture and Other Cruel, Inhuman or Degrading
        Treatment or Punishment 48, 188, 199–203, 208, 266
1985   Agreement between the Governments of the States of the Benelux Economic
        Union the Federal Republic of Germany and the French Republic on the Gradual
        Abolition of Checks at their Common Borders 33, 89
1989   Convention on the Rights of the Child 100, 212, 278
1990   Convention Implementing the Schengen Agreement of 14 June 1985 between the
        Governments of the States of the Benelux Economic Union, the Federal Republic
        of Germany and the French Republic on the Gradual Abolition of Checks at
        their Common Borders 33, 89–125
1990   Dublin Convention determining the State responsible for examining applications
        for asylum lodged in one of the Member States of the European
        Communities 3, 29, 35, 89–125
1990   International Convention on the Protection of the Rights of All Migrant Workers
        and Their Families 278, 282
1990   Treaty on Good-Neighborliness, Partnership and Cooperation between the Federal
        Republic of Germany and the Union of Soviet Socialist Republics 167
1991   Treaty on Good-Neighbourliness and Friendly Co-operation between Germany
        and Poland 167
1992   Agreement in relation to the reassimilation of German and Romanian Citizens
        between the Federal Republic of Germany and Romania 68
1992   Treaty on European Union signed in Maastricht 36, 42, 228, 245–246
1994   Partnership and Cooperation Agreement between the EC and their Member States of
        the one part, and the Russian Federation, of the other 72
1994   San Jose Declaration on Refugees and Displaced Persons. 204
1995   Council of Europe Framework Convention for the Protection of National
        Minorities. 168
1996   Treaty on Understanding, Cooperation and Good-Neighborliness between Hungary
        and Romania 168
1997   Treaty of Amsterdam amending the Treaty on European Union, the Treaties
        Establishing the European Community and Certain Related Acts 30, 34, 36, 43,
                                    61–62, 67, 71, 94, 143, 223–224, 232, 237, 245
1998   Protocol No. 11 to the European Convention for the Protection of Human Rights and
        Fundamental Freedoms 190
1999   Optional Protocol to the Convention on the Elimination of All Forms of
        Discrimination Against Women 282
2000   Charter of Fundamental Rights of the European Union 16, 205, 210, 242, 247–9
2000   Partnership Agreement between the members of the African, Caribbean and Pacific
        Group of States of the one part, and the European Community and its Member
        States, of the other part, signed in Cotonou 73, 144

2000   Protocol to Prevent, Supress and Punish Trafficking in Persons, especially
       Women and Children, supplementing the United Nations Convention against
       Transnational Organized Crime 204
2000   Treaty of Nice Amending the Treaty on European Union, The Treaties Establishing
       the European Communities and Certain Related Acts 36–38, 225, 228–229, 239
2001   Declaration reaffirming the commitment of signatory States to the 1951
       Convention. 206, 269
2001   Final Text of the Asian-African Legal Consultative Organization's 1966 Bangkok
       Principles on Status and Treatment of Refugees. 204
2001   San Remo Declaraton on the Principle of Non-Refoulement. .204
2001   Treaty of Nice Amending the Treaty on European Union, The Treaties Establishing the
       European Communities and Certain Related Acts
2002   Agreement Between the Government of Canada and the Government of the
       United States of America Regarding Asylum Claims Made at Land
       Borders 4, 48, 54, 134, 220
2002   Consolidated Versions of the Treaty on European Union and the Treaty on the
       Functioning of the European Union 36–37, 90, 223,
2002   International Law Commission, Articles on the Responsibility of States for
       Internationally Wrongful Acts 214, 216, 221
2004   Agreement between the European Community and the Government of Hong Kong
       Special Administrative Region of the People's Republic of China on the readmission
       of persons residing without authorization 75
2004   Agreement between the European Community and the Macao Special Administrative
       Region of the People's Republic of China on the readmission of persons residing
       without authorization 76
2004   Agreement between the European Community and the Swiss Confederation
       concerning the criteria and mechanisms for establishing the State responsible for
       examining a request for asylum lodged in a Member State or in Switzerland 94
2004   Agreement between the European Union, the European Community and the Swiss
       Confederation on the Swiss Confederation's association with the implementation,
       application and development of the Schengen Acquis 34
2004   Mexico Declaration and Plan of Action to Strengthen the International
       Protection of Refugees in Latin America 204
2004   Treaty establishing a Constitution for Europe 43, 225
2005   Agreement between the European Community and the Democratic Socialist Republic of
       Sri Lanka on the readmission of persons residing without authorization 76
2005   Agreement between the European Community and the Republic of Albania on the
       readmission of persons residing without authorization 76
2006   Agreement between the European Community and the Kingdom of Denmark extending
       to Denmark the provisions of Council Regulation (EC) No. 343/2003 establishing
       the criteria and mechanisms for determining the Member States by a third-country
       national and Council Regulation (EC) No. 2725/2000 concerning the establishment
       of 'Eurodac' for the comparison of fingerprints for the effective application of the
       Dublin Convention. 94
2007   Agreement between the European Community and the Russian Federation on
       readmission. 76
2007   Treaty of Lisbon Amending the Treaty on European Union and the Treaty Establishing
       the European Community 43, 144, 225, 227, 239, 245, 247
2008   Consolidated Versions of the Treaty on European Union and the Treaty on the
       Functioning of the European Union 205

List of Abbreviations

AFDI	Annuaire français de droit international
CAT	Convention Against Torture, and Other Cruel, Inhuman, or Degrading Treatment or Punishment
CDE	Cahiers de droit européen
CEDAW	Convention on the Elimination of All Forms of Discrimination Against Women
CERD	Convention on the Elimination of All Forms of Racial Discrimination
CPA	Comprehensive Plan of Action for Indo-Chinese Refugees
CPMW	International Convention on the Protection of the Rights of All Migrant Workers and Their Families
CRC	Convention on the Rights of the Child
CSR	Convention Relating to the Status of Refugees
DC	Dublin Convention determining the State responsible for examining applications for asylum lodged in one of the Member States of the European Communities
DR	Decisions and Reports of the European Commission of Human Rights
ECHR	European Convention for the Protection of Human Rights and Fundamental Freedoms
ECtHR	European Court of Human Rights
ECJ	Court of Justice of the European Communities
ECR	European Court Reports
ECRE	European Council on Refugees and Exiles
ECT	European Community Treaty
EHRR	European Human Rights Reports
EJML	European Journal of Migration and Law
EU	European Union
ExCom	Executive Committee of the UNHCR
GV	Gids Vreemdelingenrecht
Harv Hum Rts J	Harvard Human Rights Journal
ICCPR	International Covenant on Civil and Political Rights and Protocols thereto
ICJ	International Court of Justice
IGC	Inter-Governmental Consultations on Asylum, Refugee and Migration Policies in Europe, North America and Australia
IJRL	International Journal of Refugee Law
ILC	International Law Commission
ILR	International Law Reports
IMR	International Migration Review
InfAuslR	Information Ausländerrecht

IOM	International Organization for Migration
JRS	Journal of Refugee Studies
JuB	Jurisprudentie Bijlage Vreemdelingen Bulletin
JV	Jurisprudentie Vreemdelingenrecht
MJ	Maastricht Journal of European and Comparative Law
NAV	Nieuwsbrief Asiel- and Vluchtelingenrecht
NGO	Non-governmental Organization
NQHR	Netherlands Quarterly for Human Rights
OAU	Organisation of African Unity
RBDI	Revue belge de droit international
RdC	Recueil des Cours
RDE	Revue du droit des étrangers
RMCUE	Revue du Marché commun et de l'Union européenne
RMUE	Revue du Marché unique européen
RTDE	Revue trimestrielle de droit européen
RV	Rechtspraak Vreemdelingenrecht
SC	Schengen Implementing Convention
SEW	Tijdschrift voor Europees and economisch recht
TEU	Treaty on European Union
TVR	Tijdschrift voor Vreemdelingenrecht
UDHR	Universal Declaration of Human Rights
UNHCR	United Nations High Commissioner for Refugees
UNRIAA	United Nations Reports of International Arbitral Awards

Introduction

With the coming of the second world war, many eyes in imprisoned Europe turned hopefully—or desperately—towards the freedom of the Americas. Lisbon became the great embarkation point, but not everybody could get to Lisbon directly and so a tortuous round-about refugee trail sprang up: Paris to Marseilles, across the Mediterranean to Oran, then by train or auto or foot across the rim of Africa to Casablanca, in French Morocco. Here the fortunate ones, through money, or influence, or luck, might obtain exit visas and scurry to Lisbon, and from Lisbon to the New World. But the others wait in Casablanca.

(opening narrative, *Casablanca*, 1942)

Towards the end of the 1970s, States in the industrialized world saw a significant increase in the number of asylum seekers arriving on their territories. This trend became more pronounced in the 1980s and the 1990s and the number of asylum applications reached a peak of 690,000 in 1992.[1] Since then, however, this number has dramatically decreased by more than 50 per cent, to 338,300 applications in 2007.[2] There are various reasons for this reduction. One explanation points to the cessation of conflicts in many parts of the world.[3] Other likely factors are those related to the implementation of policies which effectively prevent asylum seekers from reaching the territories of industrialized countries, and in case they still manage to do so, prevent them from having access to refugee status determination procedures. In other words, this steep decrease is largely due to the fact that,

- many asylum seekers are stopped *en route* or at the border before having any opportunity to seek asylum;[4]

[1] See UNHCR, *The State of the World's Refugees 2006: Human Displacement in the New Millennium* (Oxford University Press, Oxford 2006) 36.

[2] UNHCR, Number of asylum seekers halved since 2001, March 2006, reporting that the number of asylum applications in 2005 was 331,600, the lowest since 1987; see also UNHCR, *Statistical Overview of Asylum Applications Lodged in Europe and Selected Non-European Countries*, 18 March 2008, 4. For further statistical information on asylum and refugee protection, see <http://www.unhcr.org/statistics.html>.

[3] See UNHCR, *The State of the World's Refugees 2006*, n 1 above, 10.

[4] In 2005, the mass deportation of migrants from the Italian Island of Lampedusa led to the lodging of complaints before the European Court of Human Rights. The Court requested information

- many have their application dismissed on procedural grounds;
- many prefer to remain in an irregular situation and renounce to seek asylum;[5]
- finally, many simply die during their perilous journey.[6]

Examples of policies restricting asylum include the imposition of visas on nationals from 'refugee producing' countries, carrier sanctions, interception on the high seas, and expedited procedures for manifestly unfounded and abusive claims.[7] Thus, while international cooperation in the refugee field traditionally focused on protection and assistance, the last two decades have been characterized by the emergence of transnational policies aimed at 'containing' refugee flows, above all on the European continent.[8]

The fact that people follow 'tortuous trails' to reach countries of refuge is not new.[9] In some cases, asylum seekers and refugees stay first in a country in their region of origin but decide to leave because they fear persecution or a threat to life or freedom in that country, or because they want to be reunited with relatives present elsewhere, because they lack a secure status, or are offered no educational or economic opportunities, or durable status and solutions.[10] They therefore decide to pursue their journey—usually without valid travel documents—and engage in so-called 'secondary movements' in search of protection and opportunities. According to the United Nations High Commissioner for Refugees (UNHCR), 'secondary' movements should only comprise situations in which an

---

from the Italian government on whether there were any asylum seekers among the migrants who were expelled using fast-track procedures, see 'Italy: the ECHR asks for information on Lampedusa deportations', *Statewatch News Online*, April 2005, available at: <http://www.statewatch.org>. See *Salem and ors v Italy*, Appl. Nos. 10171/05, 10601/05, 11593/05, and 17165/05 Decision of 11 May 2006.

[5] This hypothesis is supported by some estimates, which indicate that as many as 500,000 additional irregular migrants in Europe are entering or overstaying every year, see Parliamentary Assembly of the Council of Europe, Report of the Committee on Migration, Refugees and Population, 'Assessment of transit and processing centres as a response to mixed flows of migrants and asylum seekers' (hereafter, Council of Europe Report), 14 June 2007, para 1, see also para 7, which reports that the number of irregular migrants arriving in the Canary Islands rose from 4,700 in 2005 to 34,000 in 2006.

[6] See Directorate-General for External Policies of the Union Directorate B, 'Study: Analysis of the External Dimension of the EU's Asylum and Immigration Policies—Summary and Recommendations for the European Parliament', 8 June 2006, 4 (hereafter, Directorate Study); see also 'Spain: Record Number of Migrant Deaths', *Statewatch Bulletin*, Vol 15, No. 1, January–February 2005, available at: <http://www.statewatch.org>; see also Council of Europe Report, n 5 above, para 8, giving an estimate of about 7,000 deaths of migrants trying to reach Spain.

[7] See Chapter 1 Section 1.2 for a full outline of containment policies.

[8] This formulation was first used by A Shacknove in 'From Asylum to Containment' (1993) 5 *IJRL* 516.

[9] For examples of refugee routes to Europe, see <http://news.bbc.co.uk/hi/english/static/in_depth/world/2001/road_to_refuge/journey/map.stm>. For accounts of refugees' journeys, see <http://www.unhcr.org/news/NEWS/45d96dae4.html>.

[10] UNHCR, 'Convention Plus Issues Paper on Addressing Irregular Secondary Movements of Refugees and Asylum Seekers', FORUM/CG/SM/03, 11 March 2004, para 2, 15.

asylum seeker or refugee is moving from a country where he has sought protection, to another country.[11] However, the term 'secondary movements' is generally used by States and other international actors, such as the European Union, to also cover situations where asylum seekers have only transited for even a brief period in an intermediate country.

Secondary movements tend to be regarded as proof of the fraudulent or manifestly unfounded nature of an asylum claim. Many States, essentially in Europe and the industrialized world, have therefore developed practices, adopted regulations, or even agreed on international instruments designed to limit their obligations towards asylum seekers who have not arrived directly from their countries of origin. Accordingly, States may dismiss an asylum application on the ground that an asylum seeker has, should, or could have claimed asylum in another State which is regarded as safe, hence the commonly used formulation of 'safe third' country.[12] The safe third country concept thus seeks to allocate international legal obligations, primarily based on the Convention Relating to the Status of Refugees.[13] Many States have introduced 'safe third country' regulations in their domestic law, and the provisions of the 1990 Dublin Convention concluded between the Member States of the European Union and of its sequel, the so-called 'Dublin' Regulation adopted in 2003, rely on the same principle.

Allocating responsibility might seem commendable if asylum seekers can thereby be assured to have their claim examined substantively and if the manner in which responsibility is allocated does not overburden certain States. Yet, the arrangements and practices analysed in this study do not offer sufficient safeguards guaranteeing the protection of refugees' rights. Nor do they ensure a more equitable distribution of refugees amongst States, in accordance with the principle of solidarity and burden-sharing.[14] The aim of safe third country practices is to reduce the scope of a State's obligation to host refugees who are present on its territory or at its borders and have not come directly from their countries of origin. As such, these are instruments of containment; they limit States' obligations to examine an asylum claim, restrict the refugee's choice of asylum country, hinder movements from the region of origin, and increase the protection burden on first asylum States and those States situated near the country or region of origin of asylum seekers.

At the end of the 1970s and 1980s, legal scholars, such as Melander, Vierdag, and Weis, were the first to observe the development by some European States of

[11] Ibid. Note also that UNHCR explains at para 4 of the same document, that secondary movements can also include fully regular movements and that therefore, the phrase 'irregular secondary movements' is more accurate.

[12] 'Host third' and 'first country of asylum' were also often used. Under EC law, there is now a distinction between 'safe third country' and 'first country of asylum', see Chapter 2, Section 2.1.1.

[13] See Chapter 1, Section 1.1.3.

[14] J Milner, 'Burden Sharing', in M Gibney and R Hansen (eds) *Immigration and Asylum from 1900 to the Present* (ABC-CLIO, Santa Barbara 2005) defines 'burden-sharing' as the 'mechanism through which the diverse costs of granting asylum to refugees are more equitably divided among States', 56.

certain practices based on what was termed at the time the 'protection elsewhere' principle.[15] The end of the 1980s and 1990s saw compounded interest in this question, and most authors took a strongly critical stance against safe third country practices.[16] Only Hailbronner stood out as a qualified supporter, although he acknowledged that they should be implemented through formalized agreements.[17]

At the end of the 1990s, focus shifted to the development of harmonized legislation at the level of the European Union and to developments in Eastern European States, which were under great pressure to adopt similar policies as part of the negotiations on European Union accession.[18] The conclusion of the Canada–US Safe Third Country Agreement and the increasingly restrictive policies followed by Australia also generated serious criticisms by legal scholars.[19]

---

[15] G Melander, *Refugees in Orbit* (International University Exchange Fund, Geneva 1978); G Melander, 'Responsibility for Examining an Asylum Request' (1986) 20 *IMR* 220; P Weis, 'Refugees in Orbit' (1980) 10 *Israel Ybk on Human Rights* (Nijhoff, Dordrecht) 157; G Jaeger, *Study of Irregular Movements of Asylum Seekers and Refugees* (Working Group on Irregular Movements and Asylum Seekers, Geneva 1985); E W Vierdag, 'The Country of "First Asylum": Some European Aspects', in D A Martin (ed) *The New Asylum Seekers: Refugee Law in the 1980s* (Nijhoff, Dordrecht 1988) 73.

[16] M Kjaerum, 'The Concept of Country of First Asylum' (1992) 4 *IJRL* 514; J Bolten, 'From Schengen to Dublin' [1991] *Nederlands Juristenblad* 165; A Helton, 'Towards Harmonized Asylum Procedures in North America: The Proposed United States-Canada Memorandum of Understanding for Cooperation in the Examination of Refugee Status Claims from Nationals of Third Countries' (1993) 26 *Cornell Intl LJ* 737; J B Mus, '"Veilige" derde staten: het verbod van refoulement op de tocht?' [1994] *Nederlands Juristenblad* 1365; A Achermann and M Gattiker, 'Safe Third Countries: European Developments' (1995) 7 *IJRL* 19; R Byrne, 'Redesigning Fortress Europe: European Asylum Policy' [1996] *The Oxford International Review* (summer issue) 10; R Byrne and A Shacknove, 'The Safe Country Notion in European Asylum Law' (1996) 9 *Harv Hum Rts J* 185.

[17] K Hailbronner, 'The Concept of "Safe Country" and Expeditious Asylum Procedures: A Western European Perspective' (1993) 5 *IJRL* 31.

[18] See eg S Lavenex, *Safe Third Countries: Extending the EU Asylum and Immigration Policies to Central and Eastern Europe* (Central European University Press, New York 1999); D Bouteillet-Paquet, *L'Europe et le Droit d'Asile* (L'Harmattan, Paris 2001); H Battjes, 'A Balance Between Fairness and Efficiency? The Directive on International Protection and the Dublin Regulation' (2002) 4 *EJML* 159; R Byrne, 'Harmonization and Burden Redistribution in the Two Europes' (2003) 16 *JRS* 336–58; R Byrne, G Noll, and J Vevsted-Hansen, 'Understanding Refugee Law in an Enlarged European Union' (2004) *EJIL* 355–79; J-Y Carlier, 'Le développement d'une politique commune en matière d'asile', in P De Bruycker and C Dias Urbano de Sousa (eds), *The Emergence of a European Asylum Policy* (Bruylant, Bruxelles 2004) 1; U Brandl, 'Distribution of Asylum Seekers in Europe? Dublin II Regulation Determining the Responsibility for Examining an Asylum Application', in P De Bruycker and C Dias Urbano de Sousa (eds), *The Emergence of a European Asylum Policy* (Bruylant, Bruxelles 2004) 33; C Costello, 'The Asylum Procedures Directive and the Proliferation of Safe Third Country Practices: Deterrence, Deflection and the Dismantling of International Protection?' (2005) 7 *EJML* 35; C Costello, 'The European Asylum Procedures Directive in Legal Context' UNHCR New Issues in Refugee Research Paper No. 134, November 2006; O Ferguson Sidorenko, *The Common European Asylum System* (TMC Asser Press, The Hague 2007).

[19] See eg N Alburquerque Abell, 'The Safe Third Country Concept: Deflection in Europe and Its Implications for Canada' (1995) 14 *Refuge* 1, and 'Safe Country Provisions in Canada and in the European Union: A Critical Assessment' (1997) 31 *IMR* 569; C Cutler, 'The US-Canada Safe Third Country Agreement: Slamming the Door on Refugees' (2004) 11 *ILSA J Intl & Comp L* 121; A Moore, 'Unsafe in America: A Review of the US–Canada Safe Third Country Agreement' (2007) 47 *Santa Clara LR* 201, 208–9; P Mathew, 'Safe for Whom? The Safe Third Country Concepts Finds a Home in Australia', Paper given at the 7th International Research and Advisory Panel (IRAP) of the

Another strand of research has sought to analyse these developments from a wider perspective, by considering ways to comprehensively address secondary movements and the crisis of 'protection' and improve burden-sharing and solidarity.[20] Finally, a number of scholars have discussed the legality of these mechanisms under public international law,[21] which is the focus of the present volume.

The argument presented here is that safe third country practices challenge the very foundations of the international refugee regime, which is based on a collective endeavour and commitment to protect refugees, a collective responsibility of States as members of the international community which results from the unwillingness and/or inability of the country of origin to provide such protection. In essence, safe third country practices increase the risk of violations of States' obligations towards refugees, and have a negative impact on inter-State relations. By allowing States to dismiss an asylum claim on the ground that another State could be responsible, safe third country practices raise the risk of *refoulement* and of violations of other international obligations and curtail the fundamental

---

International Association for the Study of Forced Migration (IASFM) 8–12 January 2001 Johannesburg (on file with the author); S Taylor, 'Australia's "Safe Third Country" Provisions Their Impact on Australia's Fulfillment of Its Non-Refoulement Obligations' (1996) 15 *University of Tasmania LR* 196; S Taylor, 'Protection Elsewhere/Nowhere' (2006) 18 *IJRL* 283.

[20] See eg P Schuck, 'Refugee Burden-Sharing: A Modest Proposal' (1997) 22 *Yale J Intl L* 243, 276; J C Hathaway and A Neve, 'Making International Refugee Law Relevant Again: A Proposal for Collectivized and Solution-Oriented Protection' (1997) 10 *Harv Hum Rts J* 115; A Hans and A Suhrke, 'Responsibility-Sharing', in J C Hathaway (ed), *Reconceiving International Refugee Law* (Nijhoff, The Hague [etc] 1997) 83; G Noll, *Negotiating Asylum, the EU Acquis, Extraterritorial Protection and the Common Market of Deflection* (Martinus Nijhoff, The Hague [etc] 2000); E Thielemann, 'Editorial Introduction to Special Issue on European Burden-Sharing and Forced Migration' (2003) 16 *JRS* 225–35; S Kneebone and F Rawlings-Sanaei, 'Introduction: Regionalism as a Response to a Global Challenge', in S Kneebone and F Rawlings-Sanaei (eds), *New Regionalism and Asylum Seekers* (Berghahn Books, New York 2007) 1; M Gibney, 'Forced Migration, Engineered Regionalism and Justice Between States', in S Kneebone and F Rawlings-Sanaei (eds), *New Regionalism and Asylum Seekers* (Berghahn Books, New York 2007) 57; A Betts, 'Towards a Mediterranean Solution? Implications for the Region of Origin' (2006) 18 *IJRL* 652.

[21] J Crawford and P Hyndman, 'Three Heresies in the Application of the Refugee Convention' (1989) 2 *IJRL* 155; S Blay and A Zimmermann, 'Recent Changes in German Refugee Law: A Critical Assessment' (1994) 88 *AJIL* 361; R Marx, 'Non-Refoulement, Access to Procedures, and Responsibility for Determining Refugee Claims' (1995) 7 *IJRL* 96; G S Goodwin-Gill, 'The Protection of Refugees and the Safe Third Country Rule in International Law', in *Asylum Law: Report and Papers Delivered at the First International Judicial Conference on Asylum Law and Procedures Held at Inner Temple, London, 1 and 2 December, 1995* (London, 1996) 89; J Henkel, 'Völkerrechtliche Aspekte des Konzepts des sicheren Drittstaates', in K Barwig and W Brill (eds), *Aktuelle asyltechtlichen Probleme der gerichtlichen Entscheidungspraxis in Deutschland, Österreich und der Schweiz* (Nomos, Baden Baden 1996) 141; N Albuquerque Abell, 'The Compatibility of Readmission Agreements with the 1951 Convention relating to the Status of Refugees' (1999) 11 *IJRL* 60; S Legomsky, 'Secondary Refugee Movement and the Return of Asylum Seekers to Third Countries: The Meaning of Effective Protection' (2003) *IJRL* 567; H Battjes, *European Asylum Law and International Law* (Nijhoff, Leiden [etc] 2006); M-T Gil-Bazo, 'The Practice of Mediterranean States in the Context of the EU's Justice and Home Affairs External Dimension: The Safe Third Country Concept Revisited' (2006) 18 *IJRL* 571; M Foster, 'Protection Elsewhere: The Legal Implications of Requiring Refugees to Seek Protection in Another State' (2007) 28 *Michigan J of Intl L* 223.

right of individuals to seek asylum from persecution. In terms of inter-State relations, the assertion that the brief—and usually irregular—transit of an asylum seeker on a State's territory may as such be sufficient to establish the existence of a jurisdictional link between that State and the asylum seeker remains highly contentious. There is also growing concern that safe third country practices create disproportionate burdens for those States closest to the countries of origin of asylum seekers. The analysis of safe third country practices in light of States' obligations under public international law will thus suggest that safe third country practices, in their current scope and modalities of application, raise serious problems of legality.

The present study also seeks to expose major gaps existing in the supervision of States' obligations under international refugee law. At present, the Court of Justice of the European Communities is the only supranational judicial organ which is competent to rule on the interpretation of the Refugee Convention, in accordance with the provisions of Title IV of the EC Treaty as amended by the 1997 Treaty of Amsterdam. However, the geographical expansion of safe third country practices justifies the need to approach this question not only within a regional perspective, but also at the global level. The strengthening of international supervisory mechanisms is therefore advocated as a means to address the protection gaps resulting from the application of safe third country practices.

Some will comment that the feasibility of such endeavour seems particularly doubtful in the current international climate. The purpose of the present contribution, however, is not to lay down a detailed proposal for the establishment of an international refugee monitoring mechanism, but to offer a range of possible options for discussion, with a view to enhance States' compliance with their obligations under international refugee law.

Structure

The volume is divided into seven chapters. Chapters 1 to 3 retrace the origins, elaboration and implementation of safe third country practices and arrangements allocating responsibility amongst States. Chapters 4 and 5 consider their validity under public international law, and finally, Chapters 6 and 7 assess regional and international supervision of States' obligations under international refugee law.

Chapter 2 recalls the historical background to the development of responsibility allocation and safe third country practices. It begins with an overview of the fundamental concepts and instruments of international refugee law, and proceeds with a description of the changes which affected refugee flows at the end of the 1970s and led to the progressive decline of protection standards and the development of restrictive refugee policies, including an analysis of the failed UN Conference on territorial asylum and of the discussions which took place within the Executive Committee of UNHCR. Developments at the regional level are also covered, namely, the negotiations of the two draft agreements on responsibility for examining an asylum request prepared by the 'Ad Hoc Committee on the Legal Aspects of Asylum and Refugees' of the Council of Europe (CAHAR), and the gradual rise to prominence of the European Community in the asylum and migration fields.

Chapter 2 examines the operation of safe third country practices and readmission agreements. The first section identifies the key elements of safe third country practices, based on an analysis of the 2005 asylum procedures Directive as well as of relevant practice, primarily in the United Kingdom and Germany. The second section reviews the main features of readmission agreements, which are used to ensure the implementation of safe third country practices, and are a crucial component of the external dimension of the EU's migration and asylum policies. The final section consists of a brief examination of proposals on extraterritorial processing that are presented as a means to tackle secondary movements of refugees.

Chapter 3 is devoted to a study of the 2003 'Dublin' Regulation determining the State responsible for examining applications for asylum lodged in one of the Member States of the European Communities. The criteria for the determination of the responsible State, as well as the procedural aspects of the operation of the 'Dublin' regime, are analysed with a view to evaluate the Regulation's effectiveness.

Chapters 4 and 5 present an analysis of safe third country practices under international law. Two fundamental issues are addressed: the impact on inter-State relations, and on the rights of refugee and asylum seekers. Chapter 4 examines whether States should be allowed to remove an asylum seeker on the sole basis of his or her transit through another State. It then discusses the legal relevance of the principles of solidarity and burden-sharing and good-neighbourliness in relation to safe third country practices.

Chapter 5 argues that the legality of safe third country practices from the standpoint of States' international obligations towards refugees is subject to important qualifications. To this end, a detailed review of key international refugee law obligations, primarily the principle of *non-refoulement,* is conducted. The prohibition of *non-refoulement* in Article 3 of the 1984 UN Convention Against Torture and Other Cruel, Inhuman or Degrading Treatment or Punishment, and the construction of Article 3 of the European Convention on the Protection of Human Rights and Fundamental Freedoms adopted by its organs, the Commission and the Court, are then analysed. Finally, the right to seek and enjoy asylum from persecution and the right to leave one's country, as well as other relevant international legal obligations, are also examined.

Chapters 6 and 7 evaluate the scope and quality of existing supervisory mechanisms of international refugee law obligations. Chapter 6 examines the situation prevailing at the level of the European Union. The amendments brought by the Treaty of Amsterdam provide for the competence of the Court of Justice of the

European Communities to rule on the interpretation and validity of measures adopted in accordance with Title IV ECT, including asylum measures.

Chapter 7 addresses the issue of supervision at the international level. A review of supervisory mechanisms designed to monitor States' compliance with their international obligations towards refugees is presented. The review builds on a classification distinguishing between three different types of international supervision: supervision by or on behalf of international organizations; supervision by States; and supervision by individuals. The second and final section examines ways to strengthen supervisory mechanisms under international refugee law.

1

Origins and Developments of Arrangements to Allocate Responsibility for the Protection of Refugees

The international community's recognition of its collective responsibility to protect refugees originated at the end of World War I and reached its high point at the level of specific treaties with the adoption of the 1951 Convention Relating to the Status of Refugees and of its 1967 Protocol.[1]

In the 1970s, important changes in the nature and scale of refugee flows led to the emergence of an increasingly restrictive discourse in industrialized States, and to the progressive implementation of policies of containment. Thus, the 'protection elsewhere' concept, which provided that asylum should not be refused solely because it could be sought from another State except where there were close links or a connection with such other State, was gradually interpreted so as to allow States to dismiss an asylum application, on the ground that the refugee could have claimed asylum elsewhere. The development of policies seeking to limit the arrival of asylum seekers was particularly striking on the European continent, where the rights-based approach of the Council of Europe was progressively eclipsed by the European Union's security driven discourse.

This chapter begins with an overview of the fundamental concepts and instruments of the international legal framework for refugee protection and proceeds with a historical analysis of the initiatives taken at the global and regional levels to address secondary movements of refugees, including an examination of the 1977 UN Conference on territorial asylum, of the discussions within the Executive Committee of UNHCR, and of the negotiations on a convention on responsibility to examine an asylum request within the Council of Europe. The origins and development of European Union policies on asylum will complete this review.

---

[1] Convention Relating to the Status of Refugees (adopted 28 July 1951, entered into force 22 April 1954) 189 UNTS 150 (hereafter, CSR or Refugee Convention). Protocol relating to the Status of Refugees of 31 January 1967 (1967) 606 UNTS 267 No. 8791.

1.1 Fundamental Concepts

1.1.1 The international legal framework of refugee protection: historical background

The refugee question emerged as an international legal issue in the nineteenth century, with the development of extradition treaties and the principle of the non-extradition of political offenders.[2] Yet it was only at the end of World War I that the rising number of displaced populations and the uncertainty of their legal status led to the development of new instruments of protection by the international community.[3] Early legal instruments generally provided for the issuance of travel documents and applied to specific categories of refugees, on the basis of their ethnic origin, the failure of protection by the government of their country of origin, and the fact that they had not acquired the nationality of any other country.[4] The 1930s saw the adoption of additional instruments dealing with refugees from the Saar,[5] from Germany,[6] from the Sudetenland,[7] and from Austria,[8] as well as the conclusion of the first international agreement of general application.[9] The 1933 Convention Relating to the International Status of Refugees expressly restricted expulsion; it also included provisions on the enjoyment of civil rights, as well as

---

[2] M Bettati, *L'asile politique en question* (Presses universitaires de France, Paris 1985) 33.

[3] Ibid, 33.

[4] See The Arrangement with Regard to the Issue of Certificates of Identity to Russian Refugees of 5 July 1922 (1922) 13 LNTS 237 No. 355; Plan for the Issue of a Certificate of Identity to Armenian Refugees of 31 May 1924 LoN Doc C.L.72 (a) 1924; Arrangement Relating to the Issue of Identity Certificates to Russian and Armenian Refugees of 12 May 1926 (1929) 89 LNTS 47 No. 2004; Arrangement Concerning the Extension to Other Categories of Refugees of Certain Measures taken in favour of Russian and Armenian Refugees of 30 June 1928, which extended international legal protection to Assyrians, Assyro-Chaldeans, and Turks 'Friends of the Allies', (1929) 89 LNTS 63 No. 2006. For an overview of these historical developments, see J C Hathaway, 'The Evolution of Refugee Status in International Law: 1920–1950' (1984) 33 *ICLQ* 348, 350–7; for a description of the specific rights granted, see A Grahl-Madsen, 'The Emergent International Law Relating to Refugees', in *The Refugee Problem on Universal, Regional and National Level* (Institute of Public International Law and International Relations, Thessaloniki 1987) 163, 178.

[5] Plan for the Issue of a Certificate of Identity to Refugees from the Saar of 24 May 1935 (1935) LoN Official Journal 633 No. 5393.

[6] Provisional Arrangement Concerning the Status of Refugees coming from Germany of 4 July 1936 (1936–1937) 171 LNTS 75 No. 3952; Convention Concerning the Status of Refugees coming from Germany of 10 February 1938 (1938) 192 LNTS 59 No. 4461.

[7] Council Resolution on Refugees from Sudetenland of 17 January 1939 (1939) 20 LoN Official Journal 73.

[8] Additional Protocol to the Provisional Arrangement and to the Convention Concerning the Status of Refugees Coming from Germany of 14 September 1939 (1939) 198 LNTS 141 No. 4634.

[9] Convention Relating to the International Status of Refugees of 28 October 1933 (1935–1936) 159 LNTS 199 No. 3663.

social and economic rights,[10] but its significance was limited by the small number of State parties, and the formulation of broad reservations to its provisions.[11]

A flurry of international organizations were also established during this period to provide assistance to refugees. The Office of the International Commissioner for Refugees was created with a mandate on the legal status and the coordination of relief operations,[12] and replaced in 1929 by the International Nansen Office for Refugees which carried out its work under the direction of the League of Nations.[13] In 1933, a High Commission for Refugees Coming from Germany was established, which had originally an autonomous status from the League.[14] The activities of the Nansen Office and the High Commission for Refugees Coming from Germany were then taken up by the High Commission for Refugees, established within the League of Nations in 1938.[15] Following the Evian Conference of 1938, an Intergovernmental Committee on Refugees, comprising 27 State representatives, was created at the initiative of the United States, which had not joined the League of Nations,[16] to provide aid to refugees from Germany.[17]

This multiplication of international bodies continued throughout the 1940s. During World War II, refugee relief and assistance was organized through the High Commission for Refugees and the Intergovernmental Committee for Refugees, which was headed by the High Commissioner.[18] International cooperation in the refugee field was also pursued by allied States, through the establishment in 1943 of the United Nations Relief and Rehabilitation Administration (UNRRA), a temporary organization whose main task was relief assistance and the repatriation of millions of displaced persons in Europe.[19] By 1947, there remained about 633,000 refugees for whom responsibility was transferred to a new organization,[20] the International Refugee Organization (IRO).[21] In addition to this refugee load, the IRO provided assistance to refugees formerly protected by the High Commissioner of the League of Nations, the Intergovernmental Committee for Refugees, and

---

[10] L Holborn, *Refugees: A Problem of Our Time, The Work of the United Nations High Commissioner for Refugees, 1951–1972* (Scarecrow Press, Metuchen 1975) Vol I, 15.

[11] Bettati, n 2 above, 38; Holborn, n 10 above, 16–17; Grahl-Madsen, n 4 above, 180.

[12] Hathaway, n 4 above, 351.

[13] Holborn, n 10 above, 12. See also G S Goodwin-Gill, 'The Politics of Refugee Protection' (2008) 27 *RSQ* 8, 11–12.

[14] Holborn, n 10 above, 14; G Melander, 'Further Development of International Refugee Law', in *The Refugee Problem on Universal, Regional and National Level* (Institute of Public International Law and International Relations, Thessaloniki 1987) 473, 474.

[15] G Jaeger, 'Les Nations Unies et les réfugiés' [1989] *RBDI* 18, 24.

[16] Jaeger, n 15 above, 25.

[17] Grahl-Madsen, n 4 above, 181.

[18] Jaeger, n 15 above, 36.

[19] G S Goodwin-Gill and J McAdam, *The Refugee in International Law* (3rd edn, Oxford University Press, Oxford 2007) 18, 423; Jaeger, n 15 above, 37.

[20] V Türk, *Das Flüchtlingshochkommissariat der Vereinten Nationen (UNHCR)* (Dunckler & Humblot, Berlin 1992) 15.

[21] GA Res 62 (I), 15 December 1946.

to 'new' refugees of the period 1947–1950, amounting to 1.6 million people.[22] IRO's main achievement was the organization of the large-scale resettlement of about one million refugees.[23] Only 18 out of the 54 members of the United Nations continued to fund it, however, as it faced accusations that it was serving the political and economic interests of the West in the emerging cold war.[24]

1.1.2 The establishment of the United Nations High Commissioner for Refugees

In 1950, the Office of the UNHCR was established by the General Assembly as a subsidiary organ pursuant to Article 22 of the Charter, originally for a period of three years.[25] Its mandate was then extended every five years,[26] until 2004 when the time limit on UNHCR's mandate was eventually removed.[27] Today, UNHCR is assisting and protecting some 21.5 million 'persons of concern' around the world and has a budget of about US$ 1 billion,[28] for which the regular UN budget only covers UNHCR's administrative expenditures, while all other expenditures are financed through voluntary contributions.[29]

The High Commissioner is elected by the General Assembly on the nomination of the Secretary General,[30] and is under the obligation to 'follow policy directives given by the General Assembly or the Economic and Social Council',[31] to which s/he reports annually. The nature of the work carried out by the High Commissioner is described in paragraph 2 of the Statute:

The work of the High Commissioner shall be of an entirely non-political character; it shall be humanitarian and social and shall relate, as a rule, to groups and categories of refugees.

The Statute also defines who is to be protected by the Office of the High Commissioner:

Any person who is outside the country of his nationality, or if he has no nationality, the country of his former habitual residence, because he has or had a well-founded fear of persecution by reason of his race, religion, nationality or political opinion and is unable, or, because of such fear, is unwilling to avail himself of the protection of the government of the

---

[22] Jaeger, n 15 above, 41.
[23] Goodwin-Gill and McAdam, n 19 above, 424–5; Jaeger, n 15 above, 46.
[24] Goodwin-Gill and McAdam, n 19 above, 425.
[25] Para 5 of the Statute, annexed to UNGA Res 428 (V), 14 December 1950.
[26] Jaeger, n 15 above, 50.
[27] See UNGA Res 58/153, 24 February 2004, para 9.
[28] The most updated information is available at: <http://www.unhcr.org/statistics.html>; UNHCR, Annual Programme Budget 2007, UN Doc A/AC.96/1026, 1 September 2006, para 43.
[29] Para 20 of the Statute; UNHCR, Annual Programme Budget 2007, n 28 above, para 14.
[30] Para 13 of the Statute.
[31] Para 4 of the Statute.

country of his nationality, or if he has no nationality, to return to the country of his former habitual residence.[32]

This definition is similar to the definition enshrined in the Refugee Convention examined below, except for the fact that it does not contain temporal and geographical limitations.[33]

The primary functions of the new international refugee agency were intended to be the provision of international protection and the search for permanent solutions to the problems of refugees.[34] The broad language of paragraph 9 of the Statute has nonetheless allowed UNHCR to extend its functions beyond its original mandate, including preventive and in country protection.[35]

One of the key organs of the international refugee regime is the Executive Committee, established in 1957 as a formally independent body[36] to give policy directives to the High Commissioner and to States, which are presented in the form of non-binding conclusions. These 'soft law' instruments have substantially contributed to the development of the international normative framework of refugee protection,[37] as they may constitute evidence of the existence of customary law or of its emergence.[38]

1.1.3 The 1951 Geneva Convention Relating to the Status of Refugees

The Refugee Convention is the key conventional instrument relating to the protection of refugees and marked the highest point in the development of international refugee law since the first Nansen arrangement of 1922. As in the inter-war arrangements, the essential condition of refugees is their presence outside the territory of their country of origin and their lack of protection by any State.[39] However, the Convention added to these criteria the condition of a well-founded fear of persecution based on one or more of five grounds: race, religion, nationality,

---

[32] Para 6(B) of the Statute.

[33] Note also that the definition does not provide for membership to a particular social group and that the mandate also covered specific categories of refugees whose international protection was provided under the various inter-war arrangements; see para 6(A) of the Statute.

[34] See para 1 of the Statute. A more detailed examination of UNHCR's function of international protection will be carried out in Chapter 7.

[35] See UNHCR, Note on International Protection, UN Doc A/AC.96/799, 25 August 1992, para 14–16; Jaeger, n 15 above, 54–7; P Kourula, *Broadening the Edges, Refugee Definition and International Protection Revisited* (Nijhoff, Boston 1997) 177–83.

[36] See UNGA Res 1166 (XII) on international assistance to refugees within the mandate of the UN, 26 November 1957, para 5; J Sztucki, 'The Conclusions on the International Protection of Refugees Adopted by the Executive Committee of the UNHCR Programme' (1989) 1 *IJRL* 285. The Executive Committee now comprises 76 States and holds an annual plenary session; on UNHCR and the Executive Committee; see Chapter 7.

[37] Sztucki, n 36 above, 303; JC Hathaway, *The Rights of Refugees under International Law* (Cambridge University Press, Cambridge 2005) 113–14.

[38] Sztucki, n 36 above, 307; Jaeger, n 15 above, 60.

[39] P Weis, 'Legal Aspects of the 1951 Geneva Convention' (1953) 30 *BYIL* 478, 480.

political opinion, and membership of a social group. Refugee status determination is carried out by State parties which are free to institute procedures they see appropriate for this purpose.[40] Article 1 sets out the conditions for granting the status of refugee under the Convention, for the exclusion of individuals from such protection, as well for the cessation of refugee status. Article 1(A) reads:

A. For the purposes of the present Convention, the term 'refugee' shall apply to any person who:

(1) Has been considered a refugee under the Arrangements of 12 May 1926 and 30 June 1928 or under the Conventions of 28 October 1933 and 10 February 1938, the Protocol of 14 September 1939 or the Constitution of the International Refugee Organization; Decisions of non-eligibility taken by the International Refugee Organization during the period of its activities shall not prevent the status of refugee being accorded to persons who fulfil the conditions of paragraph 2 of this section;

(2) As a result of events occurring before 1 January 1951 and owing to well-founded fear of being persecuted for reasons of race, religion, nationality, membership of a particular social group or political opinion, is outside the country of his nationality and is unable or, owing to such fear, is unwilling to avail himself of the protection of that country; or who, not having a nationality and being outside the country of his former habitual residence as a result of such events, is unable or, owing to such fear, is unwilling to return to it.

As is made clear by this provision, the Convention was originally conceived to provide a legal framework for the protection of European refugees from World War II. Events of the early 1960s, in particular the struggles for independence of colonized nations, demonstrated the limits of the original instrument and the temporal and geographical limitations were removed in 1967 through the signing of an additional Protocol.[41]

The Convention lays down the rights that State parties shall accord to refugees, depending on their 'simple' presence, lawful presence, lawful residence, or habitual residence.[42] The fundamental obligations set out in Articles 31 and 33 CSR obviously apply to recognized and prima facie refugees alike, that is, on the basis of their 'simple presence', otherwise their purpose would be disregarded.[43] Article 33 expresses the core principle of the Refugee Convention: it proscribes the expulsion or return (*refoulement*) in any manner whatsoever of refugees to the frontiers of territories where their life or liberty would be at risk on the grounds laid down in Article 1. Article 31 CSR, while less fundamental, is of particular relevance for the present study as it prohibits the imposition of penalties for the illegal entry of refugees arriving directly from a territory where their life or liberty is threatened, in accordance with the terms of Article 1 CSR.

---

[40] A Grahl-Madsen, *The Status of Refugees in International Law* (Sijthoff, Leiden 1966) Vol I, 333.

[41] Jaeger, n 15 above, 79. Art 1.B(1) of the Refugee Convention specifies that 'events occurring before 1 January 1951' shall be understood to mean either 'events occurring in Europe before 1 January 1951' or 'events occurring in Europe or elsewhere before 1 January 1951'. As of 1 October 2008, the Refugee Convention and/or its 1967 Protocol had been signed by 147 States.

[42] Goodwin-Gill and McAdam, n 19 above, 524.

[43] A Grahl-Madsen, *The Status of Refugees in International Law* (Sijthoff, Leiden 1972) Vol II, 224.

Apart from the 1967 Protocol, the conventional instruments which followed the Refugee Convention were concluded at the regional level. The more notable example is the conclusion of the 1969 OAU Convention Governing the Specific Aspects of Refugee Problems in Africa, which adopted an extended definition of the refugee, taking account of the peculiarities of forced migration on this continent:[44]

The term 'refugee' shall also apply to every person who, owing to external aggression, occupation, foreign domination or events seriously disturbing public order in either part or the whole of his country of origin or nationality, is compelled to leave his place of habitual residence in order to seek refuge in another place outside his country of origin or nationality.

A broader definition of the refugee has also been endorsed in the Cartagena Declaration adopted by the representatives of Central-American countries,[45] in non-binding instruments of the Council of Europe,[46] and finally by the United Nations, inter alia, through the expansion of UNHCR's mandate.[47] Western countries have also developed alternative forms of protection, known under the generic term of complementary protection, for individuals who are in need of protection but do not fulfil the conditions set out in Article 1 CSR.[48]

1.1.4 Refugees and asylum

While a normative definition of the refugee only appeared with the emergence of nation states in the nineteenth century, the practice of granting asylum is an

---

[44] Article I(2) Convention Governing the Specific Aspects of Refugee Problems in Africa, 10 September 1969 (1976) 1001 UNTS 45 No. 14691; See Melander, 'Further Development of International Refugee Law', n 14 above, 483–6; E Arboleda, 'Refugee Definition in Africa and Latin America: The Lessons of Pragmatism' (1991) 3 *IJRL* 185; J C Hathaway, *The Law of Refugee Status* (Butterworths, Toronto 1991) 17.

[45] Para 3 of the Cartagena Declaration on Refugees (19–22 November 1984) OAS/Ser.L/V/II.66, Doc. 10, rev.1, p 190–3 reprinted in UNHCR, *Collection of International Instruments and Other Legal Texts Concerning Refugees and Displaced Persons* Vol II (UNHCR, Geneva 1995) 206.

[46] Recommendation 817 (1977) adopted on 7 October 1977 on certain aspects of the right of asylum adopted by the Parliamentary Assembly of the Council of Europe reprinted in Ad Hoc Committee of Experts on the legal aspects of territorial asylum, refugees, and stateless persons (CAHAR), *Selected Texts Concerning Territorial Asylum and Refugees Adopted within the Council of Europe*, CAHAR (98) 6, March 1998, Vol II, 18, para 11.

[47] Goodwin-Gill and McAdam, n 19 above, 29.

[48] See M Kjaerum, 'Temporary Protection in Europe in the 1990s' (1994) 6 *IJRL* 444; K Kerber, 'Temporary Protection: An Assessment of the Harmonisation of Policies of European Union Member States' (1997) 9 *IJRL* 453; J McAdam, 'The European Union Qualification Directive: The Creation of a Subsidiary Protection Regime' (2005) 17 *IJRL* 461; J McAdam, *Complementary Protection in International Refugee Law* (Oxford University Press, Oxford 2007); Council Directive 2004/83 EC of 29 April 2004 on minimum standards for the qualification and status of third country nationals as refugees or as persons who otherwise need international protection and the content of the protection granted (hereafter, qualification Directive) [2004] OJ L304/12.

ancient tradition.[49] The definition of the Institute of International Law conveys in the broadest manner the modern meaning of the concept:

The term asylum means the protection which a State grants on its territory or in some other place under the control of certain of its organs, to a person who comes to seek it.[50]

If a right to be granted asylum is recognized in some domestic legal systems,[51] international law knows only of a right to seek and enjoy asylum from persecution,[52] meaning therefore that the granting of asylum remains a discretionary act of the State.[53] This was made apparent when the drafting committee of the Refugee Convention decided that it would not address the question of asylum,[54] making only brief mention of it in the Preamble.[55] The question of asylum was submitted to the International Law Commission in 1959, and eventually transferred to the UN Commission on Human Rights, whose work led to the adoption of the 1967 UN Declaration on Territorial Asylum by the General Assembly.[56] The convening

---

[49] See A M Kamanda, *Territorial Asylum and the Protection of Political Refugees in Public International Law* (Carnegie Endowment for International Peace / UNHCR 1971) 3–34; S P Sinha, *Asylum and International Law* (Nijhoff, The Hague 1971) 3–20; L B Koziebrodski, *Le Droit d'asile* (Sijthoff, Leyden 1962) 13–24; Grahl-Madsen, *The Status of Refugees in International Law* Vol I, n 40 above, 9–12; F Morgenstern, 'The Right of Asylum' (1949) 26 *BYIL* 326; P Weis, 'The United Nations Declaration on Territorial Asylum' (1969) 7 *Canadian Ybk of Intl L* (University of British Columbia Press, Vancouver) 92, 118–20; Melander, 'Further Development of International Refugee Law', n 14 above, 476–83.

[50] Article 1, Institute of International Law, Bath Session, Annuaire 1 (1950) 167.

[51] In Germany, see J Krais and C Tausch, *Asylrecht und Asylverfahren, Rechtsstellung der Flüchtlinge, Anerkennungsverfahren, Rechtschutz Mit praktischen Materialen* (Beck, München 1995) 1–14; in France, see C Norek and F Doumic-Doublet, *Le droit d'asile en France* (Presses universitaires de France, Paris 1989) 35–8.

[52] Article 14 Universal Declaration on Human Rights GA Res 217 (III), 10 December 1948; Arts 1–4 of the Caracas Convention on Territorial Asylum, 28 March 1954 OAS Official Records, OEA/Ser.X/1 reprinted in UNHCR, *Collection of International Instruments and Other Legal Texts Concerning Refugees and Displaced Persons* (UNHCR, Geneva 1995) Vol II, 185; Art II of the 1969 OAU Convention, n 44 above; Resolution (67) 14 of the Committee of Ministers of the Council of Europe on Asylum to Persons in Danger of Persecution of 29 June 1967 reprinted in CAHAR, *Selected texts concerning territorial asylum and refugees adopted within the Council of Europe*, CAHAR (98) 6 March 1998, Vol I, 32. Note, however, that the Charter of Fundamental Rights of the European Union proclaimed on 7 December 1999 by the president of the European Commission, the president of the European Parliament, and the president of the Council of Ministers [2000] OJ C364/1, recognizes under Art 18 a right 'to be granted asylum with due respect for the rules of the Geneva Convention of 28 July 1951 and the Protocol of 31 January 1967 relating to the status of refugees and in accordance with the Treaty establishing the European Community'. On the right to seek and enjoy asylum, see Chapter 5, Section 5.2.1.

[53] Para 3 of the 1967 UN Declaration on Territorial Asylum UNGA Res 2312 (XXII), 14 December 1967; Weis, 'The United Nations Declaration on Territorial Asylum', n 49 above, 137–9.

[54] Goodwin-Gill and McAdam, n 19 above, 362.

[55] Recital 4.

[56] n 53 above; Goodwin-Gill and McAdam, n 19 above, 363; Weis, 'The United Nations Declaration on Territorial Asylum', n 49 above, 97–9.

of a conference to discuss the adoption of a convention on territorial asylum in 1977 was the last attempt at regulating asylum under international law.[57]

The concept of asylum remains nevertheless central to the refugee paradigm. As stated by Goodwin-Gill and McAdam:

> What cannot be ignored however is the close relationship existing between the issue of refugee status and the principle of *non-refoulement*, on the one hand, and the concept of asylum, on the other hand. These three elements are, as it were, all links in the chain between the refugee's flight and his attainment of a permanent solution.[58]

In fact the notion of asylum seeker is commonly used to identify refugees whose formal status has not yet been recognized. This semantic slip, which originates from domestic legal systems, reflects an approach where asylum remains the primary institution.[59]

1.2 The Refugee Situation at the End of the 1970s

The 1970s saw important changes both in the nature of refugee flows and in States' policies. Socio-economic concerns following the 1973 oil crisis,[60] combined with growing unease about the potential social tensions arising from the presence of large migrant populations and mounting security concerns related to the rise of terrorist activities, led to the adoption of more restrictive regulations throughout Europe.[61] These developments coincided with an increase in the number of refugees and a geographical spread to most parts of the world, caused by the progress of international transport and communication.[62]

In 1975, a document of the Council of Europe on de facto refugees estimated that for a total number of 30,000 refugees arriving in Europe, 26,000 refugees came from developing countries,[63] and would either arrive on their own, or use

---

[57] See below Section 1.2.2.

[58] Goodwin-Gill and McAdam, n 19 above, 357.

[59] Jaeger, n 15 above, 62.

[60] S Collinson, *Europe and International Migration* (Pinter, London 1993) 53; US Committee for Refugees, *The Asylum Challenge to Western Nations*, December 1984, 3.

[61] Collinson, n 60 above, 54; S Stanton Russell, C B Keely, and B P Christian, *Multilateral Diplomacy to Harmonize Asylum Policy in Europe: 1984–1993* (Institute for the Study of International Migration, Washington DC, 2000) 8. For an analysis of these continuing trends, see E Feller, 'Asylum, Migration and Refugee Protection: Realities, Myths and the Promise of Things to Come' (2006) 18 *IJRL* 509, 518–20.

[62] See Report to the Parliamentary Assembly of the Council of Europe on the situation of de facto refugees by M Dankert and Forni Doc. 3642, 5 August 1975, 4; A R Zohlberg, A Suhrke, and S Aguayo, *Escape from Violence, Conflict and the Refugee Crisis in the Developing World* (Oxford University Press, Oxford 1989) 229; M Gibney, 'Beyond the Bounds of Responsibility: Western States and Measures to Prevent the Arrival of Refugees', Global Migration Perspectives Paper No. 22, January 2005, 4–5.

[63] Report on the situation of de facto refugees, n 62 above; G Loescher, *Beyond Charity, International Cooperation and the Global Refugee Crisis* (Oxford University Press, Oxford 1993) 93.

illegal channels of migration.[64] According to the same document, refugees who used illegal smuggling networks would either get forged identity documents or destroy their original travel documents,[65] a phenomenon which, according to data in some European countries concerned between 50% and 80% of claimants.[66] Faced with the doubling of the number of asylum seekers between 1980–84 and 1985–89,[67] Western governments responded by further restricting the opportunity to seek asylum,[68] devising a range of policies that may be outlined as follows:

(1) Measures to restrict access to States' territories through the imposition of fines on companies transporting undocumented aliens,[69] visas on nationals from refugee producing countries,[70] the posting of immigration officers abroad,[71] and interdiction at sea;[72]

(2) Measures to restrict access to asylum procedures and judicial remedies, through the application of strict time limits for the lodging of asylum claims;[73] the

---

[64] Loescher, n 63 above, 93; Zohlberg, Suhrke, and Aguayo, n 62 above, 279.

[65] See Ad Hoc Committee of Experts on the Legal Aspects of Territorial Asylum, Refugees and Stateless Persons, Proposals concerning a draft convention on first asylum CAHAR (86) 8, 15 December 1986, 2.

[66] J-C Chesnais [et al.], *People on the Move New Migration Flows in Europe* (Council of Europe, Strabourg 1992) 59.

[67] Chesnais, n 66 above, 58. The estimated number of refugees in Europe was 676,200 in 1984 and 1,213,300 in 1989, see UNHCR, *The State of the World's Refugees 2000: Fifty Years of Humanitarian Action* (Oxford University Press, Oxford 2000), annex 3, 310.

[68] On the development of containment policies, see A Shacknove, 'From Asylum to Containment' (1993) 5 *IJRL* 516; see also J C Hathaway, 'Harmonizing for Whom? The Devaluation of Refugee Protection in the Era of European Economic Integration'(1993) 26 *Cornell Intl LJ* 719, who talks of the 'deterrent regime' 722–6 or of 'non-entrée policies'; see also J C Hathaway and J A Dent, *Refugee Rights: Report on a Comparative Survey* (York Lane Press, Toronto 1995) 13–17; M Gibney, n 62 above, 6–9.

[69] R Abeyratne 'Air Carrier Liability and Responsibility for the Carriage of Inadmissible Persons and Refugees' (1998) 10 *IJRL* 675; Council Directive 2001/51/EC Supplementing the Provisions of Article 26 of the Convention Implementing the Schengen Agreement of 14 June 1985 [2001] OJ L187/45; see also ECRE, 'Defending Refugees' Access to Protection in Europe', December 2007, 28–9.

[70] K Hailbronner, 'The Right to Asylum and the Future of Asylum Procedures in the European Community' (1990) 2 *IJRL* 341, 353; ECRE, n 69 above, 26–8; Goodwin-Gill and McAdam, n 19 above, 374. For a recent analysis of the EU's visa policies, see S Peers, *EU Justice and Home Affairs Law* (2nd edn, Oxford University Press, Oxford 2007) 151–65, spec 167.

[71] ECRE, n 69 above, 30.

[72] Interception has been defined as 'the catching, turning back, diversion and escorting back of vessels before they reach coastal waters', see R Weinzierl and U Lisson, *Border Management and Human Rights: A Study of EU Law and the Law of the Sea*, German Institute for Human Rights, December 2007, 22–3, available at: <http://www.statewatch.org/news/2008/feb/eu-study-border-management.pdf>. Hathaway and Dent, n 68 above, 16–17; S Legomsky, 'An Asylum Seeker's Bill of Rights in a Non-Utopian World' (2000) 14 *Georgetown Imm LJ* 619, 626; ECRE, n 69 above, 38–43; Parliamentary Assembly of the Council of Europe, 'Europe's "boat-people": mixed migration flows by sea into Southern Europe' 11 July 2008, paras 32–42.

[73] Legomsky, n 72 above, 627; see also *Jabari v Turkey*, Appl. No. 40035/98, Judgment of 11 July 2000, ECHR 2000-VIII.

use of the 'safe country of origin' concept;[74] accelerated procedures for manifestly unfounded and/or abusive claims;[75] and the creation of international zones in airports;[76]

(3) Adoption of a narrow interpretation of Article 1 of the Refugee Convention,[77] and elaboration of weaker forms of protection, such as temporary or subsidiary protection;[78]

(4) Support for protection in the region, if not in the country itself through the creation of safe havens;[79]

(5) Restrictions on social welfare benefits, and detention of asylum seekers arriving irregularly, as deterrent measures.[80]

While the rationale behind those measures is for a large part based on the perception that many asylum seekers are in fact economic migrants with no well-founded fear of persecution, containment policies have in effect contributed to further blurring the distinction between refugee and economic migrant, a phenomenon for which the terms asylum-migration nexus or mixed migration have been coined.[81] In other words, 'by ignoring the fundamental causes of migration and treating all

---

[74] See European Parliament, 'Asylum in the European Union: The "Safe Country of Origin Principle"', Working Paper, 1997; European Legal Network on Asylum, 'The Application of the Safe Country of Origin Concept in Europe', February 2005; C Costello, 'The Asylum Procedures Directive and the Proliferation of Safe Country Practices: Deterrence, Deflection and the Dismantling of International Protection?' (2005) 7 *EJML* 35, 39; Costello, 'The European Asylum Procedures Directive in Legal Context' UNHCR New Issues in Refugee Research Paper No. 134, November 2006.

[75] Hailbronner, n 70 above, 345; R Byrne, 'Remedies of Limited Effect: Appeals under the forthcoming Directive on EU Minimum Standards on Procedures' (2005) 7 *EJML* 71.

[76] O De Schutter, 'Privation de liberté et maintien en zone internationale' [1996] *RDE* 345; see also D Bigo (ed), *Circuler, enfermer, éloigner: zones d'attente et centres de rétention aux frontières des démocraties occidentales* (L'Harmattan, Paris 1997).

[77] See J Fitzpatrick, 'Revitalizing the 1951 Refugee Convention' (1996) 9 *Harv Hum Rts J* 229, 240–1.

[78] n 48 above.

[79] Shacknove, n 68 above, 522; K Landgren, 'Safety Zones and International Protection: A Dark Grey Area' (1995) 7 *IJRL* 443; see also Chapter 2, Section 2.3–2.4.

[80] See B Gorlick, '(Mis)perception of Refugees, State Sovereignty, and the Continuing Challenge of International Protection', in A Bayefsky (ed), *Human Rights and Refugees, Internally Displaced Persons and Migrant Workers: Essays in Memory of Joan Fitzpatrick and Arthur Helton* (Nijhoff, Leiden 2006) 65, 71; A Triche Naumik, 'International Law and Detention of US Asylum Seekers: Contrasting Matter of D-J- with the United Nations Refugee Convention' (2007) 19 *IJRL* 661; European Parliament, 'The conditions in centres for third country nationals (detention camps, open centres as well as transit centres and transit zones) with a particular focus on provisions and facilities for persons with special needs in the 25 Member States', December 2007, REF: IP/C/LIBE/IC/2006-181; see also the website of the Jesuit Refugee Service devoted to the detention of asylum seekers and irregular migrants in Europe, available at: <http://www.detention-in-europe.org>; J Hughes and F Liebaut, *Detention of Asylum Seekers in Europe: Analysis and Perspectives* (Kluwer, Dordrecht 1998). On restrictions on social benefits, see *R v Secretary of State for the Home Department ex p Adam Limbuela and Tesema* [2005] UKHL 66, paras 3–5.

[81] Feller, n 61 above, 515.

entrants with suspicion and restrictiveness, governments themselves help erode the distinction between economic and forced migrants, which is a cornerstone of their policies'.[82]

1.2.1 'Refugees in orbit'

This expression appeared for the first time in a memorandum issued by NGOs on the UN Draft Convention on territorial asylum in October 1976.[83] In an Aide-Mémoire transmitted to the Council of Europe, UNHCR explained that:

This phrase [refugees in orbit] has been used to describe the plight of refugees who, while not being rejected or returned to the country where they fear persecution, are not granted asylum in any country to which they apply and are obliged to move from one country to another.[84]

Three type of 'orbit situations' were identified: refugees who did not find asylum in any country, refugees who had been granted asylum but lost the right to reside in or return to that country without having found protection anywhere else, and finally, refugees who felt obliged to leave the country where they had been granted asylum, because their lives or liberty were under threat there.[85]

The phenomenon of 'refugees in orbit' became particularly serious in Europe, not only because of differences in States' practices, for instance, as regards the geographical limitation applied by some States or the interpretation of the refugee definition in Article 1 CSR,[86] but also because States implemented unilateral policies which enabled them to refuse to examine an asylum application on formal grounds. In other words, States began to adopt the position that asylum seekers should claim protection in the first State they reached, and that consequently, they had no choice of asylum country.[87] This reactive approach became increasingly widespread,[88] and led to the development of safe third country practices.

---

[82] S Castles, 'The Migration-Asylum Nexus and Regional Approaches', in S Kneebone and F Rawlings-Sanaei (eds), *New Regionalism and Asylum Seekers* (Berghahn Books, New York 2007) 25, 26, 30.

[83] G Melander, *Refugees in Orbit* (International University Exchange Fund, Geneva 1978) 4.

[84] CAHAR, Aide-Mémoire transmitted by the UNHCR GR/TA (76) 2, 23 November 1976, 2.

[85] Sub-Committee of the Whole on International Protection, 'Note on Asylum: Refugees Without an Asylum Country', UN Doc EC/SCP/12, 30 August 1979, para 2.

[86] See Appendix II 'Refugees in Orbit: Some Constructive Proposals' to A Grahl-Madsen, *Territorial Asylum* (Almquist & Wiksell Int and Oceana pub, Stokholm [etc] 1980) 95–7; P Weis, 'Refugees in Orbit'(1980) 10 *Israel Ybk on Human Rights* (Nijhoff, Dordrecht) 157, 159; Melander, *Refugees in Orbit*, n 83 above, 2, 107–12.

[87] G Melander, 'Responsibility for Examining an Asylum Request' (1986) 20 *IMR* 220; Melander, *Refugees in Orbit*, n 83 above, 2–5; Grahl-Madsen, *Territorial Asylum*, n 86 above, 97; E W Vierdag, 'The Country of "First Asylum": Some European Aspects', in D A Martin (ed), *The New Asylum Seekers: Refugee Law in the 1980s* (Nijhoff, Dordrecht 1988) 73.

[88] A M J Swart, *Le droit d'asile et les réfugiés—Tendances actuelles et perpectives: Les problèmes liés à l'admission des demandeurs d'asile sur le territoire des Etats membres* Rapport du Colloque de droit européen, Lund 15–17 September 1986, 3.

Aware of the necessity of solving this problem through international coopera-tion, some proposed the establishment of consultative mechanisms with ultimate referral to UNHCR.[89] Grahl-Madsen recalled the proposal to create a European Refugee Commission, whose competencies would include the interpretation of the Refugee Convention, as well as the determination of the State responsible.[90] However, international initiatives to address this question, at the level of the United Nations or within the Council of Europe, were doomed to failure.[91] Instead, a profusion of small intergovernmental groups dominated by police and home affairs experts appeared on the international scene.[92] These fora played a major role in the early design of European asylum policies, including arrangements to allocate responsibility.

1.2.2 The 1977 United Nations' conference on territorial asylum

The adoption of a Declaration by the General Assembly often constitutes the first step towards the elaboration of a binding convention. The 1967 UN Declaration on territorial asylum,[93] which contained provisions on the right of States to grant asylum, solidarity between States, and *non-refoulement*, was thus logically followed by the convening of a multilateral conference to discuss the conclusion of an inter-national convention on territorial asylum. However, the conference failed to adopt a text and only three articles of the ten originally proposed were endorsed by the Committee of the Whole.[94]

The second paragraph of draft Article 1 referred to 'orbit situations':

Asylum shall not be refused by a Contracting State solely on the ground that it could be sought from another State. However, where it appears that a person requesting asylum from a Contracting State already has a connection or close links with another State, the Contracting State may, if it appears fair and reasonable, require him first to request asylum from that State.[95]

---

[89] Melander, *Refuges in Orbit*, n 83 above, 94–106; G Melander, 'Responsibility for the Examination of an Asylum Request, Asylum Seekers vs Quota Refugees', in ECRE, *Restrictive Asylum Policy in Europe, Report of the Seminar held in Zeist, The Netherlands, 16–18 January 1985*, 1985, 19–20.

[90] Grahl-Madsen, *Territorial Asylum*, n 86 above, 99–100.

[91] It should be noted that Art II.5 of the 1969 OAU Convention was rather unique in its guarantee-ing of temporary residence to refugees without a country of asylum, pending an arrangement for resettlement, see n 44 above. However, it was also criticized for placing too heavy a burden on first countries of asylum, Weis, Refugees in Orbit, n 86 above, 162.

[92] For an overview of those groups, see Russell, Keely, and Christian, n 61 above, 44–5.

[93] n 53 above.

[94] F Leduc, 'L'asile territorial et la Conférence des Nations Unies de Genève Janvier 1977' [1977] *AFDI* 221, 239.

[95] Report of the United Nations Conference on Territorial Asylum UN Doc A/CONF.78/12, 21 April 1977.

The first sentence of the Article had already been proposed by the experts who had elaborated the draft before the Conference,[96] and was regarded by UNHCR as a significant step in the development of the international law on asylum.[97] The so-called 'protection elsewhere' clause had also been included in a Recommendation of the Parliamentary Assembly of the Council of Europe adopted in 1976.[98] Its wording was not entirely clear,[99] however, and countries of first and second asylum interpreted it differently, each group considering that it was placing too heavy a burden on them.[100]

In the end, the fiasco of the conference was attributed to the low quality of the draft proposed by the experts,[101] but above all, to the insufficient political engagement with developing countries, whose position had been overlooked by UNHCR and the Western NGOs working on the project.[102] There were also serious divergences between, on the one hand, socialist and developing countries, which insisted on the prevalence of the sovereign right to grant asylum, and some Western countries, which defended the recognition of a right to asylum.[103] Divisions even existed within the Western group, Commonwealth countries and the United States being more wary of a liberal approach to territorial asylum than Sweden, Germany, France, and Italy.[104]

Another flaw of the draft was that it was supposed to apply to individual arrivals of asylum seekers as well as to mass influx, which demand differentiated responses.[105] Also, the articles adopted by the Committee of the Whole were in fact more restrictive than the domestic provisions on asylum existing in many States at that time.[106] Yet for some, the regulation of the 'protection elsewhere' concept was viewed as an essential prerequisite before an international instrument on territorial asylum could be envisaged.[107]

---

[96] A meeting of legal experts was first organized in 1971 at the initiative of the Carnegie Endowment; see the report by Kamanda, n 49 above; P Weis, 'The Draft United Nations Convention on Territorial Asylum' (1979) 50 *BYIL* 151, 161.

[97] UNHCR, Aide-Mémoire transmitted to the Council of Europe GR/TA (76) 2 p 5, 23 November 1976.

[98] Recommendation 773 (1976) on the situation of de facto refugees adopted on 26 January 1976 by the Parliamentary Assembly of the Council of Europe, reprinted in CAHAR, n 46 above, Vol II, 9.

[99] Vierdag, n 87 above, 76.

[100] Melander, *Refugees in Orbit*, n 83 above, 35.

[101] Grahl-Madsen, *Territorial Asylum*, n 86 above 62.

[102] Leduc, n 94 above, 240; Jaeger, n 15 above, 100.

[103] Leduc, n 94 above, 225. See, eg UN Doc A/CONF.78/C.1/SR.3, 19 January 1977 for the statements of the Soviet representative, para 4 and of the representative of Bulgaria, para 9.

[104] See for the position of Sweden, UN Doc A/CONF.78/C.1/SR.3, 19 January 1977, para 39; Leduc, n 94 above, 242.

[105] Leduc, n 94 above, 225.

[106] Ibid, 255.

[107] This view was expressed during an exchange of views on territorial asylum which took place within the Council of Europe, CAHAR (84) 6, 12 October 1984, 9, para 34.

The failure of the 1977 Conference may be regarded as the first manifestation of the 'protection crisis' that is still ongoing to this day. From that time, interest in territorial asylum started to wane and most Western States did not support an early reconvening of the Conference.[108] The era of generous asylum policies had reached an end, and international attention became progressively focused on restricting access to the asylum system.

1.2.3 Conclusions of the Executive Committee of the High Commissioner's Programme

The Sub-Committee of the Whole on International Protection of the Executive Committee addressed the problem of refugees without an asylum country in 1979. Members of the Sub-Committee acknowledged that the most serious concern was that States tended simply to assume that another State was responsible for processing asylum claims.[109] It was therefore suggested that it would be more desirable to have positive criteria to determine which State is responsible.[110] The Sub-Committee also distinguished situations involving a large-scale influx of asylum-seekers and those involving individual arrivals.[111] With respect to the latter, the note on asylum submitted to the Sub-Committee of the Whole identified five different criteria of application of the 'first country of asylum':

(1) A geographical criterion exclusively based on the fact that the asylum seeker had passed through another country;

(2) A temporal criterion, based on the length of time elapsed between the departure from the country of origin and the arrival in the country where the asylum claim was lodged;

(3) A criterion based on the nature of the asylum seeker's stay in the 'first country of asylum', thus on the existence of 'relevant links', and in particular on the fact that the asylum seeker had been granted protection in that country (the 'protection elsewhere' principle);

---

[108] Weis, 'The Draft United Nations Convention on Territorial Asylum', n 96 above, 168.

[109] UNHCR, Report of the meeting of the Sub-Committee of the Whole on International Protection, UN Doc A/AC.96/571, 9 October 1979, para 11; UNHCR ExCom Conclusion No. 15 (1979) on Refugees without an Asylum Country paras (h)–(i). The growing problem of refugees in orbit was also addressed by non-governmental institutions. In 1979, the San Remo Institute for International Humanitarian Law called for the adoption of uniform criteria for defining the country responsible for examining an asylum request, see Melander, 'Further Development of International Refugee Law', n 14 above, 469, 497; Weis, Refugees in Orbit, n 86 above, 162–3 which reproduces the recommendations adopted by the Institute.

[110] Report of the meeting of the Sub-Committee of the Whole on International Protection, UN Doc A/AC.96/571, 9 October 1979, para 8, 11–12.

[111] Ibid, para 5.

(4) A criterion based on the intention of the asylum seeker;

(5) A combination of the former criteria.[112]

However, none of these criteria were specifically adopted and Conclusion No. 15 of the Executive Committee merely laid down principles which should be followed in the elaboration of these criteria. A relatively liberal approach nonetheless prevailed and both the Note on asylum presented by the High Commissioner and the Conclusion of the Executive Committee insisted that consideration should be given, as far as possible, to the wishes of the asylum seeker and that States should avoid sending an asylum seeker to a country with which she had no relevant links.[113] The principle that asylum should not be refused solely on the ground that it could be sought from another State was also reiterated.[114] Finally, the Conclusion emphasized the importance of improved cooperation between States by way of consultation mechanisms among States and with UNHCR.[115]

After a failed attempt in 1985,[116] the Executive Committee adopted a second conclusion addressing the question of States' responsibilities for protecting refugees in 1989. The difference of approach with the previous discussions was manifest, as tensions between States' interests and refugee protection were growing.[117] The High Commissioner's note offered a bleak assessment of the situation:

In carrying out these protection functions, UNHCR is working in a climate where attitudes towards refugees which [sic] are becoming increasingly less accommodating. National perceptions of the refugee problem are more and more coloured by social and economic difficulties, concern over trans-continental movements and a degree of abuse of asylum procedures by individual claimants. The result has been a resiling from responsibilities by a number of States and, in some cases, a preparedness to disregard such responsibilities completely.[118]

The restrictive attitude of States towards refugees was also apparent during the discussions. The broad message of Conclusion No. 58 is particularly revealing of

---

[112] Sub-Committee of the Whole on International Protection, 'Note on Asylum: Refugees without an asylum country', UN Doc EC/SCP/12, 30 August 1979, para 8.

[113] Ibid, para 11; para (h) (ii) and (iii) of Conclusion No. 15.

[114] Para (iv) of Conclusion No. 15.

[115] Para (v) of Conclusion No. 15.

[116] A study was prepared by Gilbert Jaeger at the request of several members of the Executive Committee; see Sub-Committee of the Whole on International Protection, 'Irregular Movements of Asylum-Seekers and Refugees', UN Doc EC/SCP/40/Rev.1, 30 September 1985; see G Jaeger, *Study of Irregular Movements of Asylum Seekers and Refugees* (Working Group on Irregular Movements and Asylum Seekers, Geneva 1985). The question was briefly referred to in ExCom General Conclusion on International Protection No. 36 (1985) para (j); see also ExCom General Conclusion on International Protection No. 50 (1988) para (n).

[117] J Henkel, 'Völkerrechtliche Aspekte des Konzepts des sicheren Drittstaates', in K Barwig and W Brill (ed), *Aktuelle asyltechtlichen Probleme der gerichtlichen Entscheidungspraxis in Deutschland, Österreich und der Schweiz* (Nomos, Baden-Baden 1996) 141, 145.

[118] UNHCR, Note on International Protection, UN Doc A/AC.96/728, 2 August 1989, para 4.

the evolution in the perception of abuse, emphasizing the responsibility of asylum seekers for irregular movements:[119]

(a) The phenomenon of refugees, whether they have been formally identified as such or not (asylum seekers), who move in an irregular manner from countries in which they have already found protection, in order to seek asylum or permanent resettlement elsewhere, is a matter of growing concern. This concern results from the destabilizing effect which irregular movements of this kind have on structured international efforts to provide appropriate solutions for refugees. Such irregular movements involve entry into the territory of another country, without the prior consent of the national authorities or without an entry visa, or with no or insufficient documentation normally required for travel purposes, or with false or fraudulent documentation. Of similar concern is the growing phenomenon of refugees and asylum seekers who wilfully destroy or dispose of their documentation in order to mislead the authorities of the country of arrival...[120]

The Executive Committee failed to address, however, the question of the implementation of restrictive entry policies towards aliens, including asylum seekers and refugees that had been raised by the High Commissioner. The Conclusion focused instead on the need to determine the cause and scope of these movements, and to ensure proper protection standards in the country where they first arrived.[121] Conclusion No. 58 went further than Conclusion No. 15 by defining effective protection, that is, the conditions for determining that a country is safe for protection purposes, based on the following criteria: protection against *non-refoulement*, the right to remain in the country, and to be treated in accordance with human rights standards.[122] On the other hand, the document did not explicitly address the situation of asylum seekers in transit, which had been most problematic in practice.

Conclusion No. 58 was also part of a broader trend, starting at the end of the 1980s, towards the progressive decline of UNHCR protection activities and the growing importance of informal international fora.[123] It is indeed at that time that a meeting was organized by Sweden, with the participation of Denmark, France, Germany, the Netherlands, Switzerland, and the United Kingdom, to discuss, among several issues, a proposal for a convention on the country of first asylum. This new forum, which Canada, Belgium, Austria, and Australia later joined, and now comprises 16 States, became known as the Intergovernmental Consultations on Asylum, Refugee and Migration Policies in Europe, North America, and Australia.[124]

---

[119] See paras (a) and (c), (h) and (i) of Conclusion No. 58 (1989).
[120] Para (a) of Conclusion No. 58 (1989).
[121] Paras (c), (d), and (e) of Conclusion No. 58.
[122] Para (f) of Conclusion No. 58.
[123] Russell, Keely, and Christian, n 61 above, 44–5.
[124] Russell, Keely, and Christian, n 61 above, 18–19. The work and activities of the Intergovernmental Consultations are not public; recent information on the IGC's activities may be found on the

1.2.4 The Council of Europe

After the failure of the 1977 UN Conference on territorial asylum, European States decided to pursue discussions on asylum within the Council of Europe. A Declaration on Territorial Asylum was adopted by the Committee of Ministers on 18 November 1977,[125] while serious discussions on the question of the 'country of first asylum' or 'protection elsewhere' principle actually started in 1981.[126] Negotiations on this topic were characterized by disagreements between first and second asylum countries on the scope of their respective obligations. It also became clearer than ever before that States' primary consideration was to deter the arrival of asylum seekers on their territory.

The first draft prepared by the CAHAR, the Ad Hoc Committee of Experts on the Legal Aspects of Territorial Asylum, Refugees and Stateless Persons,[127] provided in its Preamble that the main objective of the Convention was to establish rules in order to avoid situations where asylum seekers are unable to find a State which will examine their request, in accordance with the liberal and humanitarian traditions of the Member States of the Council of Europe,[128] and to ensure fair burden-sharing between the State parties.[129]

The basic principle adopted by the draft was that the asylum request should be examined in the State where it had been lodged. This obligation was not to be affected by the fact that,

(1) Asylum could be or could have been sought in another State;

(2) The asylum seeker had not arrived directly from the country where he alleged that he had a well-founded fear of being persecuted or had stayed in other countries during his journey to the State where the request was formulated;

(3) The asylum seeker had not complied with a requirement that a request be submitted within a specified period.[130]

This rule was subject to a number of exceptions.[131] A State party was not obliged to examine an asylum request where the asylum seeker was authorized to proceed

---

website of the Australian Department of Immigration and Citizenship, available at: <http://www.immi.gov.au/about/reports/annual/2007-08/html/outcome1/administered1-2.htm>.

[125] Reprinted in CAHAR, n 52 above, Vol I, 37; see also Recommendation 817 (1977) of the Parliamentary Assembly of the Council of Europe on certain aspects of the right to asylum, n 46 above.

[126] See statement by M-O Wiederkehr in *Report of the Seminar on the Responsibility for Examining an Asylum Request*, 1986, 18.

[127] Four successive versions of the draft were submitted: see CAHAR (81) Misc, 24 March 1981; CAHAR (82) 10, 5 November 1982, Appendix III p 15; CAHAR (83) 36 final, 19 December 1983, Appendix VIII, 30; CAHAR (84) 4 final, 22 May 1984, Appendix V, 20.

[128] CAHAR (82) 10, 5 November 1982, Appendix III, 16.

[129] CAHAR (86) 1, 17 March 1986, para 17.

[130] Article 3 CAHAR (83) 36 final, 19 December 1983, 31 and CAHAR (84) 4, 22 May 1984, 21.

[131] Article 3 of the draft, CAHAR (84) 4, 22 May 1984, Appendix V, 21.

to or return to the territory of another State party and reside there on a permanent basis.[132] Secondly, the State where the asylum request was lodged was not obliged to examine it where there existed 'strong links' with another State party.[133] The existence of strong links was determined on the basis of different elements. The first related to the legal presence of close relatives in another State party. The second was based on the fact that the asylum seeker was authorized to exercise a gainful activity in another State party, other than on a purely temporary basis, and was not subject to an expulsion order in that State party. The draft further provided for a residual provision where other strong links than those referred to existed.[134]

The third exception to the basic rule was subject to substantial modifications throughout the discussions. The 1982 draft provided that the fact that the applicant had stayed legally for at least six months in the territory of another State party would be regarded as evidence of strong links, but the Committee could not agree on this clause.[135] Following a suggestion by the Swedish expert, the later versions contained a separate Article which would apply also in case of illegal stay.[136] The State which was responsible in these cases would then be obliged to admit or readmit the asylum seeker and to examine his/her claim, provided the request of (re)admission was sent within a certain time limit.[137] Where the different criteria applied simultaneously to different States, there was a hierarchy in the criteria which would be first applied,[138] and in any of these cases, the wishes of the asylum seeker would be taken into account.[139]

The draft also provided that the obligations arising out of the agreement were not to be affected by the application of readmission agreements, to which the State was also a party,[140] on the ground that the latter were not expressly designed for refugees and asylum seekers.[141] In addition, there was a consultation clause in cases of difficulties of implementation or interpretation of the agreement.[142]

---

[132] Article 5 CAHAR (84) 4 final, 22 May 1984, Appendix V, 22. Note that the 1982 and 1983 versions separately provided that the State had no such obligation if the applicant already enjoyed asylum on the territory of another State; see Art 3 a CAHAR (82) 10, 5 November 1982, 16; Art 4 CAHAR (83) 36 final, 19 December 1983, 32.

[133] Article 4 CAHAR (82) 10, 5 November 1982, 17; Art 5 CAHAR (83) 36 final, 19 December 1983, 32; Art 6 CAHAR (84) 4, 22 May 1984, 22.

[134] Article 4 CAHAR (82) 10, 5 November 1983, 17, Art 5 CAHAR (83) 36 final, 19 December 1983, 32; Art 6.3 CAHAR (84) 4, 22 May 1984, 22.

[135] Article 4 c. CAHAR (82) 10, 5 November 1982, 17.

[136] Articles 6 and 7 CAHAR (83) 36 final, 19 December 1983, 32; Art 7 CAHAR (84) 4, 22 May 1984, 22.

[137] Article 6 CAHAR (82) 10, 5 November 1982, 18; Arts 8 and 9 CAHAR (83) 36 final, 19 December 1983, 33; Arts 8 and 9 CAHAR (84) 4, 22 May 1984, 23.

[138] Articles 6 b and 7 CAHAR (82) 10, 5 November 1982, 18; Art 10 CAHAR (84) 4, 22 May 1984, 24.

[139] Articles 6 b, 7.1, and 8 CAHAR (82) 10, 5 November 1982, 19; Art 10.2 CAHAR (84) 4, 22 May 1984, 24.

[140] Article 12 CAHAR (84) 4, 22 May 1984.

[141] CAHAR (82) 4, 15 April 1982, para 19.

[142] Article 15 CAHAR (84) 4, 22 May 1984.

Serious divergences nevertheless appeared throughout the negotiations. Experts disagreed on the fundamental question of the jurisdictional link: some regarded the existence of close links as the key criterion, while the period of stay or residence would only constitute a presumption of close links which could be rebutted.[143] As it was acknowledged that the concept of protection elsewhere had different levels of acceptance and could be understood either as asylum granted elsewhere or as permission to stay elsewhere, suggestions were made to limit the right not to examine an asylum request to the case where links existed with another contracting State.[144]

The Scandinavian and Benelux countries proposed an 'en route clause', ie that a stay of more than 30 days was sufficient to exclude the responsibility of the State where the claim had been lodged.[145] Other participants pointed out that this did not constitute a sufficient indication of a connection with the country,[146] or questioned the length of time chosen.[147] Participants also discussed whether a period of illegal stay could found the responsibility of a State. It was argued that one could not impose an obligation on States for a situation that it did not allow and of which it was unaware,[148] and that, in order to prevent orbit situations, it would be important to take into consideration the 'genuine prospect applicants for asylum had of being readmitted to the territory of the State not Party to the Agreement'.[149] In the end problems of evidence precluded the inclusion of illegal stays as one of the criteria for responsibility allocation.

Finally, some States attached importance to the fact that the agreement would provide for the possibility to return an asylum seeker to a State not party to the agreement.[150] The rationale of such an approach was that otherwise, it would discourage States from signing the agreement.[151] As noted by the Secretariat, this would, however, create uncertainties as to the existence of effective protection and it was advised that the convention should not cover such situations.[152]

Resistance to the first CAHAR draft was so strong that discussions were suspended in 1984.[153] Within the Council of Europe, as in the United Nations, divisions appeared between countries which hoped to see the 'first asylum practice'

---

[143] CAHAR (82) 4, 15 April 1982, para 22.

[144] CAHAR (84) 1, 22 February 1984, 2–3, paras 4–6.

[145] CAHAR (82) 10, 5 November 1982, 17.

[146] CAHAR (83) 20 final, 12 July 1983, 7, para 30.

[147] CAHAR (83) 20 final, 12 July 1983, para 28; CAHAR (84) 4, 22 May 1984 p 8; see also Vierdag, n 87 above, 81.

[148] CAHAR (83) 20 final, 12 July 1983, p 7, para 33.

[149] 11th meeting CAHAR (82) 4, 15 April 1982, p 5, para 23.

[150] See Art 1 CAHAR (83) 36 final, 19 December 1983, p 31; G Melander, *Report of the Seminar on the Responsibility for Examining an Asylum Request*, 1986, 11.

[151] Melander, *Report of the Seminar on the Responsibility for Examining an Asylum Request*, n 150 above, 11.

[152] CAHAR (84) 1, 22 February 1984, 4, para 7.

[153] CAHAR (84) 6, 12 October 1984, 4, para 9.

being recognized in an international instrument, and those which had not adopted such practice and feared that a convention would limit their discretionary power and that, as a result, they would have to accept a higher number of asylum seekers on their territory.[154]

On the basis of these discussions, CAHAR decided to prepare a study on the country of first asylum, in order to help clarify the contentious points which had been raised during the negotiations.[155] While experts were encouraged to reduce the number of their objections in order to have the original draft adopted with minor amendments, several alternative solutions were also put forward: the conclusion of an agreement for a limited length of time to fully measure the consequences of its implementation, the setting up of a consultation procedure in case an important increase of asylum claims in one of the State parties occurred, or the participation of a greater number of States in the agreement, accompanied by a web of bilateral readmission agreements.[156]

Discussions resumed on a different basis two years later and in 1988, CAHAR adopted a new text which was submitted to the Committee of Ministers.[157] The second draft bore much resemblance to the system of responsibility allocation set out in chapter VII of the Schengen Implementing Convention and in the Dublin Convention.[158] This constituted a paradigmatic shift, since responsibility was going to be based on the first entry of the asylum seeker in one of the State parties, whether legal or illegal.[159]

At the beginning of the discussions, Turkey and Italy expressed their opposition to the inclusion of illegal entry as a ground for responsibility.[160] There were also divergences regarding the obligation to re-admit an individual whose claim had been previously rejected between Austria, Italy, Portugal, and Spain, on the one hand, and other countries on the other, primarily Germany and the Netherlands, which considered that this obligation was in conformity with the principle of good-neighbourliness.[161] A consultation mechanism was also specifically provided in cases where there was a disproportionate number of asylum seekers for which one State party would be responsible as a result of the agreement.[162]

---

[154] Wiederkehr, n 126 above, 18.

[155] CAHAR (86) 1, 17 March 1986.

[156] CAHAR (86) 1, 17 March 1986, 7–8, paras 22–3.

[157] CAHAR (88) 9 Final Activity Report, 25 January 1989, 3, para 5.

[158] See CAHAR (88) 9 Final, 25 January 1989 Appendix I, see K Hailbronner, *Möglichkeiten und Grenzen einer Europäischen Koordinierung des Einreise- und Asylrechts* (Nomos, Baden Baden 1989) 29. On the system established under the 1990 Dublin Convention and its sequel, the Dublin Regulation, see Section 1.3.2. and 1.3.3 below and Chapter 3.

[159] Article 2 CAHAR (88) 9, 25 January 1989, Appendix I, 9.

[160] CAHAR (87) 4, 22 April 1987, 7–8, paras 33–5; Turkey expressed strong objections which were maintained throughout the discussions, see CAHAR (88) 9, 4, para 10 and the letter by the representative of Turkey to the Secretary of the CAHAR, CAHAR (88) 9 Final, Appendix IV, p 23.

[161] CAHAR (88) 9 Final, 25 January 1989, 5–6, paras 14–17; Hailbronner, n 158 above, 30.

[162] Article 8 CAHAR (88) 9 Final, 25 January 1989, Appendix I.

As with the two UNHCR conclusions, the difference between the first and second drafts reflects the dramatic evolution of asylum policies from the end of the 1970s to the early 1990s. Within a decade, concern about the protection of refugees and consideration for their wishes was progressively replaced by the objective of combating abusive claims and secondary movements. The late 1980s also signalled the end of the Council of Europe's prevalence in regional cooperation on asylum and refugees, and the growing involvement of a new major regional actor in this area, the European Union, which is examined below.

1.3 The European Union

Cooperation on asylum and migration within the European Community began in the 1980s, eventually culminating with the creation of new Community competencies in these areas under the 1997 Amsterdam Treaty. These historical developments were characterized by States' original reluctance to relinquish their prerogatives to the Community on such sensitive questions, and by the profusion of expert fora created to organize intergovernmental cooperation.[163] In terms of the objectives pursued by the European Community in seeking further powers in the asylum and immigration realm, the establishment of a European political union was overshadowed by the overriding security discourse. The central narrative of European policy makers was indeed that together with criminals and terrorists, asylum seekers raised security concerns which required the adoption of compensatory measures to the abolition of checks at internal borders.[164]

1.3.1 The European Commission's proposals

A normative milestone in the European Economic Community's involvement in asylum policy was the Single European Act signed on 17 February 1986, which provided for the establishment of a single market without internal borders where the freedom of movement of capitals, goods, services, and persons would be ensured.[165] The new Article 8a EC Treaty[166] stated that the single market was an area without internal frontiers and set the deadline of 31 December 1992 for its completion.

---

[163] For an overview of these various groups, A Cruz, 'Schengen, Groupe ad hoc Immigration et autres instances intergouvernementales européennes' Comité des Eglises auprès des Migrants en Europe, Document de travail No. 12, 1993, 2.

[164] On this question, see D Bigo, *Polices en réseaux: l'expérience européenne* (Fondation nationale des sciences politiques, Paris 1996) 101.

[165] J-P Jacqué, 'L'Acte unique européen' [1986] *RTDE* 575, 597.

[166] Article 14 of the consolidated version of the EC Treaty after the amendments introduced by the Amsterdam Treaty of 2 June 1997 [1997] OJ C340/145; on Art 8, see M Ayral, 'La suppression des contrôles aux frontières intra-communautaires' [1993] *RMUE* 13, 17.

It is on the basis of these new provisions that the European Commission pro-posed the adoption of Community instruments on asylum and migration.[167] The Commission had already prepared the ground by stating in its 1985 White Paper that the issue of free movement of persons was not exclusively economic.[168] According to the Commission, the abolition of checks at internal borders was not an essential requirement of an economic single market, but had an important sym-bolic value in the perspective of a European political union.[169] People would thus be free to move as citizens of this new Union, irrespective of whether they were acting as 'economic agents'.[170] Consequently, the Commission took the view that in the future, Member States would not be able to avail themselves of any reserva-tion based on their domestic law in the field of asylum,[171] and declared that,

… against the background of moves towards Political Union [*sic*], the need for a Community based on the rule of law means there must be a joint response to the general question of the right of asylum and not just to the specific aspect of the influx of asylum seekers and the abuse of procedures.[172]

The European Parliament shared this vision of an 'integrated legal and social area' in which asylum seekers would have identical rights.[173] Yet, the integration process was not the only reason behind the Community's interest in asylum policy. The Commission and the various intergovernmental bodies which worked on asylum and migration issues also regarded the strengthening of State cooperation as ine-luctable in order to tackle the growing numbers of asylum seekers arriving in the region.[174]

---

[167] Commission Communication on the abolition of controls at internal borders COM (88) 640 final, 7 December 1988, 5–6, 17–20; R Plender, 'Competence, European Community Law and Nationals of Non-Member States' (1990) 39 *ICLQ* 599.

[168] Commission White Paper, 'Completing the Internal Market' COM (85) 310 final, 14 June 1985, para 25, 8.

[169] J De Ruyt, *L'Acte unique européen*, (2nd edn, Université Libre de Bruxelles, Bruxelles 1989) 151; Ayral, n 166 above, 16; Bigo, n 164 above, 151; J P Donner recalls that the idea was already present in the 1972 Tindemans Report, 'Abolition of Border Controls', in H Schermers et al. (eds), *Free Movement of Persons in Europe, Legal Problems and Experiences* (Nijhoff, Dordrecht [etc] 1993) 5.

[170] De Ruyt, n 169 above, 151; This new approach was first suggested by the 'Adonnino Committee' created by the European Council of Fontainebleau in 1984, J-C Masclet, 'De la difficulté d'atteindre un objectif communautaire par des moyens qui ne le sont pas', in D Bigo (ed), *L'Europe des polices et de la sécurité intérieure* (Complexe, Bruxelles 1992) 95, 102.

[171] European Commission, Communication to the Council and the European Parliament on the Right of Asylum, SEC (91) 1857 final, 11 October 1991, 4, para 5.

[172] Discussion Paper on the right of asylum, annexed to the Commission Communication, n 171 above, 11, para 16.

[173] EP Resolution of 12 March 1987 on the right of asylum [1987] OJ C99/167, para M.

[174] Co-ordinator's Group, *Free Movement of Persons: Report to the European Council by the Co-ordinator's group* (Palma Document) CIRC 3624/89, 9 June 1989, 2, reprinted in Appendix 5 to the 22nd report of the Select Committee of the House of Lords on the European Communities, *Border Control of People: ECC Report*, session 1988–89, HL Paper 90, 55; Discussion Paper on the right of asylum, n 172 above, para 16, 11.

Among the various proposals put forward by the Commission during that time, the 1987 draft proposal for a directive regarding the approximation of laws in the field of asylum deserves closer analysis.[175] The Commission's justification for Community involvement in the matter was that inasmuch as free movement of persons should be effective for every person crossing an internal border, the Community should be competent with respect to all matters necessary for the realization of the objectives set out in Articles 3 and 8a EC Treaty, including some aspects of asylum and refugee law, despite the absence of any specific treaty provision granting competence to the Community on these issues.[176]

Title II of the draft proposal, which dealt with the determination of the State responsible for examining an asylum claim was, *mutatis mutandis*, similar to chapter VII of the Schengen Implementing Convention and the Dublin Convention. The main criteria were the granting of a visa or a residence permit by one of the Member States and the presence of a family member in a State party.[177] The possibility of departing from these rules was also provided.[178] Two principles that appeared neither in the Schengen nor the Dublin conventions were particularly interesting. First, once their status was recognized, refugees would be able to travel throughout the European Community.[179] Secondly, the proposal included the establishment of a consultative committee that would issue non-binding recommendations,[180] to ensure the harmonized application of the directive and of the procedures for recognizing refugee status in each of the Member States, which, the Commission insisted, was absolutely indispensable to the efficient and fair operation of the system.[181]

In the end, this initiative was rejected on the ground that the Community lacked competence to adopt instruments in this area and because of Member States' reluctance to give up sovereignty in these matters.[182] The United Kingdom, in particular, made it clear that it was completely opposed to the Commission's suggestion that free movement would apply equally to third country nationals residing in the Member States, and that Article 8 EC Treaty could constitute a proper legal basis for the Commission's proposals.[183] At that point, the only way forward was to leave aside the legal controversy on the scope and effect of Article 8

---

[175] On file with the author; see also Plender, n 167 above, 601–4 for a description of this draft.

[176] W de Lobkowicz, 'Quelle libre circulation des personnes en 1993' [1990] *Revue du marché commun* 93, 98.

[177] Articles 3 to 13 of the Draft Proposal.

[178] Articles 12 and 13 of the Draft Proposal.

[179] Article 25 of the Draft Proposal.

[180] Draft Decision annexed to the Draft Proposal on the establishment of a Community Committee for Asylum Questions, 74; Plender, n 167 above, 602–3.

[181] Explanatory Memorandum of the Draft Proposal, 34–5.

[182] Hailbronner, n 158 above, 21; M-P Lanfranchi, *Droit communautaire et travailleurs migrants des Etats tiers, entrée et circulation dans la Communauté européenne* (Économica, Paris 1994) 57.

[183] Greece, Ireland, and Denmark supported this view; see Lanfranchi, n 182 above, 49, 54.

EC Treaty, and concentrate on the attainment of concrete results, through the adoption of non-community instruments by intergovernmental fora.[184]

This approach was advocated in the 'Palma Document' elaborated in 1989 by the 'Co-ordinators Group', which coordinated the work of several intergovernmental groups created by Member States outside the realm of the European Community, such as the Ad Hoc Immigration Group, the Schengen, and the Trevi groups.[185] The Palma Document conveyed the view of Member States that the abolition of checks at internal borders necessitated the implementation of compensatory measures to avoid the 'negative' effects which the opening of frontiers would bring about.[186] Under this approach, the movement of asylum seekers and legal and illegal immigrants, on the one hand, and of terrorists and criminals, on the other, were conceptually blurred as negative consequences of the abolition of borders.[187] Cooperation in the field of asylum was thus seen as part of the broader policy goal of enforcing stricter controls at the external borders of the European Community.[188] In this context, a system allocating responsibility for asylum claims was regarded as one of the essential compensatory measures that had to be adopted, whereas issues such as the approximation of laws on asylum and the recognition of refugee status were only 'desirable' measures with a lower degree of urgency.[189]

1.3.2 The 1985 Schengen Agreement and the 1990 Implementing Convention

Eight months before the conclusion of the Single European Act, several Member States expressed their willingness to go forward in the creation of a single area in which EC citizens and third nationals alike would move freely.[190] France, Germany, and the Benelux countries signed on 14 June 1985 in Schengen an Agreement on the Gradual Abolition of Checks at their Common Borders.[191] This initiative was

[184] Commission Communication on abolition of checks on persons at internal borders COM (88) 640 final 7 December 1988 4, para 14; de Lobkowicz, n 176 above, 99–100.

[185] The Co-ordinators Group was established by the Council in 1988 to speed up the work needed to meet the 1992 deadline and to ensure coherence among the different intergovernmental bodies, de Lobkowicz, n 176 above, 99–100; Russell, Keely, and Christian, n 61 above, 22–3; see also Cruz for an overview of the intergovernmental groups, n 163 above.

[186] K-P Nanz, 'Free Movement of Persons according to the Schengen Convention and in the Framework of the European Union', in A Pauly (ed), *De Schengen à Maastricht: voie royale et course d'obstacles* (European Institute of Public Administration, Maastricht 1996) 61, 69; for a critical analysis of this approach, see Donner, n 169 above, 8.

[187] Palma Document, n 174 above, 5.

[188] Palma Document, n 174 above, 6–7; M Anderson et al., *Policing the European Union* (Clarendon Press, Oxford 1995) 164–6.

[189] Palma Document, n 174 above, 12.

[190] Lanfranchi, n 182 above, 63–4.

[191] The 1985 Agreement is reprinted in [2000] OJ L239/13; for a historical overview of the negotiations, see L Choceyras, 'La convention d'application de l'accord de Schengen' [1991] *AFDI* 807, 808.

presented at the time as the first stage towards the creation of the common territory of a supranational entity.[192] In fact, Italy, Portugal, Spain, Greece, and Austria later adhered to the instruments,[193] along with Sweden, Finland, and Denmark,[194] while in 1999 a cooperation agreement was signed with Iceland and Norway, around the same time as the entry into force of the Amsterdam Treaty, which provided for the integration of the Schengen *acquis* into the EU framework.[195] Switzerland was the last non-EU Member State to join the Schengen system.[196]

The 1985 text distinguished between measures applicable in the short term and in the long term. These included the adoption of measures to approximate visa policy, to combat drug trafficking and illegal immigration, to reinforce police and customs cooperation, to introduce a right of pursuit for police officers and to improve cooperation in the fields of international judicial assistance and extradition. The 1985 agreement did not mention, however, measures to determine the responsibility of a State for examining an asylum request, which were contained in chapter VII of the Implementation Convention of 19 June 1990.[197]

The Schengen Convention was conceived as a 'laboratory' for the European Community, since it enabled some Member States to achieve a Community objective, without transferring competence to the Community institutions.[198] Linkages with the EC appeared throughout the text. Only Member States of the Community could become parties to the Convention. Aliens were defined as 'any person other than a national of a Member State of the European Communities'.[199] Finally, Article 134 provided that the measures adopted should comply with EC law,[200] and conventions concluded by the Member States of the European Communities

---

[192] F Julien-Laferrière, 'L'Europe de Schengen: de la disparition des frontières aux transferts des contrôles' [1992] *Actualités législatives Dalloz* 125, 126.

[193] Italy adhered on 27 November 1990, see [2000] OJ L239/63, Spain and Portugal on 25 June 1991 [2000] OJ L239/69 and 76, Greece on 6 November 1992 [2000] OJ L239/83, and Austria on 28 April 1995 [2000] OJ L239/97.

[194] Denmark, Finland, and Sweden signed the adhesion instrument on 19 December 1996 [2000] OJ L239/97, 106 and 115.

[195] Agreement of 18 May 1999 concluded by the Council of the European Union, the Republic of Iceland and the Kingdom of Norway concerning the latter's association with the implementation, application, and development of the Schengen acquis [1999] OJ L176/36; L Bay Larsen, 'Schengen, the Third Pillar and Nordic Cooperation', in M den Boer (ed), *The Implementation of Schengen: First the Widening, Now the Deepening* (European Institute of Public Administration, Maastricht 1997) 17; K A M Bleeker, 'Opheffing van de persoonscontroles aan de binnengrenzen tussen de Schengen-Staten en Noorwegen en Ijsland' [1998] *SEW* 206. On the integration of the Schengen *acquis*, see Section 1.3.4.2 below.

[196] Agreement between the European Union, the European Community, and the Swiss Confederation on the Swiss Confederation's association with the implementation, application, and development of the Schengen Acquis, 26 October 2004 [2004] OJ L370/1.

[197] [2000] OJ L239/19.

[198] Articles 134 and 142 of the 1990 Convention; Lanfranchi, n 182 above, 65–7; J E Schutte, 'Schengen: Its Meaning for the Free Movement of Persons in Europe' (1991) 28 *CML Rev* 549, 566–7.

[199] Article 1 indent 5 of the 1990 Convention.

[200] Masclet, n 170 above, 116.

with a view to the completion of an area without internal frontiers were to replace the Convention's provisions on the same subject.[201]

1.3.3 The elaboration of the Dublin Convention

The Dublin Convention of 1990 determining the State responsible for examining applications for asylum lodged in one of the Member States of the European Communities essentially replicated the substance of chapter VII of the Schengen Implementation Convention and was drafted by the Ad Hoc Immigration Group, an intergovernmental group created in 1986 and working under the authority of the Co-ordinators' Group.[202] This forum focused on the relationship between free movement of persons and internal security.[203] It was divided into six sub-groups: admission/deportation, visas, forged documents, asylum, external borders, and refugees from the former Yugoslavia.[204]

Among the other instruments drafted by the Group, the Council of the European Union adopted in 1992 a Resolution on manifestly unfounded applications for asylum,[205] a Resolution on a harmonized approach to questions concerning host third countries,[206] as well as the Conclusions on countries where there is generally no serious risk of persecution.[207] The asylum sub-group also worked on a Convention establishing a system of digital fingerprinting of asylum seekers, the Eurodac Convention, which was eventually adopted after the entry into force of the Treaty of Amsterdam, in the form of a Regulation.[208] A convention on the crossing of external borders was also elaborated by the Ad Hoc Immigration Group, but was never signed due to a dispute between Spain and Britain on sovereignty over Gibraltar.[209]

---

[201] Article 142 of the 1990 Convention.

[202] [1997] OJ C254/1. For an analysis of the specific criteria laid down in the Dublin Convention and the Dublin Regulation, see Chapter 3 section 3.3.

[203] Bigo, *Polices en réseaux*, n 164 above, 164.

[204] Russell, Keely, and Christian, n 61 above, 20.

[205] Adopted on 30 November—1 December 1992 SN 4822/92 WGI 1282 ASIM 146, reprinted in T Bunyan (ed), *Key Texts on Justice and Home Affairs in the European Union* (Statewatch, London 1997) Vol I, 64.

[206] Adopted on 30 November—1 December 1992 SN 4823/92 WGI 1283 ASIM 147, reprinted in Bunyan, n 205 above, 63.

[207] Ibid, 66.

[208] Council Regulation (EC) 2725/2000 of 11 December 2000 concerning the establishment of 'Eurodac' for the comparison of fingerprints for the effective application of the Dublin Convention [2000] OJ L316/1; see also Council Regulation 407/2002 of 28 February 2002 laying down certain rules to implement Regulation 2725/2000 concerning the establishment of 'Eurodac' for the comparison of fingerprints for the effective application of the Dublin Convention [2002] OJ L62/1; on the Eurodac system, see Chapter 3, Section 3.4.3.

[209] D O'Keeffe, 'The Emergence of a European immigration Policy' (1995) 20 *ELR* 20, 22–3; D O'Keeffe, 'The Convention on the Crossing of the External Frontiers of the Member States', in A Pauly (ed), *De Schengen à Maastricht: voie royale et course d'obstacles* (European Institute of Public Administration, 1996) 33, 36; Plender, n 167 above, 608.

With the entry into force of the Treaty of Maastricht of 1992, the 1990 Dublin Convention together with the other acts prepared by the group became part of the European Union's cooperation in justice and home affairs, the so-called 'third pillar', by reference to the 'temple' structure of the Treaty, the second pillar dealing with common foreign and security policy, while the first pillar consisted of core Community competencies in the economic, social, and environmental areas. Under the provisions of the third pillar, cooperation on asylum and immigration was still of an intergovernmental nature, yet handled by the Community institutions.[210]

1.3.4 The Amsterdam Treaty and the 'Communitarisation' of visas, asylum, immigration, and other policies related to the movement of persons

The Amsterdam Treaty, which entered into force on 1 May 1999,[211] reflects in its intricate structure, the lack of common vision for the Union, particularly in the field of justice and home affairs. The document contains three different types of flexibility clauses, seven additional protocols and seventeen declarations of the Conference annexed to the Final Act, as well as four declarations of the Member States 'acted' by the Conference,[212] which only exacerbated the common perception that European treaties are an indecipherable legal maze.

1.3.4.1 'An area of freedom, security and justice'

Contrary to a common Community technique which had proved successful in the past, the Maastricht Treaty did not define general objectives which the Union would seek to achieve in the field of justice and home affairs.[213] Neither was there

---

[210] See Art K of the Treaty on European Union, signed at Maastricht, 7 February 1992 [1992] OJ C191/4.

[211] Treaty of Amsterdam amending the Treaty on European Union, the Treaty establishing the European Community and certain related acts, 2 June 1997 [1997] C340/1 (hereafter, Amsterdam Treaty). A consolidated version of the EC treaties was produced in 1997 to incorporate the changes made in the Amsterdam Treaty [1997] OJ C340/173 and in 2002, following the Nice Treaty [2002] OJ C325/33 (hereafter, ECT); see S Langrish, 'The Treaty of Amsterdam: Selected Highlights' (1998) 23 *ELR* 3; J-M Favret, 'Le Traité d'Amsterdam: une révision *a minima* de la "charte constitutionnelle" de l'Union européenne' [1997] *CDE* 555; C W A Timmermans, 'Het Verdrag van Amsterdam' [1997] *SEW* 344; H Labayle, 'La libre circulation des personnes dans l'Union européenne, de Schengen à Amsterdam' [1997] *L'actualité juridique—Droit administratif* 923; K Lenaerts and E De Smijter, 'Le Traité d'Amsterdam' [1998] *Journal des Tribunaux* 25. On the institutional framework of justice and home affairs cooperation under the Amsterdam Treaty, see Peers, n 70 above, 20–64; S Peers, 'From Black Market to Constitution: The Development of the Institutional Framework for EC Immigration and Asylum Law', in S Peers and N Rogers (eds), *EU Immigration and Asylum Law* (Nijhoff, Leiden [etc] 2006) 19; S Peers, 'The EU Institutions and Title IV', in S Peers and N Rogers (eds), *EU Immigration and Asylum Law* (Nijhoff, Leiden [etc] 2006) 47.

[212] H Labayle, 'Un espace de liberté, de sécurité et de justice' (1997) 33 *RTDE* 814, 816.

[213] M Petite, 'Le Traité d'Amsterdam' [1997] *RMCUE* 17, 27.

any precise timetable regarding the measures to be adopted by the Union. Article 2 TEU as modified by the Treaty of Amsterdam establishes that free movement of persons and its compensatory measures with respect to external borders, asylum, immigration, and the fight against crime are implemented in order to ensure that the Union remains and develops as 'an area of freedom, security and justice'.[214] The emphasis on the relationship with the question of fundamental rights and the respect for the rule of law is also strong,[215] Article 7 TEU constituting the ultimate guarantee of compliance with these fundamental principles.[216] Far more contentious, however, was the adoption of the so-called 'Asylum Protocol', which provides that each Member State of the European Union shall be regarded as a 'safe country of origin' by other Member States. Not only is this document of dubious legal value, but it is also regarded by many commentators as contradicting the clear terms of Article 3 CSR, which prohibits discrimination on grounds of, inter alia, country of origin.[217]

With respect to justice and home affairs, the failings of the third pillar decision-making procedure ensured large support for the 'communitarisation' of most of the third pillar policies, except for police and judicial cooperation in criminal matters.[218] Accordingly, a new title (Title IV), on 'Visas, Immigration, Asylum and other Policies related to the Free Movement of Persons' was introduced in the EC Treaty. The Treaty of Amsterdam also provided for the integration of the Schengen agreements and of their *'acquis'* into the European Union framework, already foreseen in the final provisions of the 1990 Implementing Convention.[219] The objective was to adopt a more transparent and democratic institutional framework in the field of compensatory measures to the free movement of persons, while preserving the achievements of Schengen cooperation.[220]

As regards decision-making procedures under Title IV ECT, Member States agreed on a transitory period of five years, during which the Council would adopt the measures set out in Article 63 ECT by unanimity on a proposal from the

[214] See Consolidated version of the Treaty on European Union incorporating the changes made by the Amterdam Treaty [1997] OJ C340/145 and by the Nice Treaty [2002] OJ C325/5 (hereafter, TEU). For a critique of this concept, see H Bribosia, 'Liberté, sécurité et justice: l'imbroglio d'un nouvel espace' [1998] *RMUE* 27, 30 et 42.

[215] Article 6.2 TEU.

[216] Article 7 TEU lays down a procedure which may lead to the suspension of voting rights in cases of serious and persistent human rights violations by a Member State. This clause was introduced in the prospect of the enlargement to Eastern and Central European countries.

[217] Protocol on Asylum for Nationals of Member States [1997] OJ C340/103; see Peers, n 70 above, 316–17;

[218] See J Monar, 'Justice and Home Affairs in the Treaty of Amsterdam: Reform at the Price of Fragmentation' (1998) 23 *ELR* 320, 321.

[219] See Arts 134 and 142. See Section 1.3.2 above.

[220] Labayle, n 212 above, 833; see Decision 1999/435/CE concerning the definition of the Schengen acquis for the purpose of determining the legal basis for each of the provisions or decision which constitute the acquis [1999] OJ L176/1; Decision 1999/436/CE determining the legal basis for each of the provisions or decisions which constitute the Schengen acquis [1999] OJ L176/17.

Commission or a Member State and after consulting the European Parliament.[221] The application of the co-decision procedure, which provides for the joint adoption of legislation by the Council and the European Parliament, was actually introduced earlier under Article 67(5) ECT by the Nice Treaty as a derogation to the rules applicable to the transitional period. With respect to asylum matters, Article 67(5) stated that co-decision shall be applicable during the transitional period, except with respect to burden-sharing, and 'provided that the Council has previously adopted, in accordance with paragraph 1 of this article, Community legislation defining the common rules and basic principles governing these issues'.[222] This provision became obsolete in 2004, when the Council decided unanimously to apply the co-decision procedure and qualified majority voting for the adoption of future measures in the fields of internal border controls, external border controls, freedom to travel, asylum, burden-sharing, and irregular migration.[223]

The competence accorded to the Court of Justice of the European Communities to rule on the validity and interpretation of measures adopted in accordance with Title IV[224] probably constitutes the most significant advance chartered by the Amsterdam Treaty. Yet, this progress must be tempered by the fact that Community procedures were slightly modified and that the full scope of preliminary ruling procedures is not applicable to measures adopted under Title IV.[225]

1.3.4.2 Provisions on asylum, refugees, and displaced persons (Article 63.1 and 2 ECT): harmonizing asylum laws in the European Union

Article 63 ECT lays down the measures which the Council shall adopt within a period of five years after the entry into force of the Amsterdam Treaty. In the asylum field, these measures include:

(1) The criteria and mechanisms for determining which Member States is responsible for considering an application for asylum submitted by a national of a third country in one of the Member States;

---

[221] Article 67.1 ECT; K Hailbronner, 'The New Title on Free Movement of Persons, Asylum and Immigration in the TEC', in M den Boer (ed), *Schengen, Judicial Cooperation and Policy Coordination*, (European Institute of Public Administration, Maastricht 1997) 201, 210–11.

[222] Treaty of Nice Amending the Treaty on European Union, The Treaties Establishing the European Communities and Certain Related Acts (Nice, 26 February 2001) [2001] OJ C80/1 (hereafter, Nice Treaty). Note that a Protocol annexed to the Nice Treaty also provides a change of the voting procedure to qualified majority voting from 1 May 2004 for measures on administrative cooperation between Member States or between Member States and the Commission.

[223] See Council Decision 2004/927/EC of 22 December 2004 providing for certain areas covered by Title IV of Part Three of the Treaty establishing the European Community to be governed by the procedure laid down in Article 251 of that Treaty [2004] OJ L396/5.

[224] Article 68.1 ECT.

[225] See in this respect, Chapter 6.

(2)　Minimum standards on the reception of asylum seekers in Member States;

(3)　Minimum standards with respect to the qualification of nationals of third countries as refugees;

(4)　Minimum standards on procedures in Member States for granting or withdrawing refugee status.[226]

Article 63.2 ECT also provides for the adoption of measures on minimum standards for temporary protection to displaced persons from third countries who cannot return to their country of origin and for persons who otherwise need international protection (paragraph a) and of measures promoting a balance of effort between Member States in receiving and bearing the consequences of receiving refugees and displaced persons (paragraph b). Measures defined under Article 63.2 b) ECT may be adopted after the transitory period of five years from the date of the entry into force of the Treaty.[227]

The fact that the Union is to define only minimum standards indicates that under the Amsterdam Treaty, Member States have retained a shared competence in the asylum field.[228] In policy terms, while the first sentence of Article 63 ECT reaffirms Member States' commitment to the Refugee Convention and its 1967 Protocol, the focus remains unchanged: restricting access to procedures and discouraging 'abusive' asylum seekers.[229] Moreover, the number of flexibility clauses and other exceptions has exponentially increased, and created a legal framework of unprecedented complexity and opacity.

So far, the outcomes of the harmonization process have been faithful to these goals, and particularly alarming from a protection perspective. While the Commission succeeded in meeting the objective, reiterated in the Tampere European Council Conclusions, of adopting the core legislative instruments of asylum policy in accordance with Article 63.1 ECT,[230] Member States could only

---

[226]　Article 63.1 ECT.

[227]　Article 61.1 a) ECT.

[228]　See J P H Donner, 'De derde pijler en de Amsterdaamse doolhof' [1997] *SEW* 370, 373.

[229]　Labayle, n 212 above, 851.

[230]　Tampere Conclusions adopted by the European Council on 15–16 October 1999, para 14:

'This System should include, in the short term, a clear and workable determination of the State responsible for the examination of an asylum application, common standards for a fair and efficient asylum procedure, common minimum conditions of reception of asylum seekers, and the approximation of rules on the recognition and content of the refugee status. It should also be completed with measures on subsidiary forms of protection offering an appropriate status to any person in need of such protection. To that end, the Council is urged to adopt, on the basis of Commission proposals, the necessary decisions according to the timetable set in the Treaty of Amsterdam and the Vienna Action Plan. The European Council stresses the importance of consulting UNHCR and other international organisations.'

The five core instruments of asylum harmonization are Council Directive 2005/85/EC of 1 December 2005 on minimum standards on procedures in Member States for granting and withdrawing refugee status (hereafter asylum procedures Directive) [2005] OJ L326/13; the qualification Directive, n 48 above; Council Regulation (EC) No. 343/2003 of 18 February 2003 establishing the

agree on the lowest common denominator, above all where protection standards were at stake.[231] The result is that, besides the fact that some of their provisions blatantly disregard international law, the application of EU asylum instruments has also proved terribly difficult and significant differences continue to exist between asylum processes in the Member States, leading, for instance, to serious discrepancies in the assessment of risk in specific countries of origin.[232] Such concerns are particularly serious with respect to the two core instruments that will be examined in more detail in the present study, namely, the asylum procedures Directive and the Dublin Regulation.

The next phase of 'communitarisation' will probably be even more challenging. The Hague Programme, adopted by the European Council on 5 November 2004, provides for a final evaluation of the transposition and implementation of the asylum instruments adopted during the first harmonization phase.[233] It also sets the objective of establishing a common asylum procedure and uniform status for

criteria for examining an asylum application lodged in one of the Member States by a third country national (hereafter, Dublin Regulation) [2003] OJ L50/1; Council Directive 2003/9/EC of 27 January 2003 laying down minimum standards for the reception of asylum seekers (hereafter, reception Directive) [2003] OJ L31/18; Council Directive 2001/55/EC of 20 July 2001 on minimum standards for giving temporary protection in the event of a mass influx of displaced persons and on measures promoting a balance of efforts between Member States in receiving such persons and bearing the consequences thereof (hereafter, temporary protection Directive) [2001] OJ L212/12.

[231] This outcome had been feared at the very early stages of the process, see J van der Klaauw, 'Human Rights News: European Union' (1997) 15 *NQHR* 365, 367.

[232] See eg Arts 14 and 17 qualification Directive dealing with exclusion from protection and Art 27.2(c) of the asylum procedures Directive. For an overview of the difficulties of ensuring a consistent interpretation of the qualification Directive throughout the Member States, see UNHCR, 'Asylum in the European Union: A Study of the Implementation of the Qualification Directive', November 2007; European Legal Network on Asylum, 'The Impact of the EU Qualification Directive on International Protection', October 2008. These shortcoming were also recognized by the Commission in its Green Paper, see European Commission, 'Green Paper on the future Common European Asylum System' COM (2007) 301 final, 6 June 2007 (hereafter, Commission Green Paper), 5–6; European Commission, 'Communication from the Commission to the European Parliament, the Council, the European Economic and Social Committee and the Committee of Regions: Policy Plan on Asylum, An Integrated Approach to Protection Across the EU', COM (2008) 360 final, 17 June 2008, 5–6. To address these shortcomings, it is proposed to establish a European Asylum Support Office, which would ensure greater harmonization of country of origin analysis, see in this respect European Pact on Immigration and Asylum, Doc 13440/08, 24 September 2008 which was endorsed by EU interior ministers on 25 September 2008 and formally adopted on 16 October 2008 by the 27 EU Heads of State, available at <http://www.immigration.gouv.fr/IMG/pdf/Plaquette_EN.pdf>. For scholarly criticisms of first phase instruments, see McAdam, n 48 above, on the qualification Directive, Costello, n 74 above, and Peers, *EU Justice and Home Affairs Law*, n 70 above, on both the qualification Directive and the asylum procedure Directive, 334, 341–2.

[233] Hague Programme for strengthening freedom, security, and justice in the European Union as approved by the European Council at its Brussels meeting of 5 November 2004, Doc. 16054/04, 13 December 2004 (hereafter, Hague Programme); see also European Parliament, 'Recommendation to the Council and the European Parliament on the future of the area of freedom, security and justice as well as on the measures required to enhance the legitimacy and effectiveness thereof', P6_TA(2004)0022, 14 October 2004; Council and Commission Action Plan of 10 June 2005 Implementing The Hague Programme on strengthening freedom, security and justice in the European Union [2005] OJ C198/1, point 2.3.

those who are granted refugee protection or subsidiary protection and requests the Commission to submit proposals for second phase instruments to the Council and the European Parliament with a view to their adoption before the end of 2010.[234] The Commission subsequently issued a Green Paper on the future Common European Asylum System, which acknowledges some of the shortcomings of the 'first phase' asylum instruments while pledging to fill existing gaps in the current asylum *acquis* and pursue harmonization based on high standards.[235]

As has been the case since the start of the Community's involvement in asylum policy, the tension between protection objectives and restrictive measures remains more than ever present. While proclaiming the importance of a uniform status and harmonized system of protection, The Hague Programme is more 'security-driven' than ever before, emphasizing border controls and the fight against illegal immigration, and redefining the concept of 'strengthening freedom' by including therein border checks or biometrics.[236] The prevailing objective is to pursue and reinforce the approach consisting in removing or keeping asylum seekers and refugees as far as possible from the outer borders of the European Union.[237]

1.3.4.3 *The British/Irish and Danish 'opt-outs'*

As was explained above, the United Kingdom never accepted that the implementation of Article 8a EC Treaty could lead to the abolition of checks at internal borders, and that it would enable third country nationals to move freely within the territory of the Member States of the European Community. It came then as no surprise that, during the negotiations leading to the conclusion of the Amsterdam Treaty, the UK Delegation stated that they would not endorse the 'communitarisation' of justice and home affairs.[238]

---

[234] Hague Programme, 17–18. On the Commission's earlier discussion on the establishment of a common asylum procedure and a uniform status see European Commission, 'Communication from the Commission to the Council and the European Parliament: Towards a common asylum procedure and a uniform status, valid throughout the Union, for persons granted asylum' COM (2000) 755 final, 22 November 2000; European Commission, 'A More Efficient Common European Asylum System: The Single Procedure as the Next Step' COM (2004) 503 final, 15 July 2004; European Commission, 'Communication from the Commission to the Council and the European Parliament on Strengthened Practical Cooperation: New Structures, New Approaches: Improving the Quality of Decision Making in the Common European Asylum System' COM (2006) 67 final, 17 February 2006, para 10–11.

[235] Commission Green Paper, 3; see also UNHCR, 'Response to the European Commission's Green Paper on the Future Common European Asylum System', September 2007, 6–8.

[236] Hague Programme, 12; see also T Balzacq and S Carrera, 'The Hague Programme: The Long Road to Freedom, Security and Justice', in T Balzacq and S Carrera (eds), *Security v Freedom? A Challenge for Europe's Future* (Ashgate, Aldershot 2006) 1, 5–6, 18.

[237] E Guild, 'The Europeanisation of Europe's Asylum Policy' (2006) 18 *IJRL* 630, 645.

[238] C D Ehlermann, 'Différenciation, flexibilité, coopération renforcée: les nouvelles dispositions du Traité d'Amsterdam' [1997] *RMUE* 53, 75; H Kortenberg, 'Closer Cooperation in the Treaty of Amsterdam' (1998) 35 *CML Rev* 833, 836; A G Toth, 'The Legal Effects of the Protocols relating to

Two protocols concern the United Kingdom and Ireland. The first text allows the United Kingdom to maintain checks at its frontiers notwithstanding Article 14 EC Treaty.[239] Since Ireland takes part in a 'Common Travel Area' with the United Kingdom, the provisions of the Protocol apply to Ireland as well. The second Protocol provides that the United Kingdom and Ireland 'shall not take part in the adoption of measures adopted under Title IV'.[240] However, they may still be able to 'opt in' on a specific measure adopted under Title IV,[241] and the Protocol even provides that Ireland may notify the President of the Council that it wishes to 'opt in' on the entire Title IV.[242] Ireland has indicated indeed that it signed the Protocol on Article 14 ECT because of the existence of the Common Travel Area with the United Kingdom and 'that it intends to exercise its right under Article 3 of the Protocol on the position of the United Kingdom and Ireland to take part in the adoption of measures pursuant to Title IIIa[243] of the Treaty establishing the European Community to the maximum extent compatible with the maintenance of its Common Travel Area with the United Kingdom'.[244]

The motives for the Danish 'opt-out' were different. Following the negative vote of the Danish electorate on the ratification of the Maastricht Treaty, the 1992 Edinburgh summit acknowledged the specific situation of Denmark. The Danish government was extremely wary of further European integration attempts, in particular in the realm of justice and home affairs. The Protocol annexed to the Treaty provides that Denmark will not take part in the adoption of the measures pursuant to Title IV.[245] Denmark will be able to decide whether it will implement the Council decision on the 'Schengen *acquis*', but will be bound by it under public international law as opposed to EC law.[246] In accordance with its constitutional provisions, Denmark may decide to apply fully the measures which have been adopted within Title IV EC Treaty,[247] but no power of 'opt-in' on specific measures is provided.

It still remains to be seen whether the implementation of these protocols will raise the inextricable legal and political difficulties that were predicted, such as the development of distinct '*acquis communautaires*'. Ireland and the United Kingdom

the United Kingdom, Ireland and Denmark', in T Heukels N Blokker and M Brus (eds), *The European Union after Amsterdam* (Kluwer, Cambridge 1998) 227, 233.

[239] Article 1 of the Protocol (No. 3) on the application of certain aspects of Article 14 of the Treaty establishing the European Community to the United Kingdom and Ireland [1997] OJ C340/97.

[240] Article 1 of the Protocol (No. 4) on the position of the United Kingdom and Ireland [1997] OJ C340/99.

[241] Articles 3 and 4 Protocol No. 4.

[242] Article 8 Protocol No. 4.

[243] Title IV ECT.

[244] Declaration by Ireland on Article 3 of the Protocol on the position of the United Kingdom and Ireland.

[245] Article 1 of the Protocol on the position of Denmark (No. 5) [1997] OJ C340/101.

[246] Article 5 of the Protocol on the position of Denmark.

[247] Article 7 of the Protocol on the position of Denmark.

have thus far been actively involved in the asylum legislative process. In fact, the United Kingdom has been even keener than Ireland to take part, having adopted the five core asylum instruments,[248] as well as the Eurodac Regulations[249] while Ireland actually opted out of the temporary protection Directive and of the reception Directive.[250] The situation of Denmark remains particularly peculiar, since it can only 'opt in' on measures which build upon the Schengen '*acquis*' and is bound by it as an obligation of public international law.[251]

1.3.4.4 The next stage: the Lisbon Treaty

While all of the asylum harmonization legislative instruments were eventually adopted within the deadline set by the Amsterdam Treaty, opening the way for the 'second phase' of harmonization, major challenges still lie ahead. The full ratification of the Lisbon Treaty would certainly ensure greater clarity and coherence in institutional terms, however, following the rejection of the Treaty by the Irish electorate, the process is likely to be stalled for some time.[252]

This has important implications for asylum policies, given that the Lisbon Treaty offered similar innovations in the asylum realm as the draft Constitutional Treaty, which had to be scrapped after its rejection by the French and Dutch electorate,[253] by providing for the application of the full range of standard EC judicial remedies and decision-making procedures to measures adopted pursuant to Title IV.[254] Most importantly, the Lisbon Treaty was also due to set the stage for the next phase of harmonization. Article 63 requires the adoption of a uniform status for individuals having been granted international protection, uniform standards on procedures and reception, as well as the adoption of a common system of temporary protection.[255] The inclusion of a new article providing that policies on border checks, asylum, and immigration and their implementation 'shall be governed by the principle of solidarity and fair sharing of responsibility ... between the Member States', is also an important development.[256]

---

[248] n 230 above.

[249] n 208 above.

[250] See Recital 25 of the temporary protection Directive and Recital 20 of the reception Directive.

[251] See A Dashwood, 'States in the European Union' (1998) 23 *ELR* 201, 216.

[252] BBC, Q&A: The Lisbon Treaty, 21 November 2008, available at: <http://news.bbc.co.uk/2/hi/europe/6901353.stm.>

[253] Treaty establishing a Constitution for Europe [2004] OJ C310/1.

[254] See para 67 Treaty of Lisbon Amending the Treaty on European Union and the Treaty Establishing the European Community (Lisbon, 13 December 2007) [2007] OJ C306/1 (hereafter, Lisbon Treaty) providing that Arts 67–9 of the Amsterdam Treaty shall be repealed.

[255] Article 63 Lisbon Treaty.

[256] Article 63b Lisbon Treaty.

1.4 Conclusion

This historical overview shows that while international cooperation on refugee issues originally focused on protection and humanitarian objectives, the 1970s saw the emergence of an increasingly security-driven discourse which led to the adoption by States of wide-ranging restrictions against asylum seekers and refugees. The protection of refugees' rights was thus progressively undermined by 'containment' policies devised on both a unilateral and multilateral basis. In particular, it became commonplace for States to consider that they could deny a substantive examination of an application for asylum on the sole fact that protection could be found elsewhere.

The 1977 UN Conference was the last attempt to regulate territorial asylum at the international level, its failure signalling the beginning of a 'protection crisis'. This evolution was reflected in the discussions taking place within the Executive Committee of the UNHCR and the Council of Europe. Important developments also occurred as various international and supranational institutions became prominent players in the refugee and immigration realms. In particular, the end of the 1980s witnessed the rise of the European Community as the major regional actor in the asylum field. Since the entry into force of the Treaty of Amsterdam in 1999, asylum and migration policies have been subject to the Community decision-making process and to judicial supervision by the European Court of Justice. While this has ensured greater openness and transparency, the coherence and clarity of the current legal framework still leaves much to be desired. The normative instruments adopted in the first phase of the asylum harmonization process have indeed raised multiple concerns from a refugee protection perspective. This is specifically the case of the provisions on the safe third country and of the Dublin Regulation, examined in Chapters 2 and 3.

2

Safe Third Country Practices, Readmission, and Extraterritorial Processing

Safe third country practices are based on the consideration that the State where an asylum seeker lodges his/her claim does not have an obligation to examine that claim if the asylum seeker has arrived from another country than his country of origin, which is regarded as safe. Developed to tackle secondary movements, safe third country practices were initiated by Scandinavian States in the 1980s, swiftly adopted by other States in Europe, North America, and Australia, and formally embraced by the European Union in its asylum procedures Directive of 2005.[1] The first section of the chapter identifies the key features of safe third country practices, based on an analysis of the asylum procedures Directive and examples drawn primarily from British and German jurisprudence.

Readmission agreements, which will be studied in the second part of this chapter, are a key tool in the implementation of safe third country practices. After setting out the evolution of these instruments towards the containment of asylum seekers and undocumented aliens, the main characteristics of recent readmission agreements will be described. The inclusion of readmission clauses in cooperation agreements will also be considered.

The final section will look at the latest attempts at transferring responsibility to third countries, namely, proposals for the extraterritorial processing of asylum claims and their likely impact on the international refugee regime.

---

[1] Council Directive 2005/85/EC of 1 December 2005 on minimum standards on procedures in Member States for granting and withdrawing refugee status [2005] OJ L326/13 (hereafter, asylum procedures Directive) which entered into force on 2 January 2006 and which sets the deadline of 1 December 2007 for transposition into domestic law; on the asylum procedures Directive see M Panezi, 'Legislative Development: The 2005 Asylum Procedures Directive: Developing the European Asylum Law' (2007) 13 *Columbia J of European L* 501; S Peers, *EU Justice and Home Affairs Law* (2nd edn, Oxford University Press, Oxford 2006) 335–42; O Ferguson Sidorenko, *The Common European Asylum System* (TMC Asser Press, The Hague 2007) 79–108. For a detailed account of the negotiation of the asylum procedures Directive, see D Ackers, 'The Negotiations on the Asylum Procedures Directive' (2005) 7 *EJML* 1.

2.1 Safe Third Country Practices

2.1.1 Definition

The safe third country concept may be broadly defined as a mechanism whose 'effect is to deny an asylum seeker admission to substantive asylum procedures in a particular State on the ground that he/she could request or should have requested and, if qualified, would actually be granted, asylum and protection in another country'.[2]

Formulations such as first country of asylum and host third country were also often used, but safe third country is now the most common term, reflecting 'the dramatic extension and transformation of these practices'.[3] Under the asylum procedures Directive, safe third country and first country of asylum are distinct concepts. 'Safe third country' is indeed regarded as having a broader meaning, since for many States, it also covers,

[C]ountries to which an applicant has not necessarily been in the period between leaving the country of claimed persecution and arriving in the country in which he/she is now claiming asylum, if there is a country to which that individual can nonetheless be safely sent. This may include a country which has issued him or her a valid residence permit or visa.[4]

The notion of 'first country of asylum' under the asylum procedures Directives applies when a country has recognized an asylum seeker as a refugee or provides sufficient protection to that person including protection against *non-refoulement* and is willing to readmit her/him on its territory.[5]

The safe third country concept is generally linked to Article 31.1 CSR which stipulates that,

The Contracting States shall not impose penalties, on account of their illegal entry or presence, on refugees who, coming *directly*[6] from a territory where their life or freedom was threatened in the sense of article 1, enter or are present in their territory without

---

[2] UNHCR, Note on International Protection, UN Doc A/AC.96/815, 31 August 1993, para 20. Note that in the same paragraph, UNHCR notes that a State is under no obligation to grant admission to an asylum seeker who has obtained effective protection in another State.

[3] C Costello, 'The Asylum Procedures Directive and the Proliferation of Safe Country Practices: Deterrence, Deflection and the Dismantling of International Protection?' (2005) 7 *EJML* 35, 39. See also S Legomsky, 'Secondary Refugee Movements and the Return of Asylum Seekers to Third Countries: The Meaning of Effective Protection' (2003) 15 *IJRL* 567, 616, who considers that there is only a difference of degree between the first country of asylum and the safe third country and argues that the criteria for returning an individual to a safe third country or first country of asylum should be similar given that the test should be whether effective protection will be guaranteed upon return rather than whether such protection existed in the past.

[4] Opinion of the United Kingdom Delegation, 'Sending Asylum Seekers to Safe Third Countries' (1995) 7 *IJRL* 119, 120.

[5] Article 26 of the asylum procedures Directive.

[6] Emphasis added.

authorization, provided they present themselves without delay to the authorities and show good cause for their illegal entry or presence.

This has been interpreted *a contrario* as meaning that refugees who do not directly come from a country where their life or freedom are threatened may be sent back to a country in which they have been or could have been granted protection.[7] UNHCR gave qualified support to this construction, but noted that 'because of the extended scope given by some countries to the basic concept, UNHCR prefers not to refer to the safe country or host third country notion as a principle'.[8]

2.1.2 Origins and development

Safe third country practices have been developed primarily on a unilateral basis by European States, through the adoption of legislative or administrative regulations.[9] In addition to all of the States taking part in the Dublin regime,[10] the safe third country concept is applied by many Eastern European countries and former Soviet republics.[11]

---

[7] UNHCR Executive Committee 'Background Note on the Safe Country Concept and Refugee Status' UN Doc EC/SCP/68, 26 July 1991 published in R Plender (ed), *Basic Documents on International Migration Law* (Nijhoff, The Hague [etc] 1997) 199, 201, para 12; see also S Blay and A Zimmermann, 'Recent Changes in German Refugee Law: A Critical Assessment' (1994) 88 *AJIL* 361, 365–6; K Hailbronner, 'The Concept of "Safe Country" and Expeditious Asylum Procedures: A Western European Perspective' (1993) 5 *IJRL* 31, 58–9; D Bouteillet-Paquet, 'European Harmonisation in the Field of Readmission Agreements' (1997) 1 *Intl J of Human Rights* 31, 32; R Byrne and A Shacknove, 'The Safe Country Notion in European Asylum Law' (1996) 9 *Harv Hum Rts J* 185, 189–90; Costello, 'The Asylum Procedures Directive and the Proliferation', n 3 above, 40.

[8] UNHCR, 'An Overview of Protection Issues in Western Europe: Legislative Trends and Positions Taken by UNHCR', August 1995, 11.

[9] For an overview of safe third country policies on the European continent, see N Lassen and J Hughes (eds), *Safe Third Country Policies in European Countries* (Danish Refugee Council, Copenhagen 1997); see also US Committee for Refugees, At Fortress Europe's Moat: the "Safe Third Country" Concept, July 1997; European Commission, *Study on the Law and Practice of the Safe Country Principles in the Context of the Common European Asylum System and the Goal of a Common Asylum Procedure*, 2003, available at: <http://ec.europa.eu/justice_home/doc_centre/asylum/studies/docs/safe_countries_2004_en.pdf>; R Byrne, G Noll, and J Vevsted-Hansen, 'Understanding Refugee Law in an Enlarged European Union' (2004) 15 *EJIL* 355, 360.

[10] See Chapter 3. Note that among Western European countries, France continues to oppose the application of the safe third country, except as applied pursuant to the Dublin Convention and Regulation, see in this respect, E Bousquet, 'Le droit d'asile en France: politique et réalité' UNHCR New Issues in Refugee Research Paper No. 138, December 2006, 24.

[11] See eg Art 28.1 c) of the Law on Asylum in the Republic of Albania, 14 December 1998 No. 8432 <http://www.unhcr.org/refworld/docid/3ae6b5c07.html>; in Belarus, see Art 2 of the Law of the Republic of Belarus of 23 June 2008 on Granting Refugee Status, Complementary and Temporary Protection to Foreign Citizens and Stateless Persons in the Republic of Belarus <http://www.unhcr.org/refworld/docid/493541fd2.html>; in Bosnia and Herzegovina, see Art 73.2 of the Law on Movement and Stay of Aliens and Asylum, 14 October 2003 <http://www.unhcr.org/refworld/docid/3f8fbf232.html>; in Croatia, see Art 2 of the Law on Asylum, 1 July 2004, <http://www.unhcr.org/refworld/docid/3fcc66b24.html>; in Georgia, see Art 58 of the Law of Georgia on the Legal Status of Aliens, 1 July 2006 <http://www.unhcr.org/refworld/docid/3ae6b4e58.html>; in the

While this chapter focuses on safe third country practices in Europe, it bears noting that the safe third country has also been embraced on other continents. Canada[12] and the United States[13] have introduced it in their legislation, but its implementation is conditional upon the conclusion of a specific agreement with third countries. This was done in 2002 when both countries concluded with one another an agreement regarding asylum claims made at land borders.[14] The legality of the Canada–US Safe Third Country Agreement was challenged before the Canadian courts and in November 2007, the Federal Court found it to be in violation of sections 7 and 15 of the Canadian Charter of Rights and Freedoms and that the Governor-in-Council had acted unreasonably in concluding that the United States complied with Article 33 CSR and Article 3 CAT.[15] On appeal from the Crown, the Federal Court of Appeal overturned the Federal Court judgment, while leaving the Federal Court's findings on the legality of the safe third country agreement untouched.[16] Leave to appeal the Federal Court of Appeal judgment was filed before the Supreme Court of Canada on 26 September 2008.

Former Yugoslav Republic of Macedonia, see Arts 10 and 35 of the Decree for Proclaiming the Law on Asylum and Temporary Protection, 3 August 2003 <http://www.unhcr.org/refworld/docid/3fcb36494.html>; in Moldova, see Art 22(2) of the Law on the Status of Refugees, 25 May 2000 <http://www.unhcr.org/refworld/docid/3c73a9914.html> in Montenegro, see Arts 41, 56, and 59 of the Law on Asylum, 11 July 2006 <http://www.unhcr.org/refworld/docid/48650f132.html>; in the Republic of Serbia, see Art 2 of the Law on Asylum, 1 July 2008 <http://www.unhcr.org/refworld/docid/47b46e2f9.html>; in Tajikistan, see Art 8 Law of the Republic of Tajikistan on Refugees, 10 May 2002 <http://www.unhcr.org/refworld/docid/3eda26b84.html>; in Ukraine, see Art 1 of Law of Ukraine on Refugees, 31 May 2005 <http://www.unhcr.org/refworld/docid/44a286534.html>.

[12] See s 102(2)(d) of the Immigration and Refugee Protection Act, s.c., 2001, c. 27; see also N Alburquerque Abell, 'Safe Country Provisions in Canada and in the European Union: A Critical Assessment' (1997) 31 *IMR* 569, 574–8; N Alburquerque Abell, 'The Safe Third Country Concept: Deflection in Europe and Its Implications for Canada' (1995) 14 *Refuge* 1, 5; I Lee, 'La règle du "tiers pays sûr" au regard de l'Article 12 de la Charte canadienne' (1994) 73 *La Revue du Barreau Canadien* 372, 373.

[13] Immigration and Nationality Act s 208 (a) (2) (A), as amended in 1996, see also D Anker, *Law of Asylum in the United States* (3rd edn, Refugee Law Center, Boston 1999) 453.

[14] Agreement Between the Government of Canada and the Government of the United States of America Regarding Asylum Claims Made at Land Borders (15 December 2002, entered into force on 29 December 2004), reproduced in 79 *Interpreter Releases* at 1446 et seq (23 September 2002) (hereafter, Canada–US Safe Third Country Agreement). In the United States, the agreement entered into force pursuant to Department of Homeland Security and Department of Justice regulations 69480 Federal Register Vol 69, No. 228, 29 November 2004. In Canada, final regulations were issued on 26 October 2002, see UNHCR, 'Monitoring Report: Canada–United States "Safe Third Country" Agreement 29 December 2003–28 December 2005' June 2006, 3; Department of Citizenship and Immigration, 'A Partnership for Protection Year One Review', November 2006, <http://www.cic.gc.ca/English/department/laws-policy/partnership/index.asp>; see also C Cutler, 'The US–Canada Safe Third Country Agreement: Slamming the Door on Refugees' (2004) 11 *ILSA J Intl & Comp L* 121; A Moore, 'Unsafe in America: A Review of the US–Canada Safe Third Country Agreement' (2007) 47 *Santa Clara LR* 201, 208–9.

[15] *Canadian Council for Refugees, Canadian Council of Churches, Amnesty International and John Doe v R* 2007 FC 1262, para 338.

[16] *R v Canadian Council for Refugees, Canadian Council of Churches, Amnesty International and John Doe* 2008 FCA 229, para 105.

Australia adopted safe third country regulations in 1994. This legislation applied to specific categories of asylum seekers, namely individuals 'screened out' under the Comprehensive Plan of Action for Indo-Chinese Refugees[17] and to those covered by an agreement between Australia and another country relating to persons seeking asylum.[18] The latter was implemented towards Sino-Vietnamese asylum seekers whose return was provided for under a Memorandum of Understanding with the People's Republic of China.[19] The scope of application of this legislation was then extended in 1999 and the safe third country concept is now applicable even in the absence of a specific agreement.[20] In 2000, Australia concluded a 'regional cooperation agreement' with Indonesia and the International Organization for Migration (IOM) which allows Australia to return asylum seekers to Indonesia, which is not a party to the Refugee Convention. In accordance with this arrangement, asylum seekers are 'prevented by Indonesian authorities from leaving Indonesia, but are provided with food, accommodation and emergency medical care by IOM'.[21]

[17] The Comprehensive Plan of Action provided that refugees status determination procedures would be carried out by first asylum countries and those who were recognized as refugees would be resettled in industrialized countries, see R Towle, 'Processes and Critique of the Indo-Chinese Comprehensive Plan of Action: An Instrument of Burden-Sharing?' (2006) 18 *IJRL* 537, 549–50.

[18] See s 91A-E of the 1958 Migration Act No. 62 which authorize exclusion on safe third country grounds; S Taylor, 'Australia's "Safe Third Country" Provisions: Their Impact on Australia's Fulfillment of Its Non-Refoulement Obligations' (1996) 15 *University of Tasmania LR* 196, 210–27; P Mathew, 'Safe for Whom? The Safe Third Country Concept Finds a Home in Australia', Paper presented at the 7th International Research and Advisory Panel (IRAP) of the International Association for the Study of Forced Migration (IASFM) 8–12 January 2001, Johannesburg (on file with the author); see also statement by the representative of Australia before the Executive Committee, UN Doc A/AC.96, 16 February 1996, para 71; S Taylor, 'Protection Elsewhere/Nowhere' (2006) 18 *IJRL* 283, 301, 307.

[19] Taylor, 'Australia' Safe Third Country Provisions', n 18 above, 221.

[20] See s 65–7 of the Border Protection Legislation Amendment Act No. 160, 1999 which inserted s 91M-Q in the 1958 Migration Act No. 62 and ss 36(3)–(5) Migration Act adopted in 1999 which define effective protection; see in particular s 91N(3) which provides:

The Minister may, after considering any advice received from the Office of the United Nations High Commissioner for Refugees:

    (a) declare in writing that a specified country:

        (i) provides access, for persons seeking asylum, to effective procedures for assessing their need for protection; and

        (ii) provides protection to persons to whom that country has protection obligations; and

        (iii) meets relevant human rights standards for persons to whom that country has protection obligations; ...

According to Taylor, in 2006, no declaration under that section had been made yet, n 18 above, 301. Following a decision of the High Court finding that Australia owes protection obligations to any refugee and not only to those who cannot be removed to third countries unless the legislator explicitly intends that this be the case, the law was amended so as to make it more explicit, see *NAGV and NAGW of 2002 v Minister for Immigration and Multicultural and Indigenous Affairs* [2005] HCA 6 (2005) 213 ALR 668.

[21] See Taylor, 'Protection Elsewhere', n 18 above, 295, 299 who reports that between 2000 and 2004, 3,930 asylum seekers were subject to this arrangement.

Safe third country practices even spread to the African continent,[22] where South Africa and Tanzania adopted safe third country regulations.[23] In South Africa, the authorities declared that they follow the guidelines set out in Conclusion No. 58 of the Executive Committee, but it is not clear whether this corresponds to actual implementation.[24] Other Southern African countries expressed support for the 'safe country of asylum' in order to curb irregular movements of refugees,[25] but limited evidence has been found with regard to actual practice. Botswana apparently denies asylum to all persons coming from outside the region and the authorities refuse to look at the merits of the case.[26] Member States of the Southern African Development Community met in 1995 to discuss the possible harmonization of asylum laws and procedures, with apparently little result.[27]

Attempts at regulating safe third country practices at the international level have generally failed and existing international instruments on the subject are not binding. The documents from the Executive Committee of UNHCR, namely Conclusions No. 15 and No. 58,[28] are still at this time the most relevant

---

[22] G Melander, 'Refugees in Orbit', in G Melander and P Nobel (eds) *African Refugees and the Law* (Scandinavian Institute of African Studies, Uppsala 1978) 27, 32; Lawyers Committee for Human Rights, *African Exodus: Refugee Crisis, Human Rights and the 1969 OAU Convention* (Lawyers Committee for Human Rights, New York 1995) 22–3.

[23] For The United Republic of Tanzania, see para 4(4)(d) and (e) of the Act to make provision for the enactment of the Refugees Act, National Eligibility Committee, Asylum seeker and Refugee administration and to repeal the Refugee (Control) Act and for connected matters No. 9 of 1998 published on 24 January 1999. For South Africa, see para 4(1) (d) of the 1998 Refugees Act, No. 130 (1998) 402 Government Gazette No. 19544; Departmental Circular No. 59 of 2000 on Influx of Asylum Seekers: First Country of Asylum (on file with the author).

[24] I van Beek, 'Prima facie asylum Determination in South Africa: A Description of Policy and Practice', in J Handmaker, L A de la Hunt, and J Klaaren (eds), *Perspectives on Refugee Protection in South Africa* (Lawyers for Human Rights, Pretoria 2001) 5. On practice before the entry into force of the Refugee Act, see Human Rights Watch, *'Prohibited Persons' Abuse of Undocumented Migrants, Asylum-Seekers, and Refugees in South Africa* (Human Rights Watch, New York 1998) 173.

[25] See statement by the Observer of Swaziland at the 45th session of the Executive Committee of the Office of the UNHCR, UN Doc A/AC.96/SR.494, 12 October 1994, para 68; statement by the Observer of Botswana at the 46th session, UN Doc A/AC.96/SR.505, 24 October 1995, para 32; statement by the Representative of Namibia at the 46th session, UN Doc A/AC.96/SR.504, 27 February 1996, para 54 and at the 47th session UN Doc A/AC.96/SR.512, 15 October 1996, para 4; statement by the Observer of Malawi UN Doc A/AC.96.SR.510, 15 October 1996, para 27 who called for further cooperation between UNHCR and the Southern African Development Community to tackle irregular movements of people in the region; statement by the Representative of South Africa at the 50th session, UN Doc A/AC.96/SR.538, 12 October 1999, para 31.

[26] B Geddo, 'Durable Solutions to the Refugee Problem: UNHCR's Regional Strategy for Southern Africa', in *Perspectives on Refugee Protection in South Africa*, n 24 above.

[27] I Chokuwenga, 'The Refugee Crisis: A Southern African Perspective', in J Whitman (ed), *Migrants, Citizens and the State in Southern Africa* (Macmillan, Basingstoke 2000) 117, 122; J Handmaker, 'Who Determines Policy? Promoting the Rights of Asylum in South Africa' (1999) 4 *IJRL* 290, 302; see also the proposal for a 'Regional Agreement on Appropriate Locations for Asylum Applications' suggested by M Kingsley-Nyinah, 'Asylum, Refugee Criteria and Irregular Movements in Southern Africa' (1995) 7 *IJRL* 291, 314–15.

[28] ExCom Conclusion No. 15 (1979) on refugees without an asylum country; ExCom Conclusion No. 58 (1989) on the problem of refugees and asylum seekers who move in an irregular manner from a country in which they had already found protection. Note that ExCom Conclusion No. 58 was

international texts.[29] Finally, the Council of Europe adopted a recommendation on the application of the safe third country in 1997 but it has had limited impact.[30]

Supranational processes have therefore taken the lead and the asylum procedures Directive is now the only binding instrument regulating the safe third country, aside from domestic legislations. Unfortunately, this Directive is also a prime example of the lowest common denominator approach to harmonization, and its provisions were both fiercely debated among Member States and strongly criticized by UNHCR and non-governmental organizations, which made unprecedented interventions to call for the withdrawal of the document, as they believed that its provisions would in effect deny access to protection.[31] In some respects, the previous non-binding Resolution adopted in 1992[32] went further in terms of

intended to cover the cases of asylum seekers who had already found protection and subsequently engaged in secondary movements. For an analysis of the adoption of Conclusions No. 15 and No. 58, see Chapter 1, Section 1.2.3. Additionally, an expert roundtable convened by UNHCR in 2002 adopted conclusions so as to provide more specific guidelines on the notion of effective protection, see 'Summary Conclusions on the Concept of "Effective Protection" in the Context of Secondary Movements of Refugees and Asylum Seekers', Lisbon Expert Roundtable organized by the UNHCR and the Migration Policy Institute and hosted by the Luso-American Foundation for Development, 9 and 10 December 2002 (hereafter, Lisbon Conclusions).

[29] On the legal relevance of ExCom conclusions, see J Sztucki, 'The Conclusions on the International Protection of Refugees Adopted by the Executive Committee of the UNHCR Programme' (1989) 3 *IJRL* 285, 303, and 306.

[30] Recommendation No. R (97) 22 containing guidelines on the application of the safe third country concept, adopted by the Committee of Ministers of the Council of Europe on 25 November 1997, reprinted in Ad Hoc Committee of Experts on the legal aspects of territorial asylum, refugees, and stateless persons (CAHAR) *Selected Texts Concerning Territorial Asylum and Refugees Adopted within the Council of Europe*, CAHAR (98) 6 March 1998, Vol I, 74.

[31] UNHCR Press Release, *Lubbers Calls for EU Asylum Laws not to Contravene International Law*, 29 March 2004; UNHCR Press Release, *UNHCR Regrets Missed Opportunity to Adopt High EU Asylum Standards*, 30 April 2004; ECRE, ILGA Europe, Amnesty International, Pax Christi International, Quaker Council for European Affairs, Human Rights Watch, CARITAS-Europe, Médecins sans Frontières, Churches' Commission for Migrants, Save the Children in Europe, *Call for Withdrawal of the Asylum Procedures Directive*, 22 March 2004; see also ECRE, *Amnesty International and Human Rights Watch, Refugee and Human Rights Organisations Across Europe Express their Concern at the Expected Agreement on Asylum Measures in Breach of International Law*, 28 April 2004; S Peers, 'EU Law on Asylum Procedures: An Assault on Human Rights?', *Statewatch Analysis*, November 2004, available at: <http://www.statewatch.org>.

[32] EU Resolution on a harmonized approach to questions concerning host third countries, adopted on 30 November and 1 December 1992 by Immigration Ministers, SN 4823/92 WG 1283 ASIM 147 (hereafter, EU Resolution) published in E Guild (ed), *The Developing Immigration and Asylum Policies of the European Union* (Kluwer, The Hague 1996) 161. Article 4 of the Resolution provided that Member States would seek to ensure that the principles set out in the Resolution would be incorporated into domestic law. This Resolution influenced the drafting of safe third country legislation, eg, in Germany, the United Kingdom and the Netherlands; for Germany, see Federal Ministry of the Interior, 'Recent Developments in the German law on Asylum and Aliens' (1994) 6 *IJRL* 265, 267; for the United Kingdom, see *HC Standing Committee D*, 11 January 1996, cols 64–5; for the Netherlands, see J B Mus, '"Veilige" derde staten: het verbod van refoulement op de tocht ?' [1994] *Nederlands Juristenblad* 1365.

harmonization and in providing minimum guarantees for asylum seekers than the current instrument.

In light of the limited harmonization achieved, national legislations retain particular significance in this area. The following analysis will thus be based on the text of the Directive, analysed in light of previous practice, primarily in the United Kingdom[33] and Germany.[34] Three issues will be singled out in this examination:

(a) The existence of effective protection in the third country;
(b) The existence of a link or contact between the asylum seeker and the third country and the consent of the third country to the removal of the asylum seeker;
(c) Procedural issues concerning the application of the safe third country concept.

2.1.2.1 *Effective protection*

EXCOM Conclusion No. 58 constituted the first attempt at defining what a 'safe' country is. The Conclusion provides that protection by the third country should entail permission to enter and remain safely in the country, *non-refoulement* and treatment in accordance with basic human standards until a durable solution is found, as well as absence of persecution or threats to safety or freedom.[35]

The asylum procedures Directive creates no less than three different categories which are based on slightly different criteria: the safe third country,[36] the first country of asylum,[37] and the European safe third country.[38] With respect to the

---

[33] In the United Kingdom, the safe third country concept was originally included in the Immigration Rules (as amended in November 2008) HC 395, 345 <http://www.ukba.homeoffice.gov.uk/policyandlaw/immigrationlaw/immigrationrules/part11/> and is also referred to in the 1996 Asylum and Immigration Act whose relevant provisions were further amended in 2000 and 2004; see s 2(1) and (2) of the Asylum and Immigration Act 1996.

[34] In Germany, the safe third country concept was incorporated in Art 16 of the Constitution in 1993. While the safe third country is currently exclusively implemented through the application of the Dublin Regulation examined in Chapter 3, the earlier approach adopted in German law remains of interest to understand some of the provisions of the asylum procedures Directive and the ways in which the safe third country is implemented in practice.

[35] Conclusion No. 58, n 28 above, para f) i)–ii) and g); see Lisbon Conclusions, n 28 above, para 15, which adds that there should be 'no real risk that the person would be sent by the third State to another State in which he or she would not receive effective protection or would be at risk of being sent from there on to any other State where such protection would not be available'; that there should be an express agreement to readmit the person and that there should be access to fair and efficient asylum procedures. See also the recommendations of non-governmental organizations, Amnesty International, 'Europe: Harmonisation de la politique d'asile, procédures accélérées pour les demandes d'asile "manifestement infondées" et notion de 'pays sûr', 1992, 2; ECRE, 'Safe Third Countries Myths and Realities', 1997; US Committee for Refugees, n 9 above, 33. For further discussion on the conditions of application, see also Byrne and Shacknove, n 7 above, 214; Hailbronner, n 7 above, 63.

[36] Article 27 of the asylum procedures Directive.

[37] Article 26 of the asylum procedures Directive.

[38] Article 36 of the asylum procedures Directive. Note that on 6 May 2008, the European Court of Justice annulled Art 36.3 of the asylum procedures Directive at the request of the European Parliament,

safe third country, the Directive stipulates in Article 27.1 that safety must entail respect for the following principles:

life and liberty are not threatened on account of race, religion, nationality, membership of a particular social group or political opinion;

the principle of *non-refoulement* in accordance with the Geneva Convention is respected;

the prohibition of removal, in violation of the right to freedom from torture and cruel, inhuman or degrading treatment as laid down in international law, is respected; and

the possibility exists to request refugee status and, if found to be a refugee, to receive protection in accordance with the Geneva Convention.

While these requirements are in some ways more specific than in Conclusion No. 58, the asylum procedures Directive does not specifically require that a country be a party to the 1951 Refugee Convention,[39] and only demands that there be a 'possibility' to apply for refugee status.[40] Article 26 on the first country of asylum stipulates more concisely that the asylum seeker must 'otherwise [enjoy] sufficient protection in that country, including benefiting from the principle of *non-refoulement*',[41] a language which might seek to 'dilute' the international standards referred above.[42] More stringent requirements were, on the other hand, attached to the concept of European safe third country, namely, ratification of the Refugee Convention with no geographical limitations, existing asylum procedures prescribed by law, ratification of the European Convention for the Protection of Human Rights and Fundamental Freedoms (ECHR), and compliance with its standards, including Article 13, and designation by the Council as a safe third country.[43]

having found that the Council had exceeded its powers by providing that the adoption of a safe third country list would only require consultation with the European Parliament rather than the application of the co-decision procedure provided under Art 251 ECT, see *Parliament v Council*, Case C-133/06, 6 May 2008, para 43–61. Apparently, no amendment will be presented to reintroduce the annulled provision, and this chapter will therefore not dwell on the controversial notion of 'European safe third country'. For a stringent critique of the European safe third country concept, see Costello, 'The Asylum Procedures and the Proliferation', n 3 above, 64.

[39] See ECRE, 'Information Note on the Council Directive 2005/85/EC of 1 December 2005', 23; on the requirement of accession to the 1951 Refugee Convention, see also UNHCR (London Office), 'The Safe Third Country Policy in the light of International Obligations of Countries vis-a-vis Refugees and Asylum Seekers', July 1993, para 4.2.7; cf Lisbon Conclusions, n 28 above, para 15(e) which requires at the very least a 'practice akin to the 1951 Convention and/or its 1967 Protocol'.

[40] Article 27.1(d) of the asylum procedures Directive; see Ackers, n 1 above, 21, who reports that this language was adopted at the request of some Member States which considered that even if an asylum seeker did not have the opportunity to seek asylum in a third country, the *possibility* of obtaining protection should be regarded as sufficient. Such suggestion was clearly linked to the proposals for extraterritorial processing discussed below, see Section 2.3.

[41] Note that Art 26 specifies that 'in applying the concept of first country of asylum to the particular circumstances of an applicant for asylum, Member States may take into account Art 27(1)'.

[42] C Costello, 'The European Asylum Procedures Directive in Legal Context', UNHCR New Issues in Refugee Research Paper No. 134, November 2006, 11; ECRE, Information Note, n 39 above, 22.

[43] Article 36.1 of the asylum procedures Directive; see n 38 above.

The basic principle is thus that the third State is able to grant effective protection to refugees. For example, the fact that Greece would prefer to offer temporary protection to Albanians from Kosovo rather than granting refugee status was regarded as sufficient to consider that country as safe for protection, since the applicants would not be sent to their country of origin.[44] It is also generally accepted that the third country may in turn send the asylum seeker to a 'fourth' country, provided the same criteria are applied.[45]

What is also clear is that effective protection should not be equated with absence of persecution pursuant to Article 1 of the Refugee Convention.[46] Kjaerum rightly considers that the threshold for determining the risk of violation of the asylum seeker's rights by the third country should be lower than for establishing the existence of a well-founded fear of persecution within the terms of Article 1 CSR.[47] In the early 1990s, several cases of asylum seekers who had first lodged an asylum application in Germany but left for fear of extreme-right violence against foreigners were submitted to the Court of Appeal. The court ruled that this situation did not amount to persecution and that the Secretary of State was entitled to conclude that Germany was a safe third country for the applicants, since the German government had taken all necessary measures to address this problem.[48] One could have argued, however, that the Secretary of State had not established that the protection granted in Germany was effective, because, while these acts of violence may not have amounted to persecution pursuant to Article 1 CSR, the situation did constitute a threat to the physical safety of the applicants.[49]

---

[44] *R v Secretary of State for the Home Department ex p Elshani and Berisha* [1998] *INLR* 683 (QB); see also *Canadian Council for Refugees, Canadian Council of Churches, Amnesty International and John Doe v R*, 2007 FC 1262, para 136.

[45] See the decision of the German Constitutional Court of 14 May 1996, *Bundesverfassungsgericht* (1997) 94 BVerfGE 49; in the United Kingdom, see *Huseyn Dursun v Secretary of State for the Home Department* [1993] Imm AR 169 (CA); *R v Secretary of State for the Home Department ex parte Senay Mehari Mohamed Ahmed Doreh Ali Abdi Hersi Fuat Celik Kuti Augusto* [1994] Imm AR 151 (QB); *Julia Martinas v a Special Adjudicator Secretary of State for the Home Department* [1995] Imm AR 190 (CA); *R v Special Adjudicator ex parte Vibulan Srikantharajah* [1996] Imm AR 326 (QB); see also R Byrne, 'Harmonization and Burden Redistribution in the Two Europes' (2003) 16 *JRS* 336, 350. Cf Art 3.2 of the Canada–US Safe Third Country Agreement, which expressly provides that '[t]he parties shall not remove a refugee status claimant returned to the country of last presence under the terms of this Agreement to another country pursuant to any other safe third country agreement or regulatory designation'.

[46] E W Vierdag, 'The Country of "First Asylum": Some European Aspects', in D A Martin (ed), *The New Asylum Seekers: Refugee Law in the 1980s* (Nijhoff, Dordrecht 1988) 73, 77.

[47] M Kjaerum, 'The Concept of Country of First Asylum' (1992) 4 *IJRL* 514, 518.

[48] *Balbir Singh, Gurmail Singh, Parmjit Singh, Hardeep Singh, Satpal Singh v Secretary of State for the Home Department* [1992] Imm AR 426 (CA); *Ahmed Gamel Haliq Abdulla v Secretary of State for the Home Department* [1992] Imm AR 438 (CA); see also *R v Secretary of State for the Home Department ex p Mangal Singh* [1992] Imm AR 376 (QB).

[49] See also in this regard Lisbon Conclusions, n 28 above, para 15 (b) and (h) which makes it clear that threats of physical safety or violations of the rights of asylum seekers 'with special vulnerabilities' should be considered as part as the effective protection assessment.

In recent years, European States have returned a large number of Iraqi asylum seekers to Jordan, Syria, and Turkey, which not only already host a large population of refugees, but are not parties to the Refugee Convention or, in the case of Turkey, limit its application to European refugees.[50] In other third countries, such as Morocco, the standards of protection are far from satisfactory; for instance, UNHCR is not allowed to visit detention sites.[51] Additionally, the mixed message sent by the European Union on illegal immigration and refugee protection has had unfortunate consequences. In 2006, the Moroccan police carried out operations to arrest sub-Saharan migrants in Rabat, Nador, and Oujda, possibly to show Morocco's 'goodwill' in the fight against illegal immigration. A number of these 'migrants' were in fact recognized refugees or asylum seekers whose application was being examined.[52]

Finally, what is missing from the asylum procedures Directive is the crucial requirement that the asylum seeker be treated in accordance with basic human standards.[53] Protection should indeed also encompass socio-economic conditions

---

[50] J Crosbie, 'EU States Return Iraqi Asylum Seekers', *European Voice*, 24 May 2007. See also J Crosbie, 'Iraqi Refugees Reveal Asylum Regimes Disharmony', *European Voice*, 1 March 2007; M Sperl, 'Fortress Europe and the Iraqi "intruders": Iraqi Asylum-Seekers and the EU, 2003–2007' UNHCR New Issues in Refugee Research Paper No. 144, October 2007, 5, who compares the treatment of Iraqi asylum seekers in Greece, Germany, the UK, and Sweden, the latter country being the only one to offer a generous asylum policy to this group. In the UK, 88 per cent of claims for refugee status or subsidiary protection lodged by Iraqi nationals were rejected in 2006, ibid, 7.

[51] See Directorate-General for External Policies of the Union Directorate B, 'Study: Analysis of the External Dimension of the EU's Asylum and Immigration Policies—Summary and Recommendations for the European Parliament', 8 June 2006 (hereafter, Directorate Study) 19.

[52] 'Open Letter by Moroccan, African and European Associations: "In Morocco, the Right of Men and Women are Scorned in the Name of the Protection of Europe's Borders"', *Statewatch News Online* January 2007, available at: <http://ww.statewatch.org>; see also UN News Service, 'Annan Urges Humane Treatment of Migrants Trying to Cross Morocco-Spain Border', 7 October 2005. Many of the 'migrants' who arrive in Morocco come from countries with poor human rights records including Algeria, Côte d'Ivoire, Congo, the Democratic Republic of Congo, Guinea, Iraq, Liberia, and Sudan; see A Betts, 'Towards a Mediterranean Solution? Implications for the Region of Origin' (2006) 18 *IJRL* 652, 657–8; M-T Gil-Bazo, 'The Practice of Mediterranean States in the context of the European Union's Justice and Home Affairs External Dimension. The Safe Third Country Concept Revisited' (2006) 18 *IJRL* 571, 577; J Valluy, 'Le HCR au Maroc: acteur de la politique européenne d'externalisation de l'asile' [2007] *Cahiers du Maghreb* 547, 553–6.

[53] The European Commission indicated that effective protection should include 'social and economic well-being, including as a minimum access to primary healthcare and primary education and access to the labour market or to means of subsistence sufficient to maintain an adequate standard of living', European Commission, 'Communication from the Commission to the Council and the European Parliament: Towards more accessible, equitable and managed asylum systems' COM (2003) 315 final, 3 June 2003, 6. In 2004, the Commission referred to the 'possibility to live a safe and dignified life taking into account the relevant socio-economic conditions prevailing in the host country', see European Commission, 'Communication from the Commission to the Council and the European Parliament on the managed entry in the EU of persons in need of international protection and enhancement of the protection capacity of the regions of origin: improving access to durable solutions' COM (2004) 410 final, 4 June 2004, para 45; see also *R v Secretary of State for the Home Department ex p Razgar* [2004] UKHL 27 on whether in extreme circumstances, a violation of Art 8 ECHR might prevent the removal of an individual to a certain country; *R v Special Adjudicator ex p Ullah* [2004]

of the asylum seeker in the third country.[54] These do not have to be similar to living standards in Western countries, but in accordance with Article 7 CSR, the refugee must be accorded at least similar treatment as aliens generally living in the country.[55]

2.1.2.2 Contact between the asylum seeker and the third country and consent of the third state to the removal

Conclusion No. 15, which was the first ExCom conclusion to address the question of the identification of the State responsible for examining an asylum request, recommends to take into account the duration and nature of any sojourn of the asylum seeker in another country, as well as his/her intention, and draws attention to the importance of the existence of close links between the asylum seeker and a specific country.[56] This criterion is now one that clearly distinguishes the first country of asylum concept from the safe third country concept under EU law. While the former presupposes that some form of protection already exists in a third country,[57] Article 27.1(d) of the asylum procedures Directive simply refers to the 'possibility' of requesting asylum, suggesting that removal to a third country might take place in the absence of any relevant link. Article 27.2(d) also indicates that rules requiring a connection between the person seeking asylum and the third country concerned shall be subject to national legislation of the Member States.[58] On this point, the Directive offers therefore less harmonization and adopts lower standards than the former EU Resolution, which at least required that

... the asylum seeker has already been granted protection in the third country or has had an opportunity, at the border or within the territory of the third country, to make contact with

UKHL 26, paras 21, 35, 39–49, 52, 53, 62, 67; *EM (Lebanon) v Secretary of State for the Home Department* [2008] UKHL 64.

[54] UNHCR, 'An Overview of Protection Issues in Western Europe', n 8 above, 12; ECRE, Information Note, n 39 above, 22; see also Lisbon Conclusions, n 28 above, para 15 (g) which recommends that the person should have 'access to means of subsistence sufficient to maintain an adequate standard of living'. cf *R v Secretary of State for the Home Department ex p Thangasara and R v Secretary of State for the Home Department ex p Yogathas* [2002] UKHL para 9, which holds that it can never be appropriate to compare living conditions in other countries as part of the assessment of effective protection if there is no risk of persecution or *refoulement* in that country.

[55] Kjaerum, n 47 above, 519; on the existence of material safety for asylum seekers in third countries, see Legomsky, n 3 above, 595–7; Costello, 'The Asylum Procedures Directive and the Proliferation', n 3 above, 58. See also Chapter 5 for further analysis of this specific question, Section 5.2.3.

[56] Para h), n 28 above; see also UNHCR, 'The Concept of "Protection Elsewhere"' (1995) 7 *IJRL* 123, 125; UNCHR Working Paper, 'UNHCR's three pronged proposal', June 2003, 3; see also Chapter 1, Section 1.2.3.

[57] Article 26 of the asylum procedures Directive; see also Recital 22 of the asylum procedures Directive.

[58] Note that Recital 23 of the asylum procedures Directive also refers to the existence of a 'connection to a third country as defined by national law'.

that country's authorities in order to seek their protection, before approaching the Member State in which he is applying for asylum [...].[59]

The scant interest shown in the question of the existence of a link between the asylum seeker and a third country tends to confirm the view that the application of the safe third country is seen as evidence of a 'weak substantive claim, rather than reflecting the fact that requisite protection is available elsewhere'.[60] Thus, in the United Kingdom, it has been held that the opportunity to seek asylum does not require knowledge by the asylum seeker that he or she could apply for asylum, and that it was therefore sufficient for the asylum seeker to know that he or she had left the country of alleged persecution.[61] In the same vein, the German Constitutional Court ruled that the asylum seeker can be denied protection in accordance with Article 16a of the Constitution, even if it is not possible to determine which safe third country the asylum seeker has come from, as long as he/she arrived in Germany by land.[62] This judgment confirmed the ruling of the Federal Administrative Court of 7 November 1995 concerning a Kurd from Turkey who had been hidden in a lorry and did not know which countries he had travelled through.[63] This approach constitutes a dangerous misconception of the safe third country concept whose *rationale* is the existence of effective protection *somewhere*,[64] as repeatedly asserted by UNHCR,[65] which has opposed removal to a third State on the basis of mere transit.[66]

Another common feature of the safe third country is its unilateral operation. In Britain, the immigration rules expressly provides that the Secretary of State is under no obligation to consult the authorities of the third country before the removal of the asylum applicant,[67] thereby confirming previous administrative practice.[68]

British practice has, however, shown that unilateral transfer to the safe third country on the basis of mere transit is usually unsuccessful, and frequently results in the asylum seeker being 'bounced back' to the United Kingdom, at which point some judges have ruled that the authorities should examine the asylum claim on

---

[59] Article 2(c) of the 1992 Resolution, n 32 above; Note that the Recommendation No. R (97) 22 of the Council of Europe, n 30 above, and para (2) (i) Rule 345 of HC 395, n 33 above, have a similar wording.

[60] Costello, 'The European Asylum Procedures Directive in Legal Context', n 42 above, 4; see also the similar practice followed in Australia—Taylor, 'Protection Elsewhere', n 18 above, 307–9.

[61] *R v Special Adjudicator ex p Linsam Kandasamy* [1994] Imm AR 333 (QB).

[62] BverfGE, n 45 above, 94; see also Australian practice, which would allow return to a country with which an asylum seeker has had no prior contacts, Taylor, 'Protection Elsewhere', n 18 above, 306.

[63] (1995) 100 *Entscheidungen des Bundesverwaltungsgericht* 23.

[64] Emphasis added.

[65] UNHCR, 'The Concept of "Protection Elsewhere"', n 56 above, 123.

[66] For a discussion of this practice, see Chapter 4, Section 4.1.

[67] Rule 345 of HC 395, n 33 above, para (2).

[68] See eg *Charles Maroum Bouzeid Nehmattalah Halidar Hassan Abdul Karim Chahine Imad Hussein Al-Sayed Hayder Akram v Secretary of State for the Home Department* [1991] Imm AR 204 (CA), 206.

its merits.[69] According to a decision of the Queen's Bench Division, the fact that the safe third country might send the asylum seeker back to the United Kingdom does not mean that removal from the United Kingdom violates the Refugee Convention.[70] This may be legally correct, but one ought to question whether this is the most effective way to tackle secondary movements of refugees. In a study carried out by Amnesty International in 1995, 70 per cent of the 60 asylum cases examined were eventually considered substantively by the Home Office, either after a successful appeal to the Immigration Appeals Authority, after the asylum seeker applied for judicial review, or because the asylum seeker was 'bounced back' to the United Kingdom.[71]

As it appears, the policy followed by the British authorities is to evade as far as possible their duty to protect refugees and to examine their claims. Thus, in a case concerning Lebanese citizens who had claimed asylum in the United Kingdom while in transit, the Secretary of State considered that it was Brazil, the country of destination, which was responsible for examining the claims. The decisions were quashed by the High Court, which noted that Brazil was likely to apply the first asylum principle and that 'it was perverse to set in train a process which would almost certainly result in these applicants shuttled backwards and forwards in conditions which might well involve a breach of art 3 of the European Convention on Human Rights'.[72]

One of the most problematic applications of the safe third country concept, however, occurred in a case submitted to the German Constitutional Court. The asylum claim had been rejected in Austria, on the ground that it had already been rejected in Germany. Yet, it had been dismissed there because the applicant could be removed to Austria.[73] These were commonly followed practices, according to the Danish Refugee Council, which reported that States did not usually seek assurances that the asylum seeker would be given access to asylum procedures and did not inform the 'safe State' that the denial of asylum was based on formal grounds.[74]

From a protection perspective, it has been repeatedly stressed that it is essential that the authorities seek the consent of the third State and indicate that the

---

[69] P Shah, 'Refugees and Safe Third Countries: United Kingdom, European and International Aspects' (1995) 1 *European Public Law* 259, 279. See eg *Charles Maroum Bouzeid Nehmattalah Halidar Hassan Abdul Karim Chahine Imad Hussein Al-Sayed Hayder Akram v Secretary of State for the Home Department* [1991] Imm AR 204 (CA); *R v Special Adjudicator ex parte Bekim Babatinca* [1995] Imm AR 484 (QB).

[70] *R v Secretary of State for the Home Department ex p Senay Mehari Mohamed Ahmed Doreh Ali Abdi Hersi Fuat Celik Kuti Augusto* [1994] Imm AR 151 (QB).

[71] Amnesty International, *Playing Human Pinball: Home Office Practice in 'Safe Third Countries' Asylum Cases* (1995) 21 and 26.

[72] *R v Secretary of State for the Home Department ex p Khalil Yassine, Rahma Yassine Mohammad El-Nacher Hicham Ali Hachem, Salam Bou Imad, Zoueir Bou Imad* [1990] Imm AR 354, (QB) 362.

[73] BverfGE, n 45 above, 65–6.

[74] Lassen and Hughes, n 9 above, 2.

claim has not been substantively examined, but also that the asylum seeker be fully informed of the procedure and of its consequences.[75] The asylum procedures Directive does appear to provide more stringent guarantees in this regard. Article 27.3 requires that,

When implementing a decision solely on this Article, Member States shall:

(a) inform the applicant accordingly; and
(b) provide him/her with a document informing the authorities of the third country, in the language of that country, that the application has not been examined in substance.

Article 27.4 also stipulates that, 'where the third country does not permit the applicant for asylum to enter its territory, Member States shall ensure that access to a procedure is given in accordance with the basic principles and guarantees described in Chapter II'. This falls short, however, of ensuring that the asylum seeker has access to a substantive examination of his application in the third country, as it only applies if entry into the third country is refused.[76]

2.1.2.3 Procedural issues concerning the application of the safe third country concept

As seen above, the asylum procedures Directive failed to properly harmonize essential issues such as the existence of certain links between the asylum seeker and a third country or treatment in accordance with basic human standards. In strictly procedural terms, the Directive further legitimizes many questionable domestic practices.[77]

While the 'regular' procedure includes a number of important safeguards, the Directive provides for no less than 15 grounds for 'prioritising or accelerating' examination procedures,[78] including the safe third country.[79] Additionally, Member States are allowed to keep specific border procedures, in spite of the fact that the responsibility of States for applications made at the border is exactly the same as for application made inside the country.[80] Pursuant to Article 35.3 of the asylum procedures Directive, the safeguards applying to border procedures are: the right to remain at the border or transit zones, access to an interpreter and

---

[75] See Recommendation No. R (97) 22 of the Council of Europe, n 30 above; J Kumin, 'Die Genfer Flüchtlingskonvention and asylpolitischen Entwicklungen in Deutschland and Europa', in K Barwig and W Brill (eds), *Aktuelle asylrechtliche Probleme der Gerichtlichen Entscheidungspraxis in Deutschland, Österreich und der Schweiz* (Nomos, Baden-Baden 1996) 19, 21–2.

[76] Costello, 'The Asylum Procedures Directive and the Proliferation', n 3 above, 60.

[77] Costello, 'The European Asylum Procedures Directive in Legal Context', n 42 above, 6.

[78] Article 23.4 of the asylum procedures Directive; for an analysis of the concept of manifestly unfounded claims, see R Byrne, 'Remedies of Limited Effect: Appeals under the forthcoming Directive on EU Minimum Standards on Procedures' (2005) 7 *EJML* 71, 74–5.

[79] Article 23.4(c)(ii) of the asylum procedures Directive.

[80] Article 35.2 of the asylum procedures Directive; Costello, 'The European Asylum Procedures Directive in Legal Context', n 42 above, 9.

to be immediately informed of one's rights and obligations. Basic guarantees are also maintained with regard to the conduct of the interview and consultation with legal advisers. The fact remains, however, that these restrictions will push many asylum seekers to enter illegally rather than seeking asylum at the border and will lead to late applications, which is another ground provided in the Directive for applying accelerated procedures.[81]

Obviously, many questions remain on the ways administrative authorities and the judiciary will apply and interpret this instrument. Some skewed interpretation could lead for instance to the conclusion that Member States could decide that the safe third country is a valid ground to dismiss an asylum application as both inadmissible[82] and unfounded.[83]

The major issue, however, is whether the State must carry out an individual assessment of the safety of a third country for each asylum seeker. Previously, the EU Resolution on host third countries indicated that 'fulfilment of the individual requirements [...] should be assessed by the Member State in each individual case [...].'[84] The EU Resolution on manifestly unfounded applications for asylum seemed to contradict this approach, for it allowed the examination to be based on 'objective grounds' within an admissibility procedure.[85] The latter interpretation was consistent with the *rationale* that a 'reliable general determination of safety is possible'.[86]

The issue of individual assessment was examined by the German Constitutional Court in its decision of 14 May 1996, which ruled out that the 1993 safe third country amendment led to breaches of Germany's international obligations under the Refugee Convention.[87] The main provision challenged before the court was Article 16a paragraph 2 of the Constitution which provides for an exception to the

---

[81] Article 23.4(i) of the asylum procedures Directive; see Costello, 'The European Asylum Procedures Directive in Legal Context', n 42 above, 9.

[82] Article 25.2(c) of the asylum procedures Directive. Member States may also consider an application for asylum inadmissible if a country is considered as a first country of asylum; see ECRE, Information Note, n 39 above, which disagrees 'with the inclusion of safe third country cases in the admissibility procedural stage under article 25(2). The question whether a country can be considered safe for a particular applicant needs to be dealt with in the substantive determination procedures.'

[83] Article 23.4(c)(ii) of the asylum procedures Directive; see also Costello, 'The Asylum Procedures Directive and the Proliferation', n 3 above, 49, 55.

[84] Article 2 of the EU Resolution, n 32 above; see also Recommendation No. R (97) 22 of the Council of Europe, n 30 above, which states that the criteria of application should be met in each individual case.

[85] Resolution on Manifestly Unfounded Applications for Asylum, The Council, Conclusions of the Meeting of the Ministers responsible for Immigration (London, 30 November to 1 December 1992), Doc. 10579/92 IMMIG.

[86] Hailbronner, n 7 above, 61; R Marx and K Lumpp, 'The German Constitutional Court's Decision of 14 May 1996 on the Concept of "Safe Third Countries"—A Basis for Burden-Sharing in Europe?' (1996) 8 *IJRL* 419, 423.

[87] BverfGE, n 45 above; for an account of the ruling in English, see Marx and Lumpp, n 86 above 423; B Fassbender, 'International Decisions' (1997) 91 *AJIL* 355–60; 'Five Case Abstracts', in 'Cases and Comments' (1997) 9 *IJRL* 292.

constitutional right of asylum set out in Article 16a paragraph 1. Pursuant to Article 16a paragraph 2, the right to asylum shall not be granted in the case of aliens arriving from safe third countries. These safe third countries listed in Annex I to the Asylum Procedures Act are all EU Member States as well as those States where the CSR and the ECHR are fully implemented.[88] Safe third country lists have also been adopted in other countries, such as Denmark, Finland, Holland, Sweden, Croatia, or Serbia.[89]

The court based its decision on the concept of 'normative establishment of certainty' (*normative Vergewisserung*), that is, on the principle that safety can be sufficiently established by the legislator without any individual assessment in each particular case. This means that the asylum seeker cannot rebut the presumption of safety established by law, or challenge the conditions of application defined in the statute and the information used by the legislator to determine safety.[90] The decision of removal is immediately applicable and section 51 of the Aliens Act, which incorporates the obligation of *non-refoulement* in German law, cannot be invoked.[91] In the case of EC Member States, the 'normative establishment of certainty' is not relevant and safety is established *a priori* by the Constitution. The court declared that the constitutional amendment was founded on the 'broad common legal conviction' *(wesentlichen einheitliche Rechtsüberzeugung)* of the EU Member States in the field of asylum. This approach is based on Article 6.2 TEU[92] which requires compliance with the ECHR and is regarded as a fundamental principle of the Union.[93] There are a number of exceptional cases set out in the Aliens Act where an alien may not be expelled to another State and which apply to safe third country cases including: where there is actual danger of his being subjected to torture; where there is a risk of the alien being subject to capital punishment; where the expulsion is inadmissible under the ECHR; and where

---

[88] In accordance with para 5 of Art 16 of the Constitution, the application of chapter VII of the Schengen Convention, replaced on 1 September 1997 by the Dublin Convention and on 1 September 2003 by the Dublin Regulation, takes precedence over the application of the safe third country, which means that at this point the safe third country is exclusively applied through the Dublin Regulation; see also s 26a(2) *Asylverfahrensgesetz* (asylum procedure act) as amended on 19 August 2007. The non-EU safe third countries, currently Norway and Switzerland, are listed in Annex I of the Act.

[89] D Bouteillet-Paquet, *L'Europe et le Droit d'Asile, la politique d'asile européenne et ses conséquences pour les pays d'Europe centrale* (L'Harmattan, Paris 2001) 279; for Croatia, see Art 2 of the Law on Asylum, 1 July 2004, Available at: <http://www.unhcr.org/refworld/docid/3fcc66b24.html>; for Serbia, see Art 2 of the Law on Asylum, 1 July 2008, available at: <http://www.unhcr.org/refworld/docid/47b46e2f9.html>.

[90] Marx and Lumpp, n 86 above, 424.

[91] Ibid, 423.

[92] Treaty of Amsterdam amending the Treaty on European Union, the Treaty establishing the European Community and certain related acts, 2 June 1997 [1997] C340/1 and consolidated version of the Treaty establishing the European Community incorporating the changes made by the Treaty of Amsterdam [1997] OJ C340/173.

[93] BverfGE, n 45 above, 88.

there is considerable actual risk to the person, the life, or the freedom of the alien in that State.[94]

This determination *in abstracto* is based on the assumption that the legislator is the only authority competent to decide on the complex issue of whether a third country provides effective protection. The 'normative establishment of certainty' is, however, an artificial concept which challenges the foundations of the system of human rights enforcement by domestic and international courts.[95] The 'broad common legal conviction' might seem to have a more solid legal foundation, even though until the entry into force of the Amsterdam Treaty, the Court of Justice of the European Communities was not competent to ensure compliance with Article 6.2 TEU.[96]

The German Constitutional Court's legal construction contrasts with the situation that prevailed in Britain in the 1990s. In the 60 cases examined by Amnesty International in 1995, Austria, Belgium, France, Italy, and the Netherlands had been deemed 'not safe' or 'not safe for this particular individual' by special adjudicators.[97] As stated by the House of Lords, 'if it is well known that a third country which is party to the 1951 Geneva Convention regularly sends back refugees to an authoritarian country, then the United Kingdom would violate Article 33 of the Convention if it sent a refugee to that third country'.[98]

British courts also made interesting findings on the standard of proof applicable to determine whether a third country is safe for protection. In *Gulay Canbolat*, the Court of Appeal rejected the application of the test of 'reasonable degree of likelihood' used in the determination of refugee status and ruled that 'what is required is that there should be no real risk that the asylum seeker would be sent to another country otherwise than in accordance with the Convention', adding that 'the unpredictability of human behaviour or the remote possibility of changes in administrative law or procedures which there is no reason to anticipate would not be a real risk.'[99] The court later qualified its ruling, by holding that 'the Secretary of State had only to assure himself that a country did not adopt an approach which was outside the range of response of a contracting State acting in good faith to implement its obligations under the Convention', that is, 'clearly inconsistent'

---

[94] s 53 *Ausländergesetz* (Aliens Act), available at: <http://www.unhcr.org/refworld/docid/3ae6b55a0.html>.

[95] See the critique by J Henkel, 'Völkerrechtliche Aspekte des Konzepts des sicheren Drittstaates', in J Barwig and W Brill (eds), *Aktuelle asyrechtliche Probleme der gerichtlichen Entscheidungspraxis in Deutschland, Österreich, und der Schweiz* (Nomos, Baden-Baden 1996) 141, 161–3.

[96] Since the entry into force of the Treaty of Amsterdam on 1 May 1999, Art 46 TEU grants competence to the Court for ruling on the compliance of acts of the institutions with Art 6.2 TEU.

[97] This happened before the entry into force of the Dublin Convention, Amnesty International, n 71 above, 27 and 78–85. See also *R v Special Adjudicators ex p Mehmet Turus, Adem Bostem, Awat Ammen, Adam Folly-Nostron, Selcuk Ururgul* [1996] Imm AR 388 (QB).

[98] *Bugdaycay and ors v Secretary of State for the Home Department and related appeals* [1987] All ER 1 940 (HL) 952.

[99] *Gulay Canbolat v Secretary of State for the Home Department* [1997] Imm AR 442 (CA), 450–1.

with the Convention.[100] The House of Lords rejected this approach and in the *Adan* case, it adopted a more stringent test with regard to the specific question of the interpretation of Article 1 of the Refugee Convention and found that the United Kingdom would violate its obligations under international law by sending asylum applicants to Germany and France, given these countries' interpretation of Article 1 CSR.[101]

The legislative response to these judicial pronouncements was swift. The 1996 Asylum and Immigration Act had already abolished the suspensive effect of appeals in cases of removals to an EU Member State and to Canada, Norway, Switzerland, and the United States, which had been designated by the Secretary of State in a statutory instrument.[102] The asylum seeker could, however, still challenge the decision through judicial review proceedings in the High Court. Then, right before the delivery of the aforementioned *Adan* Judgment by the House of Lords, Parliament adopted in 1999 an amendment to the Asylum and Immigration Act providing that the presumption of safety of all EU Member States, as well as Canada, Norway, Switzerland, and the United States of America, may not be rebutted and that the claimant could thus be removed without a substantive examination of his claim.[103] The House of Lords had no option but to recognize that the argument which had succeeded in the *Adan* case, was now 'effectively blocked'.[104]

Further restrictions have been introduced by the legislator in 2004,[105] leading to a considerably more complex regulatory framework under UK law. Four categories of safe third countries now exist. Three lists of countries have been adopted, while the last category is based on individual certification.[106] Included in the first list, which can only be amended by Parliament, are Member States of

---

[100] *Thayaparan Iyadurai v Secretary of State for the Home Department* [1998] Imm AR 470 (CA) 470 and 476; see also *R v Secretary of State for the Home Department ex p Lul Adan* [1999] INLR 84 (QB) 89, where in accordance with the same test, the judge dismissed the claim of a Somali national.

[101] *R v Secretary of State for the Home Department ex p Adan and R v Secretary of State for the Home Department ex p Aitseguer* [2000] 1 All ER 593 (HL). For a detailed analysis of that case, see Chapter 5, Section 5.1.1.

[102] See s 3 (2) and s 2 (3) Asylum and Immigration Act 1996 and The Asylum (Designated Countries of Destination and Designated Safe Third Countries) Order 1996, SI 1996/2671; R Dunstan, 'A Case of Ministers Behaving Badly: The Asylum and Immigration Act 1996', in F Nicholson and P Twomey (eds), *Current Issues of UK Asylum Law and Policy* (Ashgate Publications, Aldershot 1998) 52, 62–3.

[103] s 11(1)(b) of the Immigration and Asylum Act 1999 and the Asylum (Designated Safe Third Countries) Order 2000 No. 2245 as amended by the Nationality and Immigration and Asylum Act 2002 s 80; see also G Clayton, *Textbook on Immigration and Asylum Law* (2nd edn, Oxford University Press Oxford 2006) 422.

[104] *R v Secretary of State for the Home Department ex p Thangasara and R v Secretary of State for the Home Department ex p Yogathas* [2002] UKHL 36, para 11.

[105] See s 33 Asylum and Immigration (Treatment of Claimants, etc.) Act 2004 (c. 19) and Schedule 3 to the 2004 Act.

[106] Clayton, n 103 above, 422.

the European Union and Norway and Iceland for which no appeal or judicial review is available in case of removal unless the Secretary of State is persuaded that there would be a breach of a human rights obligation in doing so.[107] The second list comprises States for which removal is found to be in compliance with the Refugee Convention and the ECHR and for which there is no automatic exclusion of appeal rights but a presumption that appeals are clearly unfounded. Under the third list, third States include those that are certified to be safe for Refugee Convention purposes only, for which there is no presumption that human rights claims are unfounded but which may be certified as such. The second and third lists may be amended by the Secretary of State. In all of these cases, appeals on the assessment of safety are debarred.[108] Finally the fourth category of safe third countries comprise countries found to be safe for removal provided there is no danger of *refoulement* or persecution and for which certification must be granted on an individual basis by the Secretary of State.

Since the passing of that legislation, challenges have been brought pursuant to the Human Rights Act and in the *Nasseri* case, a High Court Judge found that the provisions related to the first list, that is, the Dublin States, violated Article 3 ECHR.[109] This judgment was overturned on 14 May 2008 by the Court of Appeal, which found that there was no general incompatibility between the relevant provision of the 2004 Act and Article 3 ECHR given the Secretary of State's monitoring of States on the list to ensure individual compliance. With respect to the question of whether removal to the country concerned in that particular case was in breach of the Human Rights Act, the court concluded that 'Greece's continued presence on the list d[id] not offend the United Kingdom's Convention obligations'.[110] Yet, the Court of Appeal emphasized that 'the list system renders the United Kingdom's compliance with ECHR Article 3 fragile' noting that,

[I]n the absence of individual examinations of the merits of individual cases by those responsible for specific executive and judicial decisions in those cases, the whole weight of compliance falls on the measures and systems in place for monitoring law and practice in the listed States, and does so in circumstances where government has no discretion to take a State off the list, but must seek main legislation. Those measures and systems will need to be muscular.[111]

It bears noting that these legislative developments took place while the asylum procedures Directive was being negotiated. It is therefore unsurprising to see that

---

[107] Clayton, n 103 above, 423, who notes that the legality of this provision under international law is in doubt. On this point, see Chapter 5.

[108] Ibid, 423, 425.

[109] *Nasseri v Secretary of State for the Home Department* [2007] EWHC 1548, para 40.

[110] *Secretary of State for the Home Department v Nasseri* [2008] EWCA Civ 464, para 41. On returns to Greece pursuant to the Dublin Regulation, see Chapter 3, Section 3.3.5.

[111] Ibid, para 42.

the Directive has not brought very significant changes with respect to this fundamental question, only further confusion. While the original Commission proposal did provide for an individual assessment based on the particular circumstances of the asylum applicant, the current text, which in part resulted from Germany's insistence to maintain the approach adopted under its municipal laws,[112] only requires Member States to lay down rules in their domestic legislation on the

methodology by which the competent authorities satisfy themselves that the safe third country concept may be applied to a particular country or to a particular applicant. Such methodology shall include case-by-case consideration of the safety of the country for a particular applicant and/or national designation of countries considered to be generally safe.[113]

The Directive nonetheless specifies that the national rules must be

in accordance with international law, allowing an individual examination of whether the third country concerned is safe for a particular applicant which, as a minimum, shall permit the applicant to challenge the application of the safe third country concept on the grounds that he/she would be subjected to torture, cruel, inhuman or degrading treatment or punishment.[114]

This latter requirement was eventually inserted in the draft to comply with international legal obligations, and prevent denying access to asylum procedures.[115] The clause falls short, however, of meeting all of the international legal obligations of States, limiting itself to requiring protection against *refoulement* under Article 3 ECHR and not under Article 33 CSR. The Directive also provided that when an applicant entered illegally into the territory of a Member State from a European safe third country, the application did not need to be examined, following thereby the German approach.[116] Thus, theoretically, an asylum applicant could be sent back to a country with asylum legislation but with a 'zero recognition rate or no operative refugee status determination procedures of an acceptable standard'.[117]

---

[112] See Ackers, n 1 above, 21–2.

[113] Article 27.2(b) of the asylum procedures Directive; cf Recital 23 of the asylum procedures Directive, which provides that Member States should apply the safe third country rules 'where this particular applicant would be safe in the third country concerned'.

[114] Article 27.2(c) of the asylum procedures Directive.

[115] Costello, 'The Asylum Procedures Directive and the Proliferation', n 3 above, 60; Ackers, n 1 above, 29–30.

[116] Article 36.1 of the asylum procedures Directive; see Ackers, n 1 above, 21–2. This provision has become inapplicable given the ECJ Judgment of 6 May 2008, n 38 above. On the respective scopes of Art 33 CSR and Art 3 ECHR, see Chapter 5, Sections 5.1.1 and 5.1.2.

[117] M Garlick, 'The EU Discussions on Extraterritorial Processing: Solutions or Conundrum' (2006) 18 *IJRL* 601, 613. As noted by Costello, 'The Asylum Procedures Directive and the Proliferation', n 3 above, 53, Art 5 of the asylum procedures Directive allows States to maintain provisions existing under domestic law but does not require them to maintain those that are more

Finally, a minimalist approach was also favoured with respect to guaranteeing the right to an effective remedy. Once again, the Directive fails to provide clear requirements on the suspensive effect of an appeal filed by an asylum seeker. While, pursuant to Article 39.1(a)(i), a generic right of appeal is recognized against decisions based on Article 25(2)—which includes decisions based on the application of the safe third country and first country of asylum—Article 39.3(a) specifies that Member States shall, where appropriate, provide for rules in accordance with their international obligations dealing with, inter alia, the suspensive effect of the appeal.[118]

2.1.3 Conclusion

The asylum procedures Directive is not only an objective failure from the standpoint of EU harmonization, but the bits which have been harmonized are in fact lowering protection standards among Member States of the European Union, and arguably violate international law and basic principles of EC constitutional law.[119] As put bluntly by Peers, 'it is doubtful that any piece of EC legislation has ever been responsible for so many human rights breaches'.[120] It is also clear that normative efforts at the international level have been wholly insufficient to control the irrepressible spread of safe third country practices, whose most questionable features are now formalized in a supranational instrument. EU policies on readmission and proposals for extraterritorial processing, analysed below, are a full part of this trend towards the internationalization of refugee 'containment'.

---

favourable, contrary to usual EU practice, see eg Council Directive 2000/78/EC of 27 November 2000 establishing a general framework for equal treatment in employment and occupation [2000] OJ L303/16 and Council Directive 2000/43/EC of 29 June 2000 implementing the principle of equal treatment between persons irrespective of racial or ethnic origin [2000] OJ L180/22, which contain the following 'standstill clause': '[t]he implementation of this Directive shall under no circumstances constitute grounds for a reduction in the level of protection against discrimination already afforded by Member States in the fields covered by this Directive'; see also on this point UNHCR, 'Response to the European Commission's Green Paper on the Future Common European Asylum System' September 2007 (hereafter, UNHCR Response to Green Paper), 6.

[118] See Ackers, n 1 above, 22–3, who explains that the negotiations of the provisions on appeal were clearly affected by Member States'—namely Spain and Germany—insistence to maintain domestic provisions and by the simultaneous adoption of domestic legislation, namely in the UK and Austria, providing further restrictions on the possibility to suspend removal in safe third country cases; see also Byrne, 'Remedies of Limited Effect', n 78 above, 76–8. See *Jabari v Turkey*, Appl. No. 40035/98, Judgment of 11 July 2000, ECHR 2000-VIII, para 50; *Conka v Belgium*, Appl. No. 51564/99, Judgment of 5 February 2002, paras 79, 82–3; *Gebremedhin v France*, Appl. No. 25389/05, Judgment of 26 April 2007, para 58, 66. The suspensive effect of appeals is addressed in more detail in Chapters 3 and 5, Sections 3.4.1 and 5.1.2.

[119] Peers, *EU Justice and Home Affairs Law*, n 1 above, 338.

[120] Ibid, 341.

2.2 Readmission Agreements

2.2.1 Definition

Readmission agreements consist of a mutual undertaking by each party to take back without formalities certain categories of persons at the other party's request.[121] Their main purpose is to combat illegal immigration, but these instruments are now used for the swift expulsion of asylum seekers as well, and are critical to the effective implementation of safe third country practices.[122] Asylum seekers often lack identity documents and third countries may refuse to take them back.[123] States have then resorted to readmission agreements to remedy this problem. The use of readmission agreements as a migration and refugee containment tool has become particularly popular and has been regarded by the European Union as one of the instruments serving its objectives with respect to its relations with third countries in the migration and asylum fields,[124] along with carrier sanctions, immigration liaison officers networks, interception at sea, and protected entry procedures.[125] Since the entry into force of the Amsterdam Treaty, the European Community is competent to adopt measures 'within the area of illegal immigration and illegal residence, including repatriation of illegal residents', which thus entails a power to conclude readmission agreements with third countries.[126]

2.2.2 Evolution of readmission agreements

Apart from the 1959 European Agreement on the Abolition of Visas for Refugees, which provided for the readmission without formalities of recognized refugees

---

[121] M Schieffer, 'The Readmission of Third-Country Nationals within Bilateral and Multilateral Frameworks', in M den Boer (ed), *Schengen, First the Widening, Now the Deepening* (European Institute of Public Administration, Maastricht 1997) 97, 100.

[122] European Parliament, *Migration and Asylum in Central and Eastern Europe* (1997) 9; Byrne, 'Harmonization and Burden Redistribution in Europe', n 45 above, 349.

[123] A Achermann and M Gattiker, 'Safe Third Countries: European Developments' (1995) 7 *IJRL* 19, 24.

[124] Communication from the Commission to the Council and the European Parliament on asylum and immigration policies, COM (94) 23 final, 23 February 1994, para 114; European Pact on Immigration and Asylum, Doc 13440/08, 24 September 2008, 7 available at <http://www.immigration. gouv.fr./IMG/pdf/Plaquette_EN.pdf>.

[125] Directorate Study, n 51 above, 11–13.

[126] See Art 63(3)(b) ECT; see also European Council, Presidency Conclusions, Tampere, 15–16 October 1999, paras 26–7, which invites the Council of Ministers to conclude readmission agreements or to include standard readmission clauses in other agreements between the European Community and relevant third countries or groups of third countries. See also M Schieffer, 'Community Readmission with Third Countries—Objectives, Substance and Current State of Negotiations' (2003) 5 *EJML* 343, 350; Peers, *EU Justice and Home Affairs Law*, n 1 above, 291.

by the State which had issued them a travel document,[127] early readmission agreements generally applied to nationals of contracting parties.[128] Because some countries required documentary proof before readmitting nationals, readmission agreements set out more flexible formalities for nationality determination.[129] These agreements also applied to third country nationals who had been granted a residence permit or an entry visa by the requested State.[130]

The hardening of Western European States' attitudes towards migrants and refugees was reflected by the increasingly restrictive provisions of the 'second-generation' readmission agreements, which were extended to illegal aliens transiting through the requested State,[131] without providing specific guarantees to protect undocumented asylum seekers. The 1990s saw a rapid expansion of readmission agreements, when Central and Eastern European countries concluded readmission agreements with Western European States, as part of the increasing cooperation in the immigration and asylum field and to prepare future accession of these countries to the European Union.[132] By the late 1990s, more than a hundred readmission agreements had been concluded between European States,[133] with Germany party to as many as 17.[134] However, agreements providing for the readmission of third country nationals were concluded by Germany only with countries which were regarded as 'safe' by the legislator.[135] Germany was also the first Western country to acknowledge that Central and Eastern European countries lacked resources to deal with important numbers of immigrants and refugees. The agreements concluded at the time with Poland and the Czech Republic thus included a financial protocol to help with the costs incurred by

---

[127] European Agreement on the Abolition of Visas for Refugees (Strasbourg, 20 April 1959) (1960) 376 UNTS 85 No. 5375.

[128] See X Denoël, 'Les accords de réadmission, du Bénélux à Schengen et au-delà' [1993] *RTDE*, 635.

[129] See eg Arts 1 and 2 of the Agreement in relation to the reassimilation of German and Romanian Citizens between the Federal Republic of Germany and Romania of 24 September 1992 (1992) 31 *ILM* 1295; Inter-governmental Consultations on Asylum, Refugee and Migration Policies in Europe, North America and Australia, 'Working Paper on Readmission Agreements' (Geneva, August 1994) 5. Readmission of nationals is sometimes refused on a discriminatory basis. Bouteillet-Paquet gives the example of Albanian Kosovars whose readmission was refused by the Yugoslav authorities at the time, which argued that they were Albanian nationals, see D Bouteillet-Paquet, 'Passing the Buck: A Critical Analysis of the Readmission Policy Implemented by the European Union and its Member States' (2003) 5 *EJML* 359, 361.

[130] Bouteillet-Paquet, *L'Europe et le droit d'asile*, n 89 above, 286.

[131] Ibid, 291.

[132] See UNHCR, *3rd International Symposium on the Protection of Refugees in Central Europe* (1997) 3 *European Series* 7; ECRE, 'Position on the Enlargement of the European Union in relation to Asylum' September 1998. On discussions concerning the asylum *acquis* in the context of the negotiations on accession, see Bouteillet-Paquet, *L'Europe et le droit d'asile*, n 89 above, 311–30.

[133] Bouteillet-Paquet, *L'Europe et le droit d'asile*, n 89 above, 227.

[134] Inter-governmental Consultations on Asylum Refugee and Migration Policies in Europe, North America and Australia, 'Inventory of Readmission Agreements as at 4 February 1998'.

[135] Schieffer, 'The Readmission of Third Country Nationals', n 121 above, 103.

the arrival of migrants.[136] However, most of the money was apparently spent on improving immigration controls, rather than on developing administrative practices to examine applications for asylum.[137] This two-prong approach, readmission accompanied by capacity-building and financial support in controlling borders and fighting illegal immigration has become the hallmark of the European Union's readmission policies.

2.2.3 Characteristics

Readmission agreements are generally bilateral[138] and most instruments lay down the procedure and time limits to be followed by the requesting and requested States.[139] Time limits for readmission of third country nationals generally vary between 48 hours and 7 days in respect of readmission at the border, which is the most common. Readmission may also be carried out through diplomatic channels, usually within 90 days.[140]

In 1994, the Council of Justice and Home Affairs of the European Union adopted a Recommendation concerning a specimen bilateral readmission agreement between a Member State and a third country,[141] which was used as a basis for negotiation of instruments of the 'second generation'. A Recommendation on the guiding principles to be followed in drawing up protocols on the implementation

---

[136] S Lavenex, *Safe Third Countries: Extending the EU Asylum and Immigration Policies to Central and Eastern Europe* (Central European University Press, New York 1999) 82.

[137] Agreement between The Czech Republic and Germany of 1 January 1995 and Agreement between Poland and Germany of 7 May 1993. Financial assistance granted to Poland within the framework of the bilateral re-admission agreement concluded with Germany, was spent for the most part on the improvement of the infrastructure of the border authorities (54.6 million DEM), and on the training of the police (42.8 million DEM). Only 0.9 million DEM was granted to the Polish Refugee Office. The Czech authorities made a similar use of this assistance, Bouteillet-Paquet, 'Study on the Readmission Agreements Signed by the Czech Republic, Hungary, Poland and Slovenia and on Instruments Available to Develop Access to Fair and Efficient Refugee Status Determination Procedures in Central European Countries', Fourth International Symposium on the Protection of Refugees in the Central European and the Baltic States, 27–29 September 1998 Bled, Slovenia (on file with the author), 24. See also ECRE, n 132 above, 12; Lavenex, n 136 above, 86 and 88.

[138] Bouteillet-Paquet, *L'Europe et le droit d'asile*, n 89 above, 287. One notable exception was the Agreement between the States parties to the Schengen agreements and Poland, published in Plender, n 7 above, 863; see also Convention on the transfer of control of persons to the external frontiers of Benelux territory of 11 April 1960 (1960) 374 UNTS 3 No. 5323; Convention concerning the Waiver of Passport Control at the Intra-Nordic Frontiers of 12 July 1957 (1959) 322 UNTS 245 No. 4660.

[139] See eg Art 9 of the Convention on the Transfer of Control of Persons to the External Frontiers of Benelux territory of 11 April 1960 and the Convention concerning the Waiver of Passport Control at the Intra-Nordic Frontiers of 12 July 1957, n 138 above.

[140] Bouteillet-Paquet, 'Study on the Readmission Agreements', n 137 above. See eg Art 3 of the Schengen-Poland agreement of 29 March 1991. For a comparison of the time limits in readmission agreements, see Intergovernmental Consultations, 'Working Paper on Readmission Agreements', n 129 above, annex 2. Note that with respect to readmission at the border, removals may take place without the alien's presence being recorded, see ECRE, *Defending Refugees' Access to Protection in Europe*, December 2007, 45.

[141] Adopted on 30 November 1994 [1996] OJ C274/20.

of readmission agreements followed in 1995.[142] Another document, called the *Draft Skeleton*,[143] was presented at a meeting of the Budapest Group[144] in September 1995 with the objective of influencing discussions on the design of a standard bilateral readmission agreement. It was never adopted but its principles were implemented in agreements between Eastern European countries.[145]

While these two instruments are both a little dated, they provide a helpful comparison of the key features of readmission instruments. The major difference between the *Draft Skeleton* and the EU recommendation lies in the treatment of third country nationals. The EU document recommended an extensive application of readmission, including in cases where it could be proved or 'validly' [*sic*] assumed that the person had entered via the external frontier of the requested State, as opposed to the common border of the contracting parties.[146] The *Draft Skeleton*, on the other hand, recommended that the requested State should only accept the readmission without formalities of the alien who had been granted permanent residence or refugee status in that State. In addition, the requesting State was asked to present evidence of the illegal crossing of the common borders by a third country national. The *Draft Skeleton* also included a provision excluding 'collective readmission', that is, readmission of groups of people without an individual examination of each person's situation, in accordance with Article 4 of Protocol No. 4 to the ECHR.[147]

The major flaw of both documents was that there was no provision on the protection to be granted to asylum seekers on the basis of States' international commitments.[148] The EU recommendation only mentioned that the 1951 Geneva Convention, its 1967 Protocol, and the ECHR should not be affected

---

[142] Adopted on 24 July 1995 [1996] OJ C274/25.

[143] 'Report on the theme of readmission agreements prepared by the Czech Republic in the framework of the Expert Group of the Budapest Group' (on file with author).

[144] The Budapest Group is an informal structure which emerged from an earlier process known as the 'Berlin process'. This group was composed of representatives of 40 Member States of the Council of Europe who discussed issues relating to immigration and asylum, with the support of IOM, the Intergovernmental Consultations and the International Centre for Migration Policy Development, S Stanton Russell, C B Keely, and B P Christian, *Multilateral Diplomacy to Harmonize Asylum Policy in Europe: 1984–1993* (Institute for the Study of International Migration, Washington DC 2000) 42.

[145] Bouteillet-Paquet, 'European Harmonisation in the Field of Readmission Agreements', n 7 above, 38.

[146] Article 2.1 of the EU recommendation, n 141 above.

[147] Protocol No. 4 to the Convention for the Protection of Human Rights and Fundamental Freedoms securing certain rights and freedoms other than those already included in the Convention and in the first Protocol thereto, ETS No. 46, 16 September 1963; see Inter-governmental Consultations, 'Comparison between the EU Specimen Bilateral Readmission Agreement and the Draft Skeleton by the Czech Republic for the Budapest Group', 28 February 1995, 2.

[148] Note that this is also the case for the more recent instrument establishing the Immigration Liaison Officers Network and for the European programme of measures to combat illegal immigration across the maritime borders of the EU; see Council Regulation (EC) No. 377/2004 of 19 February 2004 on the creation of an immigration liaison officers network, 19 February 2004; European programme of measures to combat illegal immigration across the maritime borders of the European Union, Doc. 13791/03, 21 October 2003.

by the agreement, but it neither required parties to become parties to these instruments, nor to implement them.[149] There was, in other words, no sufficient guarantee that the authorities would treat asylum applicants differently than any other illegal aliens, or any explicit commitment by the requested State to examine an asylum claim of a readmitted individual.[150] Refugee protection concerns have continued to be ignored to this day, and apparently, UNHCR and other independent observers have not been consulted in relation to the content of readmission agreements that have been recently negotiated and concluded.[151]

2.2.4 Readmission as a component of the European Union's external dimension of asylum and immigration policies

As early as 1992, the Council of the European Union advocated a common approach to the development of cooperation and migration policy. The Declaration of Edinburgh recommended that Member States 'work for bilateral or multilateral agreements with countries of origin or transit to ensure that illegal immigrants can be returned to their home countries'.[152] This policy received further support in the 1998 Action Plan of the Council and the Commission concerning the implementation of the new provisions of the Treaty of Amsterdam on the area of freedom, security, and justice, where the improvement of possibilities for the removal of illegal migrants through inter alia readmission clauses was cited as one of the measures to be taken after the entry into force of the Treaty.[153] Thus, many of the initiatives towards neighbouring countries starting in the 1990s included specific provisions concerning the readmission of third country nationals.[154]

---

[149] Article 11.1 and 11.3 of the EU recommendation, n 141 above.

[150] UNHCR has recommended that readmission agreements provide that the requesting State shall communicate the reasons for removal to the requested State, see ExCom Conclusion No. 8 (1977) 'Determination of Refugee Status'; UNHCR, 'Position on Standard Bilateral Readmission Agreements Between a Member State and a Third Country', December 1994, 2; *3rd International Symposium on the Protection of Refugees in Central Europe*, n 132 above, 31; UNHCR, Background paper No. 3, Inter-State agreements for the re-admission of third country nationals, including asylum seekers, and for the determination of the State responsible for examining the substance of an asylum claim, May 2001; see also Guild, n 32 above, 406; ECRE 'Comment on the Report and Motion for a Resolution by Mrs Claudia Roth on a Draft Council Recommendation concerning a Specimen Bilateral Readmission Agreement between a Member State of the European Union and a Third Country', September 1995.

[151] Garlick, n 117 above, 614; see also ECRE, *Defending Refugees' Access to Protection in Europe*, n 140 above, 45.

[152] See Declaration on principles governing external aspects of migration policy, Annex 5 to Part A of the Conclusions of the Edinburgh European Council, 11–12 December 1992, Bull EC 12-1992, 23. See also Communication from the Commission to the Council and the European Parliament on asylum and immigration policies, n 124 above, para 115.

[153] Action Plan of the Council and the Commission on how best to implement the provisions of the Treaty of Amsterdam on areas of freedom, security, and justice, 3 December 1998 [1999] OJ C19/1, para 38 (c) (i).

[154] See eg Common Strategy of the European Union on Russia, 4 June 1999 [1999] OJ LI57/1; European Council Common Strategy of 11 December 1999 on Ukraine [1999] OJ L331/1, para 63;

One the techniques used by the European Union has been the inclusion of a clause concerning the conclusion of readmission agreements in conventional cooperation instruments.[155] This was modelled on the 'human rights clauses' which was one of the applications of conditionality approaches that became particularly popular in the 1980s and 1990s. In the 1990s, the Council adopted two conclusions on readmission clauses in Community agreements,[156] and in mixed agreements.[157] In agreements between the EC and a third State, the clause would take the form of a declaration in the final act with the commitment of the third State to enter into readmission agreements with EC Member States, and was usually limited to the readmission of nationals. In the case of mixed agreements, that is agreements between the Community and the Member States, on the one hand, and a third State, on the other, the fight against illegal immigration was to be regarded as one of the essential objectives of the agreement, which enabled the contracting parties to suspend the treaty in case of non-compliance. The clause provided that the third State would commit to conclude an agreement for the readmission of its nationals, and of third country nationals and stateless persons, without any mention of States' obligations under the Refugee Convention or other international human rights instruments.[158] Member States agreed in any case that the insertion of these clauses should be examined on a case-by-case basis when adopting the guidelines for their negotiation.[159]

By 2003, it was estimated that over 70 countries had contracted obligations in treaties with the European Community to readmit their own nationals and to negotiate further treaties on readmission at the request of the European Community or a Member State.[160] The Cotonou Agreement concluded by the

---

OJ L331/1, para 4(c); Common Strategy of the European Council of 19 June 2000 on the Mediterranean Region [2000] OJ L183/5, para 22; Council Decision of 8 March 2001 on the principles, priorities, intermediate objectives and conditions contained in the Accession Partnership with the Republic of Turkey [2001] OJ L85/13.

[155] See eg Art 84 of the Partnership and Cooperation Agreement between the EC and their Member States of the one part, and the Russian Federation, of the other signed on 24 June 1994, COM (94) 257 final, excerpts published in Plender, n 7 above, 624 and the Joint Declaration relating to readmission annexed to the Association Agreement between the European Communities and their Member States, of the one part and the Kingdom of Morocco, of the other part signed on 26 February 1995, COM (95) 740, excerpts published in Plender, n 7 above, 639.

[156] Adopted on 20 December 1995, Bull EU 12-1995 point 1.5.3.

[157] Adopted on 4 March 1996, Bull EU 3-1996 point 1.5.6; see also Council Decision of 2 December 1999 on readmission clauses in Community agreements or mixed agreements, Council Doc. 13409/99, Bull EU 12-1999, 1.5.6. Mixed agreements cover matters which do not exclusively belong to Community competencies.

[158] Note that the mixed agreement with Morocco, n 155 above, was signed before these conclusions were adopted, hence the use of a joint declaration on readmission of State Parties' nationals.

[159] EU Bull, n 157 above.

[160] S Peers, 'Readmission agreements and EC external migration law', *EU Statewatch Analysis* No. 17, May 2003, available at: <http://www.statewatch.org/news/2003/may/12readmission.htm>.

European Community with ACP States[161] is a prime example of a multilateral development cooperation instrument in which readmission clauses have been included. Article 13 creates an obligation of readmission for the nationals of State parties to the agreement.[162] Furthermore, the agreement provides for the possibility to include third country nationals and stateless persons in the scope of bilateral readmission agreements.[163] This provision was included despite the resistance of ACP States, which considered with some reason, that the readmission of third country nationals had no basis in international law.[164]

As noted above, following the entry into force of the Amsterdam Treaty in 1999, the European Community became competent to conclude directly readmission treaties with third countries. The importance given to readmission in the external dimension of EU asylum and immigration policies was highlighted in the 1999 Conclusions of the Tampere European Council[165] as well as in subsequent conclusions adopted at Seville in 2002, where Member States called for the inclusion of a clause on compulsory readmission in the event of illegal immigration 'in any future cooperation, association or equivalent agreement which the European Union of the European Community concludes with any country'.[166] The Seville Conclusions are also remembered for the threatening tone adopted by EU Member States towards third countries with regard to the joint management of migration flows:

After full use has been made of existing Community mechanisms without success, the Council may unanimously find that a third country has shown an unjustified lack of cooperation in joint management of migration flows. In that event, the Council may, in accordance with the rules laid down in the treaties, adopt measures or positions under the Common Foreign and Security Policy and other European Union policies, while honouring the Union's contractual commitments and not jeopardising development cooperation objectives.[167]

---

[161] Partnership Agreement between the Members of the Africa, Caribbean and Pacific Group of States on the one part, and the European Community and its Member States of the other part, signed at Cotonou on 23 June 2000, available at: <http://europea.eu.int/comm/development/body/cotonou/index_en.htm>.

[162] Article 13(c)(i) and (ii).

[163] Article 13(c)(ii).

[164] 'Lomé Convention used to impose repatriation on the world's poorest countries', *Statewatch News Online*, July 2000, available at: <http://www.statewatch.org/news/jul00/01lome.htm>. Statewatch also reports that the Legal Service of the Council seemed to agree with ACP States on this point; see also G Noll, 'Return of Persons to States of Origin and Third States', in T A Aleinikoff and V Chetail (eds) *Migration and International Legal Norms* (T M C Asser, The Hague [etc] 2003) 61, 63.

[165] See n 126 above.

[166] Presidency Conclusions, Seville European Council, 21–22 June 2002, para 33.

[167] Ibid, para 36; see also Proposal for a Comprehensive Plan to Combat Illegal Immigration and Trafficking of Human Beings, [2002] OJ C142/23, para 69–71 which was followed by the submission by the Commission of a Green Paper on a Community's return policy COM (2002) 175 final, 10 April 2002, 24 in which the Commission indicated that 'enabling' clauses committing the parties to a general obligation of readmission, had been included in agreements with Algeria, Armenia, Azerbaijan, Croatia, Egypt, Georgia, Lebanon, Macedonia, and Uzbekistan.

While the language of the Thessaloniki European Council Conclusion was more restrained, it still emphasized the need to 'monitor relations with third countries which do not cooperate with the EU in combating illegal immigration', and listed among the topics of primary importance, 'the cooperation of third countries in readmission/return of their nationals and of third-country nationals'.[168]

In institutional terms, the EU High Level Working Group on Asylum and Migration, which was created in 1998 and comprises civil servants from interior, development trade and foreign ministries, had its mandate expanded in 2002 to develop a strategic approach and a coherent and integrated policy for the most important countries and regions of origin and transit of asylum seekers and migrants, including the evaluation of the possibility of concluding readmission agreements.[169] In its 2002 Communication to the Council, the Commission also presented initiatives already adopted in this area, such as the establishment of reception policies and infrastructures for asylum seekers and strengthening institutional capacities, improving border controls, and tackling illegal immigration.[170]

Similarly, the European Neighbourhood Policy launched in 2003[171] has as one of its objectives the establishment of a joint border management system that focuses on moving controls outside the EU's borders, if the partner country concerned agrees. Under such system, readmission remains one of the key tools. The European Neighbourhood Policy covers Algeria, Armenia, Azerbaijan,

---

[168] Presidency Conclusions, Thessaloniki European Council, 19–20 June 2003, para 19.

[169] *Modification of the terms of reference of the High Level Working Group on Asylum and Migration (HLWG)*, Council Document 9433/02 of 30 May 2002; Gil-Bazo, n 52 above, 581–2; 'EU: High Level Working Group on Asylum and migration: crucial body in EU's external policies', *Statewatch Bulletin*, Vol 16, No. 1 January–February 2006, available at: <http://www.statewatch.org>.

[170] European Commission, 'Integrating migration issues in the European's Union relations with third countries' COM (2002) 703 final, 3 December 2002, which led to the adoption of Regulation (EC) No. 491/2004 of the European Parliament and of the Council of 10 March 2004 establishing a programme for financial and technical assistance to third countries in the areas of migration and asylum (AENEAS) [2004] OJ L80/1 which ended in 2007; see Valluy, n 52 above, 556; see also Bouteillet-Paquet, 'Passing the Buck', n 129 above, 373, who considers that 'the orientation defined within this framework has so far produced little more than an extension of the restrictive immigration policies, rather than directing political, development, or economic cooperation from a human rights perspective to prevent root causes of economic and forced displacements'.

[171] The ENP was presented by the Commission in March 2003 and endorsed by the European Council of Thessaloniki of June 2003, see European Commission, 'Communication from the Commission to the Council and the European Parliament: Wider Europe Neighbourhood: A new framework for relations with our Eastern and Southern neighbours' COM (2003) 104 final, 11 March 2003; 'Communication from the Commission to the Council and the European Parliament: European Neighbourhood Policy Strategy Paper' COM (2004) 373 final, 12 May 2004; 'Communication from the Commission: A Strong European Neighbourhood Policy' COM (2007) 774 final, 5 December 2007. The European Commission also presented a proposal for a financial instrument to fund the ENP, which was adopted in 2006, Regulation (EC) No. 1638/2006 of the European Parliament and of the Council of 24 October 2006 laying down general provisions establishing a European Neighbourhood and Partnership Instrument, Art 2.2(q)–(r).

Belarus, Egypt, Georgia, Israel, Jordan, Lebanon, Libya, the Republic of Moldova, Morocco, the Palestinian Occupied Territory, Syria, Tunisia, and Ukraine and its implementation is carried out through the adoption of 'action plans'.[172]

The latest idea of the European Union is to assist third countries in the negotiation and implementation of their own readmission agreements or arrangements with other third countries, which while unsurprising, raises even greater concerns in terms of refugee protection.[173] Thus, after having integrated within the European Union the 'first generation' of buffer States through the last waves of enlargement, the European Union is now eager to rebuild its buffer, the reach of its non-arrival policies expanding even farther into Central Asia, North Africa, and the Middle-East.[174]

In spite of these various efforts and initiatives, it has been relatively arduous for the European Union to conclude readmission agreements with third countries.[175] Since the adoption of the Amsterdam Treaty in 1997 and the Tampere conclusions of 1999, the Council authorized the Commission to start negotiations on the conclusion of readmission agreements with 11 countries.[176] By 2007, the following agreements had been concluded: with Hong Kong in 2002,[177] with

---

[172] <http://ec.europa.eu/world/enp/howitworks_en.htm>.

[173] European Commission, 'Communication from the Commission to the European Parliament and the Council: Thematic Programme for the cooperation with third countries in the areas of migration and asylum' COM (2006) 26 final, 25 January 2006, 12.

[174] 'EU buffer states and UNHCR "processing" centres and "safe havens"', *Statewatch News Online*, June 2003, available at: <http://www.statewatch.org/news/2003/jun/07eubuffer.htm>.

[175] See Council Conclusions on the evaluation of the progress and outcome of negotiation of Community readmission agreement with third countries, Luxembourg, 12–13 June 2007, available at: <http://www.consilium.europa.eu/ueDocs/cms_Data/docs/pressData/en/jha/94617. pdf>. The conclusions note that one of the contentious points remains the readmission of third country nationals.

[176] These are Albania, Algeria, China, Hong Kong, Macao, Morocco, Pakistan, Russia, Sri Lanka, Turkey, and Ukraine; see Schieffer, 'Community Readmission with Third Countries', n 126 above, 344. The criteria used to identify 'target countries' are: migration pressure on EU; States which have signed an association or cooperation agreement (excepting States negotiating accession); adjacent States; States where a readmission agreement would 'add value' to Member States' bilateral agreements; and 'geographical balance', see Council of Ministers, criteria for the identification of third countries with which new readmission agreements need to be negotiated, Doc 7990/02, 16 April 2002. Bouteillet-Paquet notes, however, that 'the target countries are designated by the Council without taking into consideration the priorities defined by the European Commission in terms of humanitarian assistance and development', n 129 above, 371.

[177] Agreement between the European Community and the Government of Hong Kong Special Administrative Region of the People's Republic of China on the readmission of persons residing without authorization [2004] OJ L17/23. The agreement entered into force on 1 March 2004 [2004] OJ L64/38.

Macao[178] and with Sri Lanka in 2002,[179] with Albania in 2005,[180] with Russia in 2006,[181] and Bosnia and Herzegovina, the Former Yugoslav Republic of Macedonia, the Republic of Montenegro, the Republic of Serbia, Moldova, and Ukraine in 2007.[182] In 2008, the Commission reported that another negotiation was being finalized while four new mandates had been given by the Council.[183]

These instruments apply to both nationals and third country nationals or stateless persons who have illegally entered or stayed on their territory.[184] A standard clause also provides that the agreement is 'without prejudice to the rights, obligations, and responsibilities of the parties arising from international law', with no further precision, except for the agreement instruments with Albania and Russia, where specific reference to international human rights and refugee laws was included.[185]

[178] Agreement between the European Community and the Macao Special Administrative Region of the People's Republic of China on the readmission of persons residing without authorization [2004] OJ L143/99. The agreement entered into force on 1 June 2004.

[179] Agreement between the European Community and the Democratic Socialist Republic of Sri Lanka on the readmission of persons residing without authorization [2005] OJ L124/43. The agreement entered into force on 1 May 2005.

[180] Agreement between the European Community and the Republic of Albania on the readmission of persons residing without authorisation [2005] OJ L124/22. The agreement entered into force on 1 May 2006.

[181] Agreement between the European Community and the Russian Federation on readmission [2007] OJ L129/40. The agreement entered into force on 1 June 2007. Note that Russia has introduced the safe third country concept and applies it at the border with asylum seekers arriving from a Central Asian Republic deemed to be safe, see Parliamentary Assembly of the Council of Europe, 'Situation of refugees and displaced persons in the Russian Federation and some other CIS countries' Doc 10118, 25 March 2004, para 44.

[182] Council Decision on the conclusion of the Agreement between the European Community and Bosnia and Herzegovina on the readmission of persons residing without authorization, Council Doc 12196/07, 14 September 2007; Adoption of a Council Decision concerning the conclusion of the Agreement between the European Community and the Former Republic of Macedonia on the readmission of persons residing without authorization, Doc 14031/07, 26 October 2007; Council Decision on the conclusion of the Agreement between the European Community and the Republic of Montenegro on the readmission of persons residing without authorization, Council Doc 13761/07, 29 October 2007; Council Decision on the conclusion of the Agreement between the European Community and the Republic of Serbia on the readmission of persons residing without authorization, Council Doc 13758/07, 29 October 2007; Council Decision on the conclusion of the Agreement between the European Community and the Republic of Moldova on the readmission of persons residing without authorization, Council Doc 13765/07, 20 November 2007; Council Decision concerning the conclusion of the Agreement between the European Community and Ukraine on the readmission of persons, Council Doc 13763/07, 26 November 2007; See also <http://ec.europa.eu/justice_home/fsj/immigration/relations/fsj_immigration_relations_en.htm>; S Peers 'Readmission Agreements and EC External Migration Law', n 160 above.

[183] European Commission, 'Communication from the Commission to the European Parliament, the Council, the European Economic and Social Committee and the Committee of the Regions: Strengthening the Global Approach to Migration: Increasing Coordination, Coherence, Synergies' COM (2008) 611 final, 8 October 2008, 5.

[184] Schieffer, 'Community Readmission with Third Countries', n 126 above, 354. However, readmission does not apply to third country nationals or stateless persons in air transit, ibid.

[185] See Art 18.1 of the Agreement with the Russian Federation, n 181 above; Art 17.1 of the Agreement with the Republic of Albania, n 180 above; Peers, *EU Justice and Home Affairs Law*, n 1 above, 290.

The fact that the European Union does not deem it necessary to carry out consultations with these third States before mandating the Commission to proceed with negotiation may explain the difficulties it faced in concluding these instruments. Apparently, by 2003, Morocco, Pakistan, and Russia had still not agreed to start negotiations, long after the mandate to negotiate the agreement was given by the Council.[186] Negotiations with Morocco have been notably blocked by its refusal to take back third country nationals having passed through its territory before arriving in Europe.[187] The Council of Ministers then came up with a new incentive for third countries, in the form of 'visa facilitation', that is 'the simplification of visa issuing procedures for nationals of third countries under a visa obligation'.[188] The Commission had even considered that 'incentives' to third States should also include close economic cooperation, trade expansion, or development assistance.[189]

While many countries continue to consider that readmission agreements are concluded due to 'unequal power relationship and are often tantamount to burden-shifting',[190] and despite the mixed results of EU strategies, readmission remains more than ever at the core of current EU policies on illegal immigration, as evidenced by the European Pact on Immigration and Asylum adopted in October 2008.[191] The fact that, in spite of the repeated calls to make readmission agreements more protection-sensitive, the content of these instruments has not been changed, demonstrates that EU Member States are not genuinely interested

---

[186] Peers, 'Readmission Agreements and EC External Migration Law', n 160 above. Cf Schieffer, 'Community Readmission with Third Countries', n 126 above, 345; see also Peers, *EU Justice and Home Affairs Law*, n 1 above, 293.

[187] Directorate Study, n 51 above, 16; Gil-Bazo, n 52 above, 589.

[188] Council of Ministers, COREPER meeting, Doc No. 16030/05, 20 December 2005; see 'EU Roundup: Visa "facilitation", European Arrest Warrants 2005, "Check the Web" and the principle of availability', *Statewatch Bulletin*, Vol 16, No. 2, March–April 2006, available at: <http://www.statewatch.org>; cf Schieffer, 'Community Readmission with Third Countries', n 126 above, 356 who considers that visa facilitation or the lifting of visa requirements is in most cases not a realistic option; see also Council Conclusions on the evaluation of the progress and outcome of negotiation of Community readmission agreement with third countries, Luxembourg, 12–13 June 2007, available at: <http://www.consilium.europa.eu/ueDocs/cms_Data/docs/pressData/en/jha/94617.pdf>; see also European Commission, 'Communication from the Commission to the Council and the European Parliament: Report on Implementation of the Hague Programme for 2007' COM (2008) 373 final, 2 July 2008, para 29.

[189] European Commission, 'Communication from the Commission to the European Parliament and the Council in view of the European Council of Thessaloniki on the development of a common policy on illegal smuggling and trafficking of human beings, external borders and the return of illegal aliens' COM (2003) 323 final, 3 June 2003.

[190] UNHCR High Commissioner's Forum, 'Convention Plus Core Group on Addressing Irregular Secondary Movements of Refugees and Asylum-Seekers: Joint Statement by the Co-Chairs' UN Doc FORUM/2005/7, 8 November 2005, 5.

[191] European Pact on Immigration and Asylum, Council Doc 13440/08, 24 September 2008, which was endorsed by EU interior ministers on 25 September 2008 and formally adopted on 16 October 2008 by the 27 EU Heads of State, see <http://www.immigration.gouv.fr/IMG/pdf/Plaquette_EN.pdf>.

in ensuring that asylum seekers who are subject to readmission proceedings have nevertheless a real opportunity to seek protection.

2.3 Extraterritorial Processing

2.3.1 Origins

The next logical leap in 'outsourcing' border controls and refugee protection to countries of transit has been the proposal to establish systems of extraterritorial processing. The United States was the first to do so, and used its infamous base of Guantanamo to screen Haitian asylum seekers intercepted at sea in the 1980s and the 1990s.[192] Australia followed suit and implemented a scheme known as the 'Pacific Solution'. Under this system, the processing of asylum applicants who arrived illegally in Australia was carried out in Nauru and Papua New Guinea. Asylum seekers were held in detention centres funded by the Australian government and managed by IOM, until a decision on their application was made. Those granted refugee status were resettled in six countries of the region.[193]

2.3.2 European proposals for extraterritorial processing

In Europe, the idea of extraterritorial processing was first floated by Denmark in closed meetings even if it is the United Kingdom which took the initiative of a more formal proposal—supported by the Netherlands and later Italy and Spain.[194] Based on the conclusion that the current protection system is failing encourages illegal migration human smuggling, and abusive claims, the UK March Paper basically suggested that asylum procedures be relocated to transit processing centres

---

[192] Parliamentary Assembly of the Council of Europe, Report of the Committee on Migration, Refugees and Population, 'Assessment of transit and processing centres as a response to mixed flows of migrants and asylum seekers' (hereafter, Council of Europe Report), 14 June 2007, para 16; see also G Noll, 'Visions of the Exceptional: Legal and Theoretical Issues Raised by Transit Processing Centres and Protection Zones' (2003) 5 *EJML* 303, 312.

[193] Council of Europe report, n 192 above, para 17; see also S Kneebone, 'The Pacific Plan: The Provision of "Effective Protection"' (2006) 18 *IJRL* 695, 696–7. Note that in February 2008, the newly elected Australian Government decided to put an end to the 'Pacific Solution', see 'Pacific Solution Winds Up', <http://www.abc.net.au/news/stories/2008/02/08/2157322.htm>, 8 February 2008. Note, however, that asylum processing continues on Christmas Island, which is 'excised' from Australian territory and is therefore used as an 'offshore' detention centre.

[194] Noll, 'Visions of the Exceptional', n 192 above, 304–5. See Letter of Prime Minister Tony Blair to the President of the Council, Mr Costas Simitis, 10 March 2003; 'EU buffer states and UNHCR "processing" centres and "safe havens"', n 174 above; see also European Commission, 'Communication from the Commission to the Council and the European Parliament: Towards more accessible, equitable and managed asylum systems' COM (2003) 315 final, 3 June 2003, which seeks to address some of the issues raised in the British paper. Note also that prior to the March letter, the UK had presented two similar proposals which are described in detail by Noll and which also contemplated the use of military force to reduce refugee flows; see Noll, n 92 above.

in third countries to which those arriving in EU Member States and claiming asylum could be transferred to have their claims processed. Those applicants whose claims were granted would then be resettled within the European Union on the basis of a burden-sharing mechanism. The processing centres would be located outside the European Union and managed by IOM, while the screening procedure would have to be approved by UNHCR. Readmission agreements could be specially concluded to ensure the return of failed applicants to their countries of origin, unless these were to be considered unsafe, in which case temporary status could be provided for. The proposal also suggested that illegal migrants intercepted *en route* and who had a clear intention to claim asylum could be encompassed in the scheme.

The Commission, which had been requested by the European Council to further explore the UK proposals, sought to reframe the debate and centred its analysis on States' obligations under international refugee law.[195] At its meeting of Thessaloniki, the European Council essentially dismissed the UK proposal but nonetheless asked for a comprehensive report by the Commission that would include proposals for the adoption of specific measures.[196] The Commission issued a communication, which presented alternatives to extraterritorial asylum processing, such as the creation of an EU resettlement scheme and the provision of funding to support protection capacity of countries in regions of origin and of transit.[197]

In the wake of the arrival of thousands of boat people from Libya on the Italian coast in 2004, Germany and Italy launched another proposal which was part of a broader plan to provide development aid for sub-Saharan countries and ensure better treatment of asylum seekers in transit countries. It consisted in establishing 'European immigration counters' in North Africa, where individuals found to be in need of international protection would be admitted to the EU or transferred to 'safe countries in the region of origin' while those found to be 'illegal migrants' would be either returned to their countries of origin or given information on alternative migratory channels.[198] Italy has in fact implemented removals of

---

[195] European Commission, 'Towards more accessible, equitable and managed asylum systems', n 194 above.

[196] Presidency Conclusions, Thessaloniki European Council, n 168 above, para 26.

[197] European Commission, 'Communication from the Commission to the Council and the European Parliament on the managed entry in the EU of persons in need of international protection and enhancement of the protection capacity of the regions of origin: improving access to durable solutions' COM (2004) 410 final, 4 June 2004.

[198] Council of Europe report, n 192 above, paras 23–24; Directorate Study, n 51 above, 8; Garlick, n 117 above, 619–21. It is reported that at an informal meeting in Scheveningen on 30 September 2004, the EU's justice and interior ministers agreed in principle that the EU would plan to set up 'reception camps for asylum seekers' in Algeria, Tunisia, Morocco, Mauritius, and Libya, H Dietrich, 'The desert front—EU refugee camps in North Africa?' *Statewatch News Online*, March 2005, available at <http://ww.statewatch.org>.

irregular migrants, including asylum seekers, arriving on the island of Lampedusa to transit centres in Libya since 2004.[199]

In 2004, the European Council further adopted the Hague Programme Strengthening Freedom, Security and Justice in the European Union, asking the Commission to present two studies, one on joint processing of asylum application within the European Union, and another to be conducted in close cooperation with UNHCR, into 'the merits, appropriateness and feasibility of joint processing of asylum application outside the EU territory'.[200] On that basis, the Commission decided to finance feasibility studies on the externalization of procedures in Libya and Mauritania and allocated funds to 'strengthening hosting and protection capacities on the ground'.[201] The assumed objective was to establish regional protection areas where asylum seekers could have their claim processed, together with resettlement programmes for those recognized as refugees.

In the meantime, UNHCR had offered its own view on the problem, suggesting a three-pronged approach that would include improved access to solutions in the region of origin,[202] improved national asylum systems of destination States,[203] and manifestly unfounded cases processing, which would take place in 'EU-based processing centres'. The last prong replicated some of the features of the UK proposal, with some important improvements: asylum seekers coming from designated countries of origin and who are primarily economic migrants would be in closed reception centres in Member States situated at one of the external borders of the Union. Processing and simplified appeals would take place with UNHCR participation, and those in need of protection would be distributed throughout Europe, while rejected applicants would be returned through the application of readmission agreements.[204] Relevant EC regulations

---

[199] G S Goodwin-Gill and J McAdam, *The Refugee in International Law* (3rd edn Oxford University Press, Oxford 2007) 411; see also *Salem and ors v Italy*, Appl. Nos. 10171/05, 10601/05, 11593/05, and 17165/05, Decision, 11 May 2006, which provides detailed information on these policies and on living conditions of migrants and asylum seekers in Libya, 6.

[200] 'The Hague Programme for strengthening freedom, security and justice in the European Union', Presidency Conclusions, 4–5 November 2004, Council Doc 16054/04, 13 December 2004, 9; see also European Commission, 'Communication from the Commission to the Council and the European Parliament: The Hague Programme: Ten priorities for the next five year, the partnership for European renewal in the field of freedom, security and justice' COM (2005) 184 final, 10 May 2005.

[201] Council and Commission Action Plan Implementing the Hague Programme on Strengthening Freedom, Security and Justice in the EU, Doc 9778/2/05, 10 June 2005 [2005] OJ C198/1; see also Regulation No. 491/2004 of the European Parliament and of the Council of 10 March 2004 establishing a programme for financial and technical assistance to third countries in the areas of migration and asylum (AENEAS [2004] OJ L80/1).

[202] UNHCR Working Paper, 'UNHCR's three-pronged proposal', June 2003, 2–6.

[203] Ibid, 11–12.

[204] Ibid, 7–10.

and directives, such as the qualification Directive or the reception Directive, would be applicable.[205]

2.3.3 Analysis

Supporters of extraterritorial processing claim that it would be a means of controlling migration, while at the same time improving the management of refugee movements by providing clear avenues for individuals seeking protection. Unsurprisingly, these various initiatives once again triggered outrage from many sides.[206] As noted by Guild,

The link of the external dimension, which was based on making countries outside the Union responsible for human rights protection of asylum seekers, has now moved beyond making third countries responsible for refugees who have some link with their territory, to shuffling them off completely to countries through which they have never passed and which owe them no duty other than that which comes into existence by reason of the Member States' actions.[207]

Besides the fact that such schemes are fundamentally objectionable on ethical grounds, extraterritorial processing, particularly the kind proposed by the United Kingdom or Germany, raises a number of legal and practical problems.[208] In legal terms, existing proposals are evasive to say the least on the question of which State(s) or international organization(s) would be responsible for upholding international human rights and refugee law standards.[209] Secondly, the categories of individuals who might be sent to such centres remain unclear: would these

---

[205] Ibid, 8. Council Directive 2004/83/EC of 29 April 2004 on minimum standards for the qualification and status of third country nationals or stateless persons as refugees or as persons who otherwise need international protection and the content of the protection granted [2004] OJ L304/12; Council Directive 2003/9/EC of 27 January 2003 laying down minimum standards for the reception of asylum seekers [2003] OJ L31/18.

[206] See eg Appeal against the creation of camps at European borders, October 2004, available at: <http://no-camps.org>; see also Parliamentary Assembly of the Council of Europe, Draft Resolution, 13 June 2007; Human Rights Watch, 'An Unjust Vision for Europe's Refugees', 2003 available at: <http://www.asylumrights.net>; Amnesty International, 'Unlawful and Unworkable—Amnesty International's View on Proposals for Extra-Territorial Processing of Asylum Claims', 18 June 2003, available at: <http://www.amnesty.org>.

[207] E Guild, 'The Europeanization of Europe's Asylum Policy' (2006) 18 *IJRL* 631, 647.

[208] See House of Lords European Union Committee, *Handling EU asylum claims: new approaches examined*, written evidence submitted by A Hurwitz to the House of Lords European Union Committee, 11th Report of Session 2003–2004, 30 April 2004, 91; Noll, 'Visions of the Exceptional', n 192 above, 313, who refers to the discussion on reception in the region of origin within the Intergovernmental Consultations in 1994 and 1995, which dismissed the idea as morally, politically, and legally unsound.

[209] G Noll, 'Law and the Logic of Outsourcing: Offshore Processing and Diplomatic Assurances', Paper presented at the workshop on *Refugee protection in international law, contemporary challenges*, Oxford, 24 April 2006, 2–3; see also UNHCR Response to Green Paper, n 117 above, 18; Noll, 'Visions of the Exceptional, n 192 above, 326. GS Goodwin-Gill, 'Offshore Processing of Asylum Seekers: The Search for Legitimate Parameters' (2007) *UTS Law Review* 26, 29.

apply only for asylum seekers coming from certain countries (UNHCR), to all asylum applicants entering EU countries illegally, or even to illegal immigrants 'intending' to seek asylum (UK proposal)? Similar questions arise with regard to whether current proposals would also apply to asylum seekers arriving in the countries where the centres are situated.[210] Many concerns have also been expressed with respect to the standards of reception that will be offered to these asylum seekers and the States or organizations that will be responsible for running the centres.[211] How long would people stay in processing centres? What restrictions on free movement would be applicable? Would detention conditions be subject to judicial review?

Such extraterritorial processing cannot, in any event, be used to evade the application of EU refugee law, the ECHR, the Refugee Convention, and other relevant international instruments.[212] In other words, removals of asylum seekers to such a third State cannot take place unless an individual assessment has been conducted of whether that third country is safe for that asylum seeker.[213] Compliance with these protection standards could nevertheless prove quite challenging in practice, above all for those people who have not even reached the border of one of the EU Member States. In this regard, the most problematic aspect of the UK proposal and its Italian-German counterpart is that the location of the processing centres would be outside the European Union, unlike what is suggested by UNHCR. Serious questions will therefore be raised as to the effectiveness of the protection granted by the countries where processing centres would be situated.[214] The countries currently considered to host these 'protection areas' do not seem to meet basic standards of effective protection. As far as Belarus and Libya are concerned, until recently, neither had been deemed eligible to be a partner in the European Neighbourhood Policy.[215] Finally, the cost-effective

---

[210] See also in this respect, Noll, 'Visions of the Exceptional', n 192 above, 329–30.

[211] Council of Europe Report, n 192 above, paras 11, 29–33; Noll, n 209 above, 5; see also C Rodier and I Saint-Saëns, 'Contrôler et filtrer: les camps au service des politiques migratoires de l'Europe', in V Chetail (ed) *Mondialisation, migration et droits de l'homme* (Bruylant, Bruxelles 2007) 619, 655.

[212] See Hurwitz, n 208 above, paras 5–6, 92; Noll, 'Visions of the Exceptional', n 192 above, 333–4.

[213] Goodwin-Gill and Mc Adam, n 199 above, 411; see also in this respect Chapter 5, Section 5.3.

[214] Hurwitz, n 208 above, 93; Garlick, n 117 above, 623.

[215] Directorate Study, n 51 above, 15, 17–18. With regard to Libya, in spite of the fact that the European Commission and the European Parliament were aware of the appalling treatment of migrants in this country, that it is not a party the Refugee Convention, and cannot in any case be regarded as providing safety from return, the European Union engaged in 2005 in a 'long-term strategy' with Libya to combat illegal immigration from Libyan shores to its own and the Commission announced in a 2005 Communication the adoption of an EU-Libya Action Plan on illegal migration, see Directorate Study, n 51 above, 18 and European Commission, 'Communication on Priority Actions for Responding to the Challenges of Migration: First Follow-Up to Hampton Court' COM (2005) 621 final, 30 November 2005, 8–9; European Commission, 'Report on the Technical mission to Libya on Illegal migration, 27 November 2004–06 December 2005', Doc 7753/05,

rationale presented by the United Kingdom is not persuasive. Noll lists a number of cost-intensive activities that would have to be part of an extraterritorial scheme and which would not be needed under a traditional asylum system.[216] This analysis is corroborated by the fact that Australia's Pacific Solution has turned out to be far more expensive than originally thought.[217]

2.4 The Way Forward

The fact that extraterritoriality has become such a pervasive question in international legal debates may be attributed to the fading significance of the very notion of State sovereignty, which stood at the core of the Westphalian system, yet is increasingly undermined by globalization processes and supranationality. In this perspective, the appeal of extraterritorial processing may be that it conveys a notion of control, which has become elusive to many States. More cynically, it also draws the attention away from the failures of European States' immigration and integration policies.

This gradual move towards the 'extraterritorialisation' of asylum processes and the constant redefinition of territorial boundaries, partly caused by the successive waves of enlargement, raises fundamental issues of legality under international law. While it is clear indeed that extraterritoriality should not diminish the responsibility of States having recourse to such devices, the manner in which such responsibility can be enforced remains particularly problematic, and vindicates the views of those who see these schemes as a major affront to the international refugee regime.

It should be stressed, however, that given the potentially interminable chain of return that may occur as a result of its application, the safe third country raises similar concerns, which were in part addressed by the European Court of

available at: <http://www.statewatch.org/news/2005/may/eu-report-libya-ill-imm.pdf>; see also European Parliament, Resolution on progress made in 2004 in creating an area of freedom, security and justice, 8 June 2005 [2005] OJ C124 E/398, paras 24–5; 'EU: European Commission Technical Mission to Libya: Exporting Fortress Europe' *Statewatch News Bulletin*, Vol 15, No. 2, March–April 2005; Council of Europe report, n 192 above, paras 25–6; Gil-Bazo, n 52 above, 590–3; Amnesty International, 'Immigration Cooperation with Libya: The Human rights Perspective', 12 April 2005, available at: <http://www.amnesty.org>. With respect to Belarus, see Parliamentary Assembly of the Council of Europe, 'Situation of refugees and displaced persons in the Russian Federation and some other CIS countries', n 181 above, para 20, which reports that Belarus makes a wide application of its safe third country legislation, which essentially prevents asylum seekers arriving from countries bordering Belarus from having access to its asylum procedure.

[216] Noll 'Visions of the Exceptional', n 192 above, 327–8.

[217] Council of Europe report, n 192 above, para 42; Noll, 'Law and the Logic of Outsourcing', n 209 above, 3; see also Noll 'Visions of the Exceptional', n 192 above, 317, 327–8, who reports that Australia had to allocate 1 million AUD to a 'trust account' for Papua New Guinea and 20 million AUD of assistance to the government of Nauru during 2001–2002 and that the Pacific solution cost the Australian taxpayer 900 million AUD more.

Human Rights in the *T.I.* case.[218] In the current climate, many scholars and advocates continue to see the courts as the ultimate protection against a European harmonization process gone awry, and which has resulted in a substantial lowering of protection standards.[219] This tension between judicial and legislative supranational processes might, as has been the case before, be resolved in favour of the former. However, and this is where the European Union's external dimension of asylum and migration policies is particularly harmful, the jurisdictional reach of supranational judges will be relatively limited in comparison with the far-reaching 'domino effect' of safe third country and readmission policies. Judicial intervention by the ECHR or the ECJ may not suffice to repair the damage caused to refugee protection in neighbouring third countries.

To counter the impact of the European Union's export of containment policies, the only approach is to put protection back at the core of the international refugee regime. While negotiations on an agreement on irregular secondary movements notably failed under the 'Convention Plus' initiative,[220] advocates must continue pushing for an international agreement on effective protection in full compliance with the Refugee Convention and international human rights law. As will be argued in the following chapters, supervisory mechanisms currently existing under international refugee law must be reviewed with a view to bolster monitoring as a means to enhance States' compliance with international obligations.

Aside from these legal approaches, more operationally-oriented solutions have been considered, consisting in the development of new or the strengthening of existing mechanisms to address secondary and mixed movements. From an operational perspective, the first and most obvious way to address protection concerns is by ensuring robust monitoring at the borders. ECRE reports that monitoring projects are being implemented in Hungary, Bulgaria, Poland, Romania, Slovakia, Belarus, Moldova, the Russian Federation, and Ukraine.[221] In application of its 10-Point Plan of Action unveiled in July 2006 at the Euro-African Ministerial Conference on Migration and Development,[222] UNHCR has

---

[218] *T.I. v United Kingdom*, Appl. No. 43844/98, 7 March 2000, ECHR 2000-III. For a detailed analysis of that case and other human rights obligations relevant to safe third country practices, see Chapter 5, Section 5.1.2.1.2.

[219] For instance, the accession of Malta to the EU led it to adopt particularly restrictive immigration and asylum regulations, such as extended and automatic detention in camps, Directorate Study, n 51 above, 20. Amnesty International also reported that the Maltese authorities announced in 2005 that they were considering a suspension of their international obligations under the Refugee Convention, Amnesty International, 'EU regional protection programs: Enhancing protection in the region or barring access to EU territory', September 2005 available at: <http://www.amnesty.org>.

[220] See High Commissioner's Forum, 'Convention Plus Core Group on Addressing Irregular Secondary Movements of Refugees and Asylum-Seekers, Joint Statement by the Co-Chairs', UN Doc FORUM/2205/7 (8 November 2005), para 1.

[221] ECRE, *Defending Refugees' Access to Protection in Europe*, n 140 above, 48.

[222] <http://www.unhcr.org/cgi-bin/texis/vtx/news/opendoc.htm?tbl=NEWS&id=44b262dd4>. See UNHCR, Refugee Protection and Mixed Migration: A 10-Point Plan of Action, January 2007 (revised); see also UNHCR Response to Green Paper, n 117 above, 9.

adopted specific 'protection-sensitive entry management' activities, including inter alia, regular monitoring missions at main entry points of irregular arrivals; and assistance to FRONTEX[223] in developing more systematic responses to protection-related border management.[224]

In the EU Hague Programme of 2004, the Council also invited the Commission to develop EU regional protection programmes in partnership with the third countries concerned and in close consultation and cooperation with UNHCR.[225] These programmes would encompass capacity-building with a view to enhance protection capacity, access to registration and local integration and assistance for improving the local infrastructure and migration management, as well as a joint resettlement programme.[226] In 2006, pilot schemes for registering asylum seekers outside the European Union's territory were set up in Tanzania and Ukraine, described as a 'first step' towards durable solutions for those in need of international protection.[227] Future regional protection programmes are also envisaged for North Africa, Afghanistan, the Horn of Africa, and the Middle-East.[228]

Such proposals, at least with respect to the region of origin, would broadly correspond to the new 'comprehensive approaches' that were advocated by UNHCR in its 'Convention Plus' initiative.[229] While less problematic than the UK proposals, refugee advocates nonetheless expressed concern that these

[223] See Council Regulation 2007/2004/EC of 26 October 2004 establishing a European Agency for the Management of Operational Cooperation at the External Borders of the Member States of the European Union [2004] OJ L349/1; see also in this respect European Commisison, 'Communication from the Commission to the Council: Reinforcing the Management of the EU's Southern Maritime Borders' COM (2006) 733 final, 30 November 2006, paras 25–30, which suggests the establishment and management of a pool of experts from Member States' administrations, and possibly, UNHCR, to ensure the prompt identification of persons seeking international protection.

[224] UNHCR, Implementing the Ten-Point Plan of Action in Southern Europe: Activities Undertaken by UNHCR to Address Mixed Migration in the Context of the Mediterranean/Atlantic Arrivals, 2 October 2006, 4.

[225] A Memorandum of Understanding between the Commission and UNHCR was concluded on 15 February 2005.

[226] European Commission, 'Communication from the Commission to the Council and the European Parliament on regional protection programmes' COM (2005) 388 final, 1 September 2005, paras 2–3; see also UNHCR, 'UNHCR Observations on the Communication from the European Commission to the Council and the European Parliament on Regional Protection Programmes', October 2005.

[227] The 2005 Communication had targeted the region of the Western NIS countries, and the Great Lakes region of Africa, n 226 above, see paras 12–16.

[228] Ibid, para 18; see also Council of Europe Report, n 192 above, paras 49–52; European Commission, 'Communication to the European Parliament, the Council, the European Economic and Social Committee and the Committee of Regions: Policy Plan on Asylum, an Integrated Approach to Protection Across the EU' COM (2008) 360 final, 17 June 2008, 10, which indicates that other regional protection programmes are also carried out in Moldova and Belarus.

[229] On Convention Plus, see A Betts and J-F Durieux, 'Convention Plus as a Norm-Setting Exercise' (2007) 20 *JRS* 509; see also S Kneebone, C McDowell, and G Morrell, 'A Mediterranean Solution? Chances of Success' (2006) 18 *IJRL* 492–508. For a discussion of comprehensive approaches, see Chapter 4, Section 4.2.1.3.3.

'programmes could be used for curbing migration into Europe' and could potentially destabilize host countries in the region of origin.[230] Also, in the absence of sufficient details on the implementation of these programmes, it is not clear whether these will truly enhance protection rather than undermine it. The same question of whether the countries chosen for the regional protection programmes are effectively 'safe' for the purposes of the application of the safe third country will arise.[231] Concern has been specifically expressed with respect to the countries selected for the pilot project. According to a report by Human Rights Watch, asylum seekers and migrants in Ukraine are subjected to numerous abuses: extended detention, physical and mental abuse, if not forced return to countries of origin.[232] As far as Tanzania is concerned, there have been a few instances in recent years of clear violations by Tanzania of its international obligations.[233]

'Protected entry procedures' are another new initiative which has been presented by the Commission in 2003. Such procedures would enable individuals to avoid having to undertake long and perilous journeys to reach Europe by allowing persons to approach an embassy to seek asylum and by introducing 'asylum visas'.[234] While promising, the idea is not without its problems, however. First of all, such procedures would remain dependent on the good will of host States. By way of example, in 2002, a few hundred North Koreans who were able to arrive in China approached European diplomatic missions. Their reaction was to step up security at their premises rather than to provide 'asylum visas'. It then made it far more difficult for dissidents to receive protection from diplomatic representations in China.[235]

Other durable solutions, such as repatriation and resettlement, are well known and have existed alongside asylum for the last 50 years.[236] While it is true that European States have tended to neglect resettlement as a durable solution, it is

---

[230] D Cronin, 'EU to vet Asylum Claims in Africa, Ukraine', *European Voice*, 6 October 2006; Amnesty International, 'EU regional protection programs: Enhancing protection in the region or barring access to the EU territory?', n 219 above; see also Garlick, n 117 above, 625.

[231] Amnesty International points out that, since the EU failed to adopt a list of safe third countries, the assessment of 'safety' remains to be carried out by Member States, on the basis of the common criteria laid down in the EU asylum procedures Directive; Amnesty International, 'EU regional protection programs', n 219 above.

[232] Human Rights Watch, 'Ukraine: Migrants, Asylum Seekers Regularly Abused', News Release, 30 November 2005; see also G Uehling, 'Unwanted Migration: Combating and Unwittingly Creating Irregular Migration in Ukraine' UNHCR New Issues in Refugee Research Working Paper No. 109, October 2004, 3, 14; B Junker, 'Burden Sharing or Burden Shifting? Asylum and Expansion in the European Union' (2006) 20 *Georgetown Immigration LJ* 293, 312–13.

[233] Amnesty International, 'EU regional protection programs', n 219 above.

[234] Communication from the Commission on the Common Asylum Policy and the Agenda for Protection COM (2003) 152 final, 26 March 2003, 6, 9; Communication from the Commission, 'Improving Access to Durable Solutions' COM (2004) 410 final, 14 June 2004, para 14.

[235] Directorate Study, n 51 above, 14.

[236] Legomsky, n 3 above, 599–603.

important to reiterate that resettlement should not be used as a substitute but as a complement to asylum.[237]

2.5 Conclusion

Two tools have proven essential to restrict secondary movements: safe third country practices and readmission agreements. More recently, proposals on extraterritorial processing have been floated with a view to preventing further arrivals of asylum seekers on the territories of EU Member States.

As it will be further demonstrated in the next chapters, each of these tools is problematic from a refugee protection perspective. The increasingly broad scope of application of the safe third country in the asylum procedures Directive, and the numerous options left to Member States on the way they intend to apply it is legally highly questionable. By the same token, the standard clauses of readmission agreements do not spell out the specific duties of States under international refugee and human rights law. As for extraterritorial processing proposals, these raise countless concerns about refugees' protection against *refoulement*, standards of treatment, and the blurring of responsibilities that such schemes would entail.

While there is certainly no ideal way to address secondary movements, a number of relatively concrete legal and policy measures deserve to be further discussed. First, in light of the fact that this question has clearly acquired great significance well beyond the boundaries of the European Union, the possibility of adopting an international agreement that would set out strict criteria for the application of the safe third country must once again be seriously considered. Secondly, the strengthening of international monitoring mechanisms under international refugee law should also be advocated. Furthermore, a number of solutions to address the phenomenon of secondary movements are under discussion. In particular, the expansion of resettlement opportunities in the European Union and the adoption of protected entry procedures could potentially help resolve the current crisis without compromising the fundamental principles that underpin the international refugee regime.

---

[237] The Commission made proposals for enhanced protection in the region, which included the setting up of an EU-wide resettlement scheme, see 'Improving Access to Durable Solutions', n 234 above; see also Communication from the Commission to the Council and the European Parliament on regional protection programmes, n 226 above, paras 6–7. On resettlement, see Chapter 4, Section 4.2.1.3.2.

3

Allocation of Responsibility for Examining an Application for Asylum under the Dublin Regime

Under the system established in accordance with the Dublin Regulation[1] the responsibility of Member States of the European Union, as well as of Iceland, Norway, and Switzerland, to examine an asylum claim is allocated based on specific criteria which are applied in hierarchical order. Prior to the entry into force of the Regulation, similar criteria were applied by Member States of the European Union under the Dublin Convention, and before that, under chapter VII of the 1990 Schengen Convention.[2] The Dublin regime is based on the principle that State parties mutually recognize each other as safe third countries, but the asylum seeker will only be sent back after the responsible State has specifically agreed to his/her transfer. Only one State is responsible for examining an asylum application, and in principle at least, that State has an obligation to guarantee effective access to the asylum procedure.

Given the limited differences between the Schengen and Dublin conventions and the subsequent Regulation, prior jurisprudence and doctrinal analyses remain for the most part relevant. Also, the review of case-law and practice related to the Dublin Regulation confirms that the system continues to suffer from the very same flaws that had been previously identified: intricacy, formalism, cost, and protection concerns. In particular, it is clear that the harmonization efforts undertaken

---

[1] Council Regulation (EC) 343/2003 of 18 February 2003 establishing the criteria and mechanisms for determining the Member State responsible for examining an asylum application lodged in one of the Member States by a third-country national [2003] OJ L50/1 (hereafter, Dublin Regulation or DR).

[2] Dublin Convention of 15 June 1990 determining the State responsible for examining asylum applications for asylum lodged in one of the Member States of the European Communities [1997] OJ C254/1. The Dublin Convention (hereafter, DC) entered into force on 1 September 1997 for the first twelve signatories; 1 October 1997 in Sweden and Austria, and on 1 January 1998 in Finland. It replaced chapter VII of the 1990 Schengen Convention on the Application of the Schengen Agreement of 14 June 1985 relating to the Gradual Suppression of Controls at Common Frontiers, Between the Governments of State Members of the Benelux Economic Union, the Federal Republic of Germany, and the French Republic [2000] OJ L239/19 (hereafter, SC). See Chapter 1, Section 1.3.2.

by the European Union have thus far not been shown to have a sufficient impact on Member States' practices to alleviate the difficulties arising from differences in Member States' implementation of their international legal obligations towards refugees.

After discussing the scope and key objectives of the Dublin allocation system, an evaluation of the operation of the Dublin Regulation will be conducted based on State practice and case-law in several Member States.[3] The basic principles underpinning the Regulation will first be examined, followed by an analysis of the criteria listed in the Regulation to determine which State is responsible for examining an asylum claim. The procedural features of the system will then be presented, including the provisions of the Eurodac Regulation.[4] The final section will offer a critical evaluation of the Dublin regime in its current operation.

3.1 Elaboration of the Dublin Regulation

Article 63.1a) ECT provides that the Council shall adopt measures on asylum, including on 'criteria and mechanisms for determining which Member State is responsible for considering an application for asylum submitted by a national of a third country in one of the Member States'.[5] In accordance with the Vienna Action Plan, the determination of the State responsible for the examination of an asylum application was one of the short-term measures to be adopted by the Council within two years.[6]

The presentation of the proposal for a Regulation, in July 2001,[7] was preceded by intense preparatory work. The Commission first submitted a Working Paper,[8]

---

[3] Examples drawn from the jurisprudence include 'pre-Regulation' cases under the Schengen and Dublin conventions as well as Dublin Regulation cases. A more detailed analysis of pre-Regulation case-law is presented in A Hurwitz, 'The 1990 Dublin Convention: A Comprehensive Assessment' (1999) 11 *IJRL* 646.

[4] Council Regulation (EC) 2725/2000 of 11 December 2000 concerning the establishment of 'Eurodac' for the comparison of fingerprints for the effective application of the Dublin Convention [2000] OJ L316/1 (hereafter, Eurodac Regulation).

[5] Consolidated version of the Treaty establishing the European Community (hereafter, ECT) [2002] OJ C325/33.

[6] European Council, Presidency Conclusions, Tampere, 15 and 16 October 1999, published in (1999) 4 *IJRL* 738, 740; Action Plan of the Council and the Commission on how best to implement the provisions of the Treaty of Amsterdam on an area of freedom, security, and justice [1999] OJ C19/1, para 36.

[7] European Commission, Proposal for a Council Regulation establishing the criteria and mechanisms for determining the Member State responsible for examining an asylum application lodged in one of the Member States by a third-country national COM (2001) 447 final, 26 July 2001.

[8] European Commission Staff Working Paper, 'Revisiting the Dublin Convention: Developing Community Legislation for Determining which Member State is Responsible for Considering an Application for Asylum Submitted in one of the Member States' SEC (2000) 522, 21 March 2000, para 12, 38.

which was followed by an assessment of the Dublin Convention based on a detailed questionnaire sent to Member States.[9] While the Commission presented several alternatives to the present system, including one based on 'natural sharing', which it thought had significant advantages, it concluded that Member States were unlikely to accept any major changes to the basic premise of the Dublin Convention,[10] even though the explanatory memorandum acknowledged 'differences between the Member States in terms of procedures for granting refugee status, reception conditions for asylum seekers and the administration of complementary forms of protection which could affect the destination chosen by asylum seekers'.[11]

The Regulation is therefore similar in many respects to the previous Convention, with only some relatively limited amendments. Yet, the adoption of a Community instrument has important implications in terms of implementation. Regulations are directly applicable in the legal order of the Member States,[12] and do not require 'transformation' through the adoption of domestic legislation in order to apply in the domestic legal order. Thus, given that the United Kingdom has 'opted in' on the adoption of the Regulation, asylum seekers are now able to directly invoke its provisions before British courts. Secondly, enforcement and supervisory mechanisms are more sophisticated under EC law and it is now possible for the ECJ to be seized of a case related to the validity and/or interpretation of any provision of the Regulation.[13]

3.2 Principles

While the Preamble of the Regulation lists numerous objectives, such as the harmonization of asylum policies, the protection of refugees in accordance with international legal instruments, the promotion of free movement, and the efficiency of asylum processes in the European Union, the key purpose of the Dublin Regulation remains the prevention of the lodging of simultaneous or consecutive asylum applications in the Member States.[14] Additionally, the Regulation is also supposed to address 'orbit' situations by ensuring that asylum seekers have effective access to refugee status determination procedures.[15]

---

[9] European Commission Staff Working Paper, 'Evaluation of the Dublin Convention', SEC (2001) 756, 13 June 2001.

[10] 'Revisiting the Dublin Convention', n 8 above, para 59.

[11] Explanatory Memorandum to the Proposal for a Council Regulation, n 7 above, 3.

[12] Article 249 ECT.

[13] On the competence of the ECJ in the asylum field, see Chapter 6, Section 6.1.1.

[14] See Recital 1, 2, 3, 8, 15 of the Preamble.

[15] See Recitals 3–4 of the Preamble.

3.2.1 Only one State is responsible for examining an application for asylum[16]

The justification for this rule is that the Dublin regime is based on States' mutual trust in their asylum procedures.[17] If an asylum seeker has already had his/her claim dismissed in another Member State, the other Member States can immediately reject the claim.[18] For asylum seekers who lodge a claim for the first time in one of the Member States, the Regulation lays down criteria to determine which State is responsible. These objective criteria are based on the opinion that, 'the more a member-State has consented (explicitly or tacitly) to the penetration of its territory by an asylum seeker, the more it is responsible'.[19] Another characteristic of these criteria is their relative rigidity and the irrelevance of the intention of the asylum seeker in the determination of the responsible State.[20]

3.2.2 The State responsible is under the obligation to guarantee effective access to the asylum procedure[21]

One of the claims of the early supporters of the Schengen and Dublin conventions was that they represented a significant advance from a protection perspective,[22] and would put an end to 'orbit situations', as the applicant for asylum was given the assurance that his/her application would be examined by at least one Member State.[23]

---

[16] Article 3.1 DR; see also Recital 7, 3 of the Preamble.

[17] P-C Müller-Graf, 'The Dublin Convention: Pioneer and Lesson for Third-Pillar Conventions', in R Bieber and J Monar (eds), *Justice and Home Affairs in the European Union: The Development of the Third Pillar,* (European Interuniversity Press, Brussels 1995) 49, 58; K Hailbronner and C Thiery, 'Schengen II and Dublin Responsibility for Asylum Applications in Europe' (1997) 34 *CML Rev* 957, 964; L Drücke, 'Refugee Protection in the Post Cold War Europe: Asylum in the Schengen and EC Harmonization Process', in A Pauly (ed), *Les accords de Schengen: abolition des frontières intérieures ou menace pour les libertés publiques ?* (European Institute of Public Administration, Maastricht 1993) 105, 117.

[18] Rejections of an asylum claim on the ground that it has been dismissed in another State were already common before the entry into force of the Schengen Convention. See the decision of the German Constitutional Court of 14 May 1996 *Bundesverfassungsgericht* (1997) 94 BVerfGE 49, 67.

[19] W de Lobkowicz, 'The Dublin Convention: A Useful Complement to International Humanitarian Law' [1990] *European Vision* 7, 9.

[20] This was affirmed in several Dutch decisions applying the Schengen Convention, see eg 's Gravenhage 25-09-96 AWB 96/8727, (1996) 3 JuB nr 14, 30; 's Gravenhage 19-02-97 AWB 97/22 [1997] *NAV* bijlage 5, 288, para 2.4.

[21] Preamble, Recital 4; Art 16.1 DR.

[22] See eg Lobkowicz, n 19 above, 8; F Doublet et P Stéfanini, 'Le droit d'asile en Europe: La convention relative à la détermination de l'Etat responsable de l'examen d'une demande d'asile présentée auprès d'un état membre des Communautés européennes' [1991] *Revue du marché commun.* 391, 395.

[23] See Recital 4 of the Preamble; cf Recital 4 of the Preamble to the Dublin Convention, as well as Art 3.1 and Art 10.1 c) DC.

Yet, commentators pointed out that other provisions void this principle of its content. Article 2(e) DR states that the '"examination of an asylum application" means any examination of, or decision or ruling concerning, an application for asylum by the competent authorities in accordance with national law except for procedures for determining the Member State responsible in accordance with this Regulation'.[24] Given the breadth of this definition, the obligation to complete the examination does not actually entail any definite obligation of the Member States.[25] Thus, the 'prioritised' or 'accelerated' asylum procedures that may be applied in cases of unfounded or abusive applications in most European countries would clearly be included under the definition of 'examination of the application for asylum.'[26] The Commission is aware of this problem and reiterated in its 2007 Report that 'the notion of an "examination of an asylum application" as defined in the Dublin Regulation should be interpreted, without any exceptions, as implying the assessment whether the applicant in question qualifies as a refugee in accordance with the Qualification Directive'.[27]

Secondly, Article 3.3 DR specifies that any Member State shall retain the right, pursuant to its national law, to send an applicant for asylum to a third State in compliance with the provisions of the Refugee Convention. The Dublin Regulation must therefore be examined in conjunction with the provisions of the asylum procedures Directive, with respect to the notions of country of first asylum and safe third country.[28] In other words, if the Dublin system allegedly resolves 'orbit' situations within the European Union, Member States may still contribute to such situations in the rest of the world.[29]

---

[24] A similarly broad definition was given in Art 1d) DC.

[25] J Bolten, 'From Schengen to Dublin' [1991] *Nederlands Juristenblad*, 165, 173.

[26] Council Directive (EC) 2005/85 of 1 December 2005 on minimum standards on procedures in Member States for granting and withdrawing refugee status (hereafter, asylum procedures Directive) [2005] OJ L326/24, Art 23.4. See eg the practice in Greece, UNHCR, 'The Dublin II Regulation: A UNHCR Discussion Paper', April 2006 (hereafter, UNHCR Dublin II Discussion Paper), 46. See also prior to the entry into force of the asylum procedures Directive, EU Resolution on manifestly unfounded applications for asylum adopted on 30 November and 1 December 1992 by the Immigration Ministers, SN 4822/92 WGI 1282 ASIM 146, published in E Guild (ed), *The Developing Immigration and Asylum Policies of the European Union* (Kluwer, The Hague [etc] 1996) 141.

[27] European Commission, 'Report from the Commission to the European Parliament and the Council on the Evaluation of the Dublin System' COM (2007) 299 final, 6 June 2007 (hereafter, 2007 Commission Report) 6.

[28] See Art 26 of the asylum procedures Directive regarding the first country of asylum and Art 27 regarding the safe third country. Note that Art 36.3 of the asylum procedures Directive was annulled by the Court of Justice on 6 May 2008, *Parliament v Council*, Case C-133/06, 6 May 2008, para 43–61.

[29] A Achermann and M Gattiker, 'Safe Third Countries: European Developments' (1995) 7 *IJRL* 19, 23; cf K Hailbronner who considers that this approach is perfectly legitimate and in compliance with the provisions of the Refugee Convention, *Immigration and Asylum Law and Policy of the European Union* (Kluwer, The Hague [etc] 2000) 391.

3.2.3 Scope

In accordance with Article 29 DR, the Dublin Regulation entered into force on 18 March 2003 and applies to asylum applications lodged as from 1 September 2003 and from that date, to any request to take charge or take back asylum seekers, irrespective of the date on which the asylum application was made. In terms of personal scope, both the Dublin Convention and the Regulation are limited to claims lodged by third country nationals.[30] The Dublin criteria are indeed irrelevant in a situation where the asylum seeker has not entered an EU Member State from a third country and is able to move freely within the Union.

In territorial terms, the scope of the Regulation has gradually expanded so as to cover most of the European continent, including States that are not members of the European Union, or that are not taking part in the adoption of asylum policies under Title IV ECT. In 2001, the Dublin Convention became applicable to Iceland and Norway.[31] Also, given that in accordance with the Treaty of Amsterdam, Denmark does not take part in the adoption of Title IV measures, an agreement between Denmark and the European Community was concluded on 21 February 2006.[32] More recently, an agreement with the Swiss Confederation extending the application of the Dublin regime to that country entered into force.[33]

The major difficulty relates, however, to the material scope of the Dublin Regulation. In conformity with the terms of the Amsterdam Treaty, Article 2(c) DR stipulates that:

'the application for asylum', means the application made by a third-country national which can be understood as a request for international protection from a Member State, under the Geneva Convention. Any application for international protection is presumed to be an application for asylum, unless a third-country national explicitly requests another kind of protection that can be applied for separately.[34]

---

[30] Article 1 DR; see also Art 1(a) DC.

[31] Council Decision (EC) 2001/258 of 15 March 2001 concerning the conclusion of an agreement between the European community and the Republic of Iceland and the Kingdom of Norway concerning the criteria and mechanisms for establishing the State responsible for examining a request for asylum lodged in a Member State or Iceland or Norway [2001] OJ L93/38; Protocol to the agreement between the European Community and the Republic of Iceland and the Kingdom of Norway concerning the criteria and mechanisms for establishing the State responsible for examining a request for asylum lodged in a Member State or in Iceland or Norway [2006] OJ L57/16.

[32] Council Decision (EC) 2006/188 of 21 February 2006 on the conclusion of the agreement between the European Community and the Kingdom of Denmark extending to Denmark the provisions of Council Regulation (EC) No. 343/2003 establishing the criteria and mechanisms for determining the Member States by a third-country national and Council Regulation (EC) No. 2725/2000 concerning the establishment of 'Eurodac' for the comparison of fingerprints for the effective application of the Dublin Convention [2006] OJ L66/37.

[33] Agreement of 26 October 2004 between the European Community and the Swiss Confederation concerning the criteria and mechanisms for establishing the State responsible for examining a request for asylum lodged in a Member State or in Switzerland [2008] OJ L53/5.

[34] Similar terms are used in Art 1 (b) DC.

This conflation between asylum and refugee protection is not actually based on international law, which conceives asylum as a much broader concept, encompassing, yet not limited to the protection provided pursuant to the Refugee Convention.[35] Asylum should in principle also include complementary forms of protection such as subsidiary protection, which was formally recognized in the qualification Directive.[36] The European Commission explained that the reason for the exclusion of subsidiary protection from the scope of the Dublin Regulation was due to the fact that in 2003, this latter concept had not yet become part of the EU asylum *acquis*[37] and it recommended that the Dublin Regulation be amended to have its scope extended to subsidiary protection, so as to accord with subsequent legislative developments.[38] It is worth adding that should an asylum seeker seek to avoid the application of the Dublin Regulation by applying for subsidiary protection, there is a major disincentive in so doing, given that he or she would not then necessarily be able to avail her- or himself of the provisions of the reception Directive.[39] Finally, while the asylum procedures Directive specifies that its minimum standards are not applicable to the determination of the responsible Member State, it nevertheless indicates that such determination intervenes at the 'admissibility' stage of the procedure.[40]

3.3 Criteria Determining the State Responsible

The criteria to determine the responsible State are listed in order of precedence,[41] those constituting the expression of an explicit authorization to enter the 'Dublin area' before the others. The only exception to this hierarchy is the criterion related

---

[35] See Chapter 1, Section 1.1.4; see in this respect M-T Gil-Bazo, 'Refugee Status, Subsidiary Protection, and the Right to be Granted Asylum Under EC Law', UNHCR New Issues in Refugee Research Paper No. 136, November 2006, 8.

[36] Article 15 Council Directive (EC) 2004/83 of 29 April 2004 on minimum standards for the qualification and status of third country nationals or stateless persons as refugees or as persons who otherwise need international protection and the content of the protection granted (hereafter, qualification Directive) [2004] OJ L304/12.

[37] For a presentation of the various ad hoc protections in Western European States, prior to the adoption of the qualification Directive, see K Hailbronner, '*Non-Refoulement* and Humanitarian Refugees: Customary International Law or Wishful Legal Thinking ?', in D A Martin (ed), *The New Asylum Seekers: Refugee Law in the 1980s* (Martinus Nijhoff, Dordrecht 1988) 123, 136; M Kjaerum, 'Temporary Protection in Europe in the 1990s' (1994) 6 *IJRL* 444; K Kerber, 'Temporary Protection: An Assessment of the Harmonisation of Policies of European Union Member States' (1997) 9 *IJRL* 453–71; Intergovernmental Consultations on Asylum, Refugee and Migration Policies, *Report on Temporary Protection in States in Europe, North America and Australia* (Geneva 1995).

[38] 2007 Commission Report, n 27 above, 6.

[39] Article 3.4 Council Directive (EC) 2003/9 of 27 January 2003 laying down minimum standards for the reception of asylum seekers [2003] OJ L31/18 (hereafter, reception Directive).

[40] Recital 29 of the Preamble and Art 25.1 of the asylum procedures Directive.

[41] See Art 5.1 DR; Art 3.2 DC.

to the presence of family members,[42] which come first. Then comes the existence of a valid residence permit or of a visa[43] issued by one of the participating States; the frontier of the State which an applicant for asylum has irregularly crossed;[44] the State responsible for controlling the entry of the alien into the territory of the participating States;[45] the State where the asylum application was lodged when in an international transit area of an airport;[46] and finally, where no State can be designated as responsible on the basis of the previous criteria, the first State in which the application for asylum is lodged.[47]

In addition, the Regulation provides that a State has the right to examine an application for asylum even if such examination is not its responsibility. Two different cases of derogation exist. First, the State in which the application for asylum has been lodged may decide to examine the application on its own initiative, even when it is not responsible (the so-called 'sovereignty' clause).[48] Secondly, a State may request another State to examine an application for asylum for humanitarian reasons based specifically on family-related grounds, even when the latter is not responsible under the criteria laid out in the Regulation (the 'humanitarian' clause).[49]

3.3.1 Family unity

This criterion constitutes the expression of a general principle of family protection, which is also found, inter alia, in Article 8 ECHR and in the Final Act of the CSR.[50] The definition of the family in Article 2(i) DR corresponds to the Western concept of nuclear family and is similar to the one used in most European family reunification laws.[51] It is in any case the most restrictive interpretation authorized

---

[42] Articles 6–8 DR; Art 4 DC; see also Art 14 DR which provides that the State responsible is the one responsible for the largest number of asylum-seeking family members or for the application of the oldest of them, if applying the other criteria would result in the family being separated.

[43] Article 9 DR; Art 5.2 DC.

[44] Article 10 DR; Art 6 DC.

[45] Article 11 DR; Art 7 DC.

[46] Article 12 DR; the Dublin Convention had a different approach on asylum application lodged in airport transit areas, see n 78 below.

[47] Article 13 DR; Art 8 DC.

[48] Article 3.2 DR; Art 3.4 DC.

[49] Article 15 DR; Art 9 DC.

[50] See also ExCom Conclusions No. 9 (1977) and No. 24 (1981) on Family Reunification.

[51] Article 2(i) DR reads:

> (i) 'family members' means insofar as the family already existed in the country of origin, the following members of the applicant's family who are present in the territory of the Member States:
> (i) the spouse of the asylum seeker or his or her unmarried partner in a stable relationship, where the legislation or practice of the Member State concerned treats unmarried couples in a way comparable to married couples under its law relating to aliens;
> (ii) the minor children of couples referred to in point (i) or of the applicant, on condition that they are unmarried and dependent and regardless of whether they were born in or out of wedlock or adopted as defined under the national law;
> (iii) the father, mother or guardian when the applicant or refugee is a minor and unmarried.

by the UNHCR *Handbook on Procedures and Criteria for Determining Refugee Status*, which recommends that family members living in the same household, such as parents of adult children, be included for family reunion purposes.[52]

Questions related to family reunion appeared right after the entry into force of the Schengen Convention. Neither the Schengen Convention nor the Dublin Convention covered the case of family members applying for asylum in different Member States at the same time. Neither did they cover the case where a family member resided in a Member State, but had not been recognized as a refugee within the terms of Article 1 CSR, or where the family member had claimed asylum in another Member State but no decision had yet been rendered on his/her status.[53] Under the Schengen Convention, administrative authorities in the Member States had recourse to the exception in Article 29.4 (Article 3.2 DR),[54] but it was desirable to establish a uniform practice, since these situations were relatively frequent. Decisions on this matter were accordingly adopted by both the Schengen Executive Committee and the Executive Committee established under Article 18 of the Dublin Convention.[55]

The case-law dealing with family reunion under both the Schengen and Dublin Conventions provides useful insights in the ways in which family reunion provisions have been applied by national authorities. In the Netherlands, the courts were at first sympathetic towards these situations. The President of The Hague Tribunal considered, for instance, that the family reunion and humanitarian

---

Note that the original proposal suggested that family members who used to live in the same home in the country of origin and were dependent on one another were to be covered as well: see U Brandl, 'Distribution of Asylum Seekers in Europe? Dublin II Regulation Determining the Responsibility for Examining an Asylum Application', in P De Bruycker and C Dias Urbano de Sousa (eds), *The Emergence of a European Asylum Policy* (Bruylant, Bruxelles 2004) 33, 45. See also Art 4 of Directive 2003/86/EC of 22 September 2003 on the right to family reunification [2003] OJ L251/12.

[52] UNHCR, *Handbook on Procedures and Criteria for Determining Refugee Status* (reprint 1992) UN Doc HCR/1P/4/Eng/Rev.2, para 185; see also para 5 of ExCom Conclusion No. 24 (1981) and Recommendation 1327 (1997) of the Council of Europe Parliamentary Assembly adopted on 24 April 1997 on the protection and reinforcement of the human rights of refugees and asylum seekers in Europe, Art 8 (vi) (o) and (p), reprinted in Ad Hoc Committee of Experts on the legal aspects of territorial asylum, refugees and stateless persons (CAHAR) *Selected Texts Concerning Territorial Asylum and Refugees Adopted within the Council of Europe*, CAHAR (98) 6, March 1998, Strasbourg, Vol II 137.

[53] See eg *Verwaltungsgericht* 28-05-1998, InfAuslR 9/98, 416 where the judge ruled that a decision against which an appeal is pending constitutes a valid decision for the purpose of Art 35 SC, and in view of the objective of chapter VII of the Schengen Convention, which is to determine as fast as possible which State is responsible for examining the claim.

[54] See Note de la Délégation néerlandaise du 24 septembre 1996 sur la jurisprudence concernant l'application de la Convention de Schengen aux Pays-Bas SCH/II-As (96) 39 (on file with the author), 3.

[55] SCH/Com-ex (97) 4 rev. of 25 April 1997 (on file with the author); Decision No. 1/2000 of 31 October 2000 of the Committee set up by Article 18 of the Dublin Convention concerning the transfer of responsibility for family members in accordance with Article 3(4) and Article 9 of that Convention [2000] OJ L281/1; see also para 186 of the UNHCR *Handbook*, n 52 above, which recommends that the principle of family unity apply equally to cases where a family unit has been temporarily disrupted through the flight of one or more of its members.

clauses should be interpreted as allowing spouses to have their applications examined jointly.[56] The government's response to this progressive attitude was to issue administrative guidelines advising that the Secretary of State should apply the sovereignty clause only if the Netherlands was responsible for the examination of the asylum claim of at least one member of the family; the family was in a situation of humanitarian need; there was an unaccompanied minor; or where the family had travelled directly and jointly to the Netherlands.[57] Where, for instance, one of the spouses had been granted temporary protection, the clause was in principle not applied.[58] The courts have not always followed the policy of the administration, and in some cases, they found that the derogation should be applied even though there were no special circumstances as required by the government guidelines.[59] The Belgian *Conseil d'État* also adopted a compassionate attitude in some cases and censured administrative decisions on the basis of Article 8 ECHR.[60]

Given the narrow scope of the Schengen and Dublin Conventions' family unity clauses and their consequent limited use, provisions on family reunion were substantially fleshed out in the Regulation and were welcomed as one of the most positive changes brought about by the new instrument. The relevant articles of the Dublin Regulation read:

Article 6

Where the applicant for asylum is an unaccompanied minor,[61] the Member State responsible for examining the application shall be that where a member of his or her family is legally present, provided that this is in the best interest of the minor. In the absence of a family member, the Member State responsible for examining the application shall be that where the minor has lodged his or her application for asylum.

---

[56] Pres Rb Den Haag 9-4-96 96/2281 [1996] *NAV* 429.

[57] See *Vreemdelingen Circulaire* 1994 and *Werkinstructie 111*; P Boeles, 'Erkenning van gezinseenheid in geval van verschillende verantwoordelijke staten: een Belgische doorbraak' [1998] *NAV* 437, 438; Pres Rechtb's Gravenhage zp Zwolle 4-10-95 AWB 95/4126 *RV* (1995) nr 14, 46; Rechtb Den Haag 22-12-95 AWB 95/12021 [1996] *NAV* 234, 235 where the judge held that the ties between a mother and her adult sons who were residing in Holland were not close enough to justify the application of the derogation. Note that there are some decisions which take account of the intention of the spouses to travel together to the Netherlands, even if they were prevented to do so by material circumstances, in order to conclude to that the Netherlands was responsible to examine both claims: Zwolle 15-07-98 AWB 98/2578 [1998] *NAV* nr162, 748; see also Zwolle 11-10-96 AWB 96/7163 and AWB 96/7323 [1996] *NAV* 857, where the judge considered that marriage constituted sufficient evidence of the existence of a family life for the purposes of Art 8 ECHR.

[58] 'Beleid gescheiden behandeling van gezinsleden door toepassing Schengen' [1996] *NAV* 959, 960-962.

[59] See eg Zwolle 28-02-97 AWB 96/7502 (1997) 4 JuB nr21, 37; see also Pres Recht 's-Gravenhage 17-12-97 AWB 97/6172 [1998] JV nr26, 119.

[60] On a commentary of the *Conseil d'Etat* decisions, see Boeles, n 57 above, 437.

[61] The definition of 'unaccompanied minor' is found at Art 2(h) of the Dublin Regulation:

(h) 'unaccompanied minor' means unmarried persons below the age of eighteen who arrive in the territory of the Member States unaccompanied by an adult responsible for them whether by law or by custom, and for as long as they are not effectively taken into the care of such a person; it includes minors who are left unaccompanied after they have entered the territory of the Member States;

Article 7

Where the asylum seeker has a family member, regardless of whether the family was previously formed in the country of origin, who has been allowed to reside as a refugee in a Member State, that Member State shall be responsible for examining the application for asylum, provided that the persons concerned so desire.

Article 8

If the asylum seeker has a family member in a Member State whose application has not yet been the subject of a first decision regarding the substance, that Member State shall be responsible for examining the application for asylum, provided that the persons concerned so desire.

Additionally, Article 14 DR provides that:

Where several members of a family submit applications for asylum in the same Member State simultaneously, or on dates close enough for the procedures for determining the Member State responsible to be conducted together, and where the application of the criteria set out in this Regulation would lead to them being separated, the Member State responsible shall be determined on the basis of the following provisions:

(a) responsibility for examining the applications for asylum of all the members of the family shall lie with the Member State which the criteria indicate is responsible for taking charge of the largest number of family members;

(b) failing this, responsibility shall lie with the Member State which the criteria indicate is responsible for examining the application of the oldest of them.

In spite of these useful amendments and the broader language of Article 6, the Regulation still leaves out reunion with family members applying for subsidiary protection status or whose decision on status has been appealed, and with family members legally residing in a Member State but who have not been granted refugee status.

Practice under the Dublin Regulation also shows that authorities have become far less compassionate. According to recent reports, Article 6 DR is too often ignored or interpreted in an unreasonably restrictive manner. In the Netherlands, for instance, a court reversed the decision of the administrative authorities to transfer a Somali minor to Spain, where he had previously applied for asylum, even though his mother was legally residing in the Netherlands, because the asylum seeker had failed to invoke Article 6 DR at the outset of the proceedings and that this provision could not be considered at the appeal stage.[62] This case is also illustrative of the fact that in many 'Dublin' States, unaccompanied minors are not properly informed of their rights under Article 6 DR.[63]

---

[62] Judgment of the District Court The Hague of 27 January 2005, AWB 04/51294 and AWB 04/51293, UNHCR Dublin II Discussion Paper, n 26 above, 22.

[63] ECRE, 'Report on the application of the Dublin II Regulation in Europe', March 2006 (hereafter, ECRE 2006 Dublin II Report), 156, which includes a specific case-study on the treatment of separated children in the United Kingdom in order to show that 'Dublin' States routinely evade or blatantly ignore their obligations under the Dublin Regulation and international law. ECRE also

UNHCR is of the view that Article 6 DR should be regarded as overriding all of the other criteria, which is a correct interpretation, since the criteria stipulated under the Regulation apply by order of precedence.[64] Furthermore, the whole provision of Article 6 DR should be interpreted with the 'best interest of the child' in mind, in accordance with Article 3.1 of the Convention on the Rights of the Child,[65] and not only where a family member is present in a Member State, as a strict reading of the provision would seem to imply.[66]

With respect to Articles 7 and 8 DR, UNHCR identified inconsistent practice related to proof of family links and the legal status of family members.[67] In Austria, Belgium, and Sweden, documentary proof of family links is not required if personal statements are consistent and credible, while other States require documentary evidence, and even DNA evidence in some cases. While Article 7 DR seems to apply exclusively when the family member has been recognized as a refugee, authorities in the Netherlands have decided to extend it to the beneficiaries of subsidiary protection, which is in accordance with the spirit if not the letter of the qualification Directive.[68] On the other hand, a decision of a Dutch court denied the application of an Iraqi asylum seeker who sought to join her husband who had been granted citizenship after being recognized as a refugee in Sweden, because the Regulation did not apply to naturalized persons.[69] ECRE also noted that in light of the extremely rapid processing of asylum claims in some States, such as the Netherlands, the applicability of Article 8 DR is restricted.[70] Furthermore, this provision only applies at the first instance level and given that the lengthier part of the procedure is usually the appeal, its relevance is only limited.[71] Finally, practice

recommended that Art 6 DR be amended to prevent children from being removed to another State except on the basis of family reunification, providing that it is in the best interest of the child.

[64] UNHCR Dublin II Discussion Paper, n 26 above, 23, which also reports that the Greek and Hungarian authorities have received requests from other States to take charge of minors based on other Dublin criteria. The European Commission more cautiously recommends that '[w]hile the application of take back requests should not be ruled out in the case of unaccompanied minors, the best interest of the child should always prevail', 2007 Commission Report, n 27 above, 7.

[65] Convention on the Rights of the Child (adopted 20 November 1989, entered into force 2 September 1990) 1577 UNTS 3. Note however that the United Kingdom reserves the right to apply legislation relating to the entry into, stay in and departure from the United Kingdom of those who do not have the right under the law of the United Kingdom to enter and remain in the United Kingdom.

[66] UNHCR Dublin II Discussion Paper, n 26 above, 23–4. What is deemed to be in the best interest of the child may differ in each Member States, thus Luxembourg considers that reunification with a family member is always in the best interest of the child.

[67] UNHCR Dublin II Discussion Paper, n 26 above, 26.

[68] ECRE 2006 Dublin II Report, n 63 above, 159; UNHCR Dublin II Discussion Paper, n 26 above, 27.

[69] ECRE 2006 Dublin II Report, n 63 above, 159 referring to District Court of Harlem 12 April 2005 (AWB 05/13491).

[70] Ibid, 158.

[71] Brandl, n 51 above, 44.

based on Article 14 DR is scarce; only limited cases were reported by Poland and Belgium.[72]

3.3.2 Visa and residence permit

According to Article 9 DR, the State which has granted a valid residence document or issued a valid visa is responsible for the examination of the application for asylum. Provisions relating to visas envisage various situations, such as the issuance of a visa on representation, or the granting of visas or residence documents by several States.[73] These include cases where different States have issued residence permits/visas which are still valid at the time of the lodging of the asylum application[74] and where the visa/residence permit is expired.[75]

3.3.3 Illegal crossing of the territory of a Member State

Article 10

1. Where it is established, on the basis of proof or circumstantial evidence as described in the two lists mentioned in Article 18(3), including the data referred to in Chapter III of Regulation (EC) No. 2725/2000, that an asylum seeker has irregularly crossed the border into a Member State by land, sea or air having come from a third country, the Member State thus entered shall be responsible for examining the application for asylum. This responsibility shall cease 12 months after the date on which the irregular border crossing took place.

2. When a Member State cannot or can no longer be held responsible in accordance with paragraph 1, and where it is established, on the basis of proof or circumstantial evidence as described in the two lists mentioned in Article 18(3), that the asylum seeker—who has entered the territories of the Member States irregularly or whose circumstances of entry cannot be established—at the time of lodging the application has been previously living for a continuous period of at least five months in a Member State, that Member State shall be responsible for examining the application for asylum.

If the applicant has been living for periods of time of at least five months in several Member States, the Member State where this has been most recently the case shall be responsible for examining the asylum application.

Two important points must be raised with respect to this provision. First, its implementation should have been greatly improved thanks to the Eurodac system.[76] Secondly, compared with the Dublin Convention, this criterion has been modified

---

[72] UNHCR Dublin II Discussion Paper, n 26 above, 28.
[73] Article 9.2 DR. Note that Art 2(j) DR defines residence document as 'any authorization issued by the authorities of a Member State allowing a third-country national to stay on its territory, including the documents substantiating the authorization to remain in the territory under temporary protection arrangements or until the circumstances preventing a removal order from being carried out no longer apply'.
[74] Article 9.3 DR; Art 5.3(a) to (c), 5.3.(b) and 5.3.(c) DC.
[75] Article 9.4 DR; Art 5.4 DC.
[76] On Eurodac, see below Section 3.4.3.

to address the situation, seen in the Sangatte camp in France, where asylum seekers stay undetected for a relatively long period of time, that is, at least five months, on the territory of a 'Dublin' State, which becomes subsequently responsible for their illegal stay on EU territory. The so-called 'Sangatte clause' was adopted at the request of Southern EU States, primarily Greece and Italy, which considered that they should not single-handedly carry the burden of irregular arrivals in the European Union.[77]

3.3.4 Control of the entry of the alien into the territory of the Member States

Article 11 DR provides that the responsibility for examining the asylum application shall be incumbent upon the State responsible for controlling the entry of the alien into the territory of the 'Dublin' States.

Following divergent interpretations of Article 7.2 DC concerning airport transit in one of the Member States,[78] the Commission clarified that under the Dublin Convention, airport transit did not give rise to responsibility of the 'transit' State. On the other hand, British courts adopted the view that since the Dublin Convention had not been incorporated into the English legal order, the Secretary of State could decide to send the applicant to another Dublin State, if the applicant had been going through airport transit in that State.[79] Currently, only in the case where the application for asylum has been lodged in transit in an airport of a Member State, as expressly stipulated under Article 12 DR, is that State responsible. It bears noting that this is the only article where the asylum seeker is actually given the right to choose between two countries of asylum, the country of transit and the country of final destination.

3.3.5 The humanitarian and 'sovereignty' clauses

In spite of the fact that the Dublin regime provides for two different cases of derogation covering two distinct situations, these have at times been confused by practitioners.[80] The sovereignty clause allows a State to decide, on a discretionary

---

[77] M-T Gil-Bazo, 'The Practice of Mediterranean States in the Context of the EU's Justice and Home Affairs External Dimension: The Safe Third Country Concept Revisited' (2006) 18 *IJRL* 571, 578–9.

[78] The text of Art 7.2 DC reads:

Pending the entry into force of an agreement between Member States on arrangements for crossing external borders, the Member State which authorizes transit without a visa through the transit zone of its airports shall not be regarded as responsible for control on entry, in respect of travellers who do not leave the transit zone.

[79] *Behluli v Secretary of State for the Home Department* [1998] Imm AR 407.

[80] *Conseil d'État, Arrêt* No. 69.578 of 13 November 1997; UNHCR Dublin II Discussion Paper, n 26 above 34.

basis, to examine an application for asylum lodged with it, even if it is not responsible in virtue of the criteria defined in the Regulation.[81] Under the Dublin Convention, Article 3.4 provided that the application of the clause was conditional upon the agreement of the asylum seeker. However, many national authorities, such as the Aliens Office in Belgium, automatically used to apply Article 3.4 DC to process asylum claims from Romanian, Hungarian, and Polish asylum seekers, and did not usually file a request for transfer to Italy, Greece Portugal, and Spain due to considerable processing delays.[82] UNHCR condemned this practice,[83] but most officials agreed that the objective of the Dublin Convention was to ensure the efficient treatment of asylum claims and that the application of the sovereignty clause in such cases was lawful.

Such interpretation has been fully endorsed with the adoption of the Regulation, since the asylum seeker's consent is no longer required under Article 3.2 DR,[84]

---

[81] Article 3.2 DR; Art 3.4 DC, known previously as 'opt-out' clause.

[82] Interview with Mr Goriya, Head of the Schengen/Dublin section in the Aliens Office, Belgium, 7 June 1999. The assumption was that the lodging of an asylum request constituted the expression of the asylum seeker's implicit consent and that, therefore, the consent required under Art 3.4 DC had been given. The asylum seeker's consent was not required under Art 29.4 SC but an Executive Committee Decision expressly required it, SCH/II-As (93) 13 3e rev. See also *Verwaltungsgericht* Berlin 14.04.97 and 10.09.96, n.p. on the situation where the mother and first child had a French visa, and the second child was born during the asylum procedure in Germany. The judge excluded the application of the humanitarian clause by France for the infant child, since he could not have given his/her consent to the decision. A 1992 note from the Spanish Presidency comparing the provisions of the Dublin Convention and the Schengen Convention concluded that the agreement of the asylum seeker was implicit in Art 29.4 SC, since an asylum seeker generally lodges his application in the State where she/he wants to have it examined, SCH/II-As (92) 4, 3e rev. (on file with the author). This approach was supported by courts in the Netherlands, see Pres Rechtb 's-Gravenhage 10-12-97 AWB 97/6627 [1998] JV nr27, 121; on the other hand in Zwolle 05-08-98 AWB 98/3760 (1998) 5 JuB nr16, 41, the authorities acknowledged that the asylum seeker was not properly informed of the consequences of the signing of the administrative form, because of a language barrier; see also F Löper, 'The Dublin Convention on Asylum: Interpretation and Application Problems', in C Marinho (ed), *The Dublin Convention on Asylum, Its Essence, Implementation and Prospects* (European Institute of Public Administration, Maastricht 2000) 17, 19; for German practice, see Hailbronner, n 29 above, 384.

[83] Interview with Johannes van der Klaauw, Senior European Affairs Officer at the Regional Office for the Benelux Countries and the European Institutions of the UNHCR, 29 March 1999. Interview with Mr Goriya, n 82 above.

[84] One should also note that courts in the Netherlands and Germany found that the applicant for asylum could not invoke a right to have the derogation applied, see Den Haag 2-8-95 AWB 95/6192 [1995] *NAV* bijlage 21, 713; 's-Gravenhage zp Zwolle 30-01-98 AWB 97/6700 [1998] JV nr39, 171; *Verwaltungsgericht* Schwerin 03.05.96 and *Verwaltungsgericht* Gießen 25.01.1996 n.p. mentioned in W Jansen, 'Overzicht van rechtspraak naar enkele thema's van de uitvoeringsovereenkomst Schengen' (1996) 3 *Vreemdelingen Bulletin* 13; Hailbronner and Thiery, n 17 above, 973, see also H Meijers, 'Refugees in Western Europe, "Schengen" affects the entire Refugee Law' (1990) 2 *IJRL* 428, 431; T Spijkerboer, 'The Practical Effects of Schengen in Asylum Cases', in *Refugee and Asylum Law: Assessing the Scope for Judicial Protection* (Nederlands Centrum for Buitenlanders, Amsterdam 1998) 36; Hailbronner, n 29 above, 392–3. However, the authorities had to consider the arguments supporting the application of the clauses put forward by the asylum seeker. The *Conseil d'Etat* of Belgium reaffirmed this principle in numerous cases, see eg *Arrêt* No. 66.292 of 16 May 1997; *Arrêt* No. 67.538 of 22 July 1997; *Arrêt* No. 67.622 of 1 August 1997 [1997] *RDE* 215–18; *Arrêt* No. 67.710 of 14 August 1997 [1997] *RDE*, 363; for the German case-law, see C Marinho, 'The Dublin Convention

allowing thereby administrative authorities to apply the sovereignty clause where the asylum seeker can be more easily and swiftly expelled at the end of the asylum procedure, or where the application is manifestly unfounded or abusive. Studies on the implementation of the Dublin Regulation show that many Member States have made full use of the sovereignty clause to this end.[85]

The 'humanitarian' clause included in the Dublin Regulation (Article 15 DR) deals with the situation where the responsible Member State will request another Member State to take responsibility for 'humanitarian' reasons in family reunion cases. The different situations contemplated under Article 15 DR somehow codify existing practice, and correspond to the guidelines which had been adopted by the Committee established under Article 18 DC. Article 15 DR reads:

1. Any Member State, even where it is not responsible under the criteria set out in this Regulation, may bring together family members, as well as other dependent relatives, on humanitarian grounds based in particular on family or cultural considerations. In this case that Member State shall, at the request of another Member State, examine the application for asylum of the person concerned. The persons concerned must consent.

2. In cases in which the person concerned is dependent on the assistance of the other on account of pregnancy or a new-born child, serious illness, severe handicap or old age, Member States shall normally keep or bring together the asylum seeker with another relative present in the territory of one of the Member States, provided that family ties existed in the country of origin.

3. If the asylum seeker is an unaccompanied minor who has a relative or relatives in another Member State who can take care of him or her, Member States shall if possible unite the minor with his or her relative or relatives, unless this is not in the best interests of the minor.

4. Where the Member State thus approached accedes to the request, responsibility for examining the application shall be transferred to it.

5. The conditions and procedures for implementing this Article including, where appropriate, conciliation mechanisms for settling differences between Member States concerning the need to unite the persons in question, or the place where this should be done, shall be adopted in accordance with the procedure referred to in Article 27(2).

Article 8 ECHR[86] may be invoked to support the application of the sovereignty and humanitarian clauses. Article 8 ECHR generally 'presupposes' the existence of

---

Judicial Control: National Case Highlights', in C Marinho (ed), *The Dublin Convention, Its Essence, Implementation and Prospects* (European Institute of Public Administration, Maastricht 2000) 225, 242.

[85] This is the case in Finland, Germany, the Netherlands, Austria, and Norway, UNHCR Dublin II Discussion Paper, n 26 above, 31; ECRE 2006 Dublin II Report, n 63 above, 154–6.

[86] ETS No. 005; Art 8 reads:

1. Everyone has the right to respect for his private and family life, his home and his correspondence.

2. There shall be no interference by a public authority with the exercise of this right except such as is in accordance with the law and is necessary in a democratic society in the interests of national security, public safety or the economic well-being of the country, for the prevention of disorder or crime, for the protection of health or morals, or for the protection of the rights and freedoms of others.

a family, but the European Court of Human Rights later clarified that an 'intended family life did not necessarily fall outside its ambit'.[87] The court also found that 'although the essential object of article 8 is to protect the individual against arbitrary interference by the public authorities, there may in addition be positive obligations inherent in an effective "respect" for family life'.[88] The court nevertheless stressed that States enjoy a wide margin of appreciation, especially in cases involving the entry of non-nationals on their territory.[89]

While the additional provisions on family reunification may have decreased the use of the sovereignty and humanitarian clauses in family cases, the narrow definition of 'family member' under Article 2(i) DR means that the 'humanitarian' and 'sovereignty' clauses are still used in a number of family-related cases.[90] Furthermore, the notion of 'dependency' is defined relatively narrowly under Article 11.2 of the Implementing Regulation, since it indicates that 'the situations of dependency shall be assessed, as far as possible, on the basis of objective criteria such as medical certificates' and, where such evidence cannot be supplied, 'humanitarian grounds shall be taken as proven only on the basis of convincing information supplied by the persons concerned'.

Recent reports indicate that there are still widely divergent practices in the application of the sovereignty clause.[91] Some States have never applied it,[92] while other States routinely use it to prevent the separation of extended family members, such as in Austria.[93] The Commission has indicated that it will propose that the circumstances and procedures for applying the sovereignty and humanitarian clauses be clarified and that the consent of the asylum seeker be required for the application of the sovereignty clause.[94]

Much of the 'pre-Regulation' case-law remains relevant in this respect, even though it should be noted that under the Dublin Convention, there was no obligation

---

[87] See *Abdulaziz and ors v United Kingdom,* Judgment of 28 May 1985 (1985) 7 EHRR 471, para 62; see 's Gravenhage zp Zwolle 9-10-98 AWB 98/4650 [1998] JV nr 227, 1050, where the judge held that Art 4 DC did not apply to a marriage formed after the lodging of the asylum claim. ECRE reports that most of the successful challenges to 'Dublin transfers' have been based on Art 8 ECHR, ECRE 2006 Dublin II Report, n 63 above, 22.

[88] *Abdulaziz and ors,* n 87 above, para 67.

[89] Ibid, para 67; see Boeles, n 57 above, 437; See eg Den Haag 11-09-96 AWB 96/8279, n.p. cited in W Jansen, 'Overzicht van rechtspraak naar enkele thema's van de uitvoeringsovereenkomst Schengen' (1996) 3 *Vreemdelingen Bulletin* 13. Zwolle 14-06-1996 AWB 96/3460 (1996) 3 JuB nr 7, 10.

[90] The Commission laid down rules for the application of the humanitarian clause in Arts 11 to 14 of Commission Regulation (EC) No. 1560/2003 of 2 September 2003 laying down detailed rules for the application of Council Regulation (EC) 343/2003 establishing the criteria and mechanisms for determining the Member State responsible for examining an asylum application lodged in one of the Member States by a third-country national [2003] OJ L222/3 (hereafter, Implementing Regulation).

[91] 2007 Commission Report, n 27 above, 6.

[92] ECRE 2006 Dublin II Report, n 63 above, 156.

[93] UNHCR Dublin II Discussion Paper, n 26 above, 30; ECRE 2006 Dublin II Report, n 63 above, 155.

[94] 2007 Commission Report, n 27 above, 7.

for Member States to ensure the unity or reunification of dependent family relatives. The situations in which the application of the sovereignty clause have been invoked include family reunion cases, humanitarian cases, cultural grounds, procedural issues, and protection concerns.

The first category of cases has probably been the most common. For instance, the *Conseil d'État* in Belgium ordered the suspension of the decision of the Aliens Office sending to France a 19-year-old Rwandan asylum seeker whose aunt had been granted refugee status in Belgium.[95] In the Netherlands, the derogation was also used for a Bosnian man, whose sister had been granted the status of refugee and with whom he had cohabited for several years. In addition, his aunt and brother-in-law had been granted protection in the Netherlands.[96] Another case, which is anterior to the entry into force of the Dublin Convention in the United Kingdom, would have also justified the application of the sovereignty clause. A 20-year-old Rwandan woman lodged an application in the United Kingdom because her cousin, one of the only surviving members of her family, was residing in that country. The British authorities had first decided to send the woman back to Belgium but leave to apply for judicial review was eventually granted by the High Court, and the British Home Office accepted to reconsider the claim.[97]

These examples reflect the general practice of Member States, which tend to apply the sovereignty clause where removal would be in violation of Article 8 ECHR, and for unification of extended family members that may not necessarily meet the dependency requirement under the humanitarian clause. That being said, many Member States have refused to take responsibility for asylum applications in such circumstances and practice remains quite restrictive.[98] The *Conseil d'État* commonly refused to stay the execution of transfers, on the ground that there was no sufficient evidence of effective and pre-existent family ties, above all where the asylum seeker invoked the legal presence of a sibling or of another member from his/her extended family in Belgium. This was the case, for instance, for an asylum seeker whose brothers-in-law and uncle lived in Belgium,[99] for an asylum seeker whose brother had been granted refugee status in Belgium,[100] and also for

---

[95] *Arrêt* No. 75.628 of 28 August 1998, n.p.; see also *Arrêt* No. 69.232 of 28 October 1997, [1998] *NAV* bijlage 14, 501; for more recent case-law of the *Conseil d'État* relating to the application of the sovereignty clause under the Dublin Convention, see ECRE 2006 Dublin II Report, n 63 above, 166.

[96] Pres 's Gravenhage 8-12-95 AWB 95/11266 [1996] NAV bijlage 12, 73.

[97] Amnesty International, *Playing Human Pinball: Home Office Practice in 'safe third countries' asylum cases*, June 1995, 49.

[98] UNHCR Dublin II Discussion Paper, n 26 above, 34; ECRE 2006 Dublin II Report, n 63 above, 160-151. See *Verwaltungsgericht* Schwerin 03.05.96 and *Verwaltungsgericht* Gießen 25.01.1996 n.p. mentioned in W Jansen, n 84 above, 15; Zwolle 25-10-95 AWB 95/4134, (1995) 2 JuB nr16, 26; 's Gravenhage 21-12-95 AWB 95/6513 [1996] GV nr18b, 60; 's Gravenhage 4-1-96 AWB 95/12042 [1996] GV 18b, 64.

[99] *Arrêt* No. 69.158 of 24 October 1997 n.p.; see also *Arrêt* No. 69.466 of 5 November 1997 n.p.

[100] *Arrêt* No. 69.714 of 21 November 1997 n.p.

an asylum seeker who had not been in close contact with her sister who was living in Belgium.[101]

The sovereignty clause may also be used in strictly humanitarian cases: pregnant asylum applicants or those accompanied by infants, medical emergencies, and psychiatric or physiological problems.[102] For example, the *Conseil d'État* considered the case of an asylum seeker who was at serious risk of committing suicide if he were sent to his country of origin or to the responsible State which had already rejected his claim. The authorities had justified their decision by stating that the claimant could receive medical treatment in Germany.[103] The *Conseil d'État* granted the application, finding that the authorities had not properly examined whether the risk of expulsion might constitute an inhuman or degrading treatment pursuant to Article 3 ECHR.[104]

The House of Lords recently examined the case of an Iraqi asylum seeker whose application had been previously denied by Germany, which was thus responsible for taking him back under the Dublin Regulation. In light of the serious mental condition of the applicant, the House of Lords found that the Secretary of State could not have found that the claim was manifestly unfounded, and that it should have made an assessment of whether the transfer to another Member State would be detrimental to the applicant's physical and mental health, based on whether the lawful operation of immigration control would in this particular case be proportional to the harm caused to the applicant's health.[105] However, Lord Carswell insisted that, 'in order to bring himself with such an exceptional engagement of article 8 [ECHR], the applicant has to establish a very grave state of affairs, amounting to a flagrant or

---

[101] *Arrêt* No. 70.163 of 11 December 1997 n.p.; see also *Arrêt* No. 71.977 of 20 February 1998 n.p.; *Arrêt* No. 73.085 of 14 April 1998 n.p.

[102] Note de la délégation néerlandaise, n 54 above, 4–5. See 's Gravenhage 5-12-95 AWB 95/5694 [1996] GV nr18b, 69, regarding an asylum seeker with diabetes who could not be transferred to Germany; 's Gravenhage 7-10-96 AWB 96/9453 (1996) 3 JuB nr13, 29, regarding an Albanian woman who was in danger of forced prostitution if sent back to Belgium; see also 's-Gravenhage 25-03-97 AWB 97/1760 (1997) 4 JuB 42; 's-Gravenhage zp Zwolle 7-12-95 AWB 95/5371 [1996] *NAV* bijlage 10, 67, on the case of a woman who feared being sent back to Germany, because one of the guards at the camp where she was held during the war resided in that country; Zwolle 18-09-98 AWB 98/3726 [1998] *NAV* nr189, 845 concerning an adult asylum seeker whose mother was treated for cancer in the Netherlands.

[103] See *Arrêt* No. 75.497 of 31 July 1998 [1998] TVR 178.

[104] This provision was invoked in another case, which was dismissed, see *Arrêt* No. 77.706 of 17 December 1998, n.p.; see also in this respect *R v Secretary of State for the Home Department ex p Mehmet Tozlukaya* [2006] EWCA Civ 379, finding no violation of Art 3 ECHR in a decision to remove to Germany an asylum seeker with suicidal tendencies, para 72; *Bensaid v UK*, Appl. 44599/98, Judgment of 6 February 2001 (2001) 33 EHRR 205, para 37, 40 where the ECtHR held that the deterioration of an individual's mental illness including the risk of self harm could in principle fall within the scope of Art 3 ECHR.

[105] *R v Secretary of State for the Home Department ex p Razgar* [2004] UKHL 27, para 24; see also in this regard, *In the Matter of an Application by Ngozi Christiana Okoye* [2006] NIQB 14, para 14, in which the Queen's Bench dismissed the application of a Nigerian asylum seeker who was to be sent back to Italy.

fundamental breach of the article, which in effect constitutes a complete denial of his rights'.[106]

Cultural grounds have been much more rarely considered. In a decision of the administrative tribunal of Orléans, the judges took account of the existence of close cultural links with France, and in particular the fact that the applicant had joined the *Légion étrangère*.[107] The decision was overruled by the *Cour d'appel administrative,* which found that the authorities were entitled to use their discretion in the application of the derogation.[108]

Procedural arguments have also been put forward in favour of the application of the sovereignty clause. In the 'pre-Regulation' case-law, issues such as the lack of information of the asylum seeker about the possibility that another Member State might examine his/her claim and the fact that asylum claims of family members were related to one another were raised.[109] It was also argued that the passing of a reasonable deadline to transfer the asylum applicant would oblige the authorities to apply the sovereignty clause.[110] Most of these arguments have been successful in limited cases, usually when the passing of the deadline was invoked jointly with humanitarian factors.[111] Dutch courts were faced with a large number of claims invoking the obligation to inform the asylum seeker and the distinction between hearings in relation with the process of allocating responsibility and interviews to determine the asylum motives.[112] According to this jurisprudence, the authorities are entitled to interview asylum seekers on the motives of their flight in order to

---

[106] Ibid, para 72.

[107] E Aubin, 'Le juge administratif français face à l'application des Conventions de Schengen dans ses dispositions sur le droit d'asile et de Dublin relative à la détermination de l'Etat responsable de l'examen d'une demande d'asile', in C Marinho (ed), *The Dublin Convention on Asylum, Its Essence, Implementation and Prospects* (European Institute of Public Administration, Maastricht 2000) 177, 190–1.

[108] Ibid, 192.

[109] 's Gravenhage 11-09-1996 AWB 96/8273 (1996) 3 JuB nr14, 26. This argument was invoked along with the respect for family unity. See also in Belgium *Arrêt* No. 69232 of 28 October 1997 [1998] *NAV* bijlage 14, 501. See in this respect, Art 19 DR on the information that must be provided to the asylum applicant in the decision to take charge.

[110] The deadline for the transfer exclusively concerns State parties and is not an 'obligation of result', therefore it cannot be invoked by the asylum seeker for the application of the derogation, 's-Gravenhage 31-5-96 AWB 96/4192, (1996) 3 JuB nr6, 12; 's-Gravenhage zp Zwolle 30-01-98 AWB 97/6700, (1998) JV nr39, 171. The *Conseil d'Etat* gave a similar ruling in an *Arrêt* No. 69.578 of 13 November 1997 n.p. In 's-Gravenhage 1-03-96 AWB 96/1098 (1996) GV nr18b, 75 the judge ruled that the passing of the three-month deadline set out in the Schengen Executive Committee Decision of 27 June 1994 to determine which State is responsible may lead to a violation of the principles of good administration. The acceptable length of the Dublin procedure depends on several factors and cannot by itself be regarded as sufficient ground to apply Art 3.4 but should normally not last more than six months, Rechtb Den Haag 14-08-98 AWB 98/5139 [1998] *NAV* nr163, 749; see also Zwolle 27-10-98 AWB 98/4848 (1998) 5 JuB nr20, 52, ruling that the asylum seeker must be fully informed of the procedural developments of his/her case; see also ECRE 2006 Dublin II report, n 63 above, 166.

[111] Ibid; see eg 's-Gravenhage zp Zwolle 24-04-98 AWB 98/576, 98/625 [1998] JV nr96, 391.

[112] See eg 's-Gravenhage 17-11-1995 AWB 95/10607 [1995] RV nr16, 50; Zwolle 13-01-99 AWB 98/6636 (1999) 6 JuB 46; 's-Gravenhage zp Zwolle 19-01-99 AWB 98/6633 [1999] JV nr79, 279;

determine whether to adopt the derogation, but s/he must be informed that this hearing does not constitute a de facto application of the derogation, and that s/he may still be sent to the responsible State.[113]

Finally, the issue of whether the sovereignty clause may be invoked on the ground of divergent asylum policies of the Member States continues to be raised even though domestic courts have become particularly restrictive in this regard. In most cases, judges have ruled that the 'sovereignty' clause cannot not be used for such purpose, since the Dublin regime is founded on Member States' 'mutual trust' in their respective asylum policies and regulations.

Prior to the Dublin Regulation, Dutch courts had already adopted a restrictive approach, and considered that while differences in the interpretation of the refugee definition of Article 1.A(2) CSR constituted a relevant fact, a more restrictive expulsion policy might not be regarded as such.[114] In Germany, the authorities admittedly never considered objections on the basis of differences in protection standards.[115] The *Conseil d'État* of Belgium never admitted such a line of argument either, which might be due to the very short timeframe applying within the emergency procedure.[116] British courts, on the other hand, addressed this question at length, although since 1999, the legislator has considerably restricted the ability of applicants to bring protection-related challenges before the courts.[117]

Since the adoption of the Regulation, a number of countries, particularly new Member States, have been regarded as not safe for protection purposes.[118] Also, the Greek administrative practice which allows for the 'interruption' of an asylum

---

Zwolle 20-01-99 AWB 98/6948 (1999) 6 JuB nr14, 32; 's-Gravenhage zp Zwolle 17-02-99 AWB 99/172 (1999) JV nr117, 425; 's Gravenhage 26-02-99 AWB 99/425 [1999] JV nr138 519.

[113] See 's-Gravenhage 17-11-95 AWB 95/10515 [1996] GV nr18b, 41; 's Gravenhage 17-11-95 AWB 95/10544 en 95/10546 [1996] GV nr18b, 35; 's-Gravenhage 17-11-95 AWB 95/10502 (1996) GV nr18b, 48; Den Haag 4-12-95 AWB 95/10910 (1996) 3 JuB nr19, 27; Zwolle 21-12-95 AWB 95/6004 (1996) 3 JuB nr6, 10; 's-Gravenhage 17-01-96 AWB 95/12477 [1996] *NAV* bijlage 9, 312; 's-Hertogenbosch 30-01-96 AWB 95/9408 (1996) 3 JuB nr13, 26; see in the UK *R v Secretary of State for the Home Department and an Immigration Officer ex parte S* [1998] Imm AR 416 (QB).

[114] The asylum seeker was asked to prove that he would be immediately threatened with *refoulement* if sent to the third country, which is virtually impossible, T Spijkerboer, case-law note [1995] RV 54; see also *Rechtseenheidskamer* 19-12-96 AWB 96/9092, [1996] RV nr13, 47; Zwolle 7-03-97 AWB 97/56, (1997) 4 JuB nr11, 21; 's Gravenhage 20-05-98 AWB 98/3293 98/3308, (1998) 5 JuB nr15, 31.

[115] Hailbronner, n 29 above, 394–5; see also ECRE 2006 Dublin II Report, n 63 above, 166, which reports that challenges on protection grounds are not admitted in Hungary and Greece.

[116] See for instance *Arrêt* No. 75497 of 31 July 1998 [1998] TVR 178; *Arrêt* No. 75.587 of 12 August 1998 [1998] TVR 180. See also the case where the claimant argued that she did not want to be transferred to France because of France's supposed involvement in the Rwandan genocide. This claim was dismissed as meritless by the judges who found that the claimant had failed to provide evidence to support her argument, *Arrêt* No. 75.898 of 24 September 1998, n.p.

[117] See in this respect *Secretary of State for the Home Department v Nasseri*, [2008] EWCA Civ 464; see Chapters 2 and 5, Sections 2.1.2.3, 5.1.1.2 and 5.3 for a detailed analysis of the lawfulness of returns in application of the safe third country under international human rights and refugee law.

[118] Brandl, n 51 above, 61, 65.

procedure in case of 'arbitrary departure',[119] has come under the spotlight and been strongly criticized by both UNHCR and non-governmental organizations, as well as the Commission.[120] UNHCR used the example of an asylum seeker from the Darfur region in Sudan, who had applied for asylum in Greece but decided to travel to the United Kingdom after having slept in the streets of Athens for two weeks. Once the Greek authorities accepted to take him back at the request of the United Kingdom, they notified him of the interruption of his asylum procedure and that his request for re-examination of his claim based on the situation in Sudan had been rejected on the ground that it was similar to his earlier application, which had never been examined on its merits.[121] More importantly, removals to Greece have been successfully challenged in many Member States, including Austria, Finland, France, the Netherlands, Slovenia, Sweden, the United Kingdom, Italy, and Norway.[122] In two important cases in the Netherlands, the removal to Greece in accordance with the provisions of the Dublin Regulation was regarded as leading to indirect *refoulement*.[123] One of the most recent cases addressing this issue was the aforementioned *Nasseri* case where the Court of Appeal overturned a High Court's decision finding that the listing of Greece as a safe third country to which an asylum seeker could be sent in accordance with the Dublin Regulation did not offend the United Kingdom obligations under the ECHR, even though it acknowledged that 'the list system renders the UK compliance with article 3 ECHR fragile'.[124]

---

[119] According to UNHCR, 'so far only circumstances such as serious health problems, hospitalization and being forced to leave a home as a result of weather conditions have been recognized as circumstances of '*force majeure*'' justifying the re-opening of the procedure, UNHCR Dublin II Discussion Paper, n 26 above, 46. UNHCR also reports that more then 30 requests for review have been lodged, none of which have been granted; see also ECRE 2006 Dublin II Report, n 63 above, 150–1.

[120] See UNHCR, 'Note on access to the asylum procedure of asylum seekers returned to Greece, inter alia, under arrangements to transfer responsibility with respect to determining an asylum claim or pursuant to the application of the safe third country concept', November 2004, in which UNHCR indicates that the overall recognition rate for any international protection needs in Greece was 0% in the first instance in 2003 while on appeal the recognition rate was about 1%, 2. On 18 February 2008, in response to a parliamentary question, the European Commission also expressed its concern about this policy see <http://www.europarl.europa.eu/sides/getAllAnswers.do?reference=E-2007-6202&language=CS>; see also P Papadimitriou, 'The New "Dubliners": Implementation of EC Regulation 343/2003 (Dublin II) by the Greek Authorities' (2005) 18 *JRS* 299, 309, who reports that the implementation of Eurodac has led to a substantial increase of requests to take back asylum seekers who had crossed illegally into Greece, which were previously never accepted in the absence of proof of illegal crossing, ibid, 305. On Eurodac, see Section 3.4.3 below.

[121] UNHCR Dublin II Discussion Paper, n 26 above, 47; see also M Sperl, 'Fortress Europe and the Iraqi "intruders": Iraqi asylum-seekers and the EU, 2003–2007', UNHCR New Issues in Refugee Research Paper No. 144, October 2007, 6–7.

[122] ECRE 2006 Dublin II Report, n 63 above, 166. See also ECRE, 'Sharing Responsibility for Refugee Protection in Europe: Dublin Reconsidered' March 2008 (hereafter, ECRE 2008 Dublin II Report), where ECRE refers to a decision revoking transfer of an Iraqi asylum seeker from Hungary to Cyprus, 10.

[123] ECRE 2006 Dublin II Report, n 63 above, 94–5 referring to a decision of 29 September 2004 (AWB 04/30154) and to a decision of 10 February 2005 (AWB 04/57933).

[124] *Secretary of State for the Home Department v Javad Nasseri* [2008] EWCA Civ 464, paras 41–2; see also *AH(Iran) Zego (Eritrea) Kadir (Iraq) v Secretary of State for the Home Department* [2008] EWCA Civ 985; see also Chapter 2, Section 2.1.2.3.

This brief overview shows that the sovereignty and humanitarian clauses have proved useful where the Convention criteria did not provide acceptable solutions to humanitarian and family related situations.[125] However, their relatively extensive use also demonstrates the failure of a system that attempts to organize the allocation of responsibility on the basis of rigid criteria which do no take sufficient account of the intention and specific circumstances of each asylum seeker.

3.4 Procedure

The Dublin system requires a complex range of procedural rules governing the transfer to the responsible State, the presentation of evidence for the determination of the State responsible, and the identification of the asylum seeker, which are presented below.

3.4.1 Transfer of the asylum seeker to the responsible State

The request for transfer shall be lodged within three months from the date of the introduction of the asylum claim[126] and must contain information to enable the authorities of the requested State to determine whether it is responsible.[127] The asylum seeker shall be informed of the request.[128] The reply should be sent within two months of the receipt of the request.[129] Transfer must take place 'as soon as practically possible, and at the latest, within six months of acceptance of the request that charge be taken or of the decision on appeal or review where there is suspensive effect'.[130] Where transfer does not take place within six months, responsibility shall lie with the Member State in which the application for asylum was lodged.

---

[125] It is worth recalling that the power of derogation was originally provided for the countries whose constitutions recognise a right to asylum, namely France and Germany, and also to reaffirm the respect of Member States' sovereignty in such a sensitive field, Hailbronner and Thiery, n 17 above, 965; J van der Klaauw, 'The Dublin Convention, the Schengen Asylum Chapter and the Treatment of Asylum Application', in *Het Akkoord van Schengen en vreemdelingen, een ongecontroleerde grens tussen recht en beleid?* (1996) 37, 40.

[126] Article 17 DR. Note that under the Dublin Convention, the deadline was six months.

[127] Article 17.3 DR.

[128] Article 19.1 DR.

[129] Article 18.1 DR.

[130] Article 19.3 DR. Note that under Chapter VII of the Schengen Convention, the deadline was difficult to comply with and the Schengen Executive Committee held that the requested State remains responsible when the delay is due to exceptional circumstances. See 's-Gravenhage 31-5-96 AWB 96/4192 (1996) 3 JuB nr 6, 12 where the judge found that the deadline set out in the decision of the Schengen Executive Committee did not entail an 'obligation of result', and that therefore, the passing of the deadline did not render the transfer illegal, and the requesting State was not obliged to apply the derogation; see also 's-Gravenhage zp Zwolle 30-01-98 AWB 97/6700 (1998) JV nr39, 171; the *Conseil d'Etat* reached the same conclusion in an *Arrêt* No. 69.578 of 13 November 1997 n.p. On the other hand, the decision of transfer has to be notified to the asylum seeker, see *Arrêt* No. 74.163 of 8 June 1998 [1998] *RDE* 219; cf 's-Gravenhage 1-03-96 AWB 96/1098 [1996] GV nr18b 75 where the judge ruled that the passing of the three-month deadline, set out in the Schengen Executive Committee Decision of 27 June 1994 to determine which State is responsible, may lead to a violation of the principles of good administration.

However, the deadline may be extended to one year if the transfer could not be carried out due to the imprisonment of the asylum seeker or up to a maximum of 18 months if the asylum seeker absconds.[131]

The responsible State will also be obliged to readmit the asylum seeker who has withdrawn his/her application and lodged an application in another Member State, who has been found irregularly in another Member State while his application is still under consideration, or whose application has been rejected.[132] Article 18.1 DR provides in these cases that the requested State shall give an answer within two months of the date on which the request was received. These obligations cease to apply if the asylum seeker has left the territory of the Member States for a period of at least three months,[133] and if the State responsible, following the withdrawal or the rejection of the application, has taken and enforced measures to return the alien to his country of origin or to another country in which he may lawfully enter.[134] One should note, however, that while there are strict time limits to respond to requests to take back an asylum seeker, there are no such time limits for submitting requests to take back asylum seekers, which may cause hardship to asylum seekers. [135]

Under the Dublin Convention, the transfer of asylum seekers was often hindered by multiple difficulties; cases of asylum seekers disappearing before the transfer frequently occurred, while some asylum seekers preferred to withdraw their claim. This may have accounted for the strong discrepancy reported by the Commission between the number of transfers formally accepted and their actual implementation.[136] In some Member States, transfer could also be delayed by appeal procedures.[137] Officials reported transfers implemented six months or even a year after the request was accepted, by Italy, for instance. This can be problematic given that it is not clear whether the minimum reception standards provided for in the reception Directive apply to 'Dublin' applicants.[138] In some cases, asylum seekers are kept in custody as a means to facilitate transfers or detain applicants who are returned pursuant to the Dublin system.[139] Problems also occurred when an asylum seeker who was taken back by a Member State, but was

---

[131] Article 19.4 DR.

[132] Article 16.1 (c)–(e) DR.

[133] Article 16.3 DR; see also Art 8 of Decision No. 1/2000, n 55 above.

[134] Article 16.4 DR.

[135] UNHCR Dublin II Discussion Paper, n 26 above, 37; see also 2007 Commission Report, n 27 above, 8.

[136] 2007 Commission Report, n 27 above, 8.

[137] See France Terre d'Asile, 'Convention d'application de l'Accord de Schengen premier bilan de sa mise en oeuvre en Europe' (February 1996), 15.

[138] M Garlick, 'Asylum Legislation in the European Community and the 1951 Convention: Key Concerns Regarding Asylum Instruments Adopted in the "First Phase" of Harmonization', in T Balzacq and S Carrera (eds), *Security versus Freedom? A Challenge for Europe's Future* (Ashgate, Aldershot 2006) 45, 53.

[139] ECRE 2008 Dublin II Report, n 122 above, 18. See also Art 16 of the reception Directive, n 39 above.

not accompanied, did not present him/herself to the authorities of the Member State and disappeared.[140]

In terms of procedural safeguards, the Dublin Regulation stipulates that States shall inform the asylum seeker in writing and in a language s/he may be reasonably expected to understand about the application of the Regulation, its time limits and its effects.[141] While most States seem to comply with this obligation, failure to provide the required information still occurs and the quality of the information presented varies widely between Member States. In Belgium, for instance, only limited information is provided on the Dublin procedure, its applicable criteria and time limits.[142] In the Netherlands, no reference is made to the possibility of being reunited with family members.[143]

The decision not to examine an application must be notified to the asylum seeker, shall set out the grounds on which it is based, and indicate the time limits for the transfer.[144] In the United Kingdom, however, the decision of the authorities does not explain why a particular State has been found responsible for examining the claim.[145] According to UNHCR, the Netherlands is a model of good practice with regard to the details provided in this respect.[146]

While the Dublin Convention lacked any specific provision on remedies,[147] the Dublin Regulation provides that the decision not to examine an asylum application may be subject to appeal or review proceedings[148] and currently, all Member States allow for the appeal or review of Dublin decisions. However, the Regulation also indicates that,

[A]ppeal or review concerning this decision [of taking charge or taking back] shall not suspend the implementation of the transfer unless the courts or competent bodies so decided on a case by case basis if national legislation allows for this.[149]

---

[140] This situation was envisaged by the Council Conclusions of 27 May 1997 concerning the application of the Dublin Convention [1997] OJ C191/27.

[141] Article 3.4 DR.

[142] UNHCR, Dublin II Discussion Paper, n 26 above, 13.

[143] Ibid, 14.

[144] Article 19.1 and 20.1 DR.

[145] UNHCR Dublin II Discussion Paper, n 26 above, 16.

[146] Ibid, 17. The decision includes the decision to reject, the different stages of the procedure, such as the date of the interview and the date that the fingerprints were taken, the reasoning of the authorities to counter the arguments of the asylum seeker for having his/her asylum application examined in the Netherlands, the consequences of the decision, namely, that the legal stay ends at the moment of notification of the decision; and available remedies.

[147] Article 11.5 DC, which related to the transfer of the applicant for asylum to the State responsible, made brief reference to the possibility of challenging the decision. The EU Resolution of 20 June 1995 on minimal guarantees for asylum procedures [1996] OJ C274/13 provided, however, that the procedure for determining the State responsible was excluded of its scope of application, and that the safeguards applicable to this procedure would be defined by the Executive Committee established by Art 18 DC.

[148] Article 19.2 DR; Art 20.1(e).

[149] Article 19.2 and Art 20.1(e) DR. See in this respect H Battjes, 'A Balance Between Fairness and Efficiency? The Directive on International Protection and the Dublin Regulation' (2002) 4 *EJML* 159, 186,

In other words, the effectiveness of such remedies varies greatly[150] and in many Member States, it is not clear that asylum seekers are able to fully exercise their right.[151]

Currently, only Portugal guarantees the automatic suspensive effect of an appeal against Dublin decisions.[152] In most other Member States, the appeal is not automatically suspensive but suspension may be granted on a case-by-case basis.[153] In Belgium, the decision on the determination of the State responsible is joined to an *Ordre de quitter le territoire*[154] and both decisions are notified in the same official document. The asylum applicant may file a request for leave to appeal the decision of expulsion before the *Conseil du contentieux des étrangers* provided the asylum applicant proves that the enforcement of the decision would give rise to a serious, and irreparable damage.[155] In the United Kingdom, since the entry into force of new legislation reforming *inter alia* asylum proceedings, removals may be carried out regardless of the filing of an appeal if it is certified that the allegation that such removal would violate the asylum seeker's human rights is manifestly unfounded.[156] In some countries, such as Germany and France, the ability to appeal is almost inexistent since the enforcement of the decision takes place on the same day or shortly after the asylum seeker is notified of the decision.[157]

Situations where the appeal is not suspensive may give rise to a violation of Article 13 ECHR, which provides for the right to an effective remedy before a national authority against any act or decision which allegedly violates one of the provisions of the ECHR, primarily, Articles 3, 5, and 8 ECHR in the case of asylum seekers.[158] It is also worth mentioning Article 16.1 CSR, which states that the

who argues that this provision goes beyond the legal scope of the Regulation, since Art 63(1)(a) ECT does not give competence to the Community for the adoption of procedural standards in 'Dublin' appeal proceedings.

[150] For an overview of the remedies available to challenge a decision of transfer under the Dublin Convention, see Marinho, n 84 above, 228–31; UNHCR Dublin II Discussion Paper, n 26 above, 19; ECRE 2006 Dublin II Report, n 63 above, 165.

[151] See also UNHCR Dublin II Discussion Paper, n 26 above, 19.

[152] Ibid.

[153] Ibid.

[154] Order to leave the Belgian territory.

[155] Before the entry into force of the law of 15 September 2006, the Conseil d'Etat was competent to adjudicate these challenges and the case-law of the *Conseil d'Etat* of Belgium cited in this chapter arises exclusively from this procedure.

[156] G Clayton, *Textbook on Immigration and Asylum Law* (2nd edn, Oxford University Press, Oxford 2006) 423.

[157] UNHCR Dublin II Discussion Paper, n 26 above, 19–20.

[158] *Jabari v Turkey*, Appl. No. 40035/98, Judgment of 11 July 2000, ECHR 2000-VIII, para 40; *Conka v Belgium*, Appl. No. 51564/99, Judgment of 5 February 2002, paras 79, 82–3, in which the ECHR found that the lack of automatic suspensive effect of the extremely urgent procedure before the Belgian *Conseil d'Etat* did not provide an effective remedy against a breach of Art 4 of Protocol No. 4 of the ECHR; *Gebremedhin v France*, Appl. No. 25389/05, Judgment of 26 April 2007, para 58, 66, where the European Court of Human Rights found that the French asylum procedure at the border violated Art 13 ECHR due to the absence of suspensive effect of decisions summarily dismissing an asylum claim; see also H Battjes, n 149 above, 186, 190.

refugee shall have free access to courts of law on the territory of all Contracting Parties. The *Section de legislation*[159] of the *Conseil d'État* in Belgium considered that this provision also entailed an obligation to guarantee effective remedies.[160]

3.4.2 Rules of evidence

The adoption of rules of evidence to determine the responsibility of Member States was one of the most problematic issues in the implementation of the Dublin Convention. While the question was addressed in Decision No. 1/97 adopted by the Committee established in accordance with Article 18 of the Dublin Convention,[161] this issue is now directly addressed in Article 18.3 of the Regulation:

In accordance with the procedure referred to in Article 27(2) two lists shall be established and periodically reviewed, indicating the elements of proof and circumstantial evidence in accordance with the following criteria:

(a) Proof:

(i) This refers to formal proof which determines responsibility pursuant to this Regulation, as long as it not refuted by proof to the contrary.

(ii) The Member States shall provide the Committee provided for in Article 27 with models of the different types of administrative documents, in accordance with the typology established in the list of formal proofs.

(b) Circumstantial evidence:

(i) This refers to indicative elements which while being refutable may be sufficient, in certain cases, according to the evidentiary value attributed to them.

(ii) Their evidentiary value, in relation to the responsibility for examining the application for asylum shall be assessed on a case-by-case basis.

---

[159] The *Section de législation du Conseil d'État* is competent to advise the government on draft legislation.

[160] S Saroléa, 'La procédure belge de reconnaissance de la qualité de réfugié et le droit à un recours effectif' [1995] *RDE*, 542, 555. For an analysis of the scope of Art 16 CSR, see P Boeles, *Fair Immigration Proceedings in Europe* (Martinus Nijhoff, The Hague [etc] 1997) 72 and 76, who observes that the *travaux préparatoires* are silent on this issue. Some commentators consider that the scope of Art 16 also covers refugee status determination. The Dutch *Raad van State* has supported this view. In Belgium, decisions of the *Cour d'appel* of 29 June 1989 [1989] *RDE* 153 and of the *Tribunal de 1ère instance* of 24 December 1990 [1990] *RDE*, 237, also shared this interpretation, see B Bléro 'Protection constitutionelle et internationale des demandeurs d'asile, quelques considérations à propos de l'arrêt de la Cour d'arbitrage du 14 juillet 1994 annulant partiellement certaines modifications apportées au statut des réfugiés par la loi du 6 mai 1993' [1994] *Revue belge de droit constitutionnel* 241.

[161] Decision No. 1/97 of the Executive Committee established under Art 18 of the Dublin Convention concerning provisions for the implementation of the Convention [1997] OJ L281/1. Note that Recital 2 of the Preamble of the Implementing Regulation specifies that it 'should be based on the common principles, lists and forms adopted by the committee set up by Art 18 of the [Dublin] Convention, with the inclusion of amendments necessitated by the introduction of new criteria, the wording of certain provisions and of the lessons drawn from experience'.

As required under Article 18.3 of the Dublin Regulation, a list of proof and circumstantial evidence is annexed to the Implementing Regulation. The Dublin Regulation also insists on the fact that the 'requirement of proof should not exceed what is necessary for the proper application of this Regulation'[162] and that 'if there is no formal proof, the requested Member State shall acknowledge its responsibility if the circumstantial evidence is coherent, verifiable and sufficiently detailed to establish responsibility'.[163]

Under the Dublin Convention, the exclusive reliance on circumstantial evidence was generally not sufficient to convince a State to take charge of an asylum seeker.[164] Officials at the Dublin Unit of the Aliens Office of Belgium declared that they had originally accepted responsibility on the basis of indicative evidence but adopted a more restrictive attitude after experiencing refusals of transfer by administrations in other Member States.[165] In one case where there was a very detailed description of a travel route through Greece together with eight pieces of documentation, such as hotel confirmations and tickets of public transport, the Greek authorities nevertheless refused to accept the transfer of the asylum seekers.[166] Train tickets were usually refused as indicative evidence in most Member States,[167] and France apparently never accepted responsibility on the sole basis of the declarations of the asylum seeker.[168] According to Spanish officials, the only country which accepted responsibility on the basis of indicative evidence was the Netherlands.[169] Given these difficulties, the Commission has insisted again that 'Member States should apply the Dublin Regulation and its Implementing Rules in their entirety, using all means of proofs foreseen, including credible and verifiable statements of the asylum seeker'.[170]

---

[162] Article 18.4 DR. See also Art 8.1 of the Implementing Regulation on cooperation on transfers; see also Art 24 and 25 of Decision No. 1/1997, n 161 above.

[163] Article 18.5 DR.

[164] UNHCR briefing with officials working at the Zevenaar centre in Holland (on file with the author); see also 's-Gravenhage zp Zwolle 24-04-98 AWB 98/1203 [1998] JV nr97, 394 where the judge found that indicative evidence of the presence of the asylum seeker in Turkey for a period of at least three months, was sufficient to show that he had been outside the 'Dublin territory', and thus that the Netherlands was responsible; 's-Gravenhage 30-10-98 AWB 98/7771 98/7774 (1998) 5 JuB nr11, 31 where the applicants' argument that the declaration of one of them on the travel route was not a sufficient element to prove France's responsibility was rejected by the judge; see also 's-Gravenhage 30-10-98 AWB 98/7773 (1998) 5 JuB nr12, 33.

[165] Interview with Mr Goriya, n 82 above.

[166] R Bartels, 'Ein Jahr Dubliner Übereinkommen' [1998] *Der Einzelentscheider-Brief*, Nr.9, 2.

[167] Interview with Mr Goriya, n 82 above.

[168] S Kok, 'De overeenkomst van Dublin; een beschrijving en praktijk ervaringen' [1998] *NAV* 677, 685.

[169] See UNHCR briefing of meeting with Eduardo Blanes, Head of the Section of the Inadmissibility Procedures and Ms Ana Clavo and Ms Blanca Suarez of the Dublin Unit at the Office for Asylum and Refuge which is subordinated to the Department of the Director for Internal Affairs within the Spanish Ministry of Internal Affairs, 28 September 1998 (on file with the author).

[170] 2007 Commission Report, n 27 above, 8.

With regard to the obligation to share relevant information, and to provide personal data concerning the asylum seeker pursuant to Article 21 DR,[171] recent studies report many instances where State authorities have provided inaccurate or incomplete information, which may have resulted in a different Member State bearing responsibility.[172] For instance, the Dutch authorities failed to mention that the mother of a separated child who was to be transferred to Spain, was present in the Netherlands.[173]

3.4.3 Identification of the asylum seeker: the Eurodac Regulation

One of the major challenges to the effective operation of the Dublin regime is the identification of asylum seekers who hide their identity and/or country of origin, file successive applications under different names, or have already been refused asylum.[174] Article 21 DR organizes the exchange of information concerning individuals. This information may relate to personal details of the asylum applicant, travel documents, residence and routes travelled, documents issued by a Member State and so on.[175] The Regulation also provides for the possibility of forwarding information concerning the grounds of an application for asylum, and the grounds for the decision on the application. In such case, the written approval of the asylum seeker is required.[176] The asylum seeker is given the right to be informed, on request, of any data that is processed about him and if she finds that this information has been processed in breach of the Regulation or of the Directive on the protection of individuals with regard to the processing of personal data and on the free movement of such data, in particular because it is incomplete or inaccurate, she is entitled to have it corrected, erased, or blocked.[177]

The most efficient way to verify the identity of asylum seekers is to compare fingerprints, and Member States cooperation in this area existed for some years;[178] however, there were difficulties because different techniques for taking fingerprints were used. Since the general formulation of Article 15 DC did not constitute

---

[171] See Art 21 DR; Arts 8 and 13.2 Implementing Regulation.

[172] ECRE 2006 Dublin II Report, n 63 above, 163.

[173] ECRE, 2006 Dublin II Report, n 63 above, 164; see also UNHCR Dublin II Discussion Paper, n 26 above, 43–4.

[174] See eg Rechtbank 's Gravenhage 11-11-98 AWB 98/8090 [1999] *NAV* nr15, 74.

[175] Article 21.2 DR; see also Art 15.2 DC.

[176] Article 21.3 DR; see also Art 15.3 DC and Art 13 of Decision No. 1/2000, n 55 above.

[177] Article 21.9 DR, which refers to Directive 95/46/EC of 24 October 1995 of the European Parliament and the Council on the protection of individuals with regard to the processing of personal data and the free movement of such data [1995] OJ L281/31.

[178] See Art 2 of Decision No. 1/98 of 30 June 1998 adopted by the Committee established under Article 18 DC concerning provisions for the implementation of the Convention [1998] OJ L196/49; see also Zwolle 18-11-98 AWB 98/5015 [1999] JV nrS70, 235; E Brouwer, 'Eurodac: Its Limitations and Temptations' (2002) 4 *EJML* 231, 243.

a proper legal basis for the creation of a system of exchange of fingerprints,[179] the Council negotiated a draft instrument establishing the 'Eurodac' system for the comparison of fingerprints of asylum applicants whose objective is to assist in determining the Member State which is responsible for examining an application for asylum lodged in a Member State.[180] Political agreement on the proposal was found at the meeting of the Council on Justice and Home Affairs of 3 and 4 December 1998, but it was decided to 'freeze' the text until the entry into force of the Treaty of Amsterdam in order to adopt it as a community instrument.[181] The Eurodac Regulation was eventually adopted on 11 December 2000,[182] and became operational on 15 January 2003, when all Member States had made the necessary technical arrangements to ensure its proper operation.[183]

The 'Eurodac' system consists of a Central Unit established within the Commission of the European Community operating a computerized central database which records and stores fingerprints from asylum seekers.[184] States send fingerprints to the Central Unit which will compare them with fingerprints already stored.[185]

Three categories of aliens are targeted. The first covers applicants for asylum of at least 14 years of age,[186] who shall have their fingerprints taken and recorded in the central database in order to be compared with previously recorded data.[187] Additional information concerning the asylum seeker will also be entered into the database, such as the country of origin, gender, place, and date of the asylum application, the dates on which the fingerprints were taken, and on which the data were transmitted to the Central Unit and entered into the database.[188] These data will be stored for ten years from the date on which the fingerprints were taken, unless the person acquires citizenship of a Member State.[189] Those refugees whose status has been formally recognized will have their data blocked in the central database.[190]

---

[179] M Toussaint, 'Eurodac: un système informatisé européen de comparaison des empreintes digitales des demandeurs d'asile' [1999] *RMCUE* 421, 422.

[180] Draft Council Act drawing up the Convention concerning the establishment of "Eurodac" for the comparison of fingerprints of applicants for asylum, 12942/98 ASIM 236, 17 November 1998 (on file with the author).

[181] See Proposal for a Council Regulation concerning the establishment of Eurodac for the comparison of fingerprints of applicants for asylum and certain aliens of 26 May 1999 COM (1999) 260 final, based on Article 63(1)a) of the EC Treaty as amended by the Amsterdam Treaty, see spec. para 4.3 of the Explanatory Memorandum regarding the amendments to the 'frozen' texts suggested by the Commission, in order to have it adjusted to the new legal framework.

[182] The United Kingdom and Ireland participated in the adoption of the Regulation; see para (20) of the Preamble.

[183] Article 27.2 Eurodac Regulation.

[184] Para 5 of the Preamble and Art 3 Eurodac Regulation.

[185] Article 4 Eurodac Regulation.

[186] On whether the fingerprinting of minors complies with international human rights law, see Brouwer, n 178 above, 237.

[187] Article 4.1–4.3 Eurodac Regulation.

[188] Article 5 Eurodac Regulation.

[189] Articles 6 and 7 Eurodac Regulation.

[190] Article 12.1 Eurodac Regulation.

The second category comprises aliens apprehended in connection with the irregular crossing of an external border.[191] The fingerprints of any of these individuals of at least 14 years of age will be taken. These data will only be recorded for the purpose of comparison with data on applicants for asylum transmitted subsequently to the Central Unit,[192] and will be stored for two years, unless the alien has been issued a residence permit, has left the territory of the Member States, or has acquired the citizenship of a Member State.[193] In any case, upon expiry of the two-year period, the data shall be automatically erased.[194]

Finally, aliens of at least 14 years of age found illegally present in a Member State may have their fingerprints taken, to determine whether s/he has already submitted an asylum application in a Member State.[195] The data of such aliens shall not be recorded in the database and shall not be compared with the data of aliens apprehended in connection with the irregular crossing of the border.[196] After the results of the comparison have been transmitted, the Central Unit must erase the data.[197]

The purpose of adding the last two categories, which were originally not covered,[198] was to extend the use of Eurodac to cases in which the asylum seeker has not claimed asylum in the first State s/he has travelled through.[199] The idea was first floated within the Schengen Executive Committee in 1997 and reiterated in the 1998 Action Plan on the influx of migrants from Iraq and the neighbouring region.[200] However, distinguishing between these two categories will not always be easy in practice, and there was some debate during the negotiations as to what 'apprehension at the frontier' precisely means.[201] Furthermore, some commentators have questioned the legality of extending fingerprinting to these categories, given the narrow terms of the Dublin Regulation.[202]

---

[191] Article 8 Eurodac Regulation.

[192] Article 9.1 Eurodac Regulation.

[193] Article 10.2 Eurodac Regulation.

[194] Article 10.1 Eurodac Regulation.

[195] Article 11.1 Eurodac Regulation.

[196] Article 11.3 Eurodac Regulation.

[197] Article 11.5 Eurodac Regulation.

[198] See in this respect E Guild, 'The Bitter Fruits of an EU Common Asylum Policy', in T Balzacq and S Carrera (eds), *Security versus Freedom? A Challenge for Europe's Future* (Ashgate, Aldershot 2006) 61, 68.

[199] C D de Jong, 'Is there a Need for a European Asylum Policy ?', in F Nicholson and P Twomey P (eds), *Refugee Rights and Realities: Evolving International Concepts and Regimes* (Cambridge University Press, Cambridge 1999) 357, 360.

[200] Brouwer, n 178 above, 235; see EU Action Plan on the influx of migrants from Iraq and the neighbouring region adopted on 26 January 1998 Council doc 5573/98 ASIM 13 (on file with the author).

[201] Hailbronner, n 29 above, 408; see also Guild, n 198 above, 69, who reports that after arduous negotiations a statement was inserted in Council minutes after the adoption of the Eurodac Regulation providing that '[t]his provision also covers cases where an alien is apprehended beyond the external border, where he/she is still en route and there is no doubt that he/she crossed the external border irregularly'.

[202] Brouwer, n 178 above, 236, 244 who also refers to the opinion of the legal service of the Commission which considered that the inclusion within Eurodac of data of persons who crossed the border lawfully but had then been residing unlawfully was not justifiable.

The Eurodac Regulation contains detailed provisions concerning the protection of personal data, in accordance with Directive 95/46/EC of 24 October 1995 of the European Parliament and the Council on the protection of individuals with regard to the processing of personal data and on the free movement of such data.[203] Under these provisions, the Member State and the European Community might be liable for damages resulting from the illegal use of the results of the fingerprint comparisons transmitted by the Central Unit.[204] Nonetheless, some have legitimately raised the question of whether these provisions comply with the right to privacy enshrined in Article 8 ECHR,[205] and whether in accordance with the aforementioned Directive, the collection of such data is not excessive for the purposes for which it is collected and processed.[206] Additionally, the temptation to use this data for purposes other than the allocation of responsibility for asylum applications is a real, albeit not new, concern.[207] A recent UK decision finding that Eurodac evidence can be used for credibility assessment in refugee status determination procedures without infringing Article 21 DR, while not surprising, reinforces these fears.[208]

The trend towards further securitization of asylum is here again apparent. The expansion of the use of the Eurodac system as a means to prevent abuses of the asylum system as well as illegal immigration is currently on the agenda, and the Commission suggested that data related to third country nationals apprehended when illegally staying on a Member State's territory should also be stored for an initial period of two years.[209] Another suggestion of the Commission is that authorities responsible for the implementation of the Dublin Regulation have access to information on the Visa Information System and the future version of the Schengen Information System,[210] and that conversely, Member States authorities and Europol be allowed access to Eurodac.[211]

The statistics on the operation of the system collected so far indicate that the system has not had quite the expected impact. In its first report on the implementation of the Dublin Regulation, the Commission indicated that in 2005 there had

---

[203] [1999] OJ L281/31; see Art 18 of the Regulation; see Guild, n 198 above, 69–70; E Guild, 'Seeking Asylum: Storm Clouds Between International Commitments And EU Legislative Measures' (2004) 29 *ELR* 198, 210, who lists the nine principles under EC law which must be respected in order for an exception to the right to privacy to be regarded as legitimate.

[204] Article 17 Eurodac Regulation.

[205] Brouwer, n 178 above, 244.

[206] Guild, 'Seeking Asylum', n 203 above, 210.

[207] Brouwer, n 178 above, 233, 246–7.

[208] *RZ v Secretary of State for the Home Department* [2008] UKAIT 00007, paras 42–3.

[209] 2007 Commission Report, n 24 above, 11.

[210] S Peers, *EU Justice and Home Affairs Law* (2nd edn, Oxford University Press, Oxford 2006) 324; on the Visa Information System, see ibid, 165.

[211] European Commission, Communication from the Commission to the European Parliament, the Council, the European Economic and Social Committee and the Committee of Regions: Policy Plan on Asylum, An Integrated Approach to Protection Across the EU' (hereafter, 'Policy Plan on Asylum') COM (2008) 360 final, 17 June 2008, 8.

been a small decrease in the number of transactions relating to the fingerprinting of asylum applicants, a 16 per cent 'multiple application' rate, and that the number of fingerprints from individuals apprehended in connection with the irregular crossing of an external border and of third country nationals found illegally present on the territory of a Member State considerably increased, to respectively 48, 657 and 101,884 data registered in the database.[212] The Commission noted, however, that despite such increase, the number of transactions for this category remained 'surprisingly low' above all in light of the 'strong irregular migratory pressures at the external borders' and the recent enlargement of the European Union.[213] The Commission expressed concern about the effective application of the obligation to fingerprint all illegal entrants apprehended at the borders of the Union and suggested that non-compliance might be taken into consideration when reviewing the implementation of the Solidarity and Management Flows Framework Programme in 2010 and in particular the relevant distribution criteria applicable for the different funds.[214] Another issue raised by the Commission related to delays in transmission of data, which could lead to the wrong determination of the responsible Member State.[215]

3.5 Assessment

In spite of the various efforts and initiatives to improve efficiency, the overall record of the application of the Dublin regime remains unconvincing and as has been said before, the system is neither fair nor efficient.[216] In its working paper preceding the drafting of the proposal for a Regulation, the Commission indicated that in 1998, less than 2 per cent of asylum seekers who lodged a claim in the Member States were transferred in accordance with the provisions of the Convention.[217] While the 2007 Commission report on the evaluation of the Dublin system shows significant increases, with requests for transfer sent out by Member States amounting to 11.5 per cent of the total number of asylum applications in all Member States for the same period,[218] such improvement is mitigated by the fact that only 16,482 cases were actually transferred, representing only 11.5 per cent of the

---

[212] 2007 Commission Report, n 27 above, 5. Guild notes that the initial assumption for 2003 was that the number of category 2 data would be 400,000; instead, it was only 7,857, n 198 above, 72.

[213] Guild's comparison of data from the 2005 Eurodac report show that the Eurodac system led to the identification of 28,864 asylum seekers by comparing category 1 against category 1; 1,466 asylum seekers by comparing category 1 against category 2, and 5,492 asylum seekers by comparing category 1 with category 3, ibid, 74.

[214] See also Brouwer, n 178 above, 244; Brandl, n 51 above, 52.

[215] 2007 Commission Report, n 27 above, 9.

[216] Hurwitz, n 3 above, 674–6.

[217] Commission Staff Working Paper, 'Revisiting the Dublin Convention', n 8 above, para 12, 38.

[218] 2007 Commission Report, n 27 above, 4. This period under evaluation ended in 2005, ibid, 2. However, the charts show many discrepancies in the period covered for each Member State, and in some cases even, the unavailability of relevant data.

55,300 requests for transfer that were sent out by Member States, even if 72 per cent of the requests had actually been accepted.[219] The Commission also acknowledged that the analysis of statistics provided by Member States had been rendered particularly difficult because of a mismatch between the number of requests received from other Member States and the number of requests and decisions that each Member State reports to other Member States.[220]

Furthermore, according to a recent ECRE report, the Dublin system has not put an end to multiple applications, whose incidence has in fact increased, suggesting that the Dublin system might have aggravated the phenomenon of multiple claims rather than attenuated it.[221] The absurdity of the system was further demonstrated when the Commission proposed that in cases where certain Member States transfer similar numbers of asylum seekers between themselves, bilateral arrangements providing for the 'annulment' of the exchange of equal numbers of asylum seekers could be concluded, recognizing that limiting the number of transfers between two Member States 'could reduce the workload and operating costs of the departments responsible for transfers'.[222] Also startling is the fact that no financial figures on the cost of the system were submitted by the Commission, which limited itself to stating that it is the political objectives of the system which matter most to Member States.[223]

In view of the complexity of the procedure and the delays incurred in the examination of asylum claims,[224] the number of implementation instruments, and the important mobilization of resources within national administrations, one is entitled to wonder whether the Dublin system is not just an 'expensive waste of time'.[225] Notwithstanding this poor record, the Commission indicated in 2008 that Member States continue to support the current system.[226]

Early on, practitioners and administrative authorities pointed to recurring problems of application, caused by the lack of cooperation between administrations triggered by the differences in administrative culture, but more fundamentally, by the intrinsic flaws of the system. The essence of the problem is that the criteria set out in the Convention defy any sensible consideration of asylum situations. The Commission recognized that the choice of criteria was primarily political,[227] and that Member States were not yet prepared to accept a system based on the wishes of the asylum seeker, out of fear that this would lead to abuses of

[219] Ibid, 4; see also M Collyer, 'The Dublin Regulation, Influences on Asylum Destinations and the Exception of Algerians in the UK' (2004) 17 *JRS* 375, 380.
[220] 2007 Commission Report, n 27 above, 3.
[221] ECRE 2008 Dublin II Report, n 122 above, 11.
[222] 2007 European Commission Report, n 27 above, 8.
[223] Ibid, 13.
[224] Ibid, 10; see also R Marx, 'Adjusting the Dublin Convention: New Approaches to Member State Responsibility for Asylum Applications' (2001) 3 *EJML* 7, 18.
[225] Peers, *EU Justice and Home Affairs Law,* n 210 above, 321.
[226] Policy Plan on Asylum, n 211 above, 7.
[227] Commission Staff Working Paper, n 8 above, para 25.

the system.[228] In fact, the choice of the 'Dublin' criteria primarily resulted from the inability of Member States to agree on a system which would have been based on the close links existing between an asylum seeker and a certain country.[229]

The contradictions of the system are so serious, according to de Jong, that Member States with long external borders prefer a dysfunctional system to one which would make them bear the burden of most asylum seekers arriving irregularly in the European Union.[230] This ongoing atmosphere of mutual 'distrust' stands in stark contrast with the declared foundation of the system. The litmus test for the Dublin regime will be whether 'outer States' will be willing and/or able to fully implement a system, which, given the growing number of illegal arrivals, is generating an increasingly significant burden for them. It has been suggested that one of the ways to address this difficulty would be to allow for a temporary suspension of the system,[231] or even the adoption of arrangements for the reallocation of asylum seekers in certain circumstances and on a voluntary basis.[232]

A more radical overhaul would in fact be far more effective. At the time of the negotiation of the Dublin Regulation, UNHCR advocated once again that responsibility should lie primarily with the State in which the application is lodged, unless the applicant already has a connection or close links with another State, in which case it might be fairer and more reasonable that s/he request asylum there.[233] It specifically asserted that the only meaningful links that could lead to transfer to another Member State were family connections, cultural ties, knowledge of the language, possession of a residence permit, and the applicant's previous periods of residence in the State in question.[234] Giving more freedom of choice to the asylum seeker would not undermine the relative efficiency of the system and it is probable that in practice, only a small number of asylum seekers would be able to invoke the

[228] Ibid, para 28 and 29; see also para 56.

[229] M-O Wiederkehr, 'L'œuvre du Conseil de l'Europe dans le domaine du droit d'asile et des réfugiés', in Société française de droit international, *Droit d'asile et des réfugiés*, (1997) 197, 204; see also para (h) (iv) of ExCom Conclusion No. 15 (1979); and Recommendation 1327 (1997), n 52 above, para (iv); see in this respect Chapter 1, Section 1.3.1 to 1.3.3.

[230] '[T]he more successful the application of this convention will be the more complaints about its effects will be heard.' de Jong, n 199 above, 4 and 13.

[231] This was suggested by UNHCR, see UNHCR, 'Building a Europe of Asylum: UNHCR's Recommendations to France for its European Union Presidency' June 2008, 7; see also Policy Plan on Asylum, n 211 above, 9.

[232] UNHCR, 'Response to the European Community's Green Paper on the Future Common European Asylum System' September 2007, 11; Policy Plan on Asylum, n 211 above, 9.

[233] UNHCR, 'Revisiting the Dublin Convention—Some Reflections by UNHCR in Response to the Commission Staff Working Paper', January 2001.

[234] UNHCR's Observations on the European Commission's Proposal for a Council Regulation establishing the criteria and mechanisms for determining the Member State responsible for examining an asylum application lodged in one of the Member States by a third-country national (COM(2001) 447 final), February 2002; see also A Shacknove and R Byrne, 'The Safe Country Notion in European Asylum Law' (1996) 9 *Harvard Human Rights LJ* 185, 206.

existence of close links with one of the Member States.[235] Furthermore, the asylum seeker whose application is examined in a Member State where family members or members of his/her community of origin live is probably going to cost less to the community.[236] In addition, enabling members of the same family to claim asylum in the same State would have significant advantages from a procedural perspective.[237]

Finally, it is unlikely that such a revision would lead to an aggravation of the existing burden on certain Member States. On the contrary, this may improve the operation of the system, which currently imposes the greatest burden on Member States situated at the external borders,[238] resulting in a 'concentration of the burden', which clearly appeared in the statistics on the application of the Dublin Convention.[239] On the other hand, studies have shown that the choice of the asylum country is based on various considerations, such as the presence of relatives or members of the national or ethnic community in a Member State,[240] and it is unlikely that a system of 'natural responsibility allocation' would create a serious imbalance between States, which in any event could be easily addressed through the adoption of a 'safeguard' clause.

In short, aside from being a corollary measure to the abolition of controls at internal borders, the Dublin regime's main goal is to act as a deterrent and limit the freedom of asylum seekers to choose the country in which they will apply for asylum, without guaranteeing that their application will actually be examined by one of the States taking part in the system, or that harmonized standards of protection will ensure that regardless of the State where an application is examined, it will be granted equivalent consideration. It is clear indeed that the linkage between the Dublin regime and harmonization is far more tenuous than is contended by the

[235] Shacknove and Byrne, n 234 above, 206–7; see also ECRE 2008 Dublin II Report, n 122 above, 25, 27–8.

[236] Shacknove and Byrne, 234 above, 206–7.

[237] Cf the argument according to which Belgium should be responsible for examining the application of an asylum seeker whose brother had been granted the status of refugee in Belgium on the ground of the principle of good administration was dismissed by the *Conseil d'Etat, Arrêt* No. 69.714 of 21 November 1997, n.p.

[238] See the ECRE reports for 1997 and 1998. Germany for instance, accepted the transfer in 84 per cent of the requests for transfer, ie of 6,696 asylum seekers in 1997, whereas Italy only accepted 33 per cent of the requests for transfer, ie of 670 asylum seekers.

[239] G Noll, *Negotiating Asylum, the EU Acquis, Extraterritorial Protection and the Common Market of Deflection* (Martinus Nijhoff, The Hague [etc] 2000) 323–5.

[240] A Böcker and T Havinga, *Asylum Migration to the European Union: Patterns of Origin and Destination* (Office for Official Publications of the European Communities, Brussels 1997) 76–7; see also D Middleton, 'Why Asylum Seekers Seek Refuge in Particular Destination Countries: An Exploration of Key Determinants' Global Migration Perspectives Paper No. 34, May 2005, 7–25; A Munteanu, 'Secondary Movement in Romania: The Asylum-Migration Nexus' UNHCR New Issues in Refugee Research Paper No. 148, December 2007, 8–9; Collyer, n 219 above, 383–5.

Commission,[241] in particular since several States taking part in the Dublin regime are not EU Member States, are not taking part in the adoption of EC asylum measures or are subject to the jurisdiction of the ECJ and that there is currently no reason to exclude that more States might join the system in the future.

3.6 Conclusion

The shortcomings of the Dublin regime, which was subject to criticism even before the entry into force of the Convention, have been further confirmed in the implementation of the Dublin Regulation. The criteria for allocating responsibility are too rigid, which leads to practical difficulties when confronted with family or humanitarian cases. The implementation of the system for asylum seekers illegally on the territory of the State parties to the system has not been particularly effective even after the entry into force of the Eurodac Regulation. The actual transfer of the asylum seeker sets in motion a complex procedure and the asylum seeker is not always adequately informed about the implications of the whole process. The conclusion is that the Dublin regime is neither fair nor efficient, and that there is an urgent need for a reassessment of current European arrangements for the allocation of responsibility.

More fundamentally, the Dublin regime does not adequately address protection challenges, given that, besides the failings of harmonization thus far, not all of the 'Dublin' States taking part in it are engaged in that process, and that removal to a safe third country outside the 'Dublin area' is allowed. Even for those States taking part in the harmonization process, the existence of effective protection is not sufficiently guaranteed due to the lowest common denominator approach and the limited protection and procedural safeguards that have been adopted in the first generation of EU asylum instruments. While it was hoped that the new provisions introduced by the Treaty of Amsterdam would give an impetus to the development of an improved system of responsibility allocation, very limited progress has been achieved. It might in fact be said that the current trend, reflected in the suggestions to extend the application and use of Eurodac evidence and in the lowering of protection standards, points to a furthering of deterrent and containment approaches in Europe.

---

[241] Policy Plan on Asylum, n 211 above, 7. By the same token the establishment of European Asylum Support Office, contemplated in the European Pact on Immigration and Asylum, will not fully resolve protection concerns within the Dublin regime, see European Pact on Immigration and Asylum, Doc 13440/08, 24 September 2008, which was endorsed by EU interior ministers on 25 September 2008 and formally adopted on 16 October 2008 by the 27 EU Heads of State, available at <http://www.immigration.gouv.fr/IMG/pdf/Plaquette_EN.pdf>.

4

The Impact of Safe Third Country Practices on Inter-State Relations

After examining the main features of safe third country practices and related arrangements, the following two chapters will examine how these impinge on the international refugee regime. For this purpose, two distinct questions will be addressed. First, given the recognition that secondary movements have generated international 'frictions',[1] the present chapter will examine the impact of safe third country practices on inter-State relations. Chapter 5 will then assess these practices from a refugee's rights perspective, and determine the extent to which they comply with international refugee and human rights law.

The first question raised in this chapter is the extent to which a State through which an asylum seeker has previously transited or stayed should be assuming responsibility for the examination of his/her asylum application and whether such allocation of responsibility receives support under international law. The second part of the chapter will examine whether the principle of solidarity and burden-sharing and the principle of good-neighbourliness may be usefully invoked in this context.

4.1 Protection Elsewhere or Mere Transit: The Relevance and Scope of Article 31 CSR

Under general international law, a State is under no obligation to readmit aliens unless it has explicitly agreed to do so in a bilateral or multilateral instrument.[2] Safe third country practices enable States to claim that they have no obligation to examine an asylum application on the ground that the asylum seeker has not come directly from his/her State of origin. This would, by implication, mean that

---

[1] UNHCR, Informal Record: Open Meeting of States and Interested Parties on Secondary, Irregular Movements of Refugees and Asylum-Seekers (Geneva, 16 December 2003) FORUM/CG/SM/01, 21 December 2003, para 14.

[2] See G Noll, 'Return of Persons to States of Origin and Third States', in T A Aleinikoff and V Chetail (eds), *Migration and International Legal Norms* (T M C Asser, The Hague [etc] 2003) 61, 63, 66.

the State(s) that the asylum seeker has travelled through to reach his/her final destination may be regarded as responsible.

Obviously, the closer the link between an asylum seeker and a State, the greater the claim that that State should accept responsibility.[3] In this perspective, there seems to be a rather solid basis for the application of the first country of asylum, which presupposes the existence of a positive undertaking to provide protection to a refugee.[4] However, safe third country practices, most notably under the Dublin regime, may apply based on the sole fact that a State has allowed, even unwillingly, an asylum seeker to enter its territory.[5] The jurisdictional link has become even more tenuous under the asylum procedures Directive, given that Article 27.1(d) states that there must merely exist a 'possibility' to request refugee status in a third State.[6] This would seem to mean that this 'possibility' need not have existed prior to arriving in the country of final destination, that is, that the asylum seeker may not have even been on the territory of the third State.

The provision of the Refugee Convention which is usually cited in support of safe third country practices is Article 31.1 CSR.[7]

Article 31.1 CSR reads:

(1) The Contracting States shall not impose penalties, on account of their illegal entry or presence, on refugees who, coming directly from a territory where their life or freedom was threatened in the sense of Article 1, enter or are present in their territory without

---

[3] UNHCR, 'Convention Plus Issues Paper Submitted by UNHCR on Addressing Irregular Secondary Movements of Refugees and Asylum-Seekers' FORUM/CG/SM/03, 11 March 2004 (hereafter, UNHCR Issues Paper) paras 31–3, which cites family ties, lawful residence, 'or other demonstrable connections'; ExCom Conclusion No. 15, see Chapter 1, Section 1.2.3. Note also that Art 1(F) of the 1951 Geneva Convention Relating to the Status of Refugees (adopted 28 July 1951, entered into force 22 April 1954) 189 UNTS 150 (hereafter, CSR or Refugee Convention) provides that the Convention shall not apply to a person who is recognized by the competent authorities of the country in which he has taken residence as having the rights and obligations which are attached to the possession of the nationality of that country.

[4] See UNHCR, 'An Overview of Protection Issues in Western Europe: Legislative Trends and Positions Taken by UNHCR', August 1995, 11, 13; see also UNHCR, 'Summary Conclusions on the Concept of "Effective Protection" in the Context of Secondary Movements of Refugees and Asylum-Seekers', Lisbon Expert Roundtable, 9–10 December 2002 (hereafter, Lisbon Conclusions), para 10; UNHCR Issues Paper, n 3 above, para 31. On the distinction between safe third country and first country of asylum, see Chapter 2, Section 2.1.1.

[5] See Art 10 of Council Regulation (EC) 343/2003 of 18 February 2003 establishing the criteria and mechanisms for determining the Member State responsible for examining an asylum application lodged in one of the Member States by a third-country national [2003] OJ L50/1; W de Lobkowicz, 'The Dublin Convention: A Useful Complement to International Humanitarian Law' [1990] *European Vision* 7, 9; Commission Staff Working Paper, 'Revisiting the Dublin Convention: Developing Community Legislation for Determining which Member State is Responsible for Considering an Application for Asylum Submitted in one of the Member States' SEC (2000) 522, 21 March 2000, para 24; see also UK and German practice, Chapter 2, Section 2.1.2.

[6] Council Directive 2005/85/EC of 1 December 2005 on minimum standards on procedures in Member States for granting and withdrawing refugee status [2005] OJ L326/13 (hereafter, asylum procedures Directive).

[7] G S Goodwin-Gill and J McAdam, *The Refugee in International Law* (3rd edn, Oxford University Press, Oxford 2007) 151.

authorization, provided they present themselves without delay to the authorities and show good cause for their illegal entry or presence.

This clause was based on the acknowledgement that most refugees do not carry valid travel documents and the containment policies implemented in the last decades have only exacerbated this reality.[8] As noted by Lord Bingham of Cornill in the *Asfaw* case,

[I]t was recognised in 1950, and has since become even clearer, that those fleeing from persecution or threatened persecution in countries where persecution of minorities is practised may have to resort to deceptions of various kinds (possession and use of false papers, forgery, misrepresentation, etc) in order to make good their escape.[9]

Reliance on Article 31.1 CSR to justify the validity of safe third country practices is based on the following reasoning: if the prohibition of penalties applies only to refugees who come directly from a country where their life or freedom is threatened, *a contrario*, refugees who travelled through intermediate countries may be penalized.[10] States have considered by analogy that they have no duty to process an asylum claim in such a case and may return an asylum seeker to the 'intermediate' country.

Some have thus argued that the safe third country mechanism constitutes a practice developed by States, deriving from the application of Article 31.1 of the Refugee Convention. UNHCR has cautiously acknowledged that the language of Article 31.1 CSR may give credence to this interpretation.[11] As detailed in

---

[8] Goodwin-Gill and McAdam, n 7 above, 384.

[9] *R v Asfaw* [2008] UKHL 31, para 9; see also *R v Uxbridge Magistrates' Court, ex p Adimi* [2001] QB 667: 'The need for Article 31 has not diminished. Quite the contrary: although under the Convention subscribing States must give sanctuary to any refugee who seeks asylum (subject only to removal to a safe third country), they are by no means bound to facilitate his arrival. Rather they strive increasingly to prevent it. The combined effect of visa requirements and carrier's liability has made it well nigh impossible for refugees to countries of refuge without false documents.'

[10] Goodwin-Gill and McAdam, n 7 above, 266 clarify in this respect that the term 'penalties' in Art 31 CSR should be construed broadly so as to reflect the fact that its purpose is 'to proscribe sanctions on account of illegal entry or presence' and that an overly restrictive interpretation would 'circumvent the fundamental protection intended', hence, 'procedural bars on applying for asylum may constitute "penalties"' under Art 31 CSR; see also G S Goodwin-Gill, 'Article 31 of the 1951 Convention Relating to the Status of Refugees: Non-Penalization, Detention and Protection', in E Feller, V Türk, and F Nicholson (eds) *UNHCR's Global Consultations on International Protection* (Cambridge University Press, Cambridge 2003) 185, 189, 191–4, 218. This view is further supported by ExCom Conclusion No. 15 (1979) on Refugees Without an Asylum Country, para (i) and ExCom Conclusion No. 22 (1981) on Protection of Asylum-Seekers in Situations of Large-Scale Influx, para B.2(a).

[11] UNHCR, 'Executive Committee Background Note on the Safe Country Concept and Refugee Status' UN Doc EC/SCP/68, 26 July 1991 published in R Plender (ed), *Basic Documents on International Migration Law* (Nijhoff, The Hague [etc] 1997) para 12, 14. In other documents, UNHCR, while not specifically referring to Art 31.1 CSR, expressed cautious support for the safe third country notion but under certain conditions, see UNHCR, 'An Overview of Protection Issues in Western Europe', n 4 above, 11; UNHCR, Note on International Protection, UN Doc A/AC.96/815, 31 August 1993, para 20. UNHCR also applied a similar practice to 'irregular movers' in Southern Africa, see M Kingsley-Nyinah, 'Asylum, Refugee Criteria and Irregular Movements in Southern Africa' (1995) 7 *IJRL* 291, 308.

Chapter 2, the existence of these practices is corroborated by a large body of legislation and jurisprudence in many European countries and was further endorsed in the EU asylum procedures Directive.[12] Several former Soviet Republics have also adopted safe third country regulations, as well as Australia, the United States, and Canada and support for this practice is growing in Africa.[13] Finally, scholars such as Blay, Zimmermann,[14] and Hailbronner[15] have expressed the view that safe third country practices are based on a lawful interpretation of Article 31 CSR.

This claim must be evaluated in light of general rules on interpretation set out in Article 31 and 32 of the 1969 Vienna Convention on the Law of Treaties:[16]

Article 31

1. A treaty shall be interpreted in good faith in accordance with the ordinary meaning to be given to the terms of the treaty in their context and in the light of its object and purpose.

2. The context for the purpose of the interpretation of a treaty shall comprise, in addition to the text, including its preamble and annexes:

    (a) any agreement relating to the treaty which was made between all the parties in connexion with the conclusion of the treaty;

    (b) any instrument which was made by one or more parties in connexion with the conclusion of the treaty and accepted by the other parties as an instrument related to the treaty.

3. There shall be taken into account, together with the context:

    (a) any subsequent agreement between the parties regarding the interpretation of the treaty or the application of its provisions;

    (b) *any subsequent practice in the application of the treaty which establishes the agreement of the parties regarding its interpretation;*[17]

    (c) any relevant rules of international law applicable in the relations between the parties.

4. A special meaning shall be given to a term if it is established that the parties so intended.

---

[12] For an overview of safe third country practices in Europe, N Lassen and J Hughes (ed), *"Safe Third Country" Policies in European Countries* (Danish Refugee Council, Copenhagen 1997); European Commission, *Study on the Law and Practice of the Safe Country Principles in the Context of the Common European Asylum System and the Goal of a Common Asylum Procedure*, 2003: <http://ec.europa.eu/justice_home/doc_centre/asylum/studies/docs/safe_countries_2004_en.pdf>.

[13] See Chapter 2, Section 2.1.

[14] S Blay and A Zimmermann, 'Recent Changes in German Refugee Law: A Critical Assessment' (1994) 88 *AJIL* 361, 367.

[15] K Hailbronner, 'The Concept of Safe Country and Expeditious Asylum Procedures: A Western European Perspective' (1993) 5 *IJRL* 31, 58–9; R Plender, *International Migration Law* (2nd edn, Nijhoff, Dordrecht [etc] 1988) 424.

[16] (1980) 1155 UNTS 331 No.18232.

[17] Emphasis added.

Article 32

Supplementary means of interpretation

Recourse may be had to supplementary means of interpretation, including the preparatory work of the treaty and the circumstances of its conclusion, in order to confirm the meaning resulting from the application of article 31, or to determine the meaning when the interpretation according to article 31:

(a) leaves the meaning ambiguous or obscure; or
(b) leads to a result which is manifestly absurd or unreasonable.

It is clear from a plain reading of Article 31 of the 1969 Vienna Convention on the Law of Treaties that subsequent practice has a high evidentiary value in the interpretation of treaties.[18] In principle, subsequent practice may cover all of the legal acts or behaviours attributable to State parties to a Treaty, which, after its entry into force, apply its provisions.[19] It may reveal a common intention and a nascent objective of the treaty,[20] and modify a conventional rule[21] in order to adjust to new circumstances which may considerably differ from the original conditions at the time of drafting.[22] Subsequent practice may even lead to the formation of a new customary rule.[23] However, practice must be common to, or at least accepted by all of the parties to a Treaty, and be consistent and concordant in order to be regarded as authentic interpretation,[24] while practice by individual parties may on the other hand provide helpful indication of the meaning of the terms of the convention.[25]

In accordance with Articles 31 and 32 of the 1969 Vienna Convention on the Law of Treaties, discussions at the Conference of Plenipotentiaries may also be

---

[18] A D McNair, *The Law of Treaties* (Clarendon Press, Oxford 1961) 424–6.

[19] L Boisson de Chazournes, 'Qu'est-ce que la pratique en droit international?', in Société française de droit international, *La Pratique et le Droit International* (Pédone, Paris 2004) 13, 25.

[20] M K Yasseen, 'Interprétation des traités d'après la Convention de Vienne sur le droit des traités' (1976) 151 *RdC* 1, 49.

[21] Ibid, 51; I Sinclair, *The Vienna Convention on the Law of Treaties* (2nd edn, Manchester University Press, Manchester 1984) 138; K Wolfke, 'Treaties and Custom: Aspects of Interrelation', in J Klabbers and R Lefeber (eds), *Essays on the Law of Treaties: A Collection of Essays in Honour of Bert Vierdag* (Nijhoff, The Hague [etc] 1998) 31, 34.

[22] G Fitzmaurice, 'The Law and Procedure of the International Court of Justice' (1957) 33 *BYIL* 203, 224–5; M E Villiger, *Customary International Law and Treaties: A Manual on the Theory and Practice of the Interrelation of Sources* (2nd edn, Kluwer, The Hague [etc] 1997) 213; Wolfke, n 21 above, 34.

[23] Villiger, ibid.

[24] Yasseen, n 20 above, 48; T O Elias, *The Modern Law of Treaties* (Oceana Publications, Dobbs Ferry, NY 1974) 76; A Aust, *Modern Treaty Law and Practice* (Cambridge University Press, Cambridge 2000) 194; Note that subsequent practice which does not fulfil these conditions may still be used as a supplementary means of interpretation, Sinclair, n 21 above, 138.

[25] I Brownlie, *Principles of Public of International Law* (7th edn, Oxford University Press, Oxford 2008) 634; R G Wetzel and D Rauschning, *The Vienna Convention on the Law of Treaties Travaux Préparatoires* (Alfred Metzner, Frankfurt Am Main 1978) 247.

relied upon, but only as a supplementary means of interpretation.[26] The *travaux préparatoires* should be used with particular caution in the case of the Refugee Convention, given that only 26 States participated in the drafting of the Convention to which 144 States are now party.[27] While this suggests that preparatory work does not carry as much weight as subsequent practice,[28] it is nevertheless helpful to shed some light on the intentions of the drafters and their discussions on the scope and purpose of Article 31 CSR.

The provision originally presented at the Conference did not require that a refugee arrive directly from the country of origin.[29] It was the French representative who proposed to add the adverb 'directly' to the first paragraph, as he believed that there was no reason to accord the exemption of penalties for movements subsequent to the arrival in a first country where the refugee had found asylum.[30] The High Commissioner for Refugees observed that some refugees could stay in a country for a period of time and then again come under threat of persecution, or that some countries would not permit refugees to settle. The formulation of the article would then prevent them from seeking asylum elsewhere.[31]

While the French amendment was adopted, there seemed to be an agreement among delegates that the condition of direct arrival should not be construed too severely, and that it applied essentially to refugees who had found asylum.[32] Grahl-Madsen suggested therefore that the adverb 'directly' should be interpreted as meaning 'without [undue] delay'.[33] Hence, refugees in mere transit through the intermediate country, those who had stayed in the intermediate country without being regularized, or regularized in the first country but who had a well-founded fear for their life and liberty in that country should be covered by Article 31.1 CSR.[34] Similarly, Jaeger considered that the situation where an asylum seeker

---

[26] On the value of preparatory work, see G Fitzmaurice, 'Law and Procedure of the International Court of Justice' (1951) 28 *BYIL* 1, 5, 15–7; McNair, n 18 above, 411, 422–3; J Klabbers, 'International Legal Histories: The Declining Importance of *Travaux Préparatoires* in Treaty Interpretation?' (2003) 50 *NILR* 267, 268–9, 280.

[27] Note that 147 states are party to either the CSR or the 1967 Protocol, see <http://www.unhcr.org/protect/PROTECTION/3b73b0d63.pdf>; see also *Case Relating to the Territorial Jurisdiction of the International Commission of the River Oder* PCIJ (1929) Series A No. 23 (Order of 20 August 1929), 42 where the PCIJ did not take the *travaux préparatoires* into consideration, given the fact that three of the parties to the case had not taken part in the drafting conference of the Versailles Treaty.

[28] Aust, n 24 above, 199.

[29] UN Doc A/CONF.2/1 reprinted in A Takkenberg and C Tahbaz, *The Collected Travaux Préparatoires of the 1951 Geneva Convention Relating to the Status of Refugees* (Dutch Refugee Council, Amsterdam 1989) Vol III 83 and 164.

[30] UN Doc A/CONF.2/62 and A/CONF.2/SR.13, 22 November 1951 reprinted in Takkenberg and Tahbaz, n 29 above, 83 and 319.

[31] UN Doc A/CONF.2/SR.14, 22 November 1951, reprinted in Takkenberg and Tahbaz, n 29 above, 322–3.

[32] Ibid, 324.

[33] A Grahl-Madsen, *The Status of Refugees in International Law*, (Sijthoff, Leyden 1972) Vol II, 206.

[34] Grahl-Madsen, n 33 above, 206–9; see also *R v Asfaw* [2008] UKHL 31, para 11, 45–6, 51, 56; *R v Uxbridge Magistrates' Court, ex p Adimi* [2001] QB 667.

has just transited through one or several countries before reaching the country where he/she claimed asylum should be assimilated to a direct flight and therefore fall within the scope of Article 31.1 CSR.[35] UNHCR has accordingly insisted that the expression 'coming directly' 'also covers a person who transits an intermediate country for a short period of time without having applied for, or received, asylum there', that, '[n]o strict time limit can be applied to the concept "coming directly" and each case must be judged on its merits'.[36]

In light of the above, Article 31 CSR would seem to provide a rather weak authority for considering that mere transit can justify the dismissal of an asylum claim on the ground that another State is responsible. Moreover, whether current practice may be regarded as sufficiently common and consistent is far from certain.[37]

The right to return an asylum seeker to a country in which he or she has briefly transited remains indeed contentious, not only because of its impact on burden-sharing, as shall be seen below, but also because it affects the quality and effectiveness of protection to be expected from the third country.[38] One would recall that the application of the safe third country must be predicated on the existence of protection elsewhere. In this perspective, Executive Committee Conclusion No. 15 of 1979 emphasized that the duration and nature of the stay of an individual should be duly considered in determining the responsible State and the existence of 'close links'.[39] This question was, however, already subject to dissensions during the negotiations of Conclusion No. 58, ten years later. The Italian delegation stated that the Conclusion would only apply to recognized refugees under the Refugee Convention and its Protocol and to asylum seekers who have already found protection in the first country of asylum.[40] Germany, on the other hand, adopted a broader construction, considering, for example, that the term

---

[35] G Jaeger, *Study of Irregular Movements of Asylum Seekers and Refugees* (Working Group on Irregular Movements and Asylum Seekers, Geneva 1985) 9, para 33; see also Goodwin-Gill, n 10 above, 216, 218.

[36] UNHCR, 'Guidelines on Applicable Criteria and Standards Relating to the Detention of Asylum-Seekers', February 1999, para 4; UNHCR, 'Summary Conclusions: Article 31 of the 1951 Convention', Expert Round table organized by the United Nations High Commissioner for Refugees and the Graduate Institute of International Studies, Geneva, Switzerland, 8–9 November 2001, para 10(b)–(c); cf UNHCR High Commissioner's Forum, 'Convention Plus Core Group on Addressing Irregular Secondary Movements of Refugees and Asylum-Seekers: Joint Statement by the Co-Chairs', FORUM/2005/7, 8 November 2005 (hereafter, Joint Statement on Irregular Secondary Movements) 4 which refers to the view that 'inability to access protection [i]s a continuation of direct flight and hence, should be deemed to be "primary" rather than secondary movement'.

[37] Lassen and Hughes (eds), n 12 above, 1–2; S Lavenex, *Safe Third Countries: Extending the EU Asylum and Immigration Policies to Central and Eastern Europe* (Central European University Press, New York 1999) 76. See also Chapter 1, Section 1.2.4.

[38] UNHCR, 'An Overview of Protection Issues in Western Europe', n 4 above, p 13; Joint Statement on Irregular Secondary Movements, n 36 above, 4. On effective protection, see Chapters 2 and 5.

[39] ExCom Conclusion No. 15 (1979) para (g) (ii)–(iv).

[40] Statement by the delegation of Italy before ExCom, UN Doc A/AC.96/SR.442, 15 November 1989, para 127.

'permission to remain' did not necessarily mean that an individual had been granted a residence permit.[41]

In 1996, Goodwin-Gill wrote that

[T]here is certainly no consistent practice among 'sending' and 'receiving' States as would permit the conclusion that any such rule exists with respect to the return of refugees and asylum seekers to safe third countries, simply on the basis of a brief or transitory contact.[42]

Since then, however, the 'mere transit' practice has been significantly bolstered by the fact that 30 States taking part in the 'Dublin system' have agreed to take back asylum seekers on the sole basis of their illegal entry on their territory and regardless of the length of their stay or the existence of other close links.[43]

That said, the question was not fully harmonized in the 2005 asylum procedures Directive,[44] and discussions on irregular secondary movements during the 'Convention Plus' process faltered in part because of this very issue, several delegations finding that 'could have found protection' was a notion that was insufficiently clear.[45] In 2004, the House of Lords European Union Committee prudently concluded that while it felt that 'UNHCR's view that removal to a third country should not take place unless the person had already been offered effective protection there goes too far', there needed to be a 'link' between the asylum seeker and the third country where his application would be processed.[46]

---

[41] See interpretative statement by the delegation of the Federal Republic of Germany before ExCom, UN Doc A/AC.96/SR.442, 15 November 1989, para 130.

[42] G S Goodwin-Gill, 'The Protection of Refugees and the Safe Third Country Rule in International Law', in *Asylum Law: Report and papers delivered at the first international judicial conference on asylum law and procedures held at Inner Temple, London, 1 and 2 December, 1995* (London, 1996) 89, 98.

[43] Dublin Regulation, Art 10. Note for instance that prior to concluding an agreement to participate in the Dublin system, Switzerland would send back an asylum seeker to a third country provided the asylum seeker had stayed in the safe third country for at least 20 days, see M Gattiker, 'Évolution et perspectives de la notion de pays tiers sûr dans la legislation suisse sur l'asile', in V Chetail and V Gowlland-Debbas (eds), *Switzerland and the International Protection of Refugees* (Kluwer, The Hague [etc.] 2002) 129, 134–6. See also Arts 4 and 5 of the Agreement Between the Government of Canada and the Government of the United States of America Regarding Asylum Claims Made at Land Borders (15 December 2002, entered into force on 29 December 2004), reproduced in 79 Interpreter Releases at 1446 et seq (23 September 2002) (hereafter, Canada–US Safe Third Country Agreement).

[44] Article 27.2 of the asylum procedures Directive.

[45] Joint Statement on Irregular Secondary Movements, n 36 above, 4. Note also that Belarus, Moldova and Ukraine's legislations all exclude the application of the safe third country provisions when the asylum seeker has just transited through a third country's territory: in Belarus, see Art 2 of the Law of the Republic of Belarus of 23 June 2008 on Granting Refugee Status, Complementary and Temporary Protection to Foreign Citizens and Stateless Persons in the Republic of Belarus <http://www.unhcr.org/refworld/docid/493541fd2.html>; in Moldova, see Art 22(2) of the Law on the Status of Refugees, 25 May 2000, <http://www.unhcr.org/refworld/docid/3c73a9914.html>; in Ukraine, see Art 1 of Law of Ukraine on Refugees, 31 May 2005 < http://www.unhcr.org/refworld/docid/44a286534.html>.

[46] House of Lords European Union Committee, *Handling EU Asylum Claims: New Approaches Examined* 11th Report of Session 2003–2004, HL Paper 74, 30 April 2004, para 68.

There are also problems with respect to the unilateral application of safe third country practices. This is important because the existence of an agreement to readmit and to examine the asylum application would at least provide greater protection to asylum seekers. However, the UK Immigration Rules stipulate that 'the Secretary of State is under no obligation to consult the authorities of the third country or territory before the removal of an asylum applicant to that country or territory'.[47] One should also recall that readmission agreements cannot be regarded as adequately addressing this question, given that these instruments do not generally include any obligation of each party to examine the asylum application of readmitted third country nationals.[48]

Hailbronner acknowledged that the unilateral application of the safe third country concept was actually worsening the inequitable distribution of refugees among States instead of alleviating the problem, thereby also contributing to the increase in 'orbit situations'.[49] Executive Committee Conclusion No. 71 recommends the conclusion of 'agreements among States directly concerned, in consultation with UNHCR, to provide for the protection of refugees through the adoption of common criteria'.[50] The application of US and Canadian safe third country provisions is conditional upon the conclusion of an agreement, which was concluded in 2002 and entered into force in 2004.[51] On the other hand, Article 27.4 of the asylum procedures Directive limits itself to providing that 'where the third country does not permit the applicant for asylum to enter its territory, Member States shall ensure that access to a procedure is given [...]'. While the provision seeks to at least prevent 'orbit situations', it falls short of explicitly forbidding the practice of unilateral removals.

Turning to the condition of commonality, it bears noting that some State parties have been openly reluctant about the development of safe third country practices. In 1995, UNHCR acknowledged that:

The principles [...] do not in their present formulation represent a general consensus among States and cannot be expected to elicit the immediate and unqualified support of countries

---

[47] Immigration Rules (as amended in November 2008) HC 395, 345(2) <http://www.ukba.homeoffice.gov.uk/policyandlaw/immigrationlaw/immigrationrules/part11/>.

[48] UNHCR Issues Paper, n 3 above, note 23; Joint Statement on Irregular Secondary Movements, n 36 above, 5; see also ExCom Conclusion No. 15, para (h) (vi).

[49] Hailbronner, n 15 above, 59.

[50] ExCom General Conclusion on International Protection No. 71 (1993) para (k); see also ExCom Conclusion No. 15 (1979) on Refugees Without an Asylum Country, para (h); Lisbon Conclusions, n 4 above, para 12: 'States could craft bi- or multilateral arrangements, consistent with international refugee and human rights law standards, according to which asylum-seekers would be encouraged and enabled to seek international protection at the first available opportunity. This could be done by agreeing to mechanisms and criteria to allocate responsibilities for the determination of asylum applications and the provision of effective protection.' See also UNHCR Issues Paper, n 3 above, para 13.

[51] For Canada, see s 102(2)(d) of the Immigration and Refugee Protection Act s.c. 2001, c. 27; for the United States, see Immigration and Nationality Act s 208 (a)(2)(A), as amended in 1996. See Chapter 2, Section 2.1.2.

of first asylum or transit which typically wish to consider the nature and duration of an asylum seeker's presence on their territory.[52]

In 1993, the representative of Brazil voiced his concern that the application of the concept of 'protection elsewhere' 'placed increased pressure on less developed countries or those not sufficiently prepared to provide protection and assistance to refugees'.[53] The same year, Bulgaria expressed similar preoccupation.[54] Other Central and Eastern European countries claimed that the receiving State shall only accept the readmission of an asylum seeker either on a case-by-case basis, or in a general agreement,[55] but they eventually yielded to EU pressures and have had to bear increasingly stricter obligations based on the safe third country concept.[56]

Turkey is the country which has objected consistently and in the most unambiguous terms to the development of this practice and which stands to be one of the most directly affected by these policies. Already during the discussions on the second draft agreement on responsibility for examining asylum requests within the Council of Europe, it made the following statement:

It is inconceivable that Turkey, a country of transit, should be deemed responsible for examining the asylum request merely because of the first entry having been made on its territory, whether or not lawfully, for the purpose of proceeding to another country. Why should a country where the first entry has been made owing to a mere geographical coincidence be responsible for examining an asylum request subsequently made to another State?[57]

Turkey maintained this position before the Executive Committee:

The delegation of Turkey has requested that it should be made quite clear that, in the light of the discussion and wording of the draft conclusions, and as then Director of the Division of Refugee Law and Doctrine had made clear in 1985, those conclusions did not apply to refugees and asylum seekers who were merely in transit in another country. That interpretation was recorded in para. 68 of the Report of the Sub-Committee for 1985.[58]

---

[52] UNHCR, 'The Concept of "Protection Elsewhere"' (1995) 7 *IJRL* 123, 126.

[53] See statement of the representative of Brazil before ExCom, UN Doc A/AC.96/SR.485, 12 October 1993, para 2.

[54] See statement by the representative of Bulgaria before ExCom, UN Doc A/AC.96/SR.485, 12 October 1993, para 47.

[55] Lavenex, n 37 above, 94–5; D Bouteillet-Paquet, *L'Europe et le Droit d'Asile, la politique d'asile européenne et ses conséquences pour les pays d'Europe centrale* (L'Harmattan, Paris 2001) 278.

[56] On the concerns of Central and Eastern European Countries about 'burden shifting', see R Byrne, 'Harmonization and Burden Redistribution in the Two Europes' (2003) 16 *JRS* 336, 343–4, 349; see also Chapter 2, Section 2.2.2.

[57] Final Activity Report on the Draft Agreement on responsibility for examining asylum requests CAHAR (88) 9 def., 25 January 1989, para 10; the same terms were used in the letter addressed by M Fisek (Turkey) to the Secretary of CAHAR on 24 November 1988, Appendix IV to the Final Activity Report CAHAR (88) 9 def., 25 January 1989, p 23.

[58] Comment by Turkey stated by Mr Arnaout, Director of the Division of Refugee Law and Doctrine before ExCom, UN Doc A/AC.96/SR.442, 15 November 1989, para 126; see also the statement by the Representative of Turkey before ExCom, UN Doc A/AC.96/SR.456, 5 October 1990,

The position of Turkey does not seem to have significantly changed since then. Turkey has apparently been reluctant to conclude a readmission agreement with the European Union,[59] and has readmitted only a small percentage of irregular migrants from Greece.[60] Needless to say, if Turkey were to eventually join the European Union, it would then have to accept all of the asylum *acquis* including the application of the Dublin Regulation and asylum procedures Directive.

That said, there seems to be prevailing support among European States for the view that in accordance with Article 31.1 CSR, a State may not have to examine an asylum claim if a refugee has not arrived directly from his/her country of origin even if he/she has not received actual protection in the third country, including in cases of mere transit.[61] Even if there was sufficiently widespread and consistent practice in this regard, one cannot, however, infer from Article 31.1 CSR the existence of a positive obligation to examine an asylum claim.[62] Fitzmaurice stated in this respect that:

[V]iolence *is* done to the terms of a treaty [...] whenever the existence of a right, obligation, procedure, &c., not expressly provided for in the treaty or prima facie contemplated by it, and not a *necessary* consequence of the terms employed, is nevertheless read into it as not being actually incompatible, while tending to promote the objects of the treaty.[63]

Nonetheless, one should note that a 'practice or conduct may affect the legal relations of the Parties even though it cannot be said to be practice in the application of the Treaty or to constitute an agreement between them'.[64] In this perspective, subsequent practice may be regarded as an interpretative tool in treaty law, but also as an autonomous source of international law.[65]

---

paras 3–7; and the statement of the representative of Tanzania before ExCom, UN Doc A/AC.96/737, 19 October 1989, 24.

[59] Parliamentary Questions, Answer to a written question—EU external border management and Turkey, 23 July 2008 E-331/2008 <http://www.europarl.europa.eu/sides/getAllAnswers.do?reference= E-2008-3313&language=ES>.

[60] 'Greece cites Turkey's inaction on illegal migration' 7 October 2007 <http://www.greekembassy. org/embassy/Content/en/Article.aspx?office=1&folder=19&article=21768>.

[61] S Legomsky, 'Secondary Refugee Movement and the Return of Asylum Seekers to Third Countries: The Meaning of Effective Protection' (2003) 15 *IJRL* 567, 613.

[62] A similar situation in international law is that of the right to expel against the duty to readmit, the latter being generally considered not to be part of general international law, see Noll, n 2 above, p 72.

[63] Fitzmaurice, (1951) 28 *BYIL*, n 26 above, 23; see also Fitzmaurice, (1957) 33 *BYIL* n 22 above, 233; see *International Status of South West Africa* (Advisory Opinion) ICJ Reports (1950) 127, 139–40; see also Dissenting Opinion of Judge Read, *Interpretation of Peace Treaties with Bulgaria, Hungary and Romania* (Advisory Opinion 2nd phase) ICJ Reports (1950) 220, 241.

[64] Eritrea-Ethiopia Boundary Commission, *Decision Regarding Delimitation of the Border between the of State of Eritrea and the Federal Democratic Republic of Ethiopia*, 13 April 2002 <http://www.pca-cpa.org/showpage.asp?pag_id=1150>, Chapter 3, para 3.6, see also para 3.7–3.10;

[65] Boisson de Chazournes, n 19 above, 25–7, who notes, however, the International Court of Justice's diverging view on the significance and free-standing nature of subsequent practice as an interpretative tool.

While the above review shows that there is no sufficient evidence at this stage of the existence of a customary obligation to readmit an asylum seeker on the basis of mere transit, some might still argue of the existence of a regional custom, based on the provisions and practice of the Dublin regime.[66] Such a norm would, however, have to be strictly circumscribed by the obligations incurred by States under international refugee and human rights law, essentially reflected in the concept of effective protection.[67]

4.2 International Cooperation to Protect Refugees: Solidarity, Burden-Sharing, and Good-Neighbourliness

Cooperation between States is one of the defining principles of contemporary international relations,[68] as stated in the 1970 UN Declaration on Principles of International Law Concerning Friendly Relations and Cooperation among States. The Declaration affirmed that:

States have a duty to co-operate with one another, irrespective of the differences in their political, economic and social systems, in the various spheres of international relations, in order to maintain international peace and security and to promote international economic stability and progress, the general welfare of nations and international co-operation free from discrimination based on such differences.[69]

The principle of solidarity and burden-sharing[70] and the principle of good-neighbourliness are derived from this duty of cooperation. The section below examines existing State practice and international instruments, in order to evaluate the commonly held claim that safe third country practices contravene the principle of solidarity and burden-sharing. The relevance of the principle of good-neighbourliness is also discussed.

---

[66] Note, however, that 'local customs [...] depend upon a particular activity by one state being accepted by the other state (or states) as an expression of a legal obligation or right' and 'need[s] the positive acceptance of both (or all) parties to the rule', see M N Shaw, *International Law* (5th edn, Cambridge University Press, Cambridge 2003) 88, who also notes that 'this is because local customs are an exception to the general nature of customary law, which involves a fairly flexible approach to law-making by all states, and instead constitutes a reminder of the former theory of consent whereby states are bound only by what they assent to', ibid.

[67] See Chapter 5, Section 5.3.

[68] See eg Arts 55 and 56 of the UN Charter.

[69] Annexed to UNGA Res 2625 (XXV), 24 October 1970.

[70] See J Milner, 'Burden Sharing', in M Gibney and R Hansen (eds) *Immigration and Asylum from 1900 to the Present* (ABC-CLIO, Santa Barbara 2005) 56; A Hans and A Suhrke, 'Responsibility-Sharing', in J C Hathaway (ed), *Reconceiving International Refugee Law* (Nijhoff, The Hague [etc] 1997) 83, who give a detailed description of burden-sharing arrangements since the end of World War II, 83.

4.2.1 The principle of solidarity and burden-sharing

It is the appearance of newly independent States on the world scene in the 1960s which triggered interest in the concept of solidarity, associated with the promotion of a 'new morality' in international law. The principle of solidarity was thus primarily connected to the emergence of developing countries,[71] and was presented as a subset of the 'new principle of global equity whereby those nations that have the necessary means are expected to assist those that do not'.[72] In the human rights realm, international solidarity was reflected in the concern of States for the protection of human rights of all people, regardless of their nationality.[73]

Even though earlier refugee instruments stressed the relationship between the refugee and the host State, inter-State relations are widely recognized as constituting a critical element of the international refugee regime, given that it deals with the movements of persons between States.[74] The principle of solidarity has in fact underpinned international action in the refugee realm since its origins under the League of Nations.[75] As noted by the former High Commissioner, Poul Hartling:

There is hardly a single subsequent resolution of the General Assembly of the United Nations relating to the work of my Office which does not contain some reference to the importance of international solidarity in seeking solutions to the refugee problem.[76]

---

[71] J-L Fonteyne, 'Burden-Sharing: An Analysis of the Nature and Function of International Solidarity in Cases of Mass Influx of Refugees' (1983) 8 *Australian Ybk Intl L* (Butterworths, Sydney) 162, 179; see also P Alston, 'A Third Generation of Solidarity Rights: A Progressive Development or Obfuscation of International Human Rights Law?' (1987) 29 *NILR* 307, 318. The concept of 'common but differentiated responsibility' of developing and developed countries existing under international environmental law is another application of international solidarity, see P Sands, *Principles of International Environmental Law* (Cambridge University Press, Cambridge 1995) 218–19.

[72] Fonteyne, n 71 above, 179. See in this respect the figures provided by UNHCR in 2003, indicating that 'more than 35 per cent of the 20.6 million asylum-seekers, refugees and other persons of concern to UNHCR were hosted by the 41 Least Developed Countries (LDCs)' and that '[o]f the 10.5 million refugees under UNHCR's mandate, 29 per cent were hosted by Sub-Saharan Africa', ExCom Standing Committee, 'Economic and Social Impact of Massive Refugee Populations on Host Developing Countries, as well as Other Countries' UN Doc EC/54/SC/CRP.5, 18 February 2004, para 7–8.

[73] P Leuprecht, 'La solidarité internationale et les droits de l'homme', in *Congress on International Solidarity and Humanitarian Actions Organized under the Auspices of the International Red Cross and the United Nations High Commissioner for Refugees* (San Remo, Italy 1980) 27, 27–8; T van Boven, 'International Solidarity and Human Rights', in *Congress on International Solidarity and Humanitarian Actions Organized under the Auspices of the International Red Cross and the United Nations High Commissioner for Refugees* (San Remo, Italy 1980) 15, 17.

[74] R Marx, 'Non-Refoulement, Access to Procedures, and Responsibility for Determining Refugee Claims' (1995) 7 *IJRL* 383, 389; J Garvey, 'Toward a Reformulation of International Refugee Law' (1985) 26 *Harvard Intl LJ* 483, 484.

[75] P Hartling, 'International Solidarity and the International Protection of Refugees', in *Congress on International Solidarity and Humanitarian Actions Organized under the Auspices of the International Red Cross and the United Nations High Commissioner for Refugees* (San Remo, Italy 1980) 237, 238.

[76] Ibid.

This has not prevented the expression of understandable scepticism over this lofty concept. Alston noted that:

[...] solidarity has a vague, almost metaphysical meaning unless its specific implications are spelt out in each particular context in which it is used. For this reason, it can readily be abused as a means of avoiding any tangible commitment while at the same time appearing virtuous.[77]

Although this observation is related to the concept of solidarity rights, it equally applies in the refugee context. The discussion below suggests indeed that, in spite of the profusion of regional and international instruments, States have generally been reluctant to accept substantial obligations based on the principle of solidarity, in particular, a more equitable distribution of the costs incurred by the protection of refugees, in particular in relation with physical burden-sharing.

The following sections offer a review of international instruments on burden-sharing. The relation between the principle of burden-sharing and *non-refoulement* will then be briefly discussed. This will be followed by an overview of international practice, with a view to assessing the legal relevance of the principle of burden-sharing.

4.2.1.1 International instruments

The Refugee Convention focused on the relationship between the host State and the refugee, and the only reference to the question of the mutual rights and duties of States is found in the Preamble:

Considering that the grant of asylum may place unduly heavy burdens on certain countries, and that a satisfactory solution of the problem of which the United Nations has recognized the international scope and nature cannot therefore be achieved without international co-operation.[78]

With the abovementioned advent of developing countries on the world scene, international solidarity gained increased currency as illustrated by the language of the 1967 UN Declaration on Territorial Asylum,[79] which was restated in the 1969 OAU Convention:

Where a Member State finds difficulty in continuing to grant asylum to refugees, such Member State may appeal directly to other Member States and through the OAU, and such other Member States *shall*[80] in the spirit of African solidarity and international cooperation take appropriate measures to lighten the burden of the Member State granting asylum.[81]

---

[77] Alston, n 71 above, 318.

[78] See Paragraph 4 of the Preamble of the CSR.

[79] Article 2.2 of the UN Declaration on Territorial Asylum, UNGA Res 2312 (XXII), 14 December 1967.

[80] Emphasis added.

[81] See Recital 3 of the Preamble and Art II (4) of the 1969 OAU Convention Governing the Specific Aspects of Refugee Problems in Africa (20 June 1974) (1976) 1001 UNTS 45 No. 14691;

The Council of Europe Resolution on Asylum to Persons in Danger of Persecution adopted a softer formulation, recognizing the importance of solidarity and common responsibility.[82] Other regional instruments such as the Cartagena Declaration,[83] and the 1970 Addendum of the Asian-African Legal Consultative Committee[84] have also emphasized the relevance of the principle.

The importance of sharing the burden with countries receiving large numbers of refugees has been increasingly stressed by the UNHCR and its Executive Committee.[85] In 1981, Conclusion No. 22 on protection of asylum seekers in situations of large-scale influx stated that,

(1) A mass influx may place unduly heavy burdens on certain countries; a satisfactory solution of a problem, international in scope and nature, cannot be achieved without international co-operation. States shall, within the framework of international solidarity and burden-sharing, take all necessary measures to assist at their request, States which have admitted asylum seekers in large-scale influx situations.[86]

see also G Martin, 'International Solidarity and Co-operation Assistance to African Refugees: Burden-Sharing or Burden-Shifting?' (1995) 7 *IJRL* 250, 253.

[82] Article 4 of Resolution 67 (14) of 29 June 1967 adopted by the Committee of Ministers of the Council of Europe on Asylum to Persons in Danger of Persecution.

[83] Cartagena Declaration on Refugees (19–22 November 1984) OAS/Ser.L/V/II.66, doc.10, rev.1, p 190–3, reprinted in UNHCR, *Collection of International Instruments and Other Legal Texts Concerning Refugees and Displaced Persons* (UNHCR, Geneva 1995) Vol II 206.

[84] Addendum to the Principles Concerning Treatment of Refugees (27 January 1970) reprinted in UNHCR, *Collection of International Instruments and Other Legal Texts Concerning Refugees and Displaced Persons* (UNHCR, Geneva 1995) Vol II 62.

[85] See ExCom General Conclusion on International Protection No. 11 (1978) para (e); ExCom Conclusion No. 15 (1979) on refugees without an asylum country para (g); ExCom Conclusion No. 19 (1980) on Temporary Refuge para (b) (ii); ExCom General Conclusion on International Protection No. 33 (1984) para (g) (i); ExCom General Conclusion on International Protection No. 61 (1990) para (g); ExCom General Conclusion on International Protection No. 65 (1991) para (i); ExCom General Conclusion on International Protection No. 71 (1993) para (h); ExCom General Conclusion on International Protection No. 74 (1994) para (h); ExCom General Conclusion on International Protection No. 77 (1995) para (o); ExCom General Conclusion on International Protection No. 79 (1996) para (h); ExCom Conclusion No. 80 (1996) on comprehensive approaches within a protection framework para (e)(iv); ExCom General Conclusion on International Protection No. 81 (1997) para (j); ExCom Conclusion on International Protection No. 85 (1998) para (p), (o); ExCom General Conclusion on International Protection No. 87 (1999) para (c); ExCom General Conclusion on International Protection No. 89 (2000); ExCom General Conclusion on International Protection No. 90 (2001) para (f) (k); ExCom General Conclusion on International Protection No. 93 (2002), para (c); ExCom General Conclusion on International Protection No. 93 (2002); ExCom General Conclusion on International Protection No. 95 (2003) para (g); ExCom General Conclusion on International Protection No. 98 (2003) para (g); ExCom General Conclusion on International Protection No. 98 (2003); ExCom General Conclusion on International Protection No. 99 (2004) paras (e) and (k); ExCom General Conclusion on International Protection No. 100 (2004) para (j); ExCom General Conclusion on International Protection No. 102 (2005) paras (h) and (l); ExCom General Conclusion on International Protection No. 108 (2008) para (m).

[86] ExCom Conclusion No. 22 (1981) on the Situation of Asylum Seekers in Situation of Large Scale Influx section IV (1).

This was followed in 1988 by Conclusion No. 52 where the Executive Committee:

3. *Stressed* that the principle of international solidarity has a fundamental role to play in encouraging a humanitarian approach to the grant of asylum and in the effective implementation of international protection in general.

4. *Recalled* that, in all circumstances, the respect for fundamental humanitarian principles is an obligation for all members of the international community, it being understood that the principle of international solidarity is of utmost importance to the satisfactory implementation of these principles.[87]

And by Conclusion No. 77 in 1995 which,

Call[ed] on all States to manifest their international solidarity and burden-sharing with countries of asylum, in particular those with limited resources, both politically and in other tangible ways which reinforce their capacity to maintain generous asylum policies.[88]

Since 1996, the Executive Committee has repeatedly insisted on its 'commitment to uphold the principles of solidarity and burden-sharing'.[89] Burden-sharing was the main theme of the 1998 session,[90] and the Executive Committee stated then that 'international solidarity and burden-sharing are of direct importance to the satisfactory implementation of refugee protection principles [...]'.[91] The question was more recently addressed by the Executive Committee in 2004, which reaffirmed that

[T]he achievement of international cooperation in solving international problems of a humanitarian character is a purpose of the United Nations as defined in its Charter and that the 1951 Convention relating to the Status of Refugees recognizes that a satisfactory solution to refugee situations cannot be achieved without international cooperation.[92]

and that

respect by States for their protection responsibilities towards refugees is strengthened by international solidarity involving all members of the international community and [...]

[87] ExCom Conclusion No. 52 (1988) on International Solidarity and Refugee Protection para 3–4.

[88] ExCom General Conclusion on International Protection No. 77 (1995) para (o).

[89] ExCom General Conclusion on International Protection No. 79 (1996) para (h); ExCom General Conclusion on International Protection No. 81 (1997) para (j); ExCom General Conclusion on International Protection No. 85 (1998) para (o); ExCom General Conclusion on International Protection No. 87 (1999) para (c); ExCom Conclusion No. 99 (2004) paras (e) and (k); ExCom Conclusion No. 100 on International Cooperation and Burden and Responsibility Sharing in Mass Influx Situations (2004) para (j); ExCom General Conclusion on International Protection No. 102 (2005) paras (h) and (l); ExCom General Conclusion on International Protection No. 108 (2008) para (m).

[90] Executive Committee, 'Annual Theme: International Solidarity and Burden-Sharing in all its Aspects: National, Regional and International Responsibilities for Refugees', UN Doc A/AC.96/904, 7 September 1998, para 28.

[91] ExCom General Conclusion on International Protection No. 85 (1998) para (p).

[92] ExCom Conclusion No. 100 (2004) on International Cooperation and Burden and Responsibility Sharing in Mass Influx Situations, Recital 1.

the refugee protection regime is enhanced through committed international cooperation in a spirit of solidarity and responsibility and burden sharing among all States.[93]

The UN General Assembly has also consistently expressed support for the principle of solidarity and burden-sharing in its resolutions on the Office of the UNHCR.[94]

At the supranational level, the Treaty of Amsterdam provides that the Council of Ministers shall adopt measures 'promoting a balance of effort between Member States in receiving and bearing the consequences of receiving refugees and displaced persons'.[95] The European Union also adopted several instruments which affirm the importance of the principle of solidarity.[96] A strict expression of the principle can be found in Article 72 of the 2000 Cotonou Agreement, which provides that 'humanitarian assistance shall be accorded to the population in ACP States' and shall aim to 'address the needs arising from the displacement of people (refugees, displaced persons, and returnees) following natural or man-made disaster'.[97] Finally, one ought to mention the proposed article 63b of

---

[93] Ibid, Recital 2; see also UNHR Issues Paper, n 3 above, para 36.

[94] GA Res 35/41, 25 November 1980, para 3; GA Res 36/125, 14 December 1981, para 3; GA Res 37/195, 18 December 1982, para 12; GA Res 38/121, 16 December 1983, paras 5 and 10; GA Res 39/140, 14 December 1984, paras 6 and 10; GA Res 40/118, 13 December 1985, para 10s and 13; GA Res 41/124, 4 December 1986, paras 11 and 16; GA Res 42/109, 7 December 1987, paras 12 and 15; GA Res 43/117, 8 December 1988, paras 14 and 19; GA Res 44/137, 15 December 1989, paras 18 and 20; GA Res 45/140, 14 December 1990, paras 20 and 21; GA Res 46/106, 16 December 1991, paras 17 and 18; GA Res 47/105, 16 December 1992, paras 22 and 23; GA Res 48/116, 20 December 1993, paras 9 and 23; GA Res 49/169, 23 December 1994, paras 8 and 24; GA Res 50/152, 21 December 1995, para 24; GA Res 51/75, 12 December 1996, para 20; GA Res 52/103, 12 December 1997, paras 6 and 17; GA Res 52/103, 12 December 1997, paras 6 and 17; GA Res 53/125, 9 December 1998, 1999, paras 7 and 21; GA Res 54/146, 17 December 1999, paras 8 and 23; GA Res 55/74, 12 December 2000, paras 9 and 25; GA Res 55/74, 12 February 2001, para 9; GA Res 56/137, 15 February 2002, para 8; GA Res 57/187, 6 February 2003, para 9; GA Res 58/151, 24 February 2004, para 9; GA Res 59/170, 22 February 2005, para 9; GA Res 60/129, 24 January 2006, para 10; GA Res 61/137, 25 January 2007, para 9; GA Res 62/124, 24 January 2008, para 27.

[95] Article 63.2 (b) of the Treaty of Amsterdam amending the Treaty on European Union, the Treaties Establishing the European Community and Certain Related Acts, opened for signature 2 October 1997 [1997] OJ C340/173 (entered into force 1 May 1999).

[96] See eg Explanatory memorandum of the Commission presented with the Proposal for a Council Directive on minimum standards for giving temporary protection in the event of a mass influx of displaced persons and on measures promoting a balance of efforts between Member States in receiving such persons bearing the consequences thereof COM (2000) 303 final 24 May 2000, para 5.1(6) [2000] OJ C311/251; Directive 2001/55/EC of 20 July 2001 on minimum standards for giving temporary protection in the event of a mass influx of displaced persons and on measures promoting a balance of efforts between Member States in receiving and bearing the consequences thereof [2001] OJ L212/12, Recital 20 of the Preamble; Recital 2 of the Preamble of the Council Decision 2000/596/EC of 28 September 2000 establishing a European Refugee Fund [2000] OJ L252/12.

[97] Partnership Agreement between the Members of the African, Caribbean and Pacific Group of States on the one part, and the European Community and its Member States of the other part, signed in Cotonou on 23 June 2000 [2000] OJ L317/3. <http://ec.europa.eu/development/geographical/cotonouintro_en.cfm>.

the Lisbon Treaty, which, if adopted, would significantly alter the legal nature of the principle of solidarity amongst Member States of the European Union.[98]

4.2.1.2 *Burden-sharing and* non-refoulement

One of the most delicate aspects of the burden-sharing debate has to do with its relation with *non-refoulement*. In 1983, Fonteyne asserted that,

Burden-sharing, certainly in cases of large-scale refugee movements, is a virtual sine qua non for the effective operation of a comprehensive *non-refoulement* policy intended to ensure safe havens for all fugitives from political persecution or other man-made or natural disasters.[99]

Countries faced with mass influxes of refugees have certainly embraced this standpoint.[100] This approach found practical application in Southeast Asia where first asylum countries gave temporary refuge to large groups of refugees, after having received assurances of international assistance and of refugees' resettlement in other countries.[101] Similarly, Tanzania has been particularly vocal on this question before the Executive Committee, stating in 1996 that its capacity to protect refugees was conditional upon the provision of financial assistance.[102]

UNHCR has, on the other hand, affirmed that 'in principle, international solidarity and burden-sharing should not be seen as a prerequisite for meeting

---

[98] Treaty of Lisbon Amending the Treaty on European Union and the Treaty Establishing the European Community (Lisbon, 13 December 2007) [2007] OJ C306/1 (hereafter, Lisbon Treaty). Art 63b reads:

> The policies of the Union set out in this Chapter and their implementation shall be governed by the principle of solidarity and fair sharing of responsibility, including its financial implications, between the Member States. Whenever necessary, the Union acts adopted pursuant to this Chapter shall contain appropriate measures to give effect to this principle.

[99] Fonteyne, n 71 above 175; See also P Hyndman, 'Asylum and Non-Refoulement—Are these Obligations Owed to Refugees under International Law?' (1982) 57 *Philippine LJ* 43, 77; P Hyndman, 'Refugees Under International Law with a Reference to the Concept of Asylum' (1986) 60 *Australian LJ* 148, 154; G Noll, 'Prisoners' Dilemma in Fortress Europe: On the Prospects for Equitable Burden-Sharing in the European Union' (1997) 40 *German Ybk of Intl L* (Duncker & Humblot, Berlin) 405; Martin, n 81 above, 253; A Grahl-Madsen 'The Emergent International Law Relating to Refugees', in *The Refugee Problem on Universal, Regional and National Level, Institute of Public International Law and International Relations, Thessaloniki* (1987) 163, 215 who talks of a 'close connection' between *non-refoulement* and burden-sharing.

[100] Goodwin-Gill and McAdam, n 7 above, 336.

[101] Hyndman, 'Refugees Under International Law', n 99 above 148, 154; Hyndman 'Asylum and Non-Refoulement', n 99 above, 75; D Perluss and J F Hartmann, 'Temporary Refuge: Emergence of a Customary Norm' (1986) 26 *Virginia J of Intl L* 551, 587.

[102] Cited by Goodwin-Gill and McAdam, n 7 above, 338; see also the statements by Côte d'Ivoire, Pakistan, and Zimbabwe, ibid, 339.

fundamental protection obligations'.[103] EXCOM Conclusion No. 85 endorsed this view, stating that,

[The Executive Committee] recognizes that international solidarity and burden-sharing are of direct importance to the satisfactory implementation of refugee protection principles; stresses, however, in this regard, that access to asylum and the meeting by States of their protection obligations should not be dependent on burden-sharing arrangements first being in place, particularly because respect for fundamental human rights and humanitarian principles is an obligation for all members of the international community.[104]

These views may be reconciled by differentiating *non-refoulement* and its corollary, the granting of temporary refuge or 'admission', which is absolute and unconditional, from asylum understood as a more permanent protection given to refugees and predicated on the existence of effective burden-sharing.[105] EXCOM Conclusion No. 22 adopted this approach:

In situations of large-scale influx, asylum seekers should be admitted to the State in which they first seek refuge and if that State is unable to admit them on a durable basis, it should always admit them at least on a temporary basis and provide them with protection according to the principles set out below.[106]

While in actuality, State have not in the vast majority of cases made real their threats to *refoule* refugees,[107] first asylum countries have considered that such threats constitute an efficient, and sometimes their only tool, for exerting pressure on Western countries. One such incident occurred during the Kosovo crisis, when the government of Macedonia closed its borders in several instances to send

---

[103] 'Annual Theme: International Solidarity and Burden-Sharing', n 90 above, para 6; see also statement by the representative of Austria on behalf of the European Union before ExCom UN Doc A/AC.96/SR.525, 16 November 1998, para 45.

[104] ExCom General Conclusion on International Protection No. 85 (1998) para (p); See also ExCom Conclusion No. 22 (1981) para 2; ExCom Conclusion No. 100 (2004), Recital 7; Council of Europe Committee of Ministers, Recommendation No. R (2000) 9 on Temporary Protection (3 May 2000), Recital 8.

[105] G Coles, *Problems Arising from Large Numbers of Asylum-Seekers: A Study of Protection Aspects*, (International Institute of Humanitarian Law, San Remo 1981), 24; G Coles, 'Temporary Refuge and the Large Scale Influx of Refugees' [1983] *Australian Ybk of Intl L* (Butterworths, Sidney) 189, 210; Fonteyne, n 71 above, 179; Perluss and Hartman, n 101 above, 571–2, and 589; Goodwin-Gill and McAdam, n 7 above, 343–4.

[106] ExCom Conclusion No. 22 (1981) on Protection of Asylum-Seekers in Situations of Large-Scale Influx, II.A.1.

[107] Goodwin-Gill and McAdam, n 7 above, 339. These authors note, however, that '[t]he element of contingency tends to relate to what *other* rights are granted apart from *non-refoulement*, and these may depend on the level of international assistance offered', ibid. See also, for instance, the position of Turkey, which in 1990 stated that '[w]hile access to highly industrialized countries was becoming more restrictive and selective, "the others" were expected to implement an open-door policy in the face of continuous and massive inflows of refugees and displaced persons', UN Doc A/AC.96/SR.456, 5 October 1990, para 2. However, Turkey later recognized the fundamental and unconditional character of *non-refoulement*, UN Doc A/AC.96/SR.528 12 October 1998, para 23; see also J Thorburn, 'Transcending Boundaries: Temporary Protection and Burden-Sharing in Europe' (1995) 7 *IJRL* 459, 474–5; P Hyndman, 'Asylum and Non-Refoulement', n 99 above, 70.

a clear message that it could not comply with its international commitments without further support from the international community.[108] Macedonia feared that the presence of refugees might be long-lasting,[109] and on 3 April 1999, it declared that it would only allow in as many refugees as it had guarantees to take from third countries.[110] UNHCR protested against the border closures but many Western States nevertheless admitted that there were indeed serious concerns as to Macedonia's political and ethnic stability.[111] In the end, UNHCR decided to coordinate an International Humanitarian Evacuation Programme, which led to the evacuation of 92,000 refugees to 29 States.[112] The House of Commons Select Committee acknowledged that while Macedonia was not entitled to violate its international obligations, the United Kingdom 'should also have provided prompt commitments of economic assistance to meet the current crisis'.[113] Goodwin-Gill and McAdam concur that 'while as a matter of law, international protection is not *contingent* on burden-sharing, there is some acknowledgement that practical responses to alleviate the pressure on countries of first asylum may be necessary to ensure that the principle is not violated'.[114]

4.2.1.3 *International practice*

There are various ways for burden-sharing to be effected.[115] The most convenient and common is through financial transfers from developed to developing countries. A similar and more recent approach has been to provide technical assistance and support capacity-building with a view to ensuring effective protection in developing countries. The most radical and thereby least popular manner to relieve first asylum States from the heavy burden of receiving and protecting refugees, however, is physical burden-sharing through the admission and reception of refugees, primarily through resettlement processes. Finally, UNHCR has recently sought to revive interest in comprehensive approaches, through the adoption of comprehensive plans of action.

---

[108] House of Commons Select Committee on International Development, *Third Report: Kosovo: The Humanitarian Crisis*, 15 May 1999, para 46, 79; see also M Barutciski and A Suhrke, 'Lessons from the Kosovo Refugee Crisis: Innovations in Protection and Burden-Sharing' (2001) 14 *JRS* 95, 96 who argue that first asylum should not be regarded as unconditional in all cases, 108–9.

[109] A Suhrke, M Barutciski, P Sandison, and R Garlock, *The Kosovo Refugee Crisis: An Evaluation of UNHCR's Emergency Preparedness and Response* (UNHCR Evaluation and Policy Analysis Unit, Geneva 2000) 91, para 449.

[110] Keesing's (1999) 42902, 3 April 1999; see also UNHCR Kosovo Crisis Update, 19 April 1999 <http://www.reliefweb.int> (1 July 2000).

[111] Suhrke, Barutciski, Sandison, Garlock, n 109 above, 90, para 446–7.

[112] Goodwin-Gill and McAdam, n 7 above, 337.

[113] House of Commons Select Committee on International Development, n 108 above, para 48.

[114] Goodwin-Gill and McAdam, n 7 above, 339.

[115] For a description of various burden-sharing schemes, see 'Annual Theme: International Responsibility and Burden-Sharing', n 90 above, paras 16–24; Hans and Suhrke, n 70 above, 86–102.

4.2.1.3.1 Fiscal burden-sharing

Fiscal burden-sharing applies equally to situations of mass influx and to individual arrivals. It is now widely accepted as an essential component of international cooperation in the refugee field. In the context of North–South cooperation, it may be regarded as a specific facet of development aid.[116]

Fiscal burden-sharing may take various forms. Financial transfers made by industrialized States through assistance programmes of UNHCR constitute the most obvious example.[117] Given the voluntary nature of these contributions, donors are free to decide on the destination of these funds, which are usually earmarked.[118] Fiscal-sharing mechanisms have also been endorsed at the level of the European Union. The first instruments were adopted to finance specific projects to improve admission facilities and voluntary repatriation for displaced persons from the former Yugoslavia,[119] and assist in the reception and voluntary repatriation of Kosovars.[120]

Ad hoc instruments have now been replaced by a generic mechanism with the establishment in 2000 of a European Refugee Fund to support and encourage the efforts of the Member States in receiving and bearing the consequences of receiving refugees and displaced persons,[121] which was followed by the establishment

---

[116] Hartling, n 75 above, 241; A Acharya and D B Dewitt, 'Fiscal Burden Sharing', in J C Hathaway (ed) *Reconceiving International Refugee Law* (Nijhoff, The Hague [etc] 1997) 111, 128–9.

[117] See ExCom Conclusion on International Cooperation and Burden and Responsibility Sharing in Mass Influx Situations No. 100 of 2004, para (j); Statement by the representative of Austria on behalf on of the European Union before ExCom, UN Doc A/AC.96/SR.525, 13 October 1998, para 46; Statement by the representative of Denmark before ExCom UN Doc A/AC.96/SR.528, 12 October 1998, para 51; Fonteyne, n 71 above, 178.

[118] R Väyrynen, 'Funding Dilemmas in Refugee Assistance: Political Interests and Institutional Reforms in UNHCR' (2001) 35 *IMR* 143, 156–7.

[119] Joint Action of 22 July 1997 concerning the financing of specific projects in favour of asylum seekers and refugees [1997] OJ L205/5; Joint Action of 22 July 1997 concerning the financing of specific projects in favour of displaced persons who have found temporary protection in the Member States and asylum seekers [1997] OJ L205/3; Joint Action of 27 April 1998 concerning the financing of specific projects in favour of asylum seekers and refugees [1998] OJ L138/8; Joint Action of 27 April 1998 concerning the financing of specific projects in favour of displaced persons who have found temporary protection in the Member States and asylum seekers [1998] OJ L138/6; see also Proposal for a Joint Action concerning solidarity in the admission and residence of beneficiaries of the temporary protection of displaced persons COM (1998) 372 final of 26 June 1998 [1998] OJ C268/22; see G Noll, *Negotiating Asylum, The EU Acquis, Extraterritorial Protection and the Common Market of Deflection* (Nijhoff, The Hague [etc] 2000) 310.

[120] Joint Action of 26 April 1999 establishing projects and measures to provide practical support in relation to the reception and voluntary repatriation of refugees, displaced persons and asylum seekers, including emergency assistance to persons who have fled as a result of recent events in Kosovo [1999] OJ L114/2.

[121] Council Decision 2000/596/EC of 28 September 2000 establishing a European Refugee Fund [2000] OJ L/252/12 supplemented by the Commission Decision 2001/275/EC of 20 March 2001 laying down detailed rules for the implementation of Council Decision 2000/596/EC as regards the eligibility and expenditure and reports on implementation in the context of actions co-financed by the European Refugee Fund [2001] OJ L95/27. Note that the United Kingdom and Ireland participated in the adoption of the Decision. For an analysis of the first European Refugee Fund, see A Hurwitz, 'Commentaires sur la détermination de l'Etat membre responsable

of a second European Refugee Fund in 2004 for the period 2005–2010.[122] In quantitative terms, the first Fund made €216 million available over five years from 1 January 2000, while the second one made €114 million available for disbursement for the first two years, thus making available a slightly higher amount every year. The two funds have a similar scope *ratione personae*, applying to refugees, persons with subsidiary protection status and persons who apply for either type of status, as well as beneficiaries of temporary protection.

The key issue, however, is the way in which the monies are being allocated to Member States. Under the second fund, each Member States receives €300,000 per year, except those Member States which joined since 2004, which receive €500,000 per year. The remainder is broken down as follows: 30 per cent of the fund is allocated for the support of beneficiaries of international protection, that is, refugee status and subsidiary protection, while 70 per cent is devoted to the support of asylum applicants as well as persons with temporary protection status. Peers notes that compared to the first fund, there has been slight shift in the percentage allocated to Member States to support applicants for international protection and temporary protection beneficiaries.[123] This would seem to conform with the increasingly restrictive approach of the EU on asylum, since according to Peers, it 'will increase the financial incentive to reject asylum or subsidiary protection claims'.[124]

The European Union is also one of the major donors for humanitarian assistance programmes. Its contribution is mostly implemented through ECHO, the Humanitarian Aid Office of the Commission, whose budget is devoted for the most part to assistance in conflict areas, and thus to projects involving refugees and internally displaced persons.[125]

In recent years, technical assistance and capacity-building have also become a particularly popular means to operationalize burden-sharing. UNHCR's Agenda for Protection granted special prominence to capacity-building, insisting that 'investment in capacity-building has to be made a more integral part of the regular operational response to any new emergency involving refugees' and that States should 'target financial and technical assistance in a manner that boosts the

de l'examen d'une demande d'asile et la répartition des charges entre Etats membres', in C Dias Urbano de Sousa and P De Bruycker (eds) *The Emergence of a European Asylum Policy* (Bruylant, Bruxelles 2004) 71, 77.

[122] Council Decision 2004/904/EC of 2 December 2004 establishing the European Refugee Fund for the period 2005–2010 [2004] OJ L381/52.

[123] S Peers, *EU Justice and Home Affairs Law* (2nd edn Oxford University Press, Oxford 2006) 347. Note that the Commission had at the time of the adoption of the first ERF justified this approach by the fact that most of the costs related to asylum policies are incurred during the asylum procedure.

[124] Ibid, 348.

[125] G Gilbert, 'Is Europe Living Up to its Obligations to Refugees?' (2004) 15 *EJIL* 963, 964–5; see also European Commission, 'Communication from the Commission to the Council and the European Parliament on the common asylum policy and the Agenda for Protection' COM (2003) 152 final, 26 March 2003, 13.

capacity of countries of first asylum to meet basic protection needs and to provide essential services'.[126] During the 'Convention Plus' process, UNHCR asserted that,

There is a collective duty of the broader community of States, including through UNHCR, to equip States receiving or likely to receive asylum-seekers with the means to live to international standards in their treatment of refugees, both upon recognition and over time. From the perspective of international burden-sharing, those regions that host the smallest number of refugees relative to their wealth can be expected to assist those with the highest number of refugees in relation to their economies.[127]

By way of example, a 'strengthening protection capacity project' (SPCP) was adopted with a view to 'develop and pilot a comprehensive and sustainable capacity-building methodology with practical and long-term deliverables'. This methodology was implemented in Benin, Burkina Faso, Kenya, the United Republic of Tanzania, Georgia, Armenia, Azerbaijan, and Thailand.[128] Also relevant is the *Framework for Durable Solutions for Refugees and Persons of Concern* which comprises development assistance for refugees, repatriation, reintegration, rehabilitation, and reconstruction and development through local integration with a view to ensuring a more equitable share of burdens and responsibilities, the building of capacity to receive and protect refugees as well as the further development of durable solutions.[129] Other examples include the provision of training on asylum and human rights issues to customs and border officials and national border-guard trainers as part of the Border Management Central Asia Programme.[130]

The focus on capacity-building is also manifest in EU policies and reflected in the priorities of the various financial programmes adopted by the European Union in the migration and asylum fields.[131] Pilot programmes in Tanzania and the

---

[126] UNHCR, Agenda for Protection, UN Doc A/AC.96/965/Add.1, 26 June 2002, 13–14; see also UNHCR Global Consultations, 'Strengthening Protection Capacities in Host Countries' UN Doc EC/GC/01/19, September 2001; see also ExCom Conclusion No. 100 (LV) of 2004 on International Cooperation and Burden and Responsibility Sharing in Mass Influx Situations, paras (j) v and (l) iv.

[127] UNHCR Issues Paper, n 3 above, para 36.

[128] UNHCR Note on International Protection, UN Doc A/AC.96/1024, 12 July 2006, para 43; for other examples of capacity-building projects supported by UNHCR, see eg UNHCR, Note on International Protection, UN Doc A/AC.96/965, 11 September 2002, paras 54–6; see also A Betts, 'Towards a Mediterranean Solution? Implications for the Region of Origin' (2006) 18 *IJRL* 652, 664.

[129] ExCom Standing Committee, n 72 above, paras 20–1; see also UNHCR High Commissioner's Forum, 'Progress Report: Convention Plus' FORUM/2005/6, 8 November 2005, para 6; ExCom Standing Committee, 'Ensuring International Protection and Enhancing International Cooperation in Mass Influx Situations' UN Doc EC/54/SC/CRP.11, 7 June 2004, para 10.

[130] ExCom Standing Committee, UNHCR's Activities in Relation to the Asylum-Migration Nexus, UN Doc EC/58/SC/CRP.12, 4 June 2007, para 6.

[131] In 2001, the budget heading B7-667 was created to allow the adoption of preparatory activities in the field of migration and asylum, with a total of €42.5 million disbursed over three years, and projects in the Balkans, Ukraine, Russia, North Africa, Turkey, Afghanistan, and Sri Lanka, see Communication from the Commission to the European Parliament and the Council, 'Thematic Programme for the cooperation with third countries in the areas of migration and asylum', COM

Western CIS have for instance been established, with the support of UNHCR.[132] The EU also funded several UNHCR projects,[133] such as a two-year project on the improvement of refugee protection within broader migration movements in North Africa,[134] with a view to strengthen protection capacity in regions of origin.[135]

4.2.1.3.2 Physical burden-sharing

State practice relating to physical burden-sharing has been inconsistent, and while in recent years, serious efforts have been undertaken to encourage States to accept further obligations, these commitments have remained limited.

The resettlement of refugees from first asylum countries has always been one of the permanent solutions which UNHCR is called to ensure,[136] even if repatriation and voluntary returns remain the preferred outcome.[137] It consists of 'making available in a third country, on a voluntary basis, permanent residence to a refugee who is in another country'.[138] Even before UNHCR's creation, the International Refugee Organization's primary task was the resettlement of European refugees in countries such as the United States, Canada and Australia, Western European States, and Latin America.[139] Moreover, large-scale resettlement

---

(2006) 26 final, 25 January 2006 (hereafter, Communication on Thematic Programme) 6. This was followed by the adoption of the Aeneas Programme, which was adopted for the period 2004–2008 with a budget of €250 million, ibid, 5; see also Regulation (EC) No. 491/2004 of the European Parliament and of the Council of 10 March 2004 establishing a programme for financial and technical assistance to third countries in the areas of migration and asylum (AENEAS) [2004] OJ L80/1. The duration of the Aeneas Programme was shortened by two years and replaced by a thematic programme adopted for the period 2007–2013, Communication on Thematic Programme, 5. The thematic programme is meant to complement geographic strategies which also comprise financial programmes supporting, inter alia, migration and asylum activities in neighbouring countries, see Communication on Thematic Programme, 7. It will include capacity-building activities for asylum infrastructures, with a specific focus on regions of origin, ibid, 12–13. Support for capacity-building activities was also reiterated in the European Pact on Immigration and Asylum, Doc 13440/08, 24 September 2008, which was endorsed by EU interior ministers on 25 September 2008 and formally adopted on 16 October 2008 by the 27 EU Heads of State, see <http://www.immigration.gouv.fr/IMG/pdf/Plaquette_EN.pdf>.

[132] UNHCR, 2006 Note on International Protection, n 128 above, para 28.

[133] UNHCR High Commissioner's Forum, 'Chairman's Summary, Third Meeting of the High Commissioner's Forum' 1 October 2004, para 16; see also European Commission, 'Towards more Accessible, Equitable and Managed Asylum Systems' COM (2003) 315 final, 3 June 2003, 16–18.

[134] ExCom Standing Committee, UNHCR's Activities in Relation to the Asylum-Migration Nexus, UN Doc EC/58/SC/CRP.12, 4 June 2007, para 5.

[135] European Commission, 'Towards more accessible, equitable and managed asylum systems' COM (2003) 315 final, 3 June 2003, 18.

[136] The other durable solutions envisaged are voluntary repatriation and local settlement; see UNHCR Statute, paras 1 and 9; ExCom General Conclusion on International Protection No. 85 (1998) para (jj); ExCom General Conclusion on International Protection No. 90 (2001) para (k); ExCom General Conclusion on International Protection No. 95 (2003) para (i);

[137] ExCom Standing Committee, 'The Strategic Use of Resettlement', UN Doc EX/53/SC/CRP.10/Add.1, 3 June 2003, para 5.

[138] Ibid, para 6.

[139] A Suhrke, 'Burden-Sharing During Refugee Emergencies: The Logic of Collective versus National Action' (1998) 11 *JRS* 396, 404; for a full account of the resettlement operation carried out

operations took place following the Soviet intervention in Hungary and the over-throw of Salvador Allende by General Pinochet in Chile.[140] Resettlement was also implemented from 1992 to 1994 for displaced persons from the former Yugoslavia. Mass flows of people fleeing ethnic cleansing led the UNHCR to launch a second appeal in 1995, however, the response of Western countries was disappointing, and emphasis was placed on protection in the region, through the creation of safety zones.[141]

If resettlement was the least preferred solution in the 1990s, recent develop-ments seem to indicate renewed interest in this mechanism.[142] The Agenda for Protection emphasized the need for a 'strategic use' of resettlement coupled with an increase in resettlement capabilities.[143] UNHCR has accordingly strived to revive States' interest in resettlement, and add additional resettlement States to the ten 'traditional' resettlement countries.[144] As a result of these efforts, UNHCR suc-ceeded in having a dozen more countries engaging in resettlement,[145] and expressed hope that a European Union resettlement scheme would be established to enhance EU resettlement capacities.[146]

The most significant normative development on resettlement, however, was the adoption of a Multilateral Framework of Understandings on Resettlement in June 2004, which was the most tangible output arising from the 'Convention Plus' process launched by UNHCR. It lays down in a non-binding instrument, the roles and responsibilities of parties involved in resettlement processes, includ-ing specific undertakings relating to registration and documentation, selection

---

by the IRO, see L W Holborn, *The International Refugee Organization: A Specialized Agency of the United Nations, its History and Work 1946–1952* (Oxford University Press, Oxford 1956) 365; Hans and Suhrke, n 70 above, 86.

[140] Hartling, n 75 above, 241.

[141] Inter-Governmental Consultations on Asylum, Refugee, and Migration Policies in Europe, North America, and Australia, *Study of the Concept of Burden-Sharing* (1998), 30.

[142] See ExCom Standing Committee, 'New Directions for Resettlement Policy and Practice' UN Doc EC/51/SC/INF.2, 14 June 2001, para 14.

[143] UNHCR Agenda for Protection, UN Doc A/AC.96/965/Add.1, 26 June 2002, 16, 20; UNHCR Note on International Protection, UN Doc A/AC.96/975, 2 July 2003, para 39.

[144] Australia, Canada, Denmark, Finland, the Netherlands, Norway, New Zealand, Sweden, Switzerland, and the United States. Inter-Governmental Consultations, n 141 above, 31.

[145] These are Benin, Brazil, Burkina Faso, Chile, Iceland, Ireland, Paraguay, Romania, Spain, and Uruguay. UNHCR, 'Easy Guide on Refugee Resettlement Programmes', Information as of June 2001; UNHCR Note on International Protection, UN Doc A/AC.96/1038, 29 June 2007, para 62.

[146] ExCom Standing Committee, 'Progress Report on Resettlement' UN Doc EC/59/SC/CRP.11, 2 June 2008, para 7. The European Commission expressed its support for resettlement to be used as one of the tools of the EU's asylum strategy, see European Commission, 'Communication from the Commission to the Council and the European Parliament on the common asylum policy and the Agenda for protection' COM (2003) 152 final, 26 March 2003, 12, 15; European Commission, 'Towards more Accessible, Equitable and Managed Asylum Systems' COM (2003) 315 final, 3 June 2003, 19; see also European Pact on Asylum and Immigration, n 131 above, 12.

criteria, family unity, transparency, the integrity of the process and programme delivery, as well as reception and integration of refugees.[147]

It is clear, however, that resettlement will always be a solution which only a very small minority of refugees will benefit from.[148] This is illustrated by the figures presented by UNHCR in its most recent report, which indicates that in 2006, submissions for resettlement were made for over 54,000 people and over 99,000 in 2007.[149] In 2007, resettlement departures had increased by 69 per cent, from 29,500 in 2006 to about 50,000 refugees.[150] It further estimated that there were at that point 155,000 people in need of resettlement and that a significant increase in resettlement needs was foreseen for 2009,[151] while noting with concern that the number of places made available by States had fallen behind and remained at 50 per cent below the identified global needs, which would increase to 565,000 refugees.[152]

As noted by Betts and Durieux, 'the North's dislike of uncontrolled migration is not a sufficient incentive for them to accept the substantially larger numbers of resettlement places required to make physical burden-sharing look real to over-burdened host countries in the South'.[153] Even within the European Union, physical burden-sharing has remained contentious, in spite of the numerous proposals launched in the last 15 years.

Common action by the European Union to deal with mass influxes originated in the conflict of the former Yugoslavia.[154] In 1992, the ministers with responsibility for immigration adopted a Conclusion on people displaced by the conflict in the former Yugoslavia.[155] This was followed in 1993 by a Resolution on certain common guidelines as regards the admission of particularly vulnerable groups of distressed persons from the former Yugoslavia.[156] In these two documents, the primary objective was to lay down guidelines on temporary protection and there were no specific provisions on burden-sharing. In 1994, the German Presidency

---

[147] UNHCR High Commissioner's Forum, 'Multilateral Framework of Understandings on Resettlement', FORUM/2004/6, 16 September 2004, para 3; UNHCR Note on International Protection, UN Doc A/AC.96/989, 7 July 2004, para 33.

[148] 'The Strategic Use of Resettlement', n 137 above, para 5.

[149] ExCom Standing Committee, 'Progress Report on Resettlement', UN Doc EC/59/SC/CRP.11, 2 June 2008, para 3.

[150] 2008 Progress Report on Resettlement, n 149 above, para 8.

[151] Ibid.

[152] Ibid, para. 4.

[153] A Betts and J-F Durieux, 'Convention Plus as a Norm-Setting Exercise' (2007) 20 *JRS* 509, 527.

[154] On the discussions relating to burden-sharing during the war in the former Yugoslavia, see A Suhrke, n 139 above, 406–12.

[155] Adopted on 30 November 1992, published in T Bunyan (ed) *Key Texts on Justice and Home Affairs in the European Union (1976–1993)* Vol I (Statewatch, London 1998) 74.

[156] Published in E Guild (ed), *The Developing Immigration and Asylum Policies of the European Union* (Kluwer, The Hague [etc] 1996) 293.

of the European Union proposed a draft Council Resolution which established a distributive key but it did not receive sufficient support.[157]

The first instrument of general application was adopted in 1995 and reflected the evolution of Member States' approach to refugee flows.[158] First, the preamble indicated that aid to the civilian population should mainly be provided in the region, by creating safe areas and security corridors and by providing humanitarian aid. The need to provide temporary refuge was also acknowledged, but on a secondary basis. The resolution then set out very broad principles which should be followed in the context of the European Union's response to humanitarian crises. Most interesting is paragraph 4, which identified certain criteria that should be taken into consideration to determine how the burden should be shared for the admission of displaced persons on a temporary basis. These were to include:

The contribution which each Member State is making to prevention or resolution of the crisis, in particular by the supply of military resources in operations and missions ordered by the United Nations Security Council or the Organization for Security and Cooperation in Europe and by the measures taken by each Member State to afford local protection to people under threat or to provide humanitarian assistance.[159]

These criteria, which could be supplemented by further ones in light of the specificity of a given situation, illustrate the broadening of the scope of burden-sharing which began in the early 1980s in the context of the debate on the 'root causes' of refugee flows.[160] Burden-sharing would then encompass all the stages of large-scale influxes, such as prevention, relief aid, peace talks, and peace-keeping missions, as well as post-conflict reconstruction.[161] UNHCR endorsed this inclusive notion, relevant at each phase of a refugee situation, from its emergence in the country of origin, to the organization of durable solutions.[162] The focus on protection in regions of origin is part of that same trend, which seeks to dilute burden-sharing

---

[157] Inter-governmental Consultations, n 141 above, 36; Suhrke, n 139 above, 410; Noll, n 119 above 292–3.

[158] Resolution on burden-sharing with regard to admission and residence of displaced persons on a temporary basis, 25 September 1995 [1995] OJ C262/1. This resolution was supplemented by a Council Decision of 1996 on an alert and emergency procedure for burden-sharing with regard to the admission and residence of displaced persons on a temporary basis, adopted on 4 March 1996 [1996] OJ L63/10.

[159] Note that this criterion was also included in the German draft, Inter-governmental Consultations, n 141 above, 36.

[160] G Coles, 'Refugees and Human Rights' [1991] *Bulletin of Human Rights* 63, 65.

[161] Inter-Governmental Consultations. n 141 above, 13–14, 52–3. 65–9; Suhrke, n 139 above, 408–9; Betts, 'Towards a Meditteranean Solution', n 128 above, 669–70.

[162] UNHCR, 'Annual Theme: International Solidarity and Burden-Sharing', n 90 above, para 28; see also Statement by the US representative before ExCom UN Doc A/AC.96/SR.525, 13 October 1998, para 42; Statement by the Austrian representative on behalf of the European Union before ExCom, UN Doc A/AC.96/SR.525, 13 October 1998, para 43.

obligations by considerably broadening the scope of activities that might be regarded as tokens of a State's commitment.[163]

The resolutions and decisions described above were 'soft law' instruments and therefore not binding. Nevertheless, one could have reasonably expected that these guidelines and procedures would have been followed during the Kosovo crisis of 1999, which saw the largest flow of refugees in Europe since the end of World War II.[164] However, they were never implemented.[165]

In September 1998, the Commission prudently stated that it would 'keep under review the possibility of making use of the procedure established in the Council decision of 4 March 1996'.[166] However, in spite of the urging by the European Parliament to organize increased cooperation and fair burden-sharing,[167] Member States were unable to do so. There were calls made for the convening of an EU meeting on the Kosovo crisis, but in the end, the emergency aid programme dominated the agenda,[168] and the competent ministers who met on 7 April 1999 could not reach an agreement on cooperation in the reception and admission of displaced persons from Kosovo.[169]

The important financial support granted to first asylum countries—Macedonia and Albania—was in fact closely linked to the idea of containing the flows and preventing a mass influx in the EU Member States.[170] Fiscal burden-sharing was once again the answer and a Joint Action was adopted to provide practical, in fact financial support, in relation to the reception and voluntary repatriation of refugees, displaced persons and asylum seekers, including emergency assistance to persons fleeing as a result of recent events in Kosovo.[171]

---

[163] See in this respect European Commission, 'Communication from the Commission to the Council and the European Parliament on the Common Asylum Policy and the Agenda for Protection' COM (2003) 152 final, 26 March 2003, 6. See also G Noll, 'Visions of the Exceptional: Legal and Theoretical Issues Raised by Transit Processing Centres and Protection Zones' (2003) 5 *EJML* 303, 315, who reports that one of the first versions of the UK proposal for extraterritorial processing contemplated the recourse to military force to reduce refugee flows and enable returns.

[164] House of Commons Select Committee on International Development, n 108 above, para 5.

[165] See Explanatory memorandum of the Commission presented with the Proposal for a Council Directive on minimum standards for giving temporary protection, n 96 above, para 3.1.

[166] See 'Answer given by Mrs Gradin on behalf of the Commission' on 22 October 1998 to a written question No. 2682/1998 by Gerhard Hager to the Commission, 1 September 1998 [1999] OJ C96/133.

[167] EP Resolution on the Situation in Kosovo of 15 April 1999 [1999] OJ C219/4, para k.

[168] 'Chirac asks for EU meeting on Kosovo refugee crisis' AFP 31 March 1999; 'Europe scrambles to organize aid for Kosovo refugees' AFP, 31 March 1999.

[169] Explanatory memorandum of the Commission presented with the Proposal for a Council Directive on minimum standards for giving temporary protection, n 96 above, para 3.2.

[170] Suhrke, Barutciski, Sandison, Garlock, n 109 above 8, para 40. The authors report that UNHCR also preferred protection in the region, 92, para 454.

[171] See in particular Art 1 Joint Action of 26 April 1999 establishing projects and measures to provide practical support in relation to the reception and voluntary repatriation of refugees, displaced persons and asylum seekers, including emergency assistance to persons who have fled as a result of recent events in Kosovo [1999] OJ L114/2.

At the end of April 1999, German authorities expressed their fury over the lack of solidarity of France and the United Kingdom in receiving refugees.[172] According to the UNHCR Kosovo Crisis Update of 29 April 1999, Germany had accepted the evacuation of almost 10,000 Kosovars from Macedonia, France 2,000 and the United Kingdom 161.[173] The UK government justified its attitude by stating that it did not want to help Milosević in his task, and that in any case, refugees did not want to leave the region. This position was nevertheless criticized by the House of Commons Select Committee on International Development which rightly noted that the option of protection outside the region of origin should not have been excluded per se.[174]

It is against this background that the European Union adopted a Directive on minimum standards for giving temporary protection in the event of a mass influx of displaced persons and on measures promoting a balance of efforts between Member States in receiving such persons bearing the consequences thereof.[175]

The new Directive provides for both fiscal and physical burden-sharing. Fiscal burden-sharing should be based on the operation of the European Refugee Fund, which is described above.[176] With regard to physical burden-sharing, the Commission implicitly acknowledged that only the lowest level of commitment would be acceptable to some Member States. The basic principle remains that of 'double voluntary action', from the host States, and from the beneficiaries of temporary protection.[177] The Council decision, which would 'activate temporary protection' and determine the existence of a situation of mass influx, would be accompanied by declarations of Member States offering to receive displaced persons. The principle is further diluted by the provision that States do not need to quote precise figures in relation to the offer.[178] The debate surrounding the question of burden-sharing was also apparent in the documents annexed to the Directive. In a statement included in the minutes of the Council Meeting, Austria voiced its preference for a burden-sharing scheme based on precise criteria, and declared that it would determine the number of persons it can receive on the basis of a comparison between the respective populations of each Member State. Opponents to the system, primarily the United Kingdom and France, considered on the other hand that a strict repartition key would contradict the principle of

---

[172] 'German fury at "mean" Britain', *The Guardian* April 30, 1999.
[173] <http://www.reliefweb.int/rw/rwb.nsf/db900sid/OCHA-64CTBG?OpenDocument&query=UNHCR%20Kosovo%20Crisis%20Update%20of%2029%20April%201999>.
[174] House of Commons Select Committee on International Development, n 108, para 75–84.
[175] Council Directive 2001/55/EC of 20 July 2001 [2001] OJ L212/12 (hereafter, temporary protection Directive); for an analysis of the temporary protection Directive, see J-F Durieux and A Hurwitz, 'How Many Is Too Many? African and European Legal Responses to Mass Influxes of Refugees' (2004) 47 *German Yearbook of Intl Law* (Duncker & Humblot, Berlin 2005) 144–56.
[176] See above, Section 4.2.1.3.1.
[177] Explanatory memorandum of the Commission presented with the Proposal for a Council Directive on minimum standards for giving temporary protection, n 96 above, paras 4.4, 6 and 6.3, 11.
[178] Ibid, para 6.3 and Art 25.1 of the Directive.

'double voluntariness' whereby transfer to a Member State requires the consent of both the host State and the displaced person.[179]

Since then, burden-sharing has remained a prominent question in European debates on asylum, and those supporting stronger commitments seem to be slowly gaining ground. In 2003, the Commission suggested an 'integrated approach' to burden-sharing that would not be limited to financial costs but also include physical burden-sharing. It noted that, 'the European Union being a unique model of an emerging "common asylum space", if burden-sharing and responsibility-sharing cannot be successfully applied within that space, how could it possibly be expected to be to others?'[180]

In addition to the aforementioned provision on burden-sharing of the not yet ratified Lisbon Treaty, the 2008 European Pact on Immigration and Asylum expresses the agreement of the European Council to 'establish procedures in the case of a crisis in a Member State faced with a massive influx of asylum seekers, to enable the secondment of officials from other Member States'. More significantly, it also states that,

[F]or those Member States which are faced with specific and disproportionate measures pressures on their asylum systems, due in particular to their geographical or demographic situation, solidarity shall also aim to promote, on a voluntary and coordinated basis, better reallocation of beneficiaries of international protection from such Member States to others, while ensuring that asylum systems are not abused.[181]

While this language still falls short of a strict commitment, there is clearly a gradual attempt by the Commission and the Council to beef up the burden-sharing principle within the European Union.

4.2.1.3.3 Comprehensive approaches
Comprehensive approaches, and in particular, the adoption of comprehensive plans of action as a means to resolve refugee situations on the basis of solidarity and burden-sharing were developed in the 1980s. The idea was to rely on a range of durable solutions and burden-sharing devices to ensure the resolution of a specific refugee situation.[182] The adoption of comprehensive approaches was

---

[179] Durieux and Hurwitz, n 175 above, 152.

[180] European Commission, 'Towards more Accessible, Equitable and Managed Asylum Systems', COM (2003) 315 final, 3 June 2003, 17.

[181] European Pact on Immigration and Asylum, n 131 above, 12.

[182] UNHCR, 'Chairman's Summary, Third Meeting of the High Commissioner's Forum', 1 October 2004, para 19. Note that such comprehensive approaches are also reminiscent, *mutatis mutandis*, of proposals made by scholars for burden-sharing schemes, see in this respect P Schuck, 'Refugee Burden-Sharing: A Modest Proposal' (1997) 22 *Yale J Intl L* 243, 276; J C Hathaway and A Neve, 'Making International Refugee Law Relevant Again: A Proposal for Collectivized and Solution-oriented Protection' (1997) 10 *Harv Hum Rts J* 115, 188–9. The latter article proposes a complex system based on the formation of 'interest convergence groups', made of 'inner core', 'outer core', and 'situation-specific' subgroups of States depending on their level of concern for certain refugee flows, ibid, 190–6, 201, 204–7. For a critique of these proposals, see D Anker, J Fitzpatrick, and

given renewed prominence during the Global Consultations, and included in the Agenda for Protection.[183] The goal of 'Convention Plus' was to further develop such approaches through the adoption of a normative framework to deal with areas that were inadequately addressed by the Refugee Convention and its 1967 Protocol.[184]

Comprehensive plans of action are the main tools to implement such approaches. These are typically multilateral agreements among a group of stakeholders, such as countries of origin, host States, UNHCR and affected communities and refugees, providing for the resolution of a specific refuge problem through, inter alia, diplomatic and political processes, coordination mechanisms, financial assistance, capacity-building, standby arrangements, humanitarian transfer or evacuation programmes, and a mix of durable solutions.[185]

While the comprehensive plans devised for Africa and Central America, namely, the International Conferences on Assistance to Refugees in Africa (ICARA) and CIREFCA (*Conferencia Internacional sobre Refugiados, Displazados y Repatriados de Centro America*), are also usually cited,[186] the Comprehensive Plan of Action for

A Shacknove, 'Crisis and Cure: A Reply to Hathaway/Neve and Schuck' (1998) 11 *Harv Hum Rts J* 295; see also M Gibney, 'Forced Migration, Engineered Regionalism and Justice Between States', in S Kneebone and F Rawlings-Sanaei (eds), *New Regionalism and Asylum Seekers* (Berghahn Books, New York 2007) 57, 67–8.

[183] UNHCR, 'The Agenda for Protection', UN Doc. A/AC.96/965/Add.1, 26 June 2002; UNHCR High Commissioner's Forum, 'Making Comprehensive Approaches to Resolving Refugee Problems More Systematic', FORUM/2004/7, 16 September 2004, para 1.

[184] Betts and Durieux, n 153 above, 512. The three areas or 'strands' for which agreements would be negotiated with a view to complement the CSR were resettlement, irregular secondary movements and targeted development assistance, ibid.

[185] ExCom Standing Committee, 'Ensuring International Protection and Enhancing International Cooperation in Mass Influx Situations', n 129 above, paras 9–11; UNHCR, 'Making Comprehensive Approaches to Resolving Refugee Problems More Systematic', n 183 above, para 6; ExCom Conclusion No. 100 (2004) on International Cooperation and Burden and Responsibility Sharing in Mass Influx Situations, para j); see also Betts and Durieux, n 153 above, p 528.

[186] UNHCR, 'Making Comprehensive Approaches to Resolving Refugee Problems More Systematic', n 183 above, para 5. The 1982 and 1984 International Conferences on Assistance to Refugees in Africa (ICARA I and II) concentrated on raising money from extra-regional donors to implement refugee-related development projects, with limited success, see para 8 of the Recommendations from the Pan-African Conference on the Situation of Refugees in Africa, UN Doc A/AC.96/INF.158 p 7, 7–17 May 1979; para 6 (c) of the Programme of Action adopted by the Second International Conference on Assistance to Refugees in Africa UN Doc A/39/402 p 22, 9–19 April 1981, both reprinted in UNHCR, *Collection of International Instruments and Other Legal Texts Concerning Refugees and Displaced Persons* Vol II (UNHCR, Geneva 1995) 31 and 54; Programme of Action annexed to the Report of the Secretary-General on the Second International Conference on Assistance to Refugees in Africa UN Doc A/39/402, 22 August 1984, p 23; B N Stein, 'ICARA II: Burden Sharing and Durable Solutions', in J Rogge (ed) *Refugees, A Third World Dilemma* (Rowman & Littlefield, Totowa (NJ) 1987) 47, 53–6; R F Gorman, *Coping with Africa's Refugee Burden, A Time for Solutions* (Nijhoff and UNITAR, Dordrecht [etc] 1987) 14 and 22; Inter-Governmental Consultations n 141 above, 27–8; Hans and Suhrke, n 70 above, 83, 91. The International Conference on Central American Refugees (CIREFCA) was more successful and included financial burden-sharing through external assistance, while its main objective was local integration or voluntary repatriation of the refugees as part of the peaceful development of the region, see International Conference on

Indo-Chinese refugees remains the most important precedent, where large-scale physical burden-sharing, implemented through resettlement, was a key component of the operation.[187] In 1978, faced with an important arrival of 'boat people' which threatened the political and economic stability of the region, first asylum countries such as Malaysia, Thailand, Indonesia, and the Philippines decided to close their borders.[188] The international community responded to this situation by convening a first conference in 1979 to organize burden-sharing between first asylum countries and Western countries.[189] The latter accepted to participate in the resettlement of around 250,000 refugees from Vietnam and Laos, based on quotas and taking account of humanitarian and immigration parameters.[190] The numbers decreased for a few years before an important surge occurred again in 1986.[191] At that point, the number of people arriving exceeded the number of resettlement offers.[192] First asylum countries showed mounting reluctance to accept 'boat people', who they were concerned were not all going to be resettled.

In 1989, a second International Conference agreed on the implementation, under the authority of UNHCR, of a 'Comprehensive Plan of Action for Indo-Chinese Refugees' (CPA).[193] The plan put an end to the previous mechanism based on automatic resettlement from first asylum countries, and parties agreed on a cut-off date after which individuals would have to undergo a refugee status determination screening. Thus after that date, individuals needed to apply for refugee status once in the country of first asylum, and only those recognized as refugees by the authorities would be accepted for resettlement. UNHCR trained the local authorities and monitored the procedures in order to ensure a harmonized application of the CSR throughout the region.[194] The number of refugees eventually resettled was much lower than before.[195] The individuals whose claims were denied would be returned to Vietnam in accordance with the Memorandum

Central American Refugees (CIREFCA), Guatemala City, 29–31 May 1989, Declaration and concerted plan of action UN Doc CIREFCA/89/14, reprinted in Goodwin-Gill, *The Refugee in International Law*, (2nd edn, Oxford University Press, Oxford 1996) 540.

[187] UNHCR Note On International Protection, UN Doc A/AC.96/975, 2 July 2003, para 47.

[188] S A Bronée, 'The History of the Comprehensive Plan of Action' (1993) 5 *IJRL* 534, 534–5.

[189] Report of the Secretary-General on the Meeting on Refugees and Displaced persons in South-east Asia, UN Doc A/34/627 1 July 1979; A Grahl-Madsen, *Territorial Asylum* (Almquist & Wiksell International and Oceana Publications, Stockholm and London [etc] 1980) 105.

[190] Hans and Suhrke, n 70 above, 100; Inter-governmental Consultations, n 141 above, 22.

[191] Inter-governmental Consultations, ibid.

[192] Bronée, n 188 above, 536.

[193] International Conference on Indo-Chinese Refugees, Geneva 13–14 June 1989: Declaration and Comprehensive Plan of Action UN Doc A/CONF.148/2, 26 April 1989.

[194] S Bari, 'Refugee Status Determination under the Comprehensive Plan of Action (CPA): A Personal Assessment' (1992) 4 *IJRL* 487; see also R Towle, 'Processes and Critique of the Indo-Chinese Comprehensive Plan of Action: An Instrument of International Burden-Sharing?' (2006) 18 *IJRL* 537, 549–50.

[195] See eg the numbers for Indonesia, Malaysia, Thailand, and the Philippines in A Helton, 'Refugee Determination under the Comprehensive Plan of Action: Overview and Assessment' (1993) 5 *IJRL* 545, 549–50, 552, 554.

of Understanding signed between Vietnam and UNHCR.[196] The Vietnamese authorities were also asked to control clandestine departures, even though some of the persons concerned were in need of international protection. This was accompanied by an information campaign in Vietnam to explain the consequences of these changes.

The CPA was officially completed on 30 June 1996,[197] and was hailed by UNHCR as paving the way for the development of similar schemes applicable in other regions and contexts.[198] It led to the resettlement of 530,000 Vietnamese and Laotians mainly to Western countries,[199] was in effect the last example of resettlement process conducted on a large scale and coincided with the start of the crisis of asylum in the West.[200]

Some have noted that the relevance of the Indo-Chinese precedent is that it had many of the characteristics of contemporary refugee situations: mixed flows, irregular secondary movements, and protracted refugee situations.[201] It is therefore unsurprising that one of the objectives of the 'Convention Plus' initiative was to reconsider this precedent and suggest a framework for the conclusion of other comprehensive plans of action. The difficulty, however, is that the conditions that led to the adoption of the Indo-Chinese CPA were rather unique.[202] First, the country of origin was involved in the discussions and took an active role in the process. Moreover, such an arrangement would not have been possible without the leadership of the United States which felt responsible for providing protection to its former allies from Southern Vietnam.[203] UNHCR recognized as much when it stated that 'a combination of interests (those of politically and economically powerful States as well as of strategic and/or proximate States) are among the most critical factors which will influence the extent and speed of international responses to mass influx situations'.[204] Also, if large-scale resettlement was common practice until the end of the cold war, there is now preference for protection in the region,

---

[196] Inter-governmental Consultations, n 141 above, 23.

[197] See UNHCR, Note on International Protection, UN Doc A/AC.96/863, 1 July 1996, para 4.

[198] Towle, n 194 above, 569; S Kneebone and F Rawlings-Sanaei, 'Introduction: Regionalism as a Response to a Global Challenge', in S Kneebone and F Rawlings-Sanaei (eds), *New Regionalism and Asylum Seekers* (Berghahn Books, New York 2007) 1, 14.

[199] Ibid.

[200] Towle, n 194 above, 555.

[201] Kneebone and Rawlings-Sanaei, n 198 above, 17.

[202] See Towle, n 194 above, 562.

[203] Suhrke, n 139 above, 406.

[204] 'Ensuring International Protection and Enhancing International Cooperation in Mass Influx Situations', n 129 above, para 8. See also in this respect the analysis proposed by Noll, based on game theory, who argues that States do not have at present rational interests to participate in burden-sharing mechanisms, n 119 above, 329, 339, 349; G Noll, 'Risky Games? A Theoretical Approach to Burden-Sharing in the Asylum Field' (2003) 16 *JRS* 237; see also Suhrke who presents a similar argument', n 139 above, 413–14.

in order to ensure, where possible, speedy repatriation and to guarantee the right of refugees to return to their country.[205]

Other precedents remain rare.[206] In 1986, Denmark presented a proposal for a 'comprehensive international approach' based on the principle of voluntary repatriation, regional integration, and extra-regional resettlement, where resettlement quotas would be determined by a precise distributive key based on factors such as population, and Gross National Product.[207] By the same token, the suggestion made by UNHCR to consider the adoption of a second Protocol to the CSR to address mass influx situations was not followed by any concrete steps.[208]

Particularly relevant for the present discussion, is the suggestion made by UNHCR that CPAs 'could include, for example, a CPA for refugees of one or more nationalities in one particular asylum country and/or a CPA focused on a chain of countries that are affected by a refugee movement'.[209] This is based on the new approach advocated by UNHCR, which would view comprehensive approaches as 'a mix of responses and stakeholders to a given refugee problem without the inhibiting requirement or expectation that it be exhaustive in scope'.[210] While this seems an attractive proposition that could possibly help address secondary movements, the way in which this would be implemented in practice remains unclear; in particular, the extent to which this would entail extraterritorial processing was not addressed.

'Convention Plus' envisaged the conclusion of an agreement on irregular secondary movements of refugees and asylum seekers which would have ensured the provision of effective protection, guaranteed durable solutions and the better management of irregular secondary movements in a protection sensitive manner.[211] Key burden-sharing components were to be proposed by UNHCR as part of this agreement, including capacity-building, development assistance targeted

---

[205] Inter-governmental Consultations, n 141 above, 23; This was the official policy of UNHCR at the beginning of the Kosovo crisis: see Suhrke, Barutciski, Sandison, Garlock, n 109 above, 91, para 452.

[206] The 1992 International Meeting on Humanitarian Aid for Victims of the Conflict of the Former Yugoslavia) and the the 1996 CIS Regional Conference to Address the Problems of Refugees, Displaced Persons, Other Forms of Involuntary Displacement and Returnees in the Countries of the Commonwealth of Independent States and Relevant Neighbouring States are also often cited as precedents.

[207] See Inter-governmental Consultations, n 141 above, 32 and 41, for a list of criteria that may be taken into consideration for the determination of a distributive key. See also in this respect the proposal made by Grahl-Madsen, who suggested the adoption of a precise distributive key based on the gross national income per capita and the population size, *Territorial Asylum*, n 189 above, 106–14.

[208] 'Ensuring International Protection and Enhancing International Cooperation in Mass Influx Situations', n 129 above, para 12. See also in this respect T Einarsen, 'Mass Flight: The Case for International Asylum' (1995) 7 *IJRL* 551, 553, who proposed the adoption of a second Protocol to the CSR laying down a regional model of temporary protection.

[209] 'Making Comprehensive Approaches to Resolving Refugee Problems More Systematic', n 183 above, para 9.

[210] Ibid, para 10; see also Betts, 'Towards a Mediterranean Solution', n 128 above, 652.

[211] UNHCR Issues Paper, n 3 above, para 40.

to refugee populations, and resettlement.[212] However, discussions on a draft Multilateral Framework of Understandings on Addressing Irregular Secondary Movements of Refugees and Asylum Seekers were suspended in November 2005, given the lack of consensus on key elements of the generic agreement.[213] The suggestion to adopt a comprehensive plan of action for Somali refugees was no more successful.[214]

4.2.1.4 The legal relevance of the principle of solidarity and burden-sharing

On the basis of the instruments cited above, one would be tempted to suggest the existence of a strong commitment to the principle of solidarity and burden-sharing,[215] and some scholars have on that basis claimed that this principle is part of customary international law.[216] As early as 1983, Fonteyne argued that,

The widespread pattern of recognition, coupled with its repeated application in State practice, seems to leave little room indeed for doubt concerning the legal nature of the principle, and its binding character for States, at least within the framework of UN Charter law.[217]

Unfortunately, practice in the last two decades has not been conclusive in particular with respect to physical burden-sharing.[218] Resettlement arrangements do not suffice to demonstrate the existence of consistent practice. These are limited to a small number of States, and the number of refugees actually resettled remains marginal against the millions of refugees present in first asylum countries. 'Convention Plus', which sought to strengthen the existing normative framework with respect to burden-sharing provided further proof of the difficulty of securing agreement on these questions.[219] While stronger commitment to burden-sharing is now reflected

---

[212] Ibid, para 43. As explained by UNHCR elsewhere, 'resettlement opportunities in the first asylum country may assist in deterring further secondary movements by providing the prospect of a durable solution', ExCom Standing Committee, 'The Strategic Use of Resettlement', n 137 above, para 26.

[213] UNHCR High Commissioner's Forum, 'Convention Plus Core Group on Addressing Irregular Secondary Movements of Refugees and Asylum-Seekers, FORUM/2005/7, 8 November 2005, para 1.

[214] See UNHCR High Commissioner's Forum, 'Information Note: Preparatory Project for the Elaboration of a Comprehensive Plan of Action for Somali Refugees', FORUM/2004/8, 24 September 2004; UNHCR, *The State of the World's Refugees: Human Displacement in the New Millennium*, (Oxford University Press, Oxford, 2006) 59; Betts and Durieux, n 153 above, 528–9. These authors argue that the choice of the Somali situation to revive the CPA concept was ill-thought given the particular complexity of that situation.

[215] Inter-governmental consultations, n 141 above, 15.

[216] B S Chimni, 'The Principle of Burden-Sharing', in B S Chimni (ed) *International Refugee Law, A Reader* (Thousand Oaks/ Sage Publications, California [etc] 2000) 146.

[217] Fonteyne, n 71 above, 184.

[218] See Inter-governmental Consultations, n 141 above, 16; Noll, *Negotiating Asylum*, n 119 above, 350.

[219] Betts and Durieux, n 153 above, 510.

in the provisions of the Lisbon Treaty, as well as in EU secondary legislation, the analysis above shows that even in the supranational context, practice remains inconsistent.

Discussions on burden-sharing within the Executive Committee have been characterized by a sharp division between developing and developed States. The representative of Pakistan considered in 1997 that

> there was a need to implement the principle of burden-sharing between countries of origin, countries of asylum and donor States, which was accepted in the Convention and reiterated in several of the Executive Committee's conclusions.[...]. Countries of first asylum, particularly developing countries, should not be alone in bearing the burden of absorbing refugees unable to return to their homes voluntarily.[220]

The representative of India adopted an even stronger stance and stated that

> Burden-sharing did not mean that developed countries could meet their obligations only by assisting developing countries; it also implied that developed countries had to accept their responsibilities under international refugee law and refrain from unilateral practices and derogations that could contribute to a complete collapse of the international regime.[221]

The only Western State which expressly called for a more equitable distribution was Germany in 1998.[222] More relevant, however, is the fact that the Austrian delegate who was speaking on behalf of the European Union stated that burden-sharing was a political principle rather than a legal one.[223] There was nobody to challenge this statement, even if many developing States regretted it. This was also expressed by the representative of Tanzania in the following terms:

> While that concept was well established and recognized in theory, it was nonetheless a sad reality that the hiatus between theory and practice was very wide. [...] That was particularly true in respect of long-standing refugee situations and, since there was no mechanism to apportion the sharing of the burden within the international community, whatever resources that were made available to the countries of asylum remained a matter of charity, left to the discretion of individual States.[224]

---

[220] Statement before ExCom, UN Doc A/AC.96/SR.517, 3 November 1997, para 20; see also UN Doc A/AC.96/SR.527, 2 December 1998, para 12.

[221] Statement before ExCom UN Doc A/AC.96/SR.528, 12 October 1998, para 8; see also statement by the representatives of Iran, UN Doc A/AC.96/SR.525, 16 November 1998, para 51; of Uganda UN Doc A/AC.96/SR.527, 2 December 1998, para 17; and of Ivory Coast UN Doc A/AC.96/SR.529, 30 November 1998, para 18.

[222] Statement by the representative of Germany before ExCom, UN Doc A/AC.96/SR.526, 8 October 1998, para 53; see also the call by the Norwegian representative that burden-sharing be better defined UN Doc A/AC.96/SR.526, 8 October 1998, para 34; and the statement by the representative of Bangladesh, UN Doc A/AC.96/SR.519, 28 October 1997, para 20; UN Doc A/AC.96/SR.527, 2 December 1998, para 52.

[223] See Statement by the Permanent Representative of Austria on behalf of the European Union before ExCom, UN Doc A/AC.96/SR.525 16 November 1998, para 46.

[224] UN Doc A/AC.96/SR.528, 12 October 1998, para 12.

There is arguably much stronger evidence supporting the existence of an obligation of fiscal burden-sharing, although one may, like Fitzpatrick, deplore the prevalence of this form of burden-sharing as a 'questionable substitute'.[225] However, even if one may argue that such a norm exists, the central question of the more equitable distribution of funds remains unresolved. There is indeed nothing in the practice of States which may indicate the existence of an obligation to transfer funds for the purpose of refugee protection on an equitable basis. The practice of earmarking the funds transferred to UNHCR shows that States like to keep tight control of the use and destination of their money and are less concerned about ensuring that each refugee situation can be adequately addressed.

Obviously, the debate on burden-sharing has been charged with heavy ideological and geopolitical undertones, which have clouded legal analyses of the principle. The fact that burden-sharing does not at present seem to meet the customary threshold does not, however, mean that it is devoid of legal relevance. The standing of the principle of solidarity and burden-sharing under international refugee law would be best understood as belonging to the category of soft law general principles. These principles, understood as 'international prescriptions that are deemed to lack requisite characteristics of international normativity but are capable of producing legal effects',[226] have gained increasing prominence and recognition in international law.

There is indeed growing interest in soft law as an element of modern international law-making.[227] Boyle and Chinkin note for instance that 'in modern international relations [...] general norms or principles are more often found in the form of non-binding declarations or resolutions of international organisations than in the provisions of multilateral treaties'.[228] Even if these principles do not lead to the emergence of customary obligations, these authors note that they may nonetheless have legal effect and that their importance 'derives principally from the influence they may exert on the interpretation, application and development of other rules of law'.[229] The authority and legitimacy of these principles derives essentially from the endorsement of States.[230]

---

[225] J Fitzpatrick. 'Temporary Protection of Refugees: Elements of a Formalized Regime' (2000) 94 *AJIL* 279, 291.

[226] G Handl, M Reisman, B Simma, P-M Dupuy, C Chinkin, and R De La Vega, 'A Hard Look at Soft Law' (1990) 82 *American Society of International Law Proceedings* (hereafter, ASIL Proceedings), 371.

[227] See in particular A Boyle and C Chinkin, *The Making of International Law* (Oxford University Press, Oxford 2007) 211; see also C Chinkin, 'The Challenge of Soft Law: Development and Change in International Law' (1989) 38 *ICLQ* 850; J Sztucki, 'Reflections on International "Soft Law"', in J Rambers et al (eds), *Festskrift till Lars Hjerner: Studies in International Law* (Norstedts, Stockholm 1990) 549; see also J Klabbers, 'The Undesirability of Soft Law' (1998) 67 *Nordic Journal of International Law* 381; H Hillgenberg, 'A Fresh Look at Soft Law' (1999) 10 *EJIL* 499.

[228] Boyle and Chinkin, n 227 above, 222.

[229] Ibid, 223.

[230] Boyle and Chinkin, n 227 above, 224,

Furthermore, these principles are helpful in that they 'wish to promote some degree of predictability, create some expectations and a framework for future action', helping define a standard of good behaviour.[231] This conception is not dissimilar to that of regime theory, where norms, understood in their broadest meaning, contribute 'to shared understandings about the nature of an issue and so "guide", "inspire" or "justify" certain types or behaviour'.[232] Examples of international soft law include the principles of precaution and sustainable development. Lowe explains for instance that sustainable development 'is a meta-principle, acting upon other rules and principles—a legal concept exercising a kind of interstitial normativity, pushing and pulling the boundaries of true primary norms when they threaten to overlap or conflict with each other'.[233]

In situations of mass influx, the principle of solidarity and burden-sharing helps create some level of predictability and expectation, and sets a standard of good behaviour to ensure support for first asylum States. It influences the behaviour of States, inasmuch as it legitimizes calls for assistance by UNHCR and first asylum States. It serves a key function in the international regime of protection, for it is undeniable that the wide disparity in the numbers of refugees hosted by States does impact the level and quality of refugee protection in countries that have to bear the heaviest burden.[234] Even if not legally binding, in that international responsibility will not be incurred for its breach, burden-sharing is nevertheless a crucial norm under international refugee law, in fact, one of its founding principles, and, to that extent, it must necessarily have some bearing on the conduct of States and international organizations. It may even be argued that while specific commitments based on the principle of burden-sharing are desirable, the generic principle of burden-sharing would be unworkable as 'hard' law', like other similar norms which 'are [...] intentionally and functionally soft'.[235]

4.2.1.5 Safe third country practices and burden-sharing

The question one must then turn to is the extent to which safe third country practices are undercutting the principle of solidarity and burden-sharing. Before addressing this question, however, it should first be noted that the unequal burden borne by States is in part responsible for the secondary movements that Western States seek to prevent. UNHCR explained that,

[T]he phenomenon of irregular movements of refugees and asylum seekers is more likely to occur from countries which host large refugee populations or which face protracted

---

[231] ASIL Proceedings, n 226 above, 388, 390.

[232] Betts and Durieux, n 153 above, p 515, 525.

[233] A V Lowe, 'Sustainable Development and Unsustainable Arguments', in A E Boyle and D Freestone (eds), *International Law and Sustainable Development* (Oxford University Press, Oxford 1999), 31.

[234] See in this respect UNHCR Issues Paper, n 3 above, para 24.

[235] ASIL Proceedings, 375.

refugee situations. Such movements generally cause problems for the irregular movers themselves as well as for the receiving countries, since they frequently indebt themselves to people smugglers and are often compelled to employ clandestine and sometimes dangerous methods of travel. Receiving countries that wish to return such persons to their countries of first asylum, often face difficulties in establishing readmission agreements. Countries of first asylum are, in general, reluctant to enter into such agreements in view of the large numbers of refugees that they already host on their territory.[236]

Safe third country practices have also been strongly criticized for shifting even further the burden to those States closer to regions of origin.[237] As noted by Shuck:

Risk differential makes it difficult to secure agreement on, much less compliance with, the norm because it reinforces the incentives of relatively insular and hence low-risk states to avoid burden-sharing by free-riding on the self-interested efforts of the higher-risk states, leaving the latter to bear all the burdens.[238]

This is certainly the case within the European Union, where Member States such as Italy, Greece, or Poland have a much stronger interest in a proportional distributive system than Ireland or France. There is therefore clear evidence that the effective application of the Dublin system reinforces the 'risk differential' by providing that the first Member State which the asylum seeker has entered is responsible.

Paradoxically, some, including UNHCR, have regarded the Dublin regime as the only multilateral and conventional system of burden-sharing existing today, both at the European and global levels.[239] If one looks at the objectives of the Convention and Regulation, however, the organization of burden-sharing does not seem to be one of them, as was correctly pointed out by the Commission.[240] The Preamble of the Dublin Convention refers to the completion of the free movement of persons within the European Union and to the need to avoid 'orbit situations'. Another objective is to put an end to what is called 'asylum shopping'—that is, successive or simultaneous asylum applications lodged with

---

[236] UNHCR, 'Burden-Sharing—Discussion Paper Submitted By UNHCR, Fifth Annual Plenary Meeting Of The Asia-Pacific Consultations', [2001] *ISIL Yearbook of International Humanitarian and Refugee Law* 17; <http://0-www.worldlii.org.prospero.murdoch.edu.au/int/journals/ISILYBIHRL/2001/17.html>; see also UNHCR Issues Paper, n 3 above, para 24.

[237] See eg A Shacknove and R Byrne, 'The Safe Country Notion in European Asylum Law' (1996) 9 *Harv Hum Rts J* 185, 214–5; Bouteillet-Paquet, n 55 above, 291; Lassen and Hughes, n 12 above, 2 and 13.

[238] Schuck, n 182 above, 273.

[239] See Executive Committee, 'Annual Theme: International Solidarity and Burden-Sharing', n 90 above, para 24.

[240] Commission Staff Working Paper, 'Revisiting the Dublin Convention', n 5 above, para 35; European Commission, 'Communication from the Commission to the European Parliament, the Council, the European Economic and Social Committee and the Committee of the Regions: Policy Plan on Asylum, an Integrated Approach to Protection Across the EU', COM (2008) 360 final, 17 June 2008 (hereafter Commission Policy Plan on Asylum), 8.

two or more Member States—but no mention is made of burden-sharing. It seems then that from the perspective of the Member States of the European Union, the imbalance in the share borne by each Member State is of little relevance. By the same token, the 2003 Dublin Regulation only refers to the necessity to 'strike a balance between responsibility criteria in a spirit of solidarity'.[241] At the time of the drafting of the Regulation, the suggestion made by Denmark to include a safeguard clause, providing for the suspension of the Convention if the number of asylum seekers hosted by one State were to increase by more than 35 per cent above the number hosted for the last three years was dismissed.[242]

The application of the Dublin regime is not only problematic at the internal level; it also has an external dimension, given that it allows Member States to return asylum seekers to States. While regional mechanisms are often preferred because of the proximity to the conflict area, and because States involved are more likely to have a strong interest in resolving the crisis,[243] UNHCR has considered that 'any regional burden-sharing arrangements should be complementary to, not at the expense of, global burden-sharing efforts'[244] and explained that

Past experience shows that in situations of mass influx, the most successful burden-sharing arrangements are those which are not limited exclusively to countries from the region. [...] there is a danger that regional burden-sharing arrangements may lead to the creation of blocs, each with their own distinctive refugee regimes. This may result in an inequitable sharing of responsibility, with burden 'shifting' from one region to another, rather than resulting in greater harmonization of practices and procedures relating to the protection and assistance of refugees and returnees at the global level.[245]

What this also means is that while a limited application of the safe third country concept may not, on its own, raise difficulties in this respect, the situation becomes more problematic in a context where a large group of States, such as the Member States of the European Union, applies these provisions, leading to the shuffling of a large number of asylum applicants to 'outer' countries. In spite of its official support for 'genuine burden sharing',[246] the European Union is currently supporting policies which are particularly concerning in this respect, such as the initiative, as part of the European Neighbourhood Policy, to encourage

---

[241] Dublin Regulation, Recital 8, Preamble.

[242] U Brandl, 'Distribution of Asylum Seekers in Europe? Dublin II Regulation Determining the Responsibility for Examining an Asylum Application', in P De Bruycker and C Dias Urbano de Sousa (eds), *The Emergence of a European Asylum Policy* (Bruylant, Bruxelles, 2004) 33, 53. Note, however, that this suggestion has now been taken up by the Commission, see Commission Policy Plan on Asylum, n 240 above, 9.

[243] Acharya and Dewitt, n 116 above, 132.

[244] 'Annual Theme: International Solidarity and Burden-Sharing', n 90 above, para 30.

[245] Ibid, para 29; see also the similar statement of the Representative of Turkey before ExCom, UN Doc A/AC.96/SR.528, 12 October 1998, para 27.

[246] Commission of the European Communities, 'Towards More Accessible, Equitable and Managed Asylum Systems' COM (2003) 315 final, 3 June 2003.

neighbouring countries to adopt readmission policies towards their own neigh-bours, ensuring thereby that asylum seekers are moved even further away from the borders of the European Union.[247] Such an approach challenges the very foundations of the international refugee regime, of which the principle of soli-darity and burden-sharing is part. Through their attempt at evading at all costs their collective responsibility, Member States of the European Union are in effect fundamentally undermining the international refugee regime. To that extent, the principle of solidarity and burden-sharing should be construed as limiting the reach of those safe third country practices which apply on a unilateral basis and/or allow return based on mere transit. As noted by Feller,

[T]he difficulties confronting international protection stem [...] from this disconnect between rights and responsibilities. How to bridge the gap is perhaps, *the* challenge con-fronting the viability of asylum. The key to ensuring international protection for those who need it lies in the development of approaches which will achieve that balance, will bet-ter apportion responsibilities, share burdens and, ultimately, enable States to identify those to whom they owe protection, with what content and those to whom they do not.[248]

4.2.2 The principle of good-neighbourliness

Another principle which might be relevant to inter-State relationships in the refugee realm is the principle of good-neighbourliness, which deals with mutual relationships between neighbouring States.[249] The principle derives from the Latin maxim, *sic utere tuo ut alienum non laedas*.[250] It is regarded as one of the major objectives of the United Nations,[251] and is referred to in general declara-tions on friendly relations and peaceful coexistence.[252] There is a large practice of bilateral treaties on good-neighbourliness.[253] This principle has been invoked for

---

[247] Communication from the Commission to the European Parliament and the Council, Thematic Programme for the cooperation with third countries in the areas of migration and asylum, COM (2006) 26 final, 25 January 2006, 12.

[248] E Feller, 'Asylum, Migration and Refugee Protection: Realities, Myths and the Promise of Things to Come' (2006) 18 *IJRL* 509, 525.

[249] I Pop, *Voisinage et Bon Voisinage en droit international* (Pédone, Paris 1980) 26.

[250] Use your property in such a way as not to harm others.

[251] See Preamble and Art 74 of the UN Charter.

[252] UNGA Res 1236 (XII), 14 December 1957 on peaceful and neighbourly relations among States relations; UNGA Res 1301 (XIII), 10 December 1958 on measures aimed at the implementa-tion and promotion of peaceful and neighbourly relations among States; UNGA Res 2129 (XX), 21 December 1965 on actions on the regional level with a view to improving neighbourly relations among European States having different social and political systems; UNGA Res 46/62, 9 December 1991 on the development and strengthening of good-neighbourliness between States.

[253] Pop, n 249 above, 200; see eg the Treaty on Good-Neighbourliness and Friendly Co-operation between Germany and Poland of 17 June 1991, see W Czaplinski, 'Current Development: The New Polish-German Treaties and the Changing Political Structure of Europe' (1992) 86 *AJIL* 163, 167; Treaty on Good-Neighborliness, Partnership and Cooperation between the Federal Republic of Germany and the Union of Soviet Socialist Republics of 9 November 1990 (1991) 30 *ILM* 505;

the most part in international environmental law,[254] and in the context of international security.[255] Recent treaties regarding the protection of minorities also refer to it.[256]

Good-neighbourliness entails the respect by States of their obligations under public international law, above all of its basic principles.[257] The multiplication of relations between States has led to the broadening of the concept, which now also encompasses many forms of international cooperation between States, even if they are not neighbours. Nevertheless, it is an obvious reality of international life that disputes are more likely to arise between neighbouring States, hence the greater importance of cooperation.

Four basic rules of conduct may be identified within the concept of good-neighbourliness: the obligation of States not to use their territory or to allow their administrations and their nationals to act against a neighbouring State or other States;[258] the obligation of each State to take measures where there is a danger of causing damage to another State and when the cause of the damage is on the territory of the first State; the obligation to inform, or/and consult with the neighbouring State which could be affected by an action, an event, or a phenomenon taking place on the territory of the first State; finally a general rule of tolerance which good neighbours shall observe in their mutual relations.[259]

In the refugee realm, the obligations encompassed in the principle of good-neighbourliness have been usually invoked against the State of origin. Thus, the forced expulsion of people induces an 'order to enter another State irrespective of the latter's wishes and entails a violation of the sovereign equality of States.[260]

Treaty on Understanding, Cooperation and Good-Neighborliness between Hungary and Romania of 16 September 1996 (1997) 36 *ILM* 340.

[254] See M Valverde Soto, 'General Principles of International Environmental Law' (1996) 3 *ILSA Journal of Intl and Comp L* 193, 197; P N Okowa, *State Responsibility for Transboundary Air Pollution in International Law* (Oxford University Press, Oxford 2000) 65–77; *Lac Lanoux Arbitration (France v Spain)* (1957) 24 ILR 101, 130; *Trail Smelter Arbitration (USA v Canada)* (1941) 3 UNRIAA 1905.

[255] Pop, n 249 above, 255.

[256] E Defeis, 'Minority Protections and Bilateral Agreements: An Effective Mechanism' (1999) 22 *Hastings Intl & Comp LR* 291, 311; Czaplinski, n 253 above, 168; see Art 2 of the Council of Europe Framework Convention for the Protection of National Minorities of 1 February 1995 (1995) 34 *ILM* 351; Arts 14 and 15 of the Treaty on Understanding, Cooperation and Good-Neighborliness between Hungary and Romania, n 253 above, 347.

[257] Pop, n 249 above, 194–5.

[258] See also *Corfu Channel Case* (merits) ICJ Reports (1949) 4, 18, and 22.

[259] Sands, n 71 above, 197–8; see eg Principle 21 of the Stockholm Declaration, UN Conference on the Human Environment (1972) 11 *ILM* 1416, 1421, 1466.

[260] L Lee, 'The Right to Compensation: Refugees and Countries of Asylum' (1986) 80 *AJIL* 532, 555; see Projet de règlementation de l'expulsion des étrangers, Institut de droit international *Annuaire* 278–9 (1891); C Tomuschat, 'State Responsibility and the Country of Origin', in V Gowlland-Debbas (ed), *The Problem of Refugees in The Light of Contemporary International Law Issues* (Nijhoff, The Hague [etc] 1996) 59, 71; L Takkenberg, 'Mass Migration of Asylum Seekers and State Responsibility', in *The Refugee Problem on Universal, Regional and National Level* (Institute of Public International Law and International Relations, Thessaloniki 1987) 787, 797; see also W Czaplinski and P Šturma, 'La responsabilité des Etats pour les flux de réfugiés provoqués par eux' [1994] *AFDI* 156.

Sir Robert Jennings argued in 1938 that a State would incur responsibility if it treated its minorities in a manner which would adversely affect neighbouring countries.[261] This reasoning has not been followed in practice, however.[262] The preferred approach is to hold that basic human rights standards oblige States towards the international community.[263] Tomuschat argues for instance that the international community through the United Nations and in particular UNHCR, could make a claim for the costs incurred by the forced displacement of populations.[264]

Good-neighbourliness may have some bearings in the context of safe third country practices. References to this concept are found in the documents of the Council of Europe regarding the elaboration of an agreement on the responsibility for examining an asylum request.[265] The representative of Germany considered that the principle of good-neighbourliness applied in the asylum realm, for 'a country must not take action which might increase the burden of one of the other countries'. He recognized, however, that this also entailed the development of harmonized asylum laws and procedures at the European level, and an equitable distribution of recognized refugees.[266] A majority of the Council of Europe experts considered however that 'Member States should not allow the transit through their territory of persons whom they know are proceeding to another member State with the intention of entering the latter country illegally'.[267] The principle of good-neighbourliness also implied that countries which would be granting transit visas were under an obligation to verify with the competent authorities that the person could legally enter the country of destination.[268] A second argument of the representative of Germany was that a State which would let asylum seekers enter another State unlawfully after conducting an asylum procedure would violate the principle of good-neighbourliness.[269] In such circumstances, States had a duty, based on the principle of good-neighbourliness, to readmit an alien who moved from their territory to another State. Portugal, Spain, Austria, and Italy considered

---

[261] R Y Jennings, 'Some International Law Aspects of the Refugee Question' (1939) 16 *BYIL* 98, 112–13; see also R Hofmann, 'Refugee-Generating Policies and the Law of State Responsibility' (1985) 45 *Zeitschrift für Ausländisches Öffentliches Recht und Völkerrecht* 694, 706–7.

[262] See case cited by Lee, n 260 above, 561–2 and the statement by India during the crisis in East Pakistan, Keesing's Contemporary Archives July 3–10 1971 at 24 685; see also R Hofmann, n 261 above, 707.

[263] Goodwin-Gill and McAdam, n 7 above, 448; Tomuschat, n 261 above, 76–8; see also C Beyani, 'State Responsibility for the Protection and Resolution of Forced Population Displacements in International Law' (1995) 7 *IJRL* Special Issue 130, 134–5.

[264] Tomuschat, n 261 above, 78.

[265] See Chapter 1, Section 1.2.4.

[266] 21st meeting CAHAR (86) 6, 17 December 1986, para 3.

[267] Ibid, para 6.

[268] Ibid, para 8.

[269] 27th meeting of CAHAR, Final Activity report (88) 9 Final, 25 January 1989, para 15.

that this rule would adversely affect first asylum countries,[270] and that it should be conditional upon the existence of harmonized visa policies and regulations on the movement of persons.[271]

Reliance on the principle of good-neighbourliness has been limited to these instances. Yet, good-neighbourliness could provide useful arguments against the unilateral application of safe third country practices. One could claim that the removal of an asylum seeker to a third country on the basis of mere transit and which has not expressly agreed to receive and examine his/her claim infringes the principle of good-neighbourliness.[272] Hailbronner refers to the opinion of a Canadian official that the unilateral application of the safe third country concept does not conform with good-neighbourliness and international cooperation in finding solutions to the refugee problem.[273] In his study on irregular movements or refugees, Jaeger noted that orbit movements have led to tensions between neighbouring States, one suspecting the other of allowing such movements to the other State.[274] A first step would be the establishment of appropriate arrangements for the identification of refugees, through registration and documentation, in countries through which refugees travel and to ascertain the itineraries followed by refugees and asylum seekers,[275] which is one of the few points about which there seems to be agreement among States,[276] and which may be regarded as another application of the principle of good-neighbourliness.

4.3 Conclusion

The analysis conducted in this chapter illustrates the uncertainties of the norm creating process under public international law. While safe third country practices have become increasingly widespread in the last 15 years, one cannot infer therefrom that an asylum seeker should be readmitted by a State through which s/he has only transited. The second question was whether the emergence of such a practice would contradict the principle of burden-sharing and solidarity and the principle of good-neighbourliness. While non-binding, the principle of solidarity and burden-sharing is a fundamental norm underpinning the international refugee regime which reflects the collective responsibility of States to

---

[270] Final Activity Report on the Draft Agreement on Responsibility for Examining Asylum Requests CAHAR (88) 9 Final, 25 January 1989, para 14.

[271] Ibid, para 16.

[272] See Marx, n 74 above, 395 who considers this practice to be contrary to the principles which govern friendly relations between States.

[273] Hailbronner, n 15 above, 41.

[274] Jaeger, n 35 above, 42, para 172.

[275] See UNHCR Issues Paper, n 3 above, para 9, 27–9; ExCom Conclusion No. 58 (1989); ExCom Conclusion No. 91 (2001) on Registration and Asylum Seekers.

[276] Joint Statement on Irregular Secondary Movements, n 36 above, 3.

protect refugees. In this perspective, the attempt of Western countries, particularly EU countries, to evade their obligations by ensuring that refugees and asylum seekers are removed ever farther from the borders of the European Union is challenging the very foundations of the international refugee regime. It is therefore arguable that the safe third country concept contravenes the principle of solidarity and burden-sharing where applied unilaterally and on the sole basis of a transitory passage.

5

States' Obligations Towards Refugees

Safe third country practices, including the Dublin Regulation,[1] are used by States to dismiss an asylum claim when the asylum seeker has transited or has other connections with another country so long as that country can be regarded as safe. However, as has been suggested in Chapters 2 and 3, these practices raise fundamental questions in terms of States' obligations towards refugees.

This chapter will show that these regulations, arrangements, and practices pose indeed serious problems in that they significantly raise the risk of *refoulement* and of violations of other international human rights of individuals, primarily the right to seek and enjoy asylum from persecution and the right to leave one's country. Additionally, the question of the extent to which the third State should also comply with other obligations under the 1951 Convention relating to the Status of Refugees[2] or other international human rights instruments regarding basic standards of treatment must also be considered.

For the purposes of this demonstration, an analysis of the scope and nature of the *non-refoulement* principle as laid out in international refugee and human rights law will be carried out. Other human rights obligations will then be reviewed, namely the right to seek and enjoy asylum from persecution and the right to leave one's country, as well as other relevant rights recognized under international refugee law and/or human rights law. An assessment of the conditions under which a State may remove an asylum seeker to a third country under international refugee and human rights law will then be conducted.

5.1 The Obligation of *Non-Refoulement*

In the context of immigration control in continental Europe, *refoulement* is a term of art covering, in particular, summary reconduction to the frontier of those discovered to have entered illegally and summary refusal of admission of those without valid papers.

---

[1] Council Regulation (EC) No. 343/2003 of 18 February 2003 establishing the criteria and mechanisms for determining the Member State responsible for examining an asylum application lodged in one of the Member States by a third-country national [2003] OJ L50/1 (hereafter, Dublin Regulation).

[2] 1951 Geneva Convention Relating to the Status of Refugees (adopted 28 July 1951, entered into force 22 April 1954) 189 UNTS 150 (hereafter, CSR or Refugee Convention).

Refoulement is thus to be distinguished from expulsion or deportation, the more formal process whereby a lawfully resident alien may be required to leave a State, or be forcibly removed.[3]

Although the concept of *non-refoulement* emerged in the nineteenth century along with the principle of non-extradition of political offenders, the obligation of *non-refoulement* was first formulated in the 1933 Convention relating to the International Status of Refugees.[4] The principle thereafter has been recognized in the Refugee Convention, in the Convention Against Torture and in a flurry of other international instruments.[5]

5.1.1 The obligation of *non-refoulement* under international refugee law

5.1.1.1 *Nature and scope of Article 33 CSR: the prohibition of expulsion or return ('*refoulement*')*

(1) No Contracting State shall expel or return ('*refouler*') a refugee in any manner whatsoever to the frontiers of territories where his life or freedom would be threatened on account of his race, religion, nationality, membership of a particular social group or political opinion.

(2) The benefit of the present provision may not, however, be claimed by a refugee whom there are reasonable grounds for regarding as a danger to the security of the country in which he is, or who, having been convicted by a final judgment of a particularly serious crime, constitutes a danger to the community of that country.

The Refugee Convention allows no reservation to this Article[6] and it applies even in emergency situations. It is owed to any individual who fulfils the conditions of the definition of the refugee in Article 1.A CSR.[7] This includes, in accordance with the declaratory character of refugee determination, refugees awaiting a decision on

---

[3] G S Goodwin-Gill and J McAdam, *The Refugee in International Law* (3rd edn, Oxford University Press, Oxford 2007) 201; see also Art 32 CSR on expulsion of refugees lawfully on the territory of a State party. On the distinction between *refoulement* and expulsion, A Grahl-Madsen, *Commentary on the Refugee Convention 1951* (UNHCR Division of International Protection, Geneva 1997) 228, reprinted from a Draft Manuscript made by the author in 1962–1963.

[4] Convention relating to the International Status of Refugees of 28 October 1933 (1935–1936) 159 LNTS 199 No. 3663; only eight States ratified this Convention, Goodwin-Gill and McAdam, n 3 above, 202; See also Art 5(3)(a) of the Convention concerning the Status of Refugees coming from Germany (10 February 1938) (1938) 192 LNTS 59 No. 4c461.

[5] UNHCR Advisory Opinion on the Extraterritorial Application of *Non-Refoulement* Obligations under the 1951 Convention Relation to the Status of Refugees and its 1967 Protocol, 26 January 2007, available at: <http://www.unhcr.org/refworld/docid/45f17a1a4.html> 5–6 (hereafter, UNHCR Advisory Opinion); Goodwin-Gill and McAdam, n 3 above, 208–15.

[6] Article 42(1) CSR; UNHCR Advisory Opinion, n 5 above, 4.

[7] See ExCom Conclusion No. 6 on *Non-Refoulement* (1977), para (c); UNHCR Advisory Opinion, n 5 above, 2.

their status.[8] The UNHCR Executive Committee has consistently reaffirmed the 'fundamental importance' of the principle of *non-refoulement*.[9]

With respect to the exception provided under paragraph 2, its wording indicates that it applies to individuals and the *travaux préparatoires* reveal that the authors of the amendment insisted on its narrow scope.[10] Derogations from the compliance with fundamental human rights based on internal disturbance or external security concerns are common in human rights instruments, and the interpretation of these clauses adopted by domestic and international courts suggests that they should be applied restrictively,[11] even though the events of 11 September 2001 have certainly led to a broader interpretation of Article 33.2.[12]

This exception has nevertheless been construed in certain cases as allowing the *refoulement* of entire groups of refugees.[13] Moreover, Article 3.2 of the 1967 UN Declaration on territorial asylum and Article III.3 of the 1966 Principles of the Asian African Legal Consultative Committee which allow exceptions for overriding reasons of national security or in order to safeguard the population, such as in a mass influx, have been used to advocate such an expanded interpretation.[14]

---

[8] See para 28 of the *UNHCR Handbook on Procedures and Criteria for Determining Refugee Status*, (reprint 1992) UN Doc HCR/1P/4/Eng/Rev.2; ExCom Conclusion No. 6 on *Non-Refoulement* (1977), para (c); ExCom General Conclusion on International Protection No. 79 (1996), para (j); ExCom General Conclusion on International Protection No. 81 (1997), para (i).

[9] ExCom General Conclusion on International Protection No. 68 (1992), para (f); ExCom General Conclusion on International Protection No. 71 (1993), para (g); ExCom General Conclusion on International Protection No. 74 (1994), para (g); ExCom General Conclusion on International Protection No. 79 (1996), para (j); ExCom General Conclusion on International Protection No. 81 (1997), para (i), ExCom Conclusion No. 82 (1997) on Safeguarding Asylum, para (i).

[10] Grahl-Madsen, n 3 above, 234; UNHCR Advisory Opinion, n 5 above, 4; for an in-depth analysis of Art 33.2, see Goodwin-Gill and McAdam, n 3 above, 234–44.

[11] T Buergenthal and L B Sohn, *The Movement of Persons Across Borders* (American Society of International Law, Washington DC 1992) 132; on the interpretation of the exceptions to Arts 8–11 ECHR, see F Matscher, 'Methods of Interpretation of the Convention', in R St J Macdonald et al. (eds), *The European System for the Protection of Human Rights* (Nijhoff, Dordrecht [etc] 1993) 63, 66; for domestic case-law, see eg *Staat der Nederlanden v Hoge Raad Nederlands*, 13 May 1988 [1988] Nederlandse Jurisprudentie nr.910, 3133, 3139 which ruled that para 2 of Art 33 CSR should be applied on a case-by-case basis and by balancing the interest of the individual against the interest of the State. Note that the 1969 Convention on the Specific Aspects of Refugee Problems in Africa (adopted 10 September 1969, entered into force 20 June 1974) 1001 UNTS 45 (hereafter, OAU Convention) does not provide for any exception to the principle; Goodwin-Gill and McAdam, n 3 above, 234–44.

[12] Goodwin-Gill and McAdam, n 3 above, 236–7, 240–1; see also UNHCR, 'Advisory Opinion regarding the scope of the national security exception in Article 33(2)', 6 January 2006 available at: <http://www.unchr.org/refworld/docid/43de2da94.html>

[13] Buergenthal and Sohn, n 11 above, 131; J-P Fonteyne, 'Burden-Sharing: An Analysis of the Nature and Function of International Solidarity in Cases of Mass Influx of Refugees' (1983) 8 *Australian Ybk Intl L* (Butterworths, Sidney) 162, 172; K Hailbronner, '*NonRefoulement* and "Humanitarian" Refugees: Customary International Law or Wishful Legal Thinking?', in D A Martin (ed), *The New Asylum Seekers: Refugee Law in the 1980s* (Nijhoff, Dordrecht 1988) 123, 128.

[14] Article 3.2 of the 1967 UN Declaration on Territorial Asylum, UNGA Res 2312 (XXII), 14 December 1967; Art III. 3 of the 1966 Principles Concerning Treatment of Refugees of the Asian African Legal Consultative Committee, reprinted in UNHCR, *Collection of International Instruments and Other Legal Texts Concerning Refugees and Displaced Persons* (1995) Vol II 10.

As noted by Goodwin-Gill and McAdam, however, 'a mass influx alone does not justify *refoulement*; it must additionally jeopardize the safety or security of the local population, which is itself likely to be offset by an international response to the situation'.[15]

Two questions are particularly relevant for the present discussion: whether Article 33 applies extra-territorially and whether 'indirect' or chain *refoulement* is prohibited under the Refugee Convention. As far as its geographical scope is concerned, the language of Article 33 makes it clear that return is prohibited to any territory in which a risk exists regardless of whether that territory is the country of origin or another State.[16] Also uncontroversial at this point is the application of the principle to refugees at the border. As noted by UNHCR in its 2007 Advisory Opinion, *non-refoulement* is applicable to 'any form of forcible removal, including deportation, expulsion, extradition, informal transfer or 'renditions', and non-admission at the border'.[17] This was also confirmed in other international instruments, namely Article II.3 of the OAU Convention, Resolution (67)14 of the Council of Ministers of the Council of Europe on asylum to persons in danger of persecution,[18] Article 3.1 of the 1967 UN Declaration on Territorial Asylum,[19] Article III of the Principles Concerning the Treatment of Refugees adopted by the Afro-Asian Legal Consultative Committee,[20] various Executive Committee conclusions,[21] and most recently in EU legislation.[22] There is also broad consensus in the literature on this matter.[23]

---

[15] Goodwin-Gill and McAdam, n 3 above, 242.

[16] Goodwin-Gill and McAdam, n 3 above, 250.

[17] n 5 above, para 7.

[18] Reprinted in (1967) *European Yearbook* 349, 351.

[19] n 14 above.

[20] Ibid.

[21] ExCom Conclusion No. 6 (1977) on *Non-Refoulement*, para (c); ExCom Conclusion No. 22 (1981) on Protection of Asylum Seekers in Situations of Large-Scale Influx II.A.2; ExCom General Conclusion on International Protection No. 81 (1997), para (h); ExCom Conclusion No. 82 (1997) on Safeguarding Asylum, para (d) (iii).

[22] Article 21 of Council Directive 2004/83/EC of 29 April 2004 on minimum standards for the qualification and status of third country nationals or stateless persons as refugees or as persons who otherwise need international protection and the content of the protection granted [2004] OJ L304/12 (hereafter, qualification Directive); Art 3.1 of Council Directive 2005/85/EC of 1 December 2005 on minimum standards on procedures in Member States for granting and withdrawing refugee status [2005] OJ L326/13 (hereafter, asylum procedures Directive).

[23] See Goodwin-Gill and McAdam, n 3 above, 207; J Henkel, 'Völkerrechtliche Aspekte des Konzepts des sicheren Drittstaates', in K Barwig and W Brill (ed) *Aktuelle asylrechtlichen Probleme der gerichtlichen Entscheidungspraxis in Deutschland, Österreich und der Schweiz* (Nomos, Berlin 1996) 141, 149–52; Hailbronner, n 13 above, 126; W Kälin, *Das Prinzip des Non-Refoulement, Das Verbot der Zurückweisung, Ausweisung und Auslieferung in den Verfolgerstaat im Völkerrecht und im Schweizerischen Landesrecht* (Peter Land Pub., Frankfurt [etc] 1982) 105–9; P Weis, 'Territorial Asylum' (1966) 6 *Indian J of Intl L* 173, 183–4; P Hyndman, 'Asylum and Non-Refoulement—Are these Obligations Owed to Refugees under International Law?' (1982) 57 *Philippine LJ*, 43, 51; N Coleman, 'Non-Refoulement Revised, Renewed Review of the Status of the Principle of *Non-Refoulement* as Customary International Law' (2003) 5 *EJML*, 23, 42–4. Cf Grahl-Madsen, *The Status*

Yet in 1989, the representative of the United States before the Executive Committee stated that the application of *non-refoulement* at the border was a practice followed by the United States but that it did not consider that by doing so, the United States was complying with any existing principle of international law.[24] The US Supreme Court's decision in *Sale v Haitian Centers Council, Inc et al.* endorsed this view.[25] The case concerned Haitian boat people whose vessels had been intercepted in international waters by the US Coast Guard and returned to Haiti without determining whether they qualified as refugees. While the majority of the bench essentially relied on domestic law considerations to legitimize this practice, the truncated analysis of the terms of the CSR led the Court to hold that Article 33 did not have extraterritorial effect, because the wording of paragraph 2 could not apply to a refugee outside the territory and that *refoulement* exclusively referred to exclusion proceedings.[26] The court justified its interpretation by declaring that even though this application of Article 33 may violate the purpose of the provision, 'a treaty cannot impose uncontemplated extraterritorial obligations on those who ratify it through no more than its general humanitarian intent'.[27] This decision was criticized by international scholars[28] and by the dissenting judge, Justice Blackmun, who underscored that this interpretation was incompatible with basic rules on interpretation enunciated in the 1969 Vienna Convention on the Law of Treaties.[29] Moreover, the decision ignored the fact that *non-refoulement*, like many human rights obligations, applies wherever a State exercises jurisdiction, including at the border, on the high seas or on the territory of another State.[30] The US has nonetheless continued its interdiction programs unabated since then,[31]

---

of Refugees in International Law (Sijthoff, Leyden 1972) Vol II 94 who argues that *non-refoulement* only applies to people on the territory of a State party.

[24] Statement by the US representative before ExCom UN Doc A/AC.96/SR.442, 15 November 1989, paras 80–1.

[25] *Sale v Haitian Centers Council Inc.* 113 S Ct 2549 (1993). An abstract of the case, and the full text of the dissenting opinion of Justice Blackmun and the UNHCR *Amicus Curiae* was published in (1994) 6 *IJRL* 69.

[26] 113 S Ct 2549 (1993) 2563.

[27] 113 S Ct 2549 (1993) 2565.

[28] See H Hongju Koh, 'Reflections on Refoulement and Haitian Centers Council' (1994) 35 *Harvard Intl LJ* 1, 17; J C Hathaway and J A Dent, *Refugee Rights: Reports on a Comparative Survey* (York Lane Press, Toronto 1995) 10–12.

[29] Dissenting opinion, n 25 above, 73; see also H Blackmun, 'The Supreme Court and the Law of Nations' (1994) 104 *Yale LJ* 39, 43–4.

[30] UNHCR Advisory Opinion, n 5 above, para 9; see also in this respect *Armed Activities on the Territory of the Congo* (Democratic Republic of the Congo v Uganda) (Judgment), 19 December 2005, ICJ Reports No. 116, para 216; *Legal Consequences of the Construction of the Wall in the Palestinian Occupied Territory* (Advisory Opinion), 9 July 2004, ICJ Reports No. 131, para 109, 111; Goodwin-Gill and McAdam, n 3 above, 248.

[31] S Legomsky, 'The USA and the Caribbean Interdiction Program' (2006) 18 *IJRL* 677, 682, 693.

while other Western countries, such as Australia, Greece, and Italy have also engaged in interception practices.[32]

From the late 1980s onwards, the erosion of the principle of *non-refoulement* in the practice of States became a preoccupying reality. In 1990, the High Commissioner openly talked of an 'asylum crisis' and explained that,

Measures of expulsion or *refoulement* are various and include expulsion orders against refugees, forcible return of refugees to countries of origin or unsafe third countries, electrified fences to prevent entry, non-admission of stowaway asylum-seekers and push-offs of boat arrivals or interdictions on the high seas. In one case, some 9,000 boat arrivals have been towed out to sea over the last year. In another part of the world, in one case some 9,700 persons, and in another case over 31,000 persons since 1987, were forcibly returned across the land borders.[33]

In 1998, the situation remained critical:

Instances of denial of access to protection, including through closure of borders, non-admission to territory or to asylum procedures, or through direct or indirect *refoulement* and other acts seriously endangering the life and physical security of refugee and asylum-seekers, continued to occur. A similar disturbing development has been the spread of restrictive policies from one country or region to other, often distant, countries or regions.[34]

And almost 20 years later, the UNHCR once again reported that,

Many industrialized States have 'externalized' their border controls, including through interception in the territorial waters or territory of third States with the latter's permission and/or involvement. In some regions, asylum policies became increasingly control-oriented and seen as a sub-set of migration policies.[35]

---

[32] UNHCR, *The State of the World's Refugees: Human Displacement in the New Millenium* (Oxford University Press, Oxford 2006) 40; European Commission, 'Reinforcing the Management of the EU's Southern Maritime Borders' COM (2006) 733 final, 30 November 2006, para 33; Parliamentary Assembly of the Council of Europe, 'Europe's "boat-people": Mixed Migration Flows by Sea into Southern Europe' 11 July 2008, paras 32–42; see R Weinzierl and U Lisson, *Border Management and Human Rights: A Study of EU Law and the Law of the Sea*, German Institute for Human Rights, December 2007, 22–3, <http://www.statewatch.org/news/2008/feb/eu-study-border-management.pdf>

[33] UNHCR Note on International Protection, UN Doc A/AC.96/750, 27 August 1990, para 14; see also UNHCR Note on International Protection, UN Doc A/AC.96/728, 2 August 1989, para 18; UNHCR Note on International Protection, UN Doc A/AC.96/777, 9 September 1991, para 28; UNHCR Note on International Protection, UN Doc A/AC.96/815, 31 August 1993, para 12; UNHCR Note on International Protection, UN Doc A/AC.96/898, 3 July 1998, paras 12–13; ExCom General Conclusion on International Protection No. 14 (1979), para (c); ExCom General Conclusion on International Protection No. 55 (1989), para (d); ExCom General Conclusion on International Protection No. 61 (1990), para (c); ExCom General Conclusion on International Protection No. 68 (1993), para (f); ExCom General Conclusion on International Protection No. 79 (1996), para (i); ExCom General Conclusion on International Protection No. 85 (1998), para (q).

[34] UNHCR Note on International Protection, UN Doc EC/9/SC/CRP.12, 4 June 1999, para 9; see also ExCom General Conclusion on International Protection No. 89 (2000).

[35] UNHCR Note on International Protection, UN Doc A/AC.96/103, 29 June 2007, para 30, see also para 10; see also ExCom General Conclusion on International Protection No. 102 (2005), para (j).

Thus, while *refoulement* in cases of mass influx has been most pervasive in first asylum countries, developed countries have been able to use various containment devices to evade their obligation under Article 33 CSR, and prevent refugees from reaching their borders.[36] States do not officially admit that containment policies,[37] which they claim are primarily intended to prevent irregular migration, may potentially lead to a violation or avoidance of Article 33 CSR, and that consequently, they would be failing to comply in good faith with their international obligations.[38] This is particularly true of measures restricting access to the territory and of safe third country practices, which may in effect prevent refugees from benefiting from *non-refoulement* when they reach the borders of the State of destination.[39] As noted by Goodwin-Gill and McAdam, 'the duty of good faith is breached if a combination of acts and omissions has the overall effect of rendering the fulfilment of treaty obligations obsolete, or defeats the object and purpose of a treaty'.[40]

These are some of the questions that were brought before the House of Lords in the so-called 'Prague airport case', where the reach of containment policies devised by the UK government was at issue. While recognizing that *non-refoulement* applied at the border, the House of Lords held that the United Kingdom Government had not violated the Refugee Convention when it posted immigration officers at Prague Airport to 'pre-clear' passengers boarding flights for the United Kingdom, denying boarding to certain passengers including those who stated that they were intending to claim asylum in the United Kingdom or those suspected to have such intention.[41] The House of Lords found that the respondents had not left their country of origin as required by Article 1.A(2) CSR and therefore could not be said to be at the actual border of the United Kingdom.[42] It further held that the 'appellants were at all times free to travel to another country, or to travel to this country otherwise than by air from Prague'.[43] The Lords thus emphasized that this situation differed clearly from the situation at hand in

---

[36] Hathaway and Dent, n 28 above, 7.

[37] For a brief outline of containment policies, see Chapter 1 Section 1.2.

[38] UN Doc A/AC.96/SR.442, para 51 (1989); J Fitzpatrick, 'Revitalizing the 1951 Refugee Convention' (1996) 9 *Harv Hum Rts J* 229, 237; Goodwin-Gill and McAdam, n 3 above, 221–3, who note, however, the recognition by Norway that preventing access to safety and to procedures might amount to *refoulement* contrary to international law; Cf K Hailbronner, 'The Right to Asylum and the Future of Asylum Procedures in the European Community' (1990) 2 *IJRL* 341, 354, who argues that restrictions on entry are not prohibited under Art 33 CSR.

[39] Hathaway and Dent, n 28 above 14–15; see also UNHCR, Note on International Protection, UN Doc A/AC.96/951, 13 September 2001, para 11; UNHCR, Note on International Protection, UN Doc A/AC.96/975, 2 July 2003, para 13; UNHCR, Note on International Protection, UN Doc A/AC/96/989, 7 July 2004, para 25.

[40] Goodwin-Gill and McAdam, n 3 above, 337.

[41] *R v Immigration Officer at Prague Airport and ors (Respondents) ex p European Roma Rights Centre and ors (Appellants)* [2004] UKHL 55, para 4.

[42] Ibid, para 26.

[43] Ibid, para 21.

the *Sale* case, where Haitians had already left their country of origin.[44] Lord Hope of Craighead explained:

Nobody now seeks to argue that the operations which were carried out at Prague Airport were in breach of article 33, even on the most generous interpretation that could be given to it. What the Convention does is assure refugees of the rights and freedoms set out in Chapters I to V when they are in countries that are not their own. It does not require the state to abstain from controlling the movement of people outside its borders who wish to travel to it in order to claim asylum. It lacks any provisions designed to meet the additional burdens which would follow if a prohibition to that effect had been agreed to. The conclusion must be that steps which are taken to control the movements of such people who have not yet reached the state's frontier are not incompatible with the acceptance of the obligations which arise when refugees have arrived in its territory. To argue that such steps are incompatible with the principle of good faith as they defeat the object and purpose of the treaty is to argue for the enlargement of the obligations which are to be found in the Convention.[45]

While one might regret that measures limiting access to a States' territory, when implemented in the country of origin of an asylum seeker, are not covered by the terms of the Refugee Convention, it is difficult to ignore the clear language of Article 1A.(2) CSR. In this respect, this was probably not the best test case for refugee rights advocates. In addition, one of the key considerations in the judgment was that there was clearly no threat to the appellants' lives or that they were otherwise at risk of torture or inhuman degrading or cruel treatment and that in other words, their rights not to be refouled under international human rights law were not at issue in this instance.[46] Most significantly, the House of Lords was able to rely on international standards on non-discrimination and related UK legislation to condemn the government's policies and find that it had violated the appellants' rights.[47]

Whether Article 33 CSR prohibits both direct and indirect *refoulement* is on the other hand uncontroversial.[48] This may be directly deduced from the language of Article 33, which specifies that *refoulement* includes return *in any manner whatsoever*[49] to a territory where the life or liberty of the refugee is endangered.[50]

---

[44] Ibid.

[45] Ibid, para 64.

[46] Ibid, para 21; on the relevant provisions of the European Convention on Human Rights, see below, Section 5.1.2.1.

[47] Ibid, para 104.

[48] See N Albuquerque Abell, 'The Compatibility of Readmission Agreements with the 1951 Convention relating to the Status of Refugees' (1999) 11 *IJRL* 60, 71; UNHCR Advisory Opinion, n 5 above, 3; S Legomsky, 'Secondary Refugee Movement and the Return of Asylum Seekers to Third Countries: The Meaning of Effective Protection' (2003) *IJRL* 567, 614; UNHCR, 'Convention plus Issues Paper on Addressing Irregular Secondary Movements of Refugees and Asylum-Seekers', FORUM/CG/SM/03, 11 March 2004 (hereafter, UNHCR Issues Paper), para 22.

[49] Emphasis added.

[50] *Secretary of State for the Home Department v Razaq Mohd Saeid Abdu Abdel* [1992] Imm AR 152 (Trib); *R v Secretary of State for the Home Department ex p Hamid Aitsegeur* [1999] INLR 176 (QBD).

The probability of indirect *refoulement* is obviously higher in the case of removal to a country which is not a party to the Refugee Convention. British courts have held that the Secretary of State needs to ascertain whether the refugee will be admitted and protected in the country, without ruling out return to non-signatory States.[51] Conversely, the mere fact that the third country is a party to the Refugee Convention does not guarantee that refugees will receive effective protection in that State. According to Crawford and Hyndman,

[...] a State may not rely on the obligation of another State party to the Convention, even where there are good grounds for saying that the latter State is indeed under a particular obligation with respect to the refugee, if that reliance is likely to result in a violation of article 33.[52]

This was also lucidly expressed by the House of Lords in *Bugdaycay*:[53]

Suppose it is well known that country A although a signatory to the convention, regularly sends back to its totalitarian and oppressive neighbour country B those opponents of the regime in country B who are apprehended in country A following their escape across the border. Against that background, if a person arriving in the UK from country A sought asylum as a refugee from country B assuming he could establish his well-founded fear of persecution there, it would it seems to me, be as much a breach of art.33 of the convention to return him to country A as to country B.

While those principles are relatively clear and widely accepted, the implementation by States of their obligations and the procedures adopted to determine refugee status raise a number of difficult challenges.

5.1.1.2 *States' obligation to implement the Refugee Convention*

In order to grant the protection provided by the Refugee Convention, States must determine whether the asylum seeker is a refugee according to the definition given in Article 1A.(2) CSR. The Convention does not lay down any specific procedure or basic safeguards for the refugee status determination process, apart from the general obligation to cooperate with UNHCR.[54] While, as UNHCR noted, 'it is generally recognized that fair and efficient procedures are an essential element in

---

[51] *Secretary of State for the Home Department v Razaq Mohd Saeid Abdu Abdel* [1992] Imm AR 152 (Trib). This practice is also common in Scandinavian countries, see eg Communication No. 88/1997 of the Committee Against Torture *Avedes Hamayak Korban v Sweden* UN Doc CAT/C/21/D/88/1997, published in (1999) 11 *IJRL* 210 discussed below in Section 5.1.2.2.

[52] J Crawford and P Hyndman, 'Three Heresies in the Application of the Refugee Convention', (1989) 2 *IJRL* 155, 171.

[53] *Bugdaycay and ors v Secretary of State for the Home Department* [1987] All ER 1 940 (HL), 952; see also *Canadian Council for Refugees, Canadian Council of Churches, Amnesty International and John Doe v R* 2007 FC 1262, para 112.

[54] Article 35 CSR; UNHCR Sub-Committee of the Whole on International Protection, Note on Determination of Refugee Status under International Instruments submitted by the High Commissioner, UN Doc EC/SCP/5, 24 August 1977, para 11; Goodwin-Gill and McAdam, n 3 above, 450.

the full and inclusive application of the 1951 Convention outside the context of mass influx situations',[55] the fact remains that the substantive and procedural rules governing refugee status determination vary greatly among States. Moreover, there is no obligation for States to accept a decision granting refugee status issued in another State, although some legal consequences of such recognition are generally acknowledged in other States, such as the recognition of travel documents.[56] Conversely, the fact that a claim to refugee status recognition has been rejected by a State may not in principle influence adjudication in another State party.[57]

This latitude accorded to States constituted a regression compared to the system established under the International Refugee Organization, where international officers were in charge of determining eligibility for international protection, with a possibility of appeal before a Review Board.[58] Hathaway summarized the situation in the following manner:

[International Refugee Law] is effectively controlled by the authorities of the various participating national governments. This control is achieved by a combination of minimal international oversight of determination procedures, the establishment of a refugee definition that is susceptible to interpretation in accordance with divergent national interests, the explicit authorization to states to turn away persons in fear of persecution insofar as their protection creates a risk for the receiving state, and the imposition of a minimalist duty to protect that requires no commitment to the provision of enduring asylum.[59]

In accordance with the principle of good faith in the implementation of treaties, States are nevertheless under an obligation to establish procedures which will conform to the purpose of the Convention, that is, 'the proper identification of those who are refugees within the meaning of those instruments'.[60] In spite of the

[55] UNHCR Advisory Opinion, n 5 above, fn 14.

[56] Article 28 and Annex 7 CSR. See also ExCom Conclusion No. 13 (1978) and ExCom Conclusion No. 49 (1987) on Travel Documents for Refugees; see also UNHCR, Note on the extraterritorial effect of the determination of refugee status under the 1951 Convention and the 1967 Protocol Relating to the Status of Refugees, UN Doc EC/SCP/9, 21 August 1978.

[57] F Schnyder, 'Les aspects juridiques actuels du problème des réfugiés' (1965) 114 *RdC* 335, 369. In accordance with the Dublin Regulation, Member States and other States taking part in the system mutually recognize negative decisions on asylum, see Chapter 3, Section 3.2.1.

[58] Para 2 of the General Principles under Annex I of the Constitution of the International Refugee Organization of 15 December 1946 (1948) 18 UNTS 3 No. 283; see also Constitution of Review Board for Eligibility Appeals IRO GC/65 26 March 1949, reprinted in L Holborn, *The International Refugee Organization, A Specialized Agency of the United Nations, Its History and Work, 1946–1952* (Oxford University Press, Oxford 1956) 213, 204–5 and 108–10; P Weis, 'Legal Aspects of the Convention of 28 July 1951 relating to the Status of Refugees' (1953) 30 *BYIL* 478, 479.

[59] J C Hathaway, 'A Reconsideration of the Underlying Premise of Refugee Law', (1990) 31 *Harvard International LJ* 129, 174; see also C Beyani, 'The Role of Human Rights Bodies in Protecting Refugees', in A Bayefsky (ed), *Human Rights and Refugees, Internally Displaced Persons and Migrant Workers: Essays in Memory of Joan Fitzpatrick and Arthur Helton* (Nijhoff, Leiden [etc.] 2006) 269, 270–1.

[60] R Plender, 'The Present State of Research Carried out by the English-speaking Section of the Centre for Studies and Research', in *Centre for Studies & Research in International Law & International Relations 1989: The Right of Asylum* (Kluwer, Dordrecht 1989) 63, 83; see also R Marx, 'Non-Refoulement, Access to Procedures, and Responsibility for Determining Refugee Claims' (1995) 7 *IJRL* 383, 401.

existence of procedural safeguards under domestic and international law, including the guidelines issued in the *UNHCR Handbook on Procedures and Criteria for Determining Refugee Status*,[61] it is undeniable that States possess a wide margin of discretion.[62]

Given this state of affairs, some have held that the Refugee Convention requires that each State party examine in each case whether an asylum seeker fulfils the conditions set out in Article 1 CSR and whether he or she may be returned or expelled to his/her country of origin. This opinion was notably expressed in 1991 by the Dutch *Raad van State*[63] in its advice prior to the ratification of the Schengen agreements:[64]

A State cannot be bound by the decision regarding refugee status made by another State party and it would be unlawful to delegate to another State the task of determining whether an individual is a refugee according to the definition of article 1 CSR. The only authority to which such competence may be transferred is an international organization such as the UNHCR.[65]

The *Raad van State* concluded that the system laid down in the Schengen agreements had no basis in the Refugee Convention and led to its violation insofar as States would evade their fundamental obligations under the Refugee Convention. Thus, the transfer of an asylum seeker could only take place if the authorities of the first State established that this would not lead to *refoulement*, on the basis of the criteria and interpretation accepted under their own legal system.

While undeniably protection-friendly, the position of the *Raad van State* must be qualified. It is true that the transfer of an asylum seeker does not relieve a State from its obligations under international refugee law and that the absence of adequate monitoring mechanisms at the international level poses serious problems in a context where responsibility for examining an asylum claim is routinely transferred to a third State. Nevertheless, State practice shows that States' obligations towards refugees have not been construed as autonomous obligations and that States have instead sought to address refugee protection concerns through collective endeavours and international cooperation, as is in fact emphasized in the Preamble of the CSR.[66] Importantly, such interpretation of States' obligations was

---

[61] (Reprint 1992) UN Doc HCR/1P/4/Eng/Rev.2.

[62] R Plender, *International Migration Law* (Nijhoff, Dordrecht [etc] 2nd edn 1988); see also UNHCR Note on Determination of Refugee Status under International Instruments, n 54 above, paras 13 and 15–19 describing the basic requirements that any refugee status determination procedure should fulfil; Fitzpatrick, 'Revitalizing the 1951 Refugee Convention', n 38 above, 243.

[63] Opinion of the Dutch *Raad van State* ('Council of State') of 8 April 1991 No. WO2.91.0013, 8 (on file with the author); D O'Keeffe, 'The Schengen Convention: A Suitable Model for European Integration?' (1991) 11 *YEL* 185, 200.

[64] The Dublin Convention replaced chapter VII of the Schengen Implementing Convention in September 1997. The systems established under chapter VII and the Dublin Convention are *mutatis mutandis*, similar, see Chapter 1, Section 1.3.2 and 1.3.3, see also Chapter 3.

[65] Translated by the author.

[66] See Preamble of the Refugee Convention Recital 4.

shared before safe third country practices became widespread and containment policies the norm. For instance, during the early stages of the discussions within the Council of Europe regarding the determination of the responsible State, at no point did any of the States present indicate that there was an 'autonomous' obligation of States to implement the CSR.[67] Most importantly, UNHCR has never officially and categorically condemned the conclusion of arrangements allocating responsibility to address secondary movements, as is illustrated by the adoption of Executive Committee Conclusions No. 15 and No. 58.[68] UNHCR has, on the other hand, insisted on the importance that each State verify that the third State to which the asylum seeker is sent will provide effective protection to that asylum seeker.[69] Furthermore, recent UNHCR initiatives, especially 'Convention Plus', contemplated the possibility of special agreements being concluded to better regulate irregular secondary movements on the basis of a collective approach to States' obligations and a common understanding of the concept of effective protection.[70]

While the *Raad van State* adopted an overly strict understanding of States' obligations, it remains that divergences in the interpretation of the Refugee Convention have led to serious problems of compliance. A brief analysis of UK jurisprudence provides a telling example of these difficulties. In the 1998 *Kerrouche* case, the High Court of England noted that,

Although it is desirable that the approach to the interpretation of the Convention and Protocol should be the same in all countries which are signatories, this is not a realistic expectation in the absence of some supranational court which is capable of giving authoritative interpretations to the provisions of the Convention and Protocol which are binding on the signatory countries. Absent such a body, the fact that a particular country adopts an approach to the Convention which involves a difference in emphasis in the interpretation of one or more provisions from that which would be adopted under English law does not

---

[67] See Chapter 1, Section 1.2.4.

[68] ExCom Conclusion No. 15 on Refugees Without an Asylum Country (1979), ExCom Conclusion No. 58 on the problem of refugees and asylum-seekers who move in an irregular manner from a country in which they had already found protection (1989). See Chapter 1, Section 1.2.3 and Chapter 2, Section 2.1.2.

[69] UNHCR Note on International Protection, UN Doc A/AC.96/975, 2 July 2003, para 12; UNHCR Issues Paper, n 48 above, para 23; UNHCR, 'Summary Conclusions on the Concept of Effective Protection in the Context of Secondary Movements of Refugees and Asylum Seekers', Expert Roundtable, Lisbon, 9–10 December 2002 (hereafter, Lisbon Conclusions), para 12; UNHCR, 'Asylum applications and the entry into force of the Schengen implementation agreement: some observations of UNHCR', March 1995; UNHCR, 'The concept of "Protection elsewhere": a comment with reference to the above note submitted by the United Kingdom' (1995) 7 *IJRL* 123; UNHCR, Background Note on the Safe country concept and refugee status submitted by the High Commissioner to the Sub-Committee of the Whole on International Protection, UN Doc EC/SCP/68, 3 July 1991, para 12; see also ExCom General Conclusion on International Protection No. 71 (1993) para (k); ExCom General Conclusion on International Protection No. 85 (1998) para (p); ExCom General Conclusion on International Protection No. 90 (2001) para (k); ExCom General Conclusion on International Protection No. 93 (2002) para (c); Goodwin-Gill and McAdam, n 3 above, 391; E Feller, 'Asylum, Migration and Refugee Protection: Realities, Myths and the Promise of Things to Come' (2006) 18 *IJRL* 509, 528–9.

[70] A Betts and J-F Durieux, 'Convention Plus as a Norm-Setting Exercise' (2007) 20 *JRS* 509.

necessarily involve that country being regarded as one which does not adhere to the principles of the Convention and Protocol when, as in the case of France, it contends that it does so.[71]

In *Iyadurai*, Lord Woolf set out a test for determining whether the return of an asylum seeker to a third country would entail a violation of the CSR:

It is only if the meaning placed on the convention by the other municipal courts is clearly inconsistent with its international meaning that the courts in this country are entitled to conclude that the approach of the other municipal court involves a contravention of the convention. It is when the approach of the other municipal courts departs from the convention to this extent that any difference in language between that which is adopted in the other country and that which would be adopted in this country becomes significant. [72]

On this basis, the Queen's Bench Division allowed the application for judicial review of an Algerian citizen who argued that the interpretation of the CSR by French authorities was outside the range of permissible interpretation as reflected by the fact that there was a dramatic difference in the percentages of recognition of Algerians refugees between France and the United Kingdom.[73]

This and two other cases were heard by the Court of Appeal as an 'academic appeal' since the Secretary of State eventually considered substantively the three claims.[74] In its judgment, the Court of Appeal drew a distinction between the interpretation of the Refugee Convention and its application. The latter, which is a matter of fact, included differences in refugee status determination procedures and other practical obstacles, and were to be assessed on grounds of reasonableness.[75] The judgment thus noted that while State parties enjoy a 'margin of discretion' in the application of the Convention, they must interpret it in accordance with its 'true interpretation', most importantly Article 1A.(2) CSR, which is a matter of law. The Court concluded that the interpretation adopted by German and French courts, which excluded from the scope of Article 1A.(2) CSR the case of a State's failure to protect its citizens,[76] was unlawful and that the Secretary of State was not entitled to issue the certificates authorizing the removals of the asylum seekers to these countries.[77]

---

[71] *R v Special Adjudicator ex p Kerrouche* [1998] INLR 88, 92 (QB).

[72] *Thayaparan Iyadurai v Secretary of State for the Home Department* [1998] Imm AR 470 (CA) 476.

[73] *R v Secretary of State for the Home Department ex p Hamid Aitsegeur* [1999] INLR 176 (QBD).

[74] *R v Secretary of State for the Home Department ex p Lul Omar Adan, Sittampalan Subaskaran and Hamid Aitsegeur* [1999] INLR 362 (CA), also published in (1999) 11 *IJRL* 702.

[75] Ibid, 381.

[76] On the French and German approaches on the 'agent of persecution', see Goodwin-Gill and McAdam, n 3 above, 41, note 138; C Phuong, 'Persecution by Non-State Agents: Comparative Judicial Interpretations of the 1951 Refugee Convention' (2003) 4 *EJML* 521.

[77] *R v Secretary of State for the Home Department ex p Lul Omar Adan, Sittampalan Subaskaran and Hamid Aitsegeur*, n 74 above, 385 and 389.

The case was then brought before the House of Lords.[78] Lord Slynn of Hadley confirmed that the Secretary of State might not send back an asylum seeker to a State whose authorities interpret the Convention in a manner which would lead to the return of the individual to a country where he/she has a well-founded fear of persecution and when the Secretary of State considers that he/she should be protected under the Refugee Convention.[79] However, the highest court explicitly rejected the *Iyadurai* test, that is, the possibility that the Secretary of State could base its decisions on a 'list of permissible or legitimate or possible or reasonable meanings and accept that any one of those when applied would be in compliance with the Convention'.[80] Lord Steyn further explained that in accordance with basic rules on treaty interpretation, which had been followed most notably by the European Court of Justice and the European Court of Human Rights, it was necessary to look at the autonomous meaning of the treaty provision.[81] He held that,

In principle, therefore there can only be one true interpretation of a treaty. […] In practice, it is left to national courts faced with a material disagreement on an issue of interpretation, to resolve it. But in doing so it must search, untrammelled by notions of its national legal culture, for the true autonomous and international meaning of the treaty. And there can only be one true meaning.[82]

The single and true meaning of treaty obligations may actually be difficult to ascertain. In the present case, the emphasis placed on the international meaning of a treaty, unhindered by domestic legal concepts is perhaps more significant, since the existence of a right to political asylum under French and German law had, at the time, clearly influenced the interpretation of Article 1 CSR in these countries.[83] The *Adan* Judgment is also important in that it draws attention to the importance of international supervision when denial of refugee status in one country bars renewed application in another State. Thus, what may be inferred from these findings is that the absence of an adequate international supervisory framework obliges States to determine the manner in which the Refugee Convention is being interpreted in another State, and whether the interpretation of the refugee definition in another legal system would actually lead to a violation of the principle of *non-refoulement*.[84]

---

[78] *R v Secretary of State for the Home Department ex p Adan and R v Secretary of State for the Home Department ex p Aitseguer* [2000] 1 All ER 593 (HL).

[79] Ibid, 597.

[80] Ibid, 598.

[81] Ibid, 603–4.

[82] Ibid, 605.

[83] See Phuong, n 76 above; C Phuong, 'Persecution by Third Parties and European Harmonization of Asylum Policies' (2001) 16 *Georgetown Immigration LJ*, 81. Note that this interpretation has now been repealed since the adoption of the qualification Directive, which affirms at Art 6 that persecution may be carried out by non-State actors.

[84] See in this respect T Endicott, 'International Meaning: Comity in Fundamental Rights Adjudication' (2001) 13 *IJRL* 280, 291–2.

However, before the judgment was even delivered, the British government presented an amendment which was adopted by Parliament, creating an irrebuttable presumption that European States, as well as Canada and the United States, were to be regarded as safe.[85] As a result the House of Lords subsequently qualified some of its pronouncements holding that,

[T]he humane objective of the convention is to establish an orderly and internationally-agreed regime for handling asylum applications and that objective is liable to be defeated if anything other than significant differences between the law and practice of different countries are allowed to prevent the return of an applicant to the member state in which asylum was, or could have been, first claimed.[86]

The House of Lords had no option but to conclude that in one of the cases before it, the challenge based on differences of interpretation of the Refugee Convention was effectively 'blocked' because the certificate of the Secretary of State had been issued after the entry into force of the 1999 Act. However, challenges based on the Human Rights Act could still be entertained. Additional restrictions were adopted to limit challenges against safe third country decisions in 2004, which are described in Chapter 2.[87]

5.1.2 *Non-refoulement* under international human rights law

The *non-refoulement* principle has also developed in the broader realm of international human rights law, where it constitutes an application of a preventive

---

[85] Immigration and Asylum Act 1999, ss 11, 12; Asylum (Designated Safe Third Countries) Order 2000 No. 2245.

[86] *R v Secretary of State for the Home Department ex p Thangasara and R v Secretary of State for the Home Department ex p Yogathas* [2002] UKHL 36, para 9, para 11; see also *Canadian Council for Refugees, Canadian Council of Churches, Amnesty International and John Doe v R* 2007 FC 1262, para 137.

[87] s 33 Schedule 3 Asylum and Immigration (Treatment of Claimants, etc.) Act 2004 (c. 19), see Chapter 2, Section 2.1.2.3. The 2004 Act introduces further restrictions on appeals against decisions based on safe third country provisions. At this time, four categories of safe third countries exist in UK law: Member States of the EU and Norway and Iceland for which no appeal is available in case of removal; other States for which removal is found to be in compliance with the Refugee Convention and the ECHR and for which there is no automatic exclusion of appeal rights but a presumption that appeals are clearly unfounded; States which are certified to be safe for Refugee Convention purposes for which there is no presumption that human rights claims are unfounded but which may be certified as such; and finally countries found to be safe for removal provided there is no danger of *refoulement* or persecution and for which certification must be granted on an individual basis by the Secretary of State. Challenges were brought against removals to Greece pursuant to the Human Rights Act and a High Court Judge found that para 3(2) of Part 2 of Schedule 3 to the 2004 Act violated Art 3 ECHR, *Nasseri v Secretary of State for the Home Department* [2007] EWHC 1548, para 40. This judgment was overturned by the Court of Appeal on 14 May 2008, which found that there is no general incompatibility between Art 3(2)(b) and Art 3 ECHR given the Secretary of State's monitoring of States on the list to ensure individual compliance, see *Secretary of State for the Home Department v Nasseri* [2008] EWCA Civ 464, para 41.

approach to the protection of human rights.[88] One of the major differences with the Refugee Convention is that the implementation and application of relevant human rights instruments, primarily, the 1950 European Convention for the Protection of Human Rights and Fundamental Freedoms,[89] the 1966 International Covenant on Civil and Political Rights and the 1984 Convention Against Torture and Other Cruel, Inhuman or Degrading Treatment,[90] are monitored by judicial, in the case of the former convention, or quasi-judicial bodies, in the case of the last two treaties. Under these instruments, States are bound not to transfer any individual to another country if this would result in exposing that individual to serious human rights violations including arbitrary deprivation of life, torture, or other cruel, inhuman or degrading treatment for the ICCPR and ECHR, and torture for the CAT.[91] Provided such risk of ill-treatment is established, there are no acceptable grounds for exclusion, such as those provided in paragraph 2 of Article 33 and in Article 1F CSR.[92] Article 7 ICCPR has a similar scope as Article 3 ECHR, and the Human Rights Committee held in General Comment No. 20 that States were not allowed to extradite, expel, or return in any other way an individual to a country where he would face torture, or cruel, inhuman or degrading treatment or punishment.[93] However, there have been relatively few relevant individual cases before the Human Rights Committee,[94] and the present examination will

---

[88] W Suntinger, 'The Principle of Non-Refoulement: Looking Rather to Geneva than to Strasbourg?' (1995) 49 *Austrian J Publ and Intl L* 203, 224; see also UNHCR Advisory Opinion, n 5 above, 9; V Chetail, 'Le droit des réfugiés à l'épreuve des droit de l'homme: Bilan de la Cour européenne des droits de l'homme sur l'interdiction du renvoi des étrangers menacés de torture et de traitements inhumains ou dégradants' [2004] *RBDI*, 155, 168–9.

[89] ETS No. 005 (hereafter, ECHR).

[90] International Covenant on Civil and Political Rights (adopted 16 December 1966, entered into force 23 March 1976) 999 UNTS 171 (hereafter, ICCPR); Convention Against Torture and Other Cruel, Inhuman or Degrading Treatment or Punishment (adopted 10 December 1984, entered into forced 26 June 1987) 1465 UNTS 85 (hereafter, CAT).

[91] Goodwin-Gill and McAdam, n 3 above, 302, 308, 310–11, 316. On the definition of torture under CAT, see V Chetail, 'Le Comité des Nations Unies contre la torture et l'éloignement des étrangers: dix ans de jurisprudence (1994–2004)' [2006] *Revue suisse de droit international et de droit européen* 63, 76–7

[92] Article II.3 of the 1969 OAU Convention, and Art 22.8 of the 1969 American Convention on Human Rights (22 November 1969) (1970) 9 *ILM* 99, do not provide for exceptions either; see also UNHCR Advisory Opinion, n 5 above, 10–11.

[93] Human Rights Committee General Comment No. 31 on the Nature of the General Obligations Imposed on State Parties to the Covenant, UN Doc CCPR/C/21/Rev.1/Add.13, 26 May 2004, para 12 which states that any form of removal of an individual that would result in him being subject to any 'irreparable harm' such as that contemplated under Arts 6 and 7 ICCPR is prohibited; see Human Rights Committee General Comment No. 20/44 replacing General Comment No. 7 concerning prohibition of torture and cruel treatment or punishment, 10 April 1992, UN Doc HR1/HEN/1/Rev., 28 July 1994, para 9; see also Human Rights Committee General Comment No. 15 on the position of aliens under the Covenant, UN Doc CCPR/C/21/Rev.1, 19 May 1989, para 5, both reprinted in the Compilation of General Comments and General Recommendations Adopted by Human Rights Treaty Bodies UN Doc HRI/GEN/1/Rev.5, 26 April 2001, 127 and 139; UNHCR Advisory Opinion, n 5 above, 9; Goodwin-Gill and McAdam, n 3 above, 305–10.

[94] M Nowak, *CCPR Commentary* (2nd edn N P Engel, Kehl 2005) 137; S Joseph, J Schultz, and M Castan, *The ICCPR: Cases, Materials and Commentary* (2nd edn Oxford University Press,

therefore be limited to the interpretation of Article 3 adopted by the organs of the European Convention for the Protection of Human Rights and Fundamental Freedoms and to the work of the Committee Against Torture.[95]

5.1.2.1 Non-refoulement *under the European Convention on Human Rights*

The principle of *non-refoulement* is not explicitly stipulated under the ECHR. It is the interpretation of conventional obligations by its competent organs, which has led to its emergence.[96] While non-return could also arise from the violation of other Convention obligations,[97] the principle has thus far been applied for the most part with respect to Article 3, which provides that 'no one shall be subjected to torture or to inhuman or degrading treatment or punishment'. No exception or qualification is provided even in time of war or public emergency.[98] Thus, although there is no clause on the granting of asylum in the Convention, Article 3 may be called on to prevent the *refoulement*, expulsion, or extradition of an alien by a State

Oxford 2004) 231, who note that currently most cases go before the Committee Against Torture. Relevant case-law includes: *Kindler v Canada*, Communication No. 470/1991, UN Doc CCPR/C/48/D/470/1991; *Ng v Canada*, Communication No. 469/1991, UN Doc CCPR/C/49/D/469/1991; *Cox v Canada*, Communication No. 539/1993, UN Doc CCPR/C/52/D/539/1993; *ARJ v Australia*, Communication No. 692/1996, UN Doc CCPR/C/60/D/692/1996, 11 August 1997; *C v Australia*, Communication No. 900/1999, UN Doc CCPR/C/76/D/900/1999, 13 November 2002; *Ahani v Canada*, Communication No. 1051/2002, UN Doc CCPR/C/80/D/1051/2002, 29 March 2004.

[95] Note that the analysis of Art 8 ECHR is also relevant to the issue of refugees' rights in relation to safe third country policies, see Chapter 3, Section 3.3.1 and 3.3.5.

[96] Chetail, 'Le droit des réfugiés', n 88 above, 160–4.

[97] Goodwin-Gill and McAdam, n 3 above, 311; see *Mamatkulov and Askarov v Turkey*, Appl. Nos. 46827/99 and 46951/99, Judgment of 4 February 2005, (2005) 41 EHRR 494, 537–9 with respect to Art 6 ECHR; *R v Secretary of State for the Home Department ex p Razgar* [2004] UKHL 27 where at para 72, the House of Lords held that 'in principle article 8 could exceptionally be engaged by the foreseeable consequences for health of removal from the United Kingdom pursuant to an immigration decision, even if they do not amount to a violation of article 3' but that 'in order to bring himself with such an exceptional engagement of article 8 the applicant has to establish a very grave state of affairs, amounting to a flagrant or fundamental breach of the article, which in effect constitutes a complete denial of his rights'; *R v Special Adjudicator ex p Ullah* [2004] UKHL 26, para 21, 35, 39–49, 52, 53, 62, 67; *EM (Lebanon) v Secretary of State for the Home Department* [2008] UKHL 64 where the House of Lords found that the return of the applicant to Lebanon would violate Art 8 ECHR because due her status as a divorcee, she would not be able to live with her adolescent child; see also Chetail, 'Le droit des réfugiés', n 88 above, 166, 170, 181–3, who notes that the ECHR has extended this construction to Art 2 and Art 1 of Protocol No. 6 to the Convention for the Protection of Human Rights and Fundamental Freedoms concerning the Abolition of the Death Penalty of 28 April 1983, ETS No. 114, as well as, albeit more hesitantly, to Arts 6, 5, and 9 ECHR.

[98] See Art 15.2 ECHR, *Soering v United Kingdom*, Appl. No. 14038/88, Judgment of 7 July 1989, Series A no. 161, para 88; *Vilvarajah and ors v United Kingdom*, Appl. Nos. 13163/87, 13164/87, 13165/87, 13447/87, 13448/87 Judgment of 30 October 1991 Series A no. 215, para 108; *Chahal v United Kingdom*, Appl. No. 22414/93, Judgment of 25 October 1996, ECHR 1996-V 97, paras 79–80; *Ahmed v Austria*, Appl. No. 25964/94, Judgment of 17 December 1996 ECHR 1996-VI 26, para 40. This jurisprudence has been consistently reaffirmed by the European Court of Human Rights (ECtHR) in spite of the arguments of certain State parties that such a principle had to be reassessed in light of growing security concerns after the events of 11 September 2001: see in this respect, *Saadi v Italy*, Appl. No. 37201/06, ECHR 28 February 2008, para 127, 137–8.

party to a State where he or she may fear torture or inhuman and degrading treatment,[99] suggesting thereby a right to de facto asylum.[100] This interpretation was adopted early on by the Commission, which in 1961, declared that,

> [...] the Contracting States have [...] accepted to restrict the free exercise of their powers under general international law, including the power to control the entry and exit of aliens, to the extent and within the limits of the obligations which they have assumed under the Convention.[101]

This construction was further supported by the Parliamentary Assembly in Recommendation 434 (1965) on the granting of the right of asylum to European Refugees and in Recommendation 817 of 1977.[102]

A State may be held responsible for a violation of Article 3 regardless of the fact that the State where the alien fears to be returned, deported, or extradited is a party to the ECHR.[103] The fact that the latter State is a party to the ECHR will be given due consideration and create a presumption that treatment contrary to Article 3

---

[99] *Soering v United Kingdom*, n 98 above, para 87–8, 90–1; *Cruz Varas v Sweden*, Judgment of 20 March 1991 Series A, No. 201, (1992) 14 EHRR 1, para 70; *Chahal v United Kingdom*, n 98 above, para 74; *Saadi v Italy*, n 98 above, para 125, see also paras 134–6, recalling the ECtHR settled case-law on the definition of ill-treatment, torture and inhuman or degrading treatment; see also Chetail, 'Le droit des réfugiés', n 88 above,175.

[100] See T Einarsen, 'The European Convention on Human Rights and the Notion of an Implied Right to De Facto Asylum' (1990) 2 *IJRL* 361, 382–5; T Clark, 'Human Rights and Expulsion: Giving Content to the Concept of Asylum' (1992) *IJRL* 189; F Ermacora, 'Problems about the Application of the European Convention on Human Rights in Asylum Cases', in R Lawson and M de Blois (eds), *The Dynamics of the Protection of Human Rights in Europe: Essays in Honour of H G Schermers* (Nijhoff, Dordrecht [etc.] Vol III 1994) 155, 163; H Labayle, 'L'éloignement des étrangers devant la Cour européenne des droits de l'homme' [1997] *Revue française de droit administratif* 977; R Plender and N Mole, 'Beyond the Geneva Convention: Constructing a *De Facto* Right of Asylum from International Rights Instruments', in F Nicholson and P Twomey (eds), *Refugee Rights and Realities: Evolving International Concepts and Regimes* (Cambridge University Press, Cambridge 1999) 81; F Sudre, 'Le renouveau jurisprudendiel de la protection des étrangers par l'Article 3 de la Convention européenne des droits de l'homme', in H Fulchiron (ed), *Les étrangers et la Convention européenne de sauvegarde des droits de l'homme et des libertés fondamentales*, (LGDJ, Paris 1999) 61; S Karagiannis, 'Expulsion des étrangers et mauvais traitements imputables à l'Etat de destination ou à des particuliers' [1999] *Revue trimestrielle des droits de l'homme* 33; N Mole, *Asylum and the European Convention on Human Rights* (Council of Europe, Strasbourg 2002). Note that Chetail, 'Le droit des réfugiés', n 88 above, 169, 203 adds that State parties may also send back an individual to another country where there is no risk of violation of Art 3 ECHR.

[101] *X v Belgium*, Appl. No. 984/61, Decision of 29 May 1961, 6 C.D. 39, 40; *S v Federal Republic of Germany*, Appl. No. 1465/62, 65–6; *Nazin Al-Kuzbari v Federal Republic of Germany*, Appl. No. 1802/63, Decision of 26 March 1963, 36; *X v Austria and Yugoslavia*, Appl. No. 2143/64, Decision of 30 June 1964, (1964) 7 Yearbook 314, 328; see also *X v Sweden*, Appl. No. 434/58, Opinion of 30 June 1959, (1958–1959) Yearbook II 354, 372. Note that since 1 November 1998, the Commission no longer exists in accordance with Art 19 of Protocol No. 11 to the European Convention on Human Rights and Fundamental Freedoms Restructuring the Control Machinery Established Thereby, ETS No. 55.

[102] Adopted on 1 October 1965 reprinted in CAHAR, *Selected Texts Concerning Territorial Asylum and Refugees Adopted within the Council of Europe*, Vol II CAHAR (86) 6 March 1998, 3.

[103] See *T.I. v United Kingdom*, Appl. No. 43844/98, 7 March 2000, ECHR 2000-III. P van Dijk and G J H van Hoof, *Theory and Practice of the European Convention on Human Rights* (3rd edn Kluwer, The Hague [etc] 1998) 325.

would not occur in that State, yet that presumption may be reversed, albeit not easily.[104] The Court's approach has been viewed by some commentators as undermining the non-derogatory nature of Article 3 in cases of removal to a State party.[105] This contention is not completely accurate, given that, rather than affecting the very nature of Article 3, the distinction drawn by the Court essentially leads to a reversal of the burden of proof. Nonetheless, the considerably enlarged membership of the Council of Europe raises some legitimate concerns as to whether ratification of the ECHR is sufficient proof that treatment contrary to Article 3 ECHR is unlikely and that an individual will have effective access to the organs of the ECHR.

5.1.2.1.1 Applicable standard

As mentioned earlier, the scope *ratione personae* of Article 3 is broader than that of Article 33 CSR.[106] It applies to any individual who fears ill-treatment, and has been instrumental in the development of complementary forms of protection[107] in several European countries and more recently at the EU level.[108] However, the organs of the ECHR have set a high threshold for determining whether returning an individual would violate Article 3. The Court requires there to be a minimum level of severity for the treatment to fall within the scope of Article 3,[109] and treatment that is just less favourable is not sufficient.[110] Before 1999, the Commission consistently held that 'the deportation of a foreigner might, *in exceptional*

---

[104] Chetail, 'Le droit des réfugiés', n 88 above, 196–7.

[105] Ibid, 197.

[106] *Chahal v United Kingdom*, n 98 above, para 80; *Ahmed v Austria*, n 98 above, para 41.

[107] Goodwin-Gill and McAdam, n 3 above, 285; see on the impact of the Court's jurisprudence in domestic legal systems P van Dijk, 'Article 3 ECHR and Asylum Law and Policy in The Netherlands', in R Lawson and M de Blois (eds), *The Dynamics of the Protection of Human Rights in Europe: Essays in Honour of H G Schermers* (Nijhoff, Dordrecht [etc.] Vol III 1994) 123, 144;

[108] See Explanatory Memorandum to the Commission Proposal for a Council Directive laying down minimum standards for the qualification and status of third country nationals and stateless persons as refugees or as persons who otherwise need international protection COM (2001) 510 final, 12 September 2001, 5. Note that while the qualification Directive does not explicitly refer to the ECHR, Art 15(b)'s language is directly drawn from the ECHR and the Court's jurisprudence; on complementary protection, see also J McAdam, *Complementary Protection in International Refugee Law* (Oxford University Press, Oxford, 2006); H Storey, 'EU Refugee Qualification Directive: A Brave New World?' (2008) 20 *IJRL* 2.

[109] *Soering v United Kingdom*, n 98 above, para 100; *Cruz Varas v Sweden*, n 99 above, para 83; *Vilvarajah v The United Kingdom*, n 98 above, para 107; *Dulas v Turkey*, Appl. No. 25801/94, Judgment of 30 January 2001, para 52; *Denizci and ors v Cyprus*, Appl. Nos. 25316–25321/94 and 27207/95, Judgment of 23 May 2001, para 383; *Ahmet Özkan and ors v Turkey*, Appl. No. 21689/93, Judgment of 6 April 2004, para 334; *Saadi v Italy*, n 98 above, para 134. On the interpretation of the 'minimum level of severity', see van Dijk and van Hoof, n 103 above, 311–15; A Fabbricotti, 'The Concept of Inhuman or Degrading Treatment in International Law and its Application in Asylum Cases' (1998) 10 *IJRL* 637, 645; Chetail, 'Le droit des réfugiés', n 88 above, 177; K Röhl, 'Fleeing Violence and Poverty: *Non-Refoulement* Obligations under the European Convention of Human Rights', UNHCR New Issues in Refugee Research Paper No. 111, January 2005, 18.

[110] Röhl, n 109 above, 8.

circumstances,[111] raise an issue under Article 3 of the Convention where there is serious reason to believe that the deportee would be liable, in the country of destination, to treatment prohibited by this provision.'[112] In *Soering*, the Court affirmed for the first time that for return, and in this case, extradition, to be prohibited under Article 3, there should be substantial grounds for believing that the person concerned faces a real risk of being subjected to torture or to inhuman or degrading treatment or punishment.[113] While the scope of *non-refoulement* is thus rather broad, the evidentiary requirements have in practice enabled the Court to restrict its application.[114] For instance, in *Vilvarajah* the applicants had been previously threatened and some of them tortured after their removal to Sri Lanka by the United Kingdom authorities, but the Court nevertheless considered that,

The evidence before the Court concerning the background of the applicants, as well as the general situation, does not establish that their personal position was any worse than the generality of other members of the Tamil community or other young male Tamils who were returning to their country. Since the situation was still unsettled there was the possibility that they might be detained and ill-treated as appears to have occurred previously in cases of some of the applicants. A mere possibility of ill-treatment, however, in such circumstances, is not in itself sufficient to give rise to a breach of article 3.[115]

The Court thus adopted an overly restrictive and individualized approach of the real risk requirement,[116] which had some concluding that the non-derogatory character of Article 3 was inversely proportional to the number of individuals likely to benefit from it.[117] It also emphasized that if the individual has not yet been removed or deported, the existence of the 'real risk' must be assessed at the time of proceedings before the Court, as was also made clear in the *Cruz Varas* case.[118]

---

[111] Emphasis added.

[112] *A v Switzerland*, Appl. No. 11933/86 (1986) 46 DR 257, 269; see also *X v the United Kingdom* Appl. 8581/79 (1982) 29 DR 48, 54; *X v Germany*, Appl. 7216/75 (1976) 5 DR 137, 142–3; *X v Germany*, Appl. 7334/76 (1976) 5 DR 154, 155.

[113] *Soering v United Kingdom*, n 98 above, para 91; *Cruz Varas v Sweden*, n 99 above, paras 69 and 82; *Vilvarajah and ors v United Kingdom*, n 98 above, paras 107 and 115; *Chahal v United Kingdom*, n 98 above, para 74; *Ahmed v Austria*, n 98 above, para 39; *H.L.R v France*, Appl. No. 24573/94, Judgment of 29 April 1997, ECHR1997-III, para 34; *Abdurrahim Incedursun v Netherlands*, Appl. No. 33124/96, Judgment of 22 June 1999, para 27; *Jabari v Turkey*, Appl. No. 40035/98, Judgment of 11 July 2000, ECHR 2000-VIII, para 38; *Salah Sheekh v the Netherlands*, Appl. No. 1948/04, Judgment of 11 January 2007, para 135; *Saadi v Italy*, n 98 above, para 125.

[114] Einarsen, n 100 above, 373 and 384; Suntinger, n 88 above, 218; H Lambert, 'Protection against *Refoulement* from Europe: Human Rights Law Comes to the Rescue' (1999) 48 *ICLQ* 515, 517; see also Goodwin-Gill and McAdam, n 3 above, 310, 316.

[115] *Vilvarajah and ors v United Kingdom*, n 98 above, para 97.

[116] See eg *H.L.R v France*, n 113 above, para 70; *Sultani v France*, Appl. No. 45223/05, Judgment of 20 December 2007, para 67.

[117] See also Chetail, 'Le droit des réfugiés', n 88 above, 201.

[118] *Cruz Varas v. Sweden*, n 99 above, para 76; *Saadi v Italy*, n 98 above, para 133; see also *NA v The United Kingdom*, Appl. No. 25904/07, Judgment of 17 July 2008, para 112.

The reason for such a restrictive attitude is probably due to its reluctance to interfere in the sensitive fields of asylum and immigration, and to counter the 'floodgates' argument, which was raised by the United Kingdom in *Vilvarajah*.[119] The Court adopted a slightly more progressive approach in subsequent judgments, even though it is arguable that this was primarily attributable to the specific facts of these cases. In *Chahal*, where the UK authorities had ordered the deportation of a Sikh activist on national security grounds, the amount of evidence presented by the applicant, his high-profile status as a dissident, and therefore the highly individualized nature of his claim, was the key factor that led the Court to find that the United Kingdom had violated Article 3.[120] In *Ahmed*, the Court's task was facilitated by the fact that the Austrian government, which sought to expel a recognized refugee who had been convicted of criminal offences, had actually acknowledged that there had been no improvement of the situation in Somalia and that therefore the risk of ill-treatment had not ceased to exist.[121]

It is only recently that the Court seems to have embraced a less individualized approach,[122] and one may speculate that the adoption of the provisions on subsidiary protection in the qualification Directive may have played a role in this jurisprudential shift.[123] In *Salah Sheekh* and, most recently *NA*, the Court held that,

[E]xceptionally, [...] in cases where an applicant alleges that he or she is a member of a group systematically exposed to a practice of ill-treatment, the Court [considers] that the protection of Article 3 of the Convention enters into play when the applicant establishes, [...] that there are serious reasons to believe in the existence of the practice in question and his or her membership of the group concerned.[124]

In the first of these cases, it actually concluded that members of the Ashraf clan, to which the complainant belonged, were subjected in certain parts of Somalia to treatment contrary to Article 3 and found that,

[I]t might render the protection offered by that provision illusory if in addition to the fact that he belongs to the Ashraf—which the Government have not disputed [*sic*]—the applicant is required to show the existence of further special distinguishing features.[125]

---

[119] Goodwin-Gill and McAdam, n 3 above, 319; see also N Mole, *Problèmes soulevés par certains aspects de la situation actuelle des réfugiés sous l'angle de la Convention européenne des droits de l'homme* Dossiers sur les droits de l'homme No. 9 (1997) 20, citing the argument of the British government in *Vilvarajah* that this would otherwise permit the entry of a large number of persons, with serious social and economic consequences for the country.

[120] *Chahal v United Kingdom*, n 98 above, paras 87–107.

[121] *Ahmed v Austria*, n 98 above, para 44.

[122] See Chetail, 'Le droit des réfugiés', n 88 above, 201, who refers to earlier cases showing that the Court and the Commission had never fully excluded that in exceptional circumstances, the general situation in a country might prevent the removal of an individual under Art 3.

[123] See Art 15 qualification Directive.

[124] *NA v The United Kingdom*, n 118 above, para 116; see also *Salah Sheekh v The Netherlands*, n 113 above, para 148; *Saadi v Italy*, n 98 above, para 132.

[125] *Salah Sheekh v The Netherlands*, n 113 above, para 148.

5.1.2.1.2 Jurisprudence of relevance to safe third country practices

The ECHR jurisprudence on *refoulement* addresses also a substantial number of issues that are of particular significance in the context of secondary movements. In the last 30 years, 'orbit situations', the existence of arrangements providing for the readmission of an individual or allocating responsibility for the examination of an asylum claim, the method by which the existence of protection is ascertained, the value of assurances provided by a third country, as well as the extraterritorial reach of the Court's jurisdiction were all subject to the Court's scrutiny.

With respect to 'orbit situations', in the 1980s, the organs of the ECHR were faced with the question of whether the act of expelling, removing, or extraditing the individual to a State might in itself constitute ill-treatment,[126] and in particular, whether the existence of an 'orbit situation', where an individual is shuffled from country to country without receiving protection, could be regarded as leading to a violation of Article 3 ECHR.[127] In the first of such cases, the Commission examined the situation of an undocumented individual who had been arrested several times for illegally staying in Belgium and whose claim for refugee status had been rejected.[128] The authorities had each time issued orders of expulsion, to no effect. The Commission held that this situation could raise an issue under Article 3 ECHR and noted that in view of the fact that similar cases had arisen in the past, States parties might suggest ways to solve this common problem.[129] In the case of a stateless individual who had been expelled over 20 times from the Netherlands, the Commission found that a similar situation would arise 'if an alien is over a long period of time deported repeatedly from one country to another without any country taking measures to regularise his situation'.[130] The application was nevertheless rejected as manifestly ill founded, because the claimant seemed to have come back to the Netherlands of his own free will, and did not attempt to have his alleged Algerian nationality recognized by the authorities of this country, showing thereby that he was essentially responsible for his situation. It bears noting that in both cases, the 'orbit situation' had already taken place; it would be far more difficult to bring such a case on the basis of a risk of orbit situation, given the difficulty of documenting rejections at the border and the strict evidentiary requirements imposed by the Court.[131]

In *Amuur*, the Commission dismissed the claim by France that the detention of asylum seekers in international zones of airports did not constitute a deprivation of

---

[126] F G Jacobs and R C A White, *The European Convention on Human Rights* (2nd edn, Oxford University Press, Oxford 1996) 60.

[127] See in this respect, O De Schutter, 'Privation de liberté et maintien en zone internationale' [1996] *RDE* 345, 348.

[128] *Giama v Belgium*, Appl. 7612/76, (1980) 23 *Yearbook of the European Convention of Human Rights* 428, 86–8.

[129] Ibid, 94.

[130] *Harabi v the Netherlands*, Appl. No. 10798/84, 5 March 1986, 46 DR 112.

[131] Einarsen, n 100 above, 382–3.

liberty, since the applicants were free to leave the zone for any other country than France, holding that it was 'insufficient to find that the applicants had a theoretical and illusory ability to go to a third country'.[132] However, in that particular case, the claimants, who were Somali nationals, had not shown that they feared for their life or security if sent back to Syria, which had accepted to receive them.[133] The Court nevertheless endorsed the principle that the possibility of leaving the country where the applicants sought refuge would be theoretical 'if no other country offering protection comparable to the protection they expect to find in the country where they are seeking asylum is inclined or prepared to take them in'.[134] However, it went further than the Commission, considering that,

Sending the applicants back to Syria only became possible, apart from the practical problems of the journey, following negotiations between the French and Syrian authorities. The assurances of the latter were dependent on the vagaries of diplomatic relations, in view of the fact that Syria was not bound by the Geneva Convention relating to the Status of Refugees.[135]

It concluded that holding the applicants in the international zone of the airport constituted a deprivation of liberty and that Article 5(1) ECHR was therefore applicable.[136] One may infer from the above that States parties to the ECHR need to consider whether the practice of removing unilaterally asylum seekers to a third country may raise an issue under the ECHR, given the absence of formal guarantee that effective protection would be provided. Also, while the Court was obviously not competent to address this point, the fact that a State is not a party to the Refugee Convention would also significantly raise the level of guarantees required to send an asylum seeker to a third country.

In 2000, the Court was given the opportunity to directly assess the validity of safe third country practices, specifically, the 1990 Dublin Convention, in a complaint filed against the United Kingdom by an applicant who had fled from Sri Lanka to Germany where he had first claimed asylum.[137] His claim was denied and the Administrative court of Regensburg which heard his appeal, confirmed the administrative decision, holding that actions by the LTTE, the Tamil rebel group operating in the Jaffna region, could not be attributed to the State. The applicant was safe if he were to return to the South of Sri Lanka, since the government had no reasons to suspect that he was a member of the LTTE. In addition, it considered that the claim was completely fabricated, in view of the lack of precision of the story and the unconvincing evidence that was brought to support the claim.[138]

---

[132] *Amuur v France*, Appl. No. 19776/92 Judgment of 25 June 1996, ECHR 1996-III 11, para 47.
[133] Ibid, para 49.
[134] Ibid, para 48.
[135] Ibid.
[136] Ibid, para 49.
[137] *T.I. v United Kingdom*, n 103 above.
[138] Ibid, para 216.

The applicant then travelled to the United Kingdom where he lodged a second application. In accordance with the provisions of the Dublin Convention, Germany accepted to take back the applicant at the request of the UK authorities. The applicant applied for judicial review of the decision of transfer, leave was granted, but the Court of Appeal considered that the Secretary of State was entitled to conclude that Germany's interpretation of the Refugee Convention was permissible.[139] Meanwhile, the applicant was examined by a physician who certified that the applicant's allegations of torture were consistent with the descriptions given by other Sri Lankan asylum seekers and with the scars on his body. Following the Court of Appeal's decision in *Adan and ors*,[140] the counsel of the applicant requested that the Secretary of State reconsider his decision. The Secretary of State responded that since he was lodging an appeal before the House of Lords, he found it premature to do so.[141]

The applicant thus filed a complaint against the United Kingdom before the European Court of Human Rights, on the ground that his transfer to Germany would constitute a violation of Article 3 ECHR, since Germany would send him back to Sri Lanka where there were substantial grounds to believe that he would face a real risk of ill-treatment. German courts would not accept this new evidence, since it was not related to persecution attributable to the State.[142] The Court first established that

[…] the indirect removal in this case to an intermediate country, which is also a Contracting State, does not affect the responsibility of the United Kingdom to ensure that the applicant is not, as a result of its decision to expel, exposed to treatment contrary to Article 3 of the Convention. Nor can the United Kingdom rely automatically in that context on the arrangements made in the Dublin Convention concerning the attribution of responsibility between European countries for deciding asylum claims. Where States establish international organisations, or mutatis mutandis international agreements, to pursue co-operation in certain fields of activities, there may be implications for the protection of fundamental rights. It would be incompatible with the purpose and object of the Convention, if Contracting States were thereby absolved from their responsibility under the Convention in relation to the field of activity covered by such attribution.[143]

Yet, the Court made clear that it had no competence to determine the validity of the applicant's claim under the Refugee Convention, and that it would therefore focus on whether effective procedural safeguards existed under German law to prevent the applicant's removal to Sri Lanka.[144] In view of the submissions made by the German government, the Court concluded that the applicant could bring a claim under section 53(6) of Germany's Aliens Act, which grants discretionary

---

139 Ibid, para 217.
140 See n 74 above.
141 See n 103 above, para 218.
142 Ibid, para 224.
143 Ibid, para 228.
144 Ibid, para 230.

power to the authorities to suspend deportation in case of substantial danger to life, personal integrity, or liberty of an alien,[145] albeit for an initial duration of three months only, with possibility of renewal. The Court accepted Germany's contention that in spite of its discretionary terms, existing case-law provided that the authorities were under an obligation to apply it if an individual was in grave danger. The Court noted however that,

[...] while it may be that on any re-examination of the applicant's case the German authorities might still reject it, this is largely a matter of speculation and conjecture. [...] To the extent therefore that there is the possibility of such a removal, it has not been shown in the circumstances of this case to be sufficiently concrete or determinate.[146]

The Court thus concluded that the applicant did not establish that there was a real risk that Germany would expel him to Sri Lanka in breach of Article 3 ECHR, and that the United Kingdom had properly examined the existence of adequate procedural safeguards in Germany. Consequently, the United Kingdom had not violated its obligations under the Convention.

While one may regret the findings of the Court which, as often happens, establishes robust legal principles but concludes that these principles do not apply in the situation at hand, this judgment is nonetheless highly significant, as it affirmed that the operation of the Dublin Convention and of safe third country practices does not affect States' individual responsibility for the breach of human rights obligations and that a State party must therefore determine that the individual would effectively be enjoying protection against *refoulement* in the third country. Furthermore, by pointing out that it has no competence to address international refugee law violations, the court brought out the difficulties raised by the lack of proper supervisory framework with regard to the application and interpretation of the Refugee Convention in a context where States are increasingly transferring their responsibilities to protect refugees under the CSR.

The value and weight to be accorded to diplomatic assurances, which was peripherally addressed in *Amuur*, has recently been scrutinized in the so-called 'rendition' cases and is also relevant for the present discussion. In the *Saadi* case, the ECtHR found that the provision of diplomatic assurances may not be sufficient to show that return to a country would not entail a real risk of ill-treatment for an individual. Of particular interest was its holding that

the existence of domestic laws and accession to international treaties guaranteeing respect for fundamental rights in principle are not in themselves sufficient to ensure adequate protection against the risk of ill-treatment where, as in the present case, reliable sources have reported practice resorted to or tolerated by the authorities which are manifestly contrary to the principles of the Convention.[147]

---

[145] Ibid, para 231.
[146] Ibid, para 231.
[147] *Saadi v Italy*, n 98 above, para 147.

It more specifically found that the fact that diplomatic assurances would have been offered would not absolve the Court 'from the obligation to examine whether such assurances provided, in their practical application, a sufficient guarantee that the applicant would be protected against the risk of treatment prohibited by the Convention'.[148] Such construction reinforces by analogy the view that the existence of domestic legislation and accession to international treaties or the provision of formal assurances does not in and of itself constitute sufficient demonstration that an asylum seeker will enjoy effective protection in a country, when reliable sources show this not to be the case.[149] It thus militates against an abstract determination of safety through safe third country lists, bolstering instead the approach based on an individual assessment of whether effective protection would be enjoyed.

The Court's findings on procedural safeguards in relation with Article 3 ECHR are also important. In the *Jabari* case, the Court found that the 'automatic and mechanical application of [...] a short time-limit for submitting an asylum application must be considered at variance with the protection of the fundamental value embodied in Article 3 of the Convention'. On that basis, the Court concluded that Turkey had violated Article 3 ECHR by dismissing the applicant's asylum claim on formal grounds, namely, her failure to submit her application within a five-day time limit.[150] It further found a violation of Article 13 ECHR, holding that,

[G]iven the irreversible nature of the harm that might occur if the risk of torture or ill-treatment alleged materialised and the importance it attaches to Article 3, the notion of an effective remedy under Article 13 requires independent and rigorous scrutiny of a claim that there exist substantial grounds for fearing a real risk of treatment contrary to Article 3 and the possibility of suspending the implementation of the measures impugned.[151]

By implication, the absence of an 'independent' and 'rigorous' scrutiny of whether the application of the safe third country would entail a violation of Article 3 should be regarded as a breach of the right to an effective remedy under Article 13 ECHR.

A final question is the extraterritorial reach of States' obligations under the ECHR. The question has definitely gained some heightened resonance in the refugee realm, given the various proposals on extraterritorial processing of asylum claims that have been floated in recent years.[152] In this respect, the highly

---

[148] *Saadi v Italy*, n 98 above, para 148;

[149] See also in this respect UNHCR, 'Note on Diplomatic Assurances and International Refugee Protection', August 2006, para 37 available at: <http://www.unhcr.org/refworld/docid/44dc81164.html>.

[150] *Jabari v Turkey*, n 113 above, para 40.

[151] Ibid, para 50; see also *Conka v Belgium*, Appl. No. 51564/99, Judgment of 5 February 2002, paras 79, 82–3, in which the ECtHR found that the lack of automatic suspensive effect of the extremely urgent procedure before the Belgian *Conseil d'Etat* was not providing an effective remedy against a breach of Art 4 of Protocol No. 4 of the ECHR; *Gebremedhin v France*, Appl. No. 25389/05, Judgment of 26 April 2007, para 58, 66, where the ECtHR found that the French asylum procedure at the border violated Art 13 ECHR due to the absence of suspensive effect of decisions summarily dismissing an asylum claim.

[152] On extraterritorial processing, see Chapter 2, Section 2.3.

controversial *Banković* case is actually of far lesser concern than one may have assumed at first. While the finding that 'the Convention was not designed to be applied throughout the world, even in respect of the conduct of Contracting States' and that 'the desirability of avoiding a gap or vacuum in human rights protection has so far been relied on by the Court in favour of establishing jurisdiction only when the territory in question was one that, but for the specific circumstances, would normally be covered by the Convention'[153] generated heated debate, it is important to bear in mind that the situation examined in that case was particularly sensitive and unique.[154] The Court has in fact reaffirmed in subsequent cases its prior jurisprudence to the effect that for the purposes of Article 1 ECHR, the exercise of jurisdiction should extend to all persons under a State's actual authority and responsibility, whether this authority is exercised on its own territory or abroad.[155] This means that any individual removed by the authorities of a State party to extraterritorial processing centres would still be protected by the relevant provisions of the ECHR.

5.1.2.2 *Article 3 of the Convention Against Torture*

Article 3 CAT provides that,

1. No State Party shall expel, return ("refouler") or extradite a person to another State where there are substantial grounds for believing that he would be in danger of being subjected to torture.

2. For the purpose of determining whether there are such grounds, the competent authorities shall take into account all relevant considerations including, where applicable, the existence in the State concerned of a consistent pattern of gross, flagrant or mass violations of human rights.

As with the ICCPR and ECHR, the principle applies without exceptions and regardless of the character or behaviour of the individual concerned or the fact that he/she poses a danger to society in the State party.[156]

---

[153] *Banković and ors v Belgium and 16 Other Contracting States*, Appl. No. 52207/99, Admissibility Decision of 12 December 2001 (2002) 41 *ILM* 517, para 80.

[154] On *Banković*, see eg M Gondek, 'Extraterritorial Application of the European Convention on Human Rights: Territorial Focus in the Age of Globalization?', (2005) 52 *NILR* 347, 356; G Ress, 'Problems of Extraterritorial Human Rights Violations—the Jurisdiction of the European Court of Human Rights: The Banković Case' (2003) 12 *Italian Ybk of Intl L* (Napoli, Editoriale Scientifica) 51; see also more generally on extraterritorial application of international human rights law, R Wilde, Legal "black hole"?: Extraterritorial State Action and International Treaty Law on Civil and Political Rights' (2005) 26 *Michigan J of Intl Law*, 739.

[155] Gondek, n 154 above, 373–5 citing *Öcalan v Turkey*, Appl. No. 46221/99, Judgment of 12 March 2003; *Issa and ors v Turkey*, Appl. No. 31821/96, Judgment of 16 November 2004, para 71; see also in this respect the ICJ cases cited at n 30 above; *Lopez Burgos v Uruguay* Communication No. R12/52 UN Doc Supp No. 40 (A/36/40) at 176, 29 July 1981, para 12.3; Human Rights Committee, General Comment No. 31 n 93 above, para 10.

[156] See eg *Aemei v Switzerland*, Communication No. 34/1995, UN Doc CAT/C/18/D/34/1995, 29 May 1997, para 9.10; *Paez v Sweden*, Communication No. 39/1996, UN Doc CAT/C/18/D/39/

The Committee Against Torture established under Article 17 CAT examines State reports in which they present the measures adopted to ensure the implementation of the Convention provisions, including Article 3.[157] The Committee also receives individual complaints against States which have made a formal declaration under Article 22.[158] The views of the Committee, while non-binding, have nevertheless great authority and States have generally been fully compliant with the Committee's findings.[159]

In its first communication on an alleged violation of Article 3, the Committee found that in order to qualify for protection, an individual must be 'personally at risk of being subjected to torture in the country to which he or she would return'.[160] In subsequent cases, it specified that the risk must be real, foreseeable and personal without having to be 'highly probable'.[161] The Committee further clarified that the existence of a situation of 'consistent pattern of gross, flagrant or mass violations of human rights', is not required, but constitutes a significant element in the determination of the risk of torture.[162] It also indicated that while the fact that the State to which an individual would be removed is a party to the Convention and has recognized the jurisdiction of the Committee under Article 22 is a relevant factor, these factors may not in themselves be sufficient to preclude a risk of torture under Article 3.[163]

1996, 28 April 1997; *M B B v Sweden*, Communication No. 104/1988, UN Doc CAT/C/22/D/104/1998, 21 June 1999; *Arana v France*, Communication No. 63/1997, UN Doc CAT/C/23/D/63/1997, 5 June 2000, para 11.5; *Tebourski v France*, Communication No. 300/2006, UN Doc CAT/C/38/D/300/2006, 11 May 2007, para 8.2–8.3; see Chetail, 'Le Comité des Nations Unies contre la torture', n 91 above, 83–4.

[157] Article 19 of the Convention; for an overview of the Committee's functions, A Byrnes, 'The Committee Against Torture', in P Alston (ed) *The United Nations and Human Rights* (Clarendon Press, Oxford 1992) 508, 534 on the individual complaints procedure, see Chetail, 'Le Comité des Nations Unies contre la torture', n 91 above, 65.

[158] Sixty-four States have recognized the competence of the Committee Against Torture to examine individual complaints, statistical survey of individual complaints dealt with by the Committee against Torture under the procedure governed by Art 22 of the Convention Against Torture and Other Cruel, Inhuman, or Degrading Treatment or Punishment, updated on 12 August 2008. Note, however, that the United Kingdom and the three Baltic States have refused to recognize the competence of the Committee so far. <http://www2.ohchr.org/english/bodies/cat/stat3.htm>.

[159] Chetail, 'Le Comité des Nations Unies contre la torture', n 91 above, 101.

[160] *Mutombo v Switzerland*, Communication No. 13/1993 CAT/C/12/D/13/1993, 27 April 1994, para 9.3.

[161] Chetail, 'Le Comité des Nations Unies contre la torture', n 91 above, 86, 95–6.

[162] See eg *T M v Sweden*, Communication No. 228/2003, UN Doc CAT/C/31/D/228/2003, 2 December 2003, para 7.2; *Kamil Agiza v Sweden*, Communication No. 233/2003, UN Doc CAT/C/34/D/233/2003, 24 May 2005, para 13.3; *El Rgeig v Switzerland*, Communication No. 280/2005, UN Doc CAT/C/37/D/280/2005, 30 November 2006, para 7.2; *Iya v Switzerland*, Communication No. 299/2006, UN Doc CAT/C/39/D/299/2006, 26 November 2007, para 6.3.

[163] *Alan v Switzerland*, Communication No. 21/1995, UN Doc CAT/C/16/D/21/1995, 13 May 1996, para 11.5; Chetail, 'Le Comité des Nations Unies contre la torture', n 91 above, 92–3; see also *Arana v France*, n 156 above, in which the expulsion to Spain of an individual was found to amount to a violation by France of Art 3.

The requirements regarding the presentation of evidence are not as rigid as in ECtHR's proceedings and the Committee has stated that,

[…] it is aware of the concerns of the State party that the implementation of Article 3 of the Convention might be abused by asylum seekers. The Committee considers that, even if there are doubts about the facts adduced by the author, it must ensure that his security is not endangered. In order to do this, it is not necessary that all the facts invoked by the author should be proved; it is sufficient that the Committee should consider them to be sufficiently substantiated and reliable.[164]

The Committee also stressed that it renders its decision on the basis of the information which the authorities of the State party had or should have had in their possession at the time of the expulsion and that subsequent events are useful only for assessing the information which the State party actually had or could have deduced at the time of expulsion.[165]

Since its inception, the vast majority of cases before the Committee have been submitted by asylum seekers pursuant to Article 3 CAT and the Committee has therefore become in many instances the ultimate recourse in asylum cases.[166] States such as Australia, Canada, Finland, France, Sweden, and Switzerland are now the most frequent respondents before the Committee.[167] It seems that in response to this influx of cases based on Article 3, the Committee adopted stricter requirements as to the admissibility of complaints and the evidence of a risk of torture.[168]

Most of the cases examined by the Committee Against Torture have focused on the severity of the treatment which might be faced by the claimant, and on issues of credibility and burden of proof.[169] A number of cases, however, deserve further examination. The most interesting case for the present discussion is related to the

---

[164] *Mutombo v Switzerland,* Communication, n 160 above, para 9.2; *Aemei v Switzerland,* n 156 above, para 9.6; see also *Kaveh Yaragh Tala v Sweden,* Communication No. 43/1996 UN Doc CAT/C/17/D/43/1996, 15 November 1996, para 10.3; see also Chetail, 'Le Comité des Nations Unies contre la torture', n 91 above, 89, 101.

[165] See *Tebourski v France*, n 156 above, para 8.1; *Kamil Agiza v Sweden,* n 162 above, para 13.2.

[166] B Gorlick, 'The Convention and the Committee Against Torture: A Complementary Protection Regime for Refugees' (1999) 11 *IJRL* 479, 490; see also O Andrysek, 'Gaps in International Protection and the Potential for Redress through Individual Complaints Procedures' (1997) 9 *IJRL* 392, 413; Chetail, 'Le Comité des Nations Unies contre la torture', n 91 above, 96–7, 102–3.

[167] See statistical survey, n 158 above; see also Chetail, 'Le Comité des Nations Unies contre la torture', n 91 above, 66.

[168] Gorlick, n 166 above, 491.

[169] Gorlick, n 166 above, 486–91; see eg the following recent cases: *V L v Switzerland,* Communication No. 262/2005, UN Doc CAT/C/37/D/262/2005, 22 January 2007; *Iya v Switzerland,* n 162 above; *El Rgeig v Switzerland,* n 162 above; *C T and K M v Sweden,* Communication No. 279/2005, UN Doc CAT/C/37/D/279/2005, 7 December 2006; *T A v Sweden,* Communication No. 226/2003, UN Doc CAT/C/34/D/226/2003, 27 May 2005, *Falcon Rios v Canada,* Communication No. 133/1999, UN Doc CAT/C/33/D/133/1999, 17 December 2004; *M V v The Netherlands,* Communication No. 201/2002, UN Doc CAT/C/30/D/201/2002, 19 May 2003; Chetail, n 91 above, 85–98.

situation of an Iraqi national who faced forced removal from Sweden.[170] The Swedish Immigration Board and Aliens Appeal Board had rejected his asylum claim on the ground that since his wife was from Jordan and lived there, he had close links with that country and would be received there. The claimant contended that he had not been granted a residence permit when he stayed in Jordan. If removed to Jordan, the authorities would probably return him to Iraq. A UNHCR letter to the Committee confirmed that foreigners married to Jordanian women had no preferential access to residence status. Furthermore, UNHCR reported other cases of Iraqi asylum seekers who were refused entry in Jordan after being removed from Sweden or Denmark. The Swedish government argued that even though Jordan was not a party to the Refugee Convention, Jordan usually followed the principles contained in this Convention, and had signed a Memorandum of Understanding with UNHCR. However, UNHCR provided evidence that Jordan was not as welcoming for refugees who were returned from Europe and that in such cases, the refugee was likely to be returned to his country of origin. This was also confirmed by the clauses of the Memorandum of Understanding, which stipulated that it did not apply to deportees from third countries.

The Committee was exclusively asked to assess the existence of a risk of *refoulement* from Jordan to Iraq, since no one was denying the existence of a risk of torture faced by the claimant in Iraq. The Committee followed the argument of the claimant, relying on its General Comment No. 1, where it stated that the words 'another state' should also include 'any State to which the author may subsequently be expelled, returned or extradited', and considered that the claimant should not be forcibly removed to Iraq or to Jordan.[171] It also relied on the fact that while Jordan was a party to the Convention, it had not made a declaration recognizing the competence of the Committee and that if returned to Jordan, the applicant would not be able to bring a complaint before the Committee.

This case's factual background provides an interesting illustration of the reluctance of some States to readmit individuals based on the application of the safe third country. Regardless of the fact that Jordan is not a party of the CSR, which also raises questions as to Sweden's compliance with its obligations under the CSR,[172] there is here evidence of the difficulties of implementing safe third country practices and of the fact that they lead to an increasing risk of *refoulement*.

---

[170] *Avedes Hamayak Korban v Sweden*, Communication No. 88/1997, UN Doc CAT/C/21/D/88/1997, 16 November 1998, published in (1999) 11 *IJRL* 210.

[171] Ibid, para 7, 216; see para 2 of Committee Against Torture General Comment No. 1 on the Implementation of Article 3 in the context of Article 22 of the Convention Against Torture, 21 November 1997, UN Doc A/53/44, annex IX; see also Chetail, 'Le Comité des Nations Unies contre la torture', n 91 above, 99–100.

[172] It is worth noting that like the ECtHR, the Committee Against Torture has repeatedly held that it has no jurisdiction to determine whether a complainant should be granted asylum under the domestic law of a State party or whether he or she should be granted protection under the Refugee Convention, or even to determine the legal status of an individual in a State party, see Chetail, 'Le Comité des Nations Unies contre la torture', n 91 above, 103–4.

The availability and access to international remedies is also a relevant consideration in assessing whether an individual is effectively protected against *refoulement*. The case thus shows once again that the determination of such risk must be made on an individual basis rather than *in abstracto*.

The Committee was, like the European Court of Human Rights, also called to assess whether certain types of cooperation between States entailed violations of the Convention. In the *Agiza* case, it found that diplomatic assurances were not sufficient to protect an individual against a manifest risk of violation of Article 3 CAT, noting that there was no mechanism provided for their enforcement, and that, in particular, evidence had been adduced showing that Egypt had breached its assurances to guarantee a fair trial and had shown no willingness to conduct an independent investigation despite appeals from the State party's authorities at the highest levels.[173] In the same case, the Committee also made particularly important findings with respect to the remedies available in State parties. It first affirmed that 'the right to an effective remedy for a breach of the Convention underpins the entire Convention, for otherwise the protections afforded by the Convention would be rendered largely illusory' and that the 'prohibition of refoulement contained in Article 3 should be interpreted the same way to encompass a remedy for its breach, even though it may not contain on its face such a right to remedy for a breach thereof'.[174] It then found that,

[T]he right to an effective remedy contained in Article 3 requires, in this context, an opportunity for effective, independent, and impartial review of the decision to expel or remove, once that decision is made, when there is a plausible allegation that article 3 issues arise.[175]

The Committee concluded that the fact that the complainant had not been able to bring a complaint before the Committee before his removal constituted a breach of the State's obligations under Article 22.[176]

The above review confirms that under the CAT, indirect *refoulement* is as unlawful as direct removal to the country of origin, that assurances provided by the State to which an individual is removed may not be sufficient if a real risk of torture exists, and finally, that Article 3 entails the right to an effective remedy, that is, an independent, effective, and impartial review of the decision of removal, and the ability to exercise the right of complaint provided under Article 22 of the Convention.

---

[173] *Kamil Agiza v Sweden*, n 162 above, paras 13.4–13.5; see also *Arana v France*, n 156 above, para 11.5.

[174] *Kamil Agiza v Sweden*, n 162 above, para 13.6.

[175] Ibid, para 13.9.

[176] Ibid, para 13.8; see also *Brada v France*, Communication No. 195/2002, UN Doc CAT/C/34/ D/195/2002, 24 May 2005, para 13.4, where France expelled the complainant in spite of the Committee having requested interim measures to stay the complainant's expulsion; *Tebourski v France*, n 156 above, para 7.4; *Singh Sogi v Canada*, Communication No. 297/2006, UN Doc CAT/C/39/ D/297/2006, 29 November 2007, para 10.11; see also Chetail, 'Le Comité des Nations Unies contre la torture', n 91 above, 73.

5.1.3 *Non-refoulement* as a customary obligation

In order to become customary, a rule of international law must be of a fundamentally norm-creating character, there must be consistent practice by States as well as evidence of *opinio juris sive necessitatis*, an acceptance of the legally binding character of the rule,[177] often demonstrated through statements, declarations, or agreement among States. Treaty provisions may become customary if they are of a norm-creating character and if there has been wide participation in the Convention, including by States specially affected, and if there has been extensive and virtually uniform practice.[178]

As early as 1954, the Final Act of the Convention relating to the Status of Stateless Persons stipulated that Article 33 CSR was the expression of a generally accepted principle.[179] Even though this statement might have been premature,[180] *non-refoulement* is now widely recognized as a principle of customary international law.[181] There are currently 147 States bound by the conventional obligation of *non-refoulement* under the Refugee Convention and/or its 1967 Protocol. The fundamental importance of the principle has been affirmed in international conventions and declarations,[182] in conclusions of the Executive Committee of

---

[177] *North Sea Continental Shelf*, (Judgment) ICJ Reports (1969) 3, 42, paras 71–2; *Military and Paramilitary Activities in and Against Nicaragua* (Merits) ICJ Reports (1986) 14, 94, para 177.

[178] *North Sea Continental Shelf*, n 177 above, para 73–4.

[179] Convention Relating to the Status of Stateless Persons (adopted 28 September 1954, entered into force 6 June 1960) 360 UNTS 117.

[180] See Kälin, n 23 above, 66–8.

[181] UNHCR Advisory Opinion, n 5 above, para 15.

[182] See Art 22(8) of the 1969 American Convention on Human Rights; Art II. 3 of the 1969 OAU Convention, n 11 above; Art 3.1 1967 UN Declaration on Territorial Asylum, n 14 above; Resolution (67) 14 of the Committee of Ministers of the Council of Europe on Asylum to Persons in Danger of Persecution of 29 June 1967; Recommendation No. R (84) 1 adopted on 25 January 1984 by the Committee of Ministers of the Council of Europe on the Persons Satisfying the Criteria in the Geneva Convention Who Are not Formally Recognised as Refugees; Cartagena Declaration on Refugees adopted on 19–22 November 1984, OAS/Ser.L/V/II.66 doc.10, rev.1 190–3 reprinted in UNHCR, *Collection of International Instruments and Other Legal Texts Concerning Refugees and Displaced Persons* (1995) Vol II 205; Arts III.3 and III.5 of the 1966 Principles Concerning Treatment of Refugees, n 14 above; Declaration adopted on the 10th anniversary of the Cartagena Declaration: San Jose Declaration on Refugees and Displaced persons (San Jose, 5–7 December 1994); Art 45 of the Geneva Convention (IV) Relative to the Protection of Civilian Persons in Time of War (adopted 12 August 1949, entered into force 21 October 1950) 75 UNTS 287; Art 14(1) Protocol to Prevent, Suppress and Punish Trafficking in Persons, especially Women and Children, supplementing the United Nations Convention against Transnational Organized Crime, UNGA Res 55/25, 15 November 2002; Art 19(1) Protocol Against the Smuggling of Migrants by Land, Sea and Air, supplementing the United Nations Convention against Transnational Organized crime, UNGA Res 55/25, 15 November 2000; Final Text of the Asian-African Legal Consultative Organization's 1966 Bangkok Principles on Status and Treatment of Refugees, 40th Session, New Delhi (adopted 24 June 2001); San Remo Declaration on the Principle of *Non-Refoulement*, September 2001; Mexico Declaration and Plan of Action to Strengthen the International Protection of Refugees in Latin America, Mexico City, 16 November 2004; Council of Europe Convention on Action against Trafficking in Human Beings, 16 May 2005, ETS No. 197.

the UNHCR,[183] as well as in resolutions of the General Assembly of the United Nations,[184] supranational instruments,[185] national legislation of States,[186] and most recently by the House of Lords.[187] The customary character of the principle is also recognized by the most eminent scholars.[188] In 2001, States parties to the

[183] ExCom Conclusion No. 6 on *Non-Refoulement* (1977) para (a); ExCom Conclusion No. 17 on Problems of Extradition Affecting Refugees (1980) para (d); ExCom Conclusion No. 19 on Temporary Refuge (1980), para (a); ExCom Conclusion No. 22 on Protection of Asylum-Seekers in Situations of Large-Scale Influx (1981) II.A.2; ExCom General Conclusion on International Protection No. 25 (1982) para (b); ExCom General Conclusion on International Protection No. 33 (1984) para (c); ExCom Conclusion on Accession to International Instruments and Their Implementation No. 42 (1986) para (b); ExCom General Conclusion on International Protection No. 50 (1988) para (g); ExCom General Conclusion on International Protection No. 65 (1991) para (c); ExCom General Conclusion on International Protection No. 68 (1992) para (f); ExCom General Conclusion on International Protection No. 71 (1993) para (g); ExCom General Conclusion on International Protection No. 74 (1994) para (g); ExCom General Conclusion on International Protection No. 79 (1996) para (j); ExCom General Conclusion on International Protection No. 81 (1997) para (i); ExCom General Conclusion on International Protection No. 99 (2004) para (l); ExCom Conclusion on complementary forms of protection No. 103 (2005) para (m).

[184] GA Res 32/67, 8 December 1977, para 5 (c); GA Res 33/26, 29 November 1978, para 6; GA Res 34/60, 29 November 1979, para 5 (a); GA Res 35/41, 25 November 1980, para 5 (a); GA Res 36/125, 14 December 1981, para 5 (a); GA Res 37/195, 18 December 1982, para 2; GA Res 38/121, 16 December 1983, para 2; GA Res 39/140, 14 December 1984, para 2; GA Res 40/118, 13 December 1985, para 2; GA Res 41/124, 4 December 1986, para 2; GA Res 42/109, 7 December 1987, para 1; GA Res 43/117, 8 December 1988, para 1; GA Res 44/137, 15 December 1989, para 3; GA Res 45/140, 14 December 1990, para 3; GA Res 46/106, 16 December 1991, para 4; GA Res 47/105, 16 December 1992, para 4; GA Res 48/116, 20 December 1993, para 3; GA Res 49/169, 23 December 1994, para 4; GA Res 50/152, 21 December 1995, para 3; GA Res 51/75, 12 December 1996, para 3; Res 52/103, 12 September 1997, paras 3 and 5; GA Res 52/103, 9 February 1998, para 3; GA Res 53/125, 12 February 1999, para 5; GA Res 54/146, 22 February 2000, para 6; GA Res 55/74, 12 February 2001, para 6; GA Res 56/137, 19 December 2001, para 3; GA Res 57/187, 18 December 2002, para 4; GA Res 58/151, 22 December 2003, para 3; GA Res 59/170, 20 December 2004, para 3; GA Res 60/120, 16 December 2005, para 3; GA Res 60/129, 24 January 2006, para 3; GA Res 61/137, 25 January 2007, para 3; GA Res 62/124, 24 January 2008, para 4.

[185] Article 19 of the Charter of Fundamental Rights of the European Union proclaimed on 7 December 1999 by the President of the European Commission, the President of the European Parliament, and the President of the Council of Ministers [2000] OJ C364/1; para 2 of the Preamble and Art 21.1 of the qualification Directive, n 22 above; para 2 of the Preamble of the asylum procedures Directive, n 22 above; Art 78.1 of the Consolidated Versions of the Treaty on European Union and the Treaty on the Functioning of the European Union [2008] OJ C115/1 (not yet in force).

[186] See UNHCR Sub-Committee of the Whole on International Protection, Note on *Non-refoulement*, UN Doc EC/SCP/2, 23 August 1977, para 11; see also R C Sexton, 'Political Refugees, *Nonrefoulement* and State Practice: A Comparative Study' (1985) 18 *Vanderbilt J of Transnational L* 731 for an overview of legislation from the United States, Great Britain, France and Italy; Sir E Lauterpacht and D Bethlehem, 'The Scope and Content of the Principle of *Non-Refoulement*', 20 June 2001, available at: <http://www.unhcr.org/protect/PROTECTION/3b33574d1.pdf> who report that about 80 States have included the principle in their legislation, para 213; Goodwin-Gill and McAdam, n 3 above, para 218–32.

[187] *R v Immigration Officer at Prague Airport and ors (Respondents) ex p European Roma Rights Centre and ors (Appellants)*, n 41 above, para 26.

[188] P Weis, 'Legal Aspects of the Convention of 28 July 1951 relating to the Status of Refugees' (1953) 30 *BYIL* 478, 482, who recognizes the existence of a usage; Kälin, n 23 above, 72 and Hailbronner, n 13 above, 129 considered in the early 1980s that there was an emergent rule of general international law on *non-refoulement*; P Hyndman, 'Refugees Under International Law with a Reference to the Concept of Asylum' (1986) 60 *Australian LJ*, 148, 154; T Meron, *Human Rights and*

Refugee Convention, assembled at a ministerial meeting organized in the context of the Global Consultations on international protection launched by UNHCR, explicitly declared the principle of *non-refoulement* to be part of customary law.[189]

As to State practice, it is undeniable that there have been violations of this obligation in multiple instances.[190] Many 'first asylum' countries have considered that the international community should guarantee the provision of assistance and solutions for the resettlement of refugees in return for their hosting refugee populations.[191] Southeast Asian countries have for instance refused to use the term refugees for the people fleeing Laos, Kampuchea, and Vietnam, in order to avoid the reception of these populations being regarded as their recognition of a customary obligation, and they insisted that they were only receiving these people out of humanitarian concern.[192] Other well-documented incidents of *refoulement* occurred in 1991 during the first Gulf War with Turkey's decision to close its border with Iraq and at the hands of Croatia and the Former Yugoslav Republic of Macedonia during the Balkan wars of the 1990s.[193] Yet, Goodwin-Gill and McAdam note that in most cases, States have preferred to characterize their actions as 'something "other" than refoulement'.[194]

In other words, instances of violations do not significantly diminish the standing of the rule. Indeed, according to the ICJ, the infringement of a rule should not be necessarily regarded as affecting its customary character:

The Court does not consider that, for a rule to be established as customary, the corresponding practice must be in absolutely rigorous conformity with the rule. In order to deduce the existence of customary rules, the Court deems it sufficient that the conduct of

---

Humanitarian Norms as Customary Law (Clarendon Press, Oxford 1989) 97; G Stenberg, *Non-Expulsion and Non-Refoulement the Prohibition Against Removal of Refugees with Special Reference to Articles 32 and 33 of the 1951 Convention Relating to the Status of Refugees* (Iustus Förlag, Uppsala 1989) 266, 278; J C Hathaway, *The Law of Refugee Status* (Butterworths, Toronto 1991) 24–7; Nowak, n 94 above 185; Plender, *International Migration Law*, n 62 above, 431; Henkel, n 23 above, 147; K Landgren, 'Deflecting international protection by treaty: bilateral and multilateral accords on extradition, readmission and the inadmissibility of asylum requests' (1999) UNHCR New Issues in Refugee Research Paper No. 10, 2; Lauterpacht and Bethlehem, n 186 above, para 253; Goodwin-Gill and McAdam, n 3 above, 346. Cf Coleman, n 23 above, 49, who considers that the status of the principle in Asia and the Middle-East has not been definitively established, 49; K Hailbronner, 'Principles of International Law Regarding the Concept of Subsidiary Protection', in D Bouteillet-Paquet (ed), *Subsidiary Protection of Refugees in the European Union: Complementing the Geneva Convention?* (Bruylant, Brussels 2002) 3, 13; J C Hathaway, *The Rights of Refugees under International Law* (Cambridge University Press, Cambridge 2005), 360–70.

[189] Declaration reaffirming the commitment of signatory States to the 1951 Convention, 13 December 2001, para 4.

[190] See eg UNHCR, Note on International Protection submitted, UN Doc A/AC.96/898, 3 July 1998, para 10–14; see also Hathaway and Dent, n 28 above, 5.

[191] Hyndman, 'Asylum and Non-Refoulement', n 23 above, 72.

[192] D W Greig, 'The Protection of Refugees and Customary International Law' (1983) 8 *Australian Ybk of Intl L* 108, 125–7; Hyndman, 'Asylum and Non-Refoulement', n 23 above, 70–1.

[193] Goodwin-Gill and McAdam, n 3 above, 219, 227, 229–32, 347.

[194] Ibid, 352.

States should, in general, be consistent with such rules, and that instances of State conduct inconsistent with a given rule should generally have been treated as breaches of that rule, not as indications of the recognition of a new rule. If a State acts in a way prima facie incompatible with a recognized rule, but defends its conduct by appealing to exceptions or justifications contained within the rule itself, then whether or not the State's conduct is in fact justifiable on that basis, the significance of that attitude is to confirm rather than to weaken the rule.[195]

Another valid argument against those who dispute the customary nature of *non-refoulement* on the ground of lack of consistent practice is that there is a balancing relationship between *opinio juris* and State practice.[196] Schachter reckons that some international norms, such as human rights norms, are more likely to be violated and that for these types of rules, the requirement of uniform and consistent practice might be less relevant than a strong *opinio juris*, which is obviously present with regard to *non-refoulement*.[197] By the same token, the absence of open and official protests against breaches of *non-refoulement* should not be viewed as an implicit 'acquiescing' to such breaches according to Goodwin-Gill and McAdam who note that States will instead prefer to provide 'tacit support' to UNHCR's official condemnation.[198]

The determination of the existence of a customary obligation is important for several reasons. Most obviously, because States which are not parties to the Refugee Convention may nevertheless be bound by the *non-refoulement* principle. But even for those States which have ratified the Convention and/or its Protocol, the distinction between the customary and the conventional rule is important. The ICJ determined that rules which are both customary and conventional may not necessarily be completely identical, and that even if it were the case, they may be subject to different methods of interpretation and application.[199] Furthermore, customary rules are generally regarded as part of the law of the land without the need for them to be transformed by way of a legislative act.[200]

There remain, however, uncertainties regarding the precise scope of the customary obligation. While the existence of a *non-refoulement* obligation towards individuals seeking refuge does not raise major problems, the same cannot be said

---

[195] *Military and Paramilitary Activities in and Against Nicaragua* (Merits) ICJ Reports (1986) 14, para 186.

[196] O Schachter, 'Entangled Treaty and Custom', in Y Dinstein (ed) *International Law at a Time of Perplexity* (Nijhoff, London [etc] 1989) 716, 735.

[197] Schachter, n 196 above, 727; see also in this respect M Kohen, 'La pratique et la théorie des sources du droit international', in Société Française de Droit International, *La Pratique et le Droit International* (Pédone, Paris 2004) 81, 94. For a thorough review of State practice and instances of *refoulement*, see Goodwin-Gill and McAdam, n 3 above, 229–32.

[198] Goodwin-Gill and McAdam, n 3 above, 228.

[199] *Military and Paramilitary Activities in and against Nicaragua*, n 195 above, paras 176–8.

[200] Lauterpacht and Bethlehem, n 186 above, para 195.

in cases of mass influx.[201] Goodwin-Gill and McAdam point out that 'the prospect of a massive influx of refugees and asylum seekers exposes the limits of the State's obligation otherwise not to return or refuse admission to refugees'.[202] In those cases, the trade-off is often the de facto suspension of all but the most immediate and compelling protection provided by the Convention.[203] It is in fact in these situations that first asylum States, such as Turkey, Thailand, the Former Yugoslav Republic of Macedonia, Tanzania, and Pakistan have insisted on the need for international burden-sharing.[204] Yet, there is a clear and unqualified affirmation of the application of *non-refoulement* in mass influx situations in various international instruments,[205] which is supported by widespread practice.[206]

The second issue relates to the *non-refoulement* of persons not covered by the protection granted by Article 1 CSR. The expression of the principle in the Convention Against Torture and the jurisprudence of the ECtHR provides strong evidence for the existence of a customary principle protecting any person facing a risk of torture. States have, furthermore, recognized, as in Conclusion No. 79, that *non-refoulement* encompasses both the prohibition of Article 33 CSR and the prohibition of returning any person to a country where there is a substantial risk of torture.[207] Lauterpacht and Bethlehem go even further, arguing that the customary norm of *non-refoulement* applies not only to torture but also to any kind of cruel, inhuman, or degrading treatment.[208]

---

[201] See A Hurwitz, 'Mass Influx', in M Gibney and R Hansen (eds) *Immigration and Asylum from 1900 to the Present*, (ABC-CLIO Pub., Santa Barbara 2005), 393, 394.

[202] Goodwin-Gill and McAdam, n 3 above, 243, see also 229–31.

[203] Goodwin-Gill and McAdam, n 3 above, 339; see also in this respect J-F Durieux and J McAdam, '*Non-Refoulement* through Time: The Case for a Derogation Clause to the Refugee Convention in Mass Influx Emergencies' (2004) 16 *IJRL* 4, 13.

[204] See Chapter 4, Section 4.2.1.2 on the relationship between *non-refoulement* and burden-sharing; see also Goodwin-Gill and McAdam, n 3 above, 336–7.

[205] Article II.5 of the OAU 1969 Convention, n 11 above; Art 3.4 of the 1966 Principles Concerning Treatment of Refugees, n 14 above; ExCom Conclusion No. 15 (1979) on Refugees without an Asylum Country, para (f); ExCom Conclusion No. 19 (1980) on Temporary Refuge, para (b) (i); ExCom Conclusion No. 22 (1981) on Protection of Asylum Seekers in Situations of Large-scale Influx, II.A.1 and 2; see also Greig, n 192 above, 133; Hyndman, n 23 above, 75.

[206] J F Hartman, 'The Principle and Practice of Temporary Refuge: A Customary Norm Protecting Civilians Fleeing Internal Armed Conflict', in D A Martin (ed), *The New Asylum Seekers: Refugee Law in the 1980s* (Nijhoff, Dordrecht [etc.] 1988) 87, 89; D Perluss and J F Hartman, 'Temporary Refuge: Emergence of a Customary Norm' (1986) 26 *Virginia J of Intl L* 551, 558–71; the same authors nevertheless distinguish *non-refoulement* from temporary refuge, 599; see also on the terminology G J L Cole, 'Temporary Refuge and the Large Scale Influx of Refugees' (1983) 8 *Australian Ybk of Intl L* 189, 201–2; Cf Hailbronner, n 13 above, 130, 133–4; Coleman, n 23 above, 23, who argues that the status of the principle of *non-refoulement* as a non-derogable principle in cases of mass influx has become untenable.

[207] See ExCom General Conclusion on International Protection No. 79 (1996) para (j); see also ExCom General Conclusion on International Protection No. 81 (1997) para (i); ExCom Conclusion No. 82 on Safeguarding Asylum (1997) para (d) (i).

[208] Lauterpacht and Bethlehem, n 186 above, para 253; see also Goodwin-Gill and McAdam, n 3 above, 351, who note however that inhuman and degrading treatments are carefully circumscribed under international law.

To sum up, one may draw from the above that *non-refoulement* is recognized as a customary principle which applies equally in cases of mass influx as well as to individual arrivals and to anyone who meets the definition in Article 1.A(2) CSR but also to anyone at risk of torture and possibly of ill-treatment and 'irreparable harm'.

5.2 Other Human Rights Obligations

Safe third country mechanisms do not only adversely affect the protection of refugees against *non-refoulement*; other human rights obligations may be infringed, including the right to seek and enjoy asylum from persecution and the right to leave one's country, reviewed below. A number of other States' obligations under the CSR and international human rights law must also be addressed to determine the existence of effective protection in a third State.

5.2.1 The right to seek and enjoy asylum from persecution

The right to grant asylum was originally and exclusively conceived as a discretionary right of sovereign States.[209] It is a customary rule and cannot be viewed as an unfriendly act by the country of origin of the refugee.[210] Since the end of World War II, asylum has progressively shifted from an institution purely based on State sovereignty to a principle founded on human rights theory.[211] However, attempts to give a stronger basis to the concept of asylum under international law have failed so far.

Article 14 of the Universal Declaration of Human Rights provides that individuals have the right to seek and enjoy asylum from persecution.[212] Lauterpacht noted that 'the right formulated in the Convention is the right which any State indisputably possesses under international law', and he did not see what the added value of incorporating it in the Declaration was.[213] The passing allusion to the concept of asylum in the Final Act of the CSR was also indicative of its limited relevance at the time.[214]

---

[209] A Grahl-Madsen, *Territorial Asylum* (Svenska Institutet for International Rett, Stockholm 1980) 42; F Morgenstern, 'The Right of Asylum' (1949) 26 *BYIL* 326, 325; Weis, n 188 above, 481; Plender, n 62 above, 394.

[210] See Recital 4 of the Preamble of the 1967 UN Declaration on Territorial Asylum: 'Recognizing that the grant of asylum by a State to persons entitled to invoke article 14 of the Universal Declaration of Human Rights is a peaceful and humanitarian act and that, as such, it cannot be regarded as unfriendly by any other State.' See also Art 1.1 of the Declaration.

[211] L B Koziebrodski, *Le Droit d'Asile* (Sijthoff, Leyden 1962) 310, 324–5.

[212] GA Res 217 (III), 10 December 1948.

[213] H Lauterpacht, 'The Universal Declaration on Human Rights' (1948) 25 *BYIL* 354, 373; see also C Harvey, 'The Right to Seek Asylum in the European Union' [2004] *EHRLR* 17, 23.

[214] See Recommendation D of the Final Act of the United Nations Conference of Plenipotentiaries on the Status of Refugees and Stateless Persons: 'The Conference, [...] recommends that Governments

The International Law Commission of the United Nations examined the question of the right of asylum in 1959 at the request of the General Assembly, but the project was deferred and never reconsidered.[215] A proposal to include the right of asylum in the ICCPR similarly failed.[216] Article 1.2 of the 1967 UN Declaration on Territorial Asylum further confirmed the sovereign and discretionary character of the granting of asylum, subject only to the conventions or extradition treaties which bind a State.[217] The 1977 UN conference was the last and failed in its attempt to regulate territorial asylum at the international level.[218] The most recent and significant development at the normative level was the adoption of the Charter of Fundamental Rights of the European Union, proclaimed in December 1999, which provides that the right to asylum shall be guaranteed 'with due respect for the rules of the Geneva Convention of 28 July 1951 and the Protocol of 31 January 1967 relating to the status of refugees in accordance with the Treaty establishing the European Community'.[219]

None of the above initiatives, however, addressed the question of whether refugees have a choice of their country of asylum. In 1990, a ministerial statement to the British Parliament asserted that,

[I]t is an internationally accepted principle that a person fleeing persecution, who cannot avail himself of the protection of the authorities of a country of which he is a national, should normally seek asylum in the first safe country reached.[220]

Similarly, during the discussion of the asylum bill in the German Parliament in the early 1990s, it was stated that the new safe third country regulation was based on the principle that a refugee persecuted for political reasons shall seek protection in

---

continue to receive refugees in their territories and that they act in a true spirit of international cooperation in order that these refugees may find asylum and the possibility of resettlement.'

[215] GA Res 1400 (XIV), 21 November 1959; ILC Report, A/4425 (A/15/9), 1960, ch. IV(I), para 39, Ybk (1960) vii.

[216] P S Sinha, *Asylum and International Law* (Nijhoff, The Hague 1971) 71. A proposal to include a provision on the right to asylum also failed during the negotiations of the 2nd Protocol to the ECHR, K Hailbronner, *Möglichkeiten und Grenzen einer Europäischen Koordinierung des Einreise- und Asylrechts* (Nomos Verlagsgesellschaft, Baden-Baden 1989) 27–8.

[217] The exception also applies to persons persecuted for genuinely non-political crimes or for acts contrary to the purposes and principles of the United Nations, a similar formulation is found in Art 14.2 UDHR, see Lauterpacht, n 213 above; see also Art II of the OAU Convention, n 11 above; Art 12(3) of the 1981 African Charter on Human and People's Rights (1982) 21 *ILM* 58; Art 22 (7) of the 1969 American Convention on Human Rights, n 92 above.

[218] See Chapter 1, Section 1.2.2.

[219] Article 18 of the Charter of Fundamental Rights, n 185 above; see in this respect M-T Gil-Bazo, 'Refugee Status, Subsidiary Protection, and the Right to be Granted Asylum under EC Law' UNHCR New Issues in Refugee Research Paper No. 136, November 2006, 7; M-T Gil-Bazo, 'The Charter of Fundamental Rights of the European Union and the Right to be Granted Asylum in the Union's Law' (2008) 27 *Refugee Survey Quarterly 33*.

[220] *Hansard*, HC vol 177, cols 262–3 (25 July 1990); see also statement made on behalf of the European Union by the British representative at the 43rd session of the Executive Committee UN Doc A/AC/.96/SR.472, 16 November 1992, para 79.

the first State where he may possibly claim asylum.[221] While it is obvious that freedom of choice is increasingly restricted by the implementation of safe third country practices, refugees are under no such obligation in international law. The right to seek and enjoy asylum from persecution is only qualified in the two cases set out in Article 14.2 of the Universal Declaration of Human Rights, and there is at this stage no sufficient evidence of any other exception to this right.[222]

The key issue, however, is the extent to which the right to seek and enjoy asylum creates obligations for States. One may argue in this regard that States may actually abuse their right to grant (and not to grant) asylum. States would abuse their right if 'certain limits are exceeded in the course of their exercise or if they are exercised with the (sole) intention of harming others'.[223] The question is whether safe third country arrangements and other containment policies may lead to a situation where refugees would be de facto prevented from seeking asylum. The major difficulty lies in providing evidence of such behaviour. Regulating immigration is perfectly lawful under international law and the determination of 'abusive' policies is not an easy matter. Yet, it is arguable that a serious issue of good faith implementation arises when a State sends an asylum seeker to another country where the opportunity to seek and receive asylum is limited or even non-existent.[224]

There is some interesting, albeit limited, jurisprudence based on the right to seek asylum.[225] It was invoked successfully in a case relating to the interception by US Coast Guards of Haitian boat people similar to that examined by the US Supreme Court.[226] The Inter-American Commission on Human Rights, after expressing its disapproval of the US Supreme Court decision,[227] ruled that the right to seek asylum entails the right to present an asylum claim and that the

---

[221] This statement was reported in the decision of the German Constitutional Court of 14 May 1996, *Bundesverfassungsgericht* (1997) 94 BVerfGE 49, 55; see also S Blay and A Zimmermann, 'Recent Changes in German Refugee Law: A Critical Assessment' (1994) 88 *AJIL* 361, 366; The European Parliament supported on the other hand the right to choose the country of asylum, EP Resolution on the right of asylum [1987] OJ C99/167, para (h).

[222] See also n 217 above; *R v Asfaw* [2008] UKHL 31, para 19 citing Goodwin-Gill's expert opinion.

[223] G S Goodwin-Gill, 'The Right to Leave, the Right to Return and the Question of a Right to Remain', in V Gowlland-Debbas (ed) *The Problem of Refugees in The Light of Contemporary Law Issues* (Martinus Nijhoff, The Hague [etc] 1994) 93, 99. The concept of abuse of right is usually regarded as a general principle of law, B Cheng, *General Principles of Law as Applied by International Courts and Tribunals* (Cambridge University Press, Cambridge 1994) 121, Sir R Jennings and Sir A Watts (eds) *Oppenheim's International Law* (9th edn Longmans, London 1992) Vol I 38 note 5; cf I Brownlie, *Principles of Public International Law* (7th edn Clarendon Press, Oxford 2008) at 445: '[...] it may be said that the doctrine is a useful agent in the progressive development of the law, but that, as a general principle, it does not exist in positive law.'

[224] On good faith, see Goodwin-Gill and McAdam, n 3 above, 387–8.

[225] Plender and Mole, n 100 above, 81, 82.

[226] *The Haitian Centre for Human Rights et al v United States*, Case 10.675, Report No. 51/96, Inter-Am.C.H.R.,OEA/Ser.L/V/II.95 Doc. 7 rev. at 550 (1997), (1997) Inter-American Ybk on HR Vol I 936.

[227] Ibid, paras 156–7, 1046.

interdiction of Haitian boat people on international waters infringed this right.[228] The Commission agreed with the claimants that 'the United States Government's interdiction program had the effect of prohibiting the Haitians from gaining entry into The Bahamas, Jamaica, Cuba, Mexico, the Cayman Islands, or any other country in which they might seek safe haven'.[229]

5.2.2 The right to leave one's country

The right to leave may be presented as a corollary to the right to seek asylum, for the latter cannot be enjoyed if individuals are not able to leave their country of origin. The fundamental character of this right is now recognized under international human rights law,[230] but there are authorized restrictions to its enjoyment. Article 12.3 ICCPR, for instance, sets out that these limitations must be provided by law and be necessary to protect national security, public order, public health or morals, or the rights and freedoms of others.[231] In accordance with the general rules of treaty interpretation, these limitations should be construed restrictively in order to preserve the essential purpose of the Covenant, which is the protection of the fundamental rights of individuals.[232]

---

[228] Ibid, paras 161–3, 1050. Note that the Commission based its decision on Principle XXVII of the American Declaration on the Rights and Duties of Men, rather than on Art 22.7 of the 1969 American Convention on Human Rights which had been signed but not ratified by the United States at the time of the application, para 149.

[229] Ibid, para 161. The African Commission on Human and People's Rights found that the right to seek asylum entails the prohibition of the arbitrary expulsion of refugees, see Communications No. 27/89, 46/91, 49/91, 99/93 *Organisation Mondiale contre la Torture and others v Rwanda* Decision of the African Commission on Human and Peoples' Rights, 20th session October 1996 (1999) 8 Review of the African Commission on Human and People's Rights, 138, 142.

[230] See eg Art 13.2 UDHR; Art 12.2 ICCPR; Art 5(d) (ii) of the 1965 UN Convention on the Elimination of all Forms of Racial Discrimination (adopted 7 March 1966, entered into force 4 January 1969) 660 *UNTS* 195; Art 10(2) of the 1989 Convention on the Rights of the Child (adopted 20 November 1989, entered into force 2 September 1990) 1577 UNTS 3; Art 2.2 of Protocol No. 4 to the ECHR securing certain rights and freedoms other than those already included in the Convention and in the 1st Protocol thereto (15 November 1963) ETS No. 46; Art 12(2) of the 1981 African Charter of Human and People's Rights, n 217 above; and Art 22(2) of the 1969 American Convention on Human Rights, n 92 above; R Higgins, 'La liberté de circulation des personnes en droit international', in M Flory and R Higgins (eds), *Liberté de circulation des personnes en droit international* (Économica, Paris 1988) 7; H Hannum, *The Right to Leave and Return in International Law and Practice* (Nijhoff, Dordrecht [etc] 1987) 3, 7.

[231] Similar restrictions may be found in Art 29 UDHR; Art 2.3 of Protocol No. 4 to the ECHR; Art 22.2 and 22.3 of the 1969 American Convention on Human Rights, n 92 above; Art 12.2 of the 1981 African Charter on Human and People's Rights.

[232] S Jagerskiold, 'The Freedom of Movement', in L Henkin (ed), *The International Bill of Rights: The Covenant on Civil and Political Rights* (New York, Columbia University Press 1981) 166, 171–3, 178; See also Art 4 of the Strasbourg Declaration on the Right to Leave and to Return adopted on 26 November 1986; Human Rights Committee General Comment No. 27 on freedom of movement, UN Doc CCPR/C/21/Rev.1/Add.9, 2 November 1999, paras 14, 16–17; ExCom General Conclusion on International Protection No. 96 (2003) para (a).

The right to leave is also one of the constitutive elements of the right to free movement, which is emerging as an international principle, albeit in a conditional and limited form.[233] As stated by Goodwin-Gill, 'freedom to leave any country is a good in itself, but not to the point that it may be considered to impose either obligations or expectations on other States'.[234] Hailbronner supports this view, on the ground that State practice shows a clear resistance to restrictions to their right to control the entry of aliens on their territory, the only exception being cases of family reunification.[235]

Among the arsenal of containment measures adopted by States, those consisting of penalizing people who leave or help other people leave their country illegally have been the most directly antagonizing. Framed in such broad terms, such regulations would indeed seem to go beyond the scope of the exceptions allowed under international human rights law.[236] States may also incur responsibility by abetting actions of the State of origin in preventing people from leaving, for example, through the participation in joint patrols or any similar type of assistance in border control, such as those carried out by the European Union's external border's agency, FRONTEX.[237]

Secondly, and even though the right to leave is typically viewed as an obligation falling on the State of origin,[238] one could argue that since refugees are individuals

---

[233] The right to free movement entails the freedom to choose a residence and move within the borders of a State; freedom to leave a State; freedom to enter/return to a State; freedom from expulsion from a State; and freedom from exile; P Sieghart, *The International Law of Human Rights* (Clarendon Press, Oxford 1983) 178–9; see also Jagerskiold, n 232 above, 166.

[234] Goodwin-Gill, 'The Right to Leave', n 223 above, 97.

[235] K Hailbronner 'Comments on: The Right to Leave, the Right to Return and the Question of a Right to Remain', in V Gowlland-Debbas (ed), *The Problem of Refugees in The Light of Contemporary Law Issues* (Nijhoff, The Hague [etc.] 1996) 109, 113–14.

[236] See G S Goodwin-Gill, 'Migrant Rights and "Managed Migration"', in V Chetail (ed), *Mondialisation, migration et droits de l'homme: le droit international en question* (Bruylant, Brussels 2007) 161, 167, 174, citing C Rodier, 'Emigration illégale: une notion à bannir' Libération 13 juin 2006 available at: <http://www.migreurop.org/article922.html>.

[237] Weinzierl and Lisson, n 32 above, 17; see Council Regulation (EC) 2007/2004 establishing a European Agency for the Management of Operational Cooperation at the External Borders of the Member States of the European Union, [2004] OJ L349/1; see also ECRE, *Defending Refugees' Access to Protection in Europe*, December 2007, 12–13, which notes that FRONTEX reported the apprehension during one of its operations in 2007, of 1,500 migrants most of them from Albania, Afghanistan, Iraq, Pakistan, Palestine, and Somalia, without indicating whether any of these individuals intended to seek asylum. Additionally, FRONTEX has been negotiating 'working arrangements with Morocco, Mauritania, Senegal and Libya and Croatia and undertaking joint operations with some of these countries', ibid, 14. See *Xhavara and ors v Italy and Albania*, Appl. No. 39473/98, 11 January 2001, in which the ECtHR dismissed an application by Albanian nationals seeking to enter Italy irregularly. The applicants argued, inter alia, that the interdiction of their boat by an Italian vessel had violated their right to leave their country. The ECtHR held that the action of the Italian vessel was not in violation of the right to leave under Art 2.2 of Protocol No. 4 to the ECHR; see also Goodwin-Gill and McAdam, n 3 above, 383.

[238] During the cold war, Western countries focused on the violation of this right by Socialist countries; see Goodwin-Gill, 'The Right to Leave', n 223 above, 93 and 98; R Higgins, 'Recent Developments in Respect of the Right to Leave in International Law', in E D Brown and B Cheng (eds)

who cannot claim the protection of their State of origin, they are the responsibility of the international community, and each State has a duty to ensure the protection of their fundamental rights, including their right to leave their country. Goodwin-Gill and McAdam note in this respect that 'the right to leave to seek asylum from persecution may be the only aspect of the right to leave one's country in international law to impose any duty on other States'.[239]

Particularly delicate is the situation in which chain readmission takes place, which de facto prevents individuals, including potential refugees, from leaving permanently the territory of their State of origin.[240] As with the right to seek asylum, it is arguable that containment policies that fail to ensure the provision of protection to refugees actually constitute an abuse by States of their rights. As explained by Goodwin-Gill and McAdam, there might be a duty 'not to frustrate the exercise of that right in such a way as to leave individuals exposed to persecution or other violations of their human rights'.[241] This would thus entail the responsibility of all of the States participating in these readmission arrangements.[242]

5.2.3 Other relevant international refugee law and human rights obligations

While *refoulement* and related rights, namely the right to seek asylum and the right to leave one's country are of paramount importance in determining the validity of safe third country mechanisms, a wider array of international refugee and human rights law obligations must be considered for the purposes of assessing the existence of effective protection. Under the Refugee Convention, the rights granted to refugees may be categorized on the basis of the simple presence, lawful presence, lawful residence, or habitual residence of a refugee.[243] Thus at a minimum refugees 'simply present' enjoy, in accordance with the CSR, the right not to be discriminated against based on their race, religion, or country of origin; freedom of religion to the same extent as nationals of the host country; access to courts and identity papers; and non-penalization and limited restrictions on free movement.[244] Given

---

Contemporary Problems of International Law: Essays in Honour of Georg Schwartzenberger on his Eightieth Birthday (Stevens and Sons, London 1988) 138, 146.

[239] Goodwin-Gill and McAdam, n 3 above, 383.

[240] The right to leave one's country covers both temporary and permanent departure from one's country; see Art 2 of the Declaration on the Right to Leave and the Right to Return in *The Right to Leave and To Return; Papers and Recommendations of the International Colloquium held in Uppsala Sweden, 19–21 June 1972* (1976); Art 1 of the Strasbourg Declaration on the Right to Leave and to Return adopted on 26 November 1986.

[241] Goodwin-Gill and McAdam, n 3 above, 383.

[242] See in this respect Arts 16 and 47 of the International Law Commission Articles on Responsibility of States for Internationally Wrongful Acts, Res 56/83, 22 January 2002.

[243] Goodwin-Gill and McAdam, n 3 above, 524.

[244] Ibid, see Arts 3, 4, 16, 27, 31 CSR.

the declaratory nature of the status of refugee, these rights apply regardless of whether an individual has been formally recognized as a refugee. To this rather basic list of rights, one must obviously add fundamental rights recognized under international human rights treaties, such as the right to family life or the right to security and liberty.[245] Taken together, these standards have been presented as a 'bundle of rights to fair and humane treatment'.[246] UNHCR EXCOM Conclusion No. 58 refers to 'basic human standards',[247] while the Lisbon Conclusions adopted under the auspices of UNHCR suggest that in essence, effective protection should also entail 'access to means of subsistence sufficient to maintain an adequate standard of living',[248] consideration of 'special vulnerabilities' of the person concerned[249] as well as the right to privacy and family life.[250] Goodwin-Gill and McAdam adopt similarly broad language, indicating that effective guarantees would include, inter alia, 'some provision with respect to subsistence and human dignity issues, such as social assistance or access to the labour market in the interim, family unity, education of children, and so forth'.[251]

The question is whether the State of final destination, which is bound to respect these rights under relevant treaties, may send an asylum seeker to a third State, which is not a party to the relevant treaty, has entered reservations to some of these key provisions, or is not implementing its obligations.[252] This is an important consideration because, as was reflected in the findings of a survey of Somali asylum seekers, standards of treatment in the third country or first country of asylum will often be inadequate and push asylum seekers to seek better conditions elsewhere.[253]

For some, the answer is clear: the State party must comply with its obligations and cannot 'contract out' its obligations or transfer responsibility for such obligations to another State.[254] Thus 'a good faith application of Convention obligations requires that, in order to transfer a refugee to another state in accordance with the Refugee Convention, a state is under an obligation to ensure that they will enjoy

---

[245] M Foster, 'Protection Elsewhere: The Legal Implications of Requiring Refugees to Seek Protection in Another State' (2007) 28 *Michigan J of Intl L* 223, 267; Goodwin-Gill and McAdam, n 3 above, 396.

[246] Legomsky, n 48 above, 613–14.

[247] ExCom Conclusion No. 58 (1989) on the Problem of Refugees and Asylum Seekers Who Move in an Irregular Manner from a Country in Which They Already Found Protection, para (f) (ii).

[248] See Lisbon Conclusions, n 69 above, para 15 g).

[249] Ibid, para 15 h).

[250] Ibid, para 15 i).

[251] Godwin-Gill and McAdam, n 3 above, 396.

[252] See eg Legomsky, n 48 above, 386.

[253] Among the standard of treatment concerns reported in the survey are harassment by law enforcement officials, precarious living conditions, limitations on freedom of movement, prohibition of restrictions on gainful employment, lack of access to education, see J Moret, S Baglioni, D Efyonayi, *The Paths of Somali Refugees into Exile, A Comparative Analysis of Secondary Movements and Policy Responses*, SFM Studies 46, 2006, 10.

[254] Foster, n 245 above, 268–9.

the rights to which she is entitled under the Convention scheme'.[255] This view is based on a strict application of principles of international responsibility which dictate that State responsibility is at issue for direct as well as indirect breaches of international obligations.[256] At the other end of the spectrum, one finds the opinion of Lord Bingham of Cornhill in *Yogathas* who held that, 'it can never, save in extreme circumstances, be appropriate to compare an applicant's living conditions in different countries if, in each of them, he will be safe from persecution or the risk of it'.[257] A middle-ground approach is advocated by Legomsky, who suggests that a 'variable standard of proof' be applied, meaning that 'the more important the particular right, the more confident the [sending] country should have to be before it is permitted to effect a return'.[258] While certainly flexible, Legomsky acknowledges that this approach would bear clear disadvantages, namely, uncertainty, unpredictability, and risk of manipulation.[259]

The more orthodox approach in human rights terms would lead to a similar outcome as the *Raad van State*'s autonomous understanding of State obligations. While its legal logic may seem infallible, it is openly contradicted by the practice of States and the views of UNHCR. Legomsky notes that this in effect 'would disqualify a large number of countries—perhaps literally all of them' from the qualification of safety.[260] Said differently, a strict application of the abovementioned principles would basically lead to the conclusion that safe third country arrangements are essentially 'unimplementable'.

On the other hand, Lord Bingham of Cornhill's assertion overlooks the fact that asylum seekers and refugees are entitled to a wider array of rights under international law than the right not to be subject to a risk of persecution or *refoulement*, and that the question of the extent to which those rights will be guaranteed in a third country must in fact be considered in assessing the existence of effective protection. This would be the case, for instance, of discrimination on any of the grounds provided under Article 3 CSR, which may not necessarily amount to persecution but is nonetheless strictly prohibited, or to a violation of family and privacy rights under Article 8 ECHR not covered by the exceptions provided under Article 8.2 ECHR.[261] One way to resolve this difficult question could be to

---

[255] Ibid, 270.

[256] See n 242 above; see also C Phuong, 'The Concept of "effective protection" in the Context of Irregular Secondary Movements and Protection in Regions of Origin', *Global Migration Perspectives* No. 26, April 2005, 10–11 who relies on the doctrine of acquired rights to argue that by 'sending the refugee to a state where his rights are not protected, the sending state would be depriving him of his acquired rights'; GS Goodwin-Gill, 'Offshore Processing of Asylum Seekers: The Search for Legitimate Parameters' (2007) *UTS Law Review* 26, 38–9.

[257] *R v Secretary of State for the Home Department ex p Thangasara and R v Secretary of State for the Home Department ex p Yogathas* [2002] UKHL para 9.

[258] Legomsky, n 48 above, 623–4.

[259] Ibid, 624.

[260] Legosmky, n 48 above, 641.

[261] Cf the position of the House of Lords in *EM (Lebanon) v Secretary of State for the Home Department* [2008] UKHL 64, see n 97 above.

distinguish between those rights to which no reservation is allowed, and rights which can be derogated from, as is suggested by Legomsky.[262] Thus, the return of an asylum seeker to a country where he/she would not enjoy all of the rights guaranteed by the country wishing to return him or her would not be unlawful, as long as those rights may be subject to reservations.[263] This would at least ensure some level of predictability, which the 'variable standard of proof' is unlikely to guarantee.

As explained in Chapter 4, the international refugee regime is premised upon the principle of cooperation and collective responsibility of States in the protection of refugees. Furthermore, as was noted above, UNHCR has never affirmed that States' obligations under the Refugee Convention are purely autonomous. While EU Member States are now bound by the Directive on reception standards, this only partly resolves the problem.[264] Such a construction would also prevent return to a country of first asylum, which UNHCR considers to be perfectly lawful and where standards of treatment would be comparable to those in developed States.

5.3 Removal to a Safe Third Country and States' Obligations: The Content and Scope of Effective Protection

The above review shows that under conventional and general international law, a State which removes an asylum seeker to a safe third country may be held responsible for an indirect violation of the *non-refoulement* principle. This means that refugees are protected against *refoulement* even if they cannot invoke Article 31 CSR.[265] With regard to the requirement of effective protection, it is clear from domestic, supranational, and international jurisprudence, that the mere fact that the third country is a party to the CSR and/or to universal and regional human rights instruments does not constitute a sufficient guarantee that it will abide by its obligations.[266]

---

[262] Ibid, 644.

[263] Ibid, 644.

[264] Council Directive 2003/9/EC of 27 January 2003 laying down minimum standards for the reception of asylum seekers, [2003] OJ L31/18; see S Peers, *EU Justice and Home Affairs Law* (2nd edn, Oxford University Press, Oxford 2006) 324–7. Note that it is not clear that this Directive applies in 'Dublin', let alone, 'safe third country' cases.

[265] Grahl-Madsen, n 3 above, 227.

[266] See *Canadian Council for Refugees, Canadian Council of Churches, Amnesty International and John Doe v R* 2007 FC 1262, para 136. The Federal Court noted however that a presumption of compliance would apply, ibid. See also M Kagan, 'The Beleaguered Gatekeeper: Protection Challenges Posed by UNHCR Refugee Status Determination' (2006) 18 *IJRL* 1, 15.

A fortiori, the removal of a refugee to a third State not party to the CSR, which is common practice and seems to be accepted by UNHCR,[267] would seem to entail a violation of the duty to comply in good faith with one's obligations, on grounds that there is in such an instance too high a risk that the asylum seeker will not be protected and will not be given the opportunity to present his/her claim to the authorities and have it examined substantively. Even if all States are bound by a customary obligation of *non-refoulement*, the absence of adequate procedures for determining refugee status, as well as the lack of proper reception facilities, arguably raises the risk of *refoulement* and of violations of other provisions of the CSR to an unacceptable level.[268] Other commentators add that given that UNHCR is tasked with supervisory duties under Article 35 CSR, it would have greater leverage to ensure effective protection and adequately monitor legal developments in the third State, which further militates in favour of requiring third States to be parties to the CSR.[269]

The Lisbon Conclusions nevertheless provide in this respect that,

> where the return of an asylum-seeker to a third State is involved, accession to and compliance with the 1951 Convention and/or 1967 Protocol are essential, unless the destination country can demonstrate that the third State has developed a practice akin to the 1951 Convention and/or its 1967 Protocol.[270]

While seemingly restrictive, it is not fully clear from these conclusions what a 'practice akin to the 1951 Convention and/or 1967 Protocol' is. It would seem to entail the existence of domestic legislation laying down criteria for the granting of protection similar to refugee status and the procedure for claiming such status. In the author's view, any process by which protection is granted through UNHCR would not meet the 'practice akin to' standard, given the shortcomings of UNHCR refugee status determination procedures.[271] In this perspective, Legomsky's argument that there is no evidence of a clear prohibition under international law of returning individuals to third States that are not parties to the CSR, provided those individuals have access to a fair refugee status determination procedure, generally carried out by UNHCR is unpersuasive.[272] As noted by Kagan, even when UNCHR undertakes refugee status determination procedures, the government remains primarily responsible for providing protection and it is therefore 'unrealistic to expect UNHCR to itself provide effective protection through its

---

[267] See reference in Legomsky, n 48 above; Foster, n 245 above, 240.

[268] See Chapter 2.

[269] Foster, n 245 above, 240–1.

[270] Lisbon Conclusions, n 69 above, para 15 e). See also Art 27.1 (d) of the asylum procedures Directive, providing as one of the criteria 'the possibility to request refugee status and, if found to be a refugee, to receive protection in accordance with the Geneva Convention'.

[271] Kagan, n 266 above; see also M Alexander, 'Refugee Status Determination Conducted by UNHCR' (1999) 11 *IJRL* 251.

[272] Legomsky, n 48 above, 661; see also J C Hathaway, *The Rights of Refugees under International Law* n 188 above, 332–3.

mandate alone'.[273] Thus, accession and compliance with the Refugee Convention should constitute a crucial benchmark. It is in fact surprising that UNHCR has not been more insistent on this point, given its clear reluctance to mainstream refugee status determination procedures out of fear to thereby legitimize States' failure to accede to the Refugee Convention.[274] Furthermore, allowing removal to a State that is not a party to the CSR fundamentally weakens the Refugee Convention and the whole international refugee regime. There is, finally, a key policy argument favouring a principled approach. Requiring third States to become parties to the CSR would encourage European States to pressure neighbouring States that have not yet acceded to the CSR to do so without delay.[275]

The requirement that the third State be a party to the CSR is based on the consideration of the risk of threat to an individual's life and freedom. The assessment of the risk or threat of *refoulement* or of violations of other fundamental human rights faced by the refugee if sent to an intermediate country should also be determinative with respect to the modalities of removal. In this regard, the unilateral removal to a third country not only poses problems in terms of inter-State relations, as was discussed in Chapter 4, it also increases the risk of orbit situations and chain *refoulement*. Obviously, a treaty provision should not be interpreted in a manner which would lead to a violation of international law and from the standpoint of State responsibility, Goodwin-Gill and McAdam rightly note that while the State 'that actually returns a refugee to persecution or other serious harm remains primarily responsible for that act, the first State, through its act of expulsion, may be jointly liable for it'.[276] They therefore suggest that the phrases 'indirect' or 'chain' refoulement 'divert attention from the basis of liability and the nature of the act attributable to the first State'.[277] Based on the above considerations, many refugee advocates and commentators, as well as UNHCR, recommend that safe third country mechanisms be based on a written agreement between States to admit or readmit asylum seekers, providing for full compliance with the CSR, notification of UNHCR and unhindered access by UNHCR to transferred refugees and dispute settlement procedures.[278]

---

[273] Kagan, n 266 above, 12-13; see eg the situation of asylum seekers returned from Australia to Indonesia, which is not a party to the CSR, and where UNHCR undertakes refugee status determination, S Taylor, 'Protection Elsewhere/Nowhere' (2006) 18 *IJRL* 283, 297–8.

[274] On the challenges of refugee status determination procedures conducted by UNHCR, see Kagan, n 266 above, 22–3, 26.

[275] Legomsky, n 48 above, 661.

[276] Goodwin-Gill and McAdam, n 3 above, 252–3; see also Goodwin-Gill, 'Offshore Processing', n 256 above, 26, 38.

[277] Ibid.

[278] Lisbon Conclusions, n 69 above, para 12; UNHCR Issues Paper, n 48 above, para 13; Foster, n 245 above, 283–284; see also Legomsky, n 48 above, 630–2, 680; see also ExCom Conclusion No. 15 (1979) on Refugees Without an Asylum Country and ExCom General Conclusion on International Protection No. 71 (1993); cf Art 27.4 of the asylum procedures Directive, which provides that '[w]here the third country does not permit the applicant for asylum to enter its territory, Member States shall ensure that access to a procedure is given in accordance with the basic principles

An additional consideration to be drawn from the above review is that international law clearly requires that there be a case-by-case examination of whether the asylum seeker will have or has had his claim adjudicated in a proper manner in the State to which he will be removed and whether he will be protected from *refoulement* and from other fundamental human rights violations.[279] Besides the substantial international jurisprudence reviewed above, one finds further support for such holding in the principle of private international law, whereby a foreign judgment does not have automatic legal effect in another State. In *Stefan and ors*, the counsel for the Home Office relied on concepts of private international law and recognized that 'the process in the third country must be one which accords with what can broadly be stated to be the principles of natural justice.'[280] The judge agreed that the procedure in the third country should be subject to scrutiny in order to determine the existence of any serious 'procedural defect which constituted a breach of the English Court's view of substantial justice'.[281] In other words, and notwithstanding the clear preference of governments for such an approach, a determination made *in abstracto* does not meet the standard of scrutiny required to properly assess the existence of effective protection in a third State. This is a sensible approach for the basic reason that a country may be safe with respect to one particular individual or group and clearly not for another.[282] Similarly, any such determination should be subject to review or appeal in accordance with the right to an effective remedy recognized under international human rights law.[283]

and guarantees described in Chapter II'. For a discussion of the provisions of the asylum procedures Directive, see Chapter 2, Section 2.1.2.

[279] Henkel, n 23 above, 152–3. Note that Art 27.2 (b) of the asylum procedures Directive, leaves to Member States the determination of the methodology to apply to determine whether a country is safe, including through case-by-case consideration and/or national designation of countries considered to be generally safe; see also the Australian practice of returning asylum seekers to Indonesia, Taylor, n 273 above, 300; see also the Canadian Federal Court's ruling that 'the [Safe Third Country Agreement], in its application to an individual, may be "overbroad" or "arbitrary" because it applies to individuals who may be placed at risk if sent back to the U.S. and grants no discretion to the immigration officer to allow a person to make a claim in Canada where such risk exists. The analysis of the state of U.S. law, practices and policies indicates that it is not safe for all refugee claimants. Some discretion in the hands of the front line immigration official would protect refugees who would otherwise be exposed to risk of contravention of Articles 33 and 3 of the Convention or who for other individual circumstances should not be returned to the U.S.', *Canadian Council for Refugees, Canadian Council of Churches, Amnesty International and John Doe v R* 2007 FC 1262, para 310. Note, however, that this case is, at the time of writing, pending before the Supreme Court of Canada, after the Federal Court of Appeal overturned the Federal Court Judgment, see 2008 FCA 229. See also *Secretary of State for the Home Department v Nasseri* [2008] EWCA Civ 464, para 42, discussed in Chapter 2, Section 2.2.1.3.

[280] *R v Secretary of State for the Home Department and Special adjudicators ex p Tania Luiza Stefan, Andrea Anca Chiper and Marius Ionel* [1995] Imm AR 410 (QBD), 419-20.

[281] Ibid, 420; R Byrne, 'Redesigning Fortress Europe: European Asylum Policy' *The Oxford International Review* (1996 Summer Issue) 10, 13.

[282] House of Lords, *Handling EU Asylum Claims: New Approaches Examined*, European Union Committee's 11th Report of Session 2003-2004, HL Paper 74 (2004) para 66.

[283] Foster, n 245 above, 282–3. Note in this respect that Art 39 of the asylum procedures Directive provides that it is for Member States to determine 'the grounds for challenging a decision under Art 25(2) (c) in accordance with the methodology applied under Art 27(2)(b) and (c)' which would

Finally, removals to a third country should only be carried out among a group of States willing to enter into a process of closer international supervision of their asylum laws through, inter alia, the setting up of a supranational or international body with the competence to rule on the interpretation of the Refugee Convention. Many authors have emphasized that safe third country arrangements raise issues of joint responsibility and that the state sending an asylum seeker to a third country may be 'complicit' of a breach of international refugee and/or international human rights law.[284] While this is obviously true, such conclusion is not particularly helpful for the individuals affected. Traditional mechanisms of State responsibility are ill-suited to address violations of international obligations towards individuals;[285] this is the reason why international human rights bodies vested with the competence to hear individual petitions have been established.[286] In spite of their flaws, the very existence of these bodies epitomizes the evolution of the international legal system towards greater accountability of States for violations of individuals' rights.[287] The fact that refugees and stateless persons, whose status was originally created by the international community, do not have access to any specific international legal remedies to challenge States' decisions on their status based on the key treaties protecting them, is at the very least paradoxical, if not anomalous. Furthermore, the application of the safe third country within a closely integrated group of States is more likely to guarantee that equivalent levels of human rights protection would be guaranteed, including basic living standards.

5.4 Conclusion

This chapter sought to demonstrate that safe third country mechanisms are not satisfactory from the perspective of refugee protection. The analysis of the *non-refoulement* principle under international refugee and human rights law and of other human rights obligations suggests that the current implementation of these arrangements entails serious risks for refugees' rights. Given that protection standards differ so much between States, adequate implementation in compliance with international law requires that national authorities determine on an individual basis whether a third country would provide effective protection to the refugee and that removal to such a country be based on an explicit agreement, so as to guarantee

---

seem to mean that the scope of the right to appeal decisions on inadmissibility based on the assessment of safety of a country are left to Member States.

[284] See eg Goodwin-Gill and McAdam, n 3 above, 252–3; Legomsky, n 48 above, 619–20; Foster, n 245 above, 262–3. See also, Arts 16 and 47 of the ILC Arts, n 242 above.

[285] See Art 42 of the ILC Arts, n 242 above.

[286] G Cohen-Jonathan, 'Responsabilité pour atteinte aux droits de l'homme', in Société française pour le droit international (ed) *La responsabilité dans le système international* (1991) 101, 106–7; Meron, n 188 above, 138–54.

[287] See Chapter 7.

that the asylum claim will be examined on its merits and in accordance with basic procedural safeguards and international law. That country should at a minimum be party to the CSR and other key international human rights instruments. Finally, safe third country practices should be applied among States which are willing to be subject to close international supervision, preferably through quasi-judicial or judicial monitoring mechanisms.

6

Supervision at the Level of the European Union

Within the EC legal order, the Court of Justice (ECJ) has had the fundamental responsibility of guaranteeing the constitutionality of the organization's activities, and of ensuring Member States' compliance with Community law.[1] With its newly gained competence to interpret and rule on the validity of Community legislation adopted in the asylum field, the Court of Justice of the European Communities has, in effect, become the first supranational judicial organ to be granted explicit competence to rule on the interpretation of the 1951 Convention Relating to the Status of Refugees.[2] As such, the provisions of the Amsterdam Treaty constituted a landmark in the development of international refugee law.

However, one should not assume that the ECJ's intervention will substantially and necessarily contribute to the strengthening of international refugee law standards. First, there are concerns with respect to the adequacy of remedies currently available to asylum seekers and refugees under European law. Secondly, there remain many uncertainties about the EU legal framework on fundamental rights, its relation with the ECHR, and the extent to which the ECJ will consider international refugee law and human rights norms in adjudicating asylum cases.

This chapter will start by an examination of the ECJ's jurisdiction over asylum measures, including the implication of Member States' 'opt-outs', and the intervention of UNHCR in proceedings before the Court. The second section will analyse the origins and development of fundamental rights in the EU context.

---

[1] *Commentaire Mégret, Le Droit de la CEE* Vol 10 (2nd edn, Université Libre de Bruxelles, Bruxelles 1993) 3.

[2] Article 63.1 of the consolidated version of the Treaty establishing the European Community, 24 December 2002 [2002] OJ C325/33 (hereafter, ECT); 1951 Geneva Convention Relating to the Status of Refugees (adopted 28 July 1951, entered into force 22 April 1954) 189 UNTS 150 (hereafter, CSR or Refugee Convention).

6.1 The Court of Justice under the EC Treaty

6.1.1 Remedies before the European Court of Justice

Under the EC Treaty, the Court of Justice is competent:[3]

    (a) to rule at the request of the Commission,[4] or of another Member State,[5] on the alleged failure to fulfil an obligation under the Treaty;

    (b) to review the legality of Community acts;[6]

    (c) to establish a failure to act by one of the institutions;[7]

    (d) to give preliminary rulings concerning the interpretation of the Treaty and the validity and interpretation of acts of the institutions of the Community;[8]

    (e) to rule on the interpretation of Title IV or of acts of the institutions based on this title;[9]

    (f) to award damages to compensate for breaches of EC law by any Community institution or functionary;[10]

    (g) to order an interim injection in view of suspending an act being contested in the course of a principal action brought before it.[11]

Article 67.2 ECT provides that after five years following the entry into force of the Treaty of Amsterdam,

[T]he Council, acting unanimously after consulting the European Parliament, shall take a decision with a view to providing for all or parts of the areas covered by this Title to be governed by the procedure referred to in Article 251 and adapting the provisions relating to the powers of the Court of Justice.

---

[3] Note that the Court of Justice is understood here as the court system of the European Communities thus including the Court of First Instance (hereafter, CFI) established by the Single European Act and the Court of Justice as such. The jurisdiction of the CFI was originally limited to staff cases and annulment and damages actions brought in cases involving steel quotas and competition disputes. In 1994, the CFI's competence was extended to cover all actions brought by natural and legal persons against EC institutions. While the Maastricht Treaty amended the ECT allowing the Council to grant jurisdiction to the CFI over any action except for preliminary rulings, this was not done until 2004, see Council Decision (EC) No. 2004/407 of 26 April 2004 amending Articles 51 and 54 of the Protocol on the Statute of the Court of Justice [2004] OJ L132/5. The Court of Justice remains competent for annulment actions brought between EU institutions and actions brought by States seeking the annulment of EC legislative acts, see S Peers, 'The Future of the EU Judicial System and EC Immigration and Asylum Law' (2005) 7 *EJML* 263, 264–5.

[4] Article 226 ECT.

[5] Article 227 ECT.

[6] Article 230 ECT.

[7] Article 232 ECT.

[8] Article 234 ECT.

[9] Article 68.3 ECT.

[10] Article 235 ECT combined with Art 288.2 ECT.

[11] Article 243 ECT. Note that the Court has other functions which are of lesser interest to the present discussion, see Arts 235–9 ECT.

The five-year deadline passed on 1 May 2004 and in spite of the fact that in The Hague Programme of November 2004, the European Council had asked the Commission to make a proposal on the speedy and appropriate handling of requests for preliminary ruling in the areas of freedom, security, and justice,[12] no such decision seems to have been taken yet.[13] This was probably expected to be done through the ratification and entry into force of the Constitutional Treaty and afterwards, of the Treaty of Lisbon, which both provide for Article 68 ECT to be repealed, for Article 234 ECT to apply to asylum and migration policies,[14] and also included amendments to the ECJ powers under Article 230 ECT.[15] However, since the double failure to ensure the ratification by all Member States of either instrument, this issue has not yet been resolved.

For now, the only post-Amsterdam amendments relevant to the ECJ are those introduced by the 2000 Nice Treaty, which provides that the Court of First Instance shall have jurisdiction to hear and determine actions or proceedings referred to in Articles 230 and 232 ECT.[16]

6.1.1.1 *Failure to comply with the Treaty: Articles 226 and 227 ECT*

Infringement proceedings may be initiated by the Commission *proprio motu* or following a complaint lodged by an individual.[17] They are organized in four distinct phases, the first three being administrative and the fourth one being judicial in nature. The first phase consists in informal negotiations wherein the Member State is given an opportunity to put forward its position and to arrive at an agreement with the Commission. In the absence of a 'pre-contentious' settlement, the Commission in a second phase will formally notify the Member State in writing of the details of the alleged breach of European Community law. The Member State in question will generally have two months to submit its observations. Based on the Member State's submissions, the Commission has the choice

---

[12] European Council, 'The Hague Programme: Strengthening Freedom, Security and Justice in the European Union', 4–5 November 2004, Council Doc 14292/1/04 REV 1, 8 December 2004 [2004] OJ C53/1.

[13] S Peers, *EU Justice and Home Affairs Law* (2nd edn, Oxford University Press, Oxford 2006) 37.

[14] See Treaty establishing a Constitution for Europe, 16 December 2004 [2004] OJ C310/1; Art 67 of the Treaty of Lisbon Amending the Treaty on European Union and the Treaty Establishing the European Community (Lisbon, 13 December 2007) [2007] OJ C306/1 (hereafter, Lisbon Treaty).

[15] Article 214 Lisbon Treaty.

[16] See Art 2.31 of the Treaty of Nice Amending the Treaty on European Union, the Treaties Establishing the European Communities and Certain Related Acts (Nice, 26 February 2001) [2001] OJ C80/1 which entered into force on 1 February 2003 (hereafter, Nice Treaty). Note that the decisions of the Court of First Instance may be appealed to the Court of Justice on points of law only under the conditions and within the limits laid down by the Statute. See also S Peers, 'The EU Institutions and Title IV', in S Peers and N Rogers (eds), *EU Immigration and Asylum Law* (Nijhoff, Leiden [etc] 2006) 47, 76.

[17] P Craig and G De Burca, *EU Law, Text Cases & Materials* (4th edn, Oxford University Press, Oxford 2008) 429.

between either taking the case forward or closing it. If it decides to proceed with the case, the Commission, in a third phase, will deliver a reasoned opinion on the matter, which will circumscribe the scope of the dispute and set a deadline for compliance by the Member State. In most cases, a satisfactory settlement will be found. However, if the State does not comply with the opinion of the Commission, proceedings may be initiated before the Court in a fourth stage.[18] The procedure illustrates the unique role given to the Commission in the Community institutional framework as guardian of the treaties.[19]

The Commission's power under Article 226 ECT is discretionary,[20] and concern was expressed in the past over the possibility that the Commission may not bring proceedings for political reasons, or conversely, may be overzealous in its enforcement power.[21] The Court of Justice has, however, denied the possibility of bringing a claim against the Commission for failure to start infringement proceedings under Article 232 ECT.[22] Where the alleged infringement is attributable to a national court, or where the breach is an isolated incident by a Member State, which has otherwise complied with Community obligations, the Commission generally considers judicial settlement inappropriate.[23]

Thus far, the Commission has had to bring proceedings under Article 226 ECT against several Member States for failure to implement Title IV instruments, including the temporary protection Directive and the reception Directive.[24] By 2006, six judgments had been issued by the ECJ pursuant to article 230 ECT,[25]

---

[18] Ibid, 432–3.

[19] A Dashwood and R White, 'Enforcement Actions under Articles 169 and 170 EEC' (1989) 14 *ELR* 388.

[20] Case 324/82 *Commission v Belgium* [1984] ECR 1861, para 12.

[21] See also P Craig and G De Búrca, *EU Law: Text Cases and Materials*, n 17 above, 430–3, 434; Case 416/85 *Commission v United Kingdom* [1988] ECR 3127, para 8.

[22] Case 247/87 *Star Fruit Company v Commission* [1989] ECR 291, para 11.

[23] Dashwood and White, n 19 above, 402. On the possibility of infringements by national courts, see H Toner, 'Thinking the Unthinkable? State Liability for Judicial Acts after Factortame (III)' (1997) 17 *YEL* 165.

[24] Directive 2001/55/EC of 20 July 2001 on minimum standards for giving temporary protection in the event of a mass influx of displaced persons and on measures promoting a balance of efforts between Member States in receiving and bearing the consequences thereof [2001] OJ L212/12 (hereafter, temporary protection Directive); Directive 2003/9/EC laying down minimum standards for the reception of asylum seekers, 27 January 2003, [2003] L31/18 (hereafter, reception Directive). See Case C-72/06 *Commission v Greece* [2007] ECR I-57; Case C-102/06 *Commission v Austria* [2006] OJ C326/20; Case C-496/06 *Commission v Germany* [2006] OJ C326/52; Case C-389/06 *Commission v Belgium* [2006] OJ C261/18; Case C-75/06 *Commission v Portugal* [2006] OJ C86/16; Case C-47/06 *Commission v Luxembourg* [2006] OJ C60/31.

[25] Peers, *EU Justice and Home Affairs Law*, n 13 above, 40. With respect to the temporary protection Directive, see Case C-454/04 *Commission v Luxembourg*, 2 June 2005 [2005] OJ C182/18; Case C-476/04 *Commission v Greece*, 17 November 2005 [2006] OJ C22/2; Case C-455/04 *Commission v United Kingdom*, 23 February 2006 [2006] ECR I-32. With respect to Council Directive 2001/51/EC of 28 June 2001 supplementing the provisions of Article 26 of the Convention implementing the Schengen Agreement of 14 June 1985 [2001] OJ L187/45, see Case C-449/04 *Commission v Luxembourg*, 21 July 2005 [2005] OJ C217/21. With respect to Council Directive 2001/40/EC of 28 May 2001 on the mutual recognition of decisions on the expulsion of third

while seven cases brought by the Commission were eventually withdrawn,[26] most likely because Member States had eventually complied with their transposition duties.

Article 227 ECT—which allows a Member State to file a claim against another State after bringing the matter to the Commission—has been rarely used, and States prefer to refer to the Commission to start proceedings under Article 226 ECT.[27]

6.1.1.2 Review of the legality of Community acts

This procedure corresponds to the control of legality carried out by most constitutional courts.

Article 230 ECT

The Court of Justice shall review the legality of acts adopted jointly by the European Parliament and the Council, or acts of the Council, of the Commission and of the ECB, other than recommendations and opinions, and of acts of the European Parliament intended to produce legal effects vis-à-vis third parties.

It shall for this purpose have jurisdiction in actions brought by a Member State, the Council of the Commission on grounds of lack of competence, infringement of an essential procedural requirement, infringement of this Treaty or of any rule of law relating to its application, or misuse of powers.

The Court of Justice shall have jurisdiction under the same conditions in actions brought by the European Parliament, by the Court of auditors and by the ECB for the purpose of protecting their prerogatives.

Any natural or legal person may, under the same conditions, institute proceedings against a decision addressed to that person or against a decision which, although in the form of a regulation or a decision addressed to another person, is of direct and individual concern to the former.

The proceedings provided for in this article shall be instituted within two months of publication of the measure, or of its notification to the plaintiff, or in the absence thereof, of the day on which it came to the knowledge of the latter, as the case may be.[28]

---

country nationals [2001] OJ L149/34, see Case C-462/04 *Commission v Italy*, 8 September 2005 [2005] OJ C271/10; Case C-448/04 *Commission v Luxembourg*, 8 September 2005 [2005] OJ C271/1.

[26] Peers, *EU Justice and Home Affairs Law*, n 13 above, 40.

[27] This provision is, in any case, unlikely to be used in the asylum field, as States are usually reluctant to bring claims based on the violation of human rights committed by another State. On this question, see Chapter 7, Section 7.1.2.

[28] Note that Art 214 of the Lisbon Treaty, not yet in force, amends Art 230 ECT, the most relevant change relating to para 4, which would read as follows: 'any natural or legal person may, under the conditions laid down in the first and second paragraphs, institute proceedings against an act addressed to that person which is of direct and individual concern to them and against a regulatory act which is of direct concern to them and does not entail implementing measures'.

6.1.1.2.1 Reviewable acts

The list of reviewable acts specified in Article 230 ECT is not exhaustive. However, the Court made it clear that the act must be definitive, that is, constitute 'the final expression of an institution's will'.[29] It also insisted that the act must bear legal effects, according to the consistent case-law of the Court:

any measure the legal effects of which are binding on, and capable of affecting the legal interests of the applicant by bringing about a distinct change in his legal position is an act or decision which may be the subject of an action under article 230 ECT for a declaration that it is void.[30]

6.1.1.2.2 Grounds for annulment

The grounds for annulment are lack of jurisdiction, the violation of essential procedural requirements, the violation of the Treaty, or of any rule or law relating to its application, and the misuse of powers. The Court has adopted a lenient position towards the question of lack of jurisdiction in order to ensure the attainment of Community objectives,[31] and has also shown a tendency to admit any proven infringement of Community law, including general principles of Community law, common principles of Member States constitutions and international law, as falling within the realm of paragraph 2.[32] If an infringement is established, the act is annulled and becomes void,[33] and the responsible institution is required to take the measures necessary to comply with the judgment.[34]

6.1.1.2.3 Applicants

There are three categories of applicants:

- The Council, the Commission, the European Parliament[35] and Member States, which are 'privileged applicants' and may bring an action even if the act is not addressed to them.
- The Court of Auditors and the European Central Bank, which are 'semi-privileged applicants' and may lodge annulment proceedings against acts bearing legal effect only with a view to safeguarding their 'prerogatives'.

---

[29] P Mengozzi, *European Community Law From the Treaty of Rome to the Treaty of Amsterdam* (2nd edn, Kluwer, The Hague [etc] 1999) 162.

[30] Case 60/81, *International Business Machines Corporation v Commission* [1981] ECR 2639, para 9.

[31] Mengozzi, n 29 above, 166.

[32] A Arnull, *The European Union and its Court of Justice* (Oxford University Press, Oxford 1999) 33.

[33] Article 231 ECT.

[34] Article 233 ECT.

[35] The Maastricht Treaty amended Art 230 ECT by allowing the European Parliament to start proceedings, but only to defend its own prerogatives, pursuant to paragraph 3. Art 2.34 of the Nice Treaty put the European Parliament on the same footing as the other main European institutions.

- Private applicants, whose claims are adjudicated by the Court of First Instance, unlike those of the other categories of applicants, which are directly examined by the Court of Justice.[36]

In order to gain standing, private applicants are required to prove either that the act is addressed to them in relation to decisions or that they have a direct and individual interest with respect to regulations or individual acts addressed to third parties. The requirement of direct interest does not preclude further implementation of the challenged regulatory act by another EC institution or by a Member State authority but simply requires that implementation be automatic and not entail the use of discretion by the implementing authority. This requirement has been interpreted in a liberal way to the advantage of private applicants. The Court has indeed made it clear that even when legal or '*de jure*' discretion is bestowed upon the implementing authority, for example, a Member State, the private applicant can still be directly concerned by a regulatory act if the implementing authority in question has 'de facto' renounced in advance the use of such discretion.[37]

The requirement of individual interest has given rise to greater debate, because of the rather restrictive construction adopted by the Court. In *Plaumann*, the Court ruled that,

Persons other than those to whom a decision is addressed may only claim to be individually concerned if that decision affects them by reason of certain attributes which are peculiar to them or by reason of circumstances in which they are differentiated from all other persons and by virtue of these factors distinguishes them individually just as in the case of the person addressed.[38]

This jurisprudence has been followed throughout the years, with limited exceptions.[39] In *UPA*, Advocate General Jacobs had suggested that the individual concern requirement would be met when 'the measure has, or is liable to have, a substantial adverse effect on his interests'.[40] A similar reasoning was adopted in the *Jégo-Quéré case*, where the Court of First Instance found it abnormal that where the traditional test for individual concern could not be complied with and where no national implementation measure had been adopted, the only way for the private applicant to obtain judicial review over the EC act would be to breach the law so as to access national courts with a view to requesting a preliminary ruling

---

[36] Article 3 c) of Council Decision 88/591/ECSC, EEC Euratom of 24 October 1988 establishing a Court of First Instance of the European Communities [1988] OJ L319/1 and [1989] OJ L241/1 (corrigenda); for the amendments introduced by the Nice Treaty, see n 16 above.

[37] Case 11/82 *Piraiki-Patraiki v Commission* [1985] ECR 207; Mengozzi, n 29 above, 164.

[38] Case 25/62 *Plaumann & Co v Commission* [1963] ECR 95, 107.

[39] Arnull, n 32 above, 45.

[40] Case C-50/00 P *Union de Pequeños Agricultores v Council* [2002] ECR I-6677 (Advocate General's Opinion) para 102.

on the validity of the regulatory act.[41] Accordingly, the CFI put forward an alternative test of individual concern: 'a natural or legal person is to be regarded as individually concerned by a Community measure of general application that concerns him directly if the measure in question affects his legal position, in a manner which is both definite and immediate, by restricting his rights or by imposing obligations on him'. Regrettably, this test was subsequently overruled by the ECJ in both the *Jégo Quéré* and *UPA* cases where the ECJ maintained its earlier jurisprudence on individual interest.[42]

This restrictive construction will make it rather difficult to establish the existence of a direct and individual interest in challenging legislative measures on asylum and immigration matters, which by their very nature, concern a large number of people and apply to an open category of persons. Moreover, similar restrictions apply to associations of general interest.[43] In a case concerning funding accorded by the Commission for the construction of two power stations in the Canary Islands, the Court of First Instance held that,

The three applicant associations, Greenpeace, TEA and CIC, claim that they represent the general interest, in the matter of environmental protection, of people residing on Gran Canaria and Tenerife and that their members are affected by the contested decision; they do not, however, adduce any special circumstance to demonstrate the individual interest of their members as opposed to any other person residing in those areas. The possible effect on the legal position of the members of the applicant associations cannot, therefore, be any different from that alleged by the applicants who are private individuals. Consequently, in so far as the applicants in the present case who are private individuals cannot, as the Court has held [...] be considered to be individually concerned by the contested decision nor can the members of the applicant associations, as local residents of Gran Canaria and Tenerife.[44]

The conditions for *locus standi* laid down by the Court are thus stricter than those applying under administrative and constitutional law at the national level,[45] and under the case-law of the European Court of Human Rights.[46]

---

[41] Case T-177/01 *Jégo-Quéré & Cie SA v Commission* [2002] ECR II-2365 paras 22–51, spec 45.

[42] Case C-263/02 P *Commission v Jégo Quéré & Cie SA* [2004] ECR I-3425, paras 29–39; Case C-50/00 P *Union de Pequeños Agricultores v Council* [2002] ECR I-6777, paras 37–45.

[43] C Harlow, 'Access to Justice as a Human Right: The European Convention and the European Union', in P Alston (ed), *The EU and Human Rights* (Oxford University Press, Oxford 1999) 187, 197.

[44] Case T-585/93 *Stichting Greenpeace Council (Greenpeace International) and ors v Commission* [1995] ECRII-2205, para 60.

[45] D Walbroeck and A-M Verheyden, 'Les conditions de recevabilité des recours en annulation des particuliers contre les actes normatifs communautaires' (1995) 31 *CDE* 399, 404–25 who present a comparison with conditions of standing in Belgian, French, German, Italian, British, Irish, Dutch, and Greek administrative law; see also G Vandersanden, 'Pour un élargissement du droit des particuliers d'agir en annulation contre des actes autres que les décisions qui leur sont adressées' (1995) 31 *CDE* 534; C Harlow, 'Towards a Theory of Access for the European Court of Justice' (1992) 12 *YEL* 213, 229.

[46] Harlow, 'Access to Justice as a Human Right', n 43 above, 193; see also 212–13, where the author suggests the creation of a limited fund administered by the ECJ to support group

The Court has itself acknowledged that restricted standing could undermine the judicial protection of fundamental rights.[47] Conversely, various explanations have been put forward for this unusual restrictiveness of the Court,[48] one of them being the fear of a growing caseload.[49]

Another criticism of the current system relates to the privileged status of Member States and the Community institutions, which have an absolute right to intervene in proceedings between third parties before the Court,[50] while private persons are entitled to intervene only if they establish an interest in the result of any case submitted to the Court, except in cases between member States, between institutions of the Community, or between Member States and institutions of the Community.[51] This imbalance between the status of Member States—usually acting as respondents in asylum cases—and private persons or organizations ought to be corrected. One way to overcome this problem would be for refugee advocates to bring to the attention of the Commission any infringements of EC law committed by Member States.[52]

To date, only a few review proceedings have been brought before the ECJ. This might possibly be due to the fact that asylum measures have thus far been subject to unanimity voting and one might speculate that an increase in the number of such proceedings might occur for asylum measures adopted with qualified majority voting.[53] The most relevant case so far was an action brought by the European Parliament pursuant to Article 230 ECT, seeking the annulment of Articles 29.1 and 2 and 36.3 of the asylum procedures Directive before the ECJ. The ECJ granted the application, finding that in providing that the European Parliament would merely be consulted on the adoption of 'safe country' lists, the aforementioned

---

representation in public-interest actions and the development of intellectual rights for NGOs. Art 25 ECHR expressly provides for the standing of non-governmental organizations or groups of individuals.

[47] *Report of the Court of Justice on Certain Aspects of the Application of the Treaty on European Union submitted to the European Council in preparation of the IGC* (May 1995) 11.

[48] Arnull, n 32 above 27, 48.

[49] N Neuwahl, 'Article 173 Paragraph 4 EC: Past, Present and Possible Future' (1996) 21 *ELR* 17, 30.

[50] See Statute of the Court (as amended on 1 March 2008) <http://curia.europa.eu/en/instit/txt-docfr/txtsenvigueur/statut.pdf>. Article 40 of the Statute of the Court reads:

- Member States and institutions of the Communities may intervene in cases before the Court.
- The same right shall be open to any other person establishing an interest in the result of any case submitted to the Court, save in cases between Member States, between institutions of the Communities or between Member States and institutions of the Communities. [...]
- An application to intervene shall be limited to supporting the form of order sought by one of the parties.

See also Harlow, 'Access to Justice as a Human Right', n 43 above, 193.

[51] Ibid.

[52] S Peers, 'Human Rights in the EU Legal Order: Practical Relevance for EC Immigration and Asylum Law', in S Peers and N Rogers (eds), *EU Immigration and Asylum Law* (Nijhoff, Leiden [etc.] 2006) 115, 123. On the Commission's ambivalent attitude towards individual complainants in the context of infringement proceedings, see Craig and De Burca, n 17 above, 429–31.

[53] See Art 67.5 ECT; Peers, 'The EU Institutions and Title IV', n 16 above, 74.

articles infringed Article 67.5 ECT, which provides for the application of the co-decision procedure in the adoption of the measures laid down under Articles 63.1 and 2(a) ECT, once Community legislation defining the common rules and basic principles governing these issues has been adopted.[54]

6.1.1.3 Failure to act: Article 232 ECT

This remedy is available to Member States, Community institutions, and natural and legal persons where a Community institution fails to take action and infringes the Treaty or any other rule of Community law.[55] The Treaty provides that if the institution, after being called upon to act, does not react within two months, an action may be brought within a further period of two months. In spite of the different formulation between Articles 230 and 232 ECT, these should be regarded as the same legal remedy, and the strict conditions of standing also apply under the latter article.[56] No specific enforcement mechanism is provided to ensure that a judgment of the Court declaring the existence of a failure to act is complied with.

In order for the claim to be admissible, the applicant needs to show that the institution was under an obligation to act. A good example of a situation where Article 232 ECT could have been relied upon may be found under Articles 61, 62, and 63 ECT, which set out a five-year deadline for the adoption of measures in the fields of asylum, immigration, visas, and other policies relating to the free movement of persons.

6.1.1.4 Preliminary rulings: Article 68.1 ECT

The main modification introduced by the Treaty of Amsterdam concerns preliminary rulings, which have played a key part in the development of the Community legal order.[57] Following the entry into force of the Nice Treaty, Article 225 ECT was amended so as to grant jurisdiction to the Court of First Instance over preliminary reference requests 'in specific areas laid down by the Statute' of the ECJ. So far, this provision has not led to an amendment of the ECJ's Statute. Until the latter is modified, the Court itself remains the exclusive Community court with jurisdiction over preliminary rulings. This system, under which domestic courts are able to request the ECJ to give a ruling on the interpretation of the Treaty, or the

---

[54] Case C-133/06 *Parliament v Council*, 6 May 2008, [2008] OJ C158/3, paras 43–68; see also Chapter 2, Section 2.1.

[55] See Mengozzi, n 29 above, 171.

[56] Case C-107/91 *ENU v Commission* [1993] ECR I-599, para 17–18, where the Court ruled that the private applicant had a direct and individual concern to bring an action for failure to act under the EURATOM Treaty; Case T-398/94 *Kahn Scheepvart v Commission* [1997] 3 CMLR 63, where the test of individual and direct concern was applied in the same restrictive manner as under Art 230 ECT; Mengozzi, n 29 above, 171.

[57] Craig and De Bùrca, n 17 above, 460; Arnull, n 32 above, 49; Mengozzi, n 29 above, 173.

validity and interpretation of acts of the institutions, has been critical to the creation of an ongoing dialogue between the European Court and national judges, and has thereby greatly contributed to the closer integration of Community law into domestic legal systems. Moreover, this procedure provides an alternative remedy to private applicants who would not have *locus standi* under Article 230 ECT.

There are now three distinct preliminary ruling provisions under the ECT:

1. The 'standard procedure' is found under Article 234 ECT and remains unchanged.

2. In the fields of visas, immigration, asylum, and other policies related to the free movement of persons, Article 68.1 ECT allows preliminary rulings but only at the request of a national court or tribunal against whose decisions there is no judicial remedy in national law.

3. Finally, under Article 35 TEU, which was introduced into the Title dealing with police and judicial cooperation in criminal matters, the competence of the Court to give preliminary ruling is conditional upon the express acceptance of Member States.

The following analysis will focus on the second type of preliminary ruling based on relevant Article 234 ECT case-law.[58]

Article 68.1 reads as follows:

Article 234 shall apply to this Title under the following circumstances and conditions: where a question on the interpretation of this Title or on the validity or interpretation of acts of the institutions of the Community based on this Title is raised in a case pending before the court or a tribunal of a Member State against whose decisions there is no judicial remedy under national law, that court of tribunal shall, if it considers that a decision on the question is necessary to enable it to give judgment, request the Court of Justice to give a ruling thereon.

The judicial organs referred to are not only those whose decisions are never subject to appeal; the provision also covers decisions of other judicial organs, which, in specific cases, may not be appealed.[59] However, the Court has also determined that a court cannot be regarded as a court of last resort if the possibility of an appeal to a higher court exists, even though the admissibility of such an appeal must still be determined by that court.[60] In that case, the higher court might still consider whether an issue should be referred to the ECJ for preliminary ruling, including at

---

[58] See S Peers, 'Who's Judging the Watchmen? The Judicial System of the "Area of Freedom, Security and Justice"' (1998) 18 *YEL* 337, 353.

[59] On the application of Art 234.3 in the context of interlocutory proceedings for an interim order even if there is no judicial remedy available against the decision to be taken, see Case 107/76 *Hoffman-La Roche v Centrafarm* [1977] ECR 957, para 6; Joined Cases 35 and 36/82 *Morson and Jhanjan v Netherlands* [1982] ECR 3723, para 8; on the obligation of the Benelux Court to request a preliminary ruling, see Case 337/95 *Parfums Christian Dior* [1997] ECR I-6013, paras. 26–31; see Peers, 'Who's Judging', n 58 above, 356.

[60] Case C-99/00 *Lyckesog* [2002] ECR I-4839.

the admissibility stage.[61] In the United Kingdom, for instance, appeal to the House of Lords against Court of Appeal decisions may be filed, but only if leave is granted either by the Court of Appeal or by the House of Lords.

Furthermore, in many Member States, safe third country cases are adjudicated within accelerated procedures for manifestly unfounded or inadmissible claims, which usually severely restrict the right to appeal.[62] In other words, if an overly rigid understanding of the meaning of 'court of last resort' were to be adopted, most cases based on the safe third country concept might never reach the ECJ. Other hurdles are likely to appear in cases where appeals are not automatically suspensive,[63] and in countries where strict time limits have been set for appeals against dismissals.[64]

There also seems to be uncertainty as to whether the court of last resort is under an obligation to bring a question before the Court. Some authors have suggested that there is no such obligation based on the difference of wording between Article 68.2 ECT and Article 234 ECT.[65] In fact, the reverse claim may be submitted. While Article 234 ECT uses the word 'may' with regard to preliminary rulings brought by any court or tribunal, Article 68.2 ECT enunciates that courts of last resort 'shall' request a preliminary ruling.[66]

The jurisprudence of the ECJ on the scope of the obligation of courts of last resort to request a preliminary ruling provides some clarifications on this question. In *Foto-Frost*, the Court decided that while a court may regard the claim that a Community act is invalid as unfounded without referring a preliminary ruling request to it, national courts do not have the power to declare that a Community act is invalid without requesting a ruling of the ECJ.[67] The ECJ determined that the obligation to request a ruling is qualified by the circumstance that the Court

---

[61] Peers, *EU Justice and Home Affairs Law*, n 13 above, 38.

[62] For instance, in Austria, Finland, Germany, and Sweden safe third country cases are examined within accelerated procedures, see European Commission, *Study on the law and practice of the safe country principles in the context of the common European asylum system and the goal of a common asylum procedure*, 2003 (hereafter, Commission Safe Third Country Study) <http://ec.europa.eu/justice_home/doc_vcentre/asylum/studies/docs/safe_countries_2004_en.pdf>.

[63] This is for instance the case in Finland, Germany, Sweden, and the United Kingdom, see Commission Safe Third Country Study, n 62 above.

[64] This is the case for instance in Austria, see Commission Safe Third Country Study, n 62 above.

[65] H Labayle, 'La libre circulation des personnes dans l'Union européenne, de Schengen à Amsterdam' [1997] *L'actualité juridique Droit administratif* 923, 935; E Tezcan, 'La Coopération dans les domaines de la justice et des affaires intérieures dans le cadre de l'Union européenne et le Traité d'Amsterdam' (1998) 34 *CDE* 661, 673; P Wachsmann, 'Les droits de l'homme' (1997) 33 *RTDE* 883, 890.

[66] P Girerd, 'L'Article 68 CE: un renvoi préjudiciel d'interprétation et d'application incertaines' (1999) 35 *RTDE* 239, 243; H Bribosia, 'Liberté, sécurité et justice: l'imbroglio d'un nouvel espace' [1998] *RMUE* 27, 34, also support this view. The mandatory character of reference to the ECJ is also endorsed by Peers, 'Who's Judging', n 58 above, 351; N Fennelly, 'Preserving the Legal Coherence within the New Treaty, The European Court of Justice after the Treaty of Amsterdam' (1998) 5 *MJ* 185, 194; Peers, *EU Justice and Home Affairs Law*, n 13 above, 38.

[67] Case 314/85 *Foto-Frost v Hauptzollamt Lübeck-Ost* [1987] ECR 4199, para 15.

may have already ruled on the matter,[68] but most importantly, by the latitude accorded to the national court or tribunal to determine whether the ruling would be 'necessary to enable it to give a judgment'.

In the *CILFIT* case, the Court considered that a court of last resort is not obliged to refer a question if it is not relevant, that is, if the answer to the question would in no way affect the outcome of the case, or if the Court has already examined the question in a previous decision, regardless of the proceedings which gave rise to the decision, and even though the questions were not identical.[69] Even in the case where there has been no previous ruling on the same question of law, a court may decide not to submit the question to the ECJ, on the basis of the '*acte clair*' doctrine. The ECJ nevertheless set strict conditions to the application of the doctrine and insisted that the peculiarities of Community law should not be overlooked, based on the following considerations:

- First, Community legislation is drafted in many different languages, and its interpretation should be based on a comparison of these different versions;
- Secondly, some terms are specific to EC law and may not have the same meaning as a similar term used under domestic law;
- Finally, EC law should be construed in light of its objectives, and of the body of EC law as a whole.[70]

The Court has nonetheless dismissed requests for preliminary rulings, when it found that the dispute was fabricated,[71] the questions raised were regarded as hypothetical,[72] or where the national court failed to provide the factual and legislative context of the case.[73] In 1997, the Court issued a *Note for Guidance on References by National Courts for Preliminary Rulings,* which relies upon this case-law.[74]

In terms of standing, one of the great advantages of the preliminary ruling procedure is that it allows private applicants, who would not be able to show a direct and individual interest under Article 230 ECT, to challenge the validity

---

[68] In such a situation, the Court does not dismiss the request as inadmissible, but examines the question and if the question is identical to a case previously examined, the Court restates the previous ruling, see Cases 28-30/62 *Da Costa en Schaake NV, Jacob Meyer NV and Hoechst-Holland NV v Nederlandse Belastingadministratie* [1963] ECR 31, 38.

[69] Case 283/81 *Srl CILFIT and Lanificio di Gavardo SpA v Ministry of Health* [1982] ECR 3415, para 14.

[70] Ibid, paras 16–20.

[71] Case 104/79 *Foglia (Pasquale) v Mariella Novello* [1980] ECR 745, paras 10–11 and Case 244/80 *Foglia (Pasquale) v Mariella Novello* (No. 2) [1981] ECR 3045, para 18.

[72] Case C-83/91 *Wienand Meilicke v ADV/ORGA F.A. Meyer AG* [1992] ECR I-4871, paras 25 and 29–32.

[73] Case C-320–322/90 *Telemarsicabruzzo SpA v Circostel, Ministerio delle Poste e Telecommunicazioni and Ministerio della Difesa* [1993] ECR I-393, paras 6–9; Case-343/90 *Lourenco Dias v Director da Alfandega do Porto* [1992] ECR I-4673, paras 19–20.

[74] [1997] 1 *CMLRev* 78.

of a Community act.[75] However, the Court has ruled that the annulment of an act may not be pursued through the preliminary ruling procedure, if it was clear that it could have been challenged successfully under the annulment procedure of Article 230 ECT.[76] It is noteworthy that the tribunal or court may decide to request a ruling on its own initiative,[77] or rely on the *acte clair* doctrine in spite of the request of one party. In other words, the private applicant has less control over the process than in annulment or appeal proceedings. Finally, another important element is that the ECJ considers that parties other than those mentioned under Article 20 of the Statute of the Court have no rights to intervene in Article 234 proceedings, unless they have been granted leave to intervene in domestic proceedings.[78]

6.1.1.5 *Competence to rule on the interpretation of Title IV ECT*

The Council, the Commission or a Member State may request the Court of Justice to give a ruling on a question of interpretation of this Title or of acts of the institutions of the Community based on this Title. The ruling given by the Court of Justice in response to such a request shall not apply to judgments of courts and tribunals of the Member States which have become res judicata.

This provision is similar to Article 4 of the Protocol to the 1968 Brussels Convention on the jurisdiction and enforcement of judgments in civil and commercial matters, as well as to Article 300 ECT under which 'privileged parties' may seek the opinion of the Court on the conclusion of an international agreement by the Community.[79]

This competence was added to compensate for the inability of lower national courts to request preliminary rulings.[80] Instead of having to wait until a question arises before a court of last resort, the question could be presented to the Court, by a Member State, the Council or the Commission[81] but not by the European Parliament, which is regrettable.[82] The competence of the Court

---

[75] Case 294/83 *Parti écologiste 'Les Verts' v European Parliament* [1986] ECR 1339, para 23. For a critique of the Court's reasoning, see B de Witte, 'The Past and Future Role of the European Court of Justice in the Protection of Human Rights', in P Alston (ed), *The EU and Human Rights* (Oxford University Press, Oxford 1999) 859, 875–6.

[76] Case 188/92 *TWD Textilwerke Deggendorf GmbH v Germany* [1994] ECR I-833, paras 14–18.

[77] Case 283/81 *Srl CILFIT and Lanificio di Gavardo SpA v Ministry of Health* [1982] ECR 3415, para 9.

[78] Case C-181/95 *Biogen Inc v Smithkline Beecham Biologicals SA* [1997] ECR I-357.

[79] Fennelly, n 66 above, 195.

[80] K Hailbronner, 'European Immigration and Asylum law under the Amsterdam Treaty' (1998) 35 *CMLRev* 1047, 1055.

[81] Girerd, n 66 above, 247.

[82] N Fennelly, 'The Area of "Freedom, Security and Justice" and the European Court of Justice—A Personal View' (2000) 49 *ICLQ* 1, 7; A Albors-Llorens, 'Changes in the Jurisdiction of the European Court of Justice under the Treaty of Amsterdam' (1998) 35 *CML Rev* 1273, 1292.

under Article 68.3 ECT corresponds to the traditional advisory function of international courts. It should be noted, however, that Article 68.3 ECT has a restricted scope of application compared to Article 68.1 ECT, for it only applies to rulings on interpretation, excluding therefore questions on the validity of a Community measure.

6.1.2 Consequences of the British/Irish and Danish 'Opt-out'

As explained earlier, the fields of competence set out in Title IV of the Treaty are subject to protocols that deal with the peculiar position of the United Kingdom and Ireland, and of Denmark, which have 'opted out' of Title IV.[83] Article 2 of the British/Irish Protocol stipulates that decisions of the Court of Justice interpreting any measure or any provision of Title IV from which the United Kingdom and/or Ireland has opted out shall not be binding upon or applicable in the United Kingdom or Ireland.[84]

At the time of their adoption, O'Keeffe noted that 'there appears to be a real risk that a differentiation in legislation and case-law will lead to differences in judicial protection between individuals according to whether States participate in a predetermined flexibility arrangement.'[85] This question may, however, not be as problematic as it first appeared, since the United Kingdom and Ireland have opted in on most of the EU asylum instruments adopted by the Council in accordance with Article 63 ECT.[86]

6.1.3 Intervention of UNHCR in ECJ proceedings

The Treaty of Amsterdam expressly stipulates in one of its multiple declarations that '[C]onsultations shall be established with the United Nations High Commissioner for Refugees and other relevant international organizations on matters relating to asylum policy.'[87] However, the possible intervention of

---

[83] Article 69 ECT; see Chapter 1, Section 1.3.4.3.

[84] Protocol No. 4 on the Position of the United Kingdom and Ireland [1997] OJ C340/99.

[85] D O'Keeffe, 'Can the Leopard Change its Spots ? Visas, Immigration and Asylum—Following Amsterdam', in D O'Keeffe and P Twomey (eds), *Legal Issues of the Amsterdam Treaty* (Hart Publishing, Oxford 1999) 271, 284; see also A Albors-Llorens, n 82 above, 1292; Fennelly, 'Preserving the Legal Coherence within the New Treaty', n 66 above, 195; M Hedemann-Robinson, 'The Area of Freedom, Security and Justice with Regard to the UK, Ireland and Denmark: The 'Opt-in Opt-outs' under the Treaty of Amsterdam', in D O'Keeffe and P Twomey (eds), *Legal Issues of the Amsterdam Treaty* (Hart Publishing, Oxford 1999) 288, 301; A G Toth, 'The Legal Effects of the Protocols Relating to the United Kingdom, Ireland and Denmark', in T Heukels, N Blokker, and M Brus (eds), *The European Union after Amsterdam* (Kluwer Law International, The Hague [etc] 1998) 227, 243.

[86] Peers, *EU Justice and Home Affairs Law*, n 13 above, 56. See also Chapter 1, Section 1.3.4.3.

[87] Declaration Nr.17 on Article 73k of the Treaty Establishing the European Community [1997] OJ C340/134.

UNHCR in ECJ proceedings is not expressly provided for. Several avenues may nevertheless exist for UNHCR to intervene in proceedings before the Court:

- One of the Member States or a Community institution could include the opinion of UNHCR in its written statement to the Court;
- The Advocate General in charge of the case could ask UNHCR for an opinion;[88]
- In some cases, the Court has given permission to third countries to intervene,[89] and there is no reason why such permission would not be granted to UNHCR.

These solutions are nevertheless insufficient. UNHCR is expressly mandated to supervise the implementation of the Refugee Convention under Article 35 CSR, and to ensure the international protection of refugees under Article 8 of its Statute. As such, it has a unique responsibility to prevent the fragmentation of universally recognized refugee protection standards. It is highly regrettable, for instance, that UNHCR's views were not sought by the Advocate General in the *Elgafaji* case, which is about to be disposed of by the ECJ, even though some may argue that the proceedings essentially dealt with protection provided under international human rights law.[90]

UNHCR should, as a matter of principle, be allowed to intervene in any case brought before the Court involving the interpretation and/or validity of EU asylum legislation. This will require the amendment of Article 40 of the ECJ Statute,[91] for which the unanimous approval of the Council is necessary pursuant to Article 245 ECT. Another possibility would be for the ECJ to consider the possibility of allowing submissions of third parties as *amicus curiae*. These differ from intervention pursuant to Article 40 of the ECJ Statute. In the latter case, an interest must be shown by the third party while *amicus curiae* briefs are intended to assist a court and inform it on any specific question of law or fact relevant to the proceedings.

6.1.4 Assessment of existing remedies

This brief overview raises a number of questions regarding the availability and effectiveness of remedies under EC law. Of particular concern are the limited standing accorded to individuals under Article 230 ECT, the truncated preliminary ruling system existing under Article 68.1 ECT, and the restrictive understanding of third party intervention, which is bound to limit UNHCR's ability to intervene in proceedings related to EC asylum measures.

---

[88] C A Groenendijk, 'The Competence of the EC Court of Justice', in H Meijers et al. (eds), *A new immigration law for Europe?: The 1992 London and 1993 Copenhagen Rules on Immigration* (1993) 45, 50.

[89] Harlow, 'Towards a Theory', n 45 above, 221.

[90] See Case C-465/07 *Elgafaji v Staatssecretaris van Justitie* (Advocate General's Opinion), 9 September 2008.

[91] Article 40 ECJ Statute, n 50 above.

With respect to preliminary rulings, the underlying tension already existing between the ECJ's objective to promote a uniform application of Community law and the necessity of preventing a floodgate of cases is likely to be exacerbated. The reason for the limitation to courts of last resort of the power of requesting preliminary rulings was indeed underpinned by the fear of a heavy caseload and the objective of ensuring speedy procedures.[92] This has, however, had a significant impact on the ability to seek a preliminary ruling from the ECJ.[93] Peers notes in this respect that the dreaded floodgate has actually not happened,[94] and that the reform of the ECJ's rules of procedure and evidence and the restructuring of the EU judicial system implemented pursuant to the Nice Treaty was in fact meant to address the workload concern.[95] While, as noted earlier, the provisions of the Lisbon Treaty would, if implemented, ensure that standard rules on preliminary ruling also cover Title IV measures,[96] some have suggested that in the meantime, looser rules on standing that would allow individuals to bring direct challenges against EC acts before the ECJ should be considered.[97]

The approach taken by domestic courts will also be under close scrutiny. Higher courts have often been reluctant to be subject to the scrutiny of the ECJ. Some commentators suggest therefore that the *acte clair* doctrine principle be narrowed down to apply only where the court is 'certain of its interpretation beyond any possible doubt'.[98] In light of the difficulties faced by judges in asylum cases, for instance in determining the propriety of the interpretation of the Refugee Convention in another Member State, it is to be hoped that, in spite of the limitations applying in the field of asylum and immigration, the system of preliminary ruling will, once again, constitute a fundamental tool in the harmonization of laws in the European Union and in the development of an EU legal order that fully complies with international law.

---

[92] Fennelly, 'Preserving the Legal Coherence within the New Treaty', n 66 above, 194; Hailbronner, n 80 above, 1055; J-P Puissochet, 'La juridiction communautaire: son rôle dans une Union européenne élargie et transformée' in *Le Traité d'Amsterdam et les perspectives d'évolution de l'Union européenne* (Pédone, Paris 1997) 21, 31.

[93] Peers, 'The EU Institutions and Title IV', n 16 above, 75.

[94] Peers, 'The EU Institutions and Title IV', n 16 above, 76. See Case C-465/07 *M Elgafaji and N Elgafagi v Staatssecretaris van Justitie*, in which the Nederlandse Raad van State referred a case for preliminary ruling on the interpretation of Art 15(c) of Council Directive 2004/83/EC of 29 April 2004 on minimum standards for the qualification and status of third country nationals or stateless persons as refugees or as persons who otherwise need international protection and the content of the protection granted [2004] OJ L304/12 (hereafter, qualification Directive); see also, Case C-178/08 *Ahmed Adem and Hamrin Mosa Rashi v Federal Republic of Germany*, reference for a preliminary ruling from the *Bundesverwaltungsgericht* (Germany) lodged on 29 April 2008, [2008] OJ C197/5. According to Peers, by 2006, 17 applications for preliminary ruling had been brought before the ECJ in relation with Title IV ECT, see Peers, *EU Justice and Home Affairs Law*, n 13 above, 40.

[95] Peers, *EU Justice and Home Affairs Law*, n 13 above, 39 referring to Art 225a of the Nice Treaty.

[96] See Art 67 of the Lisbon Treaty which repeals Art 68 ECT.

[97] Peers, *EU Justice and Home Affairs Law*, n 13 above, 39 citing the opinion of an Advocate General in Case C-50/00 P *UPA*, n 40 above.

[98] Peers, 'Who's Judging the Watchmen', n 58 above, 353–4.

6.2 The European Court of Justice and Fundamental Rights

6.2.1 Fundamental rights as general principles of European Community Law

The development of Community measures in asylum and immigration under Title IV and of criminal and police cooperation under the third pillar puts the Court under unprecedented demand to address human rights issues. While there is no direct connection between the European Convention on Human Rights (ECHR) and the Refugee Convention, the case-law of the Strasbourg Court on Articles 3 (prohibition of torture and ill-treatment), 8 (right to privacy and family life), and 13 (right to an effective remedy) has greatly impacted refugee status determination in the Member States of the European Union. Given that asylum cases may be subject to review by both bodies, the approach adopted by the ECJ in its interpretation of the ECHR, as well as the complex relationship between the ECJ and the ECHR, should be followed closely.

The 1957 Treaty of Rome, which established the European Economic Community, did not refer to the protection of human rights;[99] it is the furthering of Community competencies which rendered the question of fundamental rights ever more significant. In order to ascertain the supremacy of Community law, the Court had to develop a doctrine on the protection of fundamental rights within the EC legal order.[100] It is in 1969 that the Court declared for the first time that fundamental rights were 'enshrined in the general principles of Community law and protected by the Court'.[101] The *International Handelsgesellshaft* case gave the Court the opportunity to explain that it would not rely on fundamental rights as formulated in national constitutions, as this would jeopardize the principle of supremacy and affect the uniformity and efficacy of Community law. It stated instead that

[…] respect for fundamental rights forms an integral part of the general principles of Community law protected by the Court of Justice. The protection of such rights, whilst inspired by the constitutional traditions common to Member States, must be ensured within the framework of the structure and objectives of the Community.[102]

In further cases, the Court went on to elaborate on the sources of fundamental rights derived by the Court. It recognized that principles enshrined in national

---

[99] De Witte, n 75 above, 863.

[100] Ibid; G Cohen-Jonathan, 'Les rapports entre la Convention européenne des Droits de l'Homme et les autres traités conclus par les Etats parties', in R Lawson and M de Blois (eds), *The Dynamics of the Protection of Human Rights in Europe: Essays in Honour of H G Schermers* Vol III (1994) 79, 93.

[101] Case 29/69 *Stauder v City of Ulm* [1969] ECR 419, para 7.

[102] Case 11/70 *Internationale Handelsgesellschaft v Einfuhr- und Vorratstelle für Getreide und Futtermittel* [1970] ECR 1125, para 4.

constitutions[103] and legislation,[104] and/or in the ECHR,[105] provided guidelines in determining the existence of such fundamental rights.[106] Since 1996, the ECJ expressly relied on the case-law of the European Court of Human Rights,[107] indicating that the Community is 'subject in effect to, if not bound formally by, the European Convention on Human Rights'.[108]

The control exercised by the ECJ to ensure respect for fundamental rights was first limited to Community acts, and was endorsed by Member States as an important tool for curbing the power of Community institutions. Supervision was eventually extended to include any Member States' action falling within the scope of Community competencies. The application by Member States of EC provisions based on the protection of human rights,[109] the enforcement and interpretation of Community rules by Member States,[110] derogation from Community rules,[111] and the treatment by Member States of EC nationals

[103] Case 44/79 *Hauer v Land Rheinland-Pfalz* [1979] ECR 3727, paras 20–2; Cases 46/87 and 227/88 *Hoechst AG v Commission* [1989] ECR 2859, paras 18 and 19.
[104] See eg the principle of lawyer/client confidentiality Case 155/79 *A.M. & S. Europe Ltd v Commission* [1982] ECR 1575, para 18.
[105] Case 4/73 *Nold v Commission* [1974] ECR 491, para 13; Case 36/75 *Rutili v Minister for the Interior* [1975] ECR 1219, para 32. The Court also referred to the ICCPR in Case 374/87 *Orkem v Commission* [1989] ECR 3283, para 31; Case C-540/03 *Parliament v Council* [2006] ECR I-05769, para 37; Opinion 2/94 *Accession by the Community to the Convention for the Protection of Human Rights and Fundamental Freedoms* [1996] ECR I-1759, para 33; R Lawson, 'Confusion and Conflict? Diverging Interpretations of the European Convention on Human Rights in Strasbourg and Luxembourg', in R Lawson and M de Blois (eds), *The Dynamics and of the Protection of Human Rights in Europe: Essays in Honour of H G Schermers* (Nijhoff, Dordrecht [etc] 1994) Vol III 219, 223; Peers, 'The EU Institutions and Title IV', n 16 above, 125–6.
[106] Note that the ECJ also recognized as general principles rights that are not explicitly provided under the ECHR such as the right to human dignity, see Case C-377/98 *Netherlands v European Parliament and Council*; Case C-36/02 *Omega Spielhallen- und Automatenaufstellungs-GmbH v Oberbürgermeisterin der Bundesstadt Bonn* [2004] ECR I-9609; Peers, 'Human Rights in the EU Legal Order', n 52 above, 120.
[107] D Spielmann, 'Human Rights Case Law in the Strasbourg and Luxembourg Courts: Conflicts, Inconsistencies, and Complementarities', in P Alston (ed), *The EU and Human Rights* (Oxford University Press, Oxford 1999) 757, 772; C Costello, 'The Bosphorus Ruling of the European Court of Human Rights: Fundamental Rights and Blurred Boundaries in Europe' (2006) 6 *Human Right LR* 87, 111–13.
[108] Case C-13/94 *P v S and Cornwall County Council*, Judgment of 30 April 2006 [1996] ECR I-02143, para 16; see also F G Jacobs, 'European Community Law and the European Convention on Human Rights', in D Curtin and T Heukels (eds), *Institutional Dynamics of European Integration* (Nijhoff, Dordrecht [etc] 1994) Vol II 561, 563. Note that while recognizing the authority of the ICCPR for the purposes of identifying general principles of EC law, the ECJ has been rather dismissive of the views of the Human Rights Committee, see Case C-249/96 *Grant v South West Trains Ltd* [1998] ECR I-621.
[109] Case 36/75 *Rutili v Minister for the Interior* [1975] ECR 1219, paras 29–32; Case 222/84 *Johnston v Chief Constable of the Royal Ulster Constabulary* [1986] ECR 1651, paras 16–19.
[110] Case 249/86 *Commission v Germany* [1989] ECR 1263, paras 10–12; Case 63/83 *R v Kent Kirk* [1984] ECR 2689, paras 21–3; Case 5/88 *Wachauf v Germany* [1989] ECR 2609, paras 17–24; Case C-2/92 *Bostock* [1994] ECR I-955, para 16; Case C-107/97 *Rombi and Arkopharma* [2000] ECR I-3367, para 65; Case C-540/03 *European Parliament v Council* [2006] ECR I-05769, para 105.
[111] Case C-260/89 *Elliniki Radiophonia Tileorassi AE v Dimotiki Etairia Pliroforissis and Sotirios Kouvelas* [1991] ECR I-2925, paras 42–5; see also Peers, 'Human Rights in the EU Legal Order', n 52 above, 115–17.

exercising Community rights have all been reviewed by the Court.[112] The Court also declared in an *obiter dictum* that it could sanction the failure by Community institutions to prevent breaches of fundamental rights,[113] providing therefore a useful basis for breaches of international human rights and refugee law resulting from the implementation of Community instruments.

According to AG Jacobs:

[...] where the review extends to measures adopted by Member States, it will be for the national courts, where appropriate after obtaining a preliminary ruling from the Court of Justice, to apply the principles derived from human rights instruments including the European Convention.[114]

For the same author, the danger of overlap and inconsistency with the function of the Strasbourg organ is exaggerated since the jurisdiction of the ECHR is subsidiary, and the application of the Convention is primarily carried out by national courts.[115]

6.2.2 The European Court of Justice and the European Court of Human Rights

In spite of apparent convergence, problems of consistency nevertheless exist. The ECJ has been criticized for overlooking human rights concerns in a few cases,[116] and there have been instances where the European Court of Human Rights adopted a divergent interpretation of an ECHR article from that of the ECJ.[117] The *Orkem* case is particularly remembered for the Advocate General's holding that,

This Court may therefore adopt, with respect to provisions of the Convention, an interpretation which does not coincide exactly with that given by the Strasbourg authorities,

---

[112] See also Art 51 of the Charter of Fundamental Rights of the European Union proclaimed on 7 December by the President of the European Commission, the President of the European Parliament, and the President of the Council of Ministers [2000] OJ C364/1 (hereafter, Charter of Fundamental Rights or CFR), which provides that the provisions of the Charter are addressed to the institutions and bodies of the Union with due regard for the principle of subsidiarity and to the Member States, only where they are implementing Union law. The commentary of the Charter nevertheless indicates that the case-law of the ECJ is not affected by this provision.

[113] Case C-68/95 *T Port GmbH & Co KG v Bundesanstalt für Landwirtschaft und Ernährung* [1996] ECR I-6065, para 40.

[114] Jacobs, n 108 above, 564.

[115] Ibid, 565.

[116] Spielmann, n 107 above, 764–6. See eg Case 136/79 *National Panasonic v Commission* [1980] ECR 2033, paras 17–22. Note, however, that there have also been cases where the ECJ gave a wider interpretation of certain rights than the ECtHR, for instance with respect to Art 6 ECHR, Peers, 'Human Rights in the EU Legal Order', n 52 above, 121; Spielmann, n 107 above, 767.

[117] Cases 46/87 and 227/88 *Hoechst AG v Commission* [1989] ECR 2859, paras 15–18 and *Niemetz v Germany* Judgment of 16 December 1992 Series A No. 251-B, paras 29–32 on whether the respect for private life extends to business premises; Case 374/87 *Orkem v Commission* [1989] ECR 3283, para 30 and *Funke v France* Judgment of 25 February 1993 Series A No. 256A, paras 41–4 on the right not to give evidence against oneself. It bears noting that at the time these two cases were decided, the ECtHR had not had the opportunity to recognize these rights, see Craig and De Burca, *EU Law*, n 17 above, 393.

in particular the European Court of Human Rights. It is not bound, so far as it does not have systematically to take into account, as regards fundamental rights under Community law, the interpretation of the Convention given by the Strasbourg authorities.[118]

Jurisprudential developments since then show that the ECJ has in fact followed ECHR standards with great care.[119] That said, the recent opinion of the Advocate General in the *Elgafaji* case is not fully reassuring on this point. In this preliminary ruling case,—the first such ruling on the qualification Directive—the question before the ECJ revolved around the interpretation of Article 15(c) of the qualification Directive, specifically, whether this provision only grants protection in cases in which Article 3 ECHR has a bearing or whether it offers supplementary protection to that offered by Article 3 ECHR.[120] In addressing the question, the Advocate General indicated that,

The answer to that question cannot be inferred from article 3 of the ECHR but must be sought principally through the prism of Article 15(c) of the Directive. Community provisions, irrespective of which provisions are concerned, are given an independent interpretation which cannot therefore vary according to and/or be dependent on developments in the case-law of the European Court of Human Rights.[121]

The Advocate General qualified this statement by noting that while 'the case-law of the European Court of Human Rights is not a binding source of interpretation of Community fundamental rights, it constitutes nonetheless a starting point for determining the content and scope of those rights within the European Union'.[122] One could not but notice, however, the perfunctory quality of the Advocate General's analysis of relevant ECHR case-law.[123]

Turning to the ECHR's perspective on the question of the EU's compliance with fundamental rights, the organs of the ECHR had usually refused to rule on violations of the Convention allegedly committed by the Community institutions or by Member States in implementing EC legislation, given that the European Community is not a party to the ECHR.[124] A jurisprudential shift occurred in the *Matthews* case—probably as a result of ECJ Opinion 2/94[125]—where the Strasbourg court declared that it was competent to rule on whether a provision of

---

[118] Joined Opinion of Mr Advocate General Darmon delivered on 18 May 1989, [1989] ECR 3283, para 140. Note that the Court of First Instance confirmed the *Orkem* jurisprudence after the *Funke* case, Case T-112/98 *Mannesmannröhren-Werke AG v Commission* [2001] ECR I-729, para 66.

[119] See eg Case C-540/03 *Parliament v Council* [2006] ECR I-05769, paras 54–6.

[120] Case C-465/07, *M Elgafaji and N Elgafaji v Staatssecretaris van Justitie*, Opinion, 9 September 2008, para 14. Article 15(c) of the qualification Directive provides that serious harm consists of 'serious and individual threat to a civilian's life or person by reason of indiscriminate violence in situations of international or internal armed conflict'.

[121] Ibid, para 19.

[122] Ibid, para 23.

[123] Only two footnotes in the Opinion refer to relevant ECHR case, see fn 3 and 9.

[124] *CFDT v European Communities*, Appl. No. 8030/77, Decision of 10 July 1978, 13 DR 231, para 3; *M & Co v Federal Republic of Germany*, Appl. No. 13258/87, 9 February 1990, 14 DR 64, 138.

[125] See below, Section 6.2.3.

the EC Treaties complied with Article 3 of Protocol No. 1 ECHR on the right to free elections.[126] The Court noted that the ECJ could not have examined the question, since the claimant disputed the validity of a treaty provision, suggesting thereby that it might exercise its jurisdiction only in such cases.[127]

The issue came back before the European Court of Human Rights in the *Bosphorus* case.[128] The question was whether Ireland, in seizing an aircraft belonging to Yugoslav Airlines on lease to a Turkish company, Bosphorus Airways,[129] had violated the latter's right to property protected under Article 1 Protocol No. 1 to the ECHR, given that the seizure was based on EU legislation implementing UN sanctions against the Federal Republic of Yugoslavia.[130]

To answer this question, the Court distinguished between situations in which the application of EC law leaves some discretion to Member States—in which case the Court will exercise its usual power of review over the acts of the State—and situations in which no such discretion exists.[131] In the latter case, the ECtHR found that its power of review would be limited to determining whether the EC offers 'equivalent protection' to the human rights protected by the ECHR.[132] Such equivalent protection could be demonstrated, according to the ECtHR, in the jurisprudence of the ECJ on fundamental rights as well as through the remedies available to individuals under EC law.[133] In these cases, compliance with the ECHR will be presumed unless there is a manifest deficiency in the level of protection accorded under EC law.[134] On the basis of this new test, the ECtHR concluded that in the case before it, the presumption applied and that no manifest deficiency in the protection existing under EC law had been established.[135]

The repercussions of this new jurisprudence in the asylum field are at this stage less significant than might appear. First, until the adoption of uniform asylum

---

[126] *Matthews v United Kingdom*, Appl. No. 24833/94, Judgment of 18 February 1999, ECHR 1999-I; paras 32–4; see in this respect I Canor, 'Primus inter pares: Who is the ultimate guardian of fundamental rights in Europe?' (2000) 25 *ELR* 3, 9–15.

[127] Canor, n 126 above, 18. Note that following the *Matthews* case, some ECJ cases gave particular deference to ECtHR case-law, see eg Case C-185/95 *Baustahlgewebe v Commission*, 17 November 1998, [1998] ECR I-8417; Case C-117/01 *KB v The National Health Service and the Secretary of State for Health* [2004] ECR I-541.

[128] *Bosphorus Hava Yollari Turism Ve Ticaret Anonim Sirketi v Ireland*, Appl. No. 45036/98, Judgment, 30 June 2005 (hereafter, *Bosphorus v Ireland*); for a thorough analysis of the Judgment see Costello, n 107 above, 97–107.

[129] *Bosphorus v Ireland*, paras 19–24.

[130] Ibid, para 107.

[131] Ibid, para 157.

[132] Ibid, para 156. Note that the 'equivalent protection' doctrine existed prior to the *Bosphorus* case and had been developed by the European Commission of Human Rights, see in this respect Costello, n 107 above, 90–3. Costello also reports that the European Commission argued before the ECtHR that the 'equivalent protection' doctrine 'should immunise EU acts from Strasbourg scrutiny due to the EU's supranationality and the autonomy of its legal order', ibid, 103–4.

[133] *Bosphorus v Ireland*, paras 159–65.

[134] Ibid, para 156; Costello, n 107 above, 102–3.

[135] *Bosphorus v Ireland*, para 165.

standards as foreseen under the Lisbon Treaty,[136] current EC secondary legislation consists for the most part of minimum standards, and Member States thus continue to enjoy wide discretion in the application of EC law. Furthermore, in light of the limited opportunity to seek a preliminary ruling from the ECJ pursuant to Article 68 ECT, the 'lower' standard of review adopted by the ECtHR should not be applicable.[137] Costello also rightly considers that the fact that certain measures are adopted in a Regulation rather than in a Directive should not be regarded as a sufficient demonstration that Member States do not enjoy discretion.[138] The Dublin Regulation is a perfect case in point, for the existence of the 'sovereignty' and humanitarian clauses leaves ample discretion to Member States in the way they apply the rules on responsibility allocation.[139]

6.2.3 Fundamental rights in European Treaties

The elaboration by the ECJ of a jurisprudence ensuring the protection of fundamental rights within the Community was endorsed by the European Parliament, the Council, and the Commission in a joint declaration on fundamental rights of 5 April 1977.[140] Successive treaty amendments have formalized the integration of fundamental rights principles into the EU legal order.[141] The Maastricht Treaty inserted a new article 6(2), which provides that,

The Union shall respect fundamental rights, as guaranteed by the European Convention for the Protection of Human Rights and Fundamental Freedoms signed in Rome on 4 November 1950 and as they result from the constitutional traditions common to the Member States, as general principles of Community law.[142]

When this provision was introduced, the competence of the ECJ to rule on its interpretation was expressly excluded under Article L TEU. Article 46 TEU modified by the Treaty of Amsterdam, now stipulates that,

The provisions of the Treaty establishing the European Community, the Treaty establishing the European Coal and Steel Community and the Treaty establishing the European Atomic Energy Community concerning the powers of the Court of Justice of the European Communities and the exercise of those powers shall apply only to the following provisions of this Treaty: [...]

---

[136] Article 63 Lisbon Treaty.
[137] See also Peers, 'Human Rights in the EU Legal Order', n 52 above, 128.
[138] Costello, n 107 above, 108–9.
[139] Ibid, 109.
[140] [1977] OJ C103/1.
[141] Preamble to the Single European Act, Art F.2 TEU (which became Art 6(2) TEU after the entry into force of the Treaty of Amsterdam).
[142] See also Art 6.3 of the Lisbon Treaty, n 14 above, which provides: '[f]undamental rights, as guaranteed by the European Convention for the Protection of Human Rights and Fundamental Freedoms and as they result from the constitutional traditions common to the Member States shall constitute general principles of the Union's law'.

(d) Article 6(2) with regard to action of the institutions, insofar as the Court has jurisdiction under the Treaties establishing the European Communities and under this Treaty; [...]

It is important to note that under that provision, the competence of the court is limited to the actions of the institutions, without any mention of compliance with fundamental rights by Member States implementing Community law.[143] This should, however, not affect existing ECJ jurisprudence.[144]

Other provisions of the Treaty refer to international human rights instruments. Article 63.1 ECT provides that the measures adopted under Title IV must be in accordance with the Refugee Convention but it exclusively applies to those measures adopted pursuant to Article 63.1 ECT. A similar provision had been introduced by the Treaty of Maastricht,[145] but at that time, the competence of the Court of Justice to rule on measures adopted under the third pillar was also expressly excluded.

Article 64 ECT stipulates, on the other hand, that,

[T]his Title shall not affect the exercise of the responsibilities incumbent upon Member States with regard to the maintenance of law and order and the safeguarding of internal security.

While 68.2 ECT states that,

[I]n any event, the Court of Justice shall not have jurisdiction to rule on any measure or decision taken pursuant to Article 62(1) relating to the maintenance of law and order and the safeguarding of internal security.[146]

This clause would also seem to cover measures of expulsion, which have in numerous cases been censured by the European Court of Human Rights. As such, the application of Article 68.2 ECT would arguably justify the application of the *Matthews* and *Bosphorus* jurisprudence by the European Court of Human Rights.[147]

In spite of all these developments, the crucial question of the formal relationship between the ECJ and the European Court of Human Rights remains unresolved.[148] In its Opinion 2/94, the ECJ considered that a Treaty amendment was the only way to enable the Community to accede to the ECHR.[149] However, accession to the ECHR has been repeatedly delayed, first by the failure of Member

---

[143] De Witte, n 75 above, 885; H Labayle, 'Un espace de liberté, de sécurité et de justice' (1997) 33 *RTDE* 814, 823.

[144] See above Sections 6.2.1 and 6.2.2.

[145] Article K.2.1 TEU.

[146] Article 62 deals with the control at external borders and the issuance of visas.

[147] See Costello, n 107 above, 117–18; see also K Lenaerts and E de Smijter, 'The Charter and the Role of the European Courts' (2001) 8 *MJ* 90, 95.

[148] Wachsmann, n 65 above, 889 and 892; V Constantinesco, 'Le renforcement des droits fondamentaux dans le Traité d'Amsterdam' in *Le Traité d'Amsterdam: Réalités et Perspectives* (1998) 33.

[149] Opinion 2/94 *Accession by the Community to the Convention for the Protection of Human Rights and Fundamental Freedoms* [1996] ECR I-1759, paras 23–36.

States to reach an agreement during the negotiations of the Amsterdam Treaty,[150] and then by the rejection of the Constitutional Treaty by the Dutch and French electorates and of the Lisbon Treaty by the Irish.[151]

6.2.4 The latest twist: the Charter of Fundamental Rights

A major development in the protection of human rights at EU level has undeniably been the adoption of the Charter of Fundamental Rights,[152] which, given the unresolved status of the Lisbon Treaty, remains at present a non-binding document.[153]

Many of the provisions of the Charter relevant to asylum are based on the ECHR and its case-law. Thus, while Article 4 CFR reproduces *verbatim* the language of Article 3 ECHR, Article 19 CFR prohibits collective expulsions as well as *refoulement* to a State where there is a serious risk that an individual would be subjected to the death penalty, torture or other inhuman or degrading treatment or punishment. Additionally, a number of articles of the Charter proclaim rights which are either not expressly recognized under the ECHR or had not been previously recognized as general principles of EC law.[154]

The most significant innovation for the purposes of the present discussion is Article 18.2 CFR, which stipulates that 'the right to asylum shall be guaranteed *with due respect*[155] for the rules of the Geneva Convention of 28 July 1951 and the Protocol of 31 January 1967 relating to the status of refugees and in accordance with the Treaty establishing the European Community'. While the insertion of the right to asylum appears to be a significant development,[156] Peers emphasizes that this right would be subject to relevant derogations in accordance

---

[150] J L Duvigneau, 'From Advisory Opinion 2/94 to the Amsterdam Treaty: Human Rights Protection in the European Union' (1998) 25 *Legal Issues of European Integration* 61, 85; Wachsmann, n 65 above, 883; de Witte, n 75 above, 890.

[151] Article 6.2 Lisbon Treaty provides that 'the Union shall accede to the European Convention for the Protection of Human Rights and Fundamental Freedoms'. This will require the conclusion of a Memorandum of Understanding with the ECtHR and Council of Europe. Also, Additional Protocol 14 to the ECHR, not yet in force, opens membership of the ECHR to the EC.

[152] n 112 above.

[153] Article 6.1 Lisbon Treaty stipulates that the Charter shall have the same legal value as the Treaties; see B de Witte, 'Legal Status of the Charter: Vital Question or Non-Issue?' (2001) 8 *MJ* 81, 84–5; see also European Commission, 'Communication on the Charter of Fundamental Rights of the European Union' COM (2000) 559 final, 13 September 2000, para 35.

[154] For instance the right to human dignity is not provided under the ECHR, while the prohibition of ill-treatment and restrictions on detention have not yet been recognized as general principles of EC law, see Peers, 'Human Rights in the EU Legal Order', n 52 above, 130; see also C McCrudden, 'Human Dignity and Judicial Interpretation of Human Rights' (2008) 19 *EJIL* 655, 683–4.

[155] Emphasis added.

[156] See M-T Gil-Bazo, 'The Charter of Fundamental Rights of the European Union and the Right to Be Granted Asylum in the Union's Law' (2008) 27 *Refugee Survey Quaterly* 33 who argues the existence of a subjective right to be granted asylum.

with Article 52.1 CFR,[157] except to the extent that it also encompasses the norm of *non-refoulement*.[158]

Despite the fact that the Charter has by now been referred to in several ECJ cases and in EC legislation,[159] and the efforts of the Commission to clarify its scope and provisions,[160] the complex relationship between EC law and the ECHR system will continue to raise delicate questions of interpretation. In this respect, Article 52.3 CFR stipulates that,

In so far as this Charter contains rights which correspond to rights guaranteed by the Convention for the Protection of Human Rights and Fundamental Freedoms, the meaning and scope of those rights shall be the same as those laid down in the said Convention. This provision shall not prevent Union law providing more extensive protection.

While Article 53 reads:

Nothing in this Charter shall be interpreted as restricting or adversely affecting human rights and fundamental freedoms as recognised, in their respective fields of application, by Union law and international law and by international agreements to which the Union, the Community or all the Member States are party, including the European Convention for the Protection of Human Rights and Fundamental Freedoms and by the Member State's constitutions.

Taken together, these two clauses seem to ensure that the protection provided under EC law cannot fall below the level guaranteed by the ECHR or other international human rights instruments,[161] including the Refugee Convention. This would also mean that the derogations allowed pursuant to Article 52.1 CFR must be understood as applying exclusively to those rights that are not recognized under the ECHR or to situations where the CFR's level of protection is increased in comparison with the ECHR or other international human rights instruments.[162]

---

[157] Article 52.1 CFR reads:

Any limitation on the exercise of the rights and freedoms recognised by this Charter must be provided for by law and respect the essence of those rights and freedoms. Subject to the principle of proportionality, limitations may be made only if they are necessary and genuinely meet objectives of general interest recognised by the Union or the need to protect the rights and freedoms of others.

[158] S Peers, 'Immigration, Asylum and the European Union Charter of Fundamental Rights' (2001) 3 *EJML* 141, 162.

[159] Case C-540/03 *Parliament v Council* [2006] ECR I-05769, para 38; Peers, 'Human Rights in the EU Legal Order', n 52 above, 129. The CFR is referred to in the reception Directive, the temporary protection Directive, the Dublin II Regulation, the qualification Directive, and the asylum procedures Directive as well as in Council Decision 2000/596/EC of 28 September 2000 establishing the European Refugee Fund.

[160] European Commission, 'Communication on compliance with the Charter of Fundamental Rights in Commission legislative proposals: Methodology for systematic and rigorous monitoring', COM (2005) 172 final, 27 April 2005, which seeks to ensure that all legislative proposals be scrutinized for full compliance with fundamental rights.

[161] Peers, 'Human Rights in the EU Legal Order', n 52 above, 131.

[162] Peers, 'Immigration, Asylum and the European Union Charter of Fundamental Rights', n 158 above, 154.

This is particularly important because the ECJ has held that fundamental rights may be subject to restrictions so long as these restrictions are proportional and reasonable.[163] The aforementioned provisions of the CFR would therefore restrict the ability of the ECJ to allow derogations to certain rights which have been regarded as suffering no exception under the ECHR, and to that extent, the Charter would strengthen legal certainty in an area in which the harmonization process has actually brought greater confusion.[164] In light of the foregoing, it is arguable that Article 19 CFR on the protection of individuals in the event of removal, expulsion, or extradition shall be interpreted in light of the case-law of the European Court of Human Rights on Article 3 ECHR, which is particularly important given, for instance, the highly contentious provisions on exclusion from international protection included in the qualification Directive.[165]

Finally, it bears noting that while the CFR is certainly a stepping stone, it does not render the question of the accession to the ECHR and in particular, the availability of remedies against violations of the ECHR by the European Union, irrelevant.[166] Most striking in all of these developments, is the tension between the efforts of the European Union to support fundamental rights and to appear as its strongest advocate before intergovernmental fora, and Member States' pressure to adopt supranational instruments which embrace an increasingly restrictive interpretation of international refugee law and human rights obligations, and sometimes openly contradict the findings of regional and international human rights bodies. In this respect, the ECJ's approach, parochial and excessively 'EU-centric' at times, is not particularly encouraging. While there are, in other words, positive developments taking place within the European Union, there is also concern that some of the crucial advances chartered in international human rights law will not be automatically received within the EU legal order.

6.3 Conclusion

Several issues will significantly impact the manner in which the ECJ will approach its new adjudicating power in the asylum field. In spite of the significant progress brought about by the Treaty of Amsterdam, there remain procedural and institutional failings, which are likely to undermine the effectiveness of the ECJ's judicial supervision. The restrictive rules on standing of private parties and on third

---

[163] See eg Case C-280/93 *Germany v Council* [1993] ECR I-4973; Case C-122/95 *Germany v Council* [1995] ECR I-973.

[164] European Commission, 'Communication on the Legal Nature of the Charter of Fundamental Rights of the European Union' COM (2000) 644 final, 11 October 2000, para 9.

[165] Article 17 qualification Directive; see in this respect M-T Gil-Bazo, 'Refugee status, subsidiary protection, and the right to be granted asylum under EC law' UNHCR New Issues in Refugee Research Paper No. 136, November 2006, 19.

[166] See also K Lenaerts and E De Smijter, 'A "Bill of Rights" for the European Union' (2001) 38 *CMLRev* 273, 297.

party intervention in proceedings before the Court pose serious problems. This is problematic in the context of asylum and immigration adjudication, where the involvement of 'litigation coalitions' may be particularly significant. Also, the role of courts of last resort with regard to preliminary ruling will be paramount to ensure a harmonized interpretation of EU asylum legislation in full compliance with international human rights and refugee law.

The Court's attitude towards the Strasbourg system and more generally, international human rights and refugee law, also leaves many doubts as to its future approach on asylum issues. While it is still too early to assess the ECJ's record in this respect, the main concern is whether the ECJ's intervention will effectively contribute to the upholding and consolidation of protection standards, which EU secondary legislation on asylum has tended to undermine.

7

International Supervision

Having highlighted the many protection challenges arising from the implementation of safe third country practices, and the limitations of EU judicial supervision, this chapter will examine whether and how monitoring and supervision of States' international obligations may be enhanced at the international level. It is argued here that to counterbalance regional integration processes which carry the potential for further erosion and fragmentation of States' international obligations, an effective response would be to strengthen international supervisory mechanisms so as to better address protection gaps and ensure a more consistent interpretation and application of international obligations.

The political sensitivity of this question demands, however, a prudent approach. The purpose here is not to present a draft instrument with a detailed description of the structure and mandate of a 'refugee monitoring body'. Rather, this contribution seeks to underscore the significance of the supervision issue with a view to improving the international legal framework of refugee protection.

The first section of the chapter examines supervisory mechanisms currently existing under international refugee law, based on a distinction between supervision carried out by international organizations, by States, and by individuals. The second part of the chapter presents an analysis of UNHCR's efforts to address protection gaps and suggests possible approaches for improving supervisory mechanisms under international refugee law.

7.1 Supervisory Mechanisms Relevant to the Protection of Refugees and Asylum Seekers

The following examination is based on a classification of international supervision proposed by Schermers and Blokker in their monograph on international institutional law.[1] These authors distinguish supervision carried out by or on behalf of an

---

[1] H G Schermers and N M Blokker, *International Institutional Law: Unity within Diversity* (3rd edn, Nijhoff, Dordrecht [etc] 1995) 867–97. This classification was also used in the paper presented by W Kälin for the 2nd Expert Roundtable in Cambridge, as part of the Global Consultations on International Protection in the context of the 50th anniversary of the 1951 Convention relating to the Status of Refugees, 'Supervising the 1951 Refugee Convention Relating to the Status of Refugees: Article 35 and Beyond', in E Feller, V Türk, and F Nicholson (eds), *Refugee Protection in International Law: UNHCR's Global Consultations on International Protection* (Cambridge University Press,

intergovernmental organization, supervision carried out by States, and supervision by individuals. These three different categories exist under international refugee law. Under the first category, the Executive Committee established by the Economic and Social Council of the United Nations controls the activities of UNHCR and makes recommendations to States. Most importantly, UNHCR has been granted wide supervisory capacities under Paragraph 8 of its Statute and Article 35 CSR.[2] UNHCR may also be able to request an advisory opinion from the International Court of Justice, with the authorization of the General Assembly. Moreover, the Human Rights Commission and its successor, the Human Rights Council, have a broad mandate which addresses the rights of all individuals, including those of asylum seekers and refugees. Supervision by States is provided under Article 38 CSR. Finally, supervision carried out by individuals is the category which, under international refugee law, remains the weakest. Although refugees are able to submit petitions to ensure the protection of some of their rights, primarily based on the principle of *non-refoulement*, under the CAT, the ICCPR and the ECHR, there is currently no international body which is competent to examine claims based on the violation of the Refugee Convention.

7.1.1 Supervision by or on behalf of the organization

7.1.1.1 The Executive Committee of the High Commissioner's programme

In 1951, the Economic and Social Council decided, in accordance with paragraph 4 of the UNHCR Statute, to set up an Advisory Committee on Refugees, which would help ECOSOC and the General Assembly manage refugee problems and provide guidelines to the High Commissioner.[3] This Committee was replaced in 1955 by the UN Refugee Fund Executive Committee,[4] which was in turn replaced by the Executive Committee of the High Commissioner's Programme in 1958.[5] It was originally given the task to advise the High Commissioner upon request on UNHCR's statutory duties and 'as to whether it is appropriate for international assistance to be provided through his office'.[6] In Resolution 1673 (XVI) of 1961,

---

Cambridge 2003) 613. Other authors distinguish between settlement of disputes between States, settlement of disputes between States and non-State actors, settlement of disputes between members and the organization, and settlement of disputes between the organization or its members and third parties, including individuals, see P Sands and P Klein, *Bowett's Law of International Institutions* (5th edn Sweet & Maxwell, London 2001) 337.

  [2] 1951 Geneva Convention Relating to the Status of Refugees (adopted 28 July 1951, entered into force 22 April 1954) 189 UNTS 150 (hereafter, CSR or Refugee Convention).

  [3] ECOSOC Res 393 B (XIII) (10 September 1951); N Singh, 'The Role and Record of Activities of the Office of the High Commissioner for Refugees', in *The Refugee Problem on Universal, Regional and International Level* (Institute of International Public Law and International Relations, Thessaloniki 1987) 325, 338.

  [4] UNGA Res 832 (IX) (21 October 1954) and ECOSOC Res 565 (XIX) (31 March 1955).

  [5] UNGA Res 1166 (XII) (26 November 1957) and ECOSOC Res 672 (XXV) (30 April 1958).

  [6] UNGA Res 1166, n 5 above, para 5(c).

the General Assembly asked the High Commissioner 'to abide by directions which that Committee might give him in regard to situations concerning refugees'.[7] A Sub-Committee of the Whole on International Protection was set up in 1975 to 'study in more detail some of the more technical aspects of the protection of refugees' and to 'focus attention on protection issues with a view to determining existing shortcomings in this field and to proposing appropriate remedies'.[8] It was then abolished in 1995 and replaced by a Standing Committee of the Whole with a general competence on protection, programme, and financial issues.

The Executive Committee holds one annual plenary session in Geneva in October. It currently has 76 members, and an important number of observers also attend the deliberations.[9] This organ contributes to the development of the international normative framework, through the adoption by consensus of conclusions on various aspects of international cooperation for the protection of refugees.[10] During its first three years of existence, the Executive Committee did not discuss protection issues,[11] but the significance of its conclusions relating to refugee protection grew significantly since its inception.[12]

The Executive Committee which was originally created to advise UNHCR often addresses its conclusions to States.[13] Each year, the Committee adopts general conclusions on international protection which, 'are a [...] compilation of very concisely and generally worded pronouncements on various current questions related to protection'.[14] It is generally recognized that conclusions adopted by the Executive Committee may participate in the emergence of *opinio juris*.[15]

---

[7] The request was repeated in Resolution 1783 (XVII) (7 December 1962).

[8] ExCom Conclusion No. 1 (1975) para (h) and ExCom Conclusion No. 2 (1976) on the Functioning of the Sub-Committee, para (i); V Türk, *Das Flüchtlingshochkommissariat der Vereinten Nationen (UNHCR)* (Duncker & Humblot, Berlin 1992) 165.

[9] The States represented are: Algeria, Argentina, Australia, Austria, Bangladesh, Belgium, Benin, Brazil, Canada, Chile, China, Colombia, Costa Rica, Côte d'Ivoire, Cyprus, Democratic Republic of the Congo, Denmark, Ecuador, Egypt, Estonia, Ethiopia, Finland, France, Germany, Ghana, Greece, Guinea, Holy See, Hungary, India, Iran, Ireland, Israel, Italy, Japan, Jordan, Kenya, Lebanon, Lesotho, Luxembourg, Madagascar, Mexico, Montenegro, Morocco, Mozambique, Namibia, Netherlands, New Zealand, Nicaragua, Nigeria, Norway, Pakistan, Philippines, Poland, Portugal, Republic of Korea, Romania, Russian Federation, Serbia, Somalia, South Africa, Spain, Sudan, Sweden, Switzerland, Thailand, The former Yugoslav Republic of Macedonia, Tunisia, Turkey, Uganda, United Kingdom, United Republic of Tanzania, United States of America, Venezuela, Yemen, and Zambia. <http://www.unhcr.org/excom/40111aab4.html>; for information on observer status, see <http://www.unhcr.org/excom/418b87ef4.html>.

[10] The Committee also adopts non-binding acts, often called decisions, on assistance matters. For an analysis of this distinction, see J Sztucki, 'The Conclusions on the International Protection of Refugees Adopted by the Executive Committee of the UNHCR Programme' (1989) 1 *IJRL* 285, 296–7.

[11] Ibid, 290.

[12] Ibid, 297.

[13] According to Sztucki, this practice started in 1972, ibid, 293.

[14] Ibid, 294.

[15] G Jaeger, 'Les Nations Unies et les réfugiés' [1989] *RBDI* 18, 60; K Hailbronner, *Immigration and Asylum Law and Policy of the European Union* (Kluwer Law International, The Hague 2000) 354.

However, not all parts of Executive Committee conclusions have a normative content,[16] and in many cases, these conclusions are, according to Sztucki, completely devoid of legal character.[17] In fact, the difficulty of adopting conclusions with a strong legal content has become particularly noticeable in recent years and continues to be a matter of great concern. In 1998, Denis McNamara, then Director of International Protection, declared that,

It was [...] disturbing that, as a result of prolonged debates during the past year which had often led to the reduction of previously agreed texts, the Executive Committee did not yet have before it a full set of agreed conclusions on protection. The asylum procedure was complicated and expensive for States and the reconciliation of protection principles and legitimate State concerns was a complex task, but refugee protection was not assisted by overzealous efforts to tip the balance towards States interests to the point where the protection content of a number of the Committee's conclusions was seriously marginalized[18]

and noted that implementation was also lagging:

The declarations and rules agreed to by the Committee or the General Assembly must be translated into supportive action by States. However, there was an increasing failure to implement or actively support the Committee's conclusions concerning, inter alia, military attacks on camps, the latter's civilian and humanitarian character, basic conditions of treatment during mass influx, responsibilities in repatriation and minimum standards for due process in determining refugee status, all of which were areas where consensus, even when achieved, had little impact on State practice.[19]

The enlargement of the Executive Committee has certainly affected the quality of its conclusions,[20] perhaps because several States now represented are not even parties to the Refugee Convention. Furthermore, Sztucki noted in 1989 that the adoption of conclusions on international protection had intensified at a time when States were progressively implementing policies of containment and the legal relevance of these instruments thus needed to be assessed with great prudence.[21]

Sztucki also noted that there had been very little follow-up by the Committee of its previous conclusions,[22] suggesting that one of the ways to enhance their value would be to have them systematically endorsed by the General Assembly.[23] In 2008, a review of the use of Executive Committee conclusions on international protection was commissioned by UNHCR. While its findings pointed to the

---

[16] Sztucki, n 10 above, 299.

[17] Ibid, 306.

[18] Statement before ExCom, UN Doc A/AC.96/SR.522, 23 October 1997, para 60.

[19] Ibid, para 62; see also statement by the representative of India supporting this statement, UN Doc A/AC.96/SR.532, 15 October 1998, para 19.

[20] New members are formally elected by the Economic and Social Council; see G Loescher, A Betts, and J Milner, *UNHCR: The Politics and Practice of Refugee Protection into the Twenty-First Century*, (Routledge, New York 2008) 77.

[21] Sztucki, n 10 above, 305–6.

[22] Ibid, 310.

[23] Ibid, 312.

general usefulness of Executive Committee conclusions, the study also reported that States expressed general disaffection with the conduct of the negotiations leading up to their adoption, were not particularly familiar with their content and were for the most part unable to provide detailed information on the use and follow up of these conclusions in their domestic legal order.[24]

This is exemplified by the fact that Conclusions No. 15 and No. 58, which are the two main international instruments addressing secondary movements have had in the end only limited impact on domestic law, above all in comparison with the 1992 non-binding Resolution adopted by the European ministers for immigration, whose guidelines influenced the drafting of national legislation in several European States.[25] By the same token, the European harmonization process as well as the European Union's efforts to export safe third country policies may have had a more profound impact on international refugee law in recent years than any of the texts adopted by the Executive Committee.

7.1.1.2 *UNHCR's function of international protection*

[...] international protection may be defined as the power, conferred by the international community to an international body, to take all necessary measures to replace the national protection of which refugees are deprived, because of their very condition.[26]

The function of international protection is at the core of UNHCR's mandate and applies to all States, whether or not they are parties to the Refugee Convention.[27] The content of international protection accorded by UNHCR should be regarded as *sui generis*.[28] It cannot be equated with diplomatic protection, for the former applies strictly while the latter is only exercised at the discretion of the State. UNHCR's role is also particularly unique within the international system, because it 'does not have to be expressly invited by States to become involved in protection matters',[29] and it has the ability to carry out protection activities throughout the world given its presence in most States.[30] As such, this function comprises an element of supranationality.[31]

---

[24] UNHCR, 'Review of the Use of UNHCR Executive Committee Conclusions on International Protection', 9 June 2008, paras 8, 23, 80–2.

[25] EU Resolution on a harmonized approach to questions concerning host third countries, adopted on 30 November and 1 December 1992 by Immigration Ministers, SN 4823/92 WG 1283 ASIM 147, (hereafter EU Resolution) published in E Guild (ed), *The Developing Immigration and Asylum Policies of the European Union*, (Kluwer, The Hague 1996) 161; see Chapter 2, Section 2.1.2.

[26] F Schnyder, 'Les aspects juridiques actuels du problème des réfugiés' (1965) 114 *RdC* 335, 423.

[27] ExCom Conclusion No. 4 (1977) para (d).

[28] Schnyder, n 26 above, 423; Türk, n 8 above, 145–6.

[29] UNHCR, 'Note on International Protection' UN Doc A/AC.96/930, 7 July 2000, para 71.

[30] See para 16 of the Statute of UNHCR, annexed to UNGA Res 428 (V),14 December 1950.

[31] S Aga Khan, 'Legal Problems relating to Refugees and Displaced Persons' (1976) 149 *RdC* 331; P Kourula, *Broadening the Edges, Refugee Definition and International Protection Revisited* (Nijhoff, The Hague 1997) 209.

Paragraph 8 of the Statute details the mandatory functions of UNHCR with regard to its international protection mandate:[32]

8. The High Commissioner shall provide for the protection of refugees falling under the competence of his Office by:

(a) Promoting the conclusion and ratification of international conventions for the protection of refugees, supervising their application and proposing amendments thereto;

(b) Promoting through special agreements with Governments the execution of any measures calculated to improve the situation of refugees and to reduce the number requiring protection;

(c) Assisting governmental and private efforts to promote voluntary repatriation or assimilation within new national communities;

(d) Promoting the admission of refugees, not excluding those in the most destitute categories, to the territories of States;

(e) Endeavouring to obtain permission for refugees to transfer their assets and especially those necessary for their resettlement;

(f) Obtaining from Governments information concerning the number and conditions of refugees in their territories and the laws and regulations concerning them;

(g) Keeping in close touch with the Governments and inter-governmental organizations concerned;

(h) Establishing contact in such manner as he may think best with private organizations dealing with refugee questions;

(i) Facilitating the co-ordination of the efforts of private organizations concerned with the welfare of refugees.

Finally, the ultimate goal is to establish durable solutions, through voluntary repatriation, local integration, or resettlement.[33]

In the first decades of operation of UNHCR, the function of protection grew in importance at the request of the General Assembly.[34] Successive resolutions reinforced the authority of UNHCR as an international agency with a special standing in the international protection of refugees and refugee assistance,[35] and extended substantially the competence *ratione personae* of the organization.[36] The legal competence of UNHCR activities has in other words different legal bases.[37]

---

[32] For a detailed analysis of this provision, see Schnyder, n 26 above, 406–16.

[33] UNHCR Statute, paras 1, 9; UNHCR, Note on International Protection, UN Doc A/AC.96/830, 7 September 1994, para 12; see also V Türk, 'Freedom from Fear: Refugees, the Broader Displacement Context and the Underlying Protection Regime', in V Chetail (ed) *Mondialisation, migration et droits de l'homme: Le droit international en question* (Bruylant, Brussels 2007) 475, 494, see also 497.

[34] See para 9 of the UNHCR Statute: 'The High Commissioner shall engage in such additional activities, including repatriation and resettlement, as the General Assembly may determine, within the limits of the resources placed at its disposal.'

[35] Schnyder, n 26 above, 396.

[36] Aga Khan, n 31 above, 287,

[37] V Türk, 'The Role of UNHCR in the Development of International Refugee Law', in F Nicholson and P Twomey (eds) *Refugee Rights and Realities: Evolving International Concepts and Regimes* (Cambridge University Press, Cambridge 1999) 153, 154.

In line with the growing inclusiveness of UNHCR's mandate, international protection now also encompasses preventive action 'to address the economic, social and political aspects of the refugee problem'.[38] This 'catch-all' notion renders a precise description of what protection currently entails delicate. UNHCR noted for instance that in cases of mass influx, a clear distinction between protection and assistance is difficult to draw.[39] This new approach was once again emphasized in the 2000 Note on International Protection of the High Commissioner[40] and approved by the Executive Committee in Conclusion No. 89:

Recognising that international protection is a dynamic and action-oriented function, carried out, in co-operation with States and other partners, to promote and facilitate admission, reception, treatment of refugees and to ensure protection-oriented solutions, towards the overall goal of enhancing respect for the rights of refugees and resolving their problems . . .[41]

7.1.1.2.1 The crisis of protection: UNHCR in the 1990s

From the mid-1980s and until the end of the 1990s, UNHCR's strategic direction led to growing concern and criticism. During that period, the organization shifted priorities so that its original function was overtaken by relief and humanitarian assistance and 'in country' protection, with the goal of eliminating the causes of refugee flows.[42] This new approach was supported by donor countries, for the budget of the UNHCR doubled between 1990 and 1995 and remained at this higher level through 2000.[43]

At the internal level, the Division of International Protection became secondary in the structure of the organization, despite UNHCR's responsibility under

---

[38] ExCom Standing Committee, 'Overview of Regional Developments', UN Doc EC/46/SC/CRP.11, 4 January 1996, para 3.

[39] Excom Standing Committee, 'Note on International Protection' UN Doc EC/50/SC/CRP.16, 9 June 2000, para 4; see also ExCom General Conclusion on International Protection No. 46 (1987) para (n) and ExCom General Conclusion on International Protection No. 61 (1990) para (e); Kourula, n 31 above, 212.

[40] UN Doc A/AC.96/930, 7 July 2000, para 4.

[41] ExCom General Conclusion on International Protection No. 89 (2000) recital 2.

[42] B Frelick, '"Preventive Protection and the Rights to Seek Asylum": A Preliminary Look at Bosnia and Croatia' (1992) 4 *IJRL* 438, 439; J C Hathaway, 'New Directions to Avoid Hard Problems: The Distortion of the Palliative Role of Refugee Protection' (1995) 8 *JRS* 288, 291–2; Anon., 'The UNHCR Note on International Protection You Won't See' (1997) 9 *IJRL* 267, 268; see also G Loescher, 'The UNHCR and World Politics: State Interests vs. Institutional Autonomy' (2001) 35 *IMR* 33, 43, 45; M Barnett, 'Humanitarianism with a Sovereign Face: UNHCR in the Global Undertow' (2001) 35 *IMR* 244, 259; S A Cunliffe and M Pugh, 'UNCHR as a Leader in Humanitarian Assistance: a Triumph of Politics Over Law ?', in F Nicholson and P Twomey (eds) *Refugee Rights and Realities: Evolving International Concepts and Regimes* (Cambridge University Press, Cambridge 1999) 175, 184–5; Loescher, Betts and Milner, n 20 above, 53.

[43] UNHCR, *The State of the World's Refugees Fifty Years of Humanitarian Action* (Oxford University Press, Oxford 2000) 167; R Väyrynen, 'Funding Dilemmas in Refugee Assistance: Political Interests and Institutional Reforms in UNHCR' (2001) 35 *IMR* 143, 157.

its Statute.[44] The involvement of UNHCR in the Bosnian and Rwandan crises in the early 1990s marked a threshold in this respect. In Bosnia, the creation of safety zones arguably prevented populations at risk from seeking asylum.[45] In Rwanda, the organization maintained its presence in spite of the militarization of refugee settlements and military attacks on the camps and its credibility was seriously endangered by its inability to fulfil its protection mandate.[46]

Thus, while there had been a multiplication of institutions involved in relief work, the protection of refugees, which had been recognized since the League of Nations as a responsibility of the international community, was weakened during the previous decade.[47] As stated by Goodwin-Gill, 'that portion of UNHCR protection work that was rooted in international law, standards and principles, has been eclipsed by so-called pragmatic approaches to refugee problems, in which everything seems to be negotiable'.[48] Furthermore, the concept of 'preventive protection' developed in the early 1990s by UNHCR[49] brought it closer to the role of human rights institutions, jeopardizing the non-political character of its mandate, which is paramount to the function of international protection.[50]

7.1.1.2.2 UNHCR's position on safe third country practices

The decline of a 'culture of protection'[51] within UNHCR may have also explained the lack of initiative and leadership of the refugee agency on safe third country practices in the 1990s. In a background note submitted to the Sub-Committee of the Whole on International Protection in 1991, the High Commissioner acknowledged that the safe third country concept could find some basis in the language of Article 31.1 of the Refugee Convention, and considered agreements such as the Dublin Convention as 'positive developments'.[52] The note mentioned that the

---

[44] G S Goodwin-Gill, 'Refugee Identity and Protection's Fading Prospect', in F Nicholson and P Twomey (eds), *Refugee Rights and Realities: Evolving International Concepts and Regimes* (Cambridge University Press, Cambridge 1999) 220, 246; The UNHCR Note on International Protection You Won't See, n 42 above, 272.

[45] M Barutciski, 'The Reinforcement of Non-Admission Policies and the Subversion of UNHCR: Displacement and Internal Assistance in Bosnia-Herzegovina (1992–94)' (1996) 8 *IJRL* 49, 89–90; Barnett, n 42 above, 265; Loescher, Betts, and Milner, n 20 above, 56.

[46] Goodwin-Gill, 'Refugee Identity and Protection's Fading Prospect', n 44 above, 230–1.

[47] Goodwin-Gill, 'Refugee Identity and Protection's Fading Prospect', n 44 above, 225.

[48] Ibid, 235.

[49] UNHCR, 'Note on International Protection' UN Doc A/AC.96/799, 25 August 1992, para 26; see also G Okoth-Obbo, 'Coping with a Complex Refugee Crisis in Africa: Issues, Problems and Constraints for Refugees and International Law', in V Gowlland-Debbas (ed), *The Problem of Refugees in the Light of Contemporary International Law Issues* (Nijhoff, The Hague 1996) 7, 10.

[50] Barutciski, n 45 above, 56; Barnett, n 42 above, 258–9; Kourula, n 31 above, 215; Frelick, n 42 above, 448.

[51] Goodwin-Gill, 'Refugee Identity and Protection's Fading Prospect', n 44 above, 247.

[52] UNHCR, 'Background Note on the Safe Country Concept and Refugee Status', UN Doc EC/SCP/68, 26 July 1991, para 14; see also UNHCR, Note on International Protection, UN Doc A/AC.96/750, 27 August 1990, para 18.

application of these mechanisms could give rise to 'difficulties',[53] but no further analysis of these practices and their protection risks was conducted.

UNHCR adopted a more principled position in later documents. It insisted on the fundamental character of the *non-refoulement* obligation and defined guidelines to ensure that readmission agreements contained provisions on refugee protection. At the same time, it considered that 'agreement among States in this context would enhance the international protection of refugees by leading to the orderly handling of asylum applications and could help reducing the misuse of asylum procedures in connection with irregular migration'.[54] In a note submitted in response to an opinion of the United Kingdom Delegation on safe third countries, it reiterated both its support for the conclusion of relevant arrangements and reaffirmed the fundamental importance of the duty of States under international refugee law,[55] while indicating that there was as yet no general consensus on this practice.[56] One particularly revealing statement indicated that,

UNHCR would agree that a third country's acceptance of responsibility for considering an asylum seeker's request can be conveyed informally, provided there is a *moral certainty*[57] that effective protection will in fact be granted.[58]

The 'certainty' that protection is guaranteed in the third country should not only be moral. It is in fact a very clear obligation under international law, namely, that States should not return an individual to any country where there is a real risk that he/she will be returned to a country that does not offer effective protection to the asylum seeker.

A more stringent formulation appeared in the 1999 UNHCR Note on International Protection, which expressed concern for the widespread misuse of the notion of safe third country, insisting that in order to establish whether an asylum seeker can be returned to a safe third country, a case-by-case examination had to be carried out, thereby condemning the use of 'safe third country lists'.[59] These statements were unfortunately watered down in the General Conclusion on International Protection of the Executive Committee, which briefly recalled that notions such as safe third country 'should be appropriately applied so as not to result in improper denial of access to asylum procedures, or to violations of the

---

[53] Background Note, n 52 above, para 15.

[54] UNHCR, 'Readmission agreements, "Protection elsewhere" and asylum policy' August 1994, 1. The same formulation is used in UNHCR, 'The Concept of Protection Elsewhere' (1995) 7 *IJRL* 123.

[55] 'The Concept of Protection Elsewhere', n 54 above, 124.

[56] Ibid, 126.

[57] Emphasis added.

[58] Ibid, 127.

[59] UNHCR, Note on International Protection, UN Doc A/AC.96/914, 7 July 1999, paras 19 and 20; see also UNHCR, Note on International Protection, UN Doc A/AC.96/898, 3 July 1998, paras 14 and 16 (c); UNHCR, Note on International Protection, UN Doc A/AC.96/815, 31 August 1993, paras 20–2.

principle of *non-refoulement*.[60] Yet again, the condemnation of the 'widespread misuse', which had been taking place for over a decade, did not lead to the formulation of concrete solutions to remedy the situation.

Many UNHCR statements throughout the 1990s reaffirmed the importance of refugee protection standards, while at the same time supporting the development of arrangements allocating responsibility between States.[61] As such, this might not have necessarily been a problem; the problem was the perfunctory quality of UNHCR's analysis.[62] While safe third country practices were being developed and exported across the European continent at a rapid pace,[63] UNHCR failed throughout the 1990s to carry out a thorough legal analysis of the problem with a view to identifying possible solutions. In 1991, the Note on International Protection stated that,

[...] UNHCR has a doctrinal responsibility to consolidate and expand the legal framework governing the status and rights of refugees. In essence, this function involves promoting, interpreting and developing the fundamental principles of refugee protection, with the goal of strengthening international commitments to receive persons crossing national borders and in need of international protection [...][64]

A year earlier, the agency had recognized that the concepts of safe country or country of transit 'lack[ed] satisfactory definition'.[65] While some may argue that UNHCR did not conduct a more thorough doctrinal analysis because it did not want to legitimize these practices, the fact remains that by disengaging from the debate, UNHCR effectively left the initiative to States and allowed the most questionable practices to thrive. In hindsight, and to conform to its doctrinal responsibilities, UNHCR would have been far more effective in its role if had been more actively involved and sought to develop a common understanding so as to provide clear legal guidelines based on full respect for existing international obligations. In failing to do so at an early stage, it arguably overlooked its own statutory obligations, lost the initiative, and was unable to reassert its moral and institutional authority when confronted with the expansion of safe third country policies.

The Executive Committee did formally encourage UNHCR to develop guiding principles on refugee protection and called on it to organize consultations

---

[60] Para (j) of ExCom General Conclusion on International Protection No. 87 (1999); Note however that para (aa) of General Conclusion on International Protection No. 85 (1998) is more strongly worded.

[61] See also 'Considerations on the "safe third country" concept' submitted by UNHCR at the EU Seminar on the Associated States as Safe Third Countries in Asylum Legislation Vienna, 8–11 July 1996.

[62] The only document which presents a more in-depth legal analysis of the question is an internal document from UNHCR's London Office, 'The "Safe Third Country" Policy in the Light of the International Obligations of Countries vis-à-vis Refugee and Asylum-Seekers' July 1993.

[63] See Chapter 2, Section 2.1.2.

[64] UNHCR, Note on International Protection, UN Doc A/AC.96/777, 9 September 1991, para 8.

[65] UNHCR, Note on International Protection, UN Doc A/AC.96/750, 27 August 1990, para 18.

on this subject. In 1991, an internal working group was convened by the High Commissioner to examine protection challenges.[66] The focus on protection was, however, diluted in a mandate that also included the analysis of preventive strategies and solutions.[67] Not a single paragraph of the findings and recommendations of the Working Group, reproduced in the Note on International Protection, dealt with secondary movements and the various arrangements adopted to prevent them. As will be explained below, it was only in the late 1990s and as a result of the Global Consultations that UNHCR sought to revive and bolster its doctrinal role and protection mandate.

7.1.1.3 Article 35 CSR

While UNHCR has an obligation to support cooperation between States for the protection of refugees, States parties to the CSR are under a similar duty to cooperate with the organization pursuant to Article 35 CSR:[68]

Co-operation of the national authorities with the United Nations

The Contracting States undertake to co-operate with the Office of the United Nations High Commissioner for Refugees, or any other agency of the United Nations which may succeed it, in the exercise of its functions, and shall in particular facilitate its duty of supervising the application of the provisions of this Convention.

In order to enable the Office of the High Commissioner or any other agency of the United Nations which may succeed it, to make reports to the competent organs of the United Nations, the Contracting States undertake to provide them in the appropriate form with information and statistical data requested concerning:

   (a) The condition of refugees,
   (b) The implementation of this Convention, and
   (c) Laws, regulations and decrees which are, or may hereafter be, in force relating to refugees.

A similar cooperation clause is found in the OAU Convention[69] and in the Cartagena Declaration.[70] It is generally submitted that this clause should be construed in a progressive manner.[71]

---

[66] See ExCom Conclusion No. 66 (1991) on the Report of the Working Group on Solutions and Protection; UNHCR, Note on International Protection, UN Doc A/AC.96/799, 25 August 1992, para 6.

[67] Ibid, paras 12 and 13.

[68] This obligation is also contained in Art II of the 1967 Protocol.

[69] Article VIII of the 1969 Convention governing the specific aspects of refugee problems in Africa (10 September 1969) (1976) 1001 UNTS 45 No. 14691.

[70] Para II of the Cartagena Declaration, (19–22 November 1984), OAS/Ser.L/V/II.66, doc.10, rev.1, p 190–3 reprinted in UNHCR, *Collection of International Instruments and Other Legal Texts Concerning Refugees and Displaced Persons* (UNHCR, Geneva 1995) Vol II 206.

[71] Türk, 'Das Flüchtlingshochkommissariat', n 8 above, 162.

Cooperation may take various forms. At a minimum, UNHCR has an advisory and consultative role in national refugee status determination procedures.[72] In many countries, UNHCR provides legal aid to individuals or groups of refugees.[73] It also provides advice on the adoption of national legislation and administrative regulations.[74] As part of these supervisory duties, UNHCR undertakes wide-ranging information gathering, pursuant to Article 35.2 CSR. However, as noted by Kälin, this never led to the development of a formal and open reporting system.[75]

In 1989, UNHCR requested information on the implementation of specific articles of the Convention and advocated the 'strengthening and expansion of co-operation' in order to facilitate its work.[76] In its report, it noted that there still existed important socio-economic,[77] legal,[78] practical, and political impediments[79] to the proper implementation of the Convention in the States parties and invited States to pursue and improve cooperation in its application.[80] Informal consultations were then carried out in 1997. Four separate issues were addressed in the report: the different interpretations of the international refugee law regulations and instruments; State reporting as a whole; the usefulness of organizing periodic dialogue with States parties; and measures of enforcement.[81]

While there has been some progress, such as domestic courts' increasing reliance on Article 35 to recognize the legal relevance of UNHCR's *Handbook*[82] and other UNHCR statements pursuant to Article 35 CSR,[83] UNHCR's supervisory functions under Article 35 CSR have remained relatively weak, and incapable of halting the erosion of international protection standards. Even though a large part of UNHCR's work in this area happens at the domestic level and consists in providing protection and advocacy in individual refugee cases, the agency could clearly have done more at the international normative level to improve State compliance

[72] ExCom Standing Committee, 'Progress Report on Informal Consultations on the Provision of International Protection to All Who Need it', UN Doc EC/47/SC/CRP.27, 30 May 1997, para 7.

[73] Ibid.

[74] Ibid.

[75] Kälin, n 1 above, 625.

[76] ExCom Sub-Committee of the Whole on International Protection, 'Implementation of the 1951 Convention and the 1967 Protocol relating to the Status of Refugees', UN Doc EC/SCP/54, 7 July 1989, para 7.

[77] Ibid, paras 10–11.

[78] Ibid, paras 13–17.

[79] Ibid, paras 18–22.

[80] Ibid, para 23.

[81] ExCom Standing Committee, 'Progress Report on Informal Consultations on the Provision of International Protection to All Who Need It', UN Doc EC/47/SC/CRP.27, 30 May 1997, para 8.

[82] UNHCR, *Handbook on Procedures and Criteria for Determining Refugee Status under the 1951 Convention and the 1967 Protocol Relating to the Status of Refugees*, HCR/IP/4/Eng/REV.1 Re-edited, Geneva, January 1992, UNHCR 1979. Available at: <http://www.unhcr.org/publ/PUBL/3d58e13b4.pdf>

[83] Kälin, n 1 above, 625–7.

with the CSR.[84] This lack of leadership on legal protection resulted in the diminished authority and influence of the agency, which, in spite of its recent valiant efforts to counter some of the most toxic aspects of EU asylum proposals, became apparent during the process leading up to the adoption of key EU legislative instruments.

Several explanations were provided for the agency's inability to take a proactive stance on these issues. The Working Group on International Refugee Policy noted in 1998 that 'as an organization which exists due to the failure of States to protect their own citizens, but at the same time, in responding to this failure, has to act through states, UNHCR's task is seen as logically unstable'.[85] The evaluation report of the Regional Bureau for Europe also noted UNHCR's difficulty in striking a balance between an NGO and a government identity,[86] while subjected to demands from both 'constituencies'. There have also been internal disagreements on the significance of the European harmonization process, which have undermined its position as a 'key interlocutor' with the European Union.[87] Finally, Loescher observes that UNHCR, concerned as it is by 'donor confidence' and the stiff competition with other international players, tends, as many other institutions, to refute criticism and avoid open acknowledgement of its failings.[88]

Clearly, a major obstacle to UNHCR's supervisory work is its dependency on voluntary contributions by donor States. This issue was discussed in 1997 within the Standing Committee of the Executive Committee, and there were divergent views on the impact of UNHCR's financial dependency on the provision of international protection.[89] It is however undeniable that the reform of the budgetary structure of the agency would improve UNHCR's standing towards States. The question was once again raised in 2003 in a report before the General Assembly, and the solutions identified consisted in broadening and diversifying UNHCR's

---

[84] D McNamara, 'Opening Address' in *UNHCR and International Refugee Protection* RSP Working Paper No. 2 June 1999, 4, 5; G S Goodwin-Gill 'Closing Address: Principles and Protection: Making it Work in the Modern World', in *UNHCR and International Refugee Protection* RSP Working Paper No. 2 June 1999, 13. Note in this respect the recent comments made by Mr Okoth-Obbo, Director of the Division of International Protection Services, who sought to emphasize UNHCR's action at the national level as being more relevant than international initiatives on supervision. These comments fail, however, to acknowledge the challenge posed by safe third country practices and the flaws of the EU system of judicial protection in the asylum field presented in Chapter 6, see UNHCR, 'Annual UNHCR/NGO Consultation', 25–26 June 2008: Thematic Session on the "Governance of Refugee Law: Suggestions and Perspectives"', 3.

[85] Working Group on International Refugee Policy, 'Report of the International Conference on the Protection Mandate of UNHCR, The Hague September 1998' (1999) 12 *JRS* 203, 205.

[86] UNHCR Evaluation and Policy Analysis, 'Implementation of UNHCR's strategy in the European Union' EVAL/04/98 July 1998 <http://www.unhcr.org/research/RESEARCH/3ae6bd480. pdf>, para 104.

[87] Ibid, paras 122 and 124–5.

[88] Loescher, n 42 above, 50.

[89] ExCom Standing Committee, 'Progress Report on Informal Consultations on the Provision of International Protection To All Who Need It', UN Doc EC/47/SC/CRP.27, 30 May 1997, para 9.

donor base and ensuring that the allocation of funding from the UN regular budget reaches a level consistent with the Office's Statute.[90] However, this does not fully address the fact that UNHCR must continue to rely on the good will of States in order to survive.

7.1.1.4 *Advisory opinion from the International Court of Justice*

In accordance with Article 65.1 of its Statute, the International Court of Justice is competent to give advisory opinions on any question of international law submitted to it by a UN body, in accordance with the UN Charter. Pursuant to Article 96 of the UN Charter, the General Assembly and the Security Council may make such a request. In addition, other UN organs and specialized agencies may do so at the authorization of the General Assembly. UNHCR contemplated the possibility of making such a request through the General Assembly, but it was eventually abandoned amid concerns about the uncertain result of such an undertaking.

7.1.1.5 *Human rights charter-based bodies*

The Commission on Human Rights of the United Nations was established in 1946 as a functional commission to the Economic and Social Council 'to make recommendations for the purpose of promoting respect for, and observance of, human rights and freedoms for all'.[91] It was composed of 53 representatives of governments and 91 observer States and has now been replaced by the 47-member Human Rights Council, which was established in 2006 as a subsidiary organ to the General Assembly.[92] Even though it does not have a specific supervisory competence in the refugee realm, the Commission on Human Rights and its successor have a broad mandate, encompassing human rights and fundamental freedoms for all.[93]

The Commission on Human Rights came up with interesting findings on the question of forced displacement. In 1997, the Sub-Commission on Prevention of Discrimination and Protection of Minorities decided to pursue its work on the right to freedom of movement and insisted on the need to further rationalize and harmonize the legal standards applicable to different types of forced displacement.[94]

---

[90] UNHCR, Report by the High Commissioner to the General Assembly on Strengthening the Capacity of the Office of the High Commissioner for Refugees to Carry out its Mandate, UN Doc. A/AC.96/980, paras 54–5, 20 August 2003, 62. In 2006, 3 per cent of UNHCR's total resources were drawn from the UN's regular budget, see UNHCR, 'Annual Programme Budget 2007', UN Doc A/AC.96/1026, 1 September 2006.

[91] Article 68 and 62.2 of the UN Charter.

[92] 'Human Rights Council', GA Res 60/251, 3 April 2006.

[93] Ibid, paras 2 and 3.

[94] Resolution on freedom of movement and population transfer, UN Doc E/CN.4/SUB.2/RES/1997/29, 28 August 1997; see also Resolution 1996/9 of the Sub-Commission on Prevention of

On 18 August 2000, the Sub-Commission adopted a Resolution on the right to seek and enjoy asylum. The Resolution recognized

[t]hat the principle of *non-refoulement* under the Convention relating to the Status of Refugees and the Protocol thereto and other human rights instruments does not imply any geographical limitation and that, accordingly, the removal of a refugee from one country to a third country which will subsequently send the refugee onward to the place of feared persecution constitutes indirect refoulement in contravention of the above-mentioned international human rights instruments.[95]

The Resolution finally requested the Special Rapporteur on the rights of non-citizens to give special attention to the situation of asylum seekers and refugees and to make practical recommendations for the further work of the Sub-Commission on this matter.[96] While more policy-oriented than legalistic, the approach of Charter-based bodies is interesting because of their emphasis on the full application of human rights standards to refugees and asylum seekers, including those set out in the Refugee Convention.

In institutional terms, the Commission also sought to bridge, or some would say, to 'mainstream' refugee issues into the human rights realm by requesting all UN bodies, including the Special Rapporteurs, Special Representatives and Working Groups of the Commission as well as the human rights treaty bodies, specialized agencies and governmental and intergovernmental bodies, to provide all relevant information on situations that generate or impact refugees and displaced persons so that it could take appropriate action in fulfilment of its mandate in consultation with the High Commissioner for Refugees.[97]

This inclusiveness also brings to light the important supervisory gaps existing in international refugee law. UNHCR recognized in 2003 that, 'the now extensive array of international human rights instruments, together with their monitoring mechanisms, offer important complementary tools for enhancing refugee protection',[98] mentioning as well the numerous conclusions touching upon refugee protection issues, and its intent to strengthen cooperation with regional human rights bodies.[99]

7.1.2 Supervision by States: Article 38 CSR

Article 38 provides that any dispute relating to the interpretation of the Refugee Convention may be brought before the International Court of Justice. In its opinion

---

Discrimination and Protection of Minorities on the right to freedom of movement, UN Doc E/CN.4/SUB.2/RES/1996/9, 25 November 1996, paras 4–7.

[95] UN Doc E/CN.4/SUB.2/RES/2000/20, 18 August 2000, preambular paragraph 11.

[96] Ibid, para 3.

[97] UNHCR, 'Human Rights and Mass Exoduses', Res 1998/49, 17 April 1998.

[98] Note on International Protection, UN Doc A/AC.96/975, 2 July 2003, para 49.

[99] Ibid, para 50.

on the *Reservations to the Genocide Convention*, the International Court of Justice noted that the Convention was 'manifestly adopted for a purely humanitarian and civilizing purpose', and that 'in such a convention the contracting States do not have any interest of their own'.[100]

The court may have then unwillingly acknowledged that States have, save in exceptional circumstances, no specific interest in ensuring the respect of human rights norms abroad.[101] While many human rights supervisory bodies provide for the settlement of inter-State disputes, the few cases where States have brought claims against other States have been motivated by strong self-interest, more than by pure humanitarian concern.[102] This is even truer in the realm of refugee protection, and in the current context, few States would be willing to call attention to them when their own behaviour may also be subject to criticism. This is probably the reason why Article 38 of the Refugee Convention has never been used by State parties,[103] and that its usefulness as a supervisory tool is therefore limited.

7.1.3 Supervision by individuals

There are currently no international remedies enabling asylum seekers and refugees to challenge the interpretation and/or application of international refugee law before a judicial or quasi-judicial body. On the other hand, many of the UN human rights treaties contain provisions which are relevant to the protection of refugees' rights and have established monitoring bodies that examine State reports as well as complaints from States and individuals.[104] As seen in Chapter 5, and aside from the key role played by regional bodies such as the ECtHR, the Committee Against Torture receives a great number of individual petitions from asylum seekers who argue that their return to their country of origin would violate Article 3 CAT.[105] UNHCR and the Executive Committee have both recognized the relevance of human rights monitoring for the strengthening of refugee rights and the work of these bodies is closely followed by UNHCR.[106]

---

[100] *Reservations to the Convention on the Prevention and Punishment of Genocide* (Advisory Opinion) ICJ Reports (1951) 14, 23.

[101] Sztucki, n 10 above, 309.

[102] Schermers and Blokker, n 1 above, 868; see also L Henkin, 'International Law: Politics, Values and Functions' (1989) 216 *RdC* Vol IV 253–4.

[103] Goodwin-Gill and J McAdam, *The Refugee in International Law* (3rd edn, Oxford University Press, Oxford 2007) 218.

[104] See eg Arts 7, 9, 12, 13 ICCPR, (adopted 16 December 1966, entered into force 23 March 1976) 999 UNTS 171; Art 3 CAT, (adopted 10 December 1984, entered into force 26 June 1987) 1465 UNTS 85.

[105] See Section 5.1.2.2.

[106] UNHCR, 'Note on International Protection', UN Doc A/AC.96/930, 7 July 2000, para 38; see also ExCom General Conclusion on International Protection No. 95 (2003) para (l), which: '*Notes* the complementary nature of international refugee and human rights law as well as the possible role of the United Nations human rights mechanisms in this area and therefore *encourages* States, as appropriate, to address the situation of the forcibly displaced in their reports to the United Nations Treaty

It is obvious, however, that these various bodies cannot ensure the protection of the whole range of rights set out under the Refugee Convention, such as the prohibition of penalties for refugees arriving illegally provided under Article 31 CSR or the prohibition of refoulement within the terms of Article 33 CSR. Above all, they have no jurisdiction to rule on the scope of application of Article 1 of the Refugee Convention, whose divergent interpretations lead to serious protection concerns in the application of safe third country practices. In this perspective, the absence of supervisory mechanism tailored to the specificity of the refugee regime and with jurisdiction to examine individual petitions remains problematic.

7.2 Future Prospects

This section seeks to identify possible strategies to improve the supervisory framework of refugee protection with a view to addressing some of the specific challenges raised by safe third country practices. Three specific approaches will be presented: the strengthening of UNHCR's supervisory and monitoring functions; the strengthening of the Executive Committee's supervisory role; and supervision by individuals through the establishment of a quasi-judicial monitoring body.[107]

7.2.1 Supervision by or on behalf of UNHCR

7.2.1.1 UNHCR's international protection mandate

In spite of its structural limitations, UNHCR still holds a cardinal position and any attempt at bolstering supervision in the international refugee realm must involve in one way or another UNHCR. The sections below examine various initiatives that have addressed directly or indirectly the question of supervision and monitoring of States' obligations, particularly in relation to secondary movements.

7.2.1.1.1 The Global Consultations and the Agenda for Protection
Since 2000, UNHCR has launched a number of initiatives with the goal to reignite support for its key function of protection. The first of such processes were the Global Consultations which were announced by the High Commissioner at the 51st session of the Executive Committee to celebrate the 50th anniversary of

---

Monitoring Bodies, and suggests that these bodies may, in turn, wish to reflect, within their mandates, on the human rights dimensions of forced displacement.'

[107] All of these options have been discussed in the legal literature and by NGOs; see K Landgren, 'Deflecting international protection by treaty: bilateral and multilateral accords on extradition, readmission and the inadmissibility of asylum requests' (1999) New Issues in Refugee Research UNHCR Working Paper No. 2, 57; Kälin, n 1 above; Working Group on International Refugee Policy, Report of the International Conference on the Protection Mandate of UNHCR, The Hague September 1998 (1999) 12 *JRS* 203, 214.

the conclusion of the CSR[108] and consisted of an 18-month process involving governments, intergovernmental and non-governmental organizations, as well as refugee experts and refugees themselves.[109] One of the key policy documents issued at the time was the 2000 Note on International Protection,[110] in which UNHCR identified four distinct protection challenges: (1) ensuring the availability and quality of asylum; (2) revitalizing the refugee protection system; (3) promoting durable solutions from a protection perspective and engaging in in-country protection activities; and (4) fostering partnerships in support of the international refugee protection system.[111]

While these four points are relatively self-explanatory, it is worth noting that UNHCR has sometimes sought to address States' growing concerns in ways that may not fit easily with the notion of protection. Thus, the second point presented in the Note tried to address issues which had emerged in the early 1990s, such as the smuggling of migrants, and abuses of the asylum system.[112] In order to respond to these challenges, UNHCR had been exploring ways to accommodate States' concerns, while at the same time trying to strengthen the existing system of international protection.[113] This more flexible approach entailed the development of systems of temporary protection,[114] and of cooperation to return persons not in need of international protection.[115] Another major facet of this strategy has been the promotion of harmonized regional approaches, above all on the European continent.[116] The question of the return of persons who are not in need of international protection was taken up in ExCom Conclusion No. 89 of 2000, which recognized the importance of comprehensive measures adopted by States in cooperation with UNHCR to ensure the fulfilment of international protection obligations towards refugees.[117] UNHCR has been involved at the level of the European Union in the work of the High Level Working Group on Asylum and Migration, and has participated in the drafting of instruments against the smuggling of migrants and trafficking in persons.[118] However, while ensuring that these

---

[108] Opening Statement by the High Commissioner, Report of the 51st session of the Executive Committee, UN Doc A/AC.96/944, 13 October 2000, Annex II, 27.

[109] See <http://www.unhcr.org/protect/3b7cea1b4.html>; see also UN Doc. A/AC.96/965/Add.1, 26 June 2002, 1, 27; see also Türk, 'Freedom from Fear', n 33 above, 508–9.

[110] Note on International Protection, UN Doc A/AC.96/930, 7 July 2000.

[111] Ibid, para 5.

[112] Ibid, paras 31–2.

[113] Ibid, para 35.

[114] Ibid, para 36.

[115] Ibid, para 37.

[116] Ibid, para 39; see also Declaration Nr. 17 on Article 73k of the Treaty Establishing the European Community [1997] OJ C340/134.

[117] Report of the 51st session of the Executive Committee of the High Commissioner's Programme UN Doc A/AC.96/944, 13 October 2000, para 9; see also the statement by the representative of Belgium at the 48th session of the Executive Committee, UN Doc A/AC.96/SR.519/Add.1, 28 November 1997, para 29.

[118] See UNHCR, Note on International Protection, UN Doc A/AC.96/930, 7 July 2000, para 37.

arrangements take into consideration the specific needs of refugees is undeniably important, this should not take priority over more core issues that were at that point still unresolved and on which UNHCR has unique expertise and authority.[119]

This is not to say that the Global Consultations did not constitute a significant achievement. They undeniably reopened a long awaited debate on the scope and meaning of refugee protection and led to the commissioning of several important expert reports,[120] some of which will have been analysed at great length in this volume. Crucially, the Global Consultations ended with the convening of a meeting of the then 141 State parties to the Refugee Convention, which adopted on 13 December 2001 a Declaration reaffirming their commitment to the principles embedded in the Convention. It also led to the adoption of the Agenda for Protection, which continues to provide the policy-framework upon which UNHCR is to develop protection-related activities, and was endorsed by the Executive Committee and welcomed by the UN General Assembly in 2002.[121]

The Agenda for Protection identified six key goals that would guide UNHCR's programme of action for the following years: strengthening implementation of the 1951 Convention and 1967 Protocol; protecting refugees within broader migration movements; sharing burdens and responsibilities more equitably and building capacities to receive and protect refugees; addressing security-related concerns more effectively; redoubling the search for durable solutions; and meeting the protecting needs of refugee women and refugee children. Each of these goals comprised long check-lists of sub-goals, of which the most relevant for the present discussion are:

- 'closer cooperation in the supervision of implementation of the 1951 Convention and 1967 Protocol',[122] which ties to the application of Article 35 CSR examined below;

---

[119] See also UNHCR, 'High Commissioner's Dialogue on Protection Challenges, Theme: Refugee Protection, Durable Solutions and International Migration, Chairman's Summary', 12 December 2007, 5; UNHCR, 'High Commissioner's Dialogue on Protection Challenges: Discussion Paper: Refugee Protection and Durable Solutions in the Context of International Migration', UN Doc. UNHCR/DPC/2007/Doc.02, 19 November 2007, para 31, 43.

[120] See eg *Refugee Protection and Migration Control: Perspectives from UNHCR and IOM*, EC/GC/01/11, 31 May 2001; J van Selm, *Access to Procedures, "Safe Third Countries". "Safe Countries of Origin" and "Time Limits"*, June 2001; Kälin, n 1 above; E Lauterpacht and D Bethlehem, *The Scope and the Content of the Principle on Non-Refoulement*, Opinion, 20 June 2001; G S Goodwin-Gill, *Article 31 of the 1951 Convention Relating to the Status of Refugees: Non-Penalization, Detention and Prosecution*, October 2001. Most of these reports were published in E Feller, V Türk, and F Nicholson (eds), *Refugee Protection in International Law: UNHCR's Global Consultations on International Refugee Protection* (Cambridge University Press, Cambridge 2003) and are also available at <http://www.unhcr.org/protect/PROTECTION/3b94e7a2a.html>; see also the various guidelines on International Protection issued by UNHCR, available at: <http://www.unhcr.org/pages/49c3646cce.html>.

[121] Both documents are included in UNHCR, 'Agenda for Protection', UN Doc. A/AC.96/965/Add.1, 26 June 2002.

[122] Ibid, 7.

- 'better identification of and proper response to the needs of asylum seekers and refugees, including access to protection within the broader context of migration management';[123]

- '[...] more precisely articulated understanding of what constitutes effective protection in countries of first asylum';[124] and finally

- 'work with States of origin, transit and destination and other partners, including IOM, on a package of measures which might be brought into play, as part of a comprehensive plan of action, for particular irregular or secondary movement situations'.[125]

With respect to the goal of protecting refugees within broader migration movements, several important activities were developed by UNHCR, such as border monitoring;[126] the training of border and immigration officials;[127] the commissioning of a study on effective protection;[128] more proactive involvement in other migration-related fora, including the Swiss 'Berne Initiative', the Inter-Governmental Consultations (IGC), and the Action Group on Asylum and Migration (AGAMI).[129]

The Agenda for Protection definitely created a momentum, triggering multiple initiatives by UNHCR. The existing time limit on the Office's mandate[130] was removed in 2004.[131] Another measure adopted in the wake of the Agenda for Protection was the establishment of the post of Assistant High Commissioner for Protection in 2004, with oversight over the division of international protection services, protection policy development, UNHCR advocacy for rule of law and implementation of standards, as well as the integration of protection priorities into management and delivery of operations by the Bureaux and in the field.[132] The rationale for such initiative was the need to strengthen UNHCR's protection work 'at a crucial time when the principles and the practice are both seriously under

[123] Ibid, 11.

[124] Ibid, 11–12.

[125] Ibid, 12.

[126] Note on International Protection, UN Doc A/AC.96/965, 11 September 2002, para 19.

[127] Ibid, para 23.

[128] Ibid, para 29; see also UNHCR, 'Summary Conclusions on the Concept of "Effective Protection" in the Context of Secondary Movements of Refugees and Asylum Seekers', Lisbon Expert Roundtable organised by the UNHCR and the Migration Policy Institute and hosted by the Luso-American Foundation for Development, 9 and 10 December 2002.

[129] UNHCR, Note on International Protection, UN Doc A/AC.96/975, 2 July 2003, para 16.

[130] UNHCR, Report by the High Commissioner to the General Assembly on Strengthening the Capacity of the Office of the High Commissioner for Refugees to Carry out its Mandate, UN Doc. A/AC.96/980, 20 August 2003, para 13.

[131] UN GA Res 58/153, 24 February 2004.

[132] UNHCR Executive Committee, Proposal to Establish an Assistant High Commissioner (Protection) Post in UNHCR, UN Doc. A/AC.96/992/Add.1, 2 September 2004. The position was approved by the Executive Committee in October 2005 and endorsed by the Secretary-General, and came into effect in February 2006 see <http://www.unhcr.org/admin/ADMIN/3b52acb48.html>.

threat', with a view to 're-aligning the place and protection in the overall priorities of UNHCR and sharpening the focus on protection in operational planning',[133] and more specifically, bolstering its supervisory role under Article 35 CSR.[134] Finally, an expert meeting convened by UNHCR in 2002 led to the adoption of conclusions on effective protection, which, while highly interesting, are of uncertain legal value.[135]

7.2.1.1.2 Regulating secondary movements: 'Convention Plus' and other initiatives

While it had been originally suggested that the various objectives laid down in the Agenda for Protection would be discussed within an 'International Protection Forum', the process floundered and another initiative was announced, known as 'Convention Plus'.[136] This new endeavour which was launched in 2002 by the then High Commissioner, Ruud Lubbers, with a view to proposing the development of new arrangements complementing the Refugee Convention, 'was intended to supplement international law on refugee protection with a normative framework for global burden-sharing'.[137] Three areas inadequately covered by the existing refugee regime were selected, for which special agreements would be discussed: resettlement, irregular secondary movements, and targeted development assistance.[138] Given the weakness of burden-sharing in the current refugee regime, 'Convention Plus' 'sought to address this gap by facilitating inter-state consensus on new norms'.[139] The idea was to adopt general normative agreements, whose principles would then be applied in Pilot Comprehensive Plans of Action (CPAs).[140]

With respect to irregular secondary movements, the process was facilitated by Switzerland and South Africa and involved over 30 participants.[141] The premise of

---

[133] Ibid, para 8.

[134] Ibid, para 4.

[135] Lisbon Expert Roundtable, see n 128 above; see S Legomsky, 'Secondary Refugee Movements and the Return of Asylum Seekers to Third Countries: The Meaning of Effective Protection' (2003) 15 *IJRL* 567.

[136] A Betts and J-F Durieux, 'Convention Plus as a Norm-Setting Exercise' (2007) 20 *JRS* 509, 512.

[137] Ibid, 509.

[138] See High Commissioner's Forum, 'Progress Report: Convention Plus', FORUM/2004/2, 20 February 2004; see Betts and Durieux, n 136 above, 510. On the use of the phrase 'irregular secondary movements', see High Commissioner's Forum, 'Convention Plus Issues Paper on Addressing Irregular Secondary Movements of Refugees and Asylum-Seekers', FORUM/CG/SM/03, 11 March 2004 (hereafter, Issues Paper) para 4.

[139] Betts and Durieux, n 136 above, 510.

[140] Ibid, 512; see also High Commissioner's Forum, 'Making Comprehensive Approaches to Resolving Refugee Problems more Systematic', FORUM/2004/7, 16 September 2004, para 6. That document specifies that a CPA could be adopted for refugees of one or more nationalities in one particular asylum country and/or for a chain of countries that are affected by a refugee movement, see para 9; see also Chapter 4, Section 4.2.1.3.3.

[141] The participants were Algeria, Australia, Austria, Brazil, Canada, China, Denmark, the Dominican Republic, Ethiopia, France, Ghana, Greece, the Holy See, India, Ireland, Italy, Japan, Latvia, Lithuania, Mexico, Morocco, the Netherlands, Norway, Oman, Romania, Slovakia, Spain, Sweden, Turkey, Uganda, the United States of America, ICVA, IOM, and OHCHR, see UNHCR,

the discussion stemmed from a recognition that the question encompassed 'a wide range of legal issues, a multitude of State actors, including host, transit and destination countries and broadly shared responsibilities among them as well as with other stakeholders'.[142] The original goals of the discussions were to ensure effective protection, providing durable solutions, and improving control of such movements in a 'protection sensitive manner', through the development of 'new tools, in the form of multilateral special agreements, to complement the 1951 Convention and its 1967 Protocol'.[143] These 'special agreements' would consist of written arrangements between UNCHR and governments, which, depending on their subject-matter, would either be drafted to be legally binding or intended to reflect an important degree of political commitment.[144] The approach was a cautious one, favouring the adoption of 'case-load specific' surveys, starting with a study of the irregular secondary movements of Somali refugees, which would then 'inform the generic work towards a special agreement'.[145]

For the purpose of the discussion, UNHCR produced an 'Issues Paper', which sought to clarify a number of legal questions in relation to irregular secondary movements. While acknowledging the concern of States, UNHCR adopted a principled stance, highlighting that one of the primary causes of those movements was attributable to serious gaps in protection,[146] and that refugees were faced with 'the uncertainty to find and to be granted protection elsewhere; and [had] no other means in this attempt than to resort to irregular means, with all the harmful consequences that this may have for them'.[147] It then went on to delineate the areas which should be covered by any agreement among States on irregular secondary movements:[148] identification and recognition of protection needs; assessment of the merits of the claim; the provision of protection pending durable solutions; and the provision of durable solutions.

UNHCR also suggested that 'agreements on ways to reduce irregular secondary movements would be best framed within comprehensive, durable solutions arrangements, into which the various strands of Convention Plus would converge'.[149] UNHCR ended its analysis by identifying seven issues which would

'Informal Record Open Meeting of States and Interested Parties on Secondary, Irregular Movements of Refugees and Asylum-Seekers' (Geneva, 16 December 2003) FORUM/CG/SM/01, 21 December 2003, para 1.

[142] Ibid, para 4.

[143] Ibid, paras 5–6.

[144] UNHCR, '"Convention Plus" Questions and Answers', 20 May 2003, para 10, available at <http://www.unhcr.org/cgi-bin/texis/vtx/protect/opendoc.pdf?tbl=PROTECTION&id=3e4b7c4b4>, see also Betts and Durieux, n 136 above, 514.

[145] High Commissioner's Forum, 'Informal Record Open Meeting of States and Interested Parties on Secondary, Irregular Movements of Refugees and Asylum-Seekers' FORUM/CG/SM/01, 21 December 2003, paras 9, 19, 22, 27.

[146] Issues Paper, n 138 above, para 15.

[147] Ibid, para 2.

[148] Ibid, paras 26–39.

[149] Ibid, para 42.

have a direct bearing on the reduction and prevention of irregular secondary movements, among which it included 'criteria for the sharing and allocation of responsibilities among States for examining refugee claims on their merits' which would 'address the ways in which responsibilities are assumed, continued and/or transferred', as well as '[m]echanisms to monitor the implementation of the agreement, evaluate its impact, and report to stakeholders' for which 'UNHCR would normally be given [...] a role consistent with its mandate'.[150]

In spite of these efforts, discussions on irregular secondary movements could not reach a successful conclusion.[151] Deliberations on a draft Multilateral Framework of Understanding on Addressing Irregular Secondary Movements of Refugees and Asylum Seekers were suspended by the facilitators of the Core Group in July 2005 to exclusively focus on finalizing the Survey of Movements of Somali refugees,[152] leading to the elaboration of a Comprehensive Plan of Action for Somali refugees which in the end received limited support.[153]

This failure was the result of important differences of view within the Core Group, essentially reflecting a North–South divide. The normative debate was indeed characterized by divergences between the North, which supported a definition of effective protection exclusively based on civil and political rights, and the principle that refugees should have found protection in a first country of asylum, so as to ensure the return of refugees to countries in their region of origin. The South, on the other hand, endorsed an approach that would also include economic and social rights and required financial aid for capacity-building, regardless of any readmission commitment.[154] These discussions unfortunately reinforced the views of many developing countries that Convention Plus was nothing more than an attempt by UNHCR to appease 'pro-containment' European States. The fact that, apart from South Africa, only Northern States were given the role of chairing each of the core groups increased the South's perception that Convention Plus was essentially a Northern initiative, in which UNHCR represented Northern interests, instead of playing the role of an even-handed facilitator.[155]

Thus, despite the consensual recognition of the need to improve responses to secondary movements, to deepen international cooperation, to address both the root causes and consequences of such movements, and to clarify and update

---

[150] Ibid, para 11.

[151] See UNHCR, 'Progress Report: Convention Plus', FORUM.2005.6, 8 November 2005, para 11.

[152] High Commissioner's Forum, 'Convention Plus Core Group on Addressing Irregular Secondary Movements of Refugees and Asylum-Seekers, Joint Statement by the Co-Chairs', FORUM/2205/7, 8 November 2005, para 1. See also J Moret, S Baglioni, and D Éfionayi-Mäder, 'The Path of Somali Refugees into Exile, A Comparative Analysis of Secondary Movements and Policy Responses', Swiss Forum for Migration and Population Studies, Studies 46, 2006, available at <http://www.migration-population.ch/fileadmin/sfm/publications/rr/s_46.pdf>.

[153] Betts and Durieux, n 136 above, 529; see also UNHCR, *The State of the World's Refugees: Human Displacement in the New Millenium* (Oxford University Press, Oxford 2006) 59.

[154] Betts and Durieux, n 136 above, 514.

[155] Ibid, 527.

international instruments,[156] the Joint Statement issued by the Co-Chairs and endorsed by all the members of the Working Group indicated that 'several members of the Core Group expressed the view that it [was] preferable to [...] launch practical initiatives in order to encourage cooperation on specific groups in concrete situations, rather than lingering on legalistic or theoretical discussions'.[157] Other members of the group were of the view that 'the multilateral framework should focus on enhancing the protection of refugees and increasing the capacity of States, particularly developing States, to provide protection effectively through close multilateral cooperation'.[158]

While this outcome was not particularly surprising, it is worth noting that the results of the 'Somali survey' pointed in fact to the importance of protection gaps in the motivations underlying refugees' irregular secondary movements, such as 'difficulties in accessing an asylum procedure that is fair, efficient and gender- and age- sensitive; difficulties in accessing registration; difficulties in obtaining a secure legal status; the risk of *refoulement* and ill treatment'.[159] Some have also noted that the selection of the Somali group for this first empirical study on irregular secondary movements was perhaps ill-conceived, given the particular challenges present in the Somali case.[160]

UNHCR's latest initiative sought to ride the momentum created by the 2006 General Assembly's High-Level Dialogue on International Migration and Development. Two policy statements were published in this context[161] as well as a 10-Point Plan of action on Refugee Protection and Mixed Migration.[162] Most relevant among the '10 points' are: protection-sensitive entry systems that would involve the training and provision of guidelines to border guards and immigration officials and the building of protection constituencies; reception arrangements including registration, profiling and referral mechanisms; and addressing secondary movements about which UNHCR recognized that, '[t]o date efforts to articulate such a strategy have failed to muster international consensus'.[163] UNHCR has

[156] High Commissioner's Forum, 'Convention Plus Core Group on Addressing Irregular Secondary Movements of Refugees and Asylum-Seekers, Joint Statement by the Co-Chairs', FORUM/2205/7, 8 November 2005, para 7.

[157] Ibid, para 4.

[158] Ibid, para 7; see also Betts and Durieux, n 136 above, 528.

[159] Ibid, para 7.

[160] Betts and Durieux, n 136 above, 532.

[161] UNHCR, 'The High-Level Dialogue on International Migration and Development: UNHCR's observations and recommendations', 28 June 2006, available at: <http://www.unhcr.org/protect/PROTECTION/48848b854.pdf>.

[162] UNHCR, 'Refugee Protection and Mixed Migration: A 10-Point Plan of Action', 1 January 2007. Note that the Plan had actually been introduced at the Euro-African Ministerial Conference on Migration and Development held in Rabat in July 2006, see ExCom Standing Committee, 'UNHCR's Activities in Relation to the Asylum-Migration Nexus', UN Doc EC/58/SC/CRP.12, 4 June 2007, para 4.

[163] UNHCR, 'Refugee Protection and Mixed Migration: A 10-Point Plan of Action', 1 January 2007, 4; see also UNHCR High Commissioner's Dialogue on Protection Challenges, 'Discussion Paper:

reiterated its call for improved monitoring since then, emphasizing the need to incorporate refugee protection safeguards in all EU border management instruments and actions, to put in place initial reception arrangements at external borders and to adopt profiling mechanisms and the deployment of Asylum Expert Teams.[164] It also provided a list of activities to address mixed migration in the context of the Mediterranean/Atlantic arrivals.[165]

7.2.1.1.3 Conclusion

All of these developments, while demonstrating UNHCR's renewed commitment to fulfil its doctrinal and protection role, have unfortunately not had yet a significant impact on the quality and level of protection provided by States. The 'action-oriented' 'caseload-specific' strategies are unlikely to suffice in order to tackle a problem which at its core, tests the very foundations of the current regime of international refugee protection. The strengthening of supervisory mechanisms under international refugee law should be considered as a complement to these strategies as it would help consolidate and develop the international normative framework for refugee protection by reconciling differing interpretations of States' obligations.

One relatively simple and easy first step would be the development of a public and more formal reporting system by UNHCR,[166] which would also avoid the pitfalls of the State reporting system existing under UN human rights treaty bodies which, as will be seen below, suffers from serious flaws.[167] The proactive efforts of UNHCR to intervene before supranational and international judicial organs and the recent publication of opinions on a number of key legal issues is also an encouraging sign that UNHCR is once again fully aware of the importance of ascertaining and reaffirming some of the most fundamental principles of refugee protection in an increasingly challenging legal context, and that it is keen to regain a leading doctrinal role in the consolidation and development of international refugee law.[168]

Refugee protection and durable solutions in the context of international migration' UN Doc UNHCR/ DPC/2007/Doc.02, 19 November 2007, which discusses how best to implement the 10-Point Plan of Action.

[164] UNHCR, 'Response to the European Commission's Green Paper on the Future Common European Asylum System', September 2007, 46–50; ExCom Standing Committee, n 162 above, para 6.

[165] UNHCR, 'Implementing the Ten-Point Plan of Action in Southern Europe: Activities Undertaken by UNHCR to Address Mixed Migration in the Context of the Mediterranean/Atlantic Arrivals', 2 October 2006; see also in this respect Chapter 2, Section 2.4.

[166] Landgren, n 107 above, 63–4.

[167] See below, Section 7.2.1.3.

[168] See eg UNHCR, 'Advisory Opinion Regarding the Scope of the National Security Exception in Article 33(2)', 6 January 2006, available at: <http://www.unchr.org/refworld/docid/43de2da94. html>; UNHCR, 'Note on Diplomatic Assurances and International Refugee Protection' August 2006, para 37 available at <http://www.unhcr.org/refworld/docid/44dc81164.html>; UNHCR, 'Advisory Opinion on the Extraterritorial Application of *Non-Refoulement* Obligations under the 1951 Convention Relation to the Status of Refugees and its 1967 Protocol', 26 January 2007,

7.2.1.2 *The Executive Committee of the High Commissioner's Programme*

The Executive Committee would seem to be the most appropriate organ currently in activity to carry out expanded supervisory tasks. It has a specialized mandate as an advisory body to UNHCR, it is formally independent and is composed of State representatives.

In his paper submitted for the Global Consultations, Kälin proposed the creation of a Sub-Committee on Review and Monitoring within the Executive Committee, which would comprise those States which are signatories to the Refugee Convention.[169] The main function of this Sub-Committee would be to monitor the implementation of the Refugee Convention and of its 1967 Protocol. For each specific situation subject to review, a team of independent experts would be appointed. The governments affected by this specific situation would submit a memorandum laying down their policy, and the difficulties encountered in the implementation of the Convention. The experts should be able, at the invitation of the government, to investigate the situation in the field and interview the various governmental and non-governmental actors involved, including refugees. The report would be presented and discussed at a public session of the Sub-Committee, which would be able to adopt observations.

This proposal was inspired by 'policy review' mechanisms such as the International Narcotic Control Board established under the Convention on Narcotic Drugs, as well as the Environmental Performance Reviews and the Development Co-operation Reviews which exist within the OECD.[170] The two main features of this mechanism are the peer-review process and the fact-finding by experts. Its advantages lie in its non-adversarial character, and its focus on overall policy achievements. In addition, it would not require an amendment of the Refugee Convention and the 1967 Protocol and could be achieved through the adoption of a Resolution by ECOSOC.[171]

While this new mechanism would already constitute a significant progress, the identified weaknesses of such a solution would be the non-binding character of the Committee's findings and above all, its limited impact on the harmonization of the Refugee Convention's application. It also bears noting that these types of mechanisms have been mostly used in rather technical areas of international cooperation, which raises some doubt as to whether they would be properly suited to more politically charged issues, such as refugee protection. The early stages of the peer-review process known as the Universal Periodic Review by the Human Rights

---

available at <http://www.unhcr.org/refworld/docid/45f17a1a4.html> 5–6. See also the statement of the Assistant High Commissioner for Protection, Erika Feller before ExCom, 8 October 2008, who suggests that the question of supervision examined during the Global Consultations should perhaps be revived, 6.

[169] Kälin, n 1 above, 664.
[170] Ibid, 646.
[171] Ibid, para 77, 34.

Council does not look extremely promising in this respect, even though it is too early to draw definitive conclusions on its impact.[172]

Finally, there might also be potential institutional difficulties to adopting such a mechanism. In view of the declining legal relevance of the conclusions adopted by the Executive Committee, there is a risk that the 'observations' will not be of much higher value and the composition of the Sub-Committee might constitute a major obstacle in this respect. A mixed composition with independent experts appointed by States, or even a committee made entirely of independent experts might ensure a higher quality of work. Another possibility would be to further institutionalize the role of non-governmental actors. Interestingly, this was done by the League of Nations, through the establishment of consultative committees whose membership included charity organizations.[173] Finally, a parameter which was not sufficiently emphasized in the proposal would be the importance of giving wide publicity to the work of the suggested sub-Committee. The suggestion to have public review sessions may not be sufficient and the role of non-governmental actors should be enhanced.[174]

With regard to the monitoring of States' international obligations beyond the 1951 Convention, Kälin suggests the appointment of Thematic Rapporteurs by the Standing Committee. The reports would be discussed with representatives from governments and non-governmental organizations. This proposal, which is inspired by the procedures existing before the former UN Commission on Human Rights and pursued by the Human Rights Council,[175] would need to be fleshed out in order to address some of their weaknesses.[176]

While these proposals are certainly interesting and worth considering, it is revealing that the 'High Commissioner's Dialogue on Protection Challenges', one of UNHCR's latest protection initiatives which seeks to provide 'a forum for high-level and participatory dialogue on protection issues, emerging global themes and challenges, as well as specific protection situations' was created outside the Executive Committee.[177] The UNHCR was at pains to assure that this initiative is not by any means meant to compete with the Executive Committee,[178] which retains key competencies relating to UNHCR's governance. Nonetheless, this might be

---

[172] 'Human Rights Council', UNGA Res 60/251, 3 April 2006, para 5(e); see also, 'Universal Periodic Review', available at: <http://www.ohchr.org/EN/HRBodies/UPR/Pages/UPRMain.aspx>.

[173] Jaeger, n 15 above, 24–5.

[174] This was also emphasized in the summary conclusions on the question of supervisory responsibility, Global Consultations, Cambridge Expert Roundtable, 9–10 July 2001 organized by the UNHCR and the Lauterpacht Research Centre for International Law, University of Cambridge.

[175] For an overview of existing thematic mandates assumed by the Human Rights Council, see <http://www2.ohchr.org/english/bodies/chr/special/themes.htm>.

[176] P Alston 'The Commission on Human Rights', in P Alston (ed) *The United Nations and Human Rights, A Critical Appraisal* (Clarendon Press, Oxford 1992) 126, 181.

[177] UNHCR, 'Concept Paper on the "High Commissioner's Dialogue on Protection Challenges"', 30 July 2007, para 2.

[178] Ibid, paras 9–10.

perceived as an acknowledgement that in its present shape and composition and given the current climate, the Executive Committee has become increasingly unable to tackle protection challenges.

7.2.1.3 Establishment of an independent body to examine State reports

An obligation to report to UNHCR and inform it about laws and regulations adopted by State parties exists under Articles 35 and 36 of the Refugee Convention, but there is no formal and open process addressing States' compliance with their obligations. Reference to the work of the UN human rights treaty monitoring bodies has been frequent in the discussions on the improvement of the supervisory framework in international refugee law, and it is therefore necessary to asssess whether these could provide a valuable model.

There are now eight monitoring bodies which have been established under human rights treaties signed under the auspices of the United Nations.[179] These bodies generally carry out three major functions: the examination of State reports, the examination of complaints brought by individuals,[180] and inter-State complaints.[181] Some of the treaty bodies have also inquiry powers.[182] The reporting procedure before UN human rights bodies requires States to submit an initial report, followed by periodic reports after a period determined in the Treaty. Treaty bodies have progressively adopted the practice of approving conclusions or recommendations which contain a general evaluation of the report. In order to assess accurately compliance with State parties, they increasingly rely on various sources, such as individual communications, general comments, documents from Charter-based bodies, reports from specialized agencies, as well as independent reports presented by NGOS.[183]

---

[179] See Art 28 ICCPR n 104 above; Art 8 CERD (adopted 7 March 1966, entered into force 4 January 1969) 660 UNTS 195; Art 17 CEDAW (adopted 18 December 1979, entered into force 3 September 1981) 1249 UNTS 13; Art 17 CAT n 104 above; Art 43 CRC (adopted 20 November 1989, entered into force 2 September 1990) 1577 UNTS 3; Art 72 CPMW (adopted 18 December 1990), annexed to UNGA Res 45/158, 30 *ILM* 1521; Art 34 of the Convention on the Rights of Persons with Disabilities (adopted 13 December 2006, entered into force 3 May 2008) annexed to UNGA Res 61/106. Note that the Committee on Economic, Social and Cultural Rights was established by the Economic and Social Council, see ECOSOC Res 1985/17 on the Review of the Composition, Organization and Administrative Arrangements of the Sessional Working Group of Governmental Experts on the Implementation of the International Covenant on Economic, Social and Cultural Rights, 28 May 1985.

[180] See below, Section 7.2.2.

[181] In view of the very small number of such complaints, this procedure will not be examined in this chapter.

[182] J Crawford, 'The UN Human Rights Treaty System: A System in Crisis', in P Alston and J Crawford (eds), *The Future of UN Human Rights Treaty Monitoring* (Cambridge University Press, Cambridge 2000) 1, 2; D McGoldrick, *The Human Rights Committee, Its Role in the Development of the International Covenant on Civil and Political Rights* (Clarendon Press, Oxford 1991) 54.

[183] I Boerefijn, *The Reporting Procedure under the Covenant on Civil and Political Rights, Practice and Procedures of the Human Rights Committee* (Hart, Oxford 1999) 201–2, 222; M R Bustelo,

Reference to the model of human rights monitoring bodies was made in the report by the Standing Committee of the Executive Committee on the provision of international protection, however, States seemed to be reluctant to adopt a system of periodic reporting, arguing that it would overpoliticize the process.[184] Landgren also suggested the establishment by the UN Economic and Social Council of a group with a specific mandate to supervise the protection of refugees' rights, in the same fashion as the Committee on Economic, Social and Cultural Rights.[185]

While there might be some merit in establishing a more formalized reporting process in the refugee field, it would be misguided to consider that the introduction of these reporting procedures would fully assuage current concerns. There is indeed unanimous agreement on the need to review the reporting system of the UN human rights regime.[186] The reporting procedure suffers from a serious backlog and many States fail to submit their reports on time, while some do not even submit them at all.[187] This led the Committee on Economic, Social and Economic Rights and the Committee on the Elimination of All Forms of Racial Discrimination to consider

---

'The Committee on the Elimination of Discrimination Against Women at the Crossroads', in P Alston and J Crawford (eds), *The Future of UN Human Rights Treaty Monitoring*, n 182 above, 79, 104–5; G Lansdown, 'The Reporting Process under the Convention on the Rights of the Child', in P Alston and J Crawford (eds), *The Future of UN Human Rights Treaty Monitoring*, n 182 above, 113, 119–20; S Leckie, 'The Committee on Economic, Social and Cultural Rights: A Catalyst for Change in a System Needing Reform', in P Alston and J Crawford (eds), *The Future of UN Human Rights Treaty Monitoring*, n 182 above, 129, 130, and 133.

[184] See ExCom Standing Committee, 'Progress Report on Informal Consultations on the Provision of International Protection to All Who Need it' UN Doc EC/47/SC/CRP.27, 30 May 1997, para 9; Landgren, n 107 above, 60.

[185] Landgren, n 107 above, 62.

[186] UN Commission on Human Rights, Resolution on effective implementation of international instruments on human rights, including reporting obligations under international instruments on human rights, UN Doc E/CN.4/RES/2000/75, 27 April 2000, paras 7–9; UNGA Res 53/138 on effective international implementation of international instruments on human rights, including reporting obligations under international obligations on human rights, 1 March 1999, paras 10–15; Report of the Secretary-General to the Commission on Human Rights on effective functioning of the bodies established pursuant to the United Nations human rights instruments UN Doc E/CN.4/1998/85, 4 February 1998, 6; UNGA Res 52/118 on effective implementation of international instruments on human rights, 23 February 1998, para 8; H Steiner, 'Individual Claims in a World of Massive Violations: What Role for the Human Rights Committee?', in P Alston and J Crawford (eds), *The Future of UN Human Rights Treaty Monitoring* (Cambridge University Press, Cambridge 2000) 15, 50; McGoldrick, n 182 above, 64 and 103; Leckie, n 183 above, 131; see also UN High Commissioner for Human Rights Secretariat, Concept paper on the High Commissioner's Proposal for a Unified Standing Treaty Body, UN Doc. HRI/MC/2006/2, 22 March 2006 (hereafter, Unified Standing Treaty Body Paper), paras 16–17.

[187] Final Report by the independent expert, Philip Alston, on enhancing the long-term effectiveness of the United Nations human rights treaty system, UN Doc E/CN.4/1997/74, 27 March 1996, paras 37–47; Bustelo, n 183 above, 84–5; Lansdown, n 183 above, 125; Leckie, n 183 above, 131; R Bank, 'Country-Oriented Procedures under the Convention Against Torture: Towards a New Dynamism', in P Alston and J Crawford (eds), *The Future of UN Human Rights Treaty Monitoring* (Cambridge University Press, Cambridge 2000) 145, 148–9; Unified Standing Treaty Body Paper, n 186 above, paras 17–19.

situations in the absence of reports by a State party, on the basis of the information at their disposal.[188] At the same time, it is clear that treaty bodies would not be able to cope with the amount of work arising from the strict respect by State of their reporting obligations, due to a lack of resources.[189]

Secondly, the quality of reporting is problematic,[190] and both Western and developing countries increasingly regard the whole process as a 'game' with very little at stake.[191] Alston acknowledged that many States just lack the political will to comply with their obligations, and therefore, that the 'cost of non-compliance should be raised'.[192]

In the wake of the UN reform process, in particular, the setting up of the Human Rights Council and the adoption by the High Commissioner for Human Rights of its Plan of action in 2005,[193] the question of how best to reform the treaty-body system resurfaced and the High Commissioner produced a concept paper on the proposal for a unified standing treaty body.[194] The paper relied also on the call by the Secretary-General to streamline and strengthen the treaty bodies' system.[195]

In its Concept Paper, the High Commissioner acknowledged the weaknesses of the current system, primarily, the fact that it is 'rarely perceived as an accessible and effective mechanism to bring about change',[196] the lack of consistency and comprehensiveness of treaty bodies' recommendations, the uneven quality of the experts appointed to these bodies and of State reports,[197] and the lack of follow up mechanisms to ensure the sustained and systematic impact of the system.[198] It nevertheless recognized the benefits of the treaty reporting system for human rights NGOs and regional organizations as well as UN agencies, including UNHCR.[199]

In order to maintain and strengthen the achievements of the reporting process while making it more effective and less burdensome, one of the first steps that it

---

[188] Boerefijn, n 183 above, 240–1; M Banton, 'Decision-Taking in the Committee on the Elimination of Racial Discrimination', in P Alston and J Crawford (eds), *The Future of UN Human Rights Treaty Monitoring* (Cambridge University Press, Cambridge 2000) 55, 66; see also Bustelo, n 183 above, 110; this solution is also advocated by Alston in his final report, n 187 above, para 45.

[189] Final Report by the independent expert, Philip Alston, n 187 above, paras 48–52; Crawford, n 182 above, 6–7; Boerefijn, n 183 above, 252.

[190] Final Report by the independent expert, Philip Alston, n 187 above, para 109; McGoldrick, n 182 above, 73; Bank, n 187 above, 150; A Boulesbaa, *The U.N. Convention on Torture and the Prospects for Enforcement* (Nijhoff, The Hague 1999) 260.

[191] M wa Mutua, 'Looking Past the Human Rights Committee: An Argument for De-marginalizing Enforcement' (1998) 4 *Buffalo Human Rights LR* 211, 229.

[192] Final Report by the independent expert, Philip Alston, n 187 above, paras 90–3.

[193] UN High Commissioner for Human Rights, 'The OHCHR Plan of Action: Protection and Empowerment', Geneva, May 2005.

[194] Unified Standing Treaty Body Paper, n 186 above.

[195] UN Secretary-General, 'In Larger Freedom: Towards Security, Development and Human Rights', UN Doc A/59/2005, 21 March 2005, para 147.

[196] Unified Standing Treaty Body Paper, n 186 above, para 21.

[197] Ibid, paras 22, 24.

[198] Ibid, para 26.

[199] Ibid, para 14.

suggests would be for treaty bodies to examine reports of State parties jointly, to formulate joint general comments or convene joint thematic working groups so as to harmonize their respective agendas, priorities, and objectives.[200]

In the long run, according to the High Commissioner, the best solution would be the establishment of a unified standing treaty body, 'comprised of permanent, full-time professionals'[201] who would produce more consistent and authoritative jurisprudence. Such body would also 'be available to victims on a permanent basis, and could respond more rapidly to grave violations', and have the ability to 'develop a strong capacity to assist State parties in their implementation of human rights obligations'.[202] The High Commissioner concluded that,

As a result of comprehensive examination of a State party's implementation of all its treaty obligations, reporting to a united standing treaty body would stimulate more effective mainstreaming of the rights of specific groups or issues in the interpretation and implementation of all human rights treaty obligations, thereby making these more visible and central.[203]

The Concept Paper finally noted that enhanced consistency would obviously have a positive impact on the interpretation of substantively similar provisions in the different instruments.[204]

While the setting up of such a single treaty body would have major advantages, it would not resolve the supervisory gaps existing under international refugee law. One notes, for instance, that among the thematic expertise identified by the High Commissioner for Human Rights, special groups include migrants and internally displaced persons, but not refugees.[205] While such omission clearly stems from current UN institutional mandates, one is entitled to question whether, in the absence of any improved supervision under the current refugee regime and as part of the efforts to streamline and rationalize the mandates of the various UN agencies, some of the legal aspects of refugee protection might not be better dealt by human rights institutions.

Reforms taking place in the human rights regime could also be a catalyst for the development of stronger supervision of States obligations under international refugee law and should be fully exploited by advocates. In particular, the suggestion made in the Concept Paper that the unified standing treaty body could be better equipped to encourage 'greater practical engagement by [UN] specialized agencies, programmes and funds in the reporting process at all phases of the reporting cycle, both at the national and at the international levels' should be seriously considered by UNHCR and refugee advocates.

---

[200] Ibid, para 20.
[201] Ibid, para 27.
[202] Ibid, para 27.
[203] Ibid, para 28; see also para 54.
[204] Ibid, para 30.
[205] OHCHR Plan of Action, n 193 above.

7.2.2 Supervision by individuals

There is no doubt that ultimately, the most effective method of supervision would be the examination of individual claims by an organ composed of independent members. However, the establishment of an international body with a competence to examine individual petitions can only be envisaged on a long-term basis. One of the main difficulties is that it would probably require the drawing up of a conventional instrument, such as an Optional Protocol to the Refugee Convention.

This idea has been suggested in various forms in the literature. In 1995, Einarsen proposed a comprehensive framework to deal with mass influx, which would include the establishment of an 'International Asylum Court'. Thus, those refugees who would be subjected to these new regulations applying in cases of mass influx would be able to file a claim before it.[206] Another suggestion was to create a monitoring body with competence to hear individual petitions, similar to those existing under UN human rights treaties,[207] such as Landgren's suggestion to establish a Committee on Refugee Protection, independent from UNHCR and with a membership of experts and individuals of high standard.[208]

In this area as well, the mechanisms existing under UN human rights treaties provide only a very imperfect model. First, treaty bodies have no fact-finding competencies, and have to rely on information provided by the parties. Secondly, the terminology used under all of these instruments, which refer to 'individual communications' rather than complaints, and to 'views' of the committees instead of decisions reflects the reluctance of States to recognize the quasi-judicial character of the functions of treaty bodies and to accept a genuine 'enforcement' mechanism.[209] The fact that the 'views' of these committees are adopted by consensus has also affected their quality: they often lack precision and clarity and offer limited legal reasoning.[210] One of the most problematic aspects of the non-judicial character of treaty bodies, however, is that there are no proper enforcement mechanisms to ensure actual compliance with their decisions.[211] Moreover, they are not widely

---

[206] T Einarsen, 'Mass Flight: The Case for International Asylum' (1995) 7 *IJRL* 551, 563.

[207] See Optional Protocol to the ICCPR, Optional Protocol to CEDAW annexed to UNGA 54/4, 6 October 1999; Art 22 CAT; Art 14.1 CERD; Art 77 CPMW; Art 1 of Optional Protocol to the Convention on the Rights of Persons with Disabilities (adopted on 13 December 2006, entered into force on 3 May 2008) annexed to UNGA Res 61/106. The Committee on the Rights of the Child has no individual complaints procedure.

[208] Landgren, n 107 above, 60.

[209] wa Mutua, n 191 above, 232; Steiner, n 186 above, 23.

[210] See the criticisms of Australia on the difficulty of complying with communications in view of their poor legal reasoning. Effective Functioning of Bodies Established Pursuant to the United Nations Human Rights Instruments Report of the Secretary-General to the Commission on Human Rights UN Doc E/CN.4/1998/85, 4 February 1998, 18; McGoldrick, n 182 above, 199.

[211] M G Schmidt, 'Individual Human Rights Complaints Procedures Based on United Nations Treaties and the Need for Reform' (1992) 41 *ICLQ* 645, 649–50; wa Mutua, n 191 above, 235; McGoldrick, n 182 above, 202.

reported and their impact on human rights adjudication at the domestic level tends to be limited.[212]

A valuable framework for further debate may be provided by Anne-Marie Slaughter and Laurence Helfer's theory of effective supranational adjudication. Their article identifies the elements that render supervision by private persons an essential tool in the human rights realm. Supranational adjudication is defined by these authors as,

[...] adjudication by a tribunal that was established by a group of states or the entire international community and that exercises jurisdiction over cases directly involving private parties—whether between a private party and a foreign government, a private party and her own government, private parties themselves, or in the criminal context, a private party and a prosecutor's office.[213]

Supranational adjudication is characterized by a higher level of compliance by States.[214] The authors identify 13 elements which help define this type of supervision, on the basis of the functioning of the ECJ and the ECHR. Some of these would be particularly important for the establishment of an efficient supervisory mechanism under international refugee law, primarily, the neutrality and demonstrated autonomy from political interests,[215] the capacity to carry out independent fact-finding,[216] the quality of legal reasoning,[217] and an incrementalist attitude in jurisprudential policy.[218] Two parameters which are not in the control of either State parties or judges are the nature of violations examined and the fact that the participating States rely on the rule of law and are responsive to their citizen's interests.[219] Those are important considerations in the refugee realm given the seriousness of the violations at stake and the fact that States will obviously not be as responsive of refugees' interests as they would be with respect to their citizens.

One must hasten to add that the international legal framework for refugee protection may not have yet reached a level of development which would render possible the establishment of a supranational mechanism. One essential feature of supranational tribunals is their 'functional capacity', that is, the financial and human resources available to carry out their mission, and the promotional activities which are related to it.[220] One only needs to look at UNHCR's fragile financial structure, and for that matter, the UN human rights regime, to foresee the hurdles of establishing such a body at the global level.

---

[212] wa Mutua, n 191 above, 236; McGoldrick, n 182 above 201; Steiner, n 186 above, 34.
[213] L R Helfer and A-M Slaughter, 'Toward a Theory of Effective Supranational Adjudication' (1997) 107 *Yale LJ* 273, 289.
[214] Ibid.
[215] Ibid, 312.
[216] Ibid, 303.
[217] Ibid, 318.
[218] Ibid, 314.
[219] Ibid, 329 and 331.
[220] Ibid, 301.

This does not mean that the suggestion of a global supervisory mechanism should be dismissed as wholly unrealistic. The very fact that the Expert Roundtable on supervisory responsibility, which was organized in the context of the Global Consultations, and thus with the support of UNHCR, envisaged the possibility of establishing a judicial body in the long term,[221] indicates that serious consideration of this question is called for. At this stage, the creation of informal forums of discussion for refugee law judges, suggested by experts, might be regarded as a first step in the right direction.

7.3 Conclusion

There are a wide variety of supervisory mechanisms existing under international refugee law, yet serious gaps exist under the current system. While UN human rights treaty bodies have been able to fill some of these protection gaps, they have no competence to interpret Articles 1 and 33 CSR and ensure compliance with the whole range of rights provided under the Refugee Convention.

The first problem relates to UNHCR's supervisory role. UNHCR has a unique mandate to ensure the international protection of refugees; however, it has not always been able to offer concrete solutions to the dilemmas raised by the uncontrollable spread of safe third country practices. In order to be successful, UNHCR needs to adopt a proactive strategy to bolster supervision so as to address the protection challenges raised by safe third country practices.

The work of the Executive Committee has also suffered from the existing tension between the practice of States and the international obligations they committed themselves to respect. The increasing difficulty in finding agreement among a large membership has hampered its work, and in particular, the legal relevance of its conclusions.

The present study attempted to contribute to the debate which was initiated in the context of the Global Consultations taking place under the auspices of UNHCR. More recent policy initiatives, such as 'Convention Plus' and the 10-Point Plan have, on the other hand, sought to provide more specific and concrete responses to protection concerns but it is argued here that these will not be sufficient to prevent the steady erosion of international standards of refugee protection. In the short term, there is a need to strengthen UNHCR's doctrinal capacities, to continue developing UNHCR monitoring capabilities at the borders, and to consider the adoption reporting or policy-review procedures within the Executive Committee or within a newly created sub-Committee. In the long term, the objective should be the establishment of an independent body competent to examine individual complaints based on violations of the Refugee Convention.

---

[221] Global Consultations, Cambridge Expert Roundtable, 9–10 July 2001, n 174 above.

Conclusion

To address secondary movements of refugees, regarded as a major problem by many States, safe third country practices have been developed and formalized in national legislations, international arrangements, and supranational instruments. These practices essentially allow a State to remove an asylum seeker to a third country without considering his or her application on its merits, provided that country is regarded as safe for refugee protection purposes. Given the continuing expansion of these practices well beyond the European continent, it is unlikely that they will disappear from the arsenal of refugee containment policies. Yet, there is no doubt that they pose serious challenges to the international legal framework for refugee protection.

Two key questions were examined in this study. The first question dealt with the impact of safe third country practices on interstate relations. One found that while there have been multiple international documents affirming the fundamental significance of the principle of burden-sharing, actual practice indicates that States are reluctant to commit to substantial obligations with respect to physical burden-sharing. There is, on the other hand, far more substantial practice in terms of financial burden-sharing, yet discussions on these questions have remained characteristically difficult, epitomizing the tension existing between developed and developing countries on the broader question of development aid. That said, even if it cannot be concluded that the principle of burden-sharing is a customary norm, its legal relevance as a soft law principle should not be underestimated. In particular, it is submitted that States' commitment, their collective responsibility to protect refugees, of which the principle of solidarity and burden-sharing is the expression, is fundamentally undermined by the application of safe third country practices whose multiplication will further concentrate the existing burden on regions of origin. It is further suggested that the principle of good-neighbourliness could actually provide a valuable parameter in order to ensure that removals of asylum seekers are not carried out on a unilateral basis and on the basis of an individual's mere transit through a State's territory, improving thereby State relations strained by current approaches to secondary movements.

Yet, it is the second question, that is, the impact of safe third country practices on refugee's rights, which raises the greatest concerns, for these practices lead at the very least to States evading their fundamental obligations under international refugee law. The application of safe third country practices in a context of widely divergent levels of protection by States entails grave risks of *refoulement*, refugees' most fundamental right. Other rights, such as the right to seek and enjoy asylum, and the right to leave one's country, are also likely to be infringed. The relative autonomy accorded to States in their interpretation of the Refugee Convention and in the adoption of basic safeguards in refugee determination procedures is no longer tenable in these circumstances. Moreover, traditional mechanisms of international responsibility are ill-suited to tackle violations of States' obligations towards individuals. In order to address this difficulty, universal and regional human rights treaties have provided for the establishment of judicial or quasi-judicial bodies, which are competent to examine complaints lodged by States or individuals. The expansion of safe third country policies therefore requires a thorough consideration of this question in the refugee realm.

International supervision of States' obligations under international refugee law needs to be given central attention. Judicial supervision at the level of the European Union is now carried out by the European Court of Justice (ECJ), which is in effect the first supranational judicial institution to rule on the interpretation of the Refugee Convention. While this undoubtedly constitutes a major advance, the lack of experience of the Court in human rights adjudication, and the ambiguous relationship existing between this institution and the European Court of Human Rights raises some questions as to the approach which will be taken on asylum issues. Furthermore, the expansion of safe third country practices beyond the European continent indicates that the jurisdiction of the ECJ will be insufficient to resolve the complex legal issues at hand. Finally, there is a danger that UNHCR's unique protection mandate and doctrinal role will be undermined, given its limited ability to intervene in ECJ proceedings.

There are a variety of supervisory mechanisms which currently exist under international refugee law. UNHCR is given supervisory powers under paragraph 8 of its Statute and Article 35 of the Refugee Convention but the agency has not been able to take full advantage of these provisions. Pressured by its key donor States, it reoriented its activities towards international relief and assistance, which led to the weakening of international protection functions in the 1990s. The Executive Committee has also seen its work hampered by the difficulty of generating agreement among an ever increasing membership added to the growing reluctance of States to endorse formulations of clear-cut legal obligations.

Recent initiatives launched by UNHCR since the 2000 Global Consultations carry some encouraging prospects that the agency's protection mandate will be bolstered and that it will once again become a proactive actor in the development and consolidation of the international normative framework for refugee protection. This renewed interest in UNHCR's protection role creates a perfect opportunity to reopen discussions on supervisory mechanisms under international refugee law. In the short term, UNHCR's international protection activities, and in particular its doctrinal role, should be strengthened and given renewed prominence. The Executive Committee could also be granted greater powers to review

States' policies, through the creation of a specialized Sub-Committee. However, for this to succeed and to ensure a lasting and effective impact on domestic actors, it will be essential to fully include non-governmental organisations and give wide publicity to these processes. In the long term, more ambitious proposals should be considered, namely, the establishment of a quasi-judicial body composed of independent members which would be competent to hear individual and inter-State petitions.

Select Bibliography

BOOKS AND MONOGRAPHS

Adelman H (ed), *Refugee policy: Canada and the United States* (1991) York Lane Press, Toronto, 455 p.

Aleinikoff T A and Chetail V (eds), *Migration and International Legal Norms* (2003) TMC Asser, The Hague.

Alston P (ed), *The United Nations and Human Rights, A Critical Appraisal* (1992) Clarendon Press, Oxford, 765 p.

—— (ed), *The EU and Human Rights* (1999) Oxford University Press, Oxford, 946 p.

—— and Crawford J (eds), *The Future of UN Human Rights Treaty Monitoring* (2000) Cambridge University Press, Cambridge, 563 p.

Anderson M, *Policing the European Union* (1995) Clarendon Press, Oxford, 331 p.

Anker D, *Law of Asylum in the United States* (3rd edn 1999) Refugee Law Center, Boston, 616 p.

Arnull A, *The European Union and its Court of Justice* (1999) Oxford University Press, Oxford, 593 p.

Aust A, *Modern Treaty Law and Practice* (2000) Cambridge University Press, Cambridge, 443 p.

Balzacq T and Carrera S (eds), *Security versus Freedom? A Challenge for Europe's Future* (2006) Ashgate, Aldershot, 313 p.

Barwig K and Brill W (eds), *Aktuelle asyltechtlichen Probleme der gerichtlichen Entschei-dungspraxis in Deutschland, Österreich und der Schweiz* (1996) Nomos, Baden-Baden, 188 p.

Battjes H, *European Asylum Law and International Law*, Nijhoff (2006) Leiden / Boston, 688 p.

Bayefsky A (ed), *Human Rights and Refugees, Internally Displaced Persons and Migrant Workers: Essays in Memory of Joan Fitzpatrick and Arthur Helton*, (2006) Nijhoff, Leiden [etc], 598 p.

Bettati M, *L'asile politique en question, un statut pour les réfugiés* (1985) Presses Universitaires de France, Paris, 203 p.

Bieber R and J Monar J (eds), *Justice and Home Affairs in the European Union: The Development of the Third Pillar* (1995) European Interuniversity Press, Brussels, 437 p.

Bigo D, (ed), *L'Europe des polices et de la sécurité intérieure* (1992) Complexe, Bruxelles, 153 p.

—— *Polices en réseaux: l'expérience européenne* (1996) Fondation nationale des sciences politiques, Paris, 358 p.

—— (ed), *Circuler, enfermer, éloigner: zones d'attente et centres de rétention aux frontières des démocraties occidentales* (1997) L'Harmattan, Paris, 185 p.

Böcker A and Havinga T, *Asylum Migration to the European Union: Patterns of Origin and Destination* (1998) Office for Official Publications of the European Communities, Brussels, 121 p.

Boeles P, *Fair Immigration Proceedings in Europe* (1997) Martinus Nijhoff, The Hague / London, 510 p.

Boerefijn I, *The Reporting Procedure under the Covenant on Civil and Political Rights, Practice and Procedures of the Human Rights Committee* (1999) Intersentia Hart, Antwerpen / Groeningen / Oxford, 417 p.

Boulesbaa A, *The U.N. Convention on Torture and the Prospects for Enforcement* (1999) Martinus Nijhoff, The Hague / London, 366 p.

Bouteillet-Paquet D, *L'Europe et le droit d'asile, la politique d'asile européenne et ses conséquences pour les pays d'Europe centrale* (2001) L'Harmattan, Paris, 396 p.

——(ed), *Subsidiary Protection of Refugees in the European Union: Complementing the Geneva Convention?* (2002) Bruylant, Bruxelles, 883 p.

Boyle A and Chinkin C, *The Making of International Law* (2007) Oxford University Press, Oxford, 288 p.

——and Freestone D (eds), *International Law and Sustainable Development: Past Achievements and Future Challenges* (2001) Oxford University Press, Oxford, 377 p.

Brown E D and Cheng B (eds), *Contemporary problems of international law: essays in honour of Georg Schwartzenberger on his eightieth birthday* (1988) Steven & Sons, London, 371 p.

Brownlie I, *Principles of Public of International Law* (5th edn 1998) Oxford University Press, Oxford, 743 p.

——*Principles of Public International Law* (7th edn 2008) Oxford University Press, Oxford, 784 p.

Buergenthal T and Sohn L B, *The Movement of Persons Across Borders* (1992) American Society of International Law, Washington DC, 193 p.

Bunyan T (ed), *Key Texts on Justice and Home Affairs in the European Union* (1997) Vol I, Statewatch Pub., London, 143 p.

Centre for Studies and research in International Law and International Relations, *Le droit d'asile* (1989) Kluwer, Dordrecht, 121 p.

Cheng B, *General Principles of Law as Applied by International Courts and Tribunals* (1994 reprinted) Cambridge University Press, Cambridge, 490 p.

——(ed), *International Law: Teaching and Practice* (1982), Stevens, London, 287 p.

Chesnais J-C [et al.], *People on the Move New Migration Flows in Europe* (1992) Council of Europe Pub., Strasbourg, 250 p.

Chetail V and Gowlland-Debbas V (eds), *Switzerland and the International Protection of Refugees* (2002) Kluwer, The Hague, 283 p.

——(ed), *Mondialisation, migration et droits de l'homme: le droit international en question* (2007) Vol II Bruylant, Bruxelles, 728 p.

Chimni B S (ed), *International Refugee Law, A Reader* (2000) Thousand Oaks, California, Sage Pub., London, 613 p.

Clayton G, *Textbook on Immigration and Asylum Law* (2nd edn, 2006) Oxford University Press, Oxford, 617 p.

Coles G, *Problems Arising from Large Numbers of Asylum-Seekers: A Study of Protection Aspects* June (1981) International Institute of Humanitarian Law, San Remo, 48 p.

Collinson S, *Europe and International Migration* (1993) Pinter, London, 189 p.

Commentaire Mégret, Le Droit de la CEE (2nd edn 1993) Vol 10, Université Libre de Bruxelles, Bruxelles, 666 p.

Congress on International Solidarity and Humanitarian Actions (1980) International Institute of Humanitarian Law, San Remo, 401 p.

Craig P and De Búrca G, *EU Law Text Cases and Materials* (2nd edn 1998) Oxford University Press, 1152 p.

——and ——*EU Law, Text Cases & Materials* (4th edn 2008) Oxford University Press, Oxford 1148 p.

Crépeau F, *Droit d'asile: de l'hospitalité aux contrôles migratoires* (1995) Bruylant, Bruxelles, 424 p.

Curtin D and Heukels T (eds), *Institutional Dynamics of European Integration, Essays in Honour of H G Schermers* (1994) Vol II, Martinus Nijhoff, Dordrecht / London, 715 p.

De Bruycker P and Dias Urbano de Sousa C (eds), *The Emergence of a European Asylum Policy* (2004) Bruylant, Bruxelles, 344 p.

Dehousse R, *The European Court of Justice: The Politics of Judicial Integration* (1998) St Martin's Press, MacMillan, Basingstoke, New York, 213 p.

den Boer M (ed), *The Implementation of Schengen: First the Widening, Now the Deepening* (1997) European Institute of Public Administration, Maastricht, 173 p.

De Ruyt J, *L'Acte unique européen: Commentaire* (2nd edn 1989) Université Libre de Bruxelles, Bruxelles, 389 p.

Dinstein Y (ed), *International Law at a Time of Perplexity: Essays in Honour of Shabtai Rosenne* (1989) Martinus Nijhoff, London / Dordrecht, 1056 p.

Elias T O, *The Modern Law of Treaties* (1974) Oceana Pub., Sijthoff, Dobbs Ferry, New York, Leiden, 272 p.

Feller F, Türk V, and Nicholson N (eds), *Refugee Protection in International Law: UNHCR's Global Consultations on International Refugee Protection* (2003) Cambridge University Press, Cambridge, 717 p.

Ferguson Sidorenko O, *The Common European Asylum System* (2007) T. M. C. Asser Press, The Hague, 241 p.

Flory M and Higgins R (eds), *Liberté de circulation des personnes en droit international* (1988) Économica, Paris, 263 p.

Fulchiron H (ed), *Les étrangers et la Convention européenne de sauvegarde des droits de l'homme et des libertés fondamentales* (1999) LGDJ, Paris, 383 p.

Gibney M and Hansen R (eds), *Immigration and Asylum from 1900 to the Present*, (2005) ABC-CLIO Pub., Santa Barbara, 1095 p.

Goodwin-Gill G S, *The Refugee in International Law* (2nd edn 1996) Oxford University Press, Oxford, 584 p.

Goodwin-Gill G S and McAdam J, *The Refugee in International Law* (3rd edn 2007) Oxford University Press, Oxford, 786 p.

Gorman R F, *Coping with Africa's Refugee Burden, A Time for Solutions* (1987) Martinus Nijhoff and UNITAR, Dordrecht / Lancaster, 206 p.

Gowlland-Debbas V (ed), *The Problem of Refugees in the Light of Contemporary International Law Issues* (1996) Martinus Nijhoff, The Hague / London, 179 p.

Grahl-Madsen A, *The Status of Refugees in International Law* (1966) Vol I, A W Sijthoff, Leyden, 499 p.

——*The Status of Refugees in International Law* (1972) Vol II, A W Sijthoff, Leyden, 482 p.

——*Territorial Asylum* (1980) Almquist & Wiksell Int. and Oceana Pub., Stockholm / London / New York, 231 p.

——*Commentary on the Refugee Convention 1951* (1997) UNHCR Division of International Protection, Geneva.

Guild E (ed), *The Developing Immigration and Asylum Policies of the European Union* (1996) Kluwer Law International, The Hague / London, 528 p.

Hailbronner K, *Möglichkeiten und Grenzen einer Europäischen Koordinierung des Einreise-und Asylrechts* (1989) Nomos Verlagsgesellschaft, Baden-Baden, 232 p.
——*Immigration and Asylum Law and Policy of the European Union* (2000) Kluwer Law International, The Hague / London, 568 p.
Handmaker J, de la Hunt L A and Klaaren J (eds), *Perspectives on Refugee Protection in South Africa* (2001) Lawyers for Human Rights, Pretoria, 76 p.
Hannum H, *The Right to Leave and Return in International Law and Practice* (1987) Martinus Nijhoff, Dordrecht / Lancaster, 189 p.
Harris D J, O'Boyle M and Warbrick C, *Law of the European Convention on Human Rights* (1995) Butterworths, London, 753 p.
Hathaway J, *The Law of Refugee Status* (1991) Butterworths, Toronto, 252 p.
——(ed), *Reconceiving International Refugee Law* (1997) Martinus Nijhoff, The Hague / London, 171 p.
——*The Rights of Refugees under International Law* (2005) Cambridge University Press, Cambridge, 1236 p.
——and Dent J A, *Refugee Rights: Report on a Comparative Survey* (1995) York Lane Press, Toronto, 82 p.
Henkin L (ed), *The International Bill of Rights: The Covenant on Civil and Political Rights* (1981) Columbia University Press, New York, 523 p.
Heukels T, Blokker N and Brus M (eds), *The European Union after Amsterdam: A Legal Analysis* (1998) Kluwer, Cambridge (MA), 335 p.
Holborn L, *The International Refugee Organization: A Specialized Agency of the United Nations, Its History and Work 1946–1952* (1956) Oxford University Press, London / New York, 805 p.
——*Refugees: A Problem of Our Time, The Work of the United Nations High Commissioner for Refugees, 1951–1972* (1975) Vol I, Metuchen (New Jersey), Scarecrow Press, 793 p.
House of Lords, *Handling EU Asylum Claims: New Approaches Examined* European Union Committee's 11th Report of Session 2003–2004, HL Paper 74 (2004) 71 p.
Human Rights Watch, *"Prohibited Persons" Abuse of Undocumented Migrants, Asylum-Seekers, and Refugees in South Africa* (1998) Human Rights Watch, New York, 236 p.
Hughes J and Liebaut F, *Detention of Asylum Seekers in Europe: Analysis and Perspectives* (1998) Kluwer, Dordrecht, 332 p.
Jacobs F G and White R C A, *The European Convention on Human Rights* (2nd edn 1996) Oxford University Press, Oxford, 469 p.
Jaeger G, *Study of Irregular Movements of Asylum Seekers and Refugees* (1985) Working Group on Irregular Movements and Asylum Seekers, Geneva, 122 p.
Joseph S, Schultz J and Castan M, *The ICCPR: Cases, Materials and Commentary* (2nd edn 2004) Oxford University Press, Oxford, 745 p.
Kälin W, *Das Prinzip des Non-Refoulement, Das Verbot der Zurückweisung, Ausweisung und Auslieferung in den Verfolgerstaat im Völkerrecht und im Schweizerischen Landesrecht* (1982) Peter Land Pub., Frankfurt/Main, Bern, 365 p.
Kamanda A M, *Territorial Asylum and the Protection of Political Refugees in Public International Law*, (1971) Colloquium on the Law of Territorial Asylum, Bellagio, 242 p.
Klabbers J and R Lefeber (eds), *Essays on the Law of Treaties: A Collection of Essays in Honour of Bert Vierdag* (1998) Martinus Nijhoff, The Hague / London, 204 p.
Kneebone S and Rawlings-Sanaei F (eds), *New Regionalism and Asylum Seekers* (2007) Berghahn Books, New York, 243 p.

Kourula P, *Broadening the Edges, Refugee Definition and International Protection Revisited* (1997) Martinus Nijhoff, Boston, 407 p.

Koziebrodski L B, *Le Droit d'Asile* (1962) Sijthoff, Leyden, 374 p.

Krais J and Tausch C, *Asylrecht und Asyl Verfahren, Rechtsstellung der Flüchtlinge, Anerkennungsverfahren, Rechtschutz mit praktischen Materialen* (1995) Beck, München, 475 p.

Lanfranchi M-P, *Droit communautaire et travailleurs migrants des Etats tiers, entrée et circulation dans la Communauté européenne*, (1994) Économica, Paris, 281 p.

Lassen N and Hughes J (eds), *'Safe Third Country Policies' in European Countries* (1997) Danish Refugee Council, Copenhagen, 167 p.

Lavenex S, *Safe Third Countries: Extending the EU Asylum and Immigration Policies to Central and Eastern Europe* (1999) Central European University Press, New York, 189 p.

Lawson R and de Blois M (eds), *The Dynamics of the Protection of Human Rights in Europe: Essays in Honour of H G Schermers* (1994) Vol III, Martinus Nijhoff, Dordrecht, London, 416 p.

Lawyers Committee for Human Rights, *African Exodus: Refugee Crisis, Human Rights and the 1969 OAU Convention* (1995) New York, 266 p.

Le Traité d'Amsterdam et les perspectives d'évolution de l'Union européenne (1997) Pédone, Paris, 110 p.

Le Traité d'Amsterdam: Réalités et Perspectives (1999) Pédone, Paris, 172 p.

Liebaut F and Hughes J, *Legal and Social Conditions for Asylum Seekers and Refugees in Western European Countries* (1997) Danish Refugee Council, Copenhagen, 246 p.

Loescher G, *Beyond Charity, International Cooperation and the Global Refugee Crisis* (1993) Oxford University Press, Oxford, New York, 260 p.

—— Betts A, and Milner J, *UNHCR: The Politics and Practice of Refugee Protection into the Twenty-First Century* (2008) Routledge, New York, 161 p.

McAdam J, *Complementary Protection in International Refugee Law* (2006) Oxford University Press, Oxford, 336 p.

Macdonald R St J et al (eds), *The European System for the Protection of Human Rights* (1993) Martinus Nijhoff, Dordrecht / London, 940 p.

McGoldrick D, *The Human Rights Committee, Its Role in the Development of the International Covenant on Civil and Political Rights* (1991) Clarendon Press, Oxford, 576 p.

McNair A D, *The Law of Treaties* (1961) Clarendon Press, Oxford, 789 p.

Marinho C (ed), *The Dublin Convention on Asylum, Its Essence, Implementation and Prospects* (2000) European Institute of Public Administration, Maastricht, 413 p.

Martin D (ed), *The New Asylum Seekers: Refugee Law in the 1980s* (1988) Martinus Nijhoff, Dordrecht, 498 p.

Meijers H et al (eds), *A new immigration law for Europe?: the 1992 London and 1993 Copenhagen Rules on Immigration* (1993) Dutch Centre for Immigrants, Utrecht, 96 p.

Melander G, *Refugees in Orbit* (1978) International University Exchange Fund, Geneva, 121 p.

—— and Nobel P (eds), *African Refugees and the Law* (1978) Scandinavian Institute of African Studies, Uppsala, 98 p.

Mengozzi P, *European Community Law From the Treaty of Rome to the Treaty of Amsterdam* (2nd edn 1999) Kluwer, The Hague / London, 325 p.

Meron T, *Human Rights and Humanitarian Norms as Customary Law* (1989) Clarendon Press, Oxford, 263 p.

Mole N, *Problèmes soulevés par certains aspects de la situation actuelle des réfugiés sous l'angle de la Convention européenne des droits de l'homme* Dossiers sur les droits de l'homme No. 9 (1997) Council of Europe, Strasbourg, 63 p.

——*Asylum and the European Convention on Human Rights* (4th edn 2007) Council of Europe Directorate General on Human Rights, Strasbourg, 149 p.

Nicholson F and Twomey P (eds), *Current Issues of UK Asylum Law and Policy* (1998) Ashgate, Aldershot, 371 p.

Nicholson F and Twomey P (eds), *Refugee Rights and Realities: Evolving International Concepts and Regimes* (1999) Cambridge University Press, Cambridge, 391 p.

Noll G, *Negotiating Asylum, the EU Acquis, Extraterritorial Protection and the Common Market of Deflection* (2000) Martinus Nijhoff, The Hague / London, 643 p.

Norek C and F Doumic-Doublet F, *Le droit d'asile en France* (1st edn 1989) Presses Universitaires de France, Paris, 127 p.

Nowak M, *UN Covenant on Civil and Political Rights: CCPR Commentary* (2nd edn 2005) Engel, Kehl [etc], 1277 p.

O'Keeffe D and Twomey P (eds), *Legal Issues of the Amsterdam Treaty* (1999) Hart, Oxford, 425 p.

Okowa P N, *State Responsibility for Transboundary Air Pollution in International Law* (2000) Oxford University Press, Oxford, 285 p.

Oppenheim L, Jennings Sir R, Jennings R Y, and Watts Sir A (eds), *Oppenheim's International Law* (9th edn 1992) Longman, London, 1584 p.

Papagianni G, *Institutional and Policy Dynamics of EU Migration Law* (2006) Nijhoff, Leiden / Boston, 392 p.

Pauly A (ed), *Les accords de Schengen: abolition des frontières intérieures ou menace pour les libertés publiques?* (1993) European Institute of Public Administration, Maastricht, 269 p.

——(ed), *De Schengen à Maastricht: voie royale et course d'obstacles* (1996) European Institute of Public Administration, Maastricht, 285 p.

Peers S, *EU Justice and Home Affairs Law* (2nd edn 2006) Oxford University Press, Oxford, 588 p.

——and Rogers N (eds), *EU Immigration and Asylum Law* (2006) Nijhoff, Leiden / Boston, 1025 p.

Plender R (ed), *International Migration Law* (2nd edn 1988) Nijhoff, Dordrecht / London, 587 p.

——*Basic Documents on International Migration Law* (2nd edn 1997) Nijhoff, The Hague / London, 896 p.

Pop I, *Voisinage et bon voisinage en droit international* (1980) Pédone, Paris, 383 p.

Rambers J et al. (eds), *Festskrift till Lars Hjerner: Studies in International Law* (1990) Norstedts Stokholm, 579 p.

Refugee and Asylum Law: Assessing the Scope for Judicial Protection (1998) Conference of the International Association of Refugee Law Judges, Nederlands Centrum voor Buitenlanders, Amsterdam, 199 p.

Rogge J (ed), *Refugees, A Third World Dilemma* (1987) Rowman & Littlefield, Totowa (NJ), 370 p.

Rubin G E, *The Asylum Challenge to Western Nations* (1984) US Committee for Refugees, Washington DC 19 p.

Sands P, *Principles of International Environmental Law* (1995) Vol I (Framework, Standards and Implementation) Manchester University Press, Manchester, 773 p.

——and Klein P, *Bowett's Law of International Institutions* (5th edn, 2001) Sweet & Maxwell, London, 610 p.

Schermers H G et al. (eds), *Free Movement of Persons in Europe, Legal Problems and Experiences* (1993) Martinus Nijhoff, Dordrecht / London, 641 p.

——and Blokker N M, *International Institutional Law: Unity within Diversity* (3rd edn 1995) Nijhoff, Dordrecht / London, 1305 p.

Shaw M, *International Law* (5th edn 2003) Cambridge University Press, Cambridge, 1288 p.

Sieghart P, *The International Law of Human Rights* (1983) Clarendon Press, Oxford, 569 p.

Sinclair I, *The Vienna Convention on the Law of Treaties* (2nd edn 1984) Manchester University Press, Manchester, 270 p.

Sinha S P, *Asylum and International Law* (1971) Martinus Nijhoff, The Hague, 366 p.

Société française pour le droit international (ed), *La responsabilité dans le système international*, Colloque du Mans (1991) Pédone, Paris, 338 p.

——*Droit d'asile et des réfugiés*, Colloque de Caen (1997) Pédone, Paris, 383 p.

——*La pratique et le droit international* (2004) Pédone, Paris, 308 p.

Stenberg G, *Non-Expulsion and Non-Refoulement, the Prohibition Against Removal of Refugees with Special Reference to Articles 32 and 33 of the 1951 Convention Relating to the Status of Refugees* (1989) Iustus Förlag, Uppsala, 309 p.

Suhrke A, Barutciski M, Sandison P, Garlock R, *The Kosovo Refugee Crisis: An Evaluation of UNHCR's Emergency Preparedness and Response* (2000) UNHCR (Evaluation and Policy Analysis Unit), Geneva 159 p.

Swart A M J, *Le droit d'asile et les réfugiés – Tendances actuelles et perspectives: Les problèmes liés à l'admission des demandeurs d'asile sur le territoire des Etats membres* Rapport du Colloque de droit européen, Lund 15–17 September 1986, 55 p.

Takkenberg A and Tahbaz C (eds), *The Collected Travaux Préparatoires of the 1951 Geneva Convention relating to the Status of Refugees* (1989) Dutch Refugee Council, Vol III, Amsterdam, 703 p.

The Refugee Problem on Universal, Regional and National Level (1987) Institute of Public International Law and International Relations, Thessaloniki, 1022 p.

Türk V, *Das Flüchtlingshochkommissariat der Vereinten Nationen (UNHCR)* (1992) Dunckler & Humblot, Berlin, 356 p.

UNHCR, *Collection of international instruments and other legal texts concerning refugees and displaced persons* (1995) Vol I (Universal Instruments) and II (Regional Instruments) Division of International Protection of the Office of the UNHCR, Geneva, 568 and 572 p.

——*Detention of Asylum Seekers in Europe* (1995) Vol 1, Regional Bureau for Europe, Geneva, 231 p.

——*3rd International Symposium on the Protection of Refugees in Central Europe*, (1997) Vol 3, Bureau for Europe, Geneva, 494 p.

——*The State of the World's Refugees, Fifty Years of Humanitarian Action* (2000) Oxford University Press, Oxford, 340 p.

——*The State of the World's Refugees: Human Displacement in the New Millennium* (2006) Oxford University Press, Oxford, 340 p.

van Dijk P and van Hoof G J H, *Theory and Practice of the European Convention on Human Rights* (3rd edn 1998) Kluwer, The Hague / London, 850 p.

Vasak K and Liskofsky S (eds), *The Right to Leave and to Return; Papers and Recommendations of the International Colloquium held in Uppsala Sweden, 19-21 June 1972* (1976) American Jewish Committee, New York, 570 p.

Villiger M E, *Customary International Law and Treaties: A Manual on the Theory and Practice of the Interrelation of Sources* (2nd edn 1997) Kluwer, The Hague / London, 346 p.

Weinzierl R and Lisson U, *Border Management and Human Rights: A Study of EU Law and the Law of the Sea* (2007) German Institute for Human Rights, Berlin, 96 p.

Wetzel R G and Rauschning D, *The Vienna Convention on the Law of Treaties Travaux Préparatoires* (1978) Alfred Metzner, Frankfurt/Main, 543 p.

Whitman J (ed), *Migrants, Citizens and the State in Southern Africa* (2000) MacMillan, Basingstoke, 286 p.

Zolberg A R, Suhrke A and Aguayo S, *Escape from Violence Conflict and the Refugee Crisis in the Developing World* (1989) Oxford University Press, Oxford, New York, 380 p.

ARTICLES, CHAPTERS, REPORTS, AND OCCASIONAL PAPERS

Abeyratne R, 'Air Carrier Liability and Responsibility for the Carriage of Inadmissible Persons and Refugees' (1998) 10 *IJRL* 675–687.

Ackers D, 'The Negotiations on the Asylum Procedures Directive' (2005) 7 *EJML* 1–33.

Ablard T and Novak A, 'L'évolution du droit d'asile en Allemagne jusqu'à la réforme de 1993' (1995) 7 *IJRL* 260–290.

Acharya A and Dewitt D B, 'Fiscal Burden Sharing' in J Hathaway (ed), *Reconceiving International Refugee Law* (1997) 111–145.

Achermann A and Gattiker M, 'Safe Third Countries: European Developments' (1995) 7 *IJRL* 19–38.

Aga Khan S, 'Legal Problems relating to Refugees and Displaced Persons' (1976) 149 *RdC* (vol 1) 287–352.

Albors-Llorens A, 'Changes in the Jurisdiction of the European court of Justice under the Treaty of Amsterdam' (1998) 35 *CML Rev* 1273–1294.

Alburquerque Abell N, 'The Safe Third Country Concept: Deflection in Europe and Its Implications for Canada' (1995) 14 *Refuge* 1–7.

——'Safe Country Provisions in Canada and in the European Union: A Critical Assessment' (1997) 31 *IMR* 569–589.

——'The Compatibility of Readmission Agreements with the 1951 Convention Relating to the Status of Refugees' (1999) 11 *IJRL* 60–83.

Alexander M, 'Refugee Status Determination Conducted by UNHCR' (1999) 11 *IJRL* 251–289.

Alston P, 'A Third Generation of Solidarity Rights: A Progressive Development or Obfuscation of International Human Rights Law?' (1987) 29 *Netherlands Intl LR* 307–322.

——'The Commission on Human Rights' in P Alston (ed), *The United Nations and Human Rights, A Critical Appraisal* (1992) 126–210.

Andrysek O, 'Gaps in International Protection and the Potential for Redress through Individual Complaints Procedures' (1997) 9 *IJRL* 392–414.

Anker D, Fitzpatrick J and Shacknove A, 'Crisis and Cure: A Reply to Hathaway/Neve and Schuck' (1998) 11 *Harvard Human Rights LJ* 295–310.

Anonymous, 'The UNHCR Note on International Protection You Won't See' (1997) 9 *IJRL* 267–273.

Arboleda E, 'Refugee Definition in Africa and Latin America: The Lessons of Pragmatism' (1991) 3 *IJRL* 185–207.

Aubin E, 'Le juge administratif français face à l'application des Conventions de Schengen dans ses dispositions sur le droit d'asile et de Dublin relative à la détermination de l'Etat responsable de l'examen d'une demande d'asile' in C Marinho (ed), *The Dublin Convention on Asylum, Its Essence, Implementation and Prospects* (2000) 177–204.

Ayral M, 'La suppression des contrôles aux frontières intra-communautaires' [1993] *RMUE* 13–44.

Balzacq T and Carrera S, 'The Hague Programme: The Long Road to Freedom, Security and Justice' in T Balzacq and S Carrera (eds), *Security v Freedom? A Challenge for Europe's Future* (2006) 1–32.

Bank R, 'Country-Oriented Procedures under the Convention Against Torture: Towards a New Dynamism' in P Alston and J Crawford (eds), *The Future of UN Human Rights Treaty Monitoring* (2000) 145–174.

Banton M, 'Decision-Taking in the Committee on the Elimination of Racial Discrimination' in P Alston and J Crawford (eds), *The Future of UN Human Rights Treaty Monitoring* (2000) 55–78.

Bari S, 'Refugee Status Determination under the Comprehensive Plan of Action (CPA): A Personal Assessment' (1992) 4 *IJRL* 487–511.

Barnett M, 'Humanitarianism with a Sovereign Face: UNHCR in the Global Undertow' (2001) 35 *IMR* 244–277.

Bartels R, 'Ein Jahr Dubliner Übereinkommen' [1998] Der Einzelentscheider-Brief, Nr.9.

Barutciski M, 'The Reinforcement of Non-Admission Policies and the Subversion of UNHCR: Displacement and Internal Assistance in Bosnia-Herzegovina (1992–94)' (1996) 8 *IJRL* 49–110.

—— 'The Development of Refugee Law and Policy in South Africa: A Commentary on the 1997 Green Paper and 1998 White Paper / Draft Bill' (1998) 10 *IJRL* 700–724.

—— and Suhrke A, 'Lessons from the Kosovo Refugee Crisis: Innovations in Protection and Burden-Sharing' (2001) 14 *JRS* 95–115.

Battjes H, 'A Balance Between Fairness and Efficiency? The Directive on International Protection and the Dublin Regulation' (2002) 4 *EJML* 159–192.

Bay Larsen L, 'Schengen, the Third Pillar and Nordic Cooperation' in M den Boer, (ed), *The Implementation of Schengen: First the Widening, Now the Deepening* (1997) 17–23.

Betts A, 'Towards a Mediterranean Solution? Implications for the Region of Origin' (2006) 18 *IJRL* 652–676.

—— and Durieux J-F, 'Convention Plus as a Norm-Setting Exercise' (2007) 20 *JRS* 509–535.

Beyani C, 'State Responsibility for the Protection and Resolution of Forced Population Displacements in International Law' (1995) 7 IJRL Special Issue 130–147.

—— 'The Role of Human Rights Bodies in Protecting Refugees' in Bayefsky A (ed), *Human Rights and Refugees, Internally Displaced Persons and Migrant Workers: Essays in Memory of Joan Fitzpatrick and Arthur Helton*, (2006) 269–281.

Blackmun H, 'The Supreme Court and the Law of Nations' (1994) 104 *Yale LJ* 39–49.

Blay S and Zimmermann A, 'Recent Changes in German Refugee Law: A Critical Assessment' (1994) 88 *AJIL* 361–72.

Bleeker K A M, 'Opheffing van de persoonscontroles aan de binnengrenzen tussen de Schengen-Staten en Noorwegen en Ijsland' [1998] *SEW* 206–209.

Bléro B, 'Protection constitutionelle et internationale des demandeurs d'asile, quelques considérations à propos de l'Arrêt de la Cour d'arbitrage du 14 juillet 1994 annulant partiellement certaines modifications apportées au statut des réfugiés par la loi du 6 mai 1993' [1994] *Revue belge de droit constitutionnel* 241–282.

Boeles P, 'Erkenning van gezinseenheid in geval van verschillende verantwoordelijke staten: een Belgische doorbraak' [1998] *NAV* 437–440.

Boisson de Chazournes L, 'Qu'est-ce que la pratique en droit international?' in Société française de droit international, *La pratique et le droit international* (2004) 13–47.

Bolten J, 'From Schengen to Dublin' [1991] Nederlands Juristenblad 165–178.

Bousquet E, 'Le droit d 'asile en France: politique et réalité', UNHR New Issues in Refugee Research Paper No. 138, December 2006, 28 p.

Bouteillet-Paquet D, 'European Harmonisation in the Field of Readmission Agreements' (1997) 1 *Intl J of Human Rights* 31–43.

—— 'Study on the Readmission Agreements Signed by the Czech Republic, Hungary,Poland and Slovenia and on Instruments Available to Develop Access to Fair and Efficient Refugee Status Determination Procedures in Central European Countries', Fourth International Symposium on the Protection of Refugees in the Central European and the Baltic States 27–29 September 1998 Bled Slovenia (on file with the author) 39 p.

—— 'Passing the Buck: A Critical Analysis of the Readmission Policy Implemented by the European Union and its Member States' (2003) 5 *EJML* 359–377.

Brandl U, 'Distribution of Asylum Seekers in Europe? Dublin II Regulation Determining the Responsibility for Examining an Asylum Application' in P De Bruycker and C Dias Urbano de Sousa (eds), *The Emergence of a European Asylum Policy* (2004) 33–69.

Bribosia H, 'Liberté, sécurité et justice: l'imbroglio d'un nouvel espace' [1998] *RMUE* 27–53.

British Institute of International and Comparative Law, 'Study on the law and practice of the safe country principles in the context of the common European asylum system and the goal of a common asylum procedure', 2003, 122 p.

Bronée S A, 'The History of the Comprehensive Plan of Action' (1993) 5 *IJRL* 534–543.

Brouwer E, 'Eurodac: Its Limitations and Temptations' (2002) 4 *EJML* 231–247.

Brownlie I, 'Problems of Specialisation' in B Cheng (ed), *International Law: Teaching and Practice* (1982) 109–113.

—— 'International Law at the Fiftieth Anniversary of the United Nations' (1995) 255 RdC 1–255.

Bruin R, 'Schengen, de neen-tenzij clausule' [1995] *NAV* 916–927.

Bustelo M R, 'The Committee on the Elimination of Discrimination Against Women at the Crossroads' in P Alston and J Crawford (eds), *The Future of UN Human Rights Treaty Monitoring* (2000) 79–111.

Byrne R, 'Redesigning Fortress Europe: European Asylum Policy' [1996] The Oxford International Review 10–16.

——'Harmonization and Burden Redistribution in the Two Europes' (2003) 16 *JRS* 336–358.

—— 'Remedies of Limited Effect: Appeals under the forthcoming Directive on EU Minimum Standards on Procedures' (2005) 7 *EJML* 71–86.

Byrne R and Shacknove A, 'The Safe Country Notion in European Asylum Law' (1996) 9 *Harv Hum Rts J* 185–228.

——Noll G, and Vevsted-Hansen J, 'Understanding Refugee Law in an Enlarged European Union' (2004) 15 *EJIL* 355–379.

Byrnes A, 'The Committee Against Torture' in P Alston (ed), *The United Nations and Human Rights* (1992) 508–546.

Canor I, 'Primus inter pares. Who is the ultimate guardian of fundamental rights in Europe ?' (2000) 25 *ELR* 3–21.

Carlier J-Y, 'Le développement d'une politique commune en matière d'asile' in P De Bruycker and C Dias Urbano de Sousa (eds), *The Emergence of a European Asylum Policy* (2004) 1.

Castles S, 'The Migration- Asylum Nexus and Regional Approaches' in S Kneebone and F Rawlings-Sanaei (eds), *New Regionalism and Asylum Seekers* (2007) 25–42.

Chetail V, 'Le droit des réfugiés à l'épreuve des droit de l'homme: Bilan de la Cour européenne des droits de l'homme sur l'interdiction du renvoi des étrangers menacés de torture et de traitements inhumains ou dégradants' [2004] *RBDI* 155–210.

—— 'Le Comité des Nations Unies contre la torture et l'éloignement des étrangers: dix ans de jurisprudence (1994–2004)' (2006) *Revue suisse de droit international et de droit européen* 63–104.

Chimni B S, 'The Geopolitics of Refugee Studies: A View from the South' (1998) 11 *JRS* 350–374.

—— 'The Principle of Burden-Sharing' in B S Chimni (ed), *International Refugee Law, A Reader* (2000) 146–151.

Chinkin C, 'The Challenge of Soft Law: Development and Change in International Law' (1989) 38 *ICLQ* 850–866.

Choceyras L, 'La Convention d'application de l'accord de Schengen' [1991] *AFDI* 807–818.

Chokuwenga I, 'The Refugee Crisis: A Southern African Perspective' in J Whitman (ed), *Migrants, Citizens and the State in Southern Africa* (2000) 117–114.

Clark T, 'Human Rights and Expulsion: Giving Content to the Concept of Asylum' (1992) 4 *IJRL* 189–204.

Cohen-Jonathan G, 'Responsabilité pour atteinte aux droits de l'homme' in Société française pour le droit international (ed), *La responsabilité dans le système international* (1991) Pédone, Paris 101–135.

—— 'Les rapports entre la Convention européenne des droits de l'Homme et les autres traités conclus par les Etats parties' in R Lawson and M de Blois (eds), *The Dynamics of the Protection of Human Rights in Europe: Essays in Honour of H G Schermers* (1994) Vol III 79–111.

Coleman N, 'Non-Refoulement Revised: Renewed Review of the Status of the Principle of Non-Refoulement as Customary International Law' (2003) 5 *EJML* 23–68.

Coles G, 'Temporary Refuge and the Large Scale Influx of Refugees' (1983) *Australian Ybk of Intl L* 189–212.

—— 'Refugees and Human Rights' [1991] *Bulletin of Human Rights* 63–73.

Collyer M, 'The Dublin Regulation, Influences on Asylum Destinations and the Exception of Algerians in the UK' (2004) 17 *JRS* 375–400.

Constantinesco V, 'Le renforcement des droits fondamentaux dans le Traité d'Amsterdam' in *Le Traité d'Amsterdam: Réalités et Perpectives* (1998) 33–48.

Costello C, 'The Asylum Procedures Directive and the Proliferation of Safe Third Country Practices: Deterrence, Deflection and the Dismantling of International Protection?' (2005) 7 *EJML* 35–69.

—— 'The Bosphorus Ruling of the European Court of Human Rights: Fundamental Rights and Blurred Boundaries in Europe' (2006) 6 *Human Right LR* 87–130.

—— 'The European Asylum Procedures Directive in Legal Context' UNHCR New Issues in Refugee Research Paper No. 134, November 2006, 23 p.

Crawford J, 'The UN Human Rights Treaty System: A System in Crisis' in P Alston and J Crawford (eds), *The Future of UN Human Rights Treaty Monitoring* (2000) 1–12.

—— and Hyndman P, 'Three Heresies in the Application of the Refugee Convention' (1989) 2 *IJRL* 155–179.

Crosbie J, 'Iraqi refugees reveal asylum regimes disharmony' *European Voice*, 1 March 2007.

—— 'EU States return Iraqi asylum seekers', *European Voice*, 24 May 2007.

Cronin D, 'EU to vet asylum claims in Africa, Ukraine' *European Voice*, 6 October 2006.

Cruz A, 'Schengen, Groupe ad hoc Immigration et autres instances intergouvernementales européennes' Comité des Eglises auprès des Migrants en Europe, *Document de travail* No. 12 (1993) 33 p.

—— 'Carriers Liability in the Member States of the European Union' Churches Commission for Migrants in Europe, Brussels, Briefing Paper No. 17 (1994) 28 p.

Cunliffe S A and Pugh M, 'UNHCR as a leader in humanitarian assistance: a triumph of politics over law?' in F Nicholson and P Twomey (eds), *Refugee rights and realities: evolving international concepts and regimes* (1999) 175–99.

Cutler C, 'The U.S.-Canada Safe Third Country Agreement: Slamming the Door on Refugees' (2004) 11 *ILSA J Intl & Comp L* 122–142.

Czaplinski W, 'Current Development: The New Polish-German Treaties and the Changing Political Structure of Europe' (1992) 86 *AJIL* 163–173.

—— 'Aliens and Refugee Law in Poland – Recent Developments' (1994) 6 *IJRL* 636–642.

—— et Šturma P, 'La responsabilité des Etats pour les flux de réfugiés provoqués par eux' [1994] *AFDI* 156–69.

Dankert P, 'Asielverlening: stroomlijning of inperking?' (1991) 45 *Internationale Spectator* 176–180.

Dashwood A, 'States in the European Union' (1998) 23 *ELR* 201–216.

—— and White R, 'Enforcement Actions under Articles 169 and 170 EEC' (1989) 14 *ELR* 388–413.

Defeis E, 'Minority Protections and Bilateral Agreements: An Effective Mechanism' (1999) 22 *Hastings Intl & Comp LR* 291–321.

Denoël X, 'Les accords de réadmission, du Bénélux à Schengen et au-delà' [1993] *Revue trimestrielle de droit européen*, 635–653.

de Jong C D, 'Is there a need for a European asylum policy ?' in Nicholson F and Twomey P (eds), *Refugee Rights and Realities: Evolving International Concepts and Regimes* (1999) 357–378.

De Schutter O, 'Privation de liberté et maintien en zone internationale' [1996] *RDE* 345–353.

de Witte B, 'The Past and Future Role of the European Court of Justice in the Protection of Human Rights' in P Alston (ed), *The EU and Human Rights* (1999) 859–897.

—— 'Legal Status of the Charter: Vital Question or Non-Issue?' (2001) 8 *MJ* 81–89.

Dietrich H, 'The desert front—EU refugee camps in North Africa?' *Statewatch News Online*, March 2005.

Donner J-P, 'Abolition of Border Controls' in H G Schermers et al. (eds), *Free Movement of Persons in Europe, Legal Problems and Experiences* (1993) 5–26.

—— 'De derde pijler en de Amsterdaamse doolhof' [1997] *SEW* 370–378.

Doublet F and Stéfanini P, 'Le droit d'asile en Europe: La convention relative à la détermination de l'Etat responsable de l'examen d'une demande d'asile présentée auprès d'un état membre des Communautés européennes' [1991] *Revue du marché commun* 391–399.

Drücke L, 'Refugee Protection in the Post Cold War Europe: Asylum in the Schengen and EC Harmonization Process' in A Pauly (ed), *Les accords de Schengen: abolition des frontières intérieures ou menace pour les libertés publiques ?* (1993) 105–169.

Dunstan R, 'A Case of Ministers Behaving Badly: The Asylum and Immigration Act 1996' in F Nicholson and P Twomey (eds), *Current Issues of UK Asylum Law and Policy* (1998) 52–72.

Durieux J-F and Hurwitz A, 'How Many Is Too Many? African and European Legal Responses to Mass Influxes of Refugee (2004) 47 *German Ybk of International Law* 105–159.

Duvigneau J L, 'From Advisory Opinion 2/94 to the Amsterdam Treaty: Human Rights Protection in the European Union' (1998) 25 *Legal Issues of European Integration* 61–91.

Ehlermann C D, 'Différenciation, flexibilité, coopération renforcée: les nouvelles dispositions du traité d'Amsterdam' [1997] *RMUE* 53–90.

Einarsen T, 'The European Convention on Human Rights and the Notion of an Implied Right to De Facto Asylum' (1990) 2 *IJRL* 360–389.

—— 'Mass Flight: The Case for International Asylum' (1995) 7 *IJRL* 551–578.

—— 'Refugee Protection Beyond Kosovo: Quo Vadis?' (2001) 14 *JRS* 119–127.

Ermacora F, 'Problems about the Application of the European Convention on Human Rights in Asylum Cases' in R Lawson R and M de Blois M (eds), *The Dynamics of the Protection of Human Rights in Europe: Essays in Honour of H G Schermers* (1994) Vol III 155–163.

Fabbricotti A, 'The Concept of Inhuman or Degrading Treatment in International Law and its Application in Asylum Cases' (1998) 10 *IJRL* 637–661.

Favret J-M, 'Le Traité d'Amsterdam: Une révision *a minima* de la "charte constitutionnelle" de l'Union européenne' [1997] *CDE* 555–605.

Federal Ministry of the Interior, 'Recent Developments in the German law on Asylum and Aliens' (1994) 6 *IJRL* 265–270.

Feller E, 'Asylum, Migration and Refugee Protection: Realities, Myths and the Promise of Things to Come' (2006) 18 *IJRL* 509–536.

Fennelly N, 'Preserving the Legal Coherence within the New Treaty: The European Court of Justice after the Treaty of Amsterdam' (1998) 5 *MJ* 185–199.

—— 'The Area of "Freedom, Security and Justice" and the European Court of Justice—A Personal View' (2000) 49 *ICLQ* 1–14.

Fernhout R, 'Schengen and the Internal Market: An Area Without Internal Frontiers.—Also Without Refugees?' (1990) 14 *Internationale Spectator* 683–689.

Fitzmaurice G, 'Law and Procedure of the International Court of Justice' (1951) 28 *BYIL* 1–28.

Fitzmaurice G, 'The Law and Procedure of the International Court of Justice' (1957) 33 *BYIL* 203–293.

Fitzpatrick Hartman J, 'The Principle and Practice of Temporary Refuge: A Customary Norm Protecting Civilians Fleeing Internal Armed Conflict' in D A Martin (ed), *The New Asylum Seekers: Refugee Law in the 1980s* (1988) 87–101.

—— 'Revitalizing the 1951 Refugee Convention' (1996) 9 *Harv Hum Rts J* 229–253.

—— 'Temporary Protection of Refugees: Elements of a Formalized Regime' (2000) 94 *AJIL* 279–306.

Fonteyne J-L, 'Burden-Sharing: An Analysis of the Nature and Function of International Solidarity in Cases of Mass Influx of Refugees' (1983) 8 *Australian Ybk Intl L* 162–188.

Foster M, 'Protection Elsewhere: The Legal Implications of Requiring Refugees to Seek Protection in Another State' (2007) 28 *Michigan J of Intl L* 223–286.

Frelick B, '"Preventive Protection" and the Rights to Seek Asylum: A Preliminary Look at Bosnia and Croatia' (1992) 4 *IJRL* 438–453.

Garlick M, 'Asylum Legislation in the European Community and the 1951 Convention: Key Concerns regarding Asylum instruments adopted in the "First Phase" of Harmonization' in T Balzacq and S Carrera (eds), *Security versus Freedom? A Challenge for Europe's Future* (2006) 45–59.

—— 'The EU Discussions on Extraterritorial Processing: Solutions or Conundrum' (2006) 18 *IJRL* 601–629.

Garvey J, 'Toward a Reformulation of International Refugee Law' (1985) 26 *Harvard Intl LJ* 483–500.

Gattiker M, 'Évolution et perspectives de la notion de pays tiers sûr dans la législation suisse sur l'asile', in V Chetail and V Gowlland-Debbas (eds), *Switzerland and the International Protection of Refugees* (2002) 129–144.

Geddo B, 'Durable Solutions to the Refugee Problem: UNHCR's Regional Strategy for Southern Africa' in J Handmaker, L A de la Hunt and J Klaaren (eds), *Perspectives on Refugee Protection in South Africa* (2001).

Gibney M, 'Beyond the bounds of responsibility: western states and measures to prevent the arrival of refugees' Global Migration Perspectives Paper No. 22, January 2005, 23 p.

—— 'Forced Migration, Engineered Regionalism and Justice Between States' in S Kneebone and F Rawlings-Sanaei (eds), *New Regionalism and Asylum Seekers* (2007) 57–77.

Gil-Bazo M-T, 'The Practice of Mediterranean States in the context of the European Union's Justice and Home Affairs External Dimension. The Safe Third Country Concept Revisited' (2006) 18 *IJRL* 571.

—— 'Refugee status, subsidiary protection, and the right to be granted asylum under EC law' UNHCR New Issues in Refugee Research Paper No. 136, November 2006.

—— 'The Charter of Fundamental Rights of the European Union and the Right to Be Granted Asylum in the Union's Law' (2008) 27 *Refugee Survey Quarterly* 33–52.

Gilbert G, 'Is Europe Living Up to its Obligations to Refugees?' (2004) 15 *EJIL* 963–987.

Girerd P, 'L'article 68 CE: un renvoi préjudiciel d'interprétation et d'application incertaines' (1999) 35 *RTDE* 239–260.

Gondek, 'Extraterritorial Application of the European Convention on Human Rights: Territorial Focus in the Age of Globalization?' (2005) 52 *Netherlands Intl L Rev* 347–387.

Goodwin-Gill G S, 'The Protection of Refugees and the Safe Third Country Rule in International Law' in *Asylum Law: Report and papers delivered at the first international judicial conference on asylum law and procedures held at Inner Temple, London, 1 and 2 December, 1995* (London, 1996) 89–108.

——'The right to leave, to return and to remain' in V Gowlland-Debbas (ed), *The Problem of Refugees in the Light of Contemporary International Law Issues* (1996) 93–108.

——'Closing address Principles and Protection: Making it Work in the Modern World' in *UNHCR and International Refugee Protection* RSP Working Paper No. 2 June 1999, 13.

——'Refugee Identity and Protection's Fading Prospect' in F Nicholson and P Twomey (eds), *Refugee Rights and Realities: Evolving International Concepts and Regimes* (1999) 220–249.

——'Article 31 of the 1951 Convention Relating to the Status of Refugees: Non-Penalization, Detention and Prosecution', in E Feller, V Türk and F Nicholson (eds), *Refugee Protection in International Law: UNHCR's Global Consultations on International Refugee Protection* (2003) 185–253.

——'Migrant Rights and "Managed Migration"' in V Chetail (ed), *Mondialisation, migration et droits de l'homme: le droit international en question* (2007) Vol II 161–187.

——'Offshore Processing of Asylum Seekers: The Search for Legitimate Parameters' (2007) *UTS Law Review* 26–40.

——'The Politics of Refugee Protection' (2008) 27 *RSQ* 8–23.

Gorlick B, 'The Convention and the Committee Against Torture: A Complementary Protection Regime for Refugees' (1999) 11 *IJRL* 479–495.

——'(Mis)perception of Refugees, State Sovereignty, and the Continuing Challenge of International Protection' in A Bayefsky (ed), *Human Rights and Refugees, Internally Displaced Persons and Migrant Workers: Essays in memory of Joan Fitzpatrick and Arthur Helton* (2006) 65–89.

Grahl-Madsen A, 'The Emergent International Law relating to Refugees' in *The Refugee Problem on Universal, Regional and National Level* (1987) 163–262.

Greig D W, 'The Protection of Refugees and Customary International Law' (1983) 8 *Australian Ybk of Intl L* 108–141.

Groenendijk C A, 'The Competence of the EC Court of Justice' in H Meijers et al. (eds), *A new immigration law for Europe?: The 1992 London and 1993 Copenhagen Rules on Immigration* (1993) 45–53.

Guild E, 'Seeking asylum: storm clouds between international commitments and EU legislative measures' (2004) 29 *ELR* 198–218.

——'The Bitter Fruits of an EU Common Asylum Policy' in T Balzacq and S Carrera (eds), *Security versus Freedom? A Challenge for Europe's Future* (2006) 61–76.

——'The Europeanisation of Europe's Asylum Policy' (2006) 18 *IJRL* 630–651.

——'The Europeanization of Europe's Asylum Policy' (2006) 18 *IJRL* 630–651.

Hailbronner K, '*Non Refoulement* and Humanitarian Refugees: Customary International or Wishful Legal Thinking ?' in D A Martin (ed), *The New Asylum Seekers: Refugee Law in the 1980s* (1988) 123–158.

——'The Right to Asylum and the Future of Asylum Procedures in the European Community' (1990) 2 *IJRL* 341–360.

——'The Concept of "Safe Country" and Expeditious Asylum Procedures: A Western European Perspective' (1993) 5 *IJRL* 31–65.

Hailbronner K, 'Comments on: The Right to Leave, the Right to Return and the Question of a Right to Remain' in V Gowlland-Debbas (ed), *The Problem of Refugees in The Light of Contemporary Law Issues* (1996) 109–118.

—— 'The New Title on Free Movement of Persons, Asylum and Immigration in the TEC' in M den Boer (ed), *Schengen, judicial cooperation and policy coordination,* (1997) 201.

—— 'European Immigration and Asylum law under the Amsterdam Treaty' (1998) 35 *CML Rev* 1047–1067.

—— 'Principles of International Law Regarding the Concept of Subsidiary Protection' in D Bouteillet-Paquet (ed), *Subsidiary Protection of Refugees in the European Union: Complementing the Geneva Convention?* (2002) 211–264.

—— and Thiery C, 'Schengen II and Dublin Responsibility for Asylum Applications in Europe' (1997) 34 *CML Rev* 957–989.

Handl G, Reisman M, Simma B, Dupuy P-M, Chinkin C, De La Vega R, 'A Hard Look at Soft Law' (1990) 82 *American Society of International Law Proceedings,* 371–395.

Handmaker J, 'Who Determines Policy? Promoting the Right of Asylum in South Africa' (1999) 11 *IJRL* 290–309.

Harrison S, 'The Law and Practice in the Application of the Dublin Convention in the United Kingdom' in C Marinho (ed), *The Dublin Convention on Asylum, Its Essence, Implementation and Prospects* (2000) 163–175.

Harvey C, 'The Right to Seek Asylum in the European Union' [2004] *European Human Rights LR* 17–36.

Hans A and Suhrke A, 'Responsibility Sharing' in J Hathaway (ed), *Reconceiving International Refugee Law* (1997) 83–109.

Harlow C, 'Towards a Theory of Access for the European Court of Justice' (1992) 12 *Ybk of European Law* 213–248.

—— 'Access to Justice as a Human Right: The European Convention and the European Union' in P Alston (ed), *The EU and Human Rights* (1999) 187–213.

Hartling P, 'International Solidarity and the International Protection of Refugees' in *Congress on International Solidarity and Humanitarian Action* (1980) 237–243.

Hathaway J, 'The Evolution of Refugee Status in International Law: 1920–1950' (1984) 33 *ICLQ* 348–380.

—— 'A Reconsideration of the Underlying Premise of Refugee Law' (1990) 31 *Harvard International LJ* 129–183.

—— 'Harmonizing for Whom? The Devaluation of Refugee Protection in the Era of European Economic Integration' (1993) 26 *Cornell Intl LJ* 719–735.

—— 'New Directions to Avoid Hard Problems: The Distortion of the Palliative Role of Refugee Protection' (1995) 8 *JRS* 288–294.

—— and Neve A, 'Making International Refugee Law Relevant Again: A Proposal for Collectivised and Solution-Oriented Protection' (1997) 10 *Harvard Hum Rts J* 115–211.

Hedemann-Robinson M, 'The Area of Freedom, Security and Justice with Regard to the UK, Ireland and Denmark: The 'Opt-in Opt-outs' under the Treaty of Amsterdam' in D O'Keeffe and P Twomey (eds), *Legal Issues of the Amsterdam Treaty* (1999) 288–302.

Helfer A R and Slaughter A-M, 'Toward a Theory of Effective Supranational Adjudication' (1997) 107 *Yale LJ* 273–391.

Helton A, 'The Detention of Asylum Seekers in the United States and Canada' in H Adelman (ed), *Refugee policy: Canada and the United States* (1991) 253–267.

—— 'Refugee Determination under the Comprehensive Plan of Action: Overview and Assessment' (1993) 5 *IJRL* 544–558.

—— 'Towards Harmonized Asylum Procedures in North America: The Proposed United States-Canada Memorandum of Understanding for Cooperation in the Examination of Refugee Status Claims from Nationals of Third Countries' (1993) 26 *Cornell Intl LJ* 737–751.

Henkel J, 'Völkerrechtliche Aspekte des Konzepts des sicheren Drittstaates' in K Barwig and W Brill (eds), *Aktuelle asyltechtlichen Probleme der gerichtlichen Entscheidungspraxis in Deutschland, Österreich und der Schweiz* (1996) 141–164.

Henkin L, 'International Law: Politics, Values and Functions' (1989) 216 *RdC* Vol IV 1–416.

Higgins R, 'La liberté de circulation des personnes en droit international' in M Flory and R Higgins (eds), *Liberté de circulation des personnes en droit international* (1988) 3–41.

—— 'Recent Developments in Respect of the Right to Leave in International Law' in E D Brown and B Cheng (eds), *Contemporary Problems of International Law: Essays in Honour of Georg Schwartzenberger on his Eightieth Birthday* (Stevens and Sons, London 1988) 138–156.

Hillgenberg H, 'A Fresh Look at Soft Law' (1999) 10 *EJIL* 499–515.

Hofmann R, 'Refugee-Generating Policies and the Law of State Responsibility' (1985) 45 *Zeitschrift für Ausländisches Öffentliches Recht und Völkerrecht* 694–713.

Hongju Koh H, 'Reflections on Refoulement and Haitian Centers Council' (1994) 35 *Harvard Intl LJ* 1–20.

Hurwitz A, 'The 1990 Dublin Convention: A Comprehensive Assessment' (1999) 11 *IJRL* 646–677.

—— 'Commentaires sur la détermination de l'Etat membre responsable de l'examen d' une demande d'asile et la répartition des charges entre Etats membres' in C Dias Urbano de Sousa and P De Bruycker (eds), *The Emergence of a European Asylum Policy* (2004) 71–86.

—— 'Mass Influx', in M Gibney and R Hansen (eds), *Immigration and Asylum from 1900 to the Present*, (ABC-CLIO Pub., Santa Barbara 2005), 393–395.

Hyndman P, 'Asylum and Non-Refoulement – Are these Obligations Owed to Refugees under International Law?' (1982) 57 *Philippine LJ* 43–77.

—— 'Refugees Under International Law with a Reference to the Concept of Asylum' (1986) 60 *Australian LJ* 148–155.

Jacobs F G, 'European Community Law and the European Convention on Human Rights' in D Curtin and T Heukels (eds), *Institutional Dynamics of European Integration, Essays in Honour of H G Schermers* (1994) Vol II 561–571.

Jacqué J-P, 'L'Acte unique européen' [1986] *RTDE* 575–605.

Jaeger G, 'Les Nations Unies et les réfugiés' [1989] *RBDI* 18–113.

Jagerskiold S, 'The Freedom of Movement' in L Henkin (ed), *The International Bill of Rights: The Covenant on Civil and Political Rights* (1981) 166–184.

Jansen W, 'Overzicht van rechtspraak naar enkele thema's van de uitvoeringsovereenkomst Schengen' (1996) 3 *Vreemdelingen Bulletin* 13–20.

Jennings R Y, 'Some International Law Aspects of the Refugee Question' (1939) 16 *BYIL* 98–114.

Julien-Laferrière F, 'L'Europe de Schengen: de la disparition des frontières aux transferts des contrôles' [1992] *Actualités législatives Dalloz* 125–130.

Junker B, 'Burden Sharing or Burden Shifting? Asylum and Expansion in the European Union' (2006) 20 *Georgetown Immigration LJ* 293–322.

Kagan M, 'The Beleaguered Gatekeeper: Protection Challenges Posed by UNHCR Refugee Status Determination' (2006) 18 *IJRL* 1–29.

Kälin W, 'Supervising the 1951 Convention on the Status of Refugees: Article 35 and Beyond', in E Feller, V Türk and F Nicholson (eds), *Refugee Protection in International Law: UNHCR's Global Consultations on International Refugee Protection* (2003) 613–667.

Karagiannis S, 'Expulsion des étrangers et mauvais traitements imputables à l'Etat de destination ou à des particuliers' (1999) *Revue trimestrielle des droits de l'homme* 33–88.

Kerber K, 'Temporary Protection: An Assessment of the Harmonisation of Policies of European Union Member States' (1997) 9 *IJRL* 453–471.

Kingsley-Nyinah M, 'Asylum, Refugee Criteria, and Irregular Movements in Southern Africa' (1995) 7 *IJRL* 291–316.

Kjaerum M, 'The Concept of Country of First Asylum' (1992) 4 *IJRL* 514–530.

——'Temporary protection in Europe in the 1990s' (1994) 6 *IJRL* 444–456.

Klabbers J, 'The Undesirability of Soft Law' (1998) 67 *Nordic Journal of International Law* 381–391.

——'International Legal Histories: The Declining Importance of *Travaux Préparatoires* in Treaty Interpretation?' (2003) 50 *NILR* 267–288.

Kneebone S, 'The Pacific Plan: The Provision of "Effective Protection"' (2006) 18 *IJRL* 696–721.

——and Rawlings-Sanaei F, 'Introduction: Regionalism as a Response to a Global Challenge' in S Kneebone and F Rawlings-Sanaei (eds), *New Regionalism and Asylum Seekers* (2007) 1–24.

——McDowell C, and Morrell G, 'A Mediterranean Solution? Chances of Success' (2006) 18 *IJRL* 492–508.

Kohen M, 'La pratique et la théorie des sources du droit international' in Société Française de Droit International, (2004) *La pratique et le droit international* 81–111.

Kok S, 'De overeenkomst van Dublin; een beschrijving en praktijk ervaringen' [1998] *NAV* 677–688.

Kortenberg H, 'Closer Cooperation in the Treaty of Amsterdam' (1998) 35 *CML Rev* 833–854.

Kumin J, 'Die Genfer Flüchtlingskonvention and asylpolitischen Entwicklungen in Deutschland and Europa' in K Barwig and W Brill *Aktuelle asylrechtliche Probleme der Gerichtlichen Entscheidungspraxis in Deutschland, Österreich und der Schweiz* (1996) 19–24.

Labayle H, 'La libre circulation des personnes dans l'Union européenne, de Schengen à Amsterdam' [1997] *L'actualité juridique Droit administratif,* 923–936.

——'L'éloignement des étrangers devant la Cour européenne des droits de l'homme' (1997) *Revue française de droit administratif,* 977–998.

——'Un espace de liberté, de sécurité et de justice' (1997) 33 *RTDE* 813–881.

Lambert H, 'Protection against *Refoulement* from Europe: Human Rights Law Comes to the Rescue' (1999) 48 *ICLQ* 515–545.

Landgren K, 'Safety Zones and International Protection: A Dark Grey Area' (1995) 7 *IJRL* 436–458.

—— 'Deflecting international protection by treaty: bilateral and multilateral accords on extradition, readmission and the inadmissibility of asylum requests' (1999) *New Issues in Refugee Research* UNHCR Working Paper No. 2, 73 p.

Langrish S, 'The Treaty of Amsterdam: Selected Highlights' (1998) 23 *ELR* 3–19.

Lankers F, 'Schengen en het intrekken van het asielverzoek' [1996] *NAV* 487–490.

Lansdown G, 'The Reporting Process under the Convention on the Rights of the Child' in P Alston and J Crawford (eds), *The Future of UN Human Rights Treaty Monitoring* (2000) 113–128.

Lauterpacht Sir E and Bethlehem D, 'The Scope and the Content of the Principle on Non-Refoulement' in E Feller, V Türk, and F Nicholson (eds), *Refugee Protection in International Law: UNHCR's Global Consultations on International Refugee Protection* (2003) 87–178.

Lauterpacht H, 'The Universal Declaration on Human Rights' (1948) 25 *BYIL* 354–381.

Lawson R, 'Confusion and Conflict? Diverging Interpretations of the European Convention on Human Rights in Strasbourg and Luxembourg' in R Lawson and M de Blois (eds), *The Dynamics and of the Protection of Human Rights in Europe: Essays in Honour of H G Schermers* (1994) Vol III 219–252.

Leckie S, 'The Committee on Economic, Social and Cultural Rights: A Catalyst for Change in a System Needing Reform' in P Alston and J Crawford (eds), *The Future of UN Human Rights Treaty Monitoring* (2000) 129–144.

Leduc F, 'L'asile territorial et la Conférence des Nations Unies de Genève, Janvier 1977' [1977] *AFDI* 221–267.

Lee I, 'La règle du "tiers pays sûr" au regard de l'article 12 de la Charte canadienne' (1994) 73 *La Revue du Barreau Canadien* 372–387.

Lee L, 'The Right to Compensation: Refugees and Countries of Asylum' (1986) 80 *AJIL* 532–567.

Legomsky S, 'An Asylum Seeker's Bill of Rights in a Non-Utopian World' (2000) 14 *Georgetown Imm LJ* 619–641.

—— 'Secondary Refugee Movements and the Return of Asylum Seekers to Third Countries: The Meaning of Effective Protection' (2003) 15 *IJRL* 567–677.

—— 'The USA and the Carribbean Interdiction Program' (2006) 18 *IJRL* 677–695.

Lenaerts K and de Smijter E, 'Le Traité d'Amsterdam' [1998] *Journal des Tribunaux* 25–36.

—— 'A "Bill of Rights" for the European Union' (2001) 38 *CML Rev* 273–300.

—— 'The Charter and the Role of the European Courts' (2001) 8 *MJ* 90–101.

Leuprecht P, 'La solidarité internationale et les droits de l'homme' in *Congress on International Solidarity and Humanitarian Actions: Organized under the Auspices of the International Red Cross and the United Nations High Commissioner for Refugees* (1980) 27–52.

Lobkowicz de L, 'Quelle libre circulation des personnes en 1993?' [1990] *Revue du marché commun* 93–102.

—— 'The Dublin Convention: A Useful Complement to International Humanitarian Law' [1990] *European Vision* 7–11.

Loescher G, 'The UNHCR and World Politics: State Interests vs. Institutional Autonomy' (2001) 35 *IMR* 33–56.

Löper F, 'The Dublin Convention on Asylum: Interpretation and Application Problems' in C Marinho (ed), *The Dublin Convention on Asylum, Its Essence, Implementation and Prospects* (2000) 17–30.

Lowe A V, 'Sustainable Development and Unsustainable Arguments' in A Boyle and D Freestone (eds), *International Law and Sustainable Development: Past Achievements and Future Challenges* (2001) 19–37.

Marinho C, 'The Dublin Convention Judicial Control: National Case Highlights' in C Marinho (ed), *The Dublin Convention, Its Essence, Implementation and Prospects* (2000) 225–277.

Martin G, 'International Solidarity and Co-operation Assistance to African Refugees: Burden-Sharing or Burden-Shifting?' (1995) 7 *IJRL* special issue 250–271.

Marx R, 'Non-Refoulement, Access to Procedures, and Responsibility for Determining Refugee Claims' (1995) 7 *IJRL* 383–406.

—— 'Adjusting the Dublin Convention: New Approaches to Member State Responsibility for Asylum Applications' (2001) 3 *EJML* 7–22.

Marx R and Lumpp K, 'The German Constitutional Court's Decision of 14 May 1996 on the Concept of "Safe Third Countries" - A Basis for Burden-Sharing in Europe?', (1996) 8 *IJRL* 419–439.

Masclet J-C, 'De la difficulté d'atteindre un objectif communautaire par des moyens qui ne le sont pas' in D Bigo (ed), *L'Europe des polices et de la sécurité intérieure* (1992) 95–121.

Mathew P, 'Safe for Whom? The Safe Third Country Concepts Finds a Home in Australia' Paper given at the 7th International Research and Advisory Panel (IRAP) of the International Association for the Study of Forced Migration (IASFM) 8–12 January 2001 Johannesburg (on file with the author) 21 p.

Matscher F, 'Methods of Interpretation of the Convention' in R St J Macdonald et al. (eds), *The European System for the Protection of Human Rights* (1993) 63–81.

McAdam J, 'The European Union Qualification Directive: The Creation of a Subsidiary Protection Regime' (2005) 17 *IJRL* 461–516.

McCrudden C, 'Human Dignity and Judicial Interpretation of Human Rights' (2008) 19 *EJIL* 655–724.

Meijers H, 'Refugees in Western Europe, "Schengen" Affects the entire Refugee Law' (1990) 2 *IJRL* 428–41.

Melander G, 'Refugees in Orbit' in G Melander and P Nobel (eds), *African Refugees and the Law* (1978) 27–40.

—— 'Responsibility for the examination of an asylum request, Asylum seekers vs Quota Refugees' in ECRE, *Restrictive Asylum Policy in Europe, Report of the Seminar held in Zeist, The Netherlands, 16–18 January 1985* (1985) 18–21.

—— *Report of the Seminar on the Responsibility for Examining an Asylum Request* (1986) 51 p.

—— 'Responsibility for Examining an Asylum Request' (1986) 20 *IMR*, 220–229.

—— 'Further Development of International Refugee Law' in *The Refugee Problem on Universal, Regional and National Level* (1987) 469–512.

Middleton D, 'Why Asylum Seekers Seek Refuge in Particular Destination Countries: An Exploration of Key Determinants' Global Migration Perspectives Paper No. 34, May 2005 67 p.

Milner J, 'Burden Sharing', in M Gibney and R Hansen (eds), *Immigration and Asylum from 1900 to the Present*, ABC-CLIO Pub., Santa Barbara (2005) 56.

Monar J, 'Justice and Home Affairs in the Treaty of Amsterdam: Reform at the Price of Fragmentation' (1998) 23 *ELR* 320–335.

Moore A, 'Unsafe in America: A Review of the US – Canada Safe Third Country Agreement' (2007) 47 *Santa Clara LR* 201–284.

Moret J, Baglioni S and Efionayi-Mäder D, 'The Path of Somali Refugees into Exile, A Comparative Analysis of Secondary Movements and Policy Responses', Swiss Forum for Migration and Population Studies, Studies 46, 2006 p. number.

Morgenstern F, 'The Right of Asylum' (1949) 26 *BYIL* 326–357.

Müller-Graf P-C, 'The Dublin Convention: Pioneer and Lesson for Third-Pillar Conventions' in R Bieber and J Monar (eds), *Justice and Home Affairs in the European Union: the Development of the Third Pillar* (1995) 49–63.

Mus J B, '"Veilige" derde staten: het verbod van refoulement op de tocht?' [1994] *Nederlands Juristenblad* 1365–1370.

Munteanu A, 'Secondary movement in Romania: the asylum-migration nexus' *UNHCR New Issues in Refugee Research* Paper No. 148, December 2007, 24 p.

McNamara D, 'Opening Address' in *UNHCR and International Refugee Protection* RSP Working Paper No. 2 June 1999, 4.

Nanz K-P, 'Free Movement of Persons according to the Schengen Convention and in the Framework of the European Union' in A Pauly (ed), *De Schengen à Maastricht: voie royale et course d'obstacles* (1996) 61–79.

Neuwahl N, 'Article 173 Paragraph 4 EC: Past, Present and Possible Future' (1996) 21 *ELR* 17–31.

Noll G, '"Prisoners" Dilemma in Fortress Europe: On the Prospects for Equitable Burden-Sharing in the European Union' (1997) 40 *German Ybk of Intl L* 405–437.

—— 'Return of Persons to States of Origin and Third States', in T A Aleinikoff and V Chetail (eds), *Migration and International Legal Norms* (2003) 61–74.

—— 'Visions of the Exceptional: Legal and Theoretical Issues Raised by Transit Processing Centres and Protection Zones' (2003) 5 *EJML* 303–341.

—— 'Law and the Logic of Outsourcing: Offshore Processing and Diplomatic Assurances', Paper presented at the workshop on *Refugee protection in international law, contemporary challenges*, Oxford, 24 April 2006.

Nys M, 'Le regroupement familial: des droits et des protections' [1996] *RDE* 493–214.

O'Keeffe D, 'The Schengen Convention: A Suitable Model for European Integration?' (1991) 11 *YEL* 185–219.

—— 'The Emergence of a European Immigration Policy' (1995) 20 *ELR* 20–36.

—— 'The Convention on the Crossing of the External Frontiers of the Member States' in A Pauly (ed), *De Schengen à Maastricht: voie royale et course d'obstacles* (1996) 33–44.

—— 'Can the Leopard Change its Spots? Visas, Immigration and Asylum – Following Amsterdam' in D O'Keeffe and P Twomey (eds), *Legal Issues of the Amsterdam Treaty* (1999) 271–288.

Okoth-Obbo G, 'Coping with a Complex Refugee Crisis in Africa: Issues, Problems and Constraints for Refugee and International Law' in V Gowlland-Debbas (ed), *The Problem of Refugees in the Light of Contemporary International Law Issues* (1996) 7–17.

Panezi M, 'Legislative Development: The 2005 Asylum Procedures Directive: Developing the European Asylum Law' (2007) 13 *Columbia J of European L* 501–512.

Papadimitriou P, 'The New "Dubliners": Implementation of EC Regulation 343/2003 (Dublin II) by the Greek Authorities' (2005) 18 *JRS* 299–318.

Peers S, 'Who's Judging the Watchmen? The Judicial System of the "Area of Freedom, Security and Justice"' (1998) 18 *YEL* 337–413.

——'EU law on asylum procedures: An assault on human rights?', Statewatch Analysis.

——'Immigration, Asylum and the European Union Charter of Fundamental Rights' (2001) 3 *EJML* 141–169.

——'Readmission agreements and EC external migration law' *Statewatch News Online*, May 2003.

——'EU law on asylum procedures: An assault on human rights?' *Statewatch Analysis*, November 2004.

——'From Black Market to Constitution: The Development of the Institutional Framework for EC Immigration and Asylum Law' in S Peers and N Rogers (eds), *EU Immigration and Asylum Law* (2006) 19–45.

——'Human Rights in the EU Legal Order: Practical Relevance for EC Immigration and Asylum Law' in S Peers and N Rogers (eds), *EU Immigration and Asylum Law* (2006) 115–137.

——'The EU Institutions and Title IV' in S Peers and N Rogers (eds), *EU Immigration and Asylum Law* (2006) 47–79.

Perluss D and Hartmann J F, 'Temporary Refuge: Emergence of a Customary Norm' (1986) 26 *Virginia J of Intl L* 551–626.

Petite M, 'Le Traité d'Amsterdam' [1997] *RMCUE* 17–52.

Phuong C, 'Persecution by Third Parties and European Harmonization of Asylum olicies' (2001) 16 *Georgetown Immigration Law Journal* 81–97.

——'Persecution by Non-State Agents: Comparative Judicial Interpretations of the 1951 Refugee Convention' (2003) 4 *EJML* 521–532.

——'The concept of "effective protection" in the context of irregular secondary movements and protection in regions of origin' *Global Migration Perspectives* Paper No. 26, April 2005 14 p.

Plender R, 'The present state of research carried out by the English-speaking section of the centre for studies and research' in Centre for Studies and Research in International Law and International Relations, *Le droit d'asile* (1989) 63–109.

——'Competence, European Community Law and Nationals of Non-Member States' (1990) 39 *ICLQ* 599–610.

——and Mole N, 'Beyond the Geneva Convention: constructing a *de facto* right of asylum from international rights instruments' in F Nicholson and P Twomey (eds), *Refugee Rights and Realities: Evolving International Concepts and Regimes* (1999) 81–105.

Puissochet J-P, 'La juridiction communautaire: son rôle dans une Union européenne élargie et transformée' in *Le Traité d'Amsterdam et les perspectives d'évolution de l'Union européenne* (1997) 21–33.

Rodier C, 'Emigration illégale: une notion à bannir' *Libération*, 13 juin 2006 available at <http://www.migreurop.org/article922.html>.

——and Saint-Saëns I, 'Contrôler et filtrer: les camps au service des politiques migratoires de l'Europe' in V Chetail (ed), *Mondialisation, migration et droits de l'homme* (2007) 619–663.

Röhl K, 'Fleeing Violence and Poverty: *Non-Refoulement* Obligations under the European Convention of Human Rights', *UNHCR Working Paper* No. 111 January 2005 35 p.

Saroléa S, 'La procédure belge de reconnaissance de la qualité de réfugié et le droit à un recours effectif' [1995] *RDE* 542–557.

Schachter O, 'Entangled Treaty and Custom' in Y Dinstein (ed), *International Law at a Time of Perplexity: Essays in Honour of Shabtai Rosenne* (1989) 716–738.

Schieffer M, 'The Readmission of Third-Country Nationals within Bilateral and Multilateral Frameworks' in M den Boer (ed), *Schengen, First the Widening, Now the Deepening* (1997) 97–108.

—— 'Community Readmission with Third Countries – Objectives, Substance and Current State of Negotiations' (2003) 5 *EJML* 343–357.

Schmidt M G, 'Individual Human Rights Complaints Procedures Based on United Nations Treaties and the Need for Reform' (1992) 41 *ICLQ* 645–659.

Schnyder F, 'Les aspects juridiques actuels du problème des réfugiés' (1965) 114 *RdC* 335–450.

Schuck P, 'Refugee Burden-Sharing: A Modest Proposal' (1997) 22 *Yale J Intl L* 243–297.

Schutte J-E, 'Schengen: Its Meaning for the Free Movement of Persons in Europe' (1991) 28 *CML Rev* 549–570.

Sexton R C, 'Political Refugees, Non-Refoulement and State Practice: A Comparative Study' (1985) 18 *Vanderbilt J of Transnational L* 731–806.

Shacknove A, 'From Asylum to Containment' (1993) 5 *IJRL* 516–533.

Shah P, 'Refugees and Safe Third Countries: United Kingdom, European and International Aspects' (1995) 1 *European Public Law* 259–288.

Singh N, 'The Role and Record of Activities of the Office of the High Commissioner for Refugees' in *The Refugee Problem on Universal, Regional and International Level* (1987) 325–394.

Sperl M, 'Fortress Europe and the Iraqi "intruders": Iraqi asylum-seekers and the EU, 2003–2007' *UNHCR New Issues in Refugee Research*, Research Paper No. 144, October 2007 19 p.

Spielmann D, 'Human Rights Case Law in the Strasbourg and Luxembourg Courts: Conflicts, Inconsistencies, and Complementarities' in P Alston (ed), *The EU and Human Rights* (1999) 757–780.

Spijkerboer T, 'The Practical Effects of Schengen in Asylum Cases' in *Refugee and Asylum Law: Assessing the Scope for Judicial Protection* (1998) 28–59.

Stanton Russell S, Keely C B, and Christian B P, *Multilateral Diplomacy to Harmonize Asylum Policy in Europe: 1984–1993*, Institute for the Study of International Migration Working Paper, Washington DC, March 2000, 68 p.

Stein B N, 'ICARA II: Burden Sharing and Durable Solutions' in J Rogge (ed), *Refugees, A Third World Dilemma* (1987) 47–59.

Steiner H, 'Individual Claims in a World of Massive Violations: What Role for the Human Rights Committee?' in P Alston and J Crawford (eds), *The Future of UN Human Rights Treaty Monitoring* (2000) 15–53.

Storey H, 'EU Refugee Qualification Directive: A Brave New World?' (2008) 20 *IJRL* 1–49.

Sudre F, 'Intervention sur la question du renforcement des droits fondamentaux dans le Traité d'Amsterdam' in *Le Traité d'Amsterdam: Réalités et Perspectives* (1999) 47–48.

—— 'Le renouveau jurisprudenciel de la protection des étrangers par l'article 3 de la Convention européenne des droits de l'homme' in Fulchiron H (ed), *Les étrangers et la Convention européenne de sauvegarde des droits de l'homme et des libertés fondamentales* (1999) 61–82.

Suhrke A, 'Burden-sharing during Refugee Emergencies: The Logic of Collective versus National Action' (1998) 11 *JRS* 396–415.

Suntinger W, 'The Principle of Non-Refoulement: Looking Rather to Geneva than to Strasbourg?' (1995) 49 *Austrian J Publ and Intl L* 203–225.

Sztucki J, 'The Conclusions on the International Protection of Refugees Adopted by the Executive Committee of the UNHCR Programme' (1989) 1 *IJRL* 285–318.

—— 'Reflections on International "Soft Law"' in J Rambers et al (eds), *Festskrift till Lars Hjerner: Studies in International Law* (1990) 549–575.

Takkenberg A, 'Mass Migration of Asylum Seekers and State Responsibility' *in The Refugee Problem on Universal, Regional and National Level* (1987) 787–802.

Taylor S, 'Australia's "Safe Third Country" Provisions: Their Impact on Australia's Fulfillment of Its Non-Refoulement Obligations' (1996) 15 *University of Tasmania LR* 196–235.

—— 'Protection Elsewhere/Nowhere' (2006) 18 *IJRL* 283–312.

Tezcan E, 'La Coopération dans les domaines de la justice et des affaires intérieures dans le cadre de l'Union européenne et le Traité d'Amsterdam' (1998) 34 *CDE* 661–681.

Timmermans C W A, 'Het Verdrag van Amsterdam' [1997] *SEW* 344–351.

Thielemann E, 'Editorial Introduction to Special Issue on European Burden-Sharing and Forced Migration' (2003) 16 *JRS* 225–235.

Thorburn J, 'Transcending Boundaries: Temporary Protection and Burden-Sharing in Europe' (1995) 7 *IJRL* 459–480.

Tomuschat C, 'State Responsibility and the Country of Origin' in V Gowlland-Debbas (ed*)*, *The Problem of Refugees in The Light of Contemporary International Law Issues* (1996) 59–79.

Toner H, 'Thinking the unthinkable? State liability for judicial acts after Factortame (III)' (1997) 17 *YEL* 165–189.

Toth A G, 'The Legal Effects of the Protocols Relating to the United Kingdom, Ireland and Denmark' in T Heukels N Blokker and M Brus (eds), *The European Union after Amsterdam: A Legal Analysis* (1998) 227–252.

Toussaint M, 'Eurodac: un système informatisé européen de comparaison des empreintes digitales des demandeurs d'asile' [1999] *RMCUE* 421–425.

Towle, 'Processes and Critique of the Indo-Chinese Comprehensive Plan of Action: an Instrument of Burden-Sharing?' (2006) 18 *IJRL* 537–570.

Triche Naumik A, 'International Law and Detention of US Asylum Seekers: Contrasting Matter of D-J- with the United Nations Refugee Convention' (2007) 19 *IJRL* 661–702.

Türk V, 'The role of UNHCR in the development of international refugee law' in F Nicholson and P Twomey (eds), *Refugee rights and realities: evolving international concepts and regimes* (1999) 153–174.

—— 'Freedom from Fear: Refugees, the Broader Displacement Context and the Underlying Protection Regime' in V Chetail (ed), *Mondialisation, migration et droits de l'homme: Le droit international en question* (2007) 475–522.

Uehling G, 'Unwanted migration: Combating and unwittingly creating irregular migration in Ukraine' *UNHCR New Issues in Refugee Research* Working Paper No. 109, October 2004, 18 p.

United Kingdom Delegation, 'Sending Asylum Seekers to Safe Third Countries' (1995) 7 *IJRL* 119–122.

Valverde Soto M, 'General Principles of International Environmental Law' (1996) 3 *ILSA Journal of Intl and Comp L* 193–209.

Valluy J, 'Le HCR au Maroc: acteur de la politique européenne d'externalisation de l'asile' [2007] *Cahiers du Maghreb* 547–575.

van Beek I, 'Prima facie asylum determination in South Africa: A description of policy and practice' in J Handmaker, L A de la Hunt and J Klaaren (eds), *Perspectives on Refugee Protection in South Africa* (2001) Online publication <http://www.lhr.org.za/refugee/book/ingrid.htm>.

van Boven T, 'International Solidarity and Human Rights' in *Congress on International Solidarity and Humanitarian Actions* (1980) 15–26.

van der Klaauw J, 'The Dublin Convention, the Schengen Asylum Chapter and the Treatment of Asylum Application', *Het Akkoord van Schengen en vreemdelingen, een ongecontroleerde grens tussen recht en beleid ?*, Verslag Studiedag OSR (1996) 37–47.

—— 'Human Rights News: European Union' (1997) 15 *NQHR* 365–379.

Vandersanden G, 'Pour un élargissement du droit des particuliers d'agir en annulation contre des actes autres que les décisions qui leur sont adressées' (1995) 31 *CDE* 535–552.

van Dijk P, 'Article 3 ECHR and Asylum Law and Policy in The Netherlands' in R Lawson and M de Blois (eds), *The Dynamics of the Protection of Human Rights in Europe: Essays in Honour of H G Schermers* (1994) Vol III 123–153.

van Selm J, 'Access to Procedures, "Safe Third Countries". "Safe Countries of Origin" and "Time Limits', Paper for the UNHCR Global Consultations, June 2001, Available at <http://www.unhcr.org/protect/PROTECTION/3b39a2403.pdf> 60 p.

Väyrynen R, 'Funding Dilemmas in Refugee Assistance: Political Interests and Institutional Reforms in UNHCR' (2001) 35 *IMR* 143–167.

Vierdag E W, 'The Country of "First Asylum": Some European Aspects' in D A Martin (ed), *The New Asylum Seekers: Refugee Law in the 1980s* (1988) 73–84.

Wachsmann P, 'Les droits de l'homme' (1997) 33 *RTDE* 883–902.

Walbroeck D and Verheyden A-M, 'Les conditions de recevabilité des recours en annulation des particuliers contre les actes normatifs communautaires' (1995) 31 *CDE* 399–441.

wa Mutua M, 'Looking Past the Human Rights Committee: An Argument for De-marginalizing Enforcement' (1998) 4 *Buffalo Human Rights LR* 211–260.

Weis P, 'Legal aspects of the Convention of 28 July 1951 relating to the status of refugees' (1953) 30 *BYIL* 478–489.

—— 'Territorial Asylum' (1966) 6 *Indian J of Intl L* 173–194.

—— 'The United Nations Declaration on Territorial Asylum' (1969) *Canadian Ybk of Intl L* 92–149.

—— 'The Draft United Nations Convention on Territorial Asylum' (1979) 50 *BYIL* 151–171.

—— 'Refugees in Orbit' (1980) 10 *Israel Ybk on Human Rights*, 157–166.

Wiederkehr M-O, Statement in *Report of the Seminar on the Responsibility for Examining an Asylum Request* (1986) 17–21.

—— 'L'œuvre du Conseil de l'Europe dans le domaine du droit d'asile et des réfugiés', in Société française pour le droit international, *Droit d'asile et des réfugiés* (1997) 197–216.

Wilde R, 'Accountability and International Actors in Bosnia and Herzegovina, Kosovo and East Timor' (2001) 7 *ILSA J Intl Comp L* 455–460.

—— 'Legal "black hole"?: extraterritorial state action and international treaty law on civil and political rights' (2005) 26 *Michigan J of Intl Law* 739–806.

Wolfke K, 'Treaties and Custom: Aspects of Interrelation' in J Klabbers and R Lefeber (eds), *Essays on the Law of Treaties: a collection of essays in honour of Bert Vierdag* (1998) 31–40.

Yasseen M K, 'Interprétation des traités d'après la Convention de Vienne sur le droit des traités' (1976) 151 *RdC* vol iii, 1–114.

DOCUMENTS FROM NON-GOVERNMENTAL ORGANIZATIONS

Amnesty International, 'Europe: Harmonisation de la politique d'asile, procédures accélérées pour les demandes d'asile 'manifestement infondées' et notion de 'pays sûr' (1992).

—— *Playing Human Pinball: Home Office Practice in 'safe third countries' asylum cases*, June 1995.

—— 'EU regional protection programs: Enhancing protection in the region or barring access to EU territory', September 2005, 3 p.

ECRE, *Restrictive Asylum Policy in Europe, Report of the Seminar held in Zeist, The Netherlands, 16–18 January 1985* (1985).

—— 'Comment on the Report and Motion for a Resolution by Mrs Claudia Roth on a Draft Council Recommendation concerning a Specimen Bilateral Readmission Agreement between a Member State of the European Union and a Third Country', September 1995.

—— 'Safe Third Countries Myths and Realities' (1997) 17 p.

—— 'Position on the implementation of the Dublin Convention in the light of lessons learned from the implementation of the Schengen Convention' December 1997.

—— 'Position on the Enlargement of the European Union in relation to Asylum' September 1998.

—— 'Unlawful and Unworkable – Amnesty International's View on Proposals for Extra-territorial Processing of Asylum Claims', 18 June 2003.

—— 'Amnesty International and Human Rights Watch, Refugee and Human Rights Organisations Across Europe Express their Concern at the Expected Agreement on Asylum Measures on breach of International Law', 28 April 2004.

—— Information Note on the Council Directive 2005/85/EC of 1 December 2005 on minimum standards on procedures in Member States on granting and withdrawing refugee status, 35 p.

—— *Defending Refugees' Access to Protection in Europe*, December 2007.

—— ILGA Europe, Amnesty International, Pax Christi International, Quaker Council for European Affairs, Human Rights Watch, CARITAS-Europe, Médecins sans Frontières, Churches' Commission for Migrants, Save the Children in Europe, 'Call for withdrawal of the Asylum Procedures Directive', 22 March 2004.

European Legal Network on Asylum, 'The Application of the Safe Country of Origin Concept in Europe', February 2005.

—— 'The Impact of the EU Qualification Directive on International Protection', October 2008.

France Terre d'Asile, 'Convention d'application de l'Accord de Schengen premier bilan de sa mise en oeuvre en Europe' February 1996.

Human Rights Watch, 'An Unjust Vision for Europe's Refugees', 2003.

——'EU buffer states and UNHCR "processing" centres and "safe havens"' Statewatch News Online, June 2003.

——'Ukraine: Migrants, Asylum Seekers Regularly Abused', News Release, 30 November 2005.

——'EU: European Commission technical mission to Libya: exporting Fortress Europe' Statewatch News Bulletin, vol 15 no 2, March-April 2005.

——'EU: High Level Working Group on Asylum and migration: crucial body in EU's external policies', Statewatch Bulletin, vol 16 no 1 January-February 2006.

——'EU Roundup: Visa "facilitation", European Arrest Warrants 2005, "Check the Web" and the principle of availability', Statewatch Bulletin, vol 16 no 2, March-April 2006.

Statewatch, 'Open Letter by Moroccan, African and European Associations: "In Morocco, the right of men and women are scorned in the name of the protection of Europe's borders"' Statewatch News Online, January 2007.

US Committee for Refugees, *The Asylum Challenge to Western Nations*, December 1984.

——At Fortress Europe's Moat: the "Safe Third Country" Concept, July 1997, 39 p.

DOCUMENTS FROM THE INTER-GOVERNMENTAL CONSULTATIONS ON ASYLUM, REFUGEE, AND MIGRATION POLICIES IN EUROPE, NORTH AMERICA, AND AUSTRALIA (IGC)

'Working Paper on Readmission Agreements' (1994).

Report on temporary protection in States in Europe, North America and Australia (1995) Geneva 263 p.

'Comparison between the EU Specimen Bilateral Readmission Agreement and the Draft Skeleton by the Czech Republic for the Budapest Group' 28 February 1995.

Report on Asylum Procedures, Overview of Policies and Practices in IGC Participating States (1997) Geneva, 449 p.

'Inventory of Readmission Agreements as at 4 February 1998'.

Study on the Concept of Burden-Sharing (1998) Geneva, 130 p.

UN DOCUMENTS

General Assembly Resolutions

Resolution 832 (IX), 21 October 1954.

Resolution 1166 (XII), 26 November 1957 on international assistance to refugees within the mandate of the United Nations.

Resolution 1236 (XII), 14 December 1957 on peaceful and neighbourly relations among States relations.

Resolution 1301 (XIII), 10 December 1958 on measures aimed at the implementation and promotion of peaceful and neighbourly relations among States.

Resolution 1783 (XVII), 7 December 1962.

Resolution 2129 (XX), 21 December 1965 on actions on the regional level with view to improving neighbourly relations among European States having different social and political systems.

Resolution 46/62, 9 December 1991 on the development and strengthening of good-neighbourliness between States.

Resolution 52/118, 23 February 1998 on effective implementation of international instruments on human rights including reporting obligations on human rights.

Resolution 53/138, 1 March 1999 on effective international implementation of international instruments on human rights, including reporting obligations under international obligations on human rights.

Resolution 56/83, 12 December 2001 on Responsibility of States for Internationally Wrongful Acts.

Resolution 56/137, 19 December 2001 on the Office of the United Nations High Commissioner for Refugees.

Resolution 57/187, 18 December 2002 on the Office of the United Nations High Commissioner for Refugees.

Resolution 58/151, 22 December 2003 on the Enlargement of the Executive Committee of the Programme of the United Nations High Commissioner for Refugees.

Resolution 59/170, 20 December 2004 on the Office of the United Nations High Commissioner for Refugees.

Resolution 60/129, 16 December 2005 on the Office of the United Nations High Commissioner for Refugees.

Resolution 61/137, 25 January 2007 on the Office of the United Nations High Commissioner for Refugees.

Resolution 62/124, 18 December 2007 on the Office of the United Nations High Commissioner for Refugees.

Economic and Social Council

Resolution 393 B (XIII), 10 September 1951.

Resolution 565 (XIX), 31 March 1955.

Resolution 672 (XXV), 30 April 1958.

Resolution 1985/17, 28 May 1985 on the Review of the Composition, Organization and Administrative Arrangements of the Sessional Working Group of Governmental Experts on the Implementation of the International Covenant on Economic, Social and Cultural Rights.

Human Rights Commission

Final Report by the independent expert, Philip Alston, on enhancing the long-term effectiveness of the United Nations human rights treaty system, UN Doc E/CN.4/1997/74, 27 March 1996.

Resolution 1996/9 of the Sub-Commission on Prevention of Discrimination and Protection of Minorities on the right to freedom of movement UN Doc E/CN.4/SUB.2/RES/1996/9, 25 November 1996.

Resolution on freedom of movement and population transfer UN Doc E/CN.4/SUB.2/RES/1997/29, 28 August 1997.

Report of the Secretary-General to the Commission on Human Rights on effective functioning of the bodies established pursuant to the United Nations human rights instruments UN Doc E/CN.4/1998/85, 4 February 1998.

Resolution 1998/49 on Human Rights and Mass Exoduses, E/CN.4/RES/1998/49, 17 April 1998.

Statistics relating to the 55th session of the Commission on Human Rights UN Doc E/CN.4/2000/8, 15 September 1999.

Resolution on Effective Implementation of international instruments on human rights, including reporting obligations under international instruments on human rights UN Doc E/CN.4/RES/2000/75, 27 April 2000.

Sub-Commission Resolution 1996/9 on the right to freedom of movement UN Doc E/CN.4/SUB.2/RES/1996/9, 18 August 2000.

Human Rights Committee

General Comment No. 15 on the position of aliens under the Covenant, UN Doc CCPR/C/21/Rev.1, 11 April 1986.

General Comment of the Human Rights Committee No. 20 replacing General Comment No. 7 concerning prohibition of torture and cruel treatment or punishment, UN Doc HR1/HEN/1/Rev., 10 March 1992.

General Comment No. 27 on freedom of movement, UN Doc CCPR/C/21/Rev.1/Add.9, 2 November 1999.

General Comment No. 31, on the nature of the general legal obligation imposed on states parties to the Covenant, UN Doc CCPR/C/21/Rev.1/Add.13, 26 May 2004.

Committee Against Torture

General Comment on the Implementation of Article 3 in the context of Article 22 of the Convention Against Torture, UN Doc, A/53/44, annex IX, 21 November 1997.

Statistical survey of individual complaints dealt with by the Committee against Torture under the procedure governed by article 22 of the Convention Against Torture and Other Cruel, Inhuman, or Degrading Treatment or Punishment, updated on 12 August 2008. <http://www2.ohchr.org/english/bodies/cat/stat3.htm>.

Miscellaneous

Report of the Secretary-General on the Meeting on Refugees and Displaced persons in South-east Asia, Geneva UN Doc A/34/627, 1 July 1979.

Recommendations from the Pan-African Conference on the Situation of Refugees in Africa, UN Doc A/AC.96/INF.158 p 7, 7–17 May 1979.

Programme of Action adopted by the Second International Conference on Assistance to Refugees in Africa UN Doc A/39/402 p 22, 9–19 April 1981.

Programme of Action annexed to the Report of the Secretary-General on the Second International Conference on Assistance to Refugees in Africa UN Doc A/39/402, 22 August 1984.

International Conference on Central American refugees (CIREFCA), Guatemala City, 29–31 May 1989, Declaration and concerted plan of action UN Doc CIREFCA/89/14.

International Conference on Indo-Chinese Refugees, Geneva 13–14 June 1989: Declaration and Comprehensive Plan of Action UN Doc A/CONF.148/2.

United Nations, Compilation of General Comments and General Recommendations Adopted by Human Rights Treaty Bodies UN Doc HRI/GEN/1/Rev.5, 26 April 2001.

UN Secretary-General, "In Larger Freedom: Towards Security, Development and Human Rights" UN Doc. A/59/2005, 21 March 2005.

UN High Commissioner for Human Rights, 'The OHCHR Plan of Action: Protection and Empowerment', Geneva, May 2005.

UNHCHR Secretariat, 'Concept paper on the High Commissioner's Proposal for a Unified Standing Treaty Body', UN Doc. HRI/MC/2006/2, 22 March 2006.

UNHCR DOCUMENTS

Executive Committee Conclusions

Conclusion No. 1 (XXVI) of 1975.

Conclusion No. 2 (XXVII) of 1976 on the Functioning of the Sub-Committee and General Conclusion on International Protection.

Conclusion No. 4 (XXVIII) of 1977 on International Instruments.

Conclusion No. 6 (XXVIII) of 1977 on *Non-Refoulement*.

Conclusion No. 8 (XXVIII) of 1977 on Determination of Refugee Status.

Conclusion No. 9 (XXVIII) of 1977 on Family Reunification.

General Conclusion on International Protection No. 11 (XXIX) of 1978.

Conclusion No. 13 (XXIX) of 1978 on Travel Documents for Refugees.

General Conclusion on International Protection No. 14 (XXX) of 1979.

Conclusion No. 15 (XXX) of 1979 on Refugees Without an Asylum Country.

Conclusion No. 17 (XXXI) of 1980 on Problems of Extradition Affecting Refugees.

Conclusion No. 19 (XXXI) of 1980 on Temporary Refuge.

Conclusion No. 22 (XXXII) of 1981 on the Situation of Asylum Seekers in Situation of Large Scale Influx.

Conclusion No. 24 (XXXII) of 1981 on Family Reunification.

General Conclusion on International Protection No. 25 (XXXIII) of 1982.

General Conclusion on International Protection No. 33 (XXXV) of 1984.

General Conclusion on International Protection No. 36 (XXXVI) of 1985.

Conclusion No. 42 (XXXVII) of 1986 on Accession to International Instruments and their Implementation.

General Conclusion on International Protection No. 46 (XXXVIII) of 1987.

Conclusion No. 49 (XXXVIII) of 1987 on Travel Documents for Refugees.

General Conclusion on International Protection No. 50 (XXXIX) of 1988.

Conclusion No. 52 (XXXIX) of 1988 on International Solidarity and Refugee Protection.

General Conclusion on International Protection No. 55 (XL) of 1989.

Conclusion No. 58 (XL) of 1989 on the Problem of Refugees and Asylum-Seekers Who Move in an Irregular Manner from a Country in which They Had Already Found Protection.

General Conclusion on International Protection No. 61 (XLI) of 1990.

General Conclusion on International Protection No. 65 (XLII) of 1991.

Conclusion No. 66 (XLII) of 1991 on the Report of the Working Group on Solutions and Protection.

General Conclusion on International Protection No. 68 (XLIII) of 1992.

General Conclusion on International Protection No. 71 (XLIV) of 1993.

General Conclusion on International Protection No. 74 (XLV) of 1994.

General Conclusion on International Protection No. 77 (XLVI) of 1995.

General Conclusion on International Protection No. 79 (XLVII) of 1996.

Conclusion No. 80 (XLVIII) of 1996 on comprehensive approaches within a protection framework.

General Conclusion on International Protection No. 81 (XLVIII) of 1997.

General Conclusion No. 82 (XLVIII) of 1997 on Safeguarding Asylum.

General Conclusion on International Protection No. 85 (XLIX) of 1998.

General Conclusion on International Protection No. 87 (L) of 1999.

General Conclusion on International Protection No. 89 (LI) of 2000.

General Conclusion No. 90 (LII) of 2001.

General Conclusion on International Protection No. 93 (LIII) of 2002.

General Conclusion on International Protection No. 98 (LIV) of 2003.

General Conclusion on International Protection No. 99 (LV) of 2004.

Conclusion on International Cooperation and Burden and Responsibility Sharing in Mass Influx Situations No. 100 (LV) of 2004.

General Conclusion on International Protection No. 102 (LVI) of 2005.

Conclusion No. 103 (LVI) of 2005 on complementary forms of protection.

General Conclusion on International Protection No. 108 (LIX) of 2008.

Sub-Committee of the Whole on International Protection and Standing Committee

Note on *Non-refoulement*, UN Doc EC/SCP/2, 23 August 1977.

Note on Determination of Refugee Status under International Instruments, UN Doc EC/SCP/5, 24 August 1977.

Note on the extraterritorial effect of the determination of refugee status under the 1951 Convention and the 1967 Protocol Relating to the Status of Refugees, UN Doc EC/SCP/9, 21 August 1978.

Note on Asylum: Refugees Without an Asylum Country, UN Doc EC/SCP/12, 30 August 1979.

Irregular Movements of Asylum-Seekers and Refugees, UN Doc EC/SCP/40/Rev.1, 30 September 1985.

Implementation of the 1951 Convention and the 1967 Protocol relating to the Status of Refugees, UN Doc EC/SCP/54, 7 July 1989.

Background Note on the Safe Country Concept and Refugee Status, UN Doc EC/SCP/68, 26 July 1991.

Overview of Regional Developments, UN Doc EC/46/SC/CRP.11, 4 January 1996.

Progress Report on Informal Consultations on the Provision of International Protection to All Who Need it, UN Doc EC/47/SC/CRP.27, 30 May 1997.

Note on International Protection submitted to the Standing Committee, UN Doc EC/9/SC/CRP.12, 4 June 1999.

Note on International Protection, UN Doc EC/50/SC/CRP.16, 9 June 2000.

21st meeting of the Standing Committee, 'New Directions for Resettlement Policy and Practice', UN Doc EC/51/SC/INF.2, 14 June 2001.

Standing Committee, 'Economic and Social Impact of Massive Refugee Populations on Host Developing Countries, as well as Other Countries', UN Doc EC/54/SC/CRP.5, 18 February 2004.

Standing Committee, 'UNHCR's Activities in Relation to the Asylum-Migration Nexus', UN Doc EC/58/SC/CRP.12, 4 June 2007.

Standing Committee, 'Ensuring International Protection and Enhancing International Cooperation in Mass Influx Situations', UN Doc EC/54/SC/CRP.11, 7 June 2004.

Standing Committee, 'Progress Report on Resettlement' UN Doc EC/59/SC/CRP.11, 2 June 2008.

Notes on International Protection and other reports submitted by the High Commissioner to the Executive Committee

Report of the meeting of the Sub-Committee of the Whole on International Protection, UN Doc A/AC.96/571, 9 October 1979.

Note on International Protection submitted by the High Commissioner at the 40th session, UN Doc A/AC.96/728, 2 August 1989.

Report of the 40th session of the Executive Committee, UN Doc A/AC.96/737, 19 October 1989.

Note on International Protection submitted by the High Commissioner at the 41st session, UN Doc A/AC.96/750, 27 August 1990.

Note on International Protection submitted by the High Commissioner at the 42nd session, UN Doc A/AC.96/777, 9 September 1991.

Note on International Protection submitted by the High Commissioner at the 43rd session, UN Doc A/AC.96/799, 25 August 1992.

Note on International Protection submitted by the High Commissioner at the 44th session, UN Doc A/AC.96/815, 31 August 1993.

Note on International Protection submitted by the High Commissioner at the 45th session, UN Doc A/AC.96/830, 7 September 1994.

Note on International Protection submitted by the High Commissioner at the 47th session, UN Doc A/AC.96/863, 1 July 1996.

Note on International Protection submitted by the High Commissioner at the 49th session, UN Doc A/AC.96/898, 3 July 1998.

49th session ExCom, 'Annual Theme: International Solidarity and Burden-Sharing in All its Aspects: National, Regional and International Responsibilities for Refugees, UN Doc A/AC.96/904, 7 September 1998.

Report of the 49th session of the Executive Committee of the High Commissioner's Programme Chairman's summing up of Agenda Item 4: Annual Theme (International Solidarity and Burden-Sharing in all its aspects: National, Regional and International Responsibilities for Refugees), UN Doc A/AC.96/911, 12 October 1998.

Note on International Protection submitted by the High Commissioner at the 50th session, UN Doc A/AC.96/914, 7 July 1999.

Note on International Protection submitted by the High Commissioner at the 51st session, UN Doc A/AC.96/930, 7 July 2000.

Report of the 51st session of the Executive committee of the High Commissioner's programme, UN Doc A/AC.96/944, 13 October 2000.

Note on International Protection submitted by the High Commissioner at the 53rd session, UN Doc A/AC.96/965, 11 September 2002.

Note on International Protection submitted by the High Commissioner at the 54th session, UN Doc A/AC.96/975, 2 July 2003.

Note on International Protection submitted by the High Commissioner at the 55th session, UN Doc A/AC/96/989, 7 July 2004.

Executive Committee of the High Commissioner's Programme, 'Proposal to Establish an Assistant High Commissioner (Protection) Post in UNHCR', UN Doc A/AC.96/992/Add.1, 2 September 2004.

Note on International Protection submitted by the High Commissioner at the 57th session, UN Doc A/AC.96/1024, 12 July 2006.

UNHCR High Commissioner's Dialogue on Protection Challenges, 'Discussion Paper: Refugee protection and durable solutions in the context of international migration', UN Doc UNHCR/DPC/2007/Doc.02, 19 November 2007.

Miscellaneous

Handbook on Procedures and Criteria for Determining Refugee Status, UN Doc HCR/1P/4/Eng/Rev.2 Geneva (reprint 1992).

UNHCR (London Office), 'The Safe Third Country Policy in the light of International Obligations of Countries vis-à-vis Refugees and Asylum Seekers', July 1993.

UNHCR 'Overview of Re-admission Agreements in Central Europe', 30 September 1993.

'Readmission agreements, "Protection elsewhere" and asylum policy', August 1994.

UNHCR, 'Position on Standard Bilateral Readmission Agreements Between a Member State and a Third Country', December 1994.

UNHCR, 'Asylum applications and the entry into force of the Schengen implementation agreement: some observations of UNHCR', March 1995.

UNHCR, 'The Concept of "Protection Elsewhere', 1995.

UNHCR, 'An Overview of Protection Issues in Western Europe: Legislative Trends and Positions Taken by UNHCR', August 1995.

'Considerations on the "safe third country" concept' submitted by UNHCR at the EU Seminar on the Associated States as Safe Third Countries in Asylum Legislation Vienna, 8–11 July 1996.

UNHCR Evaluation and Policy Analysis, 'Implementation of UNHCR's strategy in the European Union', EVAL/04/98 July 1998.

UNHCR, 'Revisiting the Dublin Convention – Some reflections by UNHCR in response to the Commission staff working paper', January 2001.

UNHCR, Background Paper No. 3, 'Inter-State agreements for the re-admission of third country nationals, including asylum seekers, and for the determination of the State responsible for examining the substance of an asylum claim', May 2001.

UNHCR, 'Global Consultations on International Protection/Third Track: Refugee Protection and Migration Control: Perspectives from UNHCR and IOM', EC/GC/01/11, 31 May 2001.

UNHCR, 'Easy Guide on Refugee Resettlement Programmes', Information as of June 2001.

UNHCR Global Consultations, 'Strengthening Protection Capacities in Host Countries' UN Doc EC/GC/01/19, September 2001.

UNHCR, 'Observations on the European Commission's Proposal for a Council Regulation establishing the criteria and mechanisms for determining the Member State responsible for examining an asylum application lodged in one of the Member States by a third-country national (COM(2001) 447 final)', February 2002.

UNHCR, 'The Agenda for Protection', UN Doc. A/AC.96/965/Add.1, 26 June 2002.

'Summary Conclusions on the Concept of "Effective Protection in the Context of Secondary Movements of Refugees and Asylum Seekers', Lisbon Expert Roundtable organised by the UNHCR and the Migration Policy Institute and hosted by the Luso-American Foundation for Development, 9 and 10 December 2002.

UNHCR, '"Convention Plus": Questions and Answers', 20 May 2003.

UNHCR, 'The Strategic Use of Resettlement (A Discussion Paper Prepared by the Working Group on Resettlement)' EC/53/SC/CRP.10/Add.1, 3 June 2003.

UNHCR Working Paper, 'UNHCR's three-pronged proposal', June 2003.

Report by the High Commissioner to the General Assembly on Strengthening the Capacity of the Office of the High Commissioner for Refugees to Carry out its Mandate, UN Doc. A/AC.96/980, 20 August 2003.

UNHCR, 'Informal Record: Open Meeting of States and Interested Parties on Secondary, Irregular Movements of Refugees and Asylum-Seekers', FORUM/CG/SM/01, 21 December 2003.

UNHCR, 'Progress Report: Convention Plus', FORUM/2004/2, 20 February 2004.

UNHCR, 'Convention Plus Issues Paper on Addressing Irregular Secondary Movements of Refugees and Asylum-Seekers', prepared by the High Commissioner's Forum, FORUM/CG/SM/03, 11 March 2004.

UNHCR Press Release, *Lubbers calls for EU asylum laws not to contravene international law*, 29 March 2004.

UNHCR Press Release, *UNHCR regrets missed opportunity to adopt high EU asylum standards*, 30 April 2004.

UNHCR, 'Making Comprehensive Approaches to Resolving Refugee Problems More Systematic', FORUM/2004/7, 16 September 2004.

'Chairman's Summary, Third Meeting of the High Commissioner's Forum' 1 October 2004.

UNHCR, 'Note on access to the asylum procedure of asylum seekers returned to Greece, inter alia, under arrangements to transfer responsibility with respect to determining an asylum claim or pursuant to the application of the safe third country concept', November 2004.

UNHCR, 'UNHCR Observations on the Communication from the European Commission to the Council and the European Parliament on Regional Protection Programmes', October 2005.

UNHCR, 'Convention Plus Core Group on Addressing Irregular Secondary Movements of Refugees and Asylum-Seekers, Joint Statement by the Co-Chairs', FORUM/2205/7, 8 November 2005.

UNHCR, 'Advisory Opinion regarding the scope of the National Security Exception in Article 33(2)', 6 January 2006.

UNHCR, 'The Dublin II Regulation: A UNHCR Discussion Paper', April 2006.

UNHCR, 'The High-Level Dialogue on International Migration and Development: UNHCR's observations and recommendations', 28 June 2006.

UNHCR, 'Monitoring Report: Canada – United States "Safe Third Country" Agreement 29 December 2003 – 28 December 2005', June 2006.

UNHCR, 'Note on Diplomatic Assurances and International Refugee Protection', August 2006.

UNHCR, 'Annual Programme Budget 2007', UN Doc A/AC.96/1026, 1 September 2006.

UNHCR, 'Implementing the Ten-Point Plan of Action in Southern Europe: Activities Undertaken by UNHCR to Address Mixed Migration in the Context of the Mediterranean/Atlantic Arrivals', 2 October 2006.

UNHCR, 'Refugee Protection and Mixed Migration: A 10-Point Plan of Action', 1 January 2007.

UNHCR, 'Refugee Protection and International Migration', 17 January 2007.

UNHCR, 'Advisory Opinion on the Extraterritorial Application of *Non-Refoulement* Obligations under the 1951 Convention Relation to the Status of Refugees and its 1967 Protocol', 26 January 2007.

UNHCR, 'UNHCR's Activities in Relation to the Asylum-Migration Nexus', paper prepared by UNHCR's Standing Committee, UN Doc EC/58/SC/CRP.12, 4 June 2007.

UNHCR, 'Concept Paper on the "High Commissioner's Dialogue on Protection Challenges"', 30 July 2007.

UNHCR, 'UNHCR's Response to the European Commission's Green Paper on the Future Common European Asylum System', September 2007.

UNHCR, 'Asylum in the European Union: A Study of the Implementation of the Qualification Directive', November 2007.

UNHCR, 'Annual UNHCR/NGO Consultation, 25–26 June 2008: Thematic Session on the "Governance of Refugee Law: Suggestions and Perspectives"'.

UNHCR, 'Building a Europe of Asylum: UNHCR's Recommendations to France for its European Union Presidency', June 2008.

COUNCIL OF EUROPE DOCUMENTS

Recommendation 434 (1965) on the granting of the right of asylum to European Refugees.

Resolution (67) 14 of the Committee of Ministers of the Council of Europe on Asylum to Persons in Danger of Persecution of 29 June 1967.

Report to the Parliamentary Assembly of the Council of Europe on the situation of de facto refugees by M Dankert and Forni Doc.3642, 5 August 1975.

Recommendation 773 (1976) on the situation of *de facto* refugees adopted by the Parliamentary Assembly of the Council of Europe.

Recommendation 817 (1977) of the Parliamentary Assembly of the Council of Europe on certain aspects of the right to asylum.

Successive drafts on an agreement on responsibility for examining an asylum request:
CAHAR (81) Misc, 24 March 1981
CAHAR (82) 10 Appendix III p 15, 5 November 1982

Successive drafts on an agreement on responsibility for examining an asylum request:
>CAHAR (83) 36 final Appendix VIII p 30, 19 December 1983
>CAHAR (84) 4 final Appendix V p 20, 22 May 1984

Recommendation No. R (84) 1 adopted on 25 January 1984 by the Committee of Ministers of the Council of Europe on the Persons Satisfying the Criteria in the Geneva Convention who are not Formally Recognised as Refugees.

Recommendation 1327 (1997) of the Council of Europe Parliamentary Assembly adopted on 24 April 1997 relating to the protection and reinforcement of the human rights of refugees and asylum seekers in Europe.

Recommendation No. R (97) 22 containing guidelines on the application of the safe third country concept, adopted by the Committee of Ministers of the Council of Europe on 25 November 1997.

Ad Hoc Committee of Experts on the legal aspects of territorial asylum, refugees and stateless persons (CAHAR) *Selected texts concerning territorial asylum and refugees adopted within the Council of Europe*, CAHAR (98) 6, Vol I and II, March 1998, Strasbourg.

Recommendation No. R (2000) 9 on Temporary Protection (3 May 2000).

Parliamentary Assembly of the Council of Europe, 'Situation of refugees and displaced persons in the Russian Federation and some other CIS countries' Doc 10118, 25 March 2004.

Parliamentary Assembly of the Council of Europe, Draft Resolution, 13 June 2007.

Parliamentary Assembly of the Council of Europe, Report of the Committee on Migration, Refugees and Population, 'Assessment of transit and processing centres as a response to mixed flows of migrants and asylum seekers', 14 June 2007.

Parliamentary Assembly of the Council of Europe, 'Europe's "boat-people": mixed migration flows by sea into Southern Europe' 11 July 2008.

EUROPEAN COMMUNITY AND EUROPEAN UNION DOCUMENTS

European Commission

White Paper: Completing the Internal Market COM (85) 310 final, 14 June 1985.

Communication on the abolition of controls at internal borders COM (88) 640 final, 7 December 1988.

Communication from the Commission to the Council and the European Parliament on the Rights of Asylum SEC (91) 1857 final, 11 October 1991.

Communication from the Commission to the Council and the European Parliament on asylum and immigration policies COM (94) 23 final, 23 February 1994.

Staff Working Paper, 'Revisiting the Dublin Convention: developing Community legislation for determining which Member State is responsible for considering an asylum application submitted in one of the Member States' SEC (2000) 522, 21 March 2000.

Communication on the Legal Nature of the Charter of Fundamental Rights of the European Union COM (2000) 644 final, 11 October 2000.

Communication from the Commission to the Council and the European Parliament, 'Towards a common asylum procedure and a uniform status, valid throughout the Union, for persons granted asylum' COM (2000) 755 final, 22 November 2000.

Staff Working Paper, 'Evaluation of the Dublin Convention' SEC (2001) 756, 13 June 2001.

Green Paper by the Commission on a Community's return policy COM (2002) 175 final, 10 April 2002.

Communication from the European Commission to the Council and European Parliament, 'Integrating migration issues in the European's Union relations with third countries' COM (2002) 703 final, 3 December 2002.

Communication from the Commission to the Council and the European Parliament, 'Wider Europe Neighbourhood: A new framework for relations with our Eastern and Southern neighbours' COM (2003) 104 final, 11 March 2003.

Communication from the Commission to the Council and the European Parliament, 'The common asylum policy and the Agenda for Protection' COM (2003) 152 final, 26 March 2003.

Communication from the Commission to the Council and the European Parliament, 'Towards more accessible, equitable and managed asylum systems' COM (2003) 315 final, 3 June 2003.

Communication from the Commission to the European Parliament and the Council in view of the European Council of Thessaloniki on the development of a common policy on illegal, smuggling and trafficking of human beings, external borders and the return of illegal aliens, COM (2003) 323 final, 3 June 2003.

Communication from the Commission to the Council and the European Parliament, 'European Neighbourhood Policy Strategy Paper' COM (2004) 373 final, 12 May 2004.

Communication from the Commission to the Council and the European Parliament, 'On the Managed Entry in the EU of Persons in Need of International Protection and Enhancement of the Protection Capacity of the Regions of Origin: Improving Access to Durable Solutions' COM (2004) 410 final, 4 June 2004.

Communication from the Commission to the Council and the European Parliament, 'On the Managed Entry in the EU of Persons in Need of International Protection and the Enhancement of the Protection Capacity of the Regions of Origin: Improving Access to Durable Solutions' COM (2004) 410 final, 14 June 2004.

Communication from the Commission to the Council and the European Parliament, 'A More Efficient Common European Asylum System: The Single Procedure as the Next Step' COM (2004) 503 final, 15 July 2004.

'Report on the Technical mission to Libya on Illegal migration, 27 November 2004–06 December 2005', Doc. 7753/05.

Communication on compliance with the Charter of Fundamental Rights in Commission Legislative Proposals: Methodology for systematic and rigorous monitoring COM (2005) 172 final, 27 April 2005.

Communication from the Commission to the Council and the European Parliament, 'The Hague Programme: Ten priorities for the next five year, the partnership for European renewal in the field of freedom, security and justice' COM (2005) 184 final, 10 May 2005.

Communication from the Commission to the Council and the European Parliament on regional protection programmes, COM (2005) 388 final, 1 September 2005.

Communication from the Commission to the Council and the European Parliament, 'Priority Actions for Responding to the Challenges of Migration: First Follow-Up to Hampton Court', COM (2005) 621 final, 30 November 2005.

Communication from the Commission to the European Parliament and the Council, Thematic Programme for the cooperation with third countries in the areas of migration and asylum COM (2006) 26 final, 25 January 2006.

'Communication from the Commission to the Council and the European Parliament on Strengthened Practical Cooperation: New Structures, New Approaches: Improving the Quality of Decision Making in the Common European Asylum System' COM (2006) 67 final, 17 February 2006.

Communication from the Commission to the Council, 'Reinforcing the Management of the EU's Southern Maritime Borders' COM (2006) 733 final, 30 November 2006.

Report from the Commission to the European Parliament and the Council on the Evaluation of the Dublin System COM (2007) 299 Final, 6 June 2007.

Communication from the Commission, 'A Strong European Neighbourhood Policy' COM (2007) 774 final, 5 December 2007.

Communication from the Commission to the European Parliament, the Council, the European Economic and Social Committee and the Committee of Regions: 'Policy Plan on Asylum, An Integrated Approach to Protection Across the EU', COM (2008) 360 final, 17 June 2008.

Communication from the Commission to the Council and the European Parliament: Report on the Implementations of the Hague Programme for 2007 COM (2008) 373 final, 2 July 2008.

Communication from the Commission to the European Parliament, the Council, the European Economic and Social Committee and the Committee of the Regions, 'Strengthening the Global Approach to Migration: Increasing Coordination, Coherence, Synergies' COM (2008) 611 final, 8 October 2008.

European Council

Co-ordinator's Group, *Free Movement of Persons: Report to the European Council by the Co-ordinator's group* (Palma Document) CIRC 3624/89, 9 June 1989.

Conclusions of the Edinburgh European Council, 11–12 December 1992, Bull EC 12–1992, 23.

Conclusions of the Tampere European Council, 15 and 16 October 1999.

Conclusions of the Seville European Council, 21–22 June 2002, Doc. No. 13463/02.

Conclusions of the Thessaloniki European Council, 19–20 June 2003, Doc. No. 11638/03.

Hague Programme for strengthening freedom, security and justice in the European Union as approved by the European Council at its Brussels meeting of 5 November 2004, Doc. 16054/04, 13 December 2004.

Council documents

Decision of 11 June 1992 setting up the CIREA SN 2781/92 WGI 1107.

Conclusions on people displaced by the conflict in the former Yugoslavia of 30 November 1992.

Conclusions on countries where there is generally no risk of persecution adopted on 30 November and 1 December 1992 by the Immigration Ministers SN 4821/92 WGI 1281 ASIM 145.

Resolution on manifestly unfounded applications for asylum adopted on 30 November and 1 December 1992 by the Immigration Ministers, SN 4822/92 WGI 1282 ASIM 146.

Resolution on a harmonised approach to questions concerning host third countries adopted on 30 November and 1 December 1992 by the Immigration Ministers SN 4823/92 WG 1283 ASIM 147.

European Union Resolution of 1 June 1993 on the Harmonisation of Policies on Family Reunification SN 2828/1/93 WGI 1497.REV 1.

Resolution on certain common guidelines as regards the admission of particularly vulnerable persons from the former Yugoslavia adopted on 1 June 1993.

Text adopted on 20 June 1994 on the circulation and confidentiality of joint reports prepared by CIREA on the situation in certain third countries [1996] OJ C274/43.

Recommendation concerning a specimen bilateral readmission agreement between a Member State and a third country adopted on 30 November 1994 [1996] OJ C274/2.

EU Resolution of 20 June 1995 on minimum guarantees for asylum procedures, [1996] OJ C274/13.

Recommendation on the guiding principles to be followed in drawing up protocols on the implementation of readmission agreements adopted on 24 July 1995 [1996] OJ C274/25.

Resolution on burden-sharing with regard to admission and residence of displaced persons on a temporary basis, adopted on 25 September 1995 [1995] OJ C262/1.

Council Conclusions of 20 December 1995 on readmission clauses in Community agreements Bull EU 12–1995 point 1.5.3.

Council Conclusions of 4 March 1996 on readmission clauses in mixed agreements, Bull EU 3–1996 point 1.5.6.

Council Decision on an alert and emergency procedure for burden-sharing with regard to the admission and residence of displaced persons on a temporary basis adopted on 4 March 1996 [1996] OJ L63/10.

Council Conclusions of 27 May 1997 concerning the application of the Dublin Convention, [1997] OJ C191/27.

Joint Action of 22 July 1997 concerning the financing of specific projects in favour of asylum seekers and refugees [1997] OJ L205/5.

Joint Action of 22 July 1997 concerning the financing of specific projects in favour of displaced persons who have found temporary protection in the Member States and asylum seekers [1997] OJ L205/3.

EU Action Plan on the influx of migrants from Iraq and the neighbouring region adopted on 26 January 1998, 5573/98.

Joint Action of 27 April 1998 concerning the financing of specific projects in favour of asylum seekers and refugees [1998] OJ L138/8.

Joint Action of 27 April 1998 concerning the financing of specific projects in favour of displaced persons who have found temporary protection in the Member States and asylum seekers [1998] OJ L138/6.

Proposal for a Joint Action concerning solidarity in the admission and residence of beneficiaries of the temporary protection of displaced persons COM (1998) 372 final, 26 June 1998 [1998] OJ C268/22.

Action plan of the Council and the Commission on how best to implement the provisions of the Treaty of Amsterdam establishing an area of freedom, security and justice adopted on 3 December 1998 [1999] OJ C19/1.

Joint Action of 26 April 1999 establishing projects and measures to provide practical support in relation to the reception and voluntary repatriation of refugees, displaced persons and asylum seekers, including emergency assistance to persons who have fled as a result of recent events in Kosovo [1999] OJ L114/2.

Council Decision (EC) No. 1999/435 of 20 May 1999 concerning the Definition of the Schengen acquis for the purpose of determining the Legal Basis for each of the provisions or decision which constitute the acquis [1999] OJ L176/1.

Decision (EC) No. 1999/436 of 20 May 1999 determining the legal basis for each of the Provisions or Decisions which constitute the Schengen acquis [1999] OJ L176/17.

Common Strategy of the European Union on Russia, 4 June 1999 [1999] OJ L157/1.

European Council Strategy of 11 December 1999 on Ukraine [1999] OJ L331/1, para 63.

Common Strategy of the European Council of 19 June 2000 on the Mediterranean Region [2000] OJ L183/5.

Council Directive (EC) 2003/43 of 29 June 2000 implementing the principle of equal treatment between persons irrespective of racial or ethnic origin [2000] OJ L180/22.

Council Decision (EC) No. 2000/596 of 28 September 2000 establishing a European Refugee Fund [2000] OJ L252/12 supplemented by the Commission Decision 2001/275/EC of 20 March 2001 laying down detailed rules for the implementation of Council Decision 2000/596/EC as regards the eligibility and expenditure and reports on implementation in the context of actions co-financed by the European Refugee Fund [2001] OJ L95/27.

Council Directive (EC) No. 2000/78 of 27 November 2000 establishing a general framework for Equal Treatment in employment and occupation [2000] OJ L303/16.

Council Regulation (EC) No. 2725/2000 of 11 December 2000 concerning the establishment of 'Eurodac' for the comparison of fingerprints for the effective application of the Dublin Convention [2000] OJ L316/1.

Council Decision of 8 March 2001 on the principles, priorities, intermediate objectives and conditions contained in the Accession Partnership with the Republic of Turkey [2001] OJ L85/13.

Council Regulation (EC) No. 539/2001 of 15 March 2001 listing the third countries whose nationals must be in possession of visas when crossing the external borders and those whose nationals are exempt from that requirement [2001] OJ L81/1.

Council Decision (EC) No. 2001/258 of 15 March 2001 concerning the conclusion of an Agreement between the European Community and the Republic of Iceland and the Kingdom of Norway concerning the criteria and mechanisms for establishing the State responsible for examining a request for asylum lodged in a Member State or Iceland or Norway [2001] OJ L93/38.

Council Directive (EC) No. 2001/40 of 28 May 2001 on the mutual recognition of decisions on the expulsion of third country nationals [2001] OJ L149/34.

Council Directive (EC) No. 2001/51 of 28 June 2001 supplementing the provisions of Article 26 of the Convention implementing the Schengen Agreement of 14 June 1985, [2001] OJ L187/45.

Council Directive (EC) No. 2001/55 of 20 July 2001 on minimum standards for giving temporary protection in the event of a mass influx of displaced persons and on measures promoting a balance of efforts between Member States in receiving such persons and bearing the consequences thereof [2001] OJ L212/12.

Council Regulation (EC) No. 2414/2001 of 7 December 2001 amending Regulation (EC) No. 539/2001 listing the third countries whose nationals must be in possession of visas when crossing the external borders of Member States and those whose nationals are exempt from that requirement [2001] L327/1.

Modification of the terms of reference of the High Level Working Group on Asylum and Migration (HLWG), Council Document 9433/02 of 30 May 2002.

Council Directive (EC) No. 2003/9 of 27 January 2003 laying down minimum standards for the reception of asylum seekers, [2003] OJ L31/18.

Council Regulation (EC) No. 343/2003 of 18 February 2003 establishing the criteria and mechanisms for determining the Member State responsible for examining an asylum application lodged in one of the Member States by a third-country national [2003] OJ L 50/1.

Council Regulation (EC) No. 453/2003 of 6 March 2003 amending Regulation (EC) No. 539/2001 listing the third countries whose nationals must be in possession of visas when crossing the external borders and those whose nationals are exempt from that requirement [2003] OJ L69/10.

Commission Regulation (EC) No. 1560/2003 of 2 September 2003 laying down detailed rules for the application of Council Regulation (EC) No. 343/2003 establishing the criteria and mechanisms for determining the Member State responsible for examining an asylum application lodged in one of the Member States by a third-country national, [2003] OJ L222/3.

Council Regulation (EC) No. 377/2004 of 19 February 2004 on the creation of an immigration liaison officers network, 19 February 2004.

Regulation (EC) No. 491/2004 of the European Parliament and of the Council of 10 March 2004 establishing a programme for financial and technical assistance to third countries in the areas of migration and asylum (AENEAS) [2004] OJ L80/1.

Agreement between the European Community and the Government of Hong Kong Special Administrative Region of the People's Republic of China on the readmission of persons residing without authorisation [2004] OJ L17/25.

Agreement between the European Community and the Macao Special Administrative Region of the People's Republic of China on the readmission of persons residing without authorisation [2004] OJ L143/99.

Council Decision (EC) No. 2004/407 of 26 April 2004 amending Articles 51 and 54 of the Protocol on the Statute of the Court of Justice, OJ [2004] L132/5.

Council Directive (EC) No. 2004/83 of 29 April 2004 on minimum standards for the qualification and status of third country nationals or stateless persons as refugees or as persons who otherwise need international protection and the content of the protection granted [2004] OJ L304/12.

Agreement between the European Union, the European Community and the Swiss Confederation on the Swiss Confederation's association with the implementation, application and development of the Schengen Acquis, 26 October 2004 [2004] OJ L370/1.

Council Regulation (EC) No. 2007/2004 of 26 October 2004 establishing a European Agency for the Management of Operational Cooperation at the External Borders of the Member States of the European Union [2004] OJ L349/1.

Council Decision (EC) No. 2004/904 of 2 December 2004 establishing the European Refugee Fund for the period 2005 to 2010 [2004] OJ L381/52.

'The Hague Programme. Strengthening Freedom, Security and Justice in the European Union', Council Document 14292/1/04 REV 1 of 8 December 2004.

Agreement between the European Community and the Republic of Albania on the readmission of persons residing without authorisation 14 April 2005 [2005] OJ L124/22.

Agreement between the European Community and the Democratic Socialist Republic of Sri Lanka on the readmission of persons residing without authorisation 4 June 2004 [2005] OJ L124/43.

Council Decision of 22 December 2004 providing for certain areas covered by Title IV of Part Three of the Treaty establishing the European Community to UK governed by the procedure laid down in Article 251 of that Treaty [2004] OJ L396/5.

Council Directive (EC) No. 2005/85 of 1 December 2005 on minimum standards on procedures in Member States for granting and withdrawing refugee status [2005] OJ L326/13.

Council and Commission Action Plan Implementing the Hague Programme on Strengthening Freedom, Security and Justice in the EU Doc 9778/2/05, 10 June 2005, [2005] OJ C198/1.

Council Decision (EC) No. 2006/188 of 21 February 2006 on the conclusion of the Agreement between the European Community and the Kingdom of Denmark extending to Denmark the provisions of Council Regulation (EC) No. 343/2003 establishing the criteria and mechanisms for determining the Member States by a third-country national and Council Regulation (EC) No. 2725/2000 concerning the establishment of 'Eurodac' for the comparison of fingerprints for the effective application of the Dublin Convention [2006] OJ L66/37.

Protocol to the Agreement between the European Community and the Republic of Iceland and the Kingdom of Norway concerning the criteria and mechanisms for establishing the State responsible for examining a request for asylum lodged in a Member State or in Iceland or Norway [2006] OJ L57/16.

Regulation (EC) No. 1638/2006 of the European Parliament and of the Council of 24 October 2006 laying down general provisions establishing a European Neighbourhood and Partnership Instrument.

Agreement between the European Community and the Russian Federation on readmission 25 May 2006 [2007] OJ L 129/40.

Council Conclusions on the evaluation of the progress and outcome of negotiation of Community readmission agreement with third countries, Luxembourg, 12–13 June 2007.

Council Decision on the conclusion of the Agreement between the European Community and Bosnia and Herzegovina on the readmission of persons residing without authorisation, Council Doc 12196/07, 14 September 2007.

Council Decision on the conclusion of the Agreement between the European Community and the Republic of Montenegro on the readmission of persons residing without authorisation, Council Doc 13761/07, 29 October 2007.

Council Decision on the conclusion of the Agreement between the European Community and the Republic of Serbia on the readmission of persons residing without authorisation, Council Doc 13758/07, 29 October 2007.

Council Decision on the conclusion of the Agreement between the European Community and the Republic of Moldova on the readmission of persons residing without authorisation, Council Doc 13765/07, 20 November 2007.

Council Decision concerning the conclusion of the Agreement between the European Community and Ukraine on the readmission of persons, Council Doc 13763/07, 26 November 2007.

Agreement between the European Community and the Swiss Confederation concerning the criteria and mechanisms for establishing the State responsible for examining a request for asylum lodged in a Member State or in Switzerland [2008] OJ L 53/5.

European Pact on Immigration and Asylum, Council Doc 13440/08, 24 September 2008.

European Parliament

European Parliament Working Paper, *Asylum in the European Union: The "Safe Country of Origin Principle"* (1997) 40 p.

Migration and Asylum in Central and Eastern Europe (1997) 71 p.

EP Resolution on the right of asylum of 12 March 1987 [1987] OJ C99/167.

EP Resolution on the Situation in Kosovo of 15 April 1999 [1999] OJ C219/4.

EP Resolution on progress made in 2004 in creating an area of freedom, security and justice, 8 June 2005 [2005] OJ C124 E/398.

EP Recommendation to the Council and the European Parliament on the future of the area of freedom, security and justice as well as on the measures required to enhance the legitimacy and effectiveness thereof, P6_TA(2004)0022, 14 October 2004.

'The conditions in centres for third country nationals (detention camps, open centres as well as transit centres and transit zones) with a particular focus on provisions and facilities for persons with special needs in the 25 Member States', December 2007, REF: IP/C/LIBE/IC/2006–181.

Schengen Executive Committee

1992 Note from the Spanish Presidency comparing the provisions of the Dublin Convention and the Schengen Convention SCH/II-As (92) 4, 3e rev (on file with the author).

Rapport annuel du 7 mai 1996 relatif au fonctionnement de la Convention d' application de Schengen pendant la période du 26 mars 1995 au 25 mars 1996 SCH/C (96) 17, 16 (on file with the author).

Note de la délégation néerlandaise du 24 septembre 1996 sur la jurisprudence concernant l'application de la Convention de Schengen aux Pays-Bas SCH/II-As (96) 39, p 6 (on file with the author).

Decision relating to responsibility-sharing for applications for asylum lodged by spouses and minors SCH/Com-ex (97) 4 rev. of 25 April 1997 (on file with the author).

Executive Committee established under article 18 of the Dublin Convention

Decision No. 1/97 of the Executive Committee established under article 18 of the Dublin Convention concerning provisions for the implementation of the Convention [1997] OJ L281/1.

Decision No. 2/97 of 9 September 1997 of the Committee set up by article 18 of the Dublin Convention, establishing the Committee's Rules of Procedure [1997] OJ L281/26.

Decision No. 1/98 of 30 June 1998 concerning provisions for the implementation of the Convention [1998] OJ L196/49.

Decision No. 1/2000 of 31 October 2000 of the Committee set up by Article 18 of the Dublin Convention concerning the transfer of responsibility for family members in accordance with article 3.4 and article 9 of the Convention [2000] OJ L281/1.

Legislative Proposals

Proposal for a Council Regulation concerning the establishment of Eurodac for the comparison of fingerprints of applicants for asylum and certain aliens COM (1999) 260 final, 26 May 1999.

Proposal for a Council Directive on minimum standards for giving temporary protection in the event of a mass influx of displaced persons and on measures promoting a balance of efforts between Member States in receiving such persons bearing the consequences thereof COM (2000) 303 final, 24 May 2000 [2000] OJ C311/251.

Proposal for a Council Directive on minimum standards on procedures in Member States for granting and withdrawing refugee status COM (2000) 578 final, 20 September 2000 [2001] OJ C62/231.

Proposal for a Council Regulation establishing the criteria and mechanisms for determining the Member State responsible for examining an asylum application lodged in one of the Member States by a third-country national COM (2001) 447 final, 26 July 2001.

Proposal for a Council Directive laying down minimum standards for the qualification and status of third country nationals and stateless persons as refugees or as persons who otherwise need international protection COM (2001) 510 final, 12 September 2001.

Miscellaneous

Protocol on the Statute of the Court of Justice, signed at Brussels on 17 April 1957, as last amended by Article 6 III (3)(c) of the Treaty of Amsterdam.

Joint Declaration on fundamental rights of the Commission, Council and European Parliament, 5 April 1977 [1977] OJ C103/1.

Council Decision 88/591/ECSC, EEC Euratom of 24 October 1988 establishing a Court of First Instance of the European Communities [1988] OJ L319/1 and [1989] OJ L241/1 (corrigenda).

Report of the Court of Justice on Certain Aspects of the Application of the Treaty on European Union submitted to the European Council in preparation of the IGC (May 1995).

EC Directive 95/46/CE of 24 October 1995 of the European Parliament and the Council on the protection of individuals with regard to the processing of personal data and on the free movement of such data.

Note for Guidance on References by National Courts for Preliminary Rulings [1997] 1 CMLR 78.

Declaration Nr.17 on article 73k of the Treaty Establishing the European Community [1997] OJ C340/134.

Protocol (No. 2) integrating the Schengen Acquis into the Framework of the European Union [1997] OJ C340/93.

Protocol (No. 3) on the application of certain aspects of article 14 of the Treaty establishing the European Community to the United Kingdom and Ireland [1997] OJ C340/97.

Protocol (No. 4) on the Position of the United Kingdom and Ireland [1997] OJ C340/99.

Protocol (No. 5) on the Position of Denmark [1997] OJ C340/101.

Proposal for a Joint Action concerning solidarity in the admission and residence of beneficiaries of the temporary protection of displaced persons COM (1998) 372 final, 26 June 1998 [1998] OJ C268/22.

Charter of Fundamental Rights of the European Union proclaimed on 7 December by the President of the European Commission, the President of the European Parliament, and the President of the Council of Ministers [2000] OJ C364/1.

Proposal for a Comprehensive Plan to Combat Illegal Immigration and Trafficking of Human Beings [2002] OJ C 142/23.

Directorate-General for External Policies of the Union Directorate B, 'Study: Analysis of the external dimension of the EU's asylum and immigration policies – Summary and recommendations for the European Parliament', 8 June 2006.

Index

access to asylum procedure, guarantee of 92–3
acte clair doctrine 235, 236, 239
Africa 15, 50, 85, 175–6
Agenda for Protection 157, 269–71
agreements *see also* readmission agreements
  comprehensive plans of action 157
  Schengen Agreement 33–5, 89
aid
  development aid 71–78, 146–150, 271
  European Union 71–78
  fiscal burden-sharing 147
  physical burden-sharing 153
airports
  airport transit 102
  detention in international zones of
      airports 194–5
amicus curiae 238
Amsterdam Treaty 36–43, 145–6, 245, 247
annulment of Community acts 228, 236
  definition of application for asylum 94
  examination of asylum procedure, definition
      of 93
  multiple applications 122
  simultaneous or consecutive applications,
      lodging of 91–2
Assistant High Commissioner for Protection,
    establishment of 270
asylum-migration nexus (mixed
    migration) 19–20
asylum procedures Directive 51–66, 87, 93,
    130, 134–5, 231–2
  Dublin Regulation 93
  effective protection 52–7
  legality of Community acts, review of 231–2
  safe third country practices 51–66, 87, 130,
      134–5
Australia
  Indonesia and International Organization for
      Migration (IOM), regional
  cooperation agreement with 49
  Pacific Solution 78, 83
  safe third country practices 49

Belgium 106–7, 109, 112
boat people 158–60, 177–8, 211–12
borders
  apprehension at the frontier 119–121
  concentrations of burden at borders 124
  Dublin Regulation 94, 124

Eurodac Regulation 117, 120
European Union 35
FRONTEX 85
  internal borders, checks at 33–5, 41
  outer borders, burdens shifting to 165
  secondary movements 85
  training of border and immigration
      officials 149, 270
Bosnia and Herzegovina 47, 76, 258
burden-sharing *see* fiscal burden-sharing;
    physical burden-sharing; solidarity and
    burden-sharing, principle of

Canada–United States Safe Third Country
    Agreement 4, 48–9, 54, 134, 220
capacity building 68–9, 146, 148–50
Cartagena Declaration 15, 141, 204, 261
Central and Eastern Europe 47, 68–70, 136
Charter of Fundamental Rights of the
    EU 205, 210, 247–9
claims processing *see* extraterritorial processing
    of claims
close links
  Council of Europe 27–9
  Dublin Regulation 123–4
  national laws 56–7
  safe third country practices 56–9, 128,
      133–4
  strong links 27–8, 56
Commission of the European Communities *see*
    European Commission
Commission on Human Rights (UN) 264–5
Committee Against Torture 189, 199–203, 266
Common European Asylum System,
    proposal for 41
complementary protection 15
comprehensive approaches 146, 156–61
  Agenda for Protection 157
  boat people 158–60
  Comprehensive Plan of Action for
      Indo-Chinese Refugees 157–60
  'Convention Plus' 159–60
  International Conferences on Assistance to
      Refugees in Africa (ICARA) 157–8
  resettlement 157–60
  solidarity and burden-sharing, principle
      of 146, 156–61
  UN High Commissioner for Refugees
      (UNHCR) 157–61, 271

consecutive applications, lodging of 91–2
Constitutional Treaty 43, 225, 247
containment policies 1–2
    abuse of rights 211–12, 214
    Council of Europe 26
    European Union 249
    examples 2, 18–20
    extraterritorial processing of claims 79–80
    historical background 18–20
    interception practices 177–8
    leave one's country, right to 213–14
    non-refoulement principle 178–80
    persecution, right to seek and enjoy asylum
        from 211–12
    Prague airport case 179–80
    readmission agreements 67–8
    safe third country practices 59–60, 129
'Convention Plus'
    comprehensive plans of action 159–60
    fiscal burden-sharing 149
    implementation of the Geneva
        Convention 1951 1951 184
    secondary movements 84, 271–3
    solidarity and burden-sharing, principle
        of 161
    UN High Commissioner for Refugees
        (UNHCR) 85–6, 271–3, 284
Convention Relating to the Status of Refugees
    1951 *see* Geneva Convention 1951
Convention Relating to the International
    Status of Refugees 1933 10–11, 174
cooperation
    Dublin Regulation 122
    international cooperation 138–70
    justice and home affairs, cooperation in (third
        pillar) 36, 37
    readmission agreements 72–8
    solidarity and burden-sharing, principle
        of 138, 139–67, 170–1
    UN Declaration on Principles of
        International Law Concerning Friendly
        Relations and Cooperation among
        States 138
    UN High Commissioner for Refugees
        (UNHCR) 181–2, 261–4
Cotonou Agreement with ACP states 72–3,
    143
Council of Europe
    Draft on responsibility allocation 26–30
    Resolution on Asylum to Persons in Danger
        of Persecution 141
    safe third country principle 26–9, 51
country of first arrival *see* safe third country
    practices
courts *see also* European Court of Justice
    Court of First Instance 225, 232

European Court of Human Rights 208,
    241–9
International Court of Justice 264–6
CSR *see* Geneva Convention 1951
customary law 138, 204–9

data protection 117, 120
de facto asylum, right to 19
definition of refugee 15–17
Denmark
    Dublin Regulation 94
    opt-out 41–3, 237
    Schengen acquis 42–3
determination of responsible state
    Dublin Convention 1990 35, 89
    Dublin Regulation 89–125
    effective protection 218–21
    'orbit' situations 21
    safe third country concept 58
developing countries
    burden-sharing 146–152
    UN conference on territorial
        assylum 1977 22
development aid 79–80, 147, 271
Dialogue on Protection Challenges 277–8
diplomatic assurances 197–8, 203
direct arrival 132–3, 137
discrimination
    nationality 37
    persecution, not amounting to 54, 216–17
documents *see* travel documents; visas
Dublin Convention 1990
    assessment 91
    criteria 95–111
    Dublin Regulation, comparison with 91, 94,
        101–2
    elaboration 35–6
    entry into territory of member state, control
        of 102
    Eurodac Regulation 117–18
    European Convention on Human
        Rights 195–6
    evidence 115–16
    family unity 97–8, 105–6
    illegal entry 101–2
    justice and home affairs, cooperation in
        (third pillar) 36
    non-refoulement principle 195–6
    Schengen Implementation
        Convention 35
    solidarity and burden-sharing, principle
        of 165–6
    sovereignty clause 103, 105–6
    third country nationals 94
    transfer of asylum seeker to responsible
        state 112–13

Dublin Regulation
  access to asylum procedure, guarantee
    of 92–3
  application for asylum, definition of 94
  assessment 121–5
  asylum and refugee , conflation of 95
  asylum procedures Directive 93
  close links 123–4
  concentrations of burden at borders 124
  cooperation 122
  criteria 89–90, 92, 95–125
  critique 122–5
  Denmark94
  derogations 96, 102–11
  determination of responsible State 89–125
  Dublin Convention, comparison with 91,
    94, 101–2
  elaboration of Regulation 90–1
  entry into territory of member state, control
    of 96, 102
  Eurodac Regulation 117–21, 125
  European Court of Justice 91
  evidence, rules of 115–17
  examination of asylum procedure, definition
    of 93
  family unity 96–111, 124–5
  fingerprinting 117–21
  Geneva Convention 1951 93, 95
  harmonization 89–91, 124–5
  hierarchical criteria 89, 95–6, 100
  humanitarian clause 96, 102–11, 125
  identification of asylum seekers 117–21
  illegal crossing of territory of a member
    state 96, 101–2
  implementation 91
  intentions of asylum seeker 92
  'orbit' situations 91, 92, 93
  preparatory work 90
  principles 91–5
  prioritised or expedited procedures 93
  procedure 111–21
  Qualification Directive 93, 94
  Reception Directive 95
  recognition of States as safe
    countries 89, 92
  refoulement 166residence permits 96, 101
  safe third country concept 3, 89, 165–7
  Schengen Convention 89–90
  scope 94–5
  simultaneous or consecutive applications,
    lodging of 91–2
  solidarity and burden-sharing, principle
    of 165–7
  sovereignty clause 96, 102–11
  subsidiary protection, exclusion of 95
  third country nationals 94
  transfer of asylum seeker to responsible
    State 111–15, 121–2, 125
  UN High Commissioner for Refugees
    (UNHCR) 258–9
  visas 96, 101

Eastern Europe 47, 136, 168–70
EC law *see* **Dublin Convention; Dublin
    Regulation; European Union**
effective protection 214, 216–22
  asylum procedures Directive 52–6
  content 217–21
  diplomatic assurances 198
  European Convention on Human
    Rights 198
  Geneva Convention 1951 217–18, 221
  good faith obligations 218
  human rights 219–21
  indirect or chain refoulement 219
  natural justice 220
  non-refoulement principle 198, 217–18
  'orbit' situations 219
  remedies 221
  safe third country practices 52–7, 217–21
  scope 217–21
  supervision 218, 221
  UN High Commissioner for Refugees
    (UNHCR) 218–19, 270
effective remedy, right to an 66, 203
**entry into territory of member State, control
    of** 96, 102
**Eurodac Regulation, identification of asylum
    seekers under the**
  apprehension at the frontier 119, 121
  Central Unit 118–19
  data protection 117, 120
  duration of retention of data 118–20
  Dublin Convention 117–18
  Dublin Regulation 117–21, 125
  Eurodac Convention 35
  exchange of information 117
  expansion of system 120
  fingerprinting 35, 101–2, 117–21
  illegal entry 101–2
  informed, right to be 117
  irregular crossing of external borders 119,
    121
  Schengen Information System 120
  statistics 120–1
  Visa Information System 120
Europe *see also* **European Convention on
    Human Rights; European Union;
    particular countries
    (eg United Kingdom)**
European Commission 30–3, 79, 86, 90, 122,
    225–226

European Convention on Human Rights
   airports, detention in international zones
      of 194–5
   Charter of Fundamental Rights of the
      EU 247–8
   de facto asylum, right to 190
   diplomatic assurances 197–8
   discrimination not amounting to
      persecution 54, 216–17
   Dublin Convention 195–6
   Dublin Regulation 106–8, 110
   effective protection 198
   equivalent protection 244
   European Court of Human Rights 208,
      241–9
   European Union 223, 240–9
   extraterritorial processing of claims 82
   extraterritoriality 82, 198–9
   family unity 96, 98, 104–5, 107–8
   inhuman or degrading treatment 188–98,
      243, 247
   justice and home affairs, cooperation in (third
      pillar) 36, 37
   liberty and security, right to 194–5
   non-refoulement principle 188–99, 208
   'orbit' situations 194
   private and family life, right to respect
      for 189, 216–17
   procedural safeguards 198
   Qualification Directive 193
   readmission agreements 70
   real risk requirement 191–3, 196–7
   rendition 197
   safe third country practices 53, 61–2, 64–5,
      194–9
   secondary movements 194
   sovereignty clause in Dublin
      Regulation 106–8, 110
   State parties, return to 190–1
   time limits, existence of short 198

**European Council on Refugees and Exiles
   (ECRE)** 84
European Court of Justice 223–39, 240–50
   acte clair doctrine 235, 236, 239
   competence 38
   Dublin Regulation 91
   European Convention on Human
      Rights 240–9
   European Court of Human Rights 241–9
   fundamental rights 230–1, 240–9, 286
   general principles of EC law 240–2, 247
   Geneva Convention 1951 240, 247–9
   intervention before the Court, right of 231
   preliminary rulings 38, 225, 232–9, 245, 250
   Qualification Directive 243
   remedies 224–29, 249

   right to asylum 247–8
   supervision 223–39, 249–50
   supremacy of EC law 240
European Neighbourhood Policy 74–5
European Refugee Fund 147–8
European Union *see also* **Dublin
      Convention 1990; Dublin Regulation;
      European Court of Justice; supervision at
      European Union level**
   acquis communautaire 42–3
   Amsterdam Treaty 36–43, 145–6, 245, 247
   annulment of Community acts 228, 236
   assistance to third countries 75
   asylum procedures Directive 51–66, 87, 93,
      130, 134–5, 231–2
   capacity building 150–1
   Charter of Fundamental Rights of the EU
      210, 247–9
   co-decision procedure 38
   Commission of the European Union 30–3,
      79, 86, 90, 122, 225–226
   Common European Asylum System,
      proposal for 41
   Constitutional Treaty 43, 225, 247
   cooperation agreements, readmission clauses
      in 72–8, 87
   Cotonou Agreement with ACP states 72–3
   Court of First Instance 225, 232
   Danish opt-out 41–3, 237
   decision-making procedure 37–8
   determination of responsible State 32, 38
   development aid 79–80
   displaced persons, minimum standards on
      temporary protection of 39
   Eurodac Convention 35, 101–2
   Eurodac Regulation 117–21, 125
   European Convention on Human
      Rights 223, 240–9
   European Neighbourhood Policy 74–5
   European Refugee Fund 147–8
   extraterritorial processing of claims 78–84
   failure to act 232
   failure to comply with EC Treaty 225–7
   fiscal burden-sharing 147–51
   free movement of persons 31–2, 233
   freedom, security and justice, area of 36–8,
      71, 225
   Geneva Convention 1951 72, 82, 84, 223,
      238, 240, 247–9
   Hague Programme 41, 80, 85, 225
   harmonization of laws 38–43, 44, 51–2, 84
   High Level Working Group on Asylum
      and Migration 74
   Humanitarian Aid Office (ECHO) 148
   illegal immigrants 73–4, 81–2, 101–2
   infringement proceedings 225–7
   internal borders, checks at 33–5, 41

intervention, right of 231, 236, 238, 249–50
Ireland
 Common Travel Area with UK 42
 opt-out by 41–3, 237
 justice and home affairs, cooperation in
  (third pillar) 36, 37
 Kosovo crisis 154–5
 legality of Community acts, review
  of 227–32
 Lisbon Treaty 43, 144, 156, 162, 225, 245, 247
 Maastricht Treaty 36–7, 42, 228, 245–246
 mass influxes 152–3
 minimum standards 39–40
 nationality discrimination 37
 Nice Treaty 38, 225, 228–229, 239
 opt-outs 41–3, 237
 physical burden-sharing 152–6
 police and criminal cooperation 240, 246
 protected entry procedures 86, 87
 Qualification Directive 93, 94, 193, 243
 readmission agreements 67–78, 80
 Reception Directive 95, 217, 226–7
 recognition of refugee status, harmonization
  for procedures for 32
 regional programmes 85–6
 safe third country practices 51–66, 86, 234
 Schengen area 33–5, 42–3, 89–90, 97–8,
  120, 183
 Schengen Information System 120
 Single European Act 30, 33
 temporary protection 39, 43, 226–7
 third country nationals 32, 72–3, 76–7
 transit processing centres 78–83
 UN High Commissioner for Refugees
  (UNHCR) 255, 268–9
 United Kingdom, opt-out by 41–3, 237
 visas
  facilitation 77
evidence
 circumstantial evidence 115–16
 Dublin Convention 115–16
 Dublin Regulation 115–17
 non-refoulement principle 188–9
 Torture Convention 201
extraterritorial processing of claims 45,
 78–83, 87
 Australia 78
 development aid 79–80
 European Convention on Human Rights 82
 European Union 78–85
 Geneva Convention 1951 82, 84
 Hague Programme 80
 illegal immigrants 81–2
 International Organization for Migration
  (IOM) 78–9
 legal and practical problems 81–4
 origins 78

standards of reception 82–3
State sovereignty 83
transit processing centres 78–83
UN High Commissioner for Refugees
 (UNHCR) 75, 80–2
extraterritoriality *see also* extraterritorial
 processing of claims
 Geneva Convention 1951 176–8
 European Convention on Human
  Rights 198–9
 non-refoulement principle 176–8

failure to comply with EC Treaty 225–7
fairness
 fair and efficient procedures 181–2
 fair and humane treatment, right to 215
family unity
 definition of family 96–7
 dependency, definition of 105
 Dublin Convention 97–8, 105–6
 Dublin Regulation 96–101, 105–107,
  124–5
 European Convention on Human
  Rights 96, 98, 104–8
 humanitarian clause 96, 102–11, 125
 Schengen Convention 97–8
 sovereignty clause in Dublin
  Regulation 102–11
 subsidiary protection 99
 UN High Commissioner for Refugees
  (UNHCR) 100
fingerprinting
 Dublin Regulation 117–21
 Eurodac Regulation 101–2, 117–21, 125
 illegal entry 101–2
first country of asylum see safe third country
 practices
fiscal burden-sharing
 allocation of funds 148
 capacity building 148–50
 'Convention Plus' 149
 development aid 146–7
 equitable distribution 163
 European Refugee Fund 147–8
 European Union 147–51, 154–5
 humanitarian assistance 148
 Kosovo Crisis 154–5
 mass influxes 144, 147
 readmission agreements 68–9
 solidarity and burden-sharing, principle
  of 144, 146–50, 163
 strengthening protection capacity project
  (SPCP) 149
 technical assistance 148–9
 temporary protection 148
 UN High Commissioner for Refugees
  (UNHCR) 149–50

France 194–5
free movement
  Dublin Convention 1990 35
  Eurodac Regulation 120
  European Union 30–2, 35, 120, 233
  leave one's country, right to 213
  third country nationals 32
freedom, security and justice, area of 36–8, 71, 225
FRONTEX 85, 213
frontiers *see* borders
fundamental rights, European Court of Justice and 240–9, 286
  Amsterdam Treaty 245, 247
  Charter of Fundamental Rights of the EU 247–9
  Constitutional Treaty 247
  containment policies 249
  EC treaties 245–7
  Dublin Regulation 245
  European Convention on Human Rights 240–9
  European Court of Human Rights 241–9
  general principles of EC law 240–2, 247
  Geneva Convention 1951 240, 247–9
  inhuman or degrading treatment 243, 247
  interpretation 243–5
  Lisbon Treaty 245, 247
  Maastricht Treaty 245
  police and criminal cooperation 240, 246
  preliminary rulings 245
  Qualification Directive 243
  remedies 249
  right to asylum 247–8
  sources of fundamental rights 240–1
  supremacy of EC law 240

general principles of EC law 240–2, 247
Geneva Convention 1951
  see also 'Convention Plus'
  Article 1 13–14, 209–10, 216
  Article 31 14, 46–7, 127–138
  Article 33 *see non-refoulement* principle
  autonomous obligations 183–4, 216–17
  Cartagena Declaration 15
  complementary protection 15
  cooperation 261–4
  customary obligations 204–9
  definition of refugee 14, 15–16
  derogations 174–5
  determination of refugee status 182–3
  discrimination not amounting to persecution 54, 216,
  Dublin Regulation 93, 95
  effective protection 217–18, 221
  emergencies 174–5

European Convention on Human Rights 196–7, 240
European Union
  extraterritorial processing of claims 82, 84
  fundamental rights 240, 247–9
  readmission agreements 72
  supervision 223, 238
extraterritorial processing of claims 82
extraterritoriality 82, 176–8
historical background 13–15
Global Consultations 267–71, 284, 286
implement Convention, State's obligation to 181–7
indirect or chain refoulement 176, 180–1
individuals, supervision by 266–7, 282–3
International Court of Justice 265–6
interpretation 21, 130–2, 184–7, 196–7, 223, 265–6, 286
mere transit 127–38
national authorities, cooperation between 261
non-refoulement principle 174–88, 204–9, 267
OAU Convention Governing the Specific Aspects of Refugee Problems in Africa 1969 15–6, 21, 140, 175–6, 188, 204, 208, 210, 261
peer review mechanisms 276–7
persecution 13–14, 209–10, 216
Prague airport case 179–80
prima facie refugees 14
'protection elsewhere' principle 127–38
Protocol 9, 14, 282–3
readmission agreements 70–2
recognized refugees 14
right to asylum 247–8
safe third country practices 3, 46–7, 53, 55–6, 58, 62–4, 258–9
Schengen agreement 183
simple presence, rights enjoyed due to 214–15
supervision 223, 238, 252, 265–7
transfers to another state 215–16
UN High Commissioner for Refugees (UNHCR) 181–2, 184, 238, 267–71, 284, 286
Vienna Convention on the Law of Treaties 130–2
Germany
  High Commission for Refugees coming from Germany 11
  individual assessment 60–2
  non-refoulement principle 61, 196–7
  safe third country practices 58, 60–2, 65
Global Consultations 267–71, 284, 286
good faith obligations 179, 182–3, 218
good neighbourliness, principle of

consult, obligation to 168
forced displacements, state of origin's
  responsibility for 169
inform, obligation to 168
international cooperation 138, 167–71
international law 167–8
mere transit 170
minorities, treatment of 169
'orbit' situations 170
readmissions 169–70
safe third country practices 138, 167–71
states of origin 168–9
Greece 109–10

Hague Programme 41, 80, 85, 225
Haitian boat people 177–8, 211–12
harmonization of laws 4–5
  Dublin Regulation 89–91, 124–5
  European Union 38–44, 51–2, 85, 89–91,
    124–5
  recognition of refugee status, harmonization
    of procedures for 32
  regional programmes 268
  safe third country practices 51–2, 56–7, 59, 66
High Commission for Refugees 11
High Commission for Refugees coming from
  Germany 11
High Commissioner for Refugees *see* UN High
  Commissioner for Refugees (UNHCR)
High-Level Dialogue on International
  Migration and Development (General
  Assembly) 274–5
historical background 10–30
  1970s, situation at the end of 17–30
  containment policies 18–20
  Convention Relating to the International
    Status of Refugees 1933 10–11
  Council of Europe 26–30
  definition of refugee 15–17
  economic migrants 19–20
  Geneva Convention 1951 13–15
  High Commission for Refugees 11
  High Commission for Refugees coming from
    Germany 11
  Intergovernmental Committee for
    Refugees 11
  International Nansen Office for Refugees 11
  International Refugee Organization (IRO),
    establishment of 11–12
  League of Nations 11
  Office of the International Commissioner for
    Refugees 11
  'refugees in orbit' 20–1
  UN conference on territorial asylum
    1977 21–3, 44
  UN High Commissioner for Refugees
    (UNHCR) 12–13, 23–5, 44

UN Relief and Rehabilitation Administration
  (UNRRA) 11
human dignity 215, 241
human rights *see also* European Convention on
  Human Rights; fundamental rights,
  European Court of Justice and
  Charter of Fundamental Rights of the
    EU 205, 210, 247–9
  Committee Against Torture 189, 199–203
  diplomatic assurances 203
  effective protection 52–56, 217–221
  effective remedy, right to an 113–115, 203
  European Convention on Human
    Rights 188–99
  evidence 201
  Human Rights Act 1998 64
  Human Rights Commission (UN) 252, 284
  Human Rights Committee 188–9
  Human Rights Council (UN) 252, 280, 284
  indirect refoulement 203
  individuals, supervision by 266, 282–3
  inhuman or degrading treatment 188–9
  International Covenant on Civil and Political
    Rights 188, 212
  leave one's country, right to 212–14
  preventive approach 187–8
  real risk requirement 200, 203
  remedies, availability of 203
  safe third country practices 55–6, 202–3
  solidarity and burden-sharing, principle
    of 139
  State's obligations 215, 216
  third countries, transfer to 188
  Torture Convention 188, 199–203
  UN charter-based bodies 264–5
humanitarian aid
  Humanitarian Aid Office (ECHO) 148
  humanitarian assistance 148
  mass influxes 153
  physical burden-sharing 153
  solidarity and burden-sharing, principle
    of 142–3
  UN High Commissioner for Refugees
    (UNHCR) 257–8
humanitarian clause in family reunion cases
  (Dublin Regulation)
  Dublin Regulation 96, 102–11, 125
  European Convention on Human
    Rights 104–5, 107–8

identification *see also* Eurodac Regulation,
  identification of asylum seekers under the;
  fingerprints
illegal crossing of territory of a member State
  Council of Europe 29
  Dublin Convention 101–2
  Dublin Regulation 96, 101–2

illegal crossing of territory of a member State
   (*cont.*)
   Eurodac system 101–2, 119, 121
   European Union 73–4, 81–2, 96, 101–2,
      119, 121
   extraterritorial processing of claims 81–2
   readmission agreements 70, 73–4
   safe third country practices 65
   Sangatte clause 102
indirect or chain readmission 176, 180–1,
      188–9, 214, 219
individuals, supervision by
   Committee Against Torture 266
   Geneva Convention 1951 266–7, 282–3
   supranational adjudication 282–3
   UN High Commissioner for Refugees
      (UNHCR) 266
Indo-Chinese refugees
   Comprehensive Plan of Action 157–60
   Vietnamese boat people 49, 158–60
**infringement proceedings (European
   Union)** 225–7
inhuman or degrading treatment 188–98, 247
interception practices 18, 177–8, 211–12
**Intergovernmental Committee for
   Refugees** 11
**Intergovernmental Consultations on Asylum,
   Refugee and Migration
Policies in Europe, North America and
   Australia** 25
**International Conferences on Assistance to
   Refugees in Africa (ICARA)** 157–8
international cooperation *see* cooperation
International Court of Justice 264–6
**International Covenant on Civil and Political
   Rights** 188, 210, 212
International Law Commission 210, 214,
      216, 221
International Nansen Office for Refugees 11
**International Organization for Migration
   (IOM)** 49, 78–9
**International Refugee Organization
   (IRO)** 11–12, 150–1, 182
international supervision 251–84, 286
   classification of international
      supervision 251–2
   Committee Against Torture 266
   future prospects 267–84
   Geneva Convention 1951 6, 252, 265–7,
      282–3
   human rights 252, 266, 282–4
   Human Rights Commission (UN) 252, 284
   Human Rights Council (UN) 252, 284
   individuals, supervision by 266–7, 282–4
   International Court of Justice 265–6
   States, by 251–2, 265–6
   supranational adjudication 282–3

Torture Convention 266
UN High Commissioner for Refugees
   (UNHCR) 252–81 267–81
interpretation
   European Court of Justice 38, 223, 236–9,
      243–5
   Geneva Convention 1951 21, 130–2,
      179–80, 223, 265–6, 286
   human rights 243–5
   'protection elsewhere' principle 9
   safe third country practices 130
**interstate relations, impact of safe third
   country practices on** 127–71, 285
   asylum procedures Directive 130, 134–5
   burden-sharing, principle of 138, 139–67,
      170–1, 285
   close links 128, 133–4
   commonality, condition of 135–6
   containment policies 129
   'direct arrival' 132–3, 137
   Geneva Convention 1951 127–38
   good neighbourliness, principle of 138,
      167–71
   international cooperation 138–70
   'mere transit' 127–38, 170
   'orbit' situations 135
   penalties 128–9
   protection elsewhere 127–38
   readmission agreements 135, 138
   non-refoulement principle 133–4
   solidarity and burden-sharing, principle
      of 138, 139–67, 170–1, 285
   Treaty interpretation 130
   Turkey 136–7
   UN Declaration on Principles of
      International Law Concerning Friendly
      Relations and Cooperation among
      States 138
   UN High Commissioner for Refugees
      (UNHCR) 129–30, 133–6
   unilateral application 135
intervention, right of 231, 236, 238, 249–50
Ireland
   Common Travel Area with UK 42
   European Union 41–3
   opt-out by 41–3, 237

Jordan 202–3
**justice and home affairs, cooperation in (third
   pillar)** 36, 37

Kosovo crisis 145–6, 154–5

League of Nations 11
leave one's country, right to 212–14, 286
   chain readmission 214
   containment measures 213–14

free movement, right to 213
International Covenant on Civil and Political
   Rights 212
readmission 214
State practice 213
legality of Community acts, review
   of 227–32
links *see* close links
Lisbon Treaty 43, 144, 156, 162, 225, 227,
   239, 245, 247
lists, adoption of 61, 63–4, 259–60
locus standi 229–32, 235–6, 249–50

Maastricht Treaty 36–7, 42, 228, 245–6
Macedonia 145–6
manifestly unfounded claims 35, 60, 234
margin of appreciation 105
mass influxes
   customary obligation 208–9
   European Union 152–3
   fiscal burden-sharing 144, 147
   humanitarian aid 153
   Kosovo crisis 145–6
   Macedonia 48, 76, 145–6
   national security 175–6
   non-refoulement principle 175–6, 179, 182,
      208–9
   physical burden-sharing 151, 162–3, 155
   solidarity and burden-sharing, principle
      of 141, 144–6, 164
   temporary protection 145, 152–3, 155
'mere transit' 57–8, 127–38, 167, 170
minorities, treatment of 169
mixed migration 19–20
monitoring
   bodies 188
   borders 84–5, 87, 270, 275
   FRONTEX 85
Morocco 55
multiple applications 122

nationality discrimination 37
natural justice 220
neighbourliness, principle of good *see* **good**
   neighbourliness, principle of
Netherlands
   family unity 97–100
   'orbit' situations 194
   sovereignty clause in Dublin
      Regulation 108–9
   transfer of asylum seeker to responsible
      state 113
Nice Treaty 36, 37, 38, 225, 228–9, 239
non-governmental organizations
   (NGOs) 263, 277–8, 280
non-refoulement principle 173–87
   see also *non-refoulement* principle,

European Convention on Human Rights
   and; refoulement
Committee Against Torture 189, 199–203
containment measures 178–80
'Convention Plus' 184
Convention Relating to the International
   Status of Refugees 1933 174
customary law 204–9, 218
determination of refugee status 182–3, 185
diplomatic assurances 203
Dublin Regulation 110
effective protection 217–18
effective remedy, right to an 203
emergencies 174–5
exceptions 175–6
extraterritoriality 176–8
fair and efficient procedures 181–2
Geneva Convention 1951 174–88, 204–9
good faith 179, 182–3
human rights 187–203
Human Rights Committee 188–9
indirect or chain refoulement 176, 180–1, 203
individuals, supervision by 267
inhuman or degrading treatment 188–9
interception practices 177–8
International Covenant on Civil and Political
   Rights 188
international refugee law, obligation
   in 174–87
mass influxes 175–6, 179, 182, 208–9
monitoring bodies 188
national security 175–6
norm-creating character 204
opinio juris 204, 207
Prague airport case 179–80
preventive approach 187–8
Principles of the Asian African Legal
   Consultative Committee 175–6
procedural safeguards 183
real risk requirement 200, 203
recognition of refugee status 182
remedies, availability of 203
resettlement 206
safe third country practices 202–3
Schengen agreement 183
scope of obligation 207–8
solidarity and burden-sharing, principle
   of 144–6
sovereignty clause in Dublin Regulation 110
State practice 204, 206–7
Stateless Persons Convention 204–5
third countries, return to 184–6, 188
Torture Convention 188, 199–203, 208–9
UN Declaration on territorial asylum 175
UN High Commissioner for Refugees
   (UNHCR) 25, 175–8, 181–2, 184,
   205, 259–61

non-refoulement principle, European
    Convention on Human Rights
    and 188–99, 208
    airports, detention in international zones
      of 194–5
    applicable standard 191–3
    de facto asylum, right to 190
    diplomatic assurances 197–8
    Dublin Convention 195–6
    effective protection 198
    extraterritoriality 198–9
    Geneva Convention 1951 196–7
    inhuman or degrading treatment 188–98
    liberty and security, right to 194–5
    'orbit' situations 194
    procedural safeguards 198
    Qualification Directive 193
    real risk requirement 191–3, 196–7
    rendition 197
    safe third country practices 194–9
    safeguards 198
    secondary movements 194
    State parties, return to 190–1
    time limits, existence of short 198
    United Kingdom 192–3, 195–6
North-South divide 273

OAU Convention Governing the Specific
    Aspects of Refugee Problems in Africa
    1969 15–6, 21, 140, 175–6, 188, 204,
    208, 210, 261
Office of the International Commissioner for
    Refugees 11
opinio juris 204, 207
opt-outs
    Denmark 41–3
    European Union 41–3
    Ireland 41–3, 237
    United Kingdom 41–3
'orbit' situations
    definition 20
    determination of responsible State 21
    Dublin Regulation 91, 92, 93
    effective protection 219
    Europe 20–1
    European Convention on Human
      Rights 195
    good neighbourliness, principle of 170
    historical background 20–1
    inhuman or degrading treatment 194
    non-refoulement principle 194
    safe third country practices 20, 135
    UN Draft Convention on territorial asylum
      1976 20
Organization of African Unity (OAU)
    Convention Governing the Specific

Aspects of Refugee Problems in Africa
    1969 15–6, 21, 140, 175–6, 188, 204,
    208, 210, 261
origins of arrangements to allocate
    responsibility 9–44

Pacific Solution (Australia) 78, 83
Palma Document 33
peer review mechanisms 276–7
persecution, right to seek and enjoy asylum
    from 209–12, 286
    abusive policies, determination of 211–12
    Charter of Fundamental Rights of the
      EU 210
    containment policies 211–12
    Council of Europe Resolution on Asylum to
      Persons in Danger
    of Persecution 141
    customary rule 209
    Geneva Convention 1951 13–14, 209–10
    interception practices 211–12
    International Covenant on Civil and Political
      Rights 210
    International Law Commission 210
    safe third country practices 54, 210–11
    State sovereignty 209
    UN Declaration on Territorial Asylum 210
    United States, interception of Haitian boat
      people by 211–12
    Universal Declaration of Human
      Rights 209, 211
physical burden-sharing 146, 150–6
    double voluntary action 155–6
    European Union 152–6
    humanitarian aid 153
    Kosovo crisis 154–5
    Lisbon Treaty 156
    mass flows 151, 152–3, 155
    resettlement 150–2
    soft law 154
    temporary protection 152–3, 155
    UN High Commissioner for Refugees
      (UNHCR) 150–5
plans of action 274–5 *see also* comprehensive
    plans of action
police and criminal cooperation 240, 246
policies restricting asylum *see* containment
    policies
policy review mechanisms 276–7, 286–7
Portugal 114
Prague airport case 179–80
preliminary rulings of European Court of
    Justice 38, 225, 232–9, 245, 250
prima facie refugees 14
principle of good neighbourliness *see* good
    neighbourliness, principle of

Principles of the Asian African Legal
    Consultative Committee 175–6
prioritised or expedited procedures 59–60, 93
procedural safeguards
    European Convention on Human
        Rights 198
    non-refoulement principle 183, 198
    transfer of asylum seeker to responsible
        state 113
processing of claims *see* extraterritorial
    processing of claims
protected entry procedures 86, 87
protected persons, definition of 12–13
'protection elsewhere' principle Council of
    Europe 26–30
    Geneva Convention 1951 127–38
    mere transit 127–38
    safe third country concept 3–4, 127–38
    UN conference on territorial asylum
        1977 22

Qualification Directive 93, 94, 193, 243

readmission agreements 45, 67–78
    assistance to third countries 75
    bilateral agreements 69–70
    capacity building 68–9
    Central and Eastern Europe 68–70
    characteristics 69–71
    collective readmission 70
    containment tool, as 67–8
    cooperation agreements, clauses in 72–8, 87
    Cotonou Agreement with ACP states 72–3
    Draft Skeleton 70
    definition 67
    European Convention on Human Rights 70
    European Neighbourhood Policy 74–5
    European Union 67–78, 80, 87
    evolution 67–9
    extraterritorial processing of claims 80
    financial support 68–9
    freedom, security and justice, area of 71
    Geneva Convention 1951 70–2
    illegal entry 70, 73–4
    mixed agreements, clauses in 72
    recommendations (EU) 69–71
    safe third country practices 67, 135, 138
    'second generation' agreements 68
    third country nationals 72–3, 76–7
    time limits 69–70
    travel documents 67–8, 77
    visa facilitation 77
readmission *see also* readmission agreements
    good neighbourliness, principle of 169–70
    indirect or chain readmission 214, 219
    leave one's country, right to 214

transfer of asylum seeker to responsible
    State 112
real risk requirement 191–3, 196–7, 200, 203
reception
    Reception Directive 95, 217, 226–7
    standards 82–3
recognition of refugee status
    Geneva Convention 1951 14
    harmonization of procedures 32
    non-refoulement principle 182
refoulement see also *non-refoulement* principle
    Dublin Regulation 89
    extraterritorial processing of claims 87
    Geneva Convention 1951 14
    indirect or chain *refoulement* 219
    inhuman or degrading treatment 64–5
    'mere transit' 133–4
    Morocco 55
    safe third country practices 55, 58–9, 64–5,
        133–4, 285–6
    solidarity and burden-sharing, principle
        of 166
Refugee Convention *see* Geneva Convention
    1951
refugee status
'refugees in orbit' *see* 'orbit' situations
remedies 113–14, 202–3, 221, 238–9, 249
rendition 197
resettlement
    Comprehensive Plan of Action for Indo-
        Chinese Refugees 158–60
    comprehensive plans of action 157–60
    Europe 86–7
    Multilateral Framework of Understandings
        on Resettlement 151–2
    physical burden-sharing 150–2
    solidarity and burden-sharing, principle
        of 146, 161–2
    statistics 152
    UN High Commissioner for Refugees
        (UNHCR) 150–2, 271
residence permits 96, 101
restrictions *see* containment policies
returns *see* *non-refoulement* principle;
    refoulement
right to asylum 190, 247–8
right to leave one's country *see* leave one's
    country, right to
Rwanda 258

safe third country practices 3, 5–6, 45–66,
    215–21 *see also* interstate relations, impact
    of safe third country practices on
    Africa 50
    appeals 64
    asylum procedures Directive 51–66, 87

safe third country practices (*cont.*)
  Australia 49
  Canada–United States Safe Third Country
    Agreement 4, 48–9
  close links 27–8
  consent of third state to removal 58–9, 134
  contact between asylum seeker and third
    country 56–9, 133–4, 198
  containment policies 26, 59–60
  Council of Europe 26–9, 51
  definition 45, 46–7, 52–3
  determination of responsible State 58
  Dublin Regulation 3, 89
  effective protection 52–6, 57, 217–21
  effective remedy, right to an 66, 113–4
  Europe 47–55
  European Convention on Human Rights 53,
    61–2, 64–5, 194–9
  European safe third country 52–3
  European Union
    asylum procedures Directive 51–66
    harmonization 51–2
    regional programmes 86
    safe countries, member states regarded as 37
    supervision 234
  first country of asylum 46, 52–3, 58
  Geneva Convention 1951 3, 46–7, 53,
    55–6, 58, 62–4
  good neighbourliness, principle of 169–70
  harmonization 51–2, 56–7, 59, 66
  individual assessment 60–2, 64–5, 220
  jurisdictional link 27–8, 133–4
  lists, adoption of 61, 63–4, 220
  mere transit 57–8, 133
  non-refoulement 5–6, 52–3, 55, 61, 194–9,
    202–3
  'orbit' situations 20
  origins and development 47–66
  procedural aspects 59–66, 133, 220
  'protection elsewhere' principle 3–4, 127
  refoulement 55, 58–9, 64–5, 176–9
  safety, presumption of 61–3
  secondary movements 45, 164–5, 285
  solidarity and burden-sharing, principle
    of 164–7
  strong links 27–8
  substantive examination of claims 58–9
  UN conference on territorial asylum
    1977 21
  UN High Commissioner for Refugees
    (UNHCR) 47, 50–2, 56–7, 258–65,
    284
  unilateral operation 57, 170, 135

Sangatte clause 102
Schengen area
  aliens, definition of 34–5

  Danish opt-out 42–3
  Dublin Regulation 89–90
  Eurodac Regulation 120
  family unity 97–8
  Geneva Convention 1951 183
  Schengen acquis 42–3
  Schengen Agreement 33–5, 183
  Schengen Implementation Convention 34–5
  Schengen Information System 120
secondary movements
  Convention Plus initiative 84, 271–3
  definition 2–3
  European Convention on Human
    Rights 194
  monitoring at borders 84–5
  Multilateral Framework of Understanding
    (draft) 273–4
  non-refoulement principle 194
  safe third country practices 45, 164–5, 285
  solidarity and burden-sharing, principle
    of 164–5
  UN High Commissioner for Refugees
    (UNHCR) 255, 261, 271–4
security
  European Union 30, 41
  historical background 44
  mass influxes 175–6
  non-refoulement principle 175–6
simple presence, rights enjoyed due to 214–15
simultaneous or consecutive applications,
    lodging of 91–2
Single European Act 30, 33
soft law 154, 163–4
solidarity and burden-sharing, principle of
  Amsterdam Treaty 145–6
  capacity building 146
  Cartagena Declaration 141
  comprehensive plans of action 146, 156–61
  Convention Plus 161
  Cotonou Agreement 143
  Council of Europe Resolution on Asylum to
    Persons in Danger of
    Persecution 141
  customary international law 161, 163
  developing countries 139, 140, 146
  Dublin Convention 165–6
  Dublin Regulation 165–7
  financial burden-sharing 68–9, 144,
    146–50, 163
  human rights 139
  international cooperation 138, 139–67,
    170–1
  international instruments 140–4
  international practice 146–54
  Kosovo crisis 145–6
  legal relevance 161–4
  Lisbon Treaty 144, 162

mass influxes 141, 144–6, 164
'mere transit' 167
non-refoulement principle 144–6
physical burden-sharing 146, 150–6, 285
refoulement 166
resettlement 146, 161–2
safe third country practices 138–67, 170–1, 285
secondary movements 164–5
soft law 163–4
technical assistance 146
temporary refuge 145
UN Declaration on Territorial Asylum 140
UN High Commissioner for Refugees (UNHCR) 141–6, 162, 164–5
South Africa 50
sovereignty clause (Dublin Regulation)
Belgium 106–7, 109
consent of asylum seeker 103–4, 105
containment policies 108–9
cultural grounds 108
Dublin Convention 103, 105–6
European Convention on Human Rights 106–8, 110
family reunion cases 105–8
Greece 109–10
humanitarian clause 102–3, 107
mental health 107–8
Netherlands 108–9
non-refoulement principle 110
procedural arguments 108
United Kingdom 109, 110
Special Rapporteur on the rights of non-citizens 265
standards *see also* minimum standards
European Union 82–3
extraterritorial processing of claims 82–3
reception 82–3
scrutiny, standards of 220
standard of living, access to adequate 215
transit processing centres 78–83
standing 229–32, 235–6, 249–50
State practice
customary obligations 204, 206–7
leave one's country, right to 213
non-refoulement principle 204, 206–7
opinio juris 207
UN High Commissioner for Refugees (UNHCR) 284
State reports, establishment of independent body to examine 278–81
State sovereignty 32–3, 83, 209
Stateless Persons Convention 204–5
States' obligations towards refugees 173–222
see also non-refoulement principle
autonomous obligation 216–17

cooperation, principle of 217
discrimination not amounting to persecution 54, 216–17
effective protection 214, 216–22
European Convention on Human Rights 216–17
fair and humane treatment, right to 215
Geneva Convention 1951 214–17, 222
human dignity 215
human rights 215, 216
leave one's country, right to 212–14, 286
persecution, right to seek and enjoy asylum from 209–12, 286
ReceptionDirective 217
simple presence, rights enjoyed due to 214–15
standard of living, access to adequate 215
subsistence, access to means of 215
third States, sending to safe 215–21
UN High Commissioner for Refugees (UNHCR) 215–16
status as refugees *see also* Geneva Convention 1951
asylum and refugee , conflation of 95
determination of refugee status 182–3, 185, 218–19, 262
harmonization 32
non-refoulement principle 182–3, 185
recognition of refugee status 32, 182
UN High Commissioner for Refugees (UNHCR), advisory and consultative role of 262
strengthening protection capacity project (SPCP) 149
strong links see also close links 27–8
subsidiary protection 95, 99
subsistence, access to means of 215
supervision *see* international supervision; supervision at European Union level
supervision at European Union level 223–50, 286
acte clair doctrine 235, 236, 239
amicus curiae 238
annulment of Community acts 228, 236
Amsterdam Treaty 245, 247
asylum procedures Directive 231–2
Charter of Fundamental Rights 245–7
Constitutional Treaty 225
containment policies 249
Court of First Instance 225, 232
Denmark, opt-out by 237
direct and individual interest 229–30
discretion 244
Dublin Regulation 245
European Convention on Human Rights 223, 240–9
European Court of Justice 223–50

supervision at European Union level (*cont.*)
  failure to act 232
  failure to comply with EC Treaty 225–7
  free movement of persons 233
  freedom, justice and security, area of 225
  fundamental rights 230–1, 240–9, 286
  general principles of EC law 240–2, 247
  Geneva Convention 1951 223, 238, 240,
    247–9
  Hague Programme 225
  infringement proceedings 225–7
  inhuman or degrading treatment 243, 247
  institutions 245–7
  interpretation 236–7, 243–5
  intervention, right of 231, 236, 238, 249–50
  Ireland, opt-out by 237
  legality of Community acts, review
    of 227–32, 234–6
  Lisbon Treaty 43, 144, 225, 227, 239, 245,
    247
  Maastricht Treaty 36, 42, 228, 245–6
  manifestly unfounded or inadmissible
    claims 234
  Nice Treaty 36–8, 225, 228–9 232, 239
  opt-outs 237
  police and criminal cooperation 240, 246
  preliminary rulings 225, 232–9, 245, 250
  Qualification Directive 243
  Reception Directive 226–7
  remedies 223–39, 249
  right to asylum 247–8
  safe third country practices 234
  standing 229–32, 235–6, 249–50
  supremacy of EC law 240
  Temporary Protection Directive 226–7
  UN High Commissioner for Refugees
    (UNHCR) 237–8
  United Kingdom, opt-out by 237
supranational adjudication 282–3
supremacy of EC law 240

Tanzania 60, 85
technical assistance 146, 148–9
temporary protection
  European Union 39, 43, 226–7
  fiscal burden-sharing 148
  infringement proceedings 226–7
  mass influxes 145, 152–3, 155
  minimum standards 39, 155
  physical burden-sharing 152–3, 155
third country nationals
  Dublin Regulation 94
  European Union 32, 72–3, 76–7
  free movement 32
  readmission agreements 72–3, 76–7
time limits, existence of short 198
Torture Convention

Committee Against Torture 189, 199–203,
  266
  customary obligation 208–9
  diplomatic assurances 203
  effective remedy, right to an 203
  evidence 201
  indirect refoulement 203
  non-refoulement principle 208–9
  real risk requirement 200, 203
  severity of treatment 201–2
  supervision 266
trafficking in persons 269
transfer of asylum seeker to responsible
  State 111–15
  appeals 112, 113–15
  Belgium 114
  Dublin Convention 112, 113
  Dublin Regulation 111–15, 121–2, 125
  informed, duty to keep asylum seeker 113,
    125
  Netherlands 113
  notification of decisions 113
  Portugal 114
  procedural safeguards 113
  readmission 112–13
  reception standards, minimum 112
  remedies 113–14
  replies, time limits for 111–12
  requests 111–12
  review 113
  suspensive effect of appeals 114–15
  time limits 111–13
  United Kingdom 114
transit processing centres 78–83
travel documents *see also* **visas**
  readmission agreements 67–8, 77
  residence permits 96, 101
  safe third country practices 129
Turkey
  'mere transit' 136–7
  protection elsewhere 136–7
  safe third country practices 136–7

UN conference on territorial asylum
  1977 21–3, 44
UN Declaration on Principles of International
  Law Concerning Friendly Relations and
  Cooperation among States 138
UN Declaration on Territorial Asylum 16–17,
  140, 175, 210
UN Draft Convention on territorial asylum
  1976 20, 140
UN High Commissioner for Refugees
  (UNHCR)
  10-Point Plan of Action 274–5
  Agenda for Protection 269–71
  allocation of responsibility arrangements 260

border monitoring 270, 275
Bosnia and Herzegovina 258
budget 12, 263–4
Commission on Human Rights (UN) 264–5
comprehensive plans of action 157–61
'Convention Plus' 85–6, 271–3, 284
cooperation between States 181–2, 261–4
determination of refugee status,
    advisory and consultative role with
    regard to 262
Dialogue on Protection Challenges 277–8
Division of International Protection 257–8
effective protection 218–19, 270
establishment 12–13
European Union 255, 268–9
Executive Committee 13, 23–5, 44, 252–5,
    259–60, 267–9, 276–8, 284, 286–7
Executive Committee conclusions 253–5,
    277
extraterritorial processing of claims 75, 80–2
fiscal burden-sharing 149–50
Geneva Convention 1951 85–6, 181–2,
    184, 238, 255, 258–81, 284, 286
Global Consultations 267–71, 284, 286
Handbook 262
High-Level Dialogue on International
    Migration and Development
    (General Assembly) 274–5
historical background 12–13, 23–5, 44
Human Rights Council 280
humanitarian protection 257–8
individuals, supervision by 266
International Court of Justice, advisory
    opinion from 264
international protection mandate 255–63,
    267–81, 284
legal competence 256–7
lists of safe countries 259–60
mandatory functions 256
national authorities, cooperation
    with 261–2
non-governmental organizations
    (NGOs) 263, 277–8, 280
non-refoulement principle 25, 175–8, 181–2,
    184, 205, 259–61
normative agreements 271
North–South divide 273
'orbit' situations 21
peer review mechanisms 276–7
preventive action 257–8, 261
protected persons, definition of 12–13
refoulement 268–9
regional programmes 75
reporting systems 275, 278–81
resettlement 150–2, 271
right to seek and enjoy asylum 265
Rwanda 258

safe third country practices 23–4, 47, 50–2,
    56–7, 129–30, 133–6, 258–65, 284
secondary movements 255, 261, 271–4
smuggling of migrants 268–9
solidarity and burden-sharing, principle
    of 141–6, 162, 164–5
Standing Committee of the Whole 253, 277
State practice 284
State reports, establishment of independent
    body to examine 278–81
States, Executive Committee conclusions
    addressed to 253–4
State's obligations 215–16
Sub-Committee of the Whole on
    International Protection 253, 258–9
Sub-Committee on Review and Monitoring,
    proposal for 276–7, 287
supervision 218, 237–8, 252–65, 266,
    267–81
Thematic Rapporteurs, appointment
    of 277
trafficking in persons 269
training of border and immigration
    officials 270
voluntary contributions, dependence
    on 263–4
UN conference on territorial asylum 21–3
UN Relief and Rehabilitation Administration
    (UNRRA) 11
United Kingdom
    Dublin Regulation 109, 110
    European Convention on Human
        Rights 192–3, 195–6
    European Union 41–3, 237
    Geneva Convention 1951 64, 179–81,
        184–7
    Human Rights Act 1998 64
    Ireland, Common Travel Area with 42
    list of countries 63–4
    non-refoulement principle 179–81, 184–7,
        192–3, 195–6
    opt-outs 41–3, 237
    Prague airport case 179–80
    presumption of safety 62–3
    safe third country practices 57–8, 62–5
    sovereignty clause in Dublin
        Regulation 109, 110
    standard of proof 62–3
    transfer of asylum seeker to responsible
        state 114
United Nations (UN)
    charter-based bodies 264–5
    Commission on Human Rights 264–5
    conference on territorial asylum 1977 21–3, 44
    Declaration on Principles of International
        Law Concerning Friendly Relations and
        Cooperation among States 138

United Nations (UN) (*cont.*)
Declaration on Territorial Asylum 16–17, 140, 175, 210
Draft Convention on territorial asylum 1976 20
High-Level Dialogue on International Migration and Development (General Assembly) 274–5
Human Rights Commission (UN) 252, 284
Human Rights Council (UN) 252, 284
Relief and Rehabilitation Administration (UNRRA) 11
United States
Canada–United States Safe Third Country Agreement 4, 48–9
Geneva Convention 1951 177–8

Haitian boat people, interception of 177–8, 211–12
non-refoulement principle 177–8
persecution, right to seek and enjoy asylum from 211–12
safe third country practices 48–9

Vietnamese boat people 49, 158–60
visas
European Union 77
Eurodac Regulation 120
European Union 86, 120
readmission agreements 77
Visa Information System 120

wishes of asylum seekers 24, 122–3